T. LEVIN
4607 KNOX RD
COLL. PK., MD.
            UM-49513

            RL

7644 CARLA RD
BALTO. 8, MD
    HU-61416

History of the American Economy

Ross M. Robertson

Indiana University

History

of the

American

Economy

SECOND EDITION

 Harcourt, Brace & World, Inc.

New York and Burlingame

SOURCES OF ILLUSTRATIONS

CHAPTER 2   **22:** The National Gallery of Art, Washington, D.C. Samuel H. Kress Collection. **25:** Alinari Art Reference Bureau (painting appears in Brera Gallery, Milan). **34:** British Museum. **38:** Rijksmuseum, Amsterdam. **46:** Museum of the City of New York.

3   **54:** Charleston Library Society. **60:** The Whaling Museum, New Bedford, Mass. **62:** Culver. **67:** Culver.

4   **83:** The Chase Manhattan Bank Money Museum. **91:** both Culver. **95:** New York Public Library.

5   **106:** Kansas State Historical Society. **121:** Culver. **122:** Library of Congress. **123:** Library of Congress.

6   **132:** New-York Historical Society. **142:** Culver. **143:** Culver. **145:** Old Print Shop, New York.

7   **150:** The Chase Manhattan Bank Money Museum. **151:** New-York Historical Society. **154:** Independence Hall, Philadelphia. **155:** The Chase Manhattan Bank Money Museum. **157:** Yale University Art Gallery. **159:** The Chase Manhattan Bank Money Museum. **168:** Culver. **172:** New-York Historical Society.

8   **192 (bottom):** Bettmann Archive. **201:** both from *The Memoirs of Samuel Slater.*

9   **208:** Library of Congress. **220:** *Harpers Weekly.*

10   **232:** Bettmann Archive. **233:** Culver. **244:** Museum of the City of New York.

11   **255:** Library of Congress. **259:** U.P.I. **269:** Library of Congress. **274:** Culver.

12   **279:** U.P.I. **281:** Union Pacific Railway Photo. **282:** *Harpers Weekly,* September 11, 1869. **288:** Illinois Central Railroad Company.

13   **310:** *Harpers Weekly,* October 16, 1869. **312:** Culver. **316:** Courtesy of the Author.

14   **339:** both American Steel and Wire Company. **341:** Library of Congress. **344:** Philadelphia Commercial Museum. **354:** Culver. **356:** Culver.

15   **362:** Courtesy of Montgomery Ward. **363:** Courtesy of Montgomery Ward. **365:** Courtesy of F. W. Woolworth Company. **367:** Culver.

16   **386:** Philadelphia Commercial Museum. **391:** Library of Congress. **393:** U.P.I. **400:** Wide World. **402:** *Harpers Weekly,* May 15, 1886. **405:** U.P.I.

17   **421:** Internal Revenue Service, Treasury Department.

18   **443:** New-York Historical Society, Bella C. Landauer Collection. **451:** Standard Oil Company (N.J.). **465:** Standard Oil Company (N.J.) photo by Corsini. **487:** United States Department of Agriculture.

19   **473:** Fairchild Aerial Surveys. **476:** Harbrace Photo. **479:** U.P.I. **489:** Standard Oil Company (N.J.).

20   **518:** U.P.I. **521:** The Franklin D. Roosevelt Library. **523:** First National City Bank.

21   **549:** United States Steel Corporation. **553:** P.F.I.

22   **571:** U.P.I. **572:** Edith Reichmann. **575:** U.P.I. **576:** Edith Reichmann. **579:** U.P.I. **584:** Fairchild Aerial Surveys. **601:** P.F.I. photo by Rotkin.

23   **613:** U.P.I. **617:** U.P.I. **624:** U.P.I.

24   **632:** U.P.I. **633:** U.P.I. **635:** Library of Congress photo by Dorothea Lange. **636:** Library of Congress photo by Dorothea Lange. **638:** U.P.I. **642:** Wide World. **658:** Stanley Rice. **659:** Wide World.

Contents

Part Two:
1789–1860

Part Three:
1861–1920

Part Four:
1921 to the Present

Maps

Charts and Graphs

Preface
to the Second Edition

One of our illustrious economic historians, a wise and gentle man, is fond of distinguishing between historians' economic historians and economists' economic historians. This sally is always good for a chuckle at academic meetings, and there is a bit of truth in it. Nevertheless, economic history is more and more becoming a single, close-knit field—much as it has been in the United Kingdom for more than a century—and I am not sure that our small fraternity any longer consists on the one hand of historians who know a little economics and on the other of economists washed in a little history.

To be sure, economic historians have in recent years paid far more attention to quantitative analysis—to measurement, if you will—than they previously did. Instead of being content to say simply more or less, they try now to say how much more and how much less. So doing, they have in the short space of a decade come up with data leading to a reassessment of old judgments about the history of the American economy. But note the word "judgment." Only rarely do facts speak for themselves. No time series, however conscientiously constructed, is a substitute for the awareness and clarity of perception that come from knowing how people worked and had fun and endured in the usually humdrum but sometimes exciting business of making a living. In any case, recent contributions to economic history have come from scholars with a tremendous heterogeneity of interest, and the results are all the better for their wide differences in method and bent.

What these results have been the reader will shortly discover, and I do not propose to spoil anyone's fun by adumbrating conclusions in the preface. It is a fair generalization that recent studies have valiantly chinked away at the mythology of history; at any rate a good many of the accepted "truths" of economic history have disappeared in the light of statistical examination. Comforting as it was to think so, pre–Civil War business cycles did not result from "excessive speculation," "reckless over-banking," or "monetary over-investment," but from sharp changes in the deficit-surplus position of the Treasury and swings in outlays on internal improvements. Slavery, as it turns out, was as profitable in the ante-bellum South as elementary economic analysis would suggest, and was not about to "fall of its own weight" in the 1850s. The concentration of American industry, at least in the first great wave, was motivated not so much by the predatory hope of monopoly power as by the fearsome excess capacities that developed as firms first competed in a national market. To take a more recent example, the Federal Reserve did not meet the oncoming economic storm of the early 1930s with easy money but with money so tight that there were serious pressures on bank reserves until it was too late for monetary policy to save the day.

This book had to be revised then for the compelling reason that we have been rewriting American economic history at a rapid rate. Of course I have taken the opportunity to bring charts, graphs, and tables very nearly up to the date of publication, simply because the book thereby becomes a better reference work for users. But these changes are relatively unimportant, and I would never have undertaken the considerable task of rewriting the first edition only to make a portion of it read like yesterday's newspaper. From the first chapter to the last the book has been entirely recast, partly as a consequence of the gain in my own knowledge but chiefly because the subject itself has grown and changed.

I hope that my former readers will consider this new book a substantial improvement over the old. Certain passages, notably those on our European origins and the economics of colonial life, have been strengthened. Others have been tightened and pulled together, particularly where the argument reportedly taxed the reader's attention. The subject of economic growth, long a favorite of historians, has in the past ten years become fashionable among economists, and I have devoted considerable space to it without explicitly treating recent growth models of dubious validity. Reader comment on these and other changes is earnestly solicited.

Like every writer, I have been sustained and supported by others. Much of my help came from scholars, many long dead or unknown to me personally, whose works appear in footnotes and in the bibliography. But there have been a few whose assistance and encouragement require some special note. My dear friend Earl J. Hamilton read the original edition and painstakingly made notes on the margins of nearly every page. Although I did not take all his advice, this new book reflects his wisdom and scholarship and is clearly much the better for his criticism. Two other friends, Douglass C. North and Harold F. Williamson, read a draft of this edition, suggesting changes that strengthened it a great deal. Forest Hill corresponded with me at length on many points, unerringly pointing up omissions that I had overlooked, and J. R. T. Hughes and Jim Potter helped me on many occasions without, I am sure, being aware of their contributions. Up to the day the last proof was read Gerald T. Dunne, lawyer turned historian, lent his Irish wit to substantive improvement and more felicitous turns of phrase. To my departmental colleagues I owe much for assistance at crucial points of the narrative, and my thanks are due David D. Martin, J. W. Milliman, Irvin M. Grossack, John P. Lewis, and Robert C. Turner.

Growing old is made less burdensome by the wonderful young people who come along to share the work load. Two graduate students, Kent Tool and Jules Levine, spent untold hours in the library and at the calculator in this cause, and Gerald W. Kuhn worked far beyond the call of duty as my research assistant. Mrs. Phyllis Darnell, with the help of Mrs. Patricia Dove, prepared the manuscript, and my secretary, Mrs. Elinor Sheehan, ably assisted me while the manuscript was in press. I am indeed grateful.

Ross M. Robertson

Bloomington, Indiana
December 1963

To my mother
Bertha Williams Robertson

and

the memory of my father
Ross Marshall Robertson

The Emerging Roles
of Economic History

He who thus considers things in their first growth and origin, whether a state or anything else, will obtain the clearest view of them.

ARISTOTLE

Young people, to whom this book is largely addressed, are not easily sold on the virtues of historical study. From their standpoint, the history they were exposed to in grade and high school often seemed irrelevant to everyday life. Kings and nobles, generals and wars, presidents and legislators, while occasionally exciting, too often arrayed themselves into long, tiresome lists. Moreover, there was a preoccupation with explaining what happened to whom, and when, rather than how and why it happened. History, too, often had a repetitious quality about it that sometimes made the past seem crystallized into a kind of mythology, to be taken several times on faith and not seriously questioned.

Yet even the unenthusiastic beginner cannot escape the impression that *some* knowledge of the past is useful. He draws on history for a sense of heritage necessary to an understanding of both his rights and his duties. Without history he is separated from the information essential to decision-making and deprived of the clues that help him untangle the complexities of the world about him. In a sense history is the source of his very identity. "In an eternal present, which is a specious present, the past is all we know. And as the past is forever slipping back, it reminds us that we too shall in time belong wholly to the past." [1]

---

[1] Herbert J. Muller, *The Uses of the Past* (New York: Oxford University Press, 1957), p. 31.

But it is as a help in solving problems that history is particularly useful, not just to professors and government officials, but to businessmen and scientists as well. Let me cite an example. On national television not long ago two famed scientists vigorously debated a question that is likely to generate heat for some time to come. The topic: What kind of expenditure should be made for civilian defense against the ravages of nuclear war? Professor Harrison Brown of the California Institute of Technology took the position that it is nonsense to attempt any large-scale construction of shelters, that the hope of mankind lies in agreement between the United States and the Soviet Union on questions of disarmament. Dr. Herman Kahn of the Hudson Institute, New York City, took the opposite view: that shelters would be effective against fallout and to some extent against nuclear blast and fire. After the opening minutes of the program it became clear to viewers that the discussion did not turn on scientific opinion. Both Brown and Kahn had been intimately connected with developments in nuclear energy. There were no differences between them on questions of scientific theory. Indeed, for almost a solid hour their discussion turned solely on historical facts. In previous wars, they asked, what was the strategy of belligerents as it affected civilian populations? What was the psychological reaction of both troops and civilians to cruel and unnecessary destruction of cities and towns? How, specifically, had Confederate soldiers reacted to Sherman's march through Georgia? What was the reaction of Londoners to *blitzkrieg*? Of the defenders of Stalingrad to German brutality? How, in general, have civilian populations behaved under the stresses of war? Is there historical evidence of degrees of civilian fear? Would nuclear blast result in panic? Or in sullen, resolute resistance?

So the discussion went for nearly an hour. The moment the two scientists got away from their laboratories and began to discuss public policy they had to resort to experience. Moreover, each discussant could assume that the other, being an educated man, was familiar with a certain recorded, more or less formal, account of experience—in short, with history. As is so often the case in literate, intelligent conversation among human beings, the search for truth ended in an appeal to history.

History does more, then, than sharpen the wits; it furnishes the vast body of information basic to a wide spectrum of public-policy decisions. Without a history a people would endure a kind of social amnesia as tragic as the loss of a personal past suffered by victims of psychic or physical shock. But history does more than provide facts. The historian worth his salt must impose some kind of organization on the facts to make them meaningful. In the chapters that follow we shall find example after example of the way in which the historian, by bringing order out of the jumble of historical events, opens the way to the solution of problems. Indeed, when he is most useful—most "practical"—the historian is either solving problems or undertaking the investigations prerequisite to ultimate problem-solving.

It is easy to exaggerate the practical values of history. Unfortunately, history repeats itself only in a limited sense, and such repetition as there is (outside the periodicity of natural phenomena) appears to teach us little. It is hard to demonstrate that men profit from the mistakes of their fore-bears, nor are historians likely to be wiser than other men. But even if history is only a frail and untrustworthy guide to prediction, it is often the only guide we have. Once again, consider how our two scientists approached the policy problem of prescribing an effective civilian-defense program.

We would sell our subject short if we failed to note three intangible values that, in varying degrees, reward those who read and write history.

1. *History is fun.* Furthermore, it becomes more enjoyable as time goes by, for the older we get the harder we try to recapture some part of our lives in nostalgic reminiscence. To be exciting, history need not be watered down as a fictionalized biography or a historical novel. Good history, taken straight, has tremendous appeal to a wide variety of readers. Fortunately, in recent years there has been a return to making history important as a literary form as well as an intellectual endeavor.

2. *Like all the liberal arts, history helps us live that "nonpractical" part of our lives to which, according to John Ciardi, the poet chiefly ministers.*[2] No sane human being is exclusively practical; we all live personal, as dis-tinguished from business or professional, lives. All of us, at one time or another, find it more important to establish some order of reality in our personal lives than to determine goals in our working lives. History, like poetry or music, on occasion helps us to understanding in a way that is non-intellectual—but no less real because it strikes directly at our consciousness.

3. *A sense of history is a great comfort.* For those who have no other faith, history may even be a substitute for religion. As we recall the great events of the past, we are impressed both with the shining achievements of mighty civilizations and with their ultimate catastrophes, with grandeur followed by final ruin. A sense of history is really a sense of participation in these high dramas, of having a part in the great flow of events that links us with those who have gone before and with others who will one day be born. This sense of belonging, of participating with the rest of humanity in the ultimate tragedy, is an antidote for the loneliness of being human.

The Merging of History and Economics

In this book we shall be concerned with a specialized historical narrative, "a longitudinal cut through the whole fabric of history," to use Professor Gay's expression.[3] It is often convenient to trace historic developments within a certain field of learning—music, science, law, and so on. Yet, as we shall

---

[2] Read, if you can, Ciardi's essay "An Ulcer, Gentlemen, Is an Unwritten Poem," reprinted in *Toward the Liberally Educated Executive* (New York: New American Library, 1960), pp. 66–69.

[3] Edwin F. Gay, "The Tasks of Economic History," *Journal of Economic History,* I (December 1941), 15.

see shortly, our endeavor to trace the economic history of the United States is more than just a convenience; it is a prerequisite to the solution of many of the policy problems that presently demand solution. But for a moment let us leave the justification of our study to consider how the two disciplines of history and economics merge.

Like any organized body of knowledge, both economics and history abstract from reality. Unaided, the human mind cannot comprehend the complexity that is our economic system. We cannot, if we would, simply look at the interrelationships among economic variables and make sense of them. It is equally apparent that history must be selective, that any attempt to record the whole of the past would be an exercise in futility. Consider, then, how economists and historians make their respective subjects manageable.

ECONOMICS

The wealth of a country consists of its resources—its people, its natural endowments, and its stock of goods. The management of these resources is a perplexing and difficult problem because resources are scarce relative to unlimited human wants. Put a little differently, there is a discrepancy between the amount of goods and services that the people in any society would *like* to have and the amount that they *can* have. Just as the members of a family must choose among alternatives when spending income, so the people in a society must make choices involving the use of resources.

We know from experience and observation that the American economy operates without much apparent guidance or direction to determine what will be produced from its resources and how output will be distributed. For example, anyone who works with young people observes their endless wrestling with the problem of choosing a career—i.e., the problem of what kind of resource they want to become. Their choices, to be sure, are not entirely determined by prospects of monetary gain; a gifted college senior may aspire to be a clergyman rather than a business executive. Nevertheless, choices of this kind are strongly influenced by ultimate financial reward.

Similarly, we are all familiar with the problem of deciding how to spend our personal incomes. How much shall go for food and how much for clothing? Should we have a better house or should we spend more on entertainment and recreation? How much should be spent on present satisfactions and how much set aside for an uncertain future? Each family and each single individual who manages his own income must endlessly make this kind of choice. Whether we like it or not, the acts we perform more than any other are those of *economizing*.

Now an economist is not primarily concerned with the *individual's* problem of scarcity, though he is well aware that the choices of individuals will add up to a total effect on the economy as a whole. The economist's attention can range from the attitudes of single human beings and the operations of individual business firms to relationships among the economies of the world. But ordinarily his chief concern is with the basic problem of scarcity as it is resolved by groups of people living together within a political boundary.[4]

People living in social groups economize by allocating limited resources among the vast array of alternatives that are human wants. Basically, an effective system of allocating resources must give quantitative answers to the following questions:

1. How much and what kind of productive (factor) services should be provided? Specifically, how many production workers, clerks, managers, doctors, teachers, and so on, are required to manufacture goods and furnish services?
2. Which enterprises shall obtain the different productive services?
3. How much of the total output of the economy should go to households for immediate use (consumption), and how much should be added to the stock of real capital (tools, machinery, and so on) for future productive effort?
4. How should the consumer goods be distributed (rationed) among consumers, and how should the additions to the stock of capital be parceled out among businesses?

History furnishes examples of what at first seem to be many different systems of allocating resources. Actually, there are two basic ways of directing the allocation process. One way is to have it centrally controlled, as in the Soviet Union, where a political commissariat makes the great decisions as to what part of the country's productive services will be devoted to providing consumer goods and services, what part will be used to make capital goods, what part allocated for space hardware, and so on. More detailed decisions are then made by lesser officials in the hierarchy, which may or may not respond to the wishes of consumers. Prices may be assigned to goods and services, but only for the purpose of keeping accounts and informing the planners.

In an enterprise economy, typified by that of the United States, the allocation of resources is accomplished by decisions made via the price system. On the one hand, households sell their services or the use of their property in the markets where resources are bought and sold, thus earning *incomes*. On the other hand, households are confronted with a battery of prices in the consumer market. The relationship between incomes and prices determines the levels of living both for individual households and for society. But in the growing, progressing American economy, choices are continuously being registered in the consumer market and telegraphed by price and quantity changes to the business sector, which reflects shifting consumer demands by changing its requirements for productive services.

---

[4] The term *economics* was not widely used until the 1870s. Before that time the expression in common use was *political economy,* a descriptive name that is once again becoming fashionable.

It would be a mistake to suppose that the price system performs its function simply by sending impulses from consumers to business. The business sector is continually at work to introduce new products and to innovate cost-reducing ways of making old ones, with resulting changes in consumer outlays. Moreover, through advertising the business community constantly strives to sway consumer preferences among goods and services and also between consumption expenditure and saving.

Indeed, the choices registered by both business managers and consumers are often made simultaneously, so that it is hard to say which decisions are causes and which effects. The important point to be comprehended is that through the pricing mechanism consumer and producer choices are translated into ultimate decisions about how resources shall be allocated. It is because prices are so vitally important that their study and observation is the chief preoccupation of the businessman and the academic economist.

In action, the American economic system is perhaps the most exciting and complex mechanism ever devised by Western civilization. Even in its most trivial manifestations the system ordinarily provides goods and services from all the parts of the world, as if by magic, just when and where they are needed. The everyday items that we all take for granted—our morning coffee and our evening newspaper, our ride to work and our television program at home, a telephone call to a friend or an air-mail letter to an office in New York—require the cooperative efforts of hundreds and even thousands of people plus the equipment with which they work. And when we wish to describe the system in all its intricate detail the task seems formidable to the point of impossibility.

At this point, the economist, like the physical scientist, must resort to theory—i.e., he must abstract from the reality of the world about him in order to see the fundamental forces at work. In devising his theories the economist encounters perplexing difficulties. Unlike the physical scientist, he cannot perform experiments in a laboratory, so he is unable to isolate and control certain variables. Nor can he get people, whose affairs are the subject of his inquiry, to submit to meaningful experimentation. So he has to fall back on the "laboratory of the mind." To get at the heart of his problems, he sets up a hypothetical model of an economy in which conditions are much simpler than those of the real world. After he has discovered central tendencies that he believes to operate in the real world, he removes his simplifying assumptions and calculates what the effect of their removal will be. For example, in ascertaining the forces that determine the price of a commodity, the theorist may assume that no changes in the value of money occur during the analysis. The assumption gets away from reality, but it greatly simplifies the problem. Later, in order to make a closer approximation to reality, the possibility of changes in the value of money may be introduced.

As long as the economist is concerned with perceiving a fundamental interplay of forces, he must construct a model, he must erect a framework.

Insofar as he abstracts from reality in order to discover principles, he is a theorist.[5]

But what does he theorize about? First, he examines the working of the mechanism by which resources are principally allocated—the _pricing system_, which (1) establishes the order of priority in which producers obtain resources and (2) rations goods among consumers. Thus, the central inquiry of economic theory has been to discover how the prices and quantities of goods are determined. In the past thirty-five years or so another problem— that of persistent and widespread unemployment of resources—has occupied the attention of economists, and a body of theory has developed to explain the paradox of idle men and idle equipment on the one hand and want on the other. To the classical theory of price, then, has been appended the theory of income and employment, an analysis that complements the theory of price determination, showing how unemployment of factors of production may exist in an economy where many people are unable to satisfy even their most pressing needs.

The broad subject of economic theory has been subdivided into a number of specialities. Some economists specialize in the theory of the firm, with its recent emphasis on problems of strategy and conflict. Others work full time at the study of monetary theory or devote their exclusive efforts to perfecting social accounting systems. Still others investigate the principles by which international trade is regulated, and there is an intricate theory of the determination of international exchange rates. But however the economist specializes, however he breaks down the job of analysis, the fact remains that there are two basic theoretical questions in economics: How are resources allocated under a market system? What forces determine the level of a nation's income?

Now whenever a subject has a body of theory, it will also have a body of applied knowledge. Thus, we often speak of "applied" or "concrete" economics. As Professor Boulding has put it, "Any subject such as economics which is 'empirical,' in the sense that it is interested in the interpretation of actual human experience, must have two parts: the construction of logical frameworks (the 'pure' subject) and the interpretation of reality by fitting the logical framework to the complex of empirical data (the 'applied' subject)." [6] There is thus a part of economics that deals with more "practical" matters. The worker in applied economics, like the theorist, has his fields of speciality. If he is an economic statistician, he compiles, organizes, and interprets current quantitative information. If he is an economic historian, he is largely concerned with the perception of change in

---

[5] We commonly hear the expression, "That's all right in theory, but it won't work in practice." This statement, if it makes sense at all, means, "If we grant your assumptions, what you say is true, but your assumptions are so abstract from reality that your analysis could never be of use in solving a real problem." If a theory is not right in practice, then the theory is wrong.

[6] Kenneth E. Boulding, "Samuelson's Foundations: The Role of Mathematics in Economics," _Journal of Political Economy_, LVI (June 1948), 190.

economic phenomena. If he is a practicing economic consultant, he furnishes policy-forming executives with business forecasts that will guide them in decision-making.

To be sure, an economist often wears two hats. He may be both theorist and problem solver, and some of the best workers in the vineyard are equally adept at constructing logical frameworks and fitting frameworks to the data. In general, though, there is a rough division of labor, economists with a theoretical bent tending to man college and university faculties while those in applied economics work on the staffs of government agencies and large business firms.[7] In government the demand for economic analysts comes largely from the Federal Reserve System, the Departments of Treasury and Commerce, and those two flourishing outfits in the Executive Office of the President—the Council of Economic Advisers and the Bureau of the Budget. Business economists, to use an expression in recent vogue, are largely employed by very large firms—of the size ordinarily found in *Fortune's* list of the top five hundred. Smaller firms are more and more coming to recognize the value of professional economic advice, but they usually get theirs on a fee basis from management consulting firms and free-lance university professors.

Wherever they work, economists rely on an almost universally accepted theoretical apparatus. The staffs of the United States Chamber of Commerce and the AFL-CIO use precisely the same definitions of the national income and product accounts. The Du Pont Company forecasts business conditions on the same basis as the Council of Economic Advisers—using data provided by Department of Commerce economists with the cooperation of the business community.

Economists are fond of saying that economics is not an exact science.[8] But neither is it guesswork. Social goals are subject to debate among economists just as they are among other occupational groups. But once he is furnished a consensus about objectives—about ends—the economist can offer, within tolerable limits of error, policy prescriptions calculated to achieve those objectives. In a word, economics is a way of thinking about the "unrelated confusion" of prices, production, and incomes that makes these phenomena intelligible and sufficiently well ordered to permit scientific prediction.

Like any scientist, the economist must ultimately answer the question: What *action* should be taken? Here an appeal must be made both to theory

---

[7] Exceptions to this generalization are economic historians, who for the most part are teachers and researchers located in the academic community, consulting on a fee basis to meet the limited market demand for their services.

[8] Economics, once a branch of "moral philosophy," had little claim to scientific status until the publication of Adam Smith's *Wealth of Nations* in 1776. For another century and a half, while economists were developing their theoretical propositions and giving them mathematical formulation, economics was on its way to being scientific. But only in the last generation or so have economists been able to attempt empirical verification of these propositions. Later, we shall have more to say about the similarities and dissimilarities among the social studies and the physical and biological sciences.

and to lessons of experience. Advisers to government officials and men of affairs cannot reason through the tangle that is the real world without some means of eliminating those facts that are least relevant. They must therefore make use of the organon of the theoretical economist. But any adviser with good sense must inevitably go back to a reading of the record. He must finally turn to economic history to check faults in reasoning and illumine paths to action.

HISTORY

The economic historian, as the name implies, is both economist and historian. As historian, what problems does he encounter? What are the trammels of historical research? Are the facts of history less securely established than the facts of the experimental sciences? To questions like these we must turn for a moment.

We use the word *history* almost every day, usually without being aware of its ambiguity. It has come to have a double meaning, for when we speak of history, we may refer to (1) the narrative of past events or (2) the events themselves. When we say, "Oh, that's past history," we are referring to events. When we say, "History proves that dictators are cruel men," we are referring to the record. The saw "Mankind makes history; historians make histories" emphasizes the dual meaning. Clearly, we are interested in the formal record. What shall we take as a working definition of the subject?

We may begin with the simple remark that history is the narrative statement of happenings in the past. But so spare an assertion does not get us very far for the simple reason that it fails to stress the terrible obligation of the historian—that he select from the whole of the known past the material for inclusion in his narrative. Another definition, perhaps too pretentious and formal for most purposes but one that points up the problem of fact selection, is the following: "History is man's formal record of actual human phenomena as consecutively manifested in the past insofar as they have been ascertained to be general, important, enduring, and true, with the legitimate deductions drawn for the pleasure and education of mankind." Note the key words: general, important, enduring, true. Obviously, history will not often be concerned with the lives of everyday individuals but with events that concern the community as a whole, events that in this sense have a high degree of importance. But who will judge the importance of these events? Why, the fact selector, of course.

So the historian, like the economist, is confronted with a jumble of facts that he must collect and put in the form of an intelligible, significant narrative. We get some notion of the difficulty of the task when we reflect that the historical fact is no longer in existence. It has happened and is gone. It can never be observed again. It can only be reconstructed from remaining evidence, chiefly in the form of documents of one sort or another, and much of the evidence is fragmentary and unreliable. But whatever the difficulties the historian must collect and organize his facts, interpret them in the light of modern interests, and present them in usable form.

It has been said that there are three phases of historical procedure. With the caution that we not jump to any conclusions about separating the historian's work into neat compartments, it may still be useful to consider these steps.

1. *Reconstruction of the historical fact.* Sometimes referred to as the "science of history," reconstruction of the historical fact may be done by people who do not write history at all—i.e., the basic researchers who nose around in attics and cellars, in court houses, in the records of business firms, and who publish their material in the form of collected letters and papers, memoirs, and journals. But no one has a monopoly of fact collection, and many historians who write at a high level of generalization, aided by scholars in sociology, political science, and anthropology, often contribute to knowledge of events.

2. *Writing the historical narrative—the "art of history."* The task is to assemble the facts so as to form a significant written record. It goes without saying that the historian must make a literary effort. Sometimes this effort is so successful that the result is a high art form. Thus, some of the towering historians—from Herodotus to Freeman—have made their mark as much because of their literary quality as because of their substantive contribution. Macaulay is still assigned in English literature classes, and many contemporary readers are even today moved by Gibbon. For a time the nineteenth-century emphasis on the literary quality of a historical work may have disappeared, but in recent years the really first-class historians have placed more stress on these values. The monograph of a young scholar, aimed at exhausting a subject of limited range, will almost surely be technical and unexciting. But at the other end of the scale, general histories, including popularizations, must cast their spell or be put aside in favor of a TV program or a summer novel.

3. *Interpretation of history—the "philosophy of history."* After the facts have been gathered and the narrative written, the record requires explanation in terms of general principles that appear to govern human conduct. The older historians sought to explain the flow of events by some grand, central motivation; they had an essentially *monistic* philosophy as opposed to the *pluralistic* philosophy of modern writers. The most common and best-known monistic theme was that history centered around political activity—about governments and the major phenomena of governments such as wars, legislative acts, and changes in rulers. College students can hardly escape familiarity with another monistic approach—the "great man" interpretation of Thomas Carlyle, who held that a few highly gifted human beings constitute the determining force in human affairs. In the nineteenth century the economic or materialistic view—that men determine the cultural, social, and political values of life while seeking to satisfy basic economic wants—gained a substantial following. There have been many other attempts

to find a single wellspring of human motivation, centering on psychology, spirituality, science or technology, the "creative mind," and geography. Gradually, however, modern historians have come to believe that the vast sweep of history cannot be explained in terms of one aspect of human activity. Modern historians take the pluralistic view that, in a physical environment more and more shaped and dominated by man himself, the human race progresses or retrogresses for a host of reasons.

But if history writing is only the result of a drastic sifting of evidence, can we ever be sure that the history we are reading is absolutely true? To this question we must make what at first seems a forlorn reply, that we can never be certain. From the tangled web of facts the historian must select some and discard others. Foremost historical scholars used to contend that the selection could be done on an "objective" basis. Yet one man's objectivity is another man's bias. No individual historian, however honorable, however magnificent his gift, can write outside the context of his own life and his own philosophy. He must include in his narrative those facts that *he* thinks are important in explaining changes that in *his* opinion are worth explaining. Whether we like it or not, history involves implicit theorizing.

Does this argument lead us to conclude that progress in historical knowledge is impossible? Of course not! History moves always toward greater clarification, to a deeper, fuller knowledge of what happened, and how, and why. This progress is possible because a succession of historians, dedicated to the job of seeking new insights and more logical explanations, endlessly rewrite history. It is this compulsion to take another look, to ask one more question, to perceive a little more clearly that makes history—in the sense of the narrative—a changing, vital subject.

ECONOMIC HISTORY

Economic history draws upon each of the two great disciplines just examined. If the general historian must go through a heroic process of selecting his material, an economic historian must winnow still further. So doing, he is not unmindful that an understanding of man's whole history is essential to a satisfactory explanation of his economic development. But most men and women interested in economics and business have not time to become historians besides. Yet they with other students of human behavior must have some clear idea of the way man has solved the age-old economic problem. Even more specifically, they may wish to know how and by what lights Americans have for more than three centuries allocated their resources. To this question the economic historian gives neither a final nor a complete answer. He nevertheless comes closest to being the specialist who can. To the patience and imagination of the historian he brings the discipline of economic theory and a certain expertness in dealing with quantitative information.

Long before there were specialists in economic history, economists were conscious of its uses. Much of Adam Smith's towering work was devoted to economic history and even to that special subject within economic history, the study of economic growth. Indeed, in the days before a national accounting system was forged, some of the great economists were forced back upon their historical knowledge to solve practical problems. Here we may recall David Ricardo's famed essay *The High Price of Bullion,* and his devastating *Reply to Bosanquet;* or reflect how, half a century later, William Stanley Jevons resolved one of the perplexing economic policy problems of the day in his *Serious Fall in the Value of Gold;* or think how, another fifty years later, Irving Fisher brought so much historical evidence to bear on the same problem in his *Purchasing Power of Money.*[9] Nor should we forget that economic history actually began, more than a century ago, as "historical economics": first, in the seminal works of a succession of gifted Germans— Wilhelm Roscher, Gustav Schmoller, Karl Knies, and finally Werner Sombart; and second, in the imaginative researches of four equally talented Englishmen—Thorold Rogers, T. E. Cliffe Leslie, William James Ashley, and Sir John Clapham.

Whatever the reasons, and they are many, the outcome of a century of inquiry in this amalgam of history and economics has been a separate field of study called economic history. We now turn to a sketch of the economic historian's work.

The Roles of the Economic Historian

As I see it, economic historians are committed to four main jobs. Some of them stick to one; others are versatile enough to tackle all four. Whatever the division of labor, someone must perform these several tasks.

1. *The traditional assignment of the economic historian is to explain changes in the* institutions *most closely connected with the business of getting a living.* In its simplest form, this work defines and describes markets, traces the behavior of sellers and buyers, and quantifies the outcome of their bargaining in time series of prices and production. But this mundane labor leads to a more exciting inquiry, the question why the present economic system and not some other should be the outcome of the past.

The working economist knows that scarcely a day passes without his having to rely on this contribution of the economic historian. Not long ago, having received an assignment from the Commission on Money and Credit, I stopped by the CMC offices in New York to discuss the proposed monograph. In the course of our conversation I asked what papers were to be furnished on the history of money and financial institutions; after all, the National Monetary Commission of two generations ago had contributed several volumes of historical material to the economist's shelves. I was informed, half in jest, that "the only history the Commission is interested in

---

[9] To see how well gifted analysts could solve problems with only rudimentary theoretical and statistical tools, students striking for an *A* might read one of the mentioned essays.

is what has happened since 1950." I thought nothing more of the conversation and went to work on my monograph about the federal lending agencies.

A few months later a telephone call from the CMC offices in New York brought an urgent request for assistance. At its most recent meeting, the full Commission had asked the head of one of its task forces to explain how the nonbank intermediaries had emerged. How, someone had asked, did life insurance companies, mutual savings banks, savings and loan associations, credit unions, and so on through the whole list of intermediaries, get their start? What were the impellents to growth of each type of institution? Did building and loan associations, for example, thrive because a few public-spirited citizens wanted to do something nice for small savers? Or was there a vulgar profit motive at work to cause these institutions to grow spectacularly in the post–World War II years? There were, of course, plenty of bits and pieces that treated these matters, and in the case of one or two of the intermediaries a full and sufficient history had been attempted. Yet no one had ever considered the question of the growth of the nonbank intermediaries as a whole. The best I could do in answer to this request was to deliver a memorandum, written hastily and without research, in less than a month. Yet even this sketchy and hastily prepared briefing provided helpful insights. Some history, in short, is better than none, though it goes without saying that a full treatment would have been much more helpful.

How did markets in mid-twentieth century perform in comparison with those of the Middle Ages? Was there ever really a kind of Golden Age of perfect competition? When did the concentration of manufacturing industry take place and why? Despite the growth of the large firm, has competition really changed from a day and age when there were many sellers of a manufactured product? Is it a change in the apparatus of competition that has led to a shifting relationship between the federal government and private economic institutions? Is our "mixed economy," which depends for a just allocation of resources largely on the price system, but partly on government, changing its mix? It is to questions of this sort that the economic historian has traditionally addressed himself.

2. *Perhaps the most fashionable subject in economics these past few years has been the study of economic growth.* The question of growth has always attracted economists, and the economic historian has considered the problem central to his own efforts.

In his presidential address before the Economic History Association, Professor Carter Goodrich wondered plaintively if the current theorists of economic growth, with their elegant analysis, had made history less important. He could quickly reassure himself. The methods of theory and of history are in this sense different: economic theory *abstracts* from reality; economic history undertakes a *selection* of variables from the complex that *is* reality. Economic theory builds models. The narrative of economic history, though admittedly a simplification, nonetheless reconstructs a world in which people live and breathe. Plainly, there are advantages of the historical method that are both intellectually satisfying and, for purposes of policy applications, more useful.

For one thing, growth theorists, by focusing almost exclusive attention on "take-off" and the variables that affect rates of change in a mature industrial economy, leave out for all practical purposes the great forces of change at work for centuries before "modern" economies emerged. To be sure, attention to the "preconditions," in Rostow's terminology, is not infrequent. But the preconditions treated by the growth theorists are almost invariably technological. Examining only science and technology, we are likely to forget the tremendous influences of art, sociology, and religion on the long course of economic events. More dangerous to our ultimate conclusions, if economic historians do not continuously re-examine the first historical interpretations, students are likely to be led into all sorts of foolish errors.

Let me cite some examples. Growth models certainly give no satisfactory explanation of the so-called rise of capitalism. Moreover, some historians have told us a lot of silly stories about the emergence of modern business, making up their own history much as economists for a century and a half made up their own psychology. Were we not told that the Renaissance was an influence on changing economies because with renaissance came interest in science and scientific applications? Yet there was really no economically significant science until well after the publication of Newton's *Principia* in 1687. Renaissance was important, yes, but for the reason that the reawakening whetted avarice by demonstrating that the best things in life are by no means free. Did not Max Weber, among others, teach that Calvinism provided capitalism with a religious rationale that, by implication at least, made this brand of Protestantism the most important single influence on the growth of "modern" economies? But the early Calvinists did not believe, as Weber asserted, in a concept of "calling" that made success in business evidence of God's blessing and thus of one's election. Quite the other way around, the early Calvinists were persuaded of the irreconcilability of God and Mammon, and only after a century and a half did they come around to a view of one's "calling" that did indeed fit the capitalist spirit. But this is only to say that what promotes growth is not any positive religious faith but a *waning of faith,* Catholic or Protestant, sufficient to permit the kind of unscrupulous conduct necessary to a powerful capitalism.[10]

In examining the problem of growth, economic history can make still another contribution not yet available from theory. Economic growth takes place within a certain social and political context. The forces that accelerated or retarded change are more likely to be discerned in their entirety

---

[10] Compare Max Weber, *The Protestant Ethic and the Spirit of Capitalism* (New York: Scribner's, 1930), with Winthrop S. Hudson, "The Weber Thesis Re-examined," *Church History,* XXX, 1 (March 1961), 88–99.

by the historian, and even the fortuitous events that played so important a part in the growth of the Western economies may be overlooked by those whose experience is largely contemporary. It would be difficult indeed to overlook the effects of World War II on such economic determinants of the postwar American economy as the rate of capital formation, the rate of saving, and the level of output. But how likely is the young theorist of today to reflect on some of the great chance happenings of the past that played an enormous part in promoting the economic growth of the United States by forcing it to gather its mid–nineteenth-century momentum?

Will he, for example, stop to think that the United States was founded after Europe had already made the change from medieval to modern times? Thus, many of the medieval rigidities (of the sort that plague the under-developed countries today) were removed, and scarcely any of them ever were transplanted. So the abundance of land not only enabled colonial Americans to feed themselves without huge drafts on their foreign exchange but made it largely unnecessary for them to throw off the shackles of feudal-istic restrictions on land tenure. Or will those who cast up the "fundamental equations" of growth stop to think that the United States was nurtured and sustained in its critical early years by the Napoleonic Wars, which stimu-lated the carrying trade of the young country, created foreign exchange to pay for capital imports, and swelled the mercantile fortunes that later sought investment outlet in the first American growth industry—cotton textiles?

More positively, economic history has lately progressed toward a unified, coherent historical narrative of the growth process. But now we are getting ahead of our story; to this matter we will return in Part Two.

3. *Economic history and its kindred subject, business history, serve to test the propositions of economic theory.*[11] Our observations about the procedures of economic theorizing caution against presuming too much for history as a testing ground of theorems, for it is impossible to isolate only the relevant historical variables. Yet a careful and judicious observa-tion of repeated phenomena may help us, with some confidence, to verify or refute propositions reached by abstract reasoning. It is in this context that economic history can offer its most valuable insights.

Economic historians of a generation and more ago were loath to accept responsibility for passing judgment on the cherished notions of the (then) contemporary theory. Today's crop of historians is not bashful about hold-ing theorems up to the white light of recorded experience. They are dis-covering, for example, that inflation is not inescapably and necessarily dis-astrous, that, quite the contrary, inflationary pressures are more often than not the signs, the symptoms, of prosperity. To be sure, a runaway inflation that destroys a value system and harms an economy is a catastrophe; but the

---

[11] At the moment a digression on the nature of business history would carry us far afield. Let us tentatively assume that business history is simply a speciality, focusing on the be-havior of the firm and its management, within the larger field of economic history. We shall have occasion to expand upon this point in later chapters.

economic historian can testify that such an inflation has occurred only once in American history—during the Revolutionary War. To take another example, it is plain enough that the combination movement in the United States was not the consequence of predatory seeking after monopoly power by robber barons; it was instead the inevitable result of legitimate defense against overcapacity and failure as small firms were bonded together in a single national market.

To make these and other judgments necessary to a wise public policy, the economic historian has to measure carefully instead of simply suggesting a rough balance of forces. To meet this need many younger men are writing a new kind of history, bringing to their generalizations a wealth of statistically reliable data obtained largely by diligent and systematic research into a hitherto neglected source of materials, the records of business firms. Thus where economic history once had to be content with "largely" and "mostly," it can oftentimes assert 60 per cent or 90 per cent.[12]

4. *Like every other historian, the specialist in economic history must at last confront his noblest task—the interpretation of the record he has forged.* Recognizing his inability to separate the economic system from the social whole, he must nonetheless assess the performance of that system in a world of conflicting ideologies. And finally he must give the best account he can of the mainsprings of the process of development, for more than half the peoples of the world require and wait on his special advice.

The scholar can never be an apologist for any social organization, nor can he honorably defend demonstrable failings of the system to which he bears allegiance. By the same token, a scrupulously fair examination of a country's economic development may be the most effective testimony to the justice and worth of its total social organization.

In the pages that follow is rewritten the history of the American economy. There would be no excuse for just another recounting of the same old facts and figures brought a few years up to a date that all too rapidly recedes into the past. There is a solid reason, though, for recasting the record, relieving it of its mythological overburden, hopefully to bear witness to the strength of a democracy that operates within the discipline of markets.

---

[12] Continuing reference will be made to works of this kind. Following are some outstanding examples: J. R. T. Hughes, *Fluctuations in Trade, Industry, and Finance* (Oxford: Clarendon Press, 1960); Lance E. Davis, J. R. T. Hughes, and Stanley Reiter, "Aspects of Quantitative Research in Economic History," *Journal of Economic History,* Vol. X, 4 (December 1960); L. E. Davis, "The New England Textile Mills and the Capital Markets: A Study of Industrial Borrowing 1840–1860," *Journal of Economic History,* Vol. XX, No. 1 (March 1960); William N. Parker, ed., *Trends in the American Economy in the Nineteenth Century,* No. 24 in Studies in Income and Wealth, National Bureau of Economic Research (Princeton: Princeton University Press, 1960); Harold F. Williamson and Arnold R. Daum, *The American Petroleum Industry* (Evanston: Northwestern University Press, 1961).

Part One:

Colonial Period

The Founding
of the Colonies

O young Mariner,
Down to the haven,
Call your companions,
Launch your vessel,
And crowd your canvas,
And, ere it vanishes
Over the margin,
After it, follow it,
Follow the Gleam.

TENNYSON

 "For the pleasing entertainment of the Polite part of Mankind, I have printed the most Beautiful Poems of Mr. Stephen Duck, the famous Wiltshire Poet," announced Fry, Stationer, Bookseller, Paper-Maker, and Rag Merchant, late of the City of London and now located in Boston. The advertisement, appearing in the Boston *Gazette*, May 1–8, 1732, was not an introductory offer, for the notice continued: "It is a full demonstration to me that the People of New England have a fine taste for Good Sense and Polite Learning, having already sold 1,200 of these Poems."

No doubt Fry was anxious to please and entertain the "Polite part of Mankind," possibly at a profit. But his advertisement contained another somewhat plainer matter that may have interested him more. It was "the common Method of the most curious merchants of Boston, to Procure their (accompt) Books from London," and Fry, for business reasons, took exception to the practice. He addressed the notice to all Gentlemen, Merchants, and Tradesmen. "This," he declared, "is to acquaint those Gentlemen, that I said Fry, will sell all sorts of Accompt-Books, done after the most accurate manner, for 20 per cent cheaper than they can have them from London."

That prepared "accompt" books, "done after the most accurate manner," were offered for sale at so early a date should occasion no more surprise than that the polite part of New England was entertained by the poems of Mr. Stephen Duck of Wiltshire. For in the beginning the American colonies were but a small part of a greatly expanded Europe—a western frontier, so to speak. The culture of the people—including double-entry bookkeeping as well as taste in poetry—was in many respects that of their former associates on the other side of the Atlantic.

Europeans migrated to the New World for many reasons. Some came because they were hired to go by statesmen or entrepreneurs at home, who variously sought great riches, the extension of Christianity, or the glory of the state. Some wished to escape the political and religious disturbances of western Europe, and others were motivated simply by a thirst for adventure, by an impelling desire to see and do new things. And, of course, there were always the unfortunates, ranging from felons to bums and tramps, who came because they were shipped over as criminals or involuntarily indentured servants.

A full and satisfactory explanation of the forces that sent the Portuguese, Spanish, Dutch, French, and English to the East and to the West, and that led eventually to the discovery of America, would require an extension in time and space beyond our compass. The major developments leading to European expansion during the fifteenth and sixteenth centuries have roots deep in the history of an earlier age; none is limited to the evolution of a social order in a particular country or on a particular continent. The area of study that would serve as an introduction to American economic development includes, at a minimum, all of western Europe and the fringes of the Mediterranean. But we are confronted with the practical problem of compressing American economic history within a few hundred pages. Although a full treatment would require a description of the economic life of Europe in the Middle Ages, we shall have to be content with only the briefest sketch before we outline the opening of the New World.

Medieval Europeans

Rome, an academic wag has remarked, petered out rather than fell. During the fifth century, as the western part of the vast empire disintegrated, its concentration of power diffused among a group of large landholders, Europe began a centuries-long existence in narrow, segmented compartments. The chief characteristic of medieval Europe was its insularity, its pathetic isolation into small political and economic units.

The span of history we call the Middle Ages stretched over more than a thousand years from the fifth to the fifteenth centuries. The longer historians examine this millennium, the more they are impressed with the fact that only carefully qualified generalizations fit the life of the times, and even the broadest generalizations are open to exceptions. Medieval economic life varied enormously from century to century, and, at any point in time, from place to place. The Dark Ages, roughly the first half of this thousand years, were never really as dark as historians once thought them to be. By the same token, the high Middle Ages, even in their most exciting manifestations of emerging culture and burgeoning trade, offer a drab and dingy comparison with western Europe of today. Nevertheless, this thousand years was marked by progress: by slow, inexorable change from political segmentation and chaos to strong national states, from almost complete cessation of commercial intercourse among the peoples of the West to a thriving, vigorous trade, and by the emergence of a middle class with means enough to afford a lively, cultural life.

Most characteristic of the first centuries of the medieval period—the Dark Ages, if you wish—was the nearly complete absence of intellectual endeavor. The world of the early Middle Ages was populated with demons, goblins, devils, werewolves—all kinds of supernatural beings—who lay waste the land, brought physical catastrophe on the people, aided thieves and seducers, and in general wreaked havoc. There was no thought, to use Muller's expression, worthy of the name of heresy. The Dark Ages lightened as men began to reason with integrity. When, square in the middle of the thirteenth century, Saint Thomas Aquinas brought rational criticism to bear on the doctrine of the Roman Catholic Church, religion itself was forced to deal with the truths of the physical world. Yet anything like a body of experimental, scientific inquiry was still a way off. Even that first flowering of man's cultural and artistic genius, the Italian Renaissance, gave little promise of a world of intellectual discipline. For the most part, intellectual renaissance simply meant reviving old errors, those of an ancient past, and such thought as we observe was little more than hunch, the organized impressions of men who looked casually about them and reported what they saw. But art—art as literature, art as sculpture, and art as painting—testified to Western man's aspirations for himself, both here and hereafter.

Like its art, the rest of medieval life was infused with Christian doctrine and teaching. It is trite to remark that Christianity was the great motivating force in Europe of the Middle Ages. The cynical may attribute the power of Christianity to an age of superstition, in which there had to be some antidote for omnipresent demons. It is nearer the truth to say that, in spite of an environment of fear and physical discomfort, men achieved in the Roman Church a spiritual quality that manifested itself in something more than the wonderful Gothic cathedrals—in a religious exaltation that fired and expanded secular life. The world of the Middle Ages witnessed Christianity in apogee; the Virgin would never again be revered as in the thirteenth century, nor would the tenets of Christianity again have such influence on the affairs of the world.

This influence is well known, but a word about it may be helpful to an understanding of the economic life of the Middle Ages. With the decline of the Roman Empire, the material as well as the spiritual power of the Church grew. During the ensuing centuries it became a great landholder, certainly the largest in Spain and what is now France. Receipts, at first in produce, became money income as the years went on, and after 1000 A.D. the papacy became the focus of the Church's economic strength. Abbot or bishop might be lord of a manor, as much a lord as a knight or baron or duke, but the lowliest priest had sanctions that no one else, not even the most exalted lay lord, could command. For in the Middle Ages Christian followers had no doubts about a real Heaven and a real Hell. They could hear angel voices and smell brimstone.

So it happened that clergy could enforce the benign form of price control known as "just price." In the Dark Ages, perhaps as late as the twelfth century in some places, just price was considered by ecclesiastical authorities to be a quality inherent in a good, a quality incorporated largely as a consequence of the quantity of labor required to produce it. As time went on, the notion of just price became far more sophisticated; indeed, by the fourteenth century it came pretty close to being what we would call a competitive price, one determined in a free market by the forces of supply and demand.[1] But whatever the time or the place, just price was meant to prevent the exercise of monopoly power by sellers who might take advantage of crop failure, shipwreck, or any other interference with the supply of a commodity. A special corollary of just price, the proscription against usury (i.e., *any* charge for the use of borrowed money) was intended to prevent the worst kind of exploitation—the charging of interest on a loan for consumption purposes, a loan that might be intended to preserve life itself. But even with regard to interest-taking, the market place imposed on the Church a more realistic view as time went on. Toward the end of the Middle Ages it was legitimate to charge interest so long as the purpose of the loan was for production rather than consumption. By 1300 both clergy and laity were knowledgeable enough to know that money was not necessarily "sterile," that it represented a command over capital goods which could in turn yield a handsome return. It was still immoral for a Christian to take interest from one who needed succor for himself or his family; it was quite another matter

---

[1] Thus as early as the thirteenth century Saint Albert Magnus could write that ". . . the just price is what a commodity may be worth according to the estimation of the market at the time of the contract." A little later, John Duns Scotus remarked that ". . . [the merchant] can justly receive a price corresponding to his trouble or industry beyond what is required for his own needs and the support of his family, and thirdly, beyond this something to cover his risks." Hear also what San Bernardine of Siena said a century later: "If, however, I am asked what price is just in buying or in selling, I answer: the just price is the one set according to the estimation of the current market, that is, according to what the goods sold are worth commonly at present in the market." But note further! "It is not licit to trade by taking into consideration the circumstances of the person with whom one deals and to sell wares dearer to wayfarers than to merchants or residents, dearer to rustics or ignorants than to well-informed citizens, or dearer to the simple than to the astute." Students wishing to write a paper on the intricacies of the rule of just price may see Saint Thomas Aquinas, *Summa Theologica*, Part II, Question LXXVII (London: Burns Oates & Washbourne, 1929), Vol. I, p. 747.

Lorenzo de Medici (as shown in Verrocchio's terra cotta bust) was the archetype of Renaissance man. Patron of Leonardo and Michelangelo and himself a poet, Lorenzo brought Florence to the peak of its economic power in the latter half of the fifteenth century.

if the borrowing was to turn a profit of 200 or 300 per cent in a single voyage.

The doctrine of just price may have inhibited economic activity for a time. It can be argued, on the other hand, that some form of price control was essential in a pre-capitalistic economy and that the rule of just price, by preventing injustice and oppression, gently nurtured a budding market system.[2] Furthermore, we should be naive to overlook the fact that in the most Catholic part of Europe—the Italian trading cities—the fortunes of banking families like the Rapondi, Peruzzi, Frescobaldi, and Medici swelled long before the end of the Middle Ages, largely on fat loan rates of 20 per cent and more.

What men think is often as important as what they do. Yet we delude ourselves when we read into philosophic or religious doctrine motivations that are simply not there.[3] It is perfectly clear that a "capitalist spirit"—or,

---

[2] The late Father Dempsey, with whom I used to discuss this point, took a much stronger position, arguing that "free" prices are possible only in a "system of individualism" that has existed for less than two centuries and is even now being strongly contested. See Bernard W. Dempsey, "Just Price in a Functional Economy," *The American Economic Review,* XXV, 3 (September 1935), 471–86.

[3] I do not mean to deny entirely the influence of the Protestant Revolt on the thought and attitudes of western Europeans. Moreover, I commend to beginning students a reading of the distinguished Tawney and Weber essays, for I remember with what pleasure and intellectual excitement I first received these great books. The fact remains that Weber began from a questionable premise, that men cannot be primarily motivated by desire for material things in the absence of some fundamental ethical formulation, such as Calvinism. And Tawney, as much as anyone else, makes it clear that the profit motive was at work long before Luther and Calvin were even born. In any case, compare Max Weber, *The Protestant Ethic and the Spirit of Capitalism* (New York: Scribner's, 1930) and Richard H. Tawney, *Religion and the Rise of Capitalism: A Historical Study* (New York: Harcourt, Brace & World, 1926).

more plainly, a deep-rooted desire to secure more of this world's goods and services—erupted in many places of western Europe at least three centuries before the Reformation as customarily defined. So much nonsense has been written about the influence of the Protestant Revolt on the rise of capitalism, that it is easy to overlook its more readily demonstrable effects: (1) the break-up of the vast church estates, the weakening of the system of tithing, and the distribution of church properties among lay lords, and (2) the shifting and moving of Protestants, persecuted or not, to different parts of the world.[4]

One of the changes that medieval man wrought was to increase the size of the political unit by which he governed himself. For one thing, the manor, that inefficient economic unit and unjust political unit, was disappearing by the middle of the thirteenth century. So crude a way of organizing society must have vanished sooner or later, but the waves of famine and pestilence that swept Europe during the first half of the fourteenth century, culminating in the Black Death of 1348, hastened the end of the manorial system. For as great numbers of peasants were killed by disease, the remainder could demand and get commutation of the old feudal payments in *kind* into *money* payments, and additional help could only be attracted by offering money wages. With the monetization of seignorial obligations, manorial organization could not endure. Whether the old feudal services were converted into *fixed* or *variable* sums of money payments, the lord of the manor sooner or later found rents and money dues lagging behind his cash requirements. By contrast, the merchant class in the increasingly large towns and cities could always adjust the prices of what they sold to their costs and so found a market system much more to their liking.

As the aristocracy were compelled to accept their land holdings as sources of cash revenue instead of a living in kind, they had to organize them better for growing cash crops and livestock. So began, as early as the thirteenth century, the "enclosure" of the common lands and the landlords' share of the arable land. The enclosure movement, though especially notable in England, was characteristic of many parts of continental Europe and continued, in waves, into the nineteenth century. Its effects were to make for a more efficient agriculture and a great landless agricultural proletariat, furthering the breakdown of the manorial system, providing a redundant supply of labor for industry and trade, and encouraging larger political units.

Often, the units that emerged were transitory and only larger territorial areas over which a noble, perhaps an aspirant to kingship, exercised an effective rule. The crucial achievement from the view of economic history was the ultimate creation of national states, large enough to permit a more efficient allocation of resources. A state might finally come into being with the eviction of a foreign ruler, as when Portugal and then Spain rid them-

---

4 Recent research suggests that even this effect was not as great as once thought. See, for example, Warren Candler Scoville, *The Persecution of Huguenots and French Economic Development, 1680–1720* (Berkeley and Los Angeles: University of California Press, 1960).

selves of the Moorish power, or when Holland established its independence of Spain and Denmark withdrew from Sweden. Or the state might be created through harsh, unceasing efforts of a powerful nobility to subject ecclesiastical and feudal jurisdictions to royal decrees and courts, as in France. Or the unification of a country, as in England, might be the consequence of a persistent competition among strong lords which, leading to ever more powerful coalitions, culminated in the ultimate power—a single king of the realm. To be sure, at least two major groups—the German and Italian—remained atomized for several centuries and for this reason came late into the struggle for colonies. But Portugal, Spain, Holland, France, and England, achieving their unity early, thereby obtained the resources to compete vigorously in the world arena.

Whatever weight we assign to religious and political forces, and however willing we may be to include in our considerations a changing faith in God and a shifting loyalty to kings, we must conclude that the forces compelling the ultimate replacement of feudalism by a market system were economic. When in the depths of the Dark Ages western Europe was ringed by hostile barbarians and the forces of Islam, Jewish traders made their slow and painful way over trails and paths to bring goods from the East and Near East to Kiev, whence German traders took them westward to those who could afford them.[5] In the darkest times the cities of southern Italy—Amalfi, Bari, Naples, Salerno, and Carindo—maintained (as outposts, we might say, of Constantinople) a vigorous trade, making terms with the Saracens and even calling at their ports. And only a little later the giant of the medieval trade, Venice, became so rich that her merchants, with the textile makers and bankers of Florence, could accumulate the resources necessary to a gestating capitalism. By the twelfth century towns in the west of Europe had expanded beyond the bounds of their old Roman walls and were spilling over into surrounding countryside. At strategic places—where rivers or trade routes joined and where defense was facilitated—new towns and cities sprang up, largely to meet the increasing money demand for products that only city dwellers could provide.

Strongest of the economic drives of the merchants of Europe was the necessity of maintaining open routes with the East. Europe had always been dependent upon Asia for luxury goods and for what to medieval Europeans came close to being necessities. Spices were used with almost unbelievable liberality by medieval cooks, whose fashion it was to embellish the flavor of monotonous food with pepper, cloves, ginger, nutmeg, and cinnamon. Where wild honey was the only local sweetener, sugar from North Africa and the Levant was in great demand. And though the drugs of those times were by no means infallible, some of them probably being worse than none at all, such relief as man might get from his ailments came largely from Asia. Some products essential to the growing textile industries of the West

---

[5] See J. Brutzkus, "Trade with Eastern Europe, 800–1200," *Economic History Review*, XIII, 1 and 2 (1943), 31–41.

Commercial splendor: Venice (here rendered by Caneletto) was almost as much an Eastern as a Western city, and for hundreds of years her commercial and naval power was a great sustaining force of Western civilization.

—chiefly dyestuffs and chemicals for fixing colors—were imported from the East. But most important were manufactured products, far superior in quality to anything available in Europe, that made up the flow of goods from East to West. Some items, like the lovely cottons and silks of India and China and the rugs of Persia, carried well; others, like glass from Damascus and porcelain from China, were likely to break and, upon their safe arrival, were prized indeed by the well-to-do of Europe.

As long as trade had to be over land, Europe could offer only products that would carry safely and that had a high value relative to their weight and bulk; woolen textiles and certain metals and minerals like arsenic, quicksilver, and copper were suitable for trade. But not until sea transportation opened the possibility of further exports to the East could the balance of payments be close to even. For this reason, gold and silver continuously drained eastward.

The three great land routes to the East ended at various points on or near the Mediterranean Sea, which continued to be the center of European medieval commerce. Recognizing the inexorable and ceaseless demand by Europeans for the products of the East and reflecting on the really formidable difficulties of transporting a sufficient variety of exports over land routes, we can see why the discovery of a sea route became inevitable as soon as a country emerged powerful enough to engineer it. Under the vigorous and imaginative leadership of Prince Dom Enrique, whose Naval Arsenal at Sagres was a fifteenth-century Cape Canaveral, Portugal from 1415 to 1460 sent one expedition after another down the western coast of Africa. Although his sailors never did find Prester John, whose mythical Christian land was as important to Henry as the passage around the southern tip of Africa, the probing researches of the Portuguese nonetheless opened new sea lanes, tapped the wealth of West Africa, and developed the caravel, a ship rugged enough to sail anywhere.

The Expanding Nations

The great bursting forth from Europe took place within a little less than thirty-five years. In 1488 Bartolomeu Dias of Portugal rounded the Cape of Good Hope and would have reached India had not a mutinous crew forced him back. In September of 1522 the *Vittoria,* last of Magellan's fleet of five ships, put in at Seville; in a spectacular achievement eighteen Europeans had circumnavigated the globe. Between these two dates there were two other voyages of no less importance. The Genoese sea captain, Cristoforo Colombo, certain that it was no more than 2,500 miles from the Canary Islands to Japan, persuaded the Spanish sovereigns, Ferdinand and Isabella, to finance his first trip. On October 12, 1492, his lookout sighted the little island of San Salvador in the Bahamas. Only a few years later Vasco da Gama, sailing for the Portuguese, reached Calicut in India via the Cape of Good Hope, to return in 1499. The early pattern was thus set, with Portugal dominant in the East and Spain supreme in the West. Even in these early years other nations were stimulated to similar efforts, but there were no immediate results of importance. Another Genoese, Giovanni Caboto, sailing for Henry VII of England, reached Newfoundland in 1497, but the English were not yet ready to profit from his discoveries. Not long after the survivors of Magellan's expedition returned home, Verrazano explored the eastern coast of North America for France, and Jacques Cartier, in the 1530s, brought back to France the first detailed information about the St. Lawrence River. But the French, like the English, were too pre-occupied with affairs at home to undertake important adventures abroad before the beginning of the seventeenth century.

After a halting start, the Spaniards established colonies on the islands of the Caribbean and then began their explorations of the mainland. Within a century after Columbus returned from his fourth voyage in 1504, the Spaniards had conquered Central America and much of the continent of South America and had explored what is now the southern United States from South Carolina to California. After the conquest of Mexico by Cortez in 1521, American treasure flowed in ever increasing quantities into Spain. When, in 1580, the Spanish king, Philip II, made good his claim to the throne of Portugal, Spanish prestige reached its zenith. Two great empires, strong in the Orient and unchallenged in the Americas, were now joined. When we reflect that no other country had as yet a single permanent settler in the New World, the gradual decline of Spanish power, so soon to begin, seems astonishing.

Spain was a colonizer, but Spanish activity in the Americas lacked a solid foundation. Spain was a country remarkably poor in resources; in the sixteenth century she had a population estimated at only 7,000,000 or 8,000,000. The main interest of the *Conquistadores* and of the rulers at home was in treasure. To be sure, there were attempts to extend agriculture and to establish manufactures in the New World, but the Spaniards remained a ruling caste, dominating the natives who did the work and holding them in political and economic bondage. Throughout the sixteenth century Spain received the output of American mines and a swelling tide of other products, including copper, dyes, hides, and naval stores, and the preoccupation of the home government was to assure as little export leakage as possible. When, toward the end of the century, Spain became involved in war with the English and began to dissipate her energies in a futile attempt to bring the Low Countries under complete subjection, she lost the advantage of being the first to expand. Even more harmful than the wars, however, was the falling off in imports of gold and silver that began after 1600 with the exhaustion of the better grade ores.[6] Spain remained strong for years and a major power for two centuries, but the future lay in the hands of the Dutch, the French, and the English.

As Spain declined Holland achieved the ascendancy. At first a nation of fishermen, she began in the sixteenth century to extend her trade to Scandinavia and the Baltic. She then turned southward and by 1600 had sent several expeditions to the East. The Dutch East India Company, started in 1602, quickly gained the ascendancy in the Spice Islands and nudged the Portuguese aside. By 1650 Holland was the chief shipping, trading, and financial nation of Europe. Her pre-eminence, however, lasted hardly a century. In large part it was the old story of too small a resource base at home and too much emphasis on the establishment of trading posts rather than colonies. In the East Indies the policy of cruel exploitation adopted by the Dutch East India Company resulted in fantastic profits, which for nearly two centuries bolstered Holland as a great entrepôt and money market. Unfortunately, the East Indian empire did not provide the strength needed in a world where, as Professor Heaton has remarked, "coal and iron were more important than spices and herrings." Yet the Netherlands' fall

---

[6] Professor Earl J. Hamilton assures me that stocks of gold and silver accumulated by the Indians were minute compared with the product of mines operated with European techniques. See Earl J. Hamilton, *American Treasure and the Price Revolution in Spain, 1501–1650* (Cambridge: Harvard University Press, 1934).

from eminence was not so much a matter of slipping back as being overtaken by two other countries with greater resources.

As it turned out, France and England became the chief competitors in the centuries-long race for supremacy. From 1608, when Champlain established Quebec, France successfully undertook explorations in America westward to the Great Lakes area, and by the end of the century had pushed southward down the Mississippi Valley to Louisiana. And in the Orient, though a latecomer, France for a time competed successfully with the English after the establishment of the French East India Company in 1664. In less than a century, however, the English defeated the French in India, as they would one day do in America. The English triumphed in both India and America because they had the most extensive permanent settlements. It is not without significance that at the beginning of the French and Indian War in 1756 there were some 60,000 French settlers in Canada as against 2,000,000 in the English colonies.

From our special point of view the most important feature of the expansion of Europe was the steady and persistent growth of settlement in the British colonies of North America. Why should the English have been so successful in their colonization? Some of the forces that impelled Englishmen to move to the new land were the same as those that motivated the nationals of other countries. There was the persistent notion that somewhere a passage to the East might be found. While the search was going on it would be helpful to have outposts to serve as bases of operations. To the English, no less than to other Europeans, the hope of finding gold and silver in America was ever present; or, if the precious metals were not to be found, then the exotic country might at least furnish spices, naval stores, wines, sugar, fur, dyes, and the other commodities that England had to import. But the English had additional strong motives that were either insignificant or nonexistent in other colonizing countries.

Unlike the leaders in some western European countries, certain Englishmen saw clearly that true colonies would eventually become important markets for the manufactures of the mother country. Toward the end of the sixteenth century this consideration became important to England. During the century her foreign trade had passed largely from the hands of foreigners into those of her own merchants. Especially significant had been the growth in exports of English woolens, paid for by her best customer, Spain, with the gold and silver that came from Mexico and Peru. But Spain became an enemy, and the need for new markets was pressing.

It was not enough, though, that merchants and statesmen should apprehend the advantages of thriving colonies. Somehow or other, common men had to be persuaded of the benefits, to them and their families, of emigration. The biggest push came from a desire to own land, still the European symbol of status and economic security, and to strive for a higher level of living than would be conceivable at home for any but the best-paid artisans. To the economic was often added a religious motivation. Unlike the Spanish,

Englishmen did not come to these shores to convert the heathen; but the New England settlers in particular wanted to worship as they saw fit, provided, of course, that those around them were of similar persuasion. In their zeal they put themselves and their families squarely into the productive process—for the most part as actual participants instead of supervisors of peons. And once a cadre of able leaders arrived in America the future of settlement was assured, for they fortuitously colonized the part of the New World that was incomparably superior to every other in climate and natural resources.

The Beginnings of Settlement

The material to be covered in the next few pages will for many be old ground, but it is well, as we start, to remind ourselves of the first facts of American history. We begin then with a brief narrative of the establishment of the colonies. All save one had their beginnings in the seventeenth century. They came into being as the result of two great waves of activity—one in the first half of the century, the other in the second half. Let us consider these waves separately, taking first the years to 1660 and then those from 1661 to 1733.

LAYING THE FOUNDATIONS, 1606–1660

Two half brothers, Sir Humphrey Gilbert and Sir Walter Raleigh, were the first Englishmen to undertake serious ventures in America. Gilbert, one of the earnest seekers after a northwest passage, went to Newfoundland in 1578 and again in 1583, but in both instances he was forced by many difficulties to give up his attempts at colonizing. In fact, Sir Humphrey lost his life on the return voyage to England after the second attempt. Raleigh, like Gilbert, was granted the right to settle in "Virginia" and to have control of the land within a radius of two hundred leagues from any colony that he might successfully establish. He actually placed two groups on the new continent. The first, which landed on the Island of Roanoke off the coast of what is now North Carolina, stayed less than a year; anything but enthusiastic about their new home, these first colonists went back to England with Sir Francis Drake in the summer of 1586. Undaunted, Raleigh solicited the financial aid of a group of wealthy Londoners, and in the following year sent his second contingent of one hundred and fifty people under the leadership of Governor John White. He had given explicit instructions that this colony was to be planted somewhere on Chesapeake Bay, but Governor White disregarded the order and landed at Roanoke. White went back to England for supplies, and when he returned after much delay in 1590, the settlers had vanished. Not a single member of the famed "lost colony" was ever found.

As long as the war with Spain continued there was little likelihood of arousing much interest in further American adventures. But with the death

Exploration: Spain and Portugal came first, then France and Holland. All ranged far in their searches, but England's later (and more modest) explorations gave rise to the most extensive permanent settlements.

of Elizabeth in 1603, the war with Spain came to an end, and Englishmen were better disposed toward venturing in a hemisphere still dominated by Spaniards. It was not long before two companies were organized for the purpose of exploring and exploiting America. In 1606 two charters were granted these companies—one to a group of Londoners and the other to merchants of the western port towns, of which Plymouth was the most important. The London Company was given the right to settle the southern part of English territory in America, and the Plymouth Company was given jurisdiction in the northern part.

So in 1607 two widely separated colonies were established, one at Sagadahoc, near the mouth of the Kennebec River in what is now Maine, the other in modern Virginia.[7] Those who survived the winter in the northern colony gave up and came home, but the colony at Jamestown became the first permanent English settlement on this continent.

Virginia. The venture nearly failed in its first years, but with the granting of a new charter in 1609 the Virginia Company was established on a firmer basis; at least there was sufficient financial backing to enable it to secure a hold. By issuing stock in the venture, its promoters were able to raise "a capital." Those who agreed to go as laborers to the new country were counted as contributing to the enterprise the value of one share of stock (£12 10s.); anyone possessing special skills might be given more than one share. It was possible for an individual to go out on a wage basis, but by far the greater number of colonists preferred the chance of participating in the profits. The project was to be run on a corporate basis for the first seven years after 1609, with all property to be divided at the end of the period share and share alike. The affairs of the company in England were guided by a treasurer and a stockholders' council with a deputy, called the governor, to be the chief officer in the colony.

If those who first came over had hopes of striking it rich, they were quickly disappointed. Gold was nowhere to be found, nor was it possible at once to produce in quantity the products so much in demand in Europe. And the individuals who made up the first contingents were not of the sort to be content with the vague possibility of gain in some distant future. Generally speaking, they were ne'er-do-wells, if not former criminals, and the harshest discipline was needed to get any work done at all.

The Virginia Colony would have failed shortly if a satisfactory export commodity had not been found. Fortunately, in 1613 tobacco seed was brought in from the West Indies, and it grew well. Here was the ideal cash crop. Virginia climate and soil were suited to its culture. It could be grown successfully by anyone equipped with the simplest tools, on land from which stumps had not been removed. The market for it in England was insatiable,

---

[7] At this time the name *Virginia* referred to all the territory claimed by the English on the North American continent. These early charters indicate that the area lay between the thirty-fourth and forty-fifth parallels, roughly between the southern portion of the Carolinas and the northernmost boundary of modern New York.

and its value was high relative to its bulk, so that the transportation problem was minimized. In 1617 perhaps 20,000 pounds of tobacco were shipped to England, a quantity that more than doubled in the next year. By this time a permanent settlement in America was assured; for though the Company itself was not a profitable operation, trade between Virginia and England amounted to some £100,000 in 1618.

Even before the end of the period of corporate effort it became the practice to allow the colonists to own small pieces of land. In 1618 the Company began to grant "headrights." Under the headright system a person emigrating at his own expense was given title to fifty acres of land for himself and an additional fifty acres for each person—man, woman, or child—whose transportation he paid. In the same year the Company ordered its governor to guarantee to the colonists the same protection of the law given Englishmen at home, and steps were taken to give the new Americans some participation in their own government.

Ironically, efforts of the Company to diversify activity in Virginia led to its undoing. The expense of enlarged undertakings was greater than past receipts or future prospects would justify. In 1625 legal proceedings to secure its dissolution were successful. In that year Virginia became a Crown colony.

Maryland. Although it breaks the chronology of events, we must here mention the founding of Virginia's sister colony, Maryland. Similar in soil and climate to the older province, Maryland's early economic life was not far different. Her colonization, however, was "proprietary" rather than "corporate." Like Gilbert and Raleigh before him, Sir George Calvert, first Lord of Baltimore, wanted a domain of his own. Failing to establish a colony in Newfoundland, he settled in Virginia, only to be asked to leave because he was a Roman Catholic. Calvert then asked Charles I for a tract of land in Virginia, a favor that the king could grant since the Company was no longer in control. In 1632, while the patent was being prepared, George Calvert died, but the grant was made to his son, Cecilius, the second Lord Baltimore. It was a huge piece of territory, extending originally from the mouth of the Potomac to New England. (A later gift to William Penn reduced it.) By the terms of the charter the proprietor could dispose of the land as he chose, the only restrictions on his power being the requirements that (1) the laws governing the colonists be in agreement with English law and that (2) the colonists be allowed to elect a legislative body in the new country.

The first group of colonists settled at St. Mary's in 1634. Although it was originally planned that Maryland would be primarily a refuge for Roman Catholics, it turned out that the rank and file of newcomers were largely Protestant. However, the large tracts of land were given for the most part to wealthy men of the Roman faith, a division that was to cause trouble later. As in Virginia, the staple crop was tobacco; consequently, Maryland's growth, except in the mountainous western part of the colony, paralleled that of her sister colony.

Massachusetts. The most familiar episode in American history is the story of the coming of the Pilgrim Fathers. This movement into New England has a special appeal largely because it was set in motion by high idealism. But the profit motive played its part; in fact, the successful colonization of the unattractive northern area would have been impossible without strong economic drives. Nevertheless, the key force was the Puritan migration.

Although the Church of England had gone through a Reformation of sorts during the sixteenth century, it remained, nearly a hundred years after Henry VIII broke with Rome, far from a "protestant" church. As modern Episcopalians are careful to point out, the Church *in* England had simply become the Church *of* England. There had certainly been no basic religious change such as Luther, Calvin, and Knox had wrought elsewhere. Yet there were in England many people who objected to the formalism of the Anglican liturgy, to the episcopal form of church government, and to the lack of concern of many parish priests for the welfare of their flocks. These people in the Church of England who insisted upon further reform were called Puritans. They were "puritanical," too, in the usual present-day sense of the word. In part they wanted to change the externals of church worship, but they were also interested in changing the moral tone of English society. This could be done, they felt, only by carrying the word of God to the people through education and vigorous preaching. The zest with which the dissenters approached their task was bound to arouse the bitter antagonism of orthodox believers. Persecution of the Puritans was bad under pious James I, the successor to Queen Elizabeth and the first of the Stuart kings. Under his son, Charles I, it became worse.

During James's reign in 1608 one group of Puritans, finding life in England intolerable, moved to Leyden in Holland. Religious freedom was found there, but life in a land of strange speech and customs was far from satisfactory. After more than ten years of exile the group applied to the Virginia Company for permission to establish a plantation in Virginia. Although the permission was obtained, it was decided for financial reasons to use the patent or public land-grant of a group of English merchants who agreed to put money into the venture. A joint-stock company was formed to carry out the proposed colonization, and the London merchants who held a large part of the stock, as well as a majority of the people who sailed on the *Mayflower,* had great hopes of financial success. As in the earlier settlement at Jamestown, all property was to be held in common for at least seven years, with a division to be made at the end of that time. There was thus a definite commercial motivation for the settlement, but it was not the paramount drive. The religious fervor of the Pilgrims provided the original impetus for the enterprise and later gave it direction and spiritual vigor.

Inadvertently, the little band landed in 1620 on the bleak Massachusetts coast, far north of its destination. Because the patent had been for a plantation in Virginia, it was necessary to arrange for another under the old Plymouth Company, reorganized as the Council for New England. It shortly

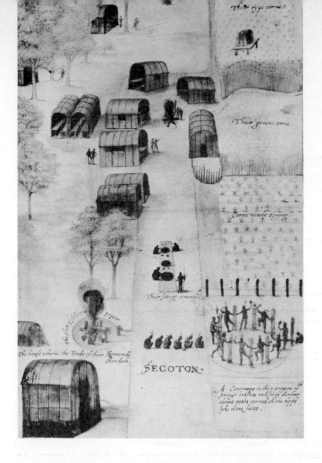

English colonists found the agricultural techniques of the Indians useful in establishing a foothold in the new continent.

became apparent that hopes of immediate and considerable profit would not materialize, and in 1626 the Pilgrims agreed to buy up the stock held by shareholders living in England.

The Plymouth Colony grew slowly and was important only as a vanguard of the New England colonists. It was to the Massachusetts Bay Company, formed in 1629, that the northern area of settlement owed a rapid and substantial growth. Under the leadership of able John Winthrop the Massachusetts Bay Colony was successful from the first. Within a year after receipt of its charter the Company had sent more than a thousand people to New England. Of the 65,000 Englishmen who came to America and the West Indies during the decade of the 1630s, some 20,000, mostly Puritans, emigrated to New England.[8]

What chiefly distinguished the Massachusetts Colony from earlier colonies was its almost complete freedom from old ties. The Massachusetts Bay Company and its charter were actually transferred to America, and very nearly complete independence from England was thus achieved. The governor, deputy governor, and "assistants" were elected by the stockholders in the colony, and these elected officials ran affairs without any interference

[8] Bernard Bailyn, *The New England Merchants in the Seventeenth Century* (Cambridge: Harvard University Press, 1955), p. 16.

from abroad. For the first time, an American group could seek its own destiny.

Of Massachusetts economic life we need say little now, but it may be well to mention here the northern system of land tenure. As the influx of people became greater, little groups from a particular locality in England tended to settle together. They would petition the General Court for a grant of land and form a "town," with a village in the center surrounded by arable fields and common woods and meadows. Such grants, sometimes as much as forty square miles in area, normally lay immediately adjacent to previously settled land, and in the North the custom grew of pushing back the frontier in a regular and orderly fashion. This method of settlement, far different from the indiscriminate location of colonists in Virginia, became a permanent part of the land system of the country to be formed a century and a half later.

Rhode Island and Connecticut. Although the Puritans had left England to escape religious intolerance, they were far from being themselves tolerant in their new home. Roger Williams, the pastor at Salem, was in 1635 banished by the General Court of Massachusetts for espousing views which, in essence, denied that even the Puritans had found the one way to salvation. Most students will recall that he established a plantation in Providence, where he was joined two years later by Anne Hutchinson and her band of dissenters. The Hutchinson group moved on to Narragansett Bay, along with others, and in 1644 a federation of the Rhode Island and Providence plantations was effected.

Meanwhile, a westward movement to the Connecticut Valley took place, and at almost the same time a colony was established at New Haven. In 1662 Connecticut was made a Crown colony, and New England, which was to constitute a well-knit economic unit, had come into being. Indeed, their unity had long since been more than economic, for in 1643 Plymouth, Massachusetts, Connecticut, and New Haven had banded together, for purposes of mutual defense, in a New England Confederacy. Of great importance to both the political and economic future of the colonies was the almost complete independence of the New Englanders in these early years. They made their own laws and traded about as they pleased. But where they pleased to trade was pretty largely determined for them by the fact that Englishmen were colonizing some distant islands that would soon become the best customers of the Puritans. To this third group of English colonies established in the New World before 1660 we turn our attention for the moment.

British West Indies. When, in 1609, a fleet was sent to take supplies to the Jamestown plantation, the flagship was wrecked on an island in the Bermudas. Three years later a settlement was made there, and these islands thus became the oldest *permanent* colonial possession of the British. By 1640 people from Bermuda were moving into the Bahamas, where they were joined a little later by adventurers from England. At about the same time a third stream of inhabitants flowed from Britain into the islands that mark the eastern end of the Caribbean Sea.

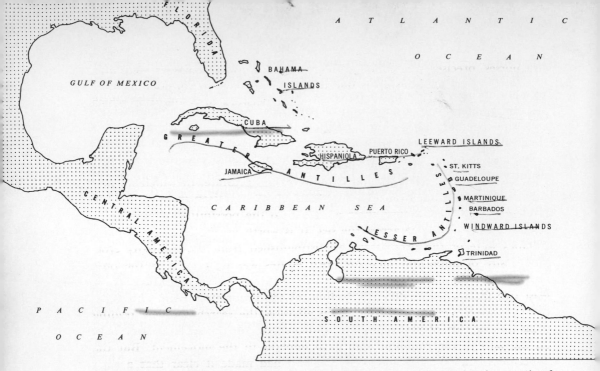

Development: Caribbean islands played a significant role in the economic growth of the American colonies through participation in the triangular trade.

The Greater Antilles—Cuba, Hispaniola, Puerto Rico, and Jamaica—were among the first American possessions of Spain (see map). The Spanish had paid little attention to the islands east of Puerto Rico that constitute the Lesser Antilles. Beginning in 1624 the English and French and, to a lesser extent, other Europeans began to gain footholds here. First, the English and French took St. Kitts, each owning about one-half of the twenty-five-mile-long island. From St. Kitts Englishmen spread into nearby islands and a few years later began to colonize Barbados at the southernmost tip of the Windward Islands. Beginning in 1635 the French took the rich islands of Martinique and Guadeloupe. By mid-century the French and English were well established in this eastern group, and the English, as a part of Cromwell's "Western Design," began to cast their eyes westward. After an unsuccessful attempt to take Hispaniola, an English fleet in 1655 captured the island of Jamaica.

The West Indies had an incredible fertility and were especially suited to the production of sugar, a commodity in great demand in seventeenth- and eighteenth-century Europe. In what high regard these islands were held, even toward the end of the colonial period, is best evidenced by the fact that there were those who felt, at the conclusion of the French and Indian War, that England should take Guadeloupe rather than Canada. What is of immediate importance, however, is the connection of the non–Spanish West Indies with the continental colonies. Specializing in the growth of tropical crops, the West Indian planters needed to import foodstuffs, lumber, and horses, precisely the commodities the New England colonies were able to furnish. This relationship is one that we shall have to consider in more detail when we come to describe the intricate network of trade upon which the prosperity of early Americans depended.

THE LATER COLONIES, 1661–1733

On the American continent there was a period of thirty years, coinciding with the English Civil Wars and Cromwell's protectorate, in which no new colonies were sent out from England. With the Restoration in 1660, English noblemen could again turn their attention to the possibility of making or re-establishing a fortune across the sea. It is worth noting that all the later colonies were of the proprietary as distinguished from the company type. The desire of important men for great estates was by no means the only impellent to colonizing in the latter half of the seventeenth century. In at least two instances the altruistic feelings of the proprietors Penn and Oglethorpe played a considerable part. In all cases the search for new trading areas on the part of merchants and ship-owners and the seeking after land on the part of the common man gave impetus to the movement. But the experiments in Virginia and New England had made it clear that a company organized for the purpose of realizing a profit within a reasonably short time could not hope to succeed financially in the long and tedious business of colonization.

It is doubtful that any of the proprietors ever reaped a reward, in pounds and shillings, commensurate with their investment. They nevertheless intended to. A proprietor always reserved to himself great tracts, which grew in value as population increased. There were some land sales, but even on lands given to settlers under the headright system an annual payment, known as a quitrent, was ordinarily paid. Quitrents, vestiges of feudal dues, were nominal per acre but if properly collected amounted to a sizeable sum on large acreages. Then, too, the owner had the revenue from his own estates, which were worked by tenants. Finally, he charged license fees for privileges of trading and even levied duties on goods coming into and going out of his province. Whatever else may have moved a Penn or a Calvert or an Ashley to action, the ultimate prospect of income was certainly not unattractive.

In the final wave of colonization there were two main thrusts—into the so-called middle colonies and into the South below Virginia. Let us complete this section by picking up a thread of the narrative that runs back to the early efforts of the Dutch in America.

New York. We might well have traced the founding of New York in the previous section, for this substantial colony began as the Dutch possession of New Netherland. The Dutch successes in the Spice Islands, which came at the turn of the seventeenth century, have already been mentioned. In its first years the Dutch East India Company persistently sought a shorter route to the East, and it was while searching for this route that Henry Hudson,

Ships like these of the fleet of the Dutch East India Company brought their owners economic leadership in the expansion of Europe.

an Englishman working for the Company, in 1609 sailed up the river that was later to bear his name. The Dutch East India Company was interested only in the Orient, but enterprising individuals from the Netherlands soon came to engage in the fur trade with the Iroquois.

The year after the Pilgrims landed in America a Dutch West India Company was formed, not so much for the purpose of colonization as to harass the Spaniards as they shipped treasure through the Caribbean. In the middle 1620s the Dutch set up forts at key points on the present sites of Albany and Manhattan. The fort established on the south end of Manhattan became the town of New Amsterdam, a center of the fur trade and a base for any Dutch ships in the area.

Contrary to the general impression, the Colony of New Netherland, which lay between New France on the north and Virginia on the south, was never outstandingly successful. The fertile lands along both sides of the Hudson were early divided into huge estates and given to wealthy Dutchmen, who ran them like feudal domains instead of trying to attract free settlers. In the area around New Amsterdam a large number of small farms were started, but trouble with the Indians precluded a productive agriculture until mid-century. The colony was ruled in autocratic fashion by a series of governors, including Peter Stuyvesant, who lacked both honesty and ability.

Neither England nor the northern colonies had ever been happy about what they considered Dutch encroachment on territory first discovered by the Cabots. As England and Holland drew apart in the seventeenth century, there was no longer any serious bar to securing New Netherland by force, especially since the colony had never been brought to sufficient strength to defend itself against attack. When in 1664 Charles II granted this area to his younger brother, the Duke of York, a small English fleet could seize it without firing a shot.

Almost a decade later the English colony of New York reverted to Dutch rule for a year or so, but with this exception steady progress was made toward the pre-eminent economic position it was to achieve within a century and a half. With the accession to the throne of the Duke of York as James II in 1685, the colony became a royal province, and thus were removed many sources of friction that had persisted when York tried to exploit it for personal profit. Agriculture quickly became more important than fur-trading; of greater significance, New York began to take advantage of its superb harbor to become a center of colonial commerce and of the shipbuilding industry.

New Jersey. The early history of New Jersey is associated with that of New York. The territory was included in the grant made by Charles II to his brother in 1664. The Duke of York almost immediately deeded the area to his friends Lord Berkeley and Sir George Carteret. When these proprietors took over, the Swedes in the valley of the Delaware and the Dutch near New Amsterdam were almost the only inhabitants; but under a liberal government colonists began to trickle in from England and, even more, from the colonies to the north. Carteret remained a proprietor, controlling East Jersey, but Berkeley disposed of his interests to the Quakers, the owners of West Jersey until governmental rights were taken over by the Crown in 1702. From the beginning, the northeastern part took on the characteristics of small industry and trade like those of New York, while the southwestern part was at first a farming region like its neighbor Pennsylvania.

Pennsylvania. The story of early Pennsylvania, like that of Massachusetts, is one most of us learn at an early age, probably because this commonwealth became the first melting-pot in America. William Penn, son of the distinguished admiral who had been helpful in getting Charles II restored to the English throne, took Pennsylvania in payment of a substantial debt owed his father by the king's brother. The grant was for all land west of the Delaware River between the fortieth and forty-third parallels, southern and northern boundaries that were disputed by other colonies for a long time.

To the consternation of his relatives and noble friends, William Penn had been converted as a young man to the Quaker faith. Quakers, it must be remembered, were considered dangerous in mid–seventeenth-century England, largely because of their pacifist beliefs. But the younger Penn, a man of great personal charm, managed to stay in the good graces of his associates and avoided disinheritance by his father, so that when his father died he became immensely wealthy. Among the properties he inherited was a part of western New Jersey, which, as we have seen, was predominantly Quaker. Penn was glad to get the much larger grant from the king, for there he could carry on his "holy experiment" in political and religious freedom. Though during the last two decades of the seventeenth century the Quaker sect was not actively persecuted, either in England or in the colonies, as it had earlier been, Penn wanted a place where Quakers could settle in peace. Even more important, he wished to provide a place where people of *all* nationalities and religions could live together in peace and harmony, where, in short, the Quaker ideal could be tested.

Colonization began in 1681; in the next year Penn himself came to the new land and forthwith selected the site of Philadelphia. A combination of cheap land and the prospect of genuine liberty quickly attracted settlers who, until 1700, were mostly English and Welsh Quakers and Germans. The colony grew rapidly, and in less than four years numbered nearly 10,000 people. The Friends tended to be the leaders and gave the colony its moral tone; usually they were given political support by the Germans, who were grateful for their new-found freedom.

Delaware. We must not forget the so-called lower counties given by the Duke of York to William Penn in 1682. Their position was anomalous throughout most of the colonial period. They were really a part of Pennsylvania until 1703, when they obtained their own assembly. Yet this, the smallest of the colonies but one, remained under the governor of Pennsylvania until Revolutionary times and was not called Delaware until then.

While the middle colonies were receiving their first strong influx of population, colonization was going on in a part of the great coastal area south of Virginia. Not until half a century after the settlement of Pennsylvania was well under way did the last of the thirteen colonies, Georgia, receive its first settlers, sent over in a final, well-intentioned experiment. We conclude our survey of the establishment of the first frontier with a consideration of these movements in the South.

The Carolinas. In the 1650s colonists began to move from Virginia into what is now North Carolina. But the story of the Carolinas really begins with the last great proprietary grant of an English king. To eight men, among them Anthony Ashley Cooper, Sir John Colleton, and Governor Berkeley of Virginia, was given all the land on the eastern seaboard from the lower Virginia border south to Florida. In 1670 the first settlement was made at Charleston, where an excellent harbor and a fertile hinterland gave promise of a bright future in both agriculture and commerce. Within a decade French Huguenots joined the original English and West Indian settlers, and, oddly, a substantial colony of Scots moved into Port Royal. South Carolina got its start by trading furs with England and naval stores with the British West Indies, but by the end of the century production of its great staple, rice, was well under way.

South Carolina was for many decades isolated from the rest of the colonies. A wide belt of forest and wasteland separated Charleston and its environs from the companion settlements to the north. The part of the Carolinas nearest Virginia (now North Carolina) was without good harbors, and the development of this region was for a long while inhibited by the impossibility of shipping the main crop, tobacco, directly to England as required by the Navigation Laws. Virginians did not look with favor on attempts to transship a competing commodity through their ports, and the illegal tobacco trade with continental Europe, via New England, was beset with difficulties.

By the end of the seventeenth century it was customary to distinguish between North and South Carolina. In 1719 South Carolina became a Crown colony, all governmental rights and ownership of unoccupied land passing to England, and North Carolina reverted to such status a decade later. Although these sister colonies were by this time not far from equal in population, North Carolina remained for a long while a poor relation.

Georgia. The thirteenth colony did not even come into existence until long after the others, save possibly New Hampshire, were firmly established political and economic entities. Like Pennsylvania and Massachusetts, Georgia was founded to assist those beset with trouble in the Old World. Dr. Thomas Bray, an Anglican clergyman noted for his good works, together with a group of associates, was persuaded by General James Edward Oglethorpe to attempt a project for the relief of men condemned to prison for debt. This particular social evil of eighteenth-century England was one that cried for remedy, because debtors might spend years in the horrible prisons of the time without hope of escape except through organized charitable institutions. As long as an individual was incarcerated, he was unable to earn anything to remove his obligation, and even if he were eventually released, his years of imprisonment might well make him unfit for a place in society. It was Oglethorpe's idea to encourage debtors to come to America where they might become responsible and even substantial citizens.

Dr. Bray and his group sought a grant of land in the Carolinas, and King George II was pleased to oblige.[9] The land lay between the Savannah and the Altamaha rivers, the original tract including considerably less territory than the modern State of Georgia. By royal charter a corporation was created that was to be governed by a group of trustees, and after twenty-one years the territory was to revert to the Crown. Financed by both private and public funds, the venture had an auspicious start. Oglethorpe himself led the first contingent of several hundred immigrants, mostly debtors, to the new country, where a fifty-acre farm awaited each colonist. Substantially larger grants were available to free settlers with families, and determined efforts were made, both on the continent and in the British Isles, to secure colonists.

---

[9] The English regarded Georgia as something of a buffer state. The Spanish were sure it was, regarding the settlement of Georgia as an evil scheme to provide a vantage point for an attack on Florida.

As a philanthropic enterprise Georgia was a modest success, but its economic development was disappointing for many decades. The climate in the low coastal country was unhealthful, yet it was in this region that the fertile land lay. Slavery was at first prohibited by the trustees so that for many years it was impossible to introduce the profitable rice and indigo culture of South Carolina, and the fifty-acre tracts given the charity immigrants were too small in any case. Not until Revolutionary times and later did Georgia, under a plantation system, come into its own. Meantime, in 1751, the colony became the property of the Crown.

The Conditions of Colonial Economic Life

Although we have mentioned the major areas of specialization in the several colonies, we shall develop the subject in more detail in the following chapter. At the moment we shall make two broad generalizations. The first is implied in what has been said, but it needs explicit statement. The second has to do with the relationship to colonial growth of the mercantile doctrines by which English statesmen were guided in the seventeenth and eighteenth centuries.

RELATIONSHIPS AMONG THE FACTORS OF PRODUCTION

The details of colonial production that we shall consider presently may fade from memory, but it will be easy to retain one basic fact about the whole of early economic life in America. This fact can be stated very simply. Land was plentiful and labor and many types of capital goods exceedingly scarce, both absolutely and relatively. This peculiar relationship among the factors of production explains many institutional growths and patterns of regional development in the colonies.

Throughout the history of the British colonies most people were dependent upon the land for a livelihood. From New Hampshire to Georgia, agriculture was the chief occupation, and such industrial and commercial activity as there was depended almost entirely upon materials extracted from the forests and the ocean. Where soil and climate were not favorable to the cultivation of one of the great staples, it was necessary to turn to fishing or trapping and to the production of ships, ship timbers, and naval stores. Despite the fact that land was seemingly limitless in extent and therefore, one would suppose, not to be especially cherished, nearly everyone wanted to be a landholder. When we reflect that, for the European, ownership of land signified wealth and position this is not hard to understand. The ever present desire for land explains why, for the first century and a half of our history, many immigrants who might have done well as artisans or as laborers in the employ of someone else tended always to turn to agriculture, thus aggravating the persistent scarcity of labor.

Especially was there a shortage of workers with highly developed skills, for artisans and trained craftsmen, in great demand in Europe, were too well off at home to be tempted even by substantially higher wages into a life of hardship at the very bounds of civilization. From the first there was an almost exclusive dependence for laborers upon the indentured servant or redemptioner, as he was called if he came from continental Europe. The indenture contract was a device that enabled people to pay for their passage to America by selling their labor for a period of time to someone in the New World. Such contracts might take a variety of forms, but law and custom made for similarity among them. Generally speaking, the prospective immigrant would sign articles of indenture binding himself to a period of service varying from two to seven years, though four years was perhaps most common. In practice the contract was signed originally with a ship-owner or his recruiting agent. As soon as the servant was delivered alive at an American port, the contract was sold to a planter or merchant. The individual who thus bound himself performed any work demanded in exchange for his keep plus certain "freedom dues," which he received at the end of the agreed period.

Who were these people who came to North America as bond servants? Hear Abbott Emerson Smith describe them:

> Many . . . were convicts from the jails, transported instead of being hanged; a few were political and military prisoners taken in war or rebellion. There were rogues, vagabonds, whores, cheats, and rabble of all descriptions, raked from the gutter and kicked out of the country. There were unfortunate French, German, and Swiss Protestants fleeing from religious persecution, starving and unhappy Irish, rack-rented Scottish farmers, poverty-stricken German peasants and artisans, brash adventurers of all sorts. People of every age and kind were decoyed, deceived, seduced, inveigled, or forcibly kidnapped and carried as servants to the plantations. There were many ordinary individuals of decent substance, and a few who were entitled by the custom of the time to be called gentlemen.[10]

Indentured servants were for the most part without skills or training. Except for convicts who had no choice, they came to America because, for one reason or another, they wanted to get away from their home country. Since there was no other way they could raise the price of their passage, which ranged between five and six pounds sterling during the entire colonial period, they were willing to sell themselves for a period of years. The life of a servant might be hard or easy depending upon the temperament of his taskmaster; the courts usually protected him from extremes of cruelty, but the forces of the law swung quickly into action to apprehend and return a servant who ran away.

More than half of all colonists who settled south of New England were servants, a statistic that suggests the powerful economic force at work to

---

[10] Abbott Emerson Smith, *Colonists in Bondage* (Chapel Hill: University of North Carolina Press, 1947), p. 3.

make their transportation and use profitable. Colonial planters would sacrifice much to secure laborers, for the labor of others made the difference between mere subsistence and affluence. Demand for labor in the colonies made a cargo of servants profitable for English merchants trading to the colonies. So private cupidity assured a colonial labor supply with almost no intervention on the part of the British government.

The alternative to white servitude—slavery—did not become important until after the middle of the seventeenth century, though slaves were imported as early as 1619. By 1700 the institution had become firmly established from Maryland southward. Slaveholding was not unknown in New England and the middle colonies, but it never took hold there for a number of reasons. The most important was climate. Whenever the labor of a man was purchased for a fixed sum of money, it was necessary that he be idle as little as possible during the year. There were few days in the South when a slave was kept from work because of the rigors of bad weather, whereas in the North outdoor work might be impossible for days on end. Also important was the fact that tobacco, then rice, and finally indigo were the staple crops of the South. Requiring much unskilled labor that could be performed under the supervision of an overseer, these crops were especially suited to cultivation by untrained men newly imported from a tropical land.

Yet north of South Carolina the demand for servants held up throughout the eighteenth century, and not until the nineteenth did the immigration of free workers completely remove the need for them, particularly in Pennsylvania. Only on the great southern plantations did the Negro supersede the servant; and even in some parts of the Deep South, as in the West Indies, servants remained in demand simply because they were white and provided some security against the blacks. In Maryland slaves never did outnumber the indentured servants, and in Virginia, though slaves outnumbered servants by 1700, shiploads of redemptioners continued to arrive throughout the eighteenth century.

Capital goods—the produced means of production—were with some notable exceptions in limited supply, especially during the first century of settlement. The exceptions were goods made from available natural resources with simple tools. The abundance of wood made it fairly easy to build houses, barns, and workshops. Wagons and carriages were largely wooden, as were farm implements, wheels, gears, and shafts. Shipyards and ways were likewise made of timber, and small ships were constructed in quantity at a very early date. But metal products were scarce, enforcing some capital rationing that for a long time held mills and other industrial facilities below optimum size. Roads and harbor works lagged behind European standards until the end of the colonial period.

The colonies could doubtless have used more capital than was ever available. The mercantilist views of English political leaders certainly resulted in legislation that hindered the export of tools and machinery from the home country. Moreover, those with funds to invest, whether English or Colonials, preferred the relatively safer investment in British firms then beginning to thrive. But after all these considerations are taken, the fact remains that the developing American colonies were relatively far better off than underdeveloped countries are today—for theirs was an age of wood and simple technology.

ENGLISH MERCANTILISM AND THE COLONIES

In the period that falls approximately between 1500 and 1800 the countries of western Europe that became nation-states were invariably influenced by a set of ideas and beliefs called, in the late eighteenth century, the "mercantile system" or "mercantilism." Mercantilist doctrine was not the creation of a particular group of thinkers; it was never set forth in systematic fashion by a "school" of economists. In fact, although there had been during this period a massive outpouring of economic literature, mostly in the form of pamphlets and small books, the first "classical" economist gained his reputation by inveighing *against* mercantilist beliefs. Nevertheless, these ideas were important because they were held by practical businessmen and statesmen who, at different times and in different countries, strongly influenced public policy.

The mercantilists wanted more than anything else to achieve power and wealth for the state. It was possible to achieve these ends, they felt, by making their own country as nearly self-sufficient as possible and by doing whatever they could to weaken the power of competing states. The means toward this end took various forms. Perhaps the best known was to secure a "favorable" balance of payments, for the experience of Spain in the sixteenth century led nearly all observers to conclude that an inflow of gold and silver was a potent help in attaining needed goods and services and in prosecuting successful wars. But balance-of-payment notions were far from the whole of good mercantilist doctrine. Great power could be fully realized by the state only if political and economic *unity* became a fact. In a day when productivity depended so much on the skill and knowledge of the individual workman, it was of primary importance that artisans be kept at home. If all the materials necessary to domestic industry were not available, they could best be obtained by establishing colonies or friendly foreign trading posts whence they could be imported. A strong merchant marine might carry the goods of foreigners and thus help to secure a favorable balance of payments, but more important, the merchant ships could be converted into men-of-war if the need arose. Nor was the attention of mercantilist leaders directed exclusively toward relations between the home country and the rest of the world. For one thing, a self-sufficient economy implied a strong and vigorous agriculture. Too, a high rate of industrial production was necessary; this meant not only the protection of old industries and the encouragement of new ones but also the enforcement of regulations that would turn the poor and the indigent to some kind of productive activity.

New Amsterdam in the seventeenth century was a minor (but promising) port city. Surrounded by relatively unproductive land, the town nevertheless combined a superb harbor with unexcelled access to the hinterland.

Mercantilists believed that these means of achieving national power could be made effective only by the passage and reasonably strict enforcement of a mass of legislation directed toward regulating the whole pattern of economic life. By the end of the fifteenth century, England had begun to pass such laws, but her mercantilist efforts did not come into full flower until after she, together with the Dutch, had successfully turned back the Spanish power. Indeed, it was largely as a consequence of English desires to surpass Holland, a nation that reached the zenith of her power during the first half of the seventeenth century, that legislation was passed which marked the beginning of an organized and consistent effort to regulate colonial trade.

Adherence to mercantilist principles was, of course, implied in the colonizing activity that began in the late 1500s. For that matter, after the first successful settlement in the New World there was no one who would argue seriously that colonies should not be regulated so as to benefit the mother country. Almost as soon as Virginia tobacco was sent in commercial quantities to England, the king laid a tax on it while agreeing to prohibit the growth of competing tobacco in England. Gradually, more and more restrictions were placed upon the carriage of cargoes shipped from the colonies in foreign vessels, and by the 1630s foreigners were legally excluded from the American trade. Furthermore, it became well established during the first few decades that certain products were to be taken to England either for sale there or for transshipment to other European countries. On the whole there seems to have been little objection to such rules and little feeling among the colonials that there was anything unjust about them.

During the English Civil War, which began in 1642 and ended in 1649, Englishmen were too bothered with their own troubles to pay much attention to regulating trade with the colonies. In this period Americans got into the bad habit of shipping goods directly to continental ports, and the Dutch made great inroads into the carrying trade. In 1651 Parliament passed the first of the so-called Navigation Acts, directed primarily at prohibiting the shipping of American products in Dutch vessels. Not until after the Restoration, however, was England in a position to enforce a strict commercial policy, and it is for this reason that we usually think of the Acts of 1660 and 1663 as the first really effective ones.

The first Navigation Acts were modified from time to time by literally hundreds of others. Though we shall pay some attention to a few crucial changes in policy, it is presently sufficient to note the three categories of restriction thus placed on colonial trade.

1. All trade between England and any of her colonies had to be carried in ships owned by English nationals or by colonials and manned by crews that were at least three-fourths English or colonial.
2. All European imports received by the colonies, with a few minor exceptions, had to come from England. This meant that any imports from continental Europe had to pass first through an English port.
3. Certain commodities, called "enumerated" articles, could be shipped only to England. Putting it formally, we sometimes say that England was made the "staple" for such products. At first the enumerated list was small, but as time went on it was expanded greatly.

The student is urged to keep these three categories of restrictions firmly in mind. While they were the cause of much loud protest on the part of the colonists, they probably did little harm. Largely because of widespread evasion by smuggling, they caused practically no disruption to established trade patterns during the remaining decades of the seventeenth century. When, in 1696, a system of admiralty courts was set up to enforce the Navigation Acts, their impact became somewhat more pronounced. Indeed, regulation of all spheres of colonial activity was henceforth to be carried on under something approaching a unified policy. But before tracing the series of events that led ultimately to revolution, we must examine the patterns of production and flows of trade that were steadily developing.

The Economic
Background of
the New Republic

Thus while around the wave-subjected soil
Impels the native to repeated toil,
Industrious habits in each bosom reign,
And industry begets a love of gain.

GOLDSMITH

The period from the founding of Jamestown to the first inauguration of President Washington is longer than the span of time from our beginnings under the Constitution to the present. Fifty years were required to secure a firm hold on the new continent, and at the end of the first century of colonial history, settlement of the eastern seaboard was far from complete. By 1660 Virginia, Maryland, and Massachusetts were established commonwealths, but the first movement of the debtors into Georgia did not take place until nearly seventy-five years later. In 1640 there were perhaps 25,000 white people in the English colonies on the mainland; in 1660 there were 80,000, and by 1690, 200,000. From this time on growth was spectacular. From over a third of a million people in 1710 the population increased to about 2,250,000 on the eve of the Revolution. In 1790 about as many people lived west of the Appalachians as had lived in the whole country a century before.

The map on p. 50 shows the extent of settlement as of 1660, 1700, and 1760. Before 1660 there was nothing to speak of south of Norfolk, and at the turn of the century a wilderness still separated Charleston and its environs from the major inhabited area in upper North Carolina. By 1760 the land hungry, rich and poor, had spread over nearly all of the coastal plain and into the piedmont. As early as 1726 Germans and Scots-Irish had begun a movement into the Shenandoah Valley, and down this and the other great valleys went ever increasing numbers seeking the cheap land to the west. Through the gaps in the mountains some turned east into the piedmont of Virginia and the Carolinas; only a few years later began a trickle to the west, particularly through the Cumberland Gap, into Kentucky and Tennessee.

Growth of population and colonization of new territory were not restricted to the eastern coast of North America. During the sixteenth century Spain had occupied northern Mexico and Florida, and while English settlement was taking place, the Spanish were moving northward into Texas, southern Arizona, and southern California. As we have mentioned, France in the seventeenth century established bases in the Lesser Antilles and Canada, and from Canada her explorers and traders pushed into the Mississippi Valley and on to the Gulf of Mexico. The three rival states were bound to clash in America, even if they had not been enemies in other parts of the world. To the general historian we must leave the descriptions of these bitter rivalries and of the resulting complex, if small-scale, wars. Following intermittent conflict between the French and the English in the northeast and along most of the western frontier, the French and Indian War resulted in the temporary downfall of the French in North America. By the Treaty of 1763 only Spain and England were left in possession of the North American continent. Spain took all of the territory west of the Mississippi, and England secured everything to the east with the exception of certain fishing rights and small islands retained by the French off Newfoundland. Furthermore, England acquired all of Florida, thus settling perennial disputes with Spain that had long disturbed the colonies of South Carolina and Georgia. It is difficult to remember that Spain, not France, gave trouble to pioneers who moved out of the original thirteen colonies into the old Southwest. Not until 1800 did France again own the Territory of Louisiana with its vital port of New Orleans, and, as everyone knows, her control did not last long.

Now let us put our attention to economic developments preceding the English policy changes that led to the Revolutionary War.

The Dominance of Agriculture

As late as the end of the eighteenth century more than nine-tenths of our people made at least a part of their living at farming. Although most families ate substantial quantities of game and seafood, it was necessary to grow the basic foodstuffs. Where unlimited amounts of fertile land were available, it would have been foolish to import in quantity items that could be produced domestically. There were difficulties to be overcome, especially the clearing of a stubborn forest, but precious transportation space had to be conserved for articles that could be produced in the colonies only at

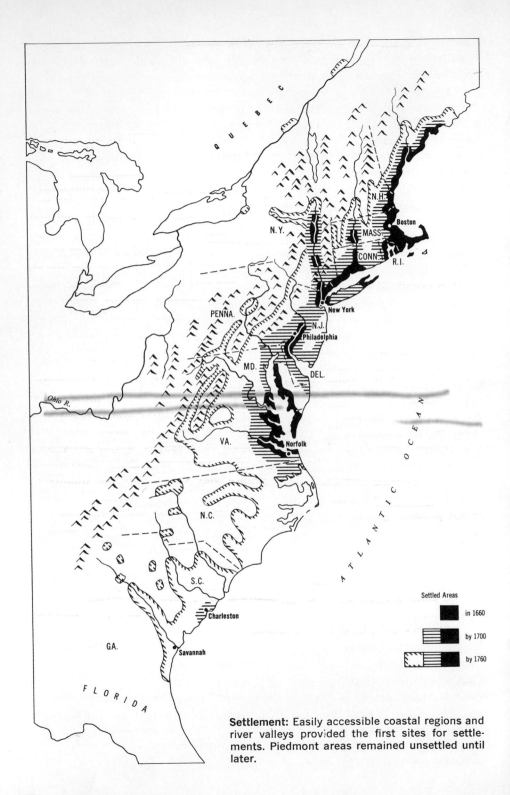

Settlement: Easily accessible coastal regions and river valleys provided the first sites for settlements. Piedmont areas remained unsettled until later.

high cost. And almost from the beginning many of the goods that had to be imported were obtained by exchanging the "commercial" crops of the southern and middle colonies.

THE SOUTHERN COLONIES

In terms of value of output southern agriculture was dominant throughout the colonial period and well into the nineteenth century. In the southern colonies we find a good example of the comparative advantage that fertile new lands possess. Almost at the outset settlers in the South started to grow tobacco that was cheaper and, before long, of better quality than that grown in most other parts of the world. Later came two other staples, rice and indigo, and just after the Revolutionary War, cotton. For nearly two and a half centuries the South was to remain tied to a few export staples, because the soil and climate of the region gave a pronounced advantage to the cultivation of crops in great demand in the industrial areas of the world.

It is not at all astonishing that, from the first, attempts should be made to secure an exportable agricultural surplus. Such a surplus meant that those who made an investment of either capital or labor would most quickly get some return, and in this instance what was good for the individual was, in the opinion of mercantilist statesmen, good for the mother country. The southern colonies especially were important to the English. Unlike the commodities of the other colonies, nothing the South exported competed with British production, either in the Isles or in the rest of the Empire. Not that the exports of Maryland, Virginia, the Carolinas, and Georgia were ideal in all respects. There was always the hope for more than ever materialized. For example, it was known that grapes would grow well in the South, and every effort was made to encourage the production of wines, then being imported from France and Spain. But the quality of American wines was so poor that serious attempts to compete with established producing areas were given up. Similarly, it was hoped that silk and hemp, two much needed fibers, might be produced in quantity, and bounties and premiums were offered for their production; but again quality was inferior and high wage rates resulted in a high-cost product.

Tobacco, as we have seen, was sent from Virginia to England within a decade after the settlement of Jamestown. The weed had been known in Europe for over a century, for sailors on the first voyages of exploration had brought back samples and descriptions of the use to which the natives put it. Despite much opposition on moral grounds, smoking had increased in popularity during the sixteenth century. It was therefore a relief to the English to find a source of supply that would make imports of tobacco from the Spanish unnecessary. Tobacco needed a long growing season and a fertile soil. Furthermore, it could be cultivated in small areas, on only partly cleared fields, and with the most rudimentary implements. All this suited the primitive Virginia community. There were two other advantages. As the culture exhausted the original fertility of a particular plot, new land was readily available, and ships could move up the rivers of the Virginia coast to load their cargoes at the plantation docks. There was one marked disadvantage, felt for a good part of the seventeenth century, in that much had to be learned about the proper curing, handling, and shipping of tobacco, and for many years the American product was inferior to the Spanish. Nevertheless, it was protected in the English market, and the fact that it was cheaper led to steady increases in the quantity taken from the market. The culture of tobacco spread northward around Chesapeake Bay and moved up the many river valleys. By the end of the seventeenth century there was some production in North Carolina.

During the early years of the seventeenth century, Spanish tobacco sold in England at an average retail price of about forty shillings a pound. When Virginia tobacco first came onto the market, it commanded between four and eight shillings a pound, and until 1627 or thereabouts there was a consensus that a price of around three shillings could be maintained. At that level the production of tobacco was so profitable that colonists could scarcely be persuaded to grow anything else, and a mining-camp spirit pervaded the Colony.[1]

All too soon the tobacco growers of Virginia encountered the problem of volatile prices that forever besets agricultural producers. By 1630 Governor Harvey complained that tobacco was fetching less than a penny a pound; and though prices in ensuing years had their ups as well as their downs, colonists resorted to all kinds of devices, including burning half of one year's crop, to maintain their incomes. An especially difficult period resulted from the increased immigration to the colonies between the outbreak of the Civil Wars and the Restoration, and only the intervention of the weather in 1667, by reducing output to nearly zero, rescued the growers from desperately low prices.

Then as now restrictions on production led to disappointing and frustrating results. If a planter were limited in the number of plants he could set out on his farm, he responded by moving more rapidly to new and fertile fields. If Virginia tried to limit the number of pounds exported, it was unlikely that Maryland and North Carolina would co-operate. Moreover, production was highly inelastic. The marketing of tobacco by consignment to merchants made for uncertainty about the price to be received, and in any case each individual planter felt that he could increase his own income by increasing his output. During the latter part of the seventeenth century and the first half of the eighteenth, there were years of relative prosperity, to be sure, but the days in which tobacco was a profitable crop for every producer were gone. It slowly became apparent that the competition would be won by large plantations and that the small planter, if he were to succeed at all, would have to specialize in high-quality tobacco or in the production of food.

[1] Lewis Cecil Gray, *History of Agriculture in the Southern United States to 1860* (Washington, D.C.: Carnegie Institution of Washington, 1933), Vol. I, pp. 259–60.

Since slaves could be worked on a more economical scale, the large unit was more efficient, and the big operator was better able to continue production in spite of extremely low prices. Because of the heights to which slave prices rose after Negroes could no longer be freely imported, nineteenth-century slavery was probably not as profitable as some plantation owners thought, but in the colonial period a slave ordinarily produced a large surplus above all the costs of his purchase and upkeep. To achieve the best results there had to be enough slaves to assure the economical use of a white manager. Thus the wealthy, or those able to secure adequate credit from English and Scottish merchants, attained an optimum scale of operation and in so doing became even wealthier and improved their credit standing further. In short, bigness begot bigness, and wealth led to wealth. We should not conclude that slaves were held only by the largest plantation owners, for the crude statistics indicate that in Revolutionary times, as later, large numbers of planters owned Negroes in lots of ten or less. Nonetheless, there was a persistent pressure in the tobacco colonies to develop an agricultural unit of large size.

About 1695 the second of the great southern staples was introduced. Although the early Virginia colonists experimented with rice and South Carolinians tried its cultivation in the first two years after settlement, success awaited the introduction of new varieties.[2] By the early 1700s rice became an established crop in the area around Charleston, although problems of irrigation had to be solved. It is possible to grow rice without intermittent flooding and draining, but the quality of the grain is hurt if this is not done. When rice was first cultivated, it was grown in the inland swamps that could be periodically flooded from the rivers, but the flooding was dependent upon uncertain stream flows. Besides, such a method could not be used on the extremely flat land that lay along the coast itself. Before long a system of flooding was devised that utilized the force of tide flows. Dikes were built along the lower reaches of the rivers, and as the tide pushed back the fresh water it could be let through gates into irrigation ditches crossing the fields.

Proper flooding was a ticklish business. It had to be done very carefully so that no salt water would be let in, and proper drainage demanded painstaking engineering. But the heavy investment of capital was worthwhile because the two major floodings could then be done at precisely the right time, and the water could be removed just as accurately. Much labor was needed, and slaves were imported at a great rate during the eighteenth century to furnish it. The "task" system of working Negroes, which gave to each man a particular piece of ground to cultivate, was used. The work was backbreaking and was carried on in hot, mosquito-infested swamps; although contemporary opinion held that the African was better able to withstand the ravages of disease and the effects of overexertion than the

---

[2] Gray, p. 278.

Colonial agriculture depended heavily on such cash crops as indigo, here being processed from fresh-cut sheaves to final drying in South Carolina.

white man, the mortality rate among Negroes was high. Despite the difficulties of producing it, until the end of the colonial period the output of rice steadily increased, its culture finally extending from below Savannah up into North Carolina.

To the profits from rice were added those of another staple—indigo. The indigo plant was successfully introduced in 1743 by a woman, Eliza Lucas, who had come from the West Indies to live on a plantation near Charleston. Almost certainly, indigo could not have been grown without the company of another staple, for its culture was demanding and the preparation of the dye required real skill. As a supplement to rice, however, it was ideal, both because the plant could be grown on high ground whereas rice grew on low ground, and because the peak work loads came at a time when the slaves were not busy in the rice fields. Indigo production, fostered by a British subsidy of sixpence a pound, added considerably to the profits of the plantation owner and thus attracted resources to the area. So it came about that when separation from England brought an end to government payments and the consequent demise of indigo growing, both capital and labor were available for the production of a new crop—short-staple cotton.[3]

In emphasizing the importance of tobacco, rice, and indigo, there is some danger of overlooking the production of other commodities in the

[3] A long-stapled variety of cotton was cultivated in the lowlands area toward the end of the colonial period. Known as Sea Island cotton, because of its adaptability to the climate and soil of the islands off the coast, this variety was in great demand for spinning into fine yarns. Furthermore, its seeds could be removed by hand with relative ease. Unfortunately, the area in which it could be grown was so narrowly restricted that it never became a significant crop.

southern colonies. Throughout the South there was a substantial output of hay and animal products and of Indian corn, wheat, and other grains. Mostly, these items, like a wide variety of fruits and vegetables, were grown in order to make the agricultural units as nearly self-sufficient as possible. Yet upland farmers, especially those of the Carolinas and Virginia, grew livestock for commercial sale, and meat, either on the hoof or in cured form, was produced in quantities for export to other colonies.

THE MIDDLE COLONIES

The land between the Potomac and the Hudson, on the whole fertile and readily tillable, was the best in the colonies for the production of food. As the seventeenth century wore on two distinct types of agricultural operation developed there. To the west, on the cutting edge of the frontier, succeeding generations continued to encounter all the difficulties that had beset the first arrivals. The trees of the forest, an ever present obstacle, had to be felled, usually after they had been girdled and allowed to die. The soil was worked with implements and tools not much different from those used by medieval Europeans. A living had literally to be wrested from the earth. But to the east of the frontier, as time went on, there developed a stable and reasonably advanced agriculture. The Dutch in New York and the Germans in Pennsylvania brought skills and methods of farming superior to those of other peoples who came from the Old World. They were encouraged from the first to grow a surplus of crops for sale in the small but growing cities of New York, Philadelphia, and Baltimore. Gradually there developed a commercial agriculture. Wheat became the important staple, and while there was a considerable output of corn, rye, oats, and barley, the economy of the region was based on the great bread grain. During the latter part of the seventeenth century a sufficient quantity of wheat and flour was being produced to permit the export of these products, particularly to the West Indies.

From the first, New Jersey and Pennsylvania contributed heavily to wheat production and in the years before the Revolution Pennsylvania became the great wheat colony. The bread colonies not only served as a granary for neighbors to the north and south; they also furnished a considerable output of fruits and vegetables, especially potatoes, and of quality livestock. And, as we shall see presently, the export of food surpluses indirectly enabled the people of this region to import manufactured products.

The kind of agricultural unit that evolved in the middle colonies later became typical of the great food belts of the Middle West. Individual farms, considerably smaller in acreage than the average plantation to the south, were of a size that could be operated by the farmer and his family with little hired help. Slaveholding was rare, for there were too many months in a year in which unskilled labor would run to waste. It was normally preferable to acquire an indentured servant as a hand; the original outlay was not great and even a young and inexperienced servant soon became worth more than his board and keep. Alternatively, the farmer could hire itinerants to work for him, but in a country where labor was scarce farm hands of this sort were likely to be marginal workers who had drifted away from the seacoast towns.

NEW ENGLAND

Vital as the agriculture of New England was to the people of the area, it furnished a relatively unimportant part of total colonial output. Generally poor soils, uneven terrain, and a hard climate led to typical "subsistence" farming—to the growth of only those crops necessary for family maintenance. Because it could be produced almost anywhere and because yields on even poor land were satisfactory, Indian corn was the chief crop. Wheat and the other cereal grains, along with the hardier vegetables, were grown for family use. Partly because of the climate and partly because of the protection from wild predators which natural barriers furnished, the Narragansett region, including the large islands off the coast, became a center of cattle and sheep raising. By the eve of the Revolution, however, New England was a net importer of food and fiber. Her destiny lay in another kind of economic endeavor; and from a very early date many of her people combined farming with other work and thus lived better than if they had been confined to the resources of their own farms.

We ought, perhaps, to say a word or two about the peculiar form of agricultural organization that persisted in New England throughout the seventeenth century. It was remarked in the last chapter that the form of land disposition was quite different there from what it was in the middle and southern sections; grants were made to groups of proprietors and allotments were then made to individuals, usually on the basis of proportionate investment. The town became not only a political unit but, in a sense, an agricultural unit as well. The result was that for upwards of a century New England agriculture had some of the characteristics of medieval land-use patterns. The homes of the villagers normally lay close to the center of the town land. Near his house each inhabitant had a small parcel of land for garden or orchard, and he ordinarily owned scattered pieces of from fifty to two hundred acres, partly arable, at varying distances from the village. Running through the center of the village there would almost invariably be a common meadow, to which each owner had rights, where livestock roamed freely. In addition there might well be common wasteland and common fields, the latter being divided into strips and allotted among the villagers. Decisions as to what crops should be grown in the common fields were made at town meetings, and while each farmer was entitled to the product grown on his own strips, the entire field became common pasture at the end of a growing season.

In eighteenth-century New England there occurred a movement similar to the English enclosures in which scattered holdings as well as strips in the common fields were consolidated. There was an important difference, however, in that in New England there was little suffering consequent upon the bringing together and fencing in of land that had been held in common. Here the process was one of slow and fairly easy adjustment among free men who, after enclosure was completed, had land sufficient for a living. In fact, because a more efficient agriculture was made possible nearly everyone benefited. In England landlords and some freemen were better off, too; there the great hardship was worked on those who had such small rights to the common fields and pastures that, upon legal division, they were left with insufficient land on which to make a living.

This quaint and outmoded method of farm organization left little imprint on modern American agriculture. But the systematic laying out of towns that began in New England was continued as the northern frontier progressed westward and had an important effect on the future American land system.

The Extractive Industries

Although most colonial Americans made their living in agriculture, a good many earned their livelihood indirectly from the land in what we should call industrial pursuits. From the forest came the furs and skins of wild animals, lumber, and naval stores. From the waters off the coast came fish and that strange mammal, the whale. Out of the ground were extracted minerals, though in small quantity during the early years. No account of colonial economic activity would be complete without some mention of these varied occupations with an output second only in value to that of agriculture.

THE FUR TRADE

The original thirteen colonies were a second-rate source of furs during most of the period before the Revolution, for the finest furs in any area were quickly taken, and the most lucrative catches were made far in advance of the frontier. Farmers nonetheless made a sideline of trapping in order to obtain cash, though for the most part they caught the muskrat and the raccoon, then, as now, the less desirable animals.

There were two centers of the fur trade. The more important was in the North, with the chief posts for a long time at Albany and Philadelphia. Traders, working through the Iroquois, tapped apparently inexhaustible supplies of luxury pelts such as beaver, mink, and fox and exported them to Europe. In the South, where the less valuable deerskin was the chief commodity, Charleston and then Augusta were the base cities. Around the southern end of the Appalachians traders pushed to the Mississippi River, dealing always with the Indians, who did most of the actual trapping.

As the search for the finer pelts continued into the interior, the French, in both the North and the South, were ever present competitors. The English were able to give the Indians more and better goods in exchange for furs,

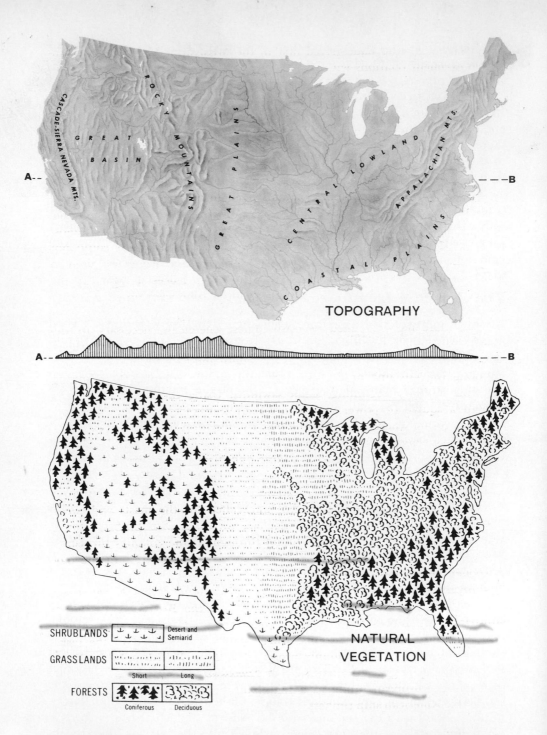

TOPOGRAPHY

NATURAL VEGETATION

SHRUBLANDS — Desert and Semiarid

GRASSLANDS — Short / Long

FORESTS — Coniferous / Deciduous

Natural Gifts: The channels of commerce and the stores of raw materials decreed by topography and natural vegetation set the first patterns from which later economic development has emerged.

but the French, who had arrived first in the Mississippi Valley, long maintained excellent relations with some tribes. With the Peace of Paris in 1763, France lost her Canadian possessions and was thus removed from the rivalry. By this time the Hudson's Bay Company in Canada had secured control of the most profitable trade; it controlled the business until John Jacob Astor and his American Fur Company again offered strong competition after 1808.

WOOD PRODUCTS

The forest itself, more than its denizens, became an economically significant object of exploitation. Colonials lived in an age of wood (see map opposite). Wood rather than minerals and metals constituted the chief fuel and the basic construction material. The agricultural population almost without exception engaged in some form of lumbering. Pioneers could not escape the necessity of felling trees to clear ground, and wood was used to build houses, barns, furniture, and in some places, fences. Frequently the timber was burned and the ashes scattered, but as time went on enterprising farmers discovered that with simple equipment they could produce potash and the more highly refined pearlash. These chemicals, necessary in the manufacture of glass and soap among other things, provided much-needed cash and were produced by households the length and breadth of the colonies.

Along the fall line of the northern and middle colonies there sprang up, from the very beginning, small sawmills. Using the water of streams as both a source of power and a means of transportation, the operators tended to locate where there was the best combination of virgin timber and handy rivers. Commercial manufacture of basic wood shapes—boards, planks, cooperage materials, etc.—began in Maine and New Hampshire, but by the end of the colonial period was a common occupation in North Carolina.

Some mills made a business of manufacturing materials for shipbuilding and ship repairs. The white pine was unexcelled for the masts and yards of sailing ships, and the white and red oak provided ship timbers of the same high quality. The pine trees found throughout the colonies furnished the raw material for the manufacture of so-called naval stores. In the day of wooden vessels naval stores—pitch, tar, and resin—were indispensable in the shipyard, mostly for protecting surfaces and caulking seams. Naval stores were in great demand in both the domestic and the British shipbuilding industries. The processes for making them required considerable skilled labor, and only in North Carolina, where slaves were trained to the tasks involved, could they be profitably produced without British subsidy. Even so, English shipwrights complained that American pitch and tar were inferior to the European products, a complaint never voiced against the incomparable American ship timbers.

SEA PRODUCTS

Although restricted pretty much to the northern colonies the occupations of fishing and whaling were of major importance in the development

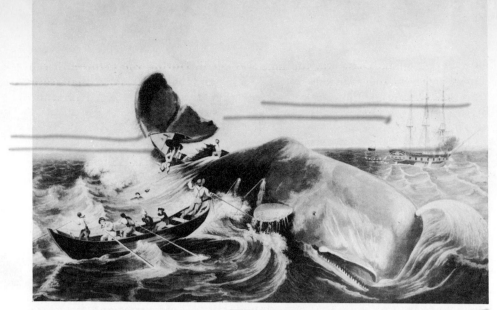

Whaling, despite its dangers, proved profitable to New Bedford sea captains and ship-owners, whose ocean experience helped them establish the China trade.

of the entire early economy. The sea gave New Englanders a commodity for which there was a ready market and in addition furnished a stimulus to shipbuilding. When Jacques Cartier sailed up the St. Lawrence River in 1534, fishermen from many European countries were already at work near the mouth of the river and had doubtless been making the hazardous journey across the North Atlantic for a long time. Originally these pioneers had operated a "wet fishery"; i.e., the catch was partly cleaned, salted down, and returned to the home country for drying. The quality of the product was much better, however, if a "shore fishery" could be established to dry fish at a nearby land base, and during the sixteenth century fishermen from Spain and Portugal, France and England attached themselves temporarily to the north coast country.

When at last a permanent settlement was made at no great distance from the banks that extended from Long Island to Newfoundland, it was only natural that the settlers should turn to deep-sea fishing. There were many splendid harbors for the small vessels and plenty of timber with which to build them. But most important, there was an insatiable market for the magnificent cod. The large, fat cod, hard to cure, were consumed at home. The best of those for export went to Catholic Europe, while the poorer grades were sent to the West Indies, where they were fed to slaves. Gloucester and Salem, Boston and Marblehead became the chief home ports of the great fishing fleets.

In colonial times whale oil was prized as both an illuminant and a lubricant, and ambergris was much sought after as a base for perfumes and whalebone as a material for stays. Whaling was therefore a small but profitable and vigorous industry. Before 1700 the whalers operated near the New England coast and the take was small. During the eighteenth century, however, they ranged far and wide, and by 1775 more than three hundred vessels of all sizes sailed from the Massachusetts ports, of which Nantucket was the great whaling center.

IRON PRODUCTION

The only mineral obtained by the colonials in any significant quantity was iron. A little copper and lead were found, and negligible amounts of coal were mined, but in the young economy iron was the chief metal and charcoal the industrial fuel. For the moment we confine our attention to the processing of the primary shapes, the "blooms" and "pigs" that were later worked up into usable finished forms. There is a certain artificial separation of our subject, for at many of the ironworks established in these early years, as now, the finishing processes were carried out by the same artisans who reduced the iron ore. It is convenient, nevertheless, to consider the reduction of iron as one of the extractive industries and the finishing of iron as a manufacturing industry.

Iron, not steel, was the common product of the colonies and, for that matter, of the rest of the world. Later we shall have to become familiar with some of the properties of steel; now it is enough to distinguish steel from wrought and cast iron. Steel is a form of iron containing carbon in amounts ranging from about 0.1 per cent to about 1.7 per cent. With a greater carbon content the product becomes cast iron. Wrought iron contains very little carbon and other impurities and is distinguishable from steel by its method of manufacture and by the presence in the final product of a certain amount of slag. Steel is malleable, very tough, and increases in brittleness and tensile strength as its carbon content becomes greater. Cast iron is extremely hard and brittle and is not malleable at any temperature. Wrought iron is tough, resists shock, does not corrode easily, and is soft enough to be worked into desired shapes. It is fairly simple to obtain wrought iron, at least in small quantities, and equally easy to obtain cast iron. The production of steel, on the other hand, presents the difficulty of adjusting the carbon content within narrow limits, and until only a century ago it was made in small quantities and for special purposes.

The colonial iron industry used methods not far different from those developed by the late Middle Ages, though by the time of the Revolution furnace sizes had increased greatly. In the seventeenth century the chief source of iron was bog ore, a sediment taken from swamps and ponds. When this sediment was treated by charcoal in a bloomery or forge, during which process the charcoal absorbed the oxygen in the ore, an incandescent sponge of metal resulted. The glowing ball of iron was removed from the forge and, white-hot, was hammered to remove the slag and leave a substantial piece of wrought iron. Output of the bloomeries was inconsiderable.

As the population moved inward, rich rock ores were discovered, and during the eighteenth century a large number of furnaces were built for

Iron manufacture, which began in Virginia, later flourished in more northerly colonies. Here is an exterior view of the casting house at Alger's Foundry near Boston.

the reduction of these ores. Pig iron could then be produced in quantity. Into the square or conical furnaces was put a mixture of rock ore, charcoal, and oyster shells or limestone, which was then ignited. Under a draft of air from bellows worked by water power the iron ore was reduced to a spongy metal which, as it settled to the bottom of the furnace, alloyed itself with large amounts of carbon and thus became what we call cast iron. Poured off into molds called pigs or sows, the resulting metal could later be remelted and cast into final form or further refined and reworked in a mill or blacksmith shop.

These rudimentary processes are important because they serve as background to an understanding of the later development of the American iron and steel industry. We shall draw on this introductory material in Chapter 14. Too, it is worth noting that, because of the simple processing required and an abundance of charcoal, the colonial iron industry was able to compete in the sale of bars and pigs with that of the British Isles. There is agreement that the number of forges and furnaces in the colonies just before the Revolution probably exceeded the number in England and Wales combined, and the annual output of wrought and cast iron was by then in the neighborhood of 30,000 tons, or about one-seventh of the world's output. But the colonies remained heavy net importers of finished iron products.

The Manufacturing Industries

It has been convenient to distinguish between the colonial extractive and manufacturing industries even though in practice one type of activity shaded into the other. Included under the heading of manufacturing are those processes by which the crude or primary materials of the extractive industries were turned into finished products. It should also be observed that the word *industry* is ordinarily used rather loosely in any description of colonial activity, for the "firms" that composed an industry were frequently heterogeneous units which might range from a household to a fairly large shop or mill. Nevertheless, output of the major categories of commodities *tended* to be produced by one of three major types of organization.

Once again we must remind ourselves of the proportions in which the factors of production were available to business enterprises. Land was abundant. Capital goods and labor were scarce. But capital was relatively less important to a manufacturing organization than it would be after the Industrial Revolution. On the other hand, labor was relatively more important; for the more complicated processes the skills of artisans rather than tools or equipment constituted the crucial agents of production. Wage rates in the colonies were much higher than they were in England, and since the less skillful and less stable operators tended to be the ones who emigrated, wage rates per unit of labor may have been twice as high as they were in the home country. Yet large amounts of household labor were available for use in those pursuits requiring little skill and simple tools. During slack periods all the members of the agrarian family worked at indoor jobs in preference to sitting around in idleness.

Farming and speculation in land offered to most people of the time the greatest hope of ultimate reward. Because of the attraction of the land, early Americans came together in only a few urban settlements as the population grew. So it resulted that large quantities of goods were made in the home for home use. In the villages and towns craftsmen tended to make those things in domestic demand that required greater skill and somewhat more expensive tools than the ordinary householder could provide. Finally, from mills and plants of varying sizes came an increasing flow of goods for the home trade and to an even greater extent for export. Now let us see specifically what kinds of goods and services were turned out by these three types of organization.

HOUSEHOLD MANUFACTURE

Before anything else the colonial household manufactured food and clothing. The finer items were imported, but household manufacture actually created a marketable surplus of some commodities. Animal products today taken for granted were the result of feverish activity on the part of all members of the family when the first cold spell came on. Meats, cured or pickled, leather, and lard were essentials that only the well-to-do could afford to buy. Wheat, rye, or Indian corn grown on the farm was ground into flour at the local gristmill, but the women of the family were required to make the plentiful weekly ration of bread and hardtack. Jellies and jams were made with enough sweetening from honey, molasses, or maple syrup to preserve them for indefinite periods in open crocks. And it must not be forgotten that the men of the family were rarely teetotalers. Beer, rum, and whiskey were easiest to make, but wines, mead, and an assortment of brandies and cordials were a specialty of some households.

The making of clothing, from the preparation of the raw fiber to the sewing of the finished garment, kept women and children busy. There was nothing fine or beautiful about the resulting product, but it covered the body. Knit goods—stockings, mittens, and sweaters—were major items of homemade apparel. Linsey-woolsey, made of flax and wool, and jeans, a combination of wool and cotton, were the standard textiles of the North and of the pioneer West. Equally indestructible, though perhaps a little easier on the skin, was fustian, a blend of cotton and flax used mostly in the South. Dress goods and fine suitings had to be brought in from England, and even for the city dweller the purchase of such luxuries might well be a rare and exciting occasion.

Those with special talents produced everything from nails and kitchen utensils to exquisite cabinets. Everywhere the men of the family participated in the construction of their own homes, though exactive woodwork and necessary masonry might be done by a specialist. These specialists, of widely varying abilities, were found in cities and at country crossroads. Let us consider their work for a moment.

THE CRAFT SHOP

Much earlier than might be supposed, artisans began to ply their trades. Some of them were true craftsmen, experts in the European tradition. What distinguished the workshop crafts from household manufactures was the fact that the former were specialized while the latter were not. Household production was for family needs and presumably required neither the full time nor attention of any member of the household. The craftsman might work in his own home, but his home was a craft shop if he earned his living at a trade.

The characteristic of "specialization," which distinguished the craftsman from the household worker, was not always a clear one in colonial America. Skilled slaves on southern plantations might devote all their time to manufacture; they were, in fact, artisans, even though their output was considered a part of the household. On the other hand, the itinerant Jack-of-all-trades, who moved from village to village selling his reasonably "expert" services, was certainly not a craftsman in the European sense. Because of the scarcity of skilled labor, individual workers often undertook to perform more processes than they would have performed in the old country; a tanner, for example, might be also a currier and a shoemaker. Furthermore, because of small local markets and consequent geographic dispersal of nearly all types of production, few workers in the same trade gathered in any particular locality. For this reason there were not many guilds or associations of craftsmen in the same trade, though as early as 1648 there were enough shoemakers in Boston to enable the General Court to incorporate them as a guild, and by 1718 tailors and cordwainers were so numerous in Philadelphia that they applied for incorporation.[4]

4 Carl Bridenbaugh, *Cities in the Wilderness* (New York: Knopf, 1955), pp. 43 and 191.

In the urban centers a great variety of skills was represented at a rather early date. In 1697, for example, fifty-one manufacturing handicrafts, besides the building trades, were followed in Philadelphia. As one authority has put it, ". . . a bare enumeration of the trades that we know were plied in the colonies indicates that varied and widely diffused handicraft manufactures then existed, in the aggregate contributing largely to colonial production, but chiefly important for the leaven of knowledge, skill and habit which they supplied for subsequent industrial development." [5]

MILLS AND YARDS

In our discussion of the extractive industries we observed that somewhat more complex organizations were required, even for rudimentary manufacture, than those of the household or of the craft shop. For want of a more precise term we shall follow common usage and speak of the mill industries. To colonials a mill was ". . . either a contrivance for grinding or any machinery operated by animal power, wind, or water." [6] Thus, mills turned out the basic wood shapes and the wrought-iron bars and iron pigs mentioned previously. Although skilled artisans or even members of households frequently made the finished wooden and iron articles, they were also produced in mills and furnaces. Again, the "reproductive" manufacturing might be done in connection with the primary manufacture or in an altogether different location. For example, furnaces for remelting iron and refining forges for making bar iron were usually attached to the smelting furnace, whereas slitting mills and plating forges were ordinarily independent establishments.

Until perhaps the middle of the eighteenth century most of the mills were crude affairs, with power furnished by the small streams found all along the middle and north Atlantic coast. Dam sites suitable for large power development were not generally used until after the Revolution, for operations were on a small scale and owners had means only for a dam and canal of minimum size. During most of the period primitive mechanisms were used; the cranks of sawmills and gristmills were probably always made of iron, but the wheels themselves and the cogs of the mill wheel were of wood, preferably hickory. So little was understood about power transmission, until fairly late, that a separate water wheel was used for each article of machinery. Shortly before the Revolution improvements were made in the application of power to milling processes, and mills along the Delaware and Chesapeake were at that time probably the finest in the world.[7] In 1770 a fair-sized gristmill would grind one hundred bushels a day; the largest ones, with several pairs of stones, might convert 75,000 bushels of grain into flour annually. The highest development of this kind of manufacture was represented by the establishment of Oliver Evans, who invented devices that enabled him

---

[5] Victor S. Clark, *History of Manufactures in the United States, 1607–1860* (Washington, D.C.: Carnegie Institution of Washington, 1916), p. 164.
[6] Clark, p. 174.   [7] Clark, p. 179.

to achieve a continuous process of manufacture from raw material to final product. In his mill, put in operation in 1782, grain was ". . . elevated mechanically to the top of the mill or warehouse, cleaned during gravity transmission to the hoppers, ground, conveyed by screw transmission and a second series of elevators to the top of the building again, cooled, bolted, and barreled during its second descent, without the intervention of any manual operation." [8] Employing only six men, mostly to close barrels, the Evans mill had an annual capacity of 100,000 bushels of grain.

We can only suggest the variety of the mill industries. Tanneries, with their bark mills, were found north and south. Paper-making establishments, common in Pennsylvania and not unusual in New England, were called mills because machinery was necessary to grind the linen rags into pulp. Textiles were essentially the product of the household, but in Massachusetts, eastern New York, and Pennsylvania there were a substantial number of mills set up for the more complicated processes of weaving and finishing. The rum distilleries of New England provided a major product for foreign trade, and breweries everywhere ministered to convivial needs. The gristmill, like the sawmill, was found everywhere in the colonies, but the largest ones eventually developed in Pennsylvania, Delaware, and New Jersey.

Even the briefest sketch of colonial productive activity must include mention of shipbuilding, certainly a major industry. In 1631 little more than a decade after the Pilgrims landed at Plymouth, a thirty-ton sloop was completed in Boston. During the seventeenth century, yards sprang up along the whole of the New England coast, but Boston and Newport led the way in shipbuilding. New York was a strong competitor until the Navigation Act of 1651 dealt her industry a crippling blow, and not until after 1720 did she make a comeback. By this time Philadelphia had a dozen major yards along the banks of the Delaware, and of the five major towns only Charleston relied on others for nearly all her merchants' ships. In the first half of the eighteenth century, output of the shipyards rose to a peak. The American industry furnished the vessels for a large domestic merchant fleet and sold a considerable number abroad, chiefly to the English. An uncontradicted estimate attributes nearly one-third of the ships in the British Merchant Marine of 1775 to American manufacture.

Many of the ships constructed were small. But whether making a square-rigged, three-masted vessel of several hundred tons, or a fishing boat of 10 tons, Americans had a marked and persistent advantage. As we have noted, timber supplies of the first quality were readily available. A great and steady demand for vessels in England enabled builders to sell their ships as fast as they could construct them, and the strength of this foreign demand helped them over the one obstacle to be surmounted—that of securing anchors, cordage, shipwares, and sailcloth, which could not be produced at home in required quantities. Thus British merchants would send over cargoes of goods to be sold in America at favorable prices. With the proceeds they

---

[8] Clark, p. 179.

The early stages of manufacturing (here shown at what was probably the Oliver Evans mill in Delaware) often made sophisticated use of primitive mechanical aids to compensate for a chronic labor scarcity.

would have a ship built to order, loaded with lumber, and sent to a southern European port or to England, where the cargo or the ship or both would be sold at a good profit. Finally, the industry attracted from both England and Holland skilled artisans who, with pride in their work, were the equal in all respects of their counterparts who remained in Europe. In general, second-rate artisans had come to this country, but not so with the ship-wrights. Furthermore, a tradition of good work was handed down from father to son so that as long as the wooden sailing ship was a major factor in transportation, America had an undeniable comparative advantage in its manufacture.[9]

Perhaps a word in summary is in order. In the chapters on business history to follow, the trends toward specialization and integration that characterize modern industry will be emphasized. Colonial production, in contrast, was distinguished by generalization and dispersion. Difficulties of land transportation led to the dispersion of plants; it was better to locate several small units near their respective markets than to set up a big one from which products would have to be sent long distances. But there was another reason for the scattering of manufacturing units. Most of these units were owned by individuals or by partners possessed of small capitals, and the state of technology caused the small plant to be most economical. In

[9] During the early colonial period the Navigation Acts effectively subsidized both English and colonial shipping. The American advantage was clear, however, before the eighteenth century was well along. See J. B. Condliffe, *The Commerce of Nations* (New York: Norton, 1950), p. 101.

addition, the source of raw material or the small stream that furnished power might "dry up" so that the entrepreneur and his plant would have to move on. Finally, mill owners refrained from too much specialization for the same reason that some craftsmen found it best to devote their talents to two or more trades. A mill owner sometimes combined under the same roof such unlike processes as sawing lumber, grinding flour, forging iron, and fulling cloth, because any one product might glut a local market.

There were some indications that bigness would be a development of the future. For one thing, the bare beginnings of a concentration of industries in certain localities could be discerned. Around Wilmington, where there was a combination of dependable water power and an abundant supply of raw material, flour mills were congregated. Near Lancaster there was a concentration of iron forges and furnaces. New England towns early became famous for their shoes and textiles.

There were hints, too, of a new type of business organization that, like the great joint-stock companies created by Europeans to exploit foreign lands, would bring together large combinations of capital. In Boston, for example, there was formed around 1751 a "Society for Encouraging Industry and Employing the Poor," an organization with a major objective of improving the lot of unfortunates and a minor objective of making profits. With stock subscriptions, a board of directors, elected officers, and a hired manager, such companies foreshadowed the corporate form of business organization.

Finally, we must call attention to a way of bringing resources together that lies somewhere in the ancestry of modern factory organization. This was the "putting-out system" or "merchant-employer system" that had been so important in both England and Germany as those countries emerged from the Middle Ages. As certain areas, for one reason or another, achieved a specialization in production, enterprising merchants began gathering the output of houses and shops under one roof. They might even "put out" raw materials, such as flax and wool, for spinning into yarn, and then gather the yarn and have it woven into cloth by another group of operators. Similarly, they might turn leather over to a number of shoemakers, who, with the help of their apprentices or of members of their families, would turn out a crude, but wearable, product for general sale. In both the textile and shoe industries entrepreneurs with large capitals frequently brought together under one roof a number of operators to help in the earlier stages of production or to carry out finishing processes.

Factory production, as we shall define it later, had not yet appeared. By the middle of the eighteenth century there were portents, however, of this organization that was later to have a unique impact upon economic life. But large-scale production had to await the development of markets, which in turn depended on a continuing growth of population, emerging regional specialization within the United States, and a firmer linkage with the Atlantic economy.

American Commerce and British Colonial Policy

Small islands not capable of protecting themselves are the proper objects for kingdoms to take under their care; but there is something very absurd in supposing a continent to be perpetually governed by an island.

THOMAS PAINE

For well over two centuries the new country was dependent upon the old for imports of manufactured goods. In the process of trading, America contributed to the prosperity of English merchants and in turn drew strength from the land whence the original settlers had come. The colonists often had to carry on complicated exchanges with other areas to obtain the much desired products of Britain, and some supplies from non-British sources were in demand for use by the colonists. Basically, though, early trade consisted of exchanging the products of the American agricultural economy for those of the English economy on its way to industrial supremacy. Because of the ever increasing demand for fabricated items, which alone could assure escape from a primitive economy, colonial merchants occupied a strategic place in the life of the times.

As a class the sedentary merchants of the northern and middle colonies were equal in importance to the planters of the South. They, with their counterparts across the ocean, furnished the drive that enabled the colonies during the eighteenth century to make substantial economic progress. Inevitably they antagonized the English merchants and thereby contributed to the strains that led to separation from the mother country. And after separation their fortunes provided much of the capital for American economic enterprise.

Money, Transportation, and Domestic Trade

Before taking up the foreign commerce of the colonies it is logical to consider the nature of domestic trade, together with the general conditions that circumscribed it. Of these conditions, the state of the money supply and the types of transportation facilities require special attention.

THE COLONIAL MONEY SUPPLY

Just before the formation of what is now the State of Tennessee, the people of that territory, wanting to break away from North Carolina, set up the State of Franklin. An act passed by the newly elected legislature reads as follows:

> Be it enacted by the General Assembly of the State of Franklin and it is hereby enacted by the authority of the same, that from the first day of January A.D. 1789, the salaries of the officers of this Commonwealth shall be as follows, to-wit:
>
> His Excellency, the Governor, per annum, 1,000 deer skins.
>
> His Honor, the Chief Justice, 500 deer skins.
>
> Attorney-General, 500 deer skins.
>
> Secretary of State, 500 raccoon skins.
>
> The Secretary of the Treasury, 450 otter skins.
>
> Each County Clerk, 300 beaver skins.
>
> Clerk of the House of Commons, 200 raccoon skins.
>
> Members of the General Assembly, per diem, three raccoon skins.
>
> Justice of the Peace fees; for signing a warrant, one muskrat skin.
>
> Ministers of the gospel for marrying the people, eight mink skins.
>
> Be it enacted by the General Assembly of the State of Franklin, that no citizen shall neglect the proper training of children in the schools. And be it further enacted that a fine of twenty mink skins shall be imposed on all those settlers who neglect sending their children to the nearest schoolteacher, etc.
>
> Enacted into a law, this 18th day of October, 1789, under the Great Seal of the State.
>
> Witness His Excellency, John Sevier, Governor.
>
> Samuel Newel, Secretary of State.[1]

We may smile at this unsophisticated way of paying public officials, but the problem it implies—that of having sufficient currency—was a pervasive one in colonial America. One of the earliest solutions was borrowed from the Indians by the first New England settlers, who used wampum for money. These polished shells, black and white, circulated for several decades after the founding of the colonies, were a legal tender for private debts in Massachusetts until 1661, and were used as money in New York as late as 1701.

---

[1] Claude A. Campbell, *The Development of Banking in Tennessee* (published by the author, 1932), pp. 14–15.

Throughout the colonies at one time or another almost every imaginable commodity was monetized. In Maryland and Virginia tobacco remained the principal medium of exchange long after its value had fallen from three shillings to a penny or two a pound; indeed the monetization of tobacco doubtless stimulated its production and so furthered the depreciation in its value. Other colonies designated as "country pay," acceptable for taxes, such items as hides, furs, tallow, cows, corn, wheat, beans, pork, fish, brandy, whiskey, and musket balls. Harried public officials were endlessly swindled by having the worst of country pay foisted off on them, but just as serious was the cost of transporting the commodities received for taxes and loss through shrinkage and deterioration.[2] What public treasuries would accept private merchants did not refuse. If Thomas Hancock, uncle of John, was to do business with country merchants of New England, he had to accept commodities, forcing them in turn on reluctant creditors, until his death in 1764.

Commodity money was used most extensively in the early days of the colonies and in areas where coins were especially scarce. By the end of the seventeenth century both specie and paper currencies were common in the five cities of the seaboard, and by the end of the eighteenth century commodities, particularly furs, were acceptable as a medium of exchange only in communities on the western frontier.

Thanks largely to illicit trading with the West Indies, the colonies before 1750 had a slightly favorable trade balance, which gradually built up the supply of specie.[3] Specie holdings reached a high point shortly after the middle of the eighteenth century. At this time stricter enforcement of British mercantilist policy led to a decline in colonial exports to the West Indies and to other European colonies to the south, the result being an outward flow of gold and silver to England. Despite this drain there may have been as much as $12 million of coin in the colonies before the outbreak of the Revolution, though Peletiah Webster, a knowledgeable economic writer and businessman of the period, set the specie figure at only $4 million.

Gold and silver coins of all the important commercial countries of Europe and their dependencies in the Western Hemisphere passed freely throughout the eastern seaboard. More important than English pieces, especially after 1700, were silver coins of the Spanish mint, struck for the most part in Mexico City and Lima and received as a consequence of lively trading with Spanish colonies. The "piece of eight," as the old Spanish peso was called, was known among English-speaking peoples as a "dollar," doubtless because it was about the size of the German *thaler*. Spanish dollars were so common that the coin was eventually adopted as the monetary unit of the United States. The fractional coin, known as the "real" or "bit," was worth

---

[2] Charles J. Bullock, *Essays on the Monetary History of the United States* (New York: Macmillan, 1900), p. 11.
[3] Specie is any monetary gold or silver, whether in the form of bullion (bars) or coin. Oddly, the word was used by some colonials to designate country pay.

about twelve and a half cents, or one-eighth of a Spanish dollar, and was important in making change.[4] Along with Spanish and English pieces, circulated in very limited amounts the Portuguese "joe," the French guinea and *louis d'or,* the Dutch guilder and *rix-dollar,* and others.

Colonial businessmen complained endlessly about the scarcity of gold and silver coin, and for a century and a half they tried hard to persuade British officials to establish separate colonial mints. It would do no good, they felt, to strike colonial coins in England, of English weight and fineness, for these would flow right back out again as a consequence of the continuing favorable British balance of payments. Because of the persistent drain of European coins, the colonists concluded that they needed a special money, with coins containing less metal than standard British coins.[5] It was for this reason that Massachusetts established a mint in 1652, striking the famed pine-tree shilling containing only seventy-two grains of silver compared with the ninety-three grains of the standard English shilling. But the experiment proved disappointing for two reasons. (1) Reduction of the silver content of the shilling did not in fact give it a higher value at home than abroad, for importers simply raised the price of English goods to correspond with the reduced bullion content of the Massachusetts coin. (2) Despite a ban on the exportation of the pine-tree shilling, out they went anyway and at approximately their actual value in silver. Though the experience of Massachusetts should have been convincing, it was not, and only heavy British opposition kept other colonies from attempting a similar remedy.

It should not surprise us to learn that the colonies turned to paper to increase their meager and undependable money supply. Paper issues, whether "bills of credit" or "loan bills," were roundly condemned by an older generation of economists and historians. The more modern view, however, is that the colonies could scarcely have gotten along without them.

In any case, settlers became accustomed to paper money at an early date. Promissory notes of well-known individuals might pass from hand to hand for several months. Bills of exchange, drawn on English merchants or various government officials in London, likewise circulated as money. Treasurers of the different colonies began to issue promissory notes in advance of tax collection or would issue written orders to officers of towns requiring the payment of obligations from local stores; like other negotiable instruments these pieces of paper would pass, on endorsement, as money.[6]

In 1690 Massachusetts issued the first bills of credit in order to pay soldiers who had returned from an unsuccessful military expedition. During the next sixty-five years at least eight other colonies followed suit to meet

---

[4] The "piece of eight" was so called in colloquial language because of the numeral *VIII* impressed on one side to indicate its value of eight *reales.* In many parts of the United States the expressions "two-bits," "four-bits," and "six-bits" are common today.

[5] See Curtis P. Nettels, *The Money Supply of the American Colonies Before 1720* (Madison: University of Wisconsin, 1934), pp. 162–78.

[6] Nettels, pp. 250–51.

financial emergencies. Bills of credit were issued with the proviso that they would be redeemed in specie at some date in the future; in the meantime they were to be accepted for taxes by the issuing colony. Such redemption provisions, though restricted, helped make the bills circulate freely as money. In some states, notably in Rhode Island, Massachusetts, Connecticut, and Virginia, the bills were overissued and their value relative to specie depreciated. The same difficulty was encountered with another type of paper, that of the publicly owned "banks" established by colonial governments.[7] These institutions, unlike anything which we should call a bank today, issued "loan bills" by lending them to individuals, usually upon the security of land or personal property. Borrowers used the bills to meet their obligations and were usually required to repay the debt, with interest, in annual installments.

A third kind of paper money, similar to that of the public loan banks, was issued by privately owned "land banks." These organizations, about which we know all too little, were associations of landowners who contributed to the bank mortgages on real property in exchange for bills, which they passed as currency. Most schemes of private entrepreneurs were short-lived, and only in Massachusetts were there repeated attempts, including the great Land Bank of 1740, to get a major institution going. But private associations were formed in at least five other colonies, and it seems likely that only Parliamentary interference in 1741 forestalled ultimate success of a private venture.

Depreciation of paper brought it into disrepute in some colonies. On the other hand, some colonies used paper money successfully. In Pennsylvania during the half-century after 1723 the paper currency of a public loan bank was carefully controlled and everyone, including the business interests, benefited from its issue.[8] Lending notes on mortgages bearing 5 per cent interest and not exceeding 50 per cent of the value of a property, the Pennsylvania Land Bank placed strict limits on the total amount of notes issued and on the amount lent to any one person. Where public and private land banks did not make their issues cautiously and with provision for redemption, the notes of the banks fell to varying discounts. The depreciation of paper relative to coin was greatest in Rhode Island, where an English shilling at one time exchanged for twenty-five shillings paper. Yet in the middle colonies and Maryland issues were so limited that eight paper shillings exchanged for a silver dollar over many decades.

Naturally, the colonies inherited from England a money system based on the pound as the unit of account.[9] On the other hand, by all odds the most common hard money in the colonial circulation was the Spanish dollar.

---

[7] Bullock reminds us that "during the entire colonial period the word 'bank' meant simply a batch of paper money." Bullock, p. 29.

[8] See Richard A. Lester, "Currency Issues to Overcome Depressions in Pennsylvania, 1723 and 1729," *Journal of Political Economy*, XLVI (June 1938), 324–75.

[9] A pound, then as now, equaled twenty shillings and there were twelve pence to the shilling.

For more than two centuries after 1600 the pound sterling contained 1,718.7 grains of fine silver, so that a shilling contained 85.93 grains of pure metal. At the beginning of the eighteenth century the Spanish piece of eight was variously estimated at between 385 and 388.5 grains of pure silver, Newton's official assay at the English mint in 1704 giving the dollar an official rating of 386.8 grains of pure metal. Thus the Spanish dollar was worth 4s. 6d. of English money.[10]

Colonial assemblies early began to play the game of competitive devaluation of currency. By raising the legal rates at which coins would pass within their own jurisdictions, they hoped to gain definite economic advantages. Colonial legislators reasoned that if the Spanish dollar were received within a colony not at 4s. 6d. but at 5s. or 6s.—or even 7s. or 8s.—pieces of eight would be attracted to the colony and would, moreover, stay there. Furthermore, a cheaper currency would be provided for the payment of debts, for colonial laws placing values on pieces of eight made them the "lawful money" of the province, and debtors could thus settle their obligations in fewer Spanish dollars than required by the earlier and lower evaluation.

As is so often the case with economic panaceas, this one worked temporarily and proved defective only after a lapse of time. The colony that made the Spanish dollar relatively more valuable within its confines could gain at least a temporary advantage in the competition for specie. Pirates were induced to bring their gold and silver to ports where its legal value was highest, and the colonies that most freely harbored pirates usually placed the highest value on pirate coin.[11] Foreign traders unquestionably were attracted to the ports of Boston, Philadelphia, New York, and Charleston partly for the reason that exchange rates were favorable. But as the supply of coin increased in any locale, prices of local products rose, so that ultimately a Spanish dollar at an arbitrarily high value would buy no more than it would have bought at its old value. Then there was always the renewed temptation to give the legal value of the dollar another hike.

The student may wonder why the English Parliament did not intervene to establish some kind of uniformity in the money of the colonies. As early as 1704, the Board of Trade attempted to equalize the rate of exchange between the colonial shilling and the Spanish dollar by obtaining a Royal Proclamation making six shillings the maximum rating of the Spanish coin. When the four leading commercial colonies defied the proclamation, Parliament passed a law of 1708 prescribing that any person in the colonies who paid or received coin at a value higher than the proclamation rate should be imprisoned six months or pay a fine of £10. Yet the law was flouted with impunity, and as late as 1782 Georgia defined a pound as a unit containing 1,547 grains of fine silver, whereas it contained 1,289 grains in Virginia, Connecticut, Rhode Island, Massachusetts, and New Hampshire and only

---

[10] Query: What was the official exchange rate between the pound sterling and the Spanish dollar?

[11] Nettels, p. 232.

966.75 grains in North Carolina and New York. As early as 1720, however, colonists had turned away from altering the value of foreign coin as an inflationary device, relying on issues of paper money to achieve their aims.

During the eighteenth century there was continuing conflict, especially in New England, over the currency question. As in every community throughout recorded history, there were advocates of "sound" money, who took the position that efforts to increase the money supply beyond the quantity of coin in circulation were both wicked and dangerous. On the whole, though, American colonists were disposed to err on the side of a rapidly increasing money stock. Primarily farmers and exporters of raw materials, Americans wanted rising prices, which meant increasing incomes and relief from debt. Farmers clearly favored the establishment of land banks so that they could obtain money at low rates of interest on their land as security. And not a few merchants, themselves debtors, joined with the agrarians to urge continuing paper issues. At last the Crown had to settle the controversy, largely, however, at the instigation of English rather than colonial merchants. By the Currency Act of 1751 the New England colonies were prohibited from issuing further bills of credit and from allowing new land banks to be organized. Further, existing note issues were to be retired as they came due. More important, from the point of view of its ultimate political consequences, was the Currency Act of 1764, which extended the provision of the earlier law to all the colonies. Directed chiefly at Virginia, which had just issued £250,000 in bills of credit, it caused planters and merchants in all the southern colonies to howl in protest, while British merchants, who objected that debts due in specie were being paid in paper money issued in great quantity during the French and Indian War, nodded approval. Coming as it did during a severe postwar depression, the law aroused much animosity.

One of the most perplexing problems to confront the founding fathers was the establishment of a uniform, efficient currency. Indeed, the conflict between the advocates of "cheap" and "sound" money was to continue, much as it had begun in colonial days, for more than a century after the beginnings of the new Republic.

TRANSPORTATION AND COMMUNICATION

During the seventeenth century, communication and commerce among the important centers of colonial America were mostly by sea. At first Americans settled where there were reasonably good harbors or along navigable streams for the obvious reason that these were the easiest places to get to. Before 1700, roads were little more than paths, and land travel was both difficult and dangerous. Even as the eighteenth century progressed the wise traveler went by coastwise vessel when possible. Benjamin Franklin, it will be remembered, transferred his residence from Boston to Philadelphia by sea. The schooner, a two- or three-masted fore-and-aft-rigged ship developed in New England, made the best of adverse winds and also economized man-

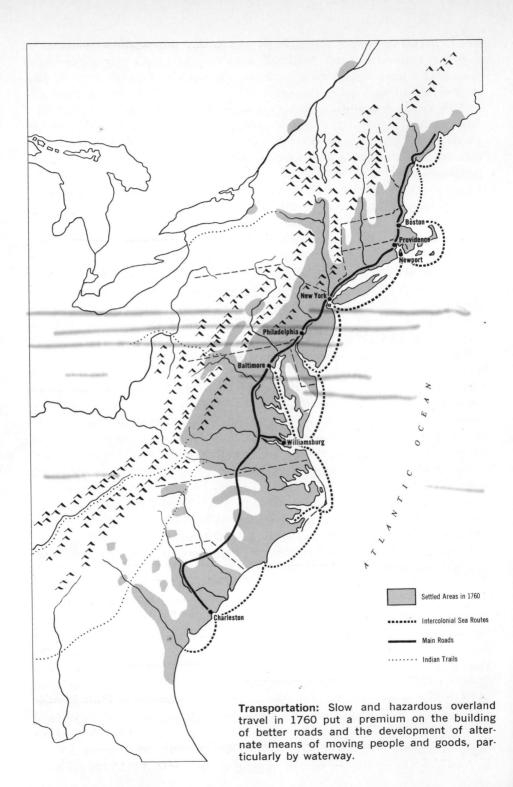

Transportation: Slow and hazardous overland travel in 1760 put a premium on the building of better roads and the development of alternate means of moving people and goods, particularly by waterway.

Settled Areas in 1760

Intercolonial Sea Routes

Main Roads

Indian Trails

Boston
Providence
Newport
New York
Philadelphia
Baltimore
Williamsburg
Charleston

ATLANTIC OCEAN

power; it and the sloop, of like construction but with a single mast, were used in the coastwise trade. In certain regions special types of craft evolved; typical of these was the sharpie of the Chesapeake Bay area which was adapted to shallow waters.

Two factors continued to favor sea travel between the colonies. One was the excessive cost of land transportation. The other was the bulky nature of the commodities produced in the colonial period. But as the population increased, people were forced to move toward the interior, away from the waterways, and some land travel was always necessary. Communities, as soon as they could afford the considerable expense, linked with those nearby. During the eighteenth century something like a road system emerged. By 1760 (see map) a road of sorts ran from Boston through Providence, New York, Philadelphia, Baltimore, and thence to Charleston. Forbes Road crossed Pennsylvania to Pittsburgh, and the Wilderness Road furnished a highway through the Shenandoah Valley. Roads that were little more than trails connected the back country with points on the fall line of the rivers, whence goods and passengers could be carried by boat to the ocean; but from the major port towns reasonably good roads might penetrate fifty miles into the interior.

From contemporary descriptions we gather that the condition of even the highroads was wretched except during dry seasons. In fact, travel in some areas was easiest when heavy snow packed down to fill the worst holes and cover the major obstacles. Until rather late in the colonial period the most comfortable means of passenger travel was by horseback, and nearly all freight was carried by pack trains of perhaps a dozen or more horses. As the eighteenth century wore on, the stagecoach could travel over the better roads, and in the decade before the Revolution one could travel by stage from New York to Philadelphia in two days. For freight carriage the Conestoga wagon, forerunner of the later "covered wagon," proved a reasonably efficient and reliable innovation, but like its passenger counterpart it was limited to use on fairly level, well-kept roads.

It follows that communication was slow and expensive. By the late seventeenth century, postal service had been established for the main urban centers, with rates charged on a basis of weight and distance carried. The early mails were under the jurisdictions of the colonial governments, but in 1710 an American system was established under the English post office. During Benjamin Franklin's term as deputy postmaster (1753–75) the system made great strides forward. Post riders made more frequent trips and traveled both night and day. Newspapers were admitted to the mails, and charges were reduced, with a consequent increase in the use of the service. Even so, it still took six days for a letter to go from Boston to Philadelphia, and as late as 1760 there were only eight mails a year from Philadelphia to points south of the Potomac River. Rates remained so high that letters were frequently given to travelers or to the masters of ships for delivery.

At the time of the Revolution, it took about three weeks for news of importance to spread throughout the colonies to the chief settlements. Those who lived on the frontier might wait much longer to hear of major events, and they were almost completely isolated from reports on such mundane matters as the state of markets. But facilities in America were not much worse than those of the Old World. Even in the highly developed economies of western Europe communication was still slow and uncertain. Bluff-bowed sailing ships took from four to six weeks in the Atlantic crossing. The colonial economy was shaped in part by the difficulties of overland travel and the slowness of communication, but these hindrances were common to all the peoples of the eighteenth-century world.

DOMESTIC TRADE

The briefest sketch of the home trade of the colonies will suffice. We can generalize about domestic commerce, though we cannot make definite statistical estimates as to its volume. Back-country people traded their pitifully small agricultural surpluses for the necessities they could not produce themselves—salt, medicines, ammunition, cotton yarn, tea or coffee, and the like. In the villages and towns households were not so self-sufficient. Even the wealthiest homes produced a part of the goods of everyday consumption; yet wherever people lived in community groups the advantages of specialization were too obvious to be overlooked.

In the complex of domestic colonial trading, two fundamental interchanges stand out. One was the flow of goods between country and town. Herein lay the basis for (1) an expansion in the fortunes of the more substantial merchants and (2) the perpetuation of the low economic status of many of the small landholders who constituted a large part of the population. It became common practice for the town merchant to extend credit to farmers, either directly or through the so-called country traders who served as middlemen. Advances were made for the purposes of obtaining both capital equipment, such as tools and building hardware, and the supplies necessary for day-to-day existence. At the end of a growing season the farmer brought his produce to town to discharge his debts, only to find that all other farmers were doing the same thing. Prices of farm products were depressed at harvest time, but the prices of next year's supplies, along with interest rates, reflected the seasonally heavy demand for both manufactured goods and money. In times of seriously depressed agricultural prices the farmer might end the year with a substantial indebtedness, and two or three bad years on end could result in foreclosure and the loss of his farm with its improvements. The outcome was that many farmers, giving up at last, moved farther west, and merchants took title to the better-situated farms in the older areas.

A second important characteristic of the domestic trade was the comparatively great volume of the coastwise commerce. Early in the seventeenth century the Dutch of New Amsterdam had seen the possibilities of profit in distributing the products of Europe along the coast in exchange for tobacco, furs, grain, and fish, which were then sent to Holland. After the Dutch lost power in North America their hold on the trade declined, and New Englanders, together with enterprising merchants of New York and Philadelphia, took over.

The entrepôt trade started by the Dutch continued; Boston, New York, and Philadelphia, each dominant in its own trading area, became important centers in the exchange of European for colonial goods. Gradually the northern traders extended their operations to the south, and while the direct trade of the plantations with Great Britain remained primary, there was a substantial exchange of staples of the South for those of the North. Such commerce arose partly in connection with the West Indian trade, to be discussed shortly. It was natural that vessels passing southern ports and plantation wharves should put in to see if they could pick up or sell some additional cargo. Perhaps more important, as time went on, were the off-season trips of Yankee fishermen. "During the winter," one writer tells us, "when there was little fishing carried on, the owners of small fishing-sloops would load their craft with salt, rum, sugar, molasses, iron and wooden ware, hats, caps, cloth, handkerchiefs, and stockings, which they carried to the southern colonies and peddled from place to place, returning early in the spring with a valuable lot of pitch and tar and supplies of corn and pickled pork. These trading expeditions of the fisherman were private ventures entirely, which offered a good opportunity to secure a profit even during the winter season from the investment in fishing craft." [12]

In money value of products exchanged, the coastwise commerce was less than the foreign trade with either Britain or the West Indies, but in physical volume it was equal to each of these major branches. Just before the Revolution more than one-third of the tonnage entering and clearing the ports of Massachusetts, the leading commercial colony, was for the colonial trade. In the South the coastwise commerce was much less important, but even there perhaps one-fifth of the tonnage entered and cleared was for the coastwise trade. [13]

Foreign Trade

The most important characteristic of colonial foreign commerce was the predominance of the South as producer of the great staples. These staples (tobacco, rice, and indigo) plus naval stores were what Englishmen under the mercantile system wanted in the way of imports. If we look at the trade figures for the beginning of the eighteenth century or just before the Revolution, we are struck with the overwhelming importance of southern exports to England as compared with those of the other colonies. In the first decade of the century southern exports to England were roughly four times

[12] E. R. Johnson, et al., History of Domestic and Foreign Commerce of the United States (Washington, D.C.: Carnegie Institution of Washington, 1915), pp. 169–70.
[13] Johnson, pp. 171–72.

Colonial Trade: Direct trade with England involved the shipment of lumber, fish, and naval stores (turpentine, especially) from New England to England in return for manufactured goods of various sorts. The southern colonies, meantime, in trade for the same kind of manufactured goods, sent rice, indigo, tobacco, and naval stores.

those of New England, New York, and Pennsylvania. Half a century later, during the decade of the 1760s, the proportion was still about the same, though by this time the Carolinas contributed much more than they had contributed earlier. Southern imports from England, on the other hand, were only slightly greater than those of the northern colonies in the first decade of the century. During the 1760s the imports of New England, New York, and Pennsylvania exceeded those of the South by some £300,000 sterling.

The trade of Virginia, Maryland, the Carolinas, and Georgia was essentially a *direct* trade with England. There were some exceptions. About half of the rice crop, for instance, was allowed to go directly to the south of Europe. Toward the end of the period the plantation owners were beginning to ship a significant amount of provisions to the West Indies. Yankee traders were forever coming south to exchange their own goods for those of the plantations, and these in turn were shipped to England. Nevertheless, the major path of colonial export commerce ran straight from the chief ports of the South to those of Great Britain. Tobacco alone amounted in money value to well over one-fourth of American exports, and nearly all of it went to England. The part of the rice crop that went to England plus the whole of the indigo output accounted for perhaps one-eighth of total exports. It is not hard to see why the southern colonies found favor in mercantilist eyes.

Once northern commerce had achieved some degree of maturity, roughly one-fourth of New England's exports went to England and about two-thirds went to the West Indies. New York sent perhaps half the money value of her goods to Great Britain, with the remaining half divided between southern Europe and the West Indies. Pennsylvania sent very little to Great Britain, her exports being divided between southern Europe and the West Indies. From New England went fish, lumber, ships, whale oil, whalebone, meat, livestock, and naval stores. The middle colonies shipped some of these

Triangular Trade: Africa, the West Indies, and America depended on each other here. New England sent rum to Africa; Africa sent slaves and gold to the Caribbean; these islands sent on gold and molasses to New England; and the northern colonies sent back cloth, livestock, and foodstuffs to the islands of the West Indies.

items, but their specialty lay in furnishing provisions, especially wheat and wheat flour, bread, and pickled and cured meats.

The trade of the North, unlike that of the South, involved more than a simple exchange of staple commodities for finished goods that would be put to immediate use. Northern commerce is epitomized in the famous colonial trade triangles, though pentagons and even hexagons of trade were common. Best known of the triangles was one that began as a two-way exchange of fish, timber, livestock, and provision, shipped from the ports of New England, New York, and Pennsylvania, for rum, molasses, and sugar of the West Indies. Molasses was converted into rum by American distilleries, and the dark, heavy liquor, together with rum already imported from the islands, was sent to the African coast to buy slaves. Slaves were in turn brought back to the ports of Richmond and Charleston or to the West Indies. In a second triangle a ship might take a cargo from Philadelphia, New York, or Newport, exchange it at Jamaica or St. Kitts for molasses and sugar, go on to England and trade for textiles and ironware, and return to the home port. A third great triangle started with the shipment of fish, lumber, and wheat products to Spain, Portugal, and the Wine Islands. Salt, fruits, and wine could then be taken to England and exchanged for manufactured goods, which were then returned to America. But the southern European trade could consist of two-way transactions, since the Navigation Acts permitted the direct importation of certain of the commodities obtained there.

In the decade before the Declaration of Independence, Great Britain was the best customer and chief source of supply of the colonies. In 1769, for example, the colonies sent something over half their exports to England, just over one-fourth to the West Indies, and about one-fifth to southern Europe. Three-fifths of the total value of imports came from England, something less than two-fifths from the West Indies, and most of the small balance from Africa. During the eighteenth century the volume of trade with Great Britain, as measured by combined value of exports and imports, grew steadily. In the first decade of the century the figure averaged something over £550,000 sterling annually; in the decade of the 1760s it was in excess of £2,800,000 sterling per annum, a five-fold increase. During the latter ten-year period England's trade with the American colonies was somewhat greater than its trade with India, about the same as the trade with Ireland, but significantly *less* than the trade with the British West Indies. The American possessions overseas, from the British point of view, had become worthwhile customers and reliable sources of materials, but they were far from being the sole concern of either the merchants or the politicians of England.

Colonial foreign trade led to an emerging business class that adumbrated today's "big" businessman. To be sure, the heterogeneous mass of colonial trade—ranging from hardware to fine textiles, from exquisite china to ship fittings, and from the pathetic white servants of western Europe to the wretched blacks of Africa—required a variety of merchandising outlets to reach the final buyer. Throughout the nearly two centuries of colonial history various merchant types developed. There were itinerant merchants, usually masters of vessels, who ranged the world's oceans, buying and selling for their own account or the accounts of the other owners of shipshares. In the major seaboard towns there developed commodity wholesalers, who specialized in bringing together large lots of such goods as tobacco, cotton, hides, and lumber that had to be graded and packed or baled before shipping. From an early date we have records of a special type of businessman who, acting as agent for sellers or buyers of goods, was reimbursed on a commission basis; dealing largely in farm products, the commission men worked on small capitals to gather commodities that would be sold to processors or exporters.

Ultimately, though, nearly every colonial businessman had to deal with the great sedentary merchants who, from mid–seventeenth century on, became as a class the dominant businessmen of the colonies. Accepting great risks and working imaginatively and skillfully under conditions of poor communication, hazardous transportation, and an uncertain money supply, the sedentary merchants nevertheless flourished and increased in power and influence. Cooperating with an English merchant who served as agent or correspondent, some of the great colonial merchants dealt in many commodities and some specialized in one or two. They relied greatly on credit extended them by their English counterparts, usually for periods of one year, and they expected their English agents to present bills of exchange for payment, maintain and account for pound sterling balances, and even make remittances to English creditors. The sedentary merchants in turn performed many of these services for their own customers in the colonies, extending credit for periods of from six months to a year, accepting bills, making payments, and keeping running accounts. In this atmosphere of mutual faith and trust was laid the foundation on which American business would be

This Connecticut forty-shilling note was issued in 1776. Congress had already authorized the issue of Continental notes, and state and Continental emissions of paper money would total approximately $400 million during the years of the Revolutionary War.

done—a free-wheeling confidence that both suppliers and customers would fulfill commitments and meet obligations when they came due.

The sedentary merchants exerted influence out of all proportion to their numbers, for at the peak of their affluence in 1770 there could not all told have been more than two or three hundred of them, most of whom resided in the port towns of Boston, Newport, New York, Philadelphia, and Charleston. In part, the success of these early entrepreneurs, many of whom became millionaires, was attributable to mark-ups of from 100 to 200 per cent on goods for which there was tremendous demand in an underdeveloped country. All of the really successful ones apparently had that mysterious, ephemeral quality called the "trading temperament," which is really a combination of guts and brains allotted to all too few men. But there were other requisites to success, not the least of which were connections with the right people in England, a major voice in colonial councils, and rapport with appointed English functionaries in the colonies.[14] The measure of Andrew Belcher's success, writes Bailyn, ". . . was less his eventual wealth or the fact that his equipage at the governor's reception in 1702 included a Negro footman, than that twelve years after serving as master on one of Samuel Sewall's vessels he had become the main provisioner of the royal ships that touched at Boston harbor."[15]

Whatever the reasons for their varied successes, achieved in one generation or two or three, the merchant aristocracy dominated the social, economic,

[14] Bernard Bailyn, *The New England Merchants in the Seventeenth Century* (Cambridge: Harvard University Press, 1955), p. 189.
[15] Bailyn, p. 189.

and political life of the cities and provinces north of Maryland. Not that there was precise social equality among the important households; though the Hancocks of Massachusetts were as rich as the Apthorps, there was a social gap between the families that not even John could close. The great names even today have an exciting ring, no matter what their status in colonial society: the Gardiners, Bowdoins, Faneuils, and Olivers in Massachusetts; the Pepperells in Maine and the Partridges and Sherburns in New Hampshire; the Ayraults, Lopezes, Bernons, and Malbones in Rhode Island; the DeLanceys, Livingstones, and Beekmans in New York; and the Schippens, Cadwaladers, Powels, Morrises, and Whartons in Philadelphia. Because the trade of Maryland and Virginia was dominated by British merchants, who placed their hired agents in the colonies, the independent American merchant did not become established in these colonies until just before the Revolution. But in the South, despite the stigma attached to mundane trading by the rich planters, the Huguenot Henry Laurens made a fortune as a wholesale commission man before acquiring his estates; and the Manigaults and de Saussures were at least as rich as the Gadsdens and Rutledges.

Standing as they did at the very center of the foreign-trade marts, the sedentary merchants had more to say about American resource allocation in the eighteenth century than any other group. Moreover, they were acquiring the fortunes that could provide a good part of the capital required for manufacturing when commerce alone would not satisfy the drive to success. Perhaps most important, the political ambitions of these towering figures, whose politics fed and supported their economics, most certainly assured a break with England when the break should prove profitable.

British Regulation of Americans

THE OLD COLONIAL POLICY

In the preceding chapter mention was made of mercantilist doctrine, and some stress was laid on the provisions of the early Navigation Acts. The aim of these laws was three-fold: to protect and encourage English and colonial shipping, to see to it that major colonial imports from Europe should come from British ports, and to make sure that the bulk of desired colonial products—the enumerated articles—should be sent to England.

The first of the Acts of Trade and Navigation, the ones of 1651, 1660, and 1663, introduced no new concepts concerning the relationship of colonies to the mother country. Colonial settlers and investors had always been aware of the restrictions that would be placed on their economic activity; the rules of the game were known to everyone. Rule changes were made gradually and, up to 1763, in such a way that no serious complaint was forthcoming from American colonists. Articles were added to the enumerated list over a long period of time. At first the list consisted entirely of southern continental and West Indian products, most important of which were tobacco, sugar, cotton, dyewood, and indigo. Rice and molasses were not added until 1704. Naval stores were put on the list by laws of 1705 and 1729, furs and skins in 1721. Whenever enumeration worked obvious and unreasonable hardship, relief might be granted. For example, the requirement that rice be sent to England added so much to shipping and handling costs that the American product, despite its superior quality, was priced out of its markets in southern Europe. Consequently, laws passed in the 1730s allowed rice to be shipped directly to ports south of Cape Finisterre, a promontory in northwestern Spain.

Commodities were listed because they were needed by English manufacturers or because they were expected to yield a substantial customs revenue. However, the requirement of shipping to English ports was less onerous than might be supposed. First, because of general ties of blood and language and, more specifically, because credit contacts were more easily established, Americans would have dealt largely with English merchants in any case. Second, duties charged on commodities that were largely re-exported, such as tobacco, were remitted entirely or in large part. Third, bounties were paid on some of the listed articles. Fourth, it was permissible to ship certain items on the list from one colony directly to another for the purpose of furnishing supplies. Finally, the laws could be evaded through smuggling, and with the exception of molasses, such evasion was probably neither more nor less common than it was for Europe generally in the seventeenth and eighteenth centuries.

With respect to imports, the effect of the Navigation Acts was to distort somewhat, but not to influence materially, the flows of trade. The fact that goods had to be funneled through England doubtless added to costs and restricted trade. Again, though, traditional ties would have worked anyway to make Americans the best customers of British merchants. Furthermore, hardship cases were relieved by providing for direct shipment to America of commodities like salt and wine from ports south of Cape Finisterre.

If the American market was to be reserved for Englishmen, was it not necessary to prevent certain types of manufacture in the new country? British manufacturers thought so and tried to convince members of Parliament that competitive colonial production should be prohibited. A law of 1699 made illegal the export of colonial wool, woolen yarn, and finished wool products to any foreign country or even to other colonies. Later, Americans were forbidden to make for export hats from beaver fur. Toward mid-century there was a controversy in England over the question of regulation of iron manufactures, the upshot of which was that after 1750 pig and bar iron were admitted into England duty free while the making of finished iron products was absolutely forbidden. That no more prohibitive laws than these were passed against colonial manufacture indicates the lack of concern for the threat of American competition. Laws against manufactures were loosely enforced; they were restrictive and a cause of annoyance, but they did not seriously affect the course of early industrial development.

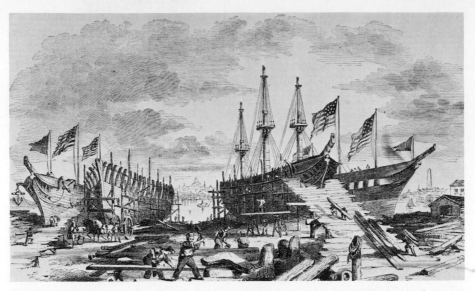

Largely because of ready supplies of first-class timber and excellent naval stores, colonial shipbuilders early enjoyed a tremendous comparative advantage in international trade.

The economic controls imposed by England on her colonies were less strict than those imposed by other European countries on theirs, and the controls were less harsh for Americans than for other colonies within the Empire. But let us not misapprehend the trend of enforcement of the old colonial policy. Regulation of the external trade of the colonies was progressively strengthened before 1763. From 1675 on, governors were supplied with staffs of officials to aid in enforcement; after the general reorganization of 1696 the powers of these officials were sufficient to provide for commercial regulation as tight as possible, considering the amount of smuggling that went on.

The only law flaunted with impunity was the Molasses Act of 1733, an act which, if enforced, would have disrupted one of the major exchanges and brought on serious political upheaval. Before 1700 the northern colonies had traded primarily with the British possessions in the West Indies. As time went on, however, British planters did not provide a sufficient market for northern goods, while the sugar and molasses of the French islands became cheaper than those of the English. During the same years English planters in the sugar islands were being hurt by the requirement that cane products be shipped to the home country before being re-exported. In an effort to protect British West Indian holdings, Parliament was prevailed upon to impose high duties on *foreign* (i.e., mostly French) sugar, molasses, and rum imported into the English colonies. Strict levying of these duties and prevention of smuggling would have led to lower prices for northern staples and serious curtailment of all trade involving rum. For the northern colonists there would have been no way out, because they had to sell their fish, provisions, lumber, and rum in order to pay for English goods. Rather than accept economic annihilation the northerners carried on their trade as usual. Instead of facing the issue resolutely, English officials made no serious attempts at enforcement. Some thirty years later, after the matter had been raised time and again, the Sugar Act of 1764 made the decision against the American colonists in favor of the West Indian planters. This decision, as we shall see, helped to bring on revolution.

THE NEW COLONIAL POLICY

The events that led to the American Revolution fall into better order if we keep in mind the central theme underlying them: *Mercantilist policy, imposed on an essentially self-governing people for a hundred and fifty years, led finally to a constitutional conflict that could be solved only on the battlefield.* The revolutionary crisis was a political crisis, but the stresses and strains that led to fear and hatred of the British had economic origins. Britain's "new" colonial policy was only an extension of the old, with this difference—the new policy was adopted with every intention of enforcing both its spirit and its letter. Furthermore, those in high places insisted, at almost precisely the wrong psychological moments, upon taking punitive action that could only compound the bitterness already stirred up.

The series of critical events began with the English victory over the French in 1763. The Seven Years' War had been a struggle for empire, of course, but it had also been a fight for the protection of the American colonies. And the colonials had not been of much help in furnishing either troops or material, to say nothing of the hurtful trade they had carried on with the French in both Canada and the West Indies. Englishmen were in no mood to spare the feelings of an upstart people who had committed the cardinal sin of ingratitude. Besides, the war had put a heavy burden on the English Treasury, and it seemed no more than right that the American colonists should be required to contribute to the support of garrisons that would still be required on their frontier.

George Grenville, the English prime minister, decided to station a British force of some 10,000 men in the North American possessions at an estimated expense of £350,000. To help pay the cost of keeping the troops, Parliament passed two laws that would yield perhaps one-third of this amount. Of these two laws the Sugar Act of 1764 had more far-reaching implications, for it contained provisions that served the ends of all the major English economic interests and at the same time threatened American business in most of the colonies. But the Stamp Act of 1765, really much less inclusive, led to a boiling up of political tempers that in a very real sense started the Revolutionary crisis.

The most important clauses of the Sugar Act were those that levied taxes on imports of non-British products of the West Indies. The duty on foreign molasses was actually *lowered* from 6d. to 3d. a gallon, a whopping reduction from the rate set by the old Molasses Act, but provision was made for strict collection of the tax. Revenue was one object of the act, but almost as important was the desire to protect British West Indian planters, who were well represented in Parliament, from the competition of their neighbors. Nor was this all. The Sugar Act added to the list of enumerated articles several raw materials demanded by British manufacturers, among which were important exports of the northern and middle colonies. Finally, this comprehensive law removed most of the tariff rebates (drawbacks) hitherto allowed on European goods passing through English ports and even placed new duties on foreign textiles that competed with English products.

The Stamp Act, on the other hand, served no ends of mercantile policy. It was simply a money-raiser, a law requiring that stamps varying in cost from half a penny to several pounds be affixed to legal documents, contracts, newspapers and pamphlets, and even playing cards and dice. The colonists objected loudly on the grounds that the act levied an "internal" tax as distinguished from the traditional "external" taxes—i.e., duties collected on goods coming into the country. When the English ministers refused to recognize this distinction, the colonists further objected that the tax had been levied by a distant Parliament in which not a single colonial representative sat. And they complained that both the Sugar Act and the Stamp Act required the tax revenues to be remitted to England for disbursement, a procedure that meant a further drain of precious specie and a constant reduction in the amount of goods that could be imported. When it became apparent that strict enforcement would accompany such measures, a howling tumult of resistance arose. An articulate, able leadership for anti-British agitation was furnished by lawyers and printers, who were especially infuriated by the Stamp Act.

There followed a decade of trouble characterized by alternating periods of colonial insubordination, British concessions, renewed attempts to raise revenues, further resistance—and, at last, punitive action taken by the British in anger at what was felt to be rank disloyalty. The so-called Stamp Act Congress met in New York in 1765, passed resolutions of fealty, and proceeded to organize a boycott of English goods. "Nonimportation associations" were established throughout the colonies, and the volume of imports from Britain declined swiftly. English merchants were so sharply affected that they demanded repeal of the Stamp Act, and they were joined by political leaders like Edmund Burke and William Pitt, whose sympathies lay with the colonists. Parliament repealed the Stamp Act and reduced the duty on foreign molasses from 3d. to 1d. a gallon.

But the British obstinately maintained the *right* of the mother country to tax her colonies. The other sugar duties stayed on, and a Declaratory Act affirmed the right of Parliament to legislate in all matters concerning Americans. Nevertheless, there was rejoicing, both in the colonies and England, for it was felt that differences would now be reconciled. Yet even then the Quartering Act of 1765 had been on the statute books a year. With its stipulations that for British troops stationed within a colony the assembly would provide barracks, some provisions, and part of the military transport, this law was to prove especially irksome to New York, where soldiers would be concentrated on their way to the West. Much worse was to come, however. George Grenville had been dismissed from the ministry in 1765, largely because King George III disliked him, and he was replaced as Chancellor of the Exchequer by Charles Townshend, who, in 1767, secured the passage of several measures identified with his name. Because the great English landowners were persistently clamoring for relief from their heavy property taxes, Townshend tried once again to raise revenues in America. He felt that if the colonials objected to "internal" taxes, they should have some of the "external" variety. Duties were levied on such important articles of consumption as tea, glass, paper, red and white lead, and colors for paint.

Although these were definitely cost-of-living items, the colonists might have accepted taxes on them calmly if measures had not been passed to put real teeth in the law. One of the Townshend Acts provided for an American Customs Board, another provided for the issuance by colonial courts of the hated general search warrants known as writs of assistance, and another established courts of admiralty to try smuggling cases in the colonies. At a single stroke the British ministry succeeded once again in antagonizing a wide cross section of the American populace. Again resistance flared, taking the form of both peaceful petitions and mob violence. Once more the nonimportation agreements, especially effective in the port towns, were imposed. In the southern colonies, except for Charleston, boycotts were not very successful because trade with Britain was not highly centralized. Nevertheless, American imports fell by late 1769 to perhaps one-third of their normal level, and once again there was pressure from Englishmen to change policy. For the second time Parliament appeared to give in to colonial demands. In 1770 all the Townshend duties except the one on tea were repealed, and, though some of the most distasteful of the Townshend Acts remained on the books, all but the hotheads in the colonies felt that a peaceful settlement was possible. Trade was resumed and a new level of prosperity was reached in 1771.

Reasonable calm prevailed until 1773. Then the whole ugly business exploded again over what must seem to us an inconsequential matter. The English East India Company, in which many politically powerful people had an interest, had run into financial difficulties. To bail it out, Parliament had granted the company a loan of public funds and in addition had passed the Tea Act of 1773, permitting an altogether new method of handling the sales of tea. Up to this time the Company, which enjoyed a monopoly of the trade with India, had sold tea to English wholesalers who in turn sold it to jobbers who sent it to America. Here the tea was turned over to colonial wholesalers who at last distributed it to the retailers. All in all, a lot of people had received income from this series of transactions; besides, duties had been collected on the product when it came into England and upon its arrival in America. Now the Tea Act allowed the East India Company to take tea directly to the colonies, thus eliminating the British duty and some costs of handling. The housewife got cheaper tea, the Company would presumably sell more at a lower price, and everybody would be happy. Only everybody was not happy. Those who had made a good thing of smuggling Dutch tea were now undersold. The colonial tax was still collected, a real sore point. Most important, the American importer was now out of the picture, and American merchants were alarmed. If the tea wholesaler could be by-passed, would it not be possible to wipe out the businesses of other merchants? Could not other companies in Great Britain be granted monopoly control of other commodities until eventually Americans would be reduced to keeping small shops and selling at retail what their foreign masters imported for them? Would not just a few pro-British agents, who would handle the necessary distribution processes, grow rich while staunch Americans grew poor? The answers seemed clear to nearly everyone engaged in business. From wealthy merchants in Boston to shopkeepers in hamlets, there was a swift and violent reaction. Tea in the port towns was sent back to England or destroyed in varied ways, of which the method used at the Boston Tea Party was the most spectacular. Many colonists were shocked at this wanton destruction of private property, but their reaction was nothing compared with the indignation that swelled in Britain.

The result was the bitter and punitive legislation known as the Intolerable Acts. These four measures, together with the Quebec Act to be discussed shortly, could lead only to a complete and final break with the mother country. Passed in the early summer of 1774, the Intolerable Acts (1) closed the Port of Boston to all shipping until the East India Company should be paid for its tea, (2) permitted British officials charged with crimes committed while enforcing British laws to be tried in another colony or in Britain, (3) revised the charter of Massachusetts so as to make certain cherished rights dependent upon the arbitrary decision of the Crown-appointed governor, and (4) provided for the quartering of troops in the city of Boston in a manner especially obnoxious to the citizens. In the ensuing months the political agitation reached new heights of violence. Economic sanctions were again invoked. For the third time nonimportation agreements were put into effect, and the delegates to the First Continental Congress voted not to trade with England or the West Indies unless concessions were made. By this time, however, legislative enactments were of little importance. The crisis was moral and political. Americans would not yield until their basic freedoms were restored, and Englishmen would make no peace until the colonists should relent. The shots of April 19, 1775, were inevitable.

The events leading to revolution centered about a basic conflict between English mercantile policy on the one hand and the need for expansion of the northern colonial merchants on the other. Earlier, though, we pointed out (1) the importance of the southern planter in the total pattern of colonial economic life and (2) the basically agrarian nature of the colonial

Angered colonists invited themselves to a tea party, as they called it, to show their English brethren what they thought of English mercantile policies.

Monday Morning, December 27, 1773.

THE Tea-Ship being arrived, every Inhabitant who wishes to preserve the Liberty of America, is desired to meet at the STATE-HOUSE, This Morning, precisely at TEN o'Clock, to advise what is best to be done on this alarming Crisis.

population. How, then, may we account for the willingness of the wealthy Southerner and of the poor farmer generally to support the rebellion of the merchant class with apparently unallied economic interests? There was again an underlying, inescapable economic motivation. Just as English mercantilism tended, after 1763, to inhibit the growth of trade, so English land policy took a turn that placed a block in the way of agricultural movement.

Before 1763 British policy had been calculated to encourage the rapid development of the West. In the interests of trade, English merchants wanted the new country to fill up as rapidly as possible. Moreover, rapid settlement extended the frontier and thus helped strengthen opposition to France and Spain. By 1763, however, the need to build up the frontier against a foreign power had disappeared. By this time, too, other considerations became important. First, the British felt it wise to contain the population well within the seaboard area where the major investments had been

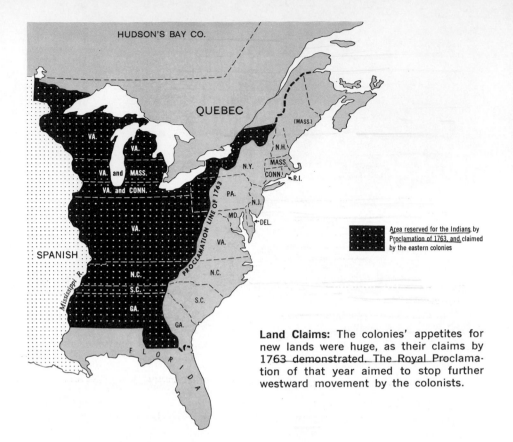

Land Claims: The colonies' appetites for new lands were huge, as their claims by 1763 demonstrated. The Royal Proclamation of that year aimed to stop further westward movement by the colonists.

made and where political control would be easier. Second, the fur trade was now under the complete control of the British, and it was deemed unwise to have frontiersmen moving in to stir up trouble with the Indians. Third, wealthy Englishmen were purchasing western land in great tracts, and there was pressure to "save" some of the good land for these investors. Finally, placing the western lands under direct control of the Crown would obtain for the British Treasury needed revenues from sales and quitrents.

For a number of reasons, then, many people in England counseled prudence in the disposition of unsettled lands. Events on the frontier forced a temporary decision. Angry over injustices, real and fancied, and fearful that the settlers were coming over the mountains to encroach upon their hunting grounds, the northern Indians under Chief Pontiac rebelled. Colonial and regular troops put down the uprising, but only after seven of the nine British garrisons west of Niagara were destroyed. Everyone knew that the red men would be a continuing threat unless they were pacified. Primarily as a temporary solution to the Indian problem, the king issued the Royal Proclamation of 1763 (see map) which, in effect, drew a line beyond which

HUDSON'S BAY CO.

QUEBEC

NOVA SCOTIA

(MASS.)

N.H.

MASS.

N.Y.

CONN.

R.I.

ADDED TO QUEBEC 1774*

PA.

N.J.

MD.

DEL.

VA.

SPANISH

RESERVED FOR THE INDIANS*

N.C.

Mississippi R.

S.C.

GA.

FLORIDA

Reassignment: The Quebec Act of 1774 gave the Indians what had earlier been claimed by various colonies, and at the same time nearly doubled Quebec's area.

* Claimed by the colonies

colonials were not to go without express permission. Governors could no longer grant patents to land lying west of the sources of rivers that flowed into the Atlantic; anyone seeking such a grant had to go directly to the king. At the same time the fur trade was brought under centralized control, and no trader was to cross the mountains without permission.

A few years later the policy of keeping settlement under the supervision of the British was reaffirmed, though it became apparent that the western boundary line would not remain rigidly fixed. In 1768 the Proclamation Line was shifted westward, and treaties with the Indians made large tracts available to speculators. In 1774, the year in which the Intolerable Acts were passed, two actions of the British made it clear that temporary expedients had evolved into permanent policy. First, a royal proclamation tightened the terms on which land would pass into private hands. Grants were no longer to be free; instead, tracts were to be sold at public auction in lots of from 100 to 1,000 acres at a minimum price of 6d. an acre. Quitrents were to be more than double their old rate. Even more serious was the passage of the Quebec Act (see map), which moved the boundaries of

Quebec to the Ohio River and the Mississippi River, thus destroying the western claims of Massachusetts, Connecticut, and Virginia. The fur trade was henceforth to be regulated by the governor of Quebec, and the Indian boundary line was to run as far south as Georgia.

Not everyone in the colonies suffered from the new land policy. Rich land speculators, politically powerful enough to obtain special grants from the king, found the new regulations restrictive but not ruinous. Indeed, great holders of ungranted lands *east* of the mountains, like the Penns and the Calverts, or of huge tracts already granted but not yet settled, stood to benefit from the rise in values caused by the British embargo on westward movement. Similarly, the farmers of the old, established agricultural areas might gain in two ways: (1) the competition from the produce of the new lands would not be so severe and (2) it would be harder for agricultural laborers to get farms of their own with the result that hired hands would be cheaper.

The real pressure was exerted on the planters in the tobacco colonies and on the frontier farmers, both of whom were dependent for prosperity on free western land. The difficulties of the plantation owners arose largely as a consequence of the system of marketing tobacco, their major crop. London merchants normally sent their vessels to America to get the tobacco and carry it back for sale in the European market. The commodity was *consigned* to the merchant, who served as *agent* for the grower; he sold the tobacco, deducted all costs, made purchases of British goods for the account of the plantation owner, and sent the supplies (together with any cash balance due) on the ship that went to get the next year's crop. In some years tobacco prices were so low in England that the sales of a planter's crop barely covered the cost of freight, insurance, duties, handling charges and commissions. But if there were no proceeds to pay for goods that had been ordered, it was no matter. The merchants were glad to lend money; after all, they did not want the planters to stop growing tobacco. On such loans there was, of course, an interest charge, usually at a rate of 6 per cent or more per annum, and the next year's crop constituted security for the loan. If prices were high in the succeeding year, well and good; if they were not, the debt simply increased. Sometimes it became necessary to convert loans made against crops into long-term loans secured by mortgages on land and slaves. As early as 1700 there was complaint about these debt burdens; by 1775 annual interest charges were a severe drain on the income of planters.

The withdrawal of free western lands threatened to cut off their hope of eventual escape from the burden of debt. Many tideland owners had for years been able to meet their obligations by realizing appreciation in values of their western holdings, holdings they had obtained for practically nothing. In the years before 1770 more and more planters were turning to this kind of investment, some, like George Washington, in anticipation of shifting from tobacco to wheat-growing. British land policy, then, not

VIEW OF THE TOWN OF BOSTON WITH SEVERAL SHIPS OF WAR IN THE HARBOUR.

Boston's natural endowments helped the city attain a place of prominence as a trading and shipping center; but the mountains to the west inhibited access to the hinterland, and Boston ultimately fell behind New York in the commercial rivalry between the two great ports.

mercantile policy, tended to sway the sympathies of this important economic group to the side of the merchant class of the North.

Similarly, the frontier farmer usually took an anti-British stand because he thought his chances better under a government that would be more liberal in disposing of land. Although poor agrarians did not have dollar stakes in western land comparable to those of large fur traders, land speculators, and planters, they were nonetheless concerned. Those unable to pay their debts often lost their farms through foreclosure, and a British policy that inhibited westward movement angered the frontiersmen and tended to align them against the British and with the aristocratic Americans, on whom they otherwise lost no love. The Currency Act of 1764 likewise frustrated and annoyed this debtor group; for though prices actually rose moderately in the ensuing decade, farmers were persuaded that their lot worsened with the moderate contraction of paper money that occurred. Finally, the repeated trade stoppages that followed the nonintercourse agreements worked against the small farmer by lowering the prices of such surplus as he had to sell. As much as anything, a vague, scarcely articulated feeling that any change would be an improvement drove the mass of farmers to the support of revolution.

Part Two:

1789–1860

The Revolution that began officially on April 19, 1775, dragged on for more than six bitter years. From a vantage point two centuries distant we can see that the war foreshadowed a massive upheaval in the Western world, for it precipitated a chain reaction of revolutions, great and small. But to the embattled colonials it was simply a conflict fought in the righteous cause of securing freedom from illegal British intervention in American affairs. Paradoxically, the Revolution never did have the support of a substantial popular majority. Perhaps a third of the colonists remained loyal to England, and another third did little or nothing to help the cause, often trafficking with the enemy and profiteering by selling provisions and supplies to American troops at exorbitant prices. In varying numbers and in widely scattered theaters, foot soldiers slogged wearily back and forth in heartbreaking campaigns that got nowhere. Although seamen were few and sea battles were for the most part indecisive, it is an irony of history that the Revolution was finally won with naval strength, as the French fleet under DeGrasse drove off the British men-of-war and bottled up poor Cornwallis at Yorktown.

In retrospect it seems astonishing that the Americans could have won their freedom. The British were hampered, of course, by extended lines of communication and supply, and their military leadership was marked on occasion by surpassing ineptness. Moreover, the French, not because they loved Americans but because they hated Englishmen, opportunistically jumped in with help that proved decisive. And despite the grave weakness of the American government, it had a persistent vitality and flexibility that deluded friend and enemy alike. Yet in the black year of 1780 only the spirit and dogged courage of those who deeply believed in independence could keep the cause alive. The next year marked the turning point of the war, for after five years of noisy argument the Articles of Confederation were ratified, and new order was imposed on the administration of the nation's affairs.

To be sure, there was still disruptive division among American leaders as to what kind of government should ultimately be adopted. One group wanted no stronger central government than the Articles provided, preferring to cast their lots and fortunes with the individual states. Another group, made up on the whole of less fiery revolutionaries, took the view that a strong central government, with power to coerce the states, should be quickly established. Until the end of the war those who preferred a strong government were largely in control of the nation's affairs; but when news of a favorable peace arrived in 1783, many of the strongest leaders went home to their own pursuits, leaving the administration largely in charge of the weak-government advocates. For several years the most able men in American life seemed to drift into preoccupation with their own interests. Only John Jay, the Secretary for Foreign Affairs, remained a tower of strength.

But problems too great to be surmounted by the states acting individually pressed inexorably for strong rather than weak union. The new nation was treated by the great powers with a disdain that bordered on contempt. Britain, annoyed because Americans refused to pay prewar British creditors and restore confiscated Tory property as provided in the peace treaty, arrogantly excluded the United States from valuable commercial privileges and refused to withdraw troops from frontier posts on American soil. Spain tried to close the lower Mississippi to American traffic. Even France refused to extend the courtesies traditionally offered a sovereign government.

Internally the most pressing problems were financial. Fortunately for postwar Confederation officials the money cost of the Revolutionary War was largely written off. Between 1775 and 1781 the war was financed by the issue of paper money in amounts great enough to result in a galloping inflation, the only one ever experienced in America save in the Confederate South. Nearly $400 million in continental money, quartermaster and commissary certificates of the central government, and paper money of the states were issued to defray wartime expenses. These various issues were for all practical purposes repudiated by the middle of 1783, the effect being that of a tax on those who held the depreciating currency while it fell in value. Only a relatively small foreign and domestic debt, totaling less than $40 million, remained; but the question of responsibility for its repayment remained a thorny one, for political leaders assumed that the political agency that paid the debt would ultimately hold the balance of power. More important was the fact that Congress had no independent income, relying for funds on catch-as-catch-can contributions of the states levied roughly in proportion to their several populations. Nor were the states without their own fiscal problems. By 1786 no less than seven of them were issuing their own paper, and debtor groups in the other six were clamoring for similar issues. Although the issuing states, with the exception of Rhode Island, acted responsibly, perhaps no other course of events so frightened conservatives as increasing control of the money supply by the states.

The United States under the Articles of Confederation was by no means the weak and hopelessly inefficient organization some historians have led us to believe. After all, the Congress did manage to finance a central government through a trying period, painstakingly working to settle a multitude of obligations incurred during the war. The leadership was strong enough to effect an imaginative and nearly permanent settlement of the perplexing western question. Barriers to trade among the states were exceptions rather than the rule. As early as 1783 even those who wanted a weak central government began to make concessions that would strengthen the power of Congress, and by 1786 most of the vehement opponents of a strong central government knew that genuine union was inevitable. Virginia called the Annapolis Convention ostensibly to settle questions of trade regulations among the states. Yet even before the delegates came to Annapolis, only to recommend to Congress that another convention be called to decide a broader range of problems, it was clear that American leadership was moving toward unity. The convention that met in Philadelphia in 1787 could ignore its instructions to amend the Articles of Confederation and instead create a new government only because the great Constitutional question debated so heatedly since 1775 was at last settled in the minds of a majority. The new Constitution, providing for a great common market and a central government strong enough to assure adequate investment in social overhead capital, was a necessary condition for the unimpeded growth of the American economy.

The Westward Movement Before 1862

An equilibrium of agriculture, manufacture, and commerce, is certainly become essential to our independence. Manufactures, sufficient for our own consumption (and no more). Commerce sufficient to carry the surplus produce of agriculture, beyond our own consumption, to a market for exchanging it for articles we cannot raise (and no more). These are the true limits of manufacture and commerce. To go beyond is to increase our dependence on foreign nations, and our liability to war.

THOMAS JEFFERSON

 Despite the transcendant desire of Europeans for land, for nearly a century and a half it remained plentiful within easy distance of the seacoast. Eventually, though, the first colonies became crowded. Newcomers, if they would settle outside the towns, had to go to the frontier, a twisting, shifting line beyond which lay a vast, unoccupied territory. In even greater numbers migrant farmers kept turning and pushing west for opportunity and fortune. Out of this constant frontier movement a new man appeared, the pioneer or frontiersman, who lasted until the frontier disappeared late in the nineteenth century.

The psychology of the peregrinating frontiersman may still be with us, as witness our transient population today; and his daring, adventurous spirit may be challenged by opportunities no less exciting, whether in or out of space. But before the Civil War the pioneer was the hero at the cutting edge of progress. It was his willingness to undertake great risk, for himself and his family, that made possible the first rapid exploitation of America's natural resources.

Land Growth: The purchase of Louisiana marked the beginning of the continental expansion of the United States, culminating in the purchase of a nonadjacent Alaska in 1867 and the annexation of a seaward archipelago (Hawaii) in 1898.

The Acquisition and Disposal of the Public Domain

The United States began with a solid mass of land extending from the Atlantic coast to the Mississippi River and from the Great Lakes to, but not including, Florida and West Florida. Except for some unimportant reserves, the seven of the original thirteen states with land claims west of the Appalachians more or less reluctantly yielded these claims to the central government. Between 1802, when Georgia, the last of the states to cede, gave over her rights to western land, and 1898, when the formal annexation of Hawaii took place, the United States took very nearly its present physical form through eight main acquisitions.

1. The Territory of Louisiana, acquired in 1803 by purchase from France.
2. Florida, acquired in 1819 by purchase from Spain. A few years previously the United States had annexed the narrow strip of land that constituted West Florida.
3. The Republic of Texas, annexed as a state in 1845. The Republic of Texas had been established nine years previously after the victory of the American settlers over the Mexicans.
4. The Oregon Country, annexed by treaty with Great Britain in 1846. Spain and Russia were original claimants to this area, but they had long since dropped out. By a treaty of 1818 the United States and

Great Britain had agreed to a joint occupation of the Oregon Country and British Columbia; the treaty of 1846 set the dividing line at the forty-ninth parallel.

5. The Mexican Cession, acquired by conquest from Mexico in 1848.
6. The Gadsden Purchase, acquired from Mexico in 1853.
7. The Alaskan Purchase, acquired from Russia in 1867.
8. The Hawaiian Annexation, formally ratified in 1898.

In half a century the United States obtained a continental area of 3,000,000 square miles, of which 1,400,000,000 acres (72% of the total) constituted the public domain.[1] In 1862, two-thirds of this vast area was still in the possession of the government, but the method of disposal was agreed upon long before. The decisions of our forbears regarding federal land policy have their consequences in the present.

THE LAND ORDINANCES OF 1785 AND 1787

After victory in the Revolution the Congress of the Confederation had to make three decisions regarding the disposal of public land. (1) Was the New England or southern land system to prevail? (2) Should the government exact high revenues from the sale of land, or should cheap land be made available to everyone? (3) What was to be the political relationship of newly settled areas to the original colonies?

Two major land systems had developed during the colonial period. The New England system of "township planting" provided for laying out townships, for subdivision of townships into carefully surveyed tracts, and for auction sale of tracts to settlers. In the eighteenth century it was usual to establish townships, often six miles square, in tiers. The opening of new townships proceeded with regularity from settled to unsettled land, gaps of unsettled land appeared infrequently, and no one could own land not previously surveyed. The contrasting southern system provided for no rectangular surveys. In the South a settler simply selected what appeared to be a choice plot of unappropriated land and had the county surveyor mark it off for him. He paid no attention to the relationship of his tract to other pieces of property, and the legal description of his tract was made with reference to more or less permanent natural objects such as stones, trees, and streams.

Two fundamentally different points of view emerged about the terms on which land should be made available, and a debate started that was not to end for several decades. Those who advocated a "conservative" policy were in favor of selling the public lands in large tracts, at high prices, and for cash. The proponents of a "liberal" policy were in favor of putting land within the reach of everyone by making it available in small parcels, at low prices, and on credit terms.

---

[1] In addition, Alaska contains more than 365,000 square miles, most of it still in the public domain, and Hawaii added 4,100 square miles, none of it in the public domain.

As is nearly always the case when economic questions are discussed, arguments were advanced on two planes—the plane of unselfish, public interest and the plane of selfish, private interest. On the higher, national-interest plane, the conservatives contended that natural resources ought to be disposed of in a way that would yield substantial revenues—revenues that would be spent to further the interests of the people as a whole. The liberals argued that every man had a right to a piece of land and that the spirit of democracy could best be preserved by affording everyone who wished an opportunity to make his way on a farm of his own. They said that there could never be economic oppression of Americans if a poor man could always avoid that oppression by moving to the West. On a lower level the conservatives argued, not always for publication, that a rag-tag population in the West would be a continuing spawning place of political unrest. Furthermore, the values of real property in the East would tend to be weaker if land were readily available in the West, and the level of wages in the East would be persistently higher if a part of the labor force were forever escaping to a new life. Needless to say, the liberal forces were largely composed of people more interested in furthering their personal interests than in preserving democracy. The western settler, the eastern laborer, and the land speculator stood together for cheap land because they would gain financially from cheap land.

Problems of land disposal could not be divorced from politics. Likewise the decision regarding the status of areas to be settled in the future was one that involved a great political principle. Were these areas to remain in colonial dependence, subject to profitable exploitation of the original thirteen states? Or were they to be admitted into a union of states on a basis of equality? Answers to these questions would test the foresight and selflessness of Americans, who had themselves escaped the dominance of a mother country.

There was no pressure on the Congress of the Confederation to provide a system for regulating public lands until 1784, by which time Virginia and New York had relinquished claims to the southern part of the territory lying northwest of the Ohio River. In that year a Congressional committee of five, headed by Thomas Jefferson, proposed a system based upon a rectangular survey. It is noteworthy that three of the five members were southerners who, despite their origins, recognized the value of the New England method of settlement. No action was taken in 1784, but a year later another committee, composed of a member from each state, worked over the report of the previous year and offered a carefully considered proposal. With minor changes this proposal was passed as the Land Ordinance of 1785.[2]

Insofar as the ordinance set a *physical* basis for disposing of the public

---

[2] *Journals of the Continental Congress* (Washington, D.C.: U.S. Government Printing Office, 1933), XXVIII, 375.

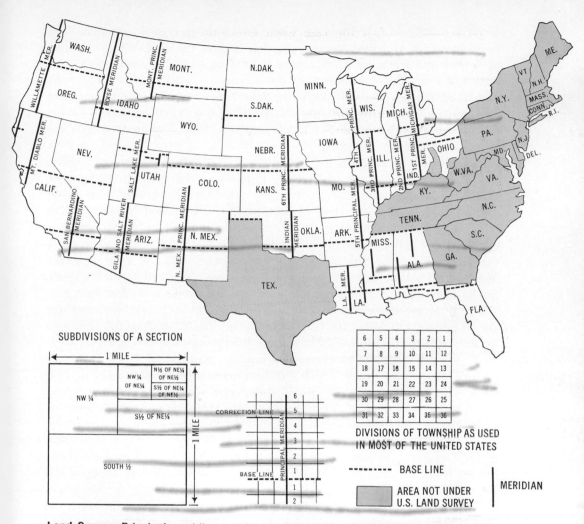

Land Survey: Principal meridians and base lines made possible precise apportioning of newly opened territories into sections and easily described subdivisions of sections, thus simplifying later property transfers.

lands its effects were permanent. Government surveyors were to establish, on unsettled land, horizontal lines called *base lines* and vertical lines called *principal meridians.* The first of the principal meridians was to be in what is now the State of Ohio, and the first surveys covered land north of the Ohio River not included in the "reserves." Eventually all of the land in the United States was included in the survey except the original thirteen states and Vermont, Kentucky, Tennessee, parts of Ohio, and Texas. As the survey moved westward, other principal meridians were established, the second being in what is now Indiana, the third in what is now Illinois, and so on. The student may locate on the map shown above the other principal meridians and the base lines perpendicular to them. The insets show how tiers of townships, called ranges, were laid out to the east and to the west of a principal meridian. The ranges were designated by a number and a direction from the meridian, and the townships within each range were numbered north and south from the base line. Each township, being six miles square, contained thirty-six square miles numbered as shown. In the Ordinance of 1785 a square mile was called a "lot," but in later acts the term *section* came to be used.

The Ordinance reflected the prevalent conservative view that public land should be a major source of revenue. Provisions relating to minimum size of tracts, prices, and terms were severe. Alternate townships were to be sold as a whole, the other half of the townships to be sold by sections. All sales, at public auction, were to be for a minimum price of $1 per acre, terms strictly cash. Thus, the smallest possible outlay was the $640 necessary to buy a section, an expenditure beyond the means of most pioneers. Moreover, a square mile of land was more than the small farmer wanted, for he would do well to clear and cultivate ten acres or so his first year, and a quarter-section was as much as a man could handle without the aid of grown children. Only individuals of means and land companies formed by large investors could purchase land under the first law.

Two years later the Congress took up the problem of establishing the *political* principles under which the settlement of the West was to take place. The Ordinance of 1787 provided that the Northwest Territory should be organized as a district to be run by a governor and judges appointed by the Congress.[3] As soon as it should contain 5,000 male inhabitants of voting age, a territorial legislature was to be elected and a nonvoting delegate sent to the Congress. At least three and not more than five states were to be created from this territory; when any one of the established divisions of the Territory should have a population of 60,000 inhabitants, it was to be admitted to the Union as a state on a basis of complete equality with the older states. Contained in the Ordinance were certain guarantees of civil and religious liberties, together with a prohibition of slavery in the Territory. *The main principle, however, was that of eventual equality of status for the new areas.* The age-old source of trouble between colony and mother country was thus removed by a simple though unprecedented device—that of making the colonies extensions of the mother country that would be allowed to become socially and politically equal.

THE LAND ACTS, 1796–1862

For a decade after the passage of the Land Ordinance of 1785, pioneering in the area north of the Ohio River was restricted by Indian trouble as well as by the high price of government land. The British, who persisted in maintaining posts on American territory in the Northwest, for

---

[3] *Journals of the Continental Congress* (Washington, D.C.: U.S. Government Printing Office, 1933), XXXII, 314.

years incited the Indians to make war upon American settlers. By a treaty of 1794 the British agreed to evacuation of the posts in the Northwest, and in August of that year "Mad Anthony" Wayne and his forces defeated the Indians at the Battle of Fallen Timbers. A peace treaty signed with the Indian braves in 1795 gave the white man the area in the southeastern corner of the Territory and certain "islands" of land around fortified outposts. The time was now ripe for the establishment of a land policy by the Congress of the United States.

The Land Act of 1796 represented another victory for the conservative view. A system of rectangular survey, substantially the same as the one established by the Ordinance of 1785, was made permanent. The minimum purchase allowed by the Act of 1796 was still 640 acres, but the minimum price per acre was raised to $2, the only concession to the cheap-land advocates being a credit provision that permitted half of the purchase price to be deferred for a year. Only a small amount of land was sold under this act before Congress in 1800 changed the minimum acreage to 320 and permitted the buyer, after a cash payment of one-half, to pay one-fourth in two years and the final fourth in four years. A law of 1804 further lowered the minimum purchase to 160 acres. In 1820, the minimum purchase was reduced to 80 acres and the price per acre to $1.25, but the credit provisions, which had resulted in losses to the government, were repealed. The liberal forces had by 1820 clearly won the battle. Twelve years later the minimum purchase was reduced to 40 acres, so that in 1832 a pioneer could get a start with a $50 expenditure for his farm. By this time pressures for *free* land, which had been exerted from the first, were beginning to get legislative results.

The individual brave enough to risk his own life and the lives of his family in a pioneering venture was not usually deterred from action by legal niceties. From the beginning, settlers had tended to go past the areas that had been surveyed and announced for sale. As the decades passed and as the West became "crowded," this tendency to pick a tract in unopened areas increased. Unauthorized settlement, or "squatting," resulted from (1) attempts of the pioneers to find better soils and (2) the hope that they could take choice land and make it a going proposition before they were billed for it.

Squatting was illegal, of course, but it was an offense hard to combat. Moreover, there were those who argued that by occupation and improvement of the land the squatter gained rights against all comers—"cabin rights" or "corn rights" or "tommyhawk rights," as they were variously called on the frontier. At first federal troops tried to drive squatters from unsurveyed land, but successes were only temporary. Gradually the government came to view this pioneer law-breaking less and less seriously. Against those who would purchase the squatter's land when it came up for public sale, informal but effective measures were taken by the squatters themselves, who formed protective associations as soon as they settled in a particular locality.

Wagon trains like this one on the main street of Manhattan, Kansas, in 1860 fed the steady stream of migrants to western America and its expansive lands.

When the public auction of land in that locality was held, the members of the protective association let it be known that there had better be no competitive bidding for land pre-empted by them. The appearance of well-armed frontiersmen at the auction ordinarily convinced city slickers and big land buyers that it would be unwise to bid. Even in places where there was no organized action, the individual who found his farm bought out from under him could often charge handsomely for the "improvements" he had made, and frontier courts were inclined to uphold his "rights."

As early as 1820 Congress began to give relief to squatters, and after 1830 scarcely a year went by in which pre-emption rights were not granted to settlers in certain areas. In 1841 a general Pre-emption Act, called the "Log Cabin Bill" by its proponents, was passed. This law granted to anyone settling on land that was surveyed, but not yet put up for sale, the right to purchase 160 acres at the minimum price when the auction should be held. No one could outbid the settler and secure the land, provided the squatter could raise the $200 necessary to buy his quarter section. Technically, squatting on *unsurveyed* land was still illegal; because of this fact and because there was still no outright grant of land, the westerner (and anyone else who stood to make money by buying land and waiting for it to rise in value) was not satisfied. Nevertheless, the land policy of the country was about as liberal as could be consistent with the requirement that the public domain be a continuing source of revenue.

Pressure remained on Congress to reduce the price of "islands" of less desirable land passed over in the first surges to the West. In 1854 the Graduation Act provided for the graduated reduction of the minimum purchase price of such tracts, so that if land remained unsold for as long as thirty years it could be had for as little as 12½ cents an acre. A remarkable gobbling up of such pieces took place, attesting to the fact that people were willing to gamble a little on probable appreciation of even the most unpromising real estate.

In the 1850s, as agitation for free land continued, it became apparent that the passage of a homestead law was inevitable. Southerners, who had at one time favored free grants to actual settlers, became violently opposed as time went on. The 160-acre farm usually proposed by homestead supporters was not large enough to make the working of slaves economical, and it seemed obvious to southern Congressmen that homesteading would fill the West with antislavery people. On the other hand, many northern Congressmen, who would normally have had leanings toward a conservative policy, joined forces with the westerners because they, too, knew that free land meant free states.

In 1860, a Homestead Act was passed, but Buchanan, fearing that it would precipitate secession, vetoed it. Two years later, with southerners out of Congress, the Homestead Act of 1862 became law. Henceforth, any head of a family or anyone over twenty-one could have 160 acres of public land upon the payment of small fees. The only stipulation was that the homesteader should either live on his place or cultivate it for five years. A not unimportant provision was that, should he decide not to meet the five-year requirement, he might obtain full title to the land by simply paying the minimum price of $1.25 an acre.

Although much land was to pass into private hands under the Homestead Act of 1862, it was not the boon to the downtrodden that it was expected to be. Most of the first-class land had by this time been taken up. Furthermore, it was so easy to get around the provisions of the law that land-grabbers used it, along with the acts that still provided for outright purchase, to build up great holdings. And by 1862 the frontier had reached the edge of the dry country, where a 160-acre farm was too small to provide a living for a man and his family.

The Migrations to the West

In the discussion of the colonial period we noted that by the middle of the eighteenth century pioneers were moving across the Appalachian Mountains. By 1790 perhaps a quarter of a million people lived within the mountain valleys or to the west, and the trickle of movement had become a small stream. There were two eighteenth-century routes to the West. The more important was the one that passed through the Cumberland Gap and thence into either Kentucky or Tennessee; the other was across southern Pennsylvania to Pittsburgh and on down the Ohio River. Even as the movement to the West was gaining momentum, pioneering was still going on in Pennsylvania and New York, and to the north in Vermont, New Hampshire, and Maine.

The frontier, as technically defined in the census reports, was an area in which there were more than two and less than six people per square mile. On the map shown below have been drawn from census data the frontier lines for 1800, 1820, 1840, and 1860. The line for 1800 indicates a wedge driven into the West, the point being in western Kentucky. Sixty years later, the line ran in a southerly direction from a point in the middle of Minnesota, with a noticeable bulge into Nebraska and Kansas territories and a definite drift into Texas. At the moment we are interested in seeing *how* the frontier line was pushed into the shape and general position it had in 1860, but in addition to learning the paths of movement, we shall have to learn something of the *why* of the westward thrust.

Moving Frontier: Census data from 1800 onward chronicled the constant westward flow of population. The "frontier," its profile determined by natural attractions and a few man-made and physiographic obstacles, was a magnet for the venturesome.

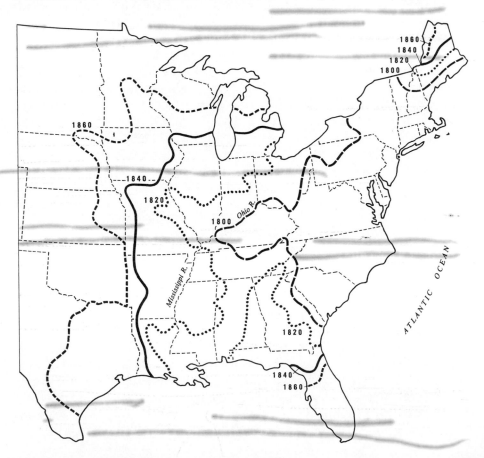

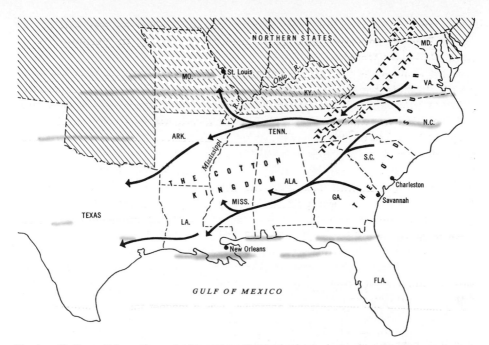

Moving Cotton: Exhaustion of old cotton fields had much to do with the westward movement of cotton civilization after the War of 1812 and up to the onset of the Civil War.

THE SOUTHERN MIGRATION

At the time of the Revolution the three great traditional staples had given the southern colonies an unquestioned economic superiority in the new land. But the war with Great Britain and separation from the mother country had serious consequences. Markets were lost or seriously impaired during the hostilities, and some of them were never regained. Indigo production was worst hit, for the British turned to the East Indies for supplies and, of course, no longer paid a bounty on the American product. Rice remained nearly constant in output until around 1820, when it began to increase in importance; its culture was limited, however, to a small coastal area and could not be significant in southern development. The great blow was the decline in tobacco production. During the 1790s tobacco continued to head the list of American exports in dollar value, but the turn of the century marked the beginning of serious difficulties. The Embargo Acts and the War of 1812 enabled the product of both the West and the East Indies to gain a place in world markets, and meanwhile high duties imposed by European countries encouraged production in Europe, where the great demand was. World prices fell so that tobacco could be grown profitably in America only on virgin lands. Production moved westward—to Tennessee, Kentucky, Missouri, and even into southern Ohio. Not until the

1850s were North Carolina and Virginia to regain something of their old importance as tobacco-producing states.

It is well known that in cotton lay the hope—or, if you wish, the tragedy —of the South. Obtaining their supplies of raw cotton from the Far East, Englishmen had turned to the manufacture of cotton cloth in the late seventeenth century. The inventions that came a hundred years or so later— the steam engine, the spinning jenny, the water frame, the spinning mule, and the power loom—all gave rise to an enormous demand for cotton fiber. The phase of the industrial revolution that made possible the application of power to textile manufacturing came at just the right time to stimulate and encourage the planting of cotton wherever it could be grown profitably. In the southern United States the conditions for a profitable agriculture based on cotton were nearly ideal. Only some way of separating the green seed from the short-staple "upland cotton" had to be devised. One of the contributions of the Yankee genius, Eli Whitney, was the invention of a gin that enabled a good hand to clean fifty pounds of cotton a day. With the application of power to the gin, there was no limit to the amount of fiber that could be produced.

On the humid coasts of Georgia and South Carolina planters who had grown indigo turned to cotton; even the rice fields were partially changed to the new staple. The culture moved up to North Carolina and Virginia and over the mountains to the beautiful rolling country of middle Tennessee. In the early 1800s the piedmont of Georgia and South Carolina became the important center, and by 1820 these states were vying for first place, with South Carolina slightly in the lead.

Beginning with the end of the War of 1812, the really important shift in cotton production was to the West (see map on p. 109). Almost unerringly, the settlers hit first the most fertile soils of the "Black Belt," extending from Georgia in an arc through Alabama into northeastern Mississippi. A second major cotton-growing area lay in the rich bottom land of the lower Mississippi River and its tributaries. In this extremely fertile soil the cotton even tended to grow a longer fiber. The culture spread into western Tennessee and eastern Arkansas. A jump into Texas then foretold the future trend of cotton production.

By 1840 the early cotton-producing states had been left behind. In 1860 Alabama, Mississippi, and Louisiana were far in the lead, with Mississippi, then in the number one position, producing more than Georgia and South Carolina together. The shift in the realm of King Cotton was to have the most far-reaching consequences upon the economy of the South.

Just before the Civil War there could be no doubt that cotton was indeed king. The great staple accounted for more than half the dollar value of United States exports, a value nearly ten times as great in foreign trade as its nearest competitor, the wheat and wheat flour of the North. At home, cotton planters furnished the raw materials for the textile manufacturers of the North, who by 1860 were selling half again as much cotton cloth as wool cloth. The amount of the national income generated by cotton manufacturers was greater at this time than that generated by the iron industry. Little wonder that the aristocratic Southerner could scarcely envisage a North, or even a world, without his chief product.

There was both a *push* and a *pull* to the new lands of the South. The push had begun in colonial times as tidewater lands began to lose the natural fertility the staples required. The small farmer, impelled by hardship, had moved into the piedmont. The shift had been especially pronounced in Virginia and North Carolina, whence struggling families tended to sift through the Cumberland Gap into Tennessee and Kentucky. The frontiersman—the professional pioneer—was next pulled into the rich new cotton country, mostly from Georgia and South Carolina, but partly from Tennessee and even Kentucky. Following closely came the yeoman farmer; almost simultaneously—and this is what clearly distinguishes the southern migration—came the planter, the man of substance, with his great household establishment and his slaves. The planter had sufficient means to acquire large acreages, and the small householder could compete in the best agricultural areas only with difficulty. The rich man was at an obvious advantage in the public land auctions; and the pioneer and the farmer with a slave or two were continually tempted to sell out to the plantation owner, for the price the latter could offer netted a profit for "improving" the land.

A farmer class of some numerical importance nevertheless developed in the South, even though many farmers sold out to planters and moved on across the Mississippi River, sometimes going north as well as west. Some of the least able retreated to the mountains or drifted into the barren pine belts that constitute much of the land area in the Deep South. But it was the plantation owner, so unimportant numerically and so very important as the aristocratic determiner of southern economic development, who was to be in complete charge of the South's undoing.

THE NORTHERN MIGRATION

The first settlements in Ohio were made by those who came down the Ohio River from Pittsburgh. These people were joined by pioneers who, having stopped for a while in Tennessee and Kentucky, moved north and west into Ohio, southern Indiana, and southern Illinois. The northern parts of these states did not attract the southerners, who filled in the valleys of rivers that ran into the Ohio River. While the movement from the South was going on, the exodus from New England began, at first into northern New Hampshire and Vermont, then into western New York, where pioneers from Pennsylvania and New Jersey were also settling.

During the early 1800s the movement across the top of the country gained momentum, and at the quarter-century mark people from the New England and middle Atlantic states were pouring into the northern counties of Ohio and Indiana and into southern Michigan. By 1850, lower Michigan

Land speculation—"holding for a rise"—became a lively offshoot of the westward surge of population. Here a Kansas land office provides a center of speculative activity.

had been pretty well taken over, and the best lands in northern Illinois and southern Wisconsin were settled. On the eve of the Civil War the pioneers were pushing the northwestern tip of the frontier into central Minnesota, most of Iowa was behind the frontier line, and the handsome country of eastern Kansas was being taken up. Only in Texas did the frontier line of 1860 bulge farther to the west than it did in Kansas. By this time California had been a state for a decade, and Oregon had been admitted the year before, but the vast area between the western frontier and the coast was not to be completely settled for another half-century.

Southerners, then, moving across the Ohio River, were the chief influence in the lower part of the old Northwest. New Englanders, when the Erie Canal made transportation easy, were dominant in the Great Lakes region, but they were joined by another stream that originated in the middle Atlantic states. For the most part, families moved singly, though sometimes as many as fifty to a hundred would move together. As the frontier pushed westward, the pioneers on the cutting edge were frequently the same people who had broken virgin soil but a short way back and only a few years previously. Or they were the grown children of men and women who had once participated in the conquest of the wilderness.

Throughout this early period there was an ever increasing influx of land-hungry people from abroad. From 1789 to the close of the War of 1812 not more than 250,000 people had immigrated from Europe. With the final defeat of Napoleon and the coming of peace abroad, immigration went on apace. From 500,000 people in the 1830s, the flow increased to 1,500,000 in the forties and to 2,500,000 in the fifties. For the most part, the newcomers were from the north of Europe. Germans and Irish predominated, but there were many from England, Scotland, Switzerland, and the Scandinavian countries. Of these peoples, the Germans tended more than any others to go directly to the lands of the West. They provided a fairly well-educated and extremely able population that was to have a pronounced effect upon the economic life of the states of the northwest and of Iowa and Missouri. Some immigrants from the other groups entered into the agricultural migration, but most were absorbed into the eastern city populations.

Whatever may have been the place of origin of the pioneer, his older way of earning a living was probably easier than the new one he chose. Early nineteenth-century life in the West was hard, and the difficulties to be surmounted were the same ones that had confronted the American colonists. For the firstcomers there could be little more than a bare existence. Housing was cramped and drafty, clothing was crude, and there was little social life. Isolation may have protected pioneer families against contagion, but once sickness struck there was little to do but let nature take its course. The arduous work of clearing the land was done slowly; at first wild plants and animals had to supplement the food brought along for subsistence, and it might take a generation to clear land for a 160-acre farm. Only gradually did the pioneer homestead begin to produce a surplus for sale; meanwhile, with the help of neighbors, timber could be converted into a livable house and useful barn, and it was not hard to build a livestock herd. The proportion of the family's work leading to immediate consumption was limited by the necessity of providing for the future; but clearing, building, and fencing were thought of as investment, and there was a sense of "building up the place." It early became a part of American folkways to keep an eye on the market for homesteads and to have in mind a price at which to sell and move on. As Professor John Ise used to remark, the farmer more than anyone else relied for a living on the unearned increment—on appreciation of capital values as population increased. Eventually the settler had a choice of selling and realizing on his investment or of staying on a workable, money-making farm.

It might be thought that when the prairies were reached the job of getting land into cultivation would be easier, but the problems were still enormous. As a matter of fact, the first settlers, thinking that land on which trees did not grow was infertile, tended to skirt the grasslands of Indiana and Illinois. After 1845, with substantial rises in world prices of grain and with railroad communication established to the East, the pioneer farmer was led to undertake the difficult task of plowing the thick and heavily matted prairie sod. Wood for buildings, fences, and fuel were scarce, but on the whole it was less expensive to break sod than to fell trees and remove stumps. A sod house was probably more comfortable, winter and summer, than a log cabin; but the treelessness of the plains made for exposure to the elements that the settlers in the river bottoms and forested areas did not have to suffer.

The North, like the South, had its staples—wheat, corn, and livestock. Animals furnished the first important cash product of the Northwest. Early in the 1800s hogs were driven overland from Ohio to the urban centers of the East or else were sent south by boat for sale to the plantations. Cattle, too, were driven in great herds to the East, there to be sold for immediate slaughter or for further fattening. But it was not long before the pioneer farmer could market his hogs fairly close to home. Very early, slaughtering and meat-packing centers arose in the West, and by the 1830s Cincinnati was the most important pork-processing city in the country. Cured beef, unlike cured pork, is not as good to eat as the fresh meat; consequently, cattle drives to the East continued until mid-century, when adequate railroad service brought an end to them.

Hog-raising implied corn-growing. For a while hogs might be turned into the forest to feed on the mast, the acorns and nuts that fell from the trees. But to produce a good grade of pork, feeding is necessary, and corn is the ideal feed crop. Corn can be grown almost anywhere, provided there is adequate rainfall. It had been cultivated in all the original colonies and throughout the South, and as late as 1840 Kentucky, Tennessee, and Virginia were first in corn production. Within twenty years, it was apparent that the states to the northwest would be the corn leaders, though the Corn Belt as we know it today was not clearly marked out.[4] On the eve of the Civil War Illinois, Ohio, Missouri, and Indiana led in corn production, and it appeared that Iowa, Kansas, and Nebraska would one day rank far ahead of Kentucky and Tennessee, then in fifth and sixth place.

Wheat was to be the great commercial crop of the North. The attraction of new lands for this basic cereal was tremendous. Wheat could not come into its own, however, until facilities were available for transporting it in quantity to the urban centers of the East, and as late as 1850 Pennsylvania and New York ranked first and third, respectively, in the production of this crop. Ohio, which had become a commercial producer in the thirties, was second. During the next decade the shift of wheat production to the West was remarkable. By 1860, Illinois, Indiana, and Wisconsin had gone into the lead, and the five states carved from the Northwest Territory produced roughly half of the nation's output of the bread grain. The major wheat-growing areas were not yet finally established; the final shift to the West of this important crop will be described in Chapter 11.

The northern migration forced changes on the agriculture of the north-

---

4 For the advantages of corn growing to the western pioneer see Paul W. Gates, *The Farmer's Age: Agriculture, 1815–1860* (New York: Holt, Rinehart and Winston, 1960), p. 169. Only a peck of seed corn, yielding as much as fifty bushels, planted an acre and could be transported far more easily than two bushels of seed wheat, weighing 120 pounds, that might bring in only fifteen to eighteen bushels to the acre.

eastern states. For a quarter of a century after the ratification of the Constitution, agriculture in New England, save for a few localities, was exceptionally primitive, production by the individual farm unit of practically everything needed for the household being the rule. With the growing industrialization of New England after 1810, production for urban markets became possible, and the result was a great improvement in the lot of the farmer. Between 1810 and 1840 farmers in the middle states continued to grow the products for which their localities had traditionally been suited, and Pennsylvania and New York remained major wheat producers until mid-century. But the opening of the Erie Canal in the 1820s and the extension of the railroads beyond the Alleghenies in the 1840s meant that products of the rich western lands would flow in ever increasing amounts to the East. Western competition caused the northeastern farmer to reduce his cultivation of grain, and only dairy cattle remained important in animal production. Specialization in truck garden and dairy products for city people and hay for city horses came to characterize the agriculture of this region, and those who could not adapt to the changing demand moved to the city or went west.

Slavery and the Plantation Economy

Under pressure of popular opinion, the New England and middle states by 1800 had prohibited the holding of slaves.[5] Also by 1800 all the original states had forbidden the *foreign* slave trade. South Carolina shortly afterward repealed her law against the importation of Negroes, but in 1807 the federal government prohibited the foreign slave trade, effective the next year. After 1807 slaves were smuggled into the South, and when the value of slaves soared in the two decades before the Civil War, slave smugglers increased their activity proportionately. The number of Negroes illegally brought in from abroad has been variously estimated, but probably not less than 250,000 adults were in this way added to the slave population between 1800 and 1860.

Northern emancipation and federal prohibition of the foreign slave trade did little to remove slavery as a major political and economic issue. Southerners, striving always to maintain equality of voting power in the Senate, fought through a series of compromises that enabled them to extend the institution they deemed necessary to survival. In 1819 the balance was even, with eleven slave and eleven free states. By the Missouri Compromise of 1820 (see map), Missouri was admitted as a slave state and Maine as a free state, with the condition that slavery should thereafter be prohibited in the territory of the Louisiana Purchase north of 36° 30'. For nearly thirty

---

[5] The emancipation of slaves in these two regions was sometimes "gradual"—i.e., the minor children of freed Negroes under some laws did not achieve a legal free status until they reached the age of twenty-one. By 1821 the institution of slavery ended north of Mason and Dixon's line.

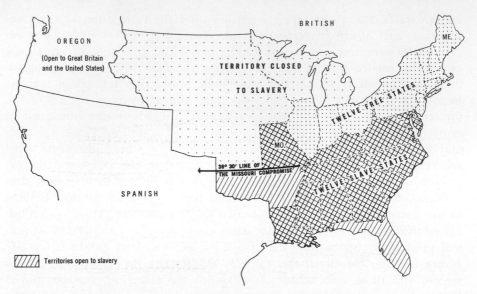

OREGON
(Open to Great Britain
and the United States)

BRITISH

ME.

TERRITORY CLOSED
TO SLAVERY

TWELVE FREE STATES

MO.

36° 30' LINE OF
THE MISSOURI COMPROMISE

TWELVE SLAVE STATES

SPANISH

///// Territories open to slavery

Missouri Compromise: Growing sectional acrimony was hopefully to be a thing of the past after this 1820 enactment. For a time, a truce did prevail.

years states were admitted to the Union in pairs, one slave and one free, so that in 1850 there were fifteen free and fifteen slave states. As of this date slavery had been prohibited in the Northwest Territory, in the territory of the Louisiana Purchase north of 36° 30′, and in the Oregon Territory, vast areas in which the slave system would not be profitable anyway. Violent controversy arose over the basis of admission of prospective states contained in the area ceded to the United States by Mexico. The terms of the Mexican Cession required that the territory remain permanently free, yet the Congress in 1848 had rejected the Wilmot Proviso, which would have prohibited slavery in the Southwest, where its extension was economically feasible. The end of the matter was that California was admitted as a free state in 1850. The territories of Utah and New Mexico were organized, and slaveholding was to be permitted there, with the final decision to be made by the territorial population upon application for admission to the Union.

Further events of the 1850s appeared for a time to portend ultimate victory for the South in the matter of slavery extension. The Kansas-Nebraska Act of 1854 (map, p. 117) in effect repealed the Missouri Compromise by providing for "popular sovereignty" in the hitherto unsettled portions of the Louisiana Purchase. The Dred Scott decision of a states' rights Supreme Court went even further and declared that Congress could not prohibit slavery in the territories. And all the while, Southerners, desperately eager to inhibit the movement of small farmers into territories where slavery could not possibly flourish, successfully resisted passage of a Homestead Act.

Yet legislative successes could be achieved only so long as Democrats from the North and Northwest were willing to ally themselves with South-

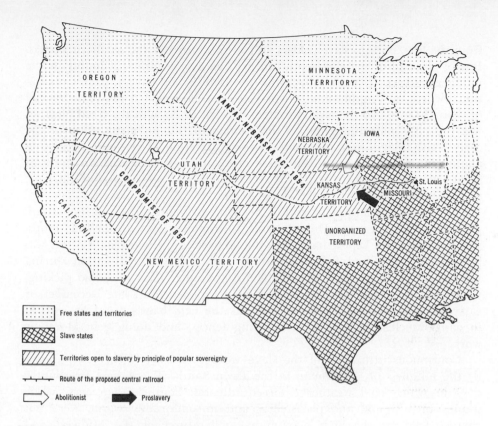

Free states and territories

Slave states

Territories open to slavery by principle of popular sovereignty

Route of the proposed central railroad

Abolitionist   Proslavery

New Settlements: The Compromise of 1850 and the Kansas–Nebraska Act of 1854 were further attempts to keep sectional strife from erupting into warfare. The concept of "popular sovereignty" introduced in this act led to conflict in Kansas.

erners. Toward the end of the fifties the antislavery movement in the North became irresistible. In large part the movement was led by those who opposed the servitude of any man on purely ethical grounds, but altruistic motives were reinforced by economic interests. Farmers of the Northwest came to resist the extension of the plantation system for fear of the resulting competition of large units with their small ones. And as transportation to eastern centers improved, the produce of the Northwest flowed to the middle states and to Europe. The people of the Northwest found their interests to be more closely akin to those of the eastern industrialist than of the southern planter. The Republican party, founded in the mid-fifties, capitalized on this shift in economic interests to weaken and destroy the old political alignments. The election of Lincoln in 1860 presented to the southern oligarchy the alternatives of submission or secession. Secession would be followed by a foolish and unnecessary war.

THE ECONOMICS OF SLAVERY

Slavery in America got its start in colonial days because of the extreme scarcity of labor. There seems little question that the system was profitable from the first, both to slave traders and to producers of the southern staples. But by the end of the eighteenth century there were growing doubts in the minds of tobacco planters about the profitability of slavery. Many plantation owners in Virginia and North Carolina expressed a desire to be rid of their charges, and the social problem of what to do with the freed Negroes was the only major deterrent to their emancipation in many areas of the early South. Slaves were profitable in the cultivation of rice and, beginning about 1795, of sugar cane. But these crops, though produced on units of great size, were grown in restricted areas and would not by themselves have maintained the vitality of the slave system.

The rapid expansion of cotton growing prevented the possible disappearance of slavery in the United States. In combination with the food crops, cotton production kept a hand busy for almost the whole year. Cotton was planted in April and required careful and persistent cultivation during most of the growing season. The bolls did not ripen all at once and picking, which began in September, might not be completed until late December or early January. During the winter months the field hands could be worked in gangs at clearing new land, building fences, and doing general repair work.

Continuous utilization of the slave work force was further encouraged by the mildness of the climate in the Deep South. There were few winter days in which cold weather enforced idleness. Southern summers, while unpleasantly humid and persistently and uncomfortably warm, were not characterized by the high maximum temperatures of the Midwest and Southwest. Except for the rice and sugar coasts there were no serious health hazards, and the Negro was in an environment less enervating than that to which his ancestors in equatorial Africa had been accustomed. The soft climate required minimum outlays on housing and clothing to maintain physical well-being. The profitability of slavery was largely a matter of latitude.

There was considerable variation in the number of acres required to keep a hand busy. If we count garden land and woodlands in addition to arable fields, the number of acres per field hand varied from fifteen to forty acres, the amount of land per slave depending upon the quality of the land. Poor Alabama pine land might require thirty-five to forty acres per hand, whereas fifteen acres of clear Mississippi alluvium would be more than the very best workers could handle.[6] By 1850 the rule of thumb was established that on land of good quality ten acres of cotton and ten acres of corn would keep an average hand fully occupied.

Negroes were employed on agricultural units of all sizes, but it was the plantation, as distinguished from the farm, that provided the economic

---

[6] For further detailed estimates see Alfred H. Conrad and John R. Meyer, "The Economics of Slavery in the Ante Bellum South," *Journal of Political Economy*, LXVI (April 1958), 100–01.

Table 5-1

Percentage Distribution of Slaveholding
Families According to Number of
Slaves Held, 1790 and 1850

Number of slaves	Percentage of families	
	1790	1850
1	24.5	17.4
2 and under 5	30.5	29.5
5 and under 10	22.0	24.4
10 and under 20	14.3	17.4
20 and under 50	6.4	9.1
50 and under 100	1.0	1.7
100 and under 200	0.2	0.4
200 and under 300	a	0.1
300 and over	a	a
Unknown		1.0

SOURCE: *Compendium of the Seventh Census*
(Washington, D.C.: A. O. P. Nicholson,
Public Printer, 1854), Table XC, p. 95.

a Less than one-tenth of 1 per cent.

Table 5-2

Estimated Average Slave Prices
in Georgia, Selected Years,
1828–1860

Year	Average price of prime field hands
1828	$ 700
1835	900
1837	1,300
1839	1,000
1840	700
1844	600
1848	900
1851	1,050
1853	1,200
1859	1,600
1860	1,800

SOURCE: U. B. Phillips, "The Economic
Cost of Slaveholding in the Cotton
Belt," *Political Science Quarterly*, XX,
2 (1905), 267.

basis of the slave system.[7] U. B. Phillips has suggested that a plantation was a unit that worked a minimum of twenty field hands, the smallest number of slaves over which it would be profitable to put an overseer. If we estimate twenty acres of arable land to a hand, a cotton plantation would contain not less than four hundred acres under cultivation. Waste and woodland would add to the total acreage so that the smallest plantation would scarcely run under seven hundred or eight hundred acres. At the other extreme there were huge units, especially in the cane-growing region of southeastern Louisiana, containing from 20,000 to 40,000 acres, with five hundred or more slaves.

It will be noted from Table 5-1 that in 1850, almost at the height of the plantation's economic importance, not far from half of the slaveholding families held four slaves or less. Yet this group of slaveholders owned only 10 per cent of the slaves. If we consider a unit employing twenty or more slaves to be of plantation size, it is a reasonable estimate that about one-half

[7] The word *plantation* has long been used, and is still used, to denote any large-scale agricultural unit employing large numbers of workers under the systematic control of a single manager. In this broad sense plantations are not confined to any particular region or period, nor is it essential that the work force be unfree or limited to the people of a particular race. For example, plantations existed in seventeenth-century America with a work force composed of indentured servants, and plantations are operated today under sharecropping or using the labor of migrant workers. But the large units of the ante-bellum South remain the archetype of plantation. For a full treatment of these matters, see Paul S. Taylor, "Plantation Agriculture in the United States: Seventeenth to Twentieth Centuries," *Land Economics*, XXX, 2, 141–52.

of the slave population lived on these large units. Roughly one-fourth of the slaves belonged to the substantial farmers and small planters who owned between ten and nineteen.[8]

For more than a century historians and economists have debated the question of the profitability of slavery to the ante-bellum southern land-owner. The fact that the system continued its inexorable movement into new cane and cotton land plus the persistent rise in slave prices (Table 5-2) in the decades before 1860 furnish strong evidence that slavery was profitable, all costs considered, in the newer regions. Many writers have alleged, on the other hand, that the slave system was cumbersome and inefficient and that within a generation it would have "toppled of its own weight."

The profitability of slavery to any particular owner depended in part, of course, upon how lucky or how shrewd he was in purchasing his human assets. From 1790 to 1860 the price of a prime field hand (in current dollars) rose from $250 or $300 to $1,800 or more. Slave prices fluctuated greatly with variations in agricultural prices. Those who bought when slaves were cheap could make large capital gains. Those who acquired their help at the top of the market would find themselves in financial straits if cotton or sugar prices began to fall, and their difficulties might lead to insolvency if the slaves were purchased with borrowed money.

If we neglect differences in entrepreneurial capability among slaveowners and consider the South as a whole, the evidence strongly supports the proposition that funds invested in slaves and nonslave capital, including land and equipment, earned a return as high as they would have in alternative employments. Conrad and Meyer conclude that realized returns on prime field hands ranged from 2.2 per cent to 13.0 per cent, with returns of from 4.5 per cent to 8.0 per cent being typical. The return to capital invested in a prime field wench was probably somewhat greater if she produced from five to ten marketable children in her lifetime.[9] Though spectacularly large earnings were made by some planters and others clearly failed to cover their costs, the run of plantation owners were able to secure a return equal to the average rate of interest—in the neighborhood of 6 per cent—in ante-bellum decades.

In order to keep the system going, it was necessary for the plantations in the Old South and the border states to maintain a supply of slaves by producing and exporting them to the major cotton-growing regions. Had free importation of Negroes been permitted, so as to increase the supply, the price per head would have been reduced and slaves would have returned a

[8] Interested students wishing to pursue the matter further should refer to the *Compendium of the Seventh Census* (Washington, D.C.: A. O. P. Nicholson, Public Printer, 1854), pp. 82–95. The table giving the percentage distribution of slaveholding families according to number of slaves held was computed directly from Table XC, p. 95, of the *Compendium*. Figures showing number of slaves by size of holding unit can be derived only after assuming an average number of slaves owned by each unit. The approximations given above will not involve serious errors.

[9] Conrad and Meyer, pp. 106–07.

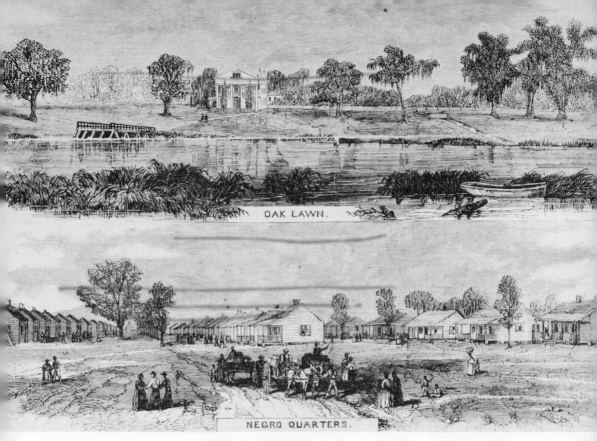

OAK LAWN.

NEGRO QUARTERS.

The plantation economy was seen in idealized terms by some: neat, well-kept homes and gardens, tidy and well-ventilated slave quarters.

surplus over all costs throughout the South (and very likely in many parts of the newly opened West). As it was, prices of field hands and wenches were bid so high in the productive cane- and cotton-growing areas that slaves in the old regions could not earn the going rate of return on funds invested in them and the other capital inputs. Slaveholding in the upper South would thus have disappeared had it not been for the lucrative business of exporting slaves to the Deep South. Many planters in the states of Kentucky, Virginia, and North Carolina readily admitted that the sale of slaves into areas farther south was an important source of income. Clearly this income led to the production of an intermediate good, slave labor, and kept the border states and the Old South in political alliance with the cotton South.

THE SOCIAL AND ECONOMIC CONSEQUENCES OF SLAVERY

We are less concerned with the economic feasibility of the slave system for the separate agricultural unit than with the long-run effects of the system on the South. What kind of a heritage did slavery leave the fifteen states in which the institution was important?

In the first place, slavery left the South with a population, Negro and white, that had little or no opportunity to acquire the good things of life. In 1860 there were about 4,000,000 Negroes and 8,000,000 whites in the South. In large areas Negroes constituted well over half the population. Later we shall see how this mass of people, thrown on their own by a landless emancipation, could only remain in abject poverty. Perhaps as many as 5,000,000 of the 8,000,000 whites were scarcely any better off. As the plantation system spread westward, the less desirable and worn-out lands were left to very small holders and poor whites.[10]

If slavery and the plantation economy kept a large part of the native white population in poverty, it quite as effectively prevented the infusion of new blood by inhibiting immigration from Europe. It was not a repugnance to the South's "peculiar institution" that kept the European migrant away, for immigration did not increase after emancipation. Europeans tended to settle in the latitudes where most of the incoming ships set them down and where the climate was not unlike that of home. But the main deterrent to locating in the South was plain lack of opportunity; the immigrant feared that he would one day find himself a "poor white." By 1860

[10] The literature is full of references to "worn-out" land. Although some land in the Old South and the border states was irreparably damaged by erosion, much of it was worn out only in the sense that it had lost a natural fertility that had not been replaced by applications of fertilizer. But in nineteenth-century America fertilizer was such a relatively expensive capital input that it was more economical to move to farther distant new land than to apply it.

Slaves themselves were not always happy to shrug off their ill fortune, as this somber group portrait suggests.

The technological breakthrough that revitalized the plantation economy was the cotton gin, invented by the New England schoolmaster and innovating genius, Eli Whitney.

only 3.4 per cent of the southern population was foreign-born, compared with a foreign-born population in the central states of 17 per cent and in New England of 15 per cent.

The slave system effectively prevented a normal accumulation of real capital in the South and consequently delayed industrialization. We should not jump to the conclusion that the Negro could not be trained for industrial or commercial jobs, for a man's color has nothing to do with his inherent capabilities. Even in pre–Civil War days some fortunate slaves became skilled craftsmen, and slaves were employed in cotton factories, coal mines, iron-works, lumber mills, and railroads. But there was no point in incurring the costs of training slaves for industrial occupations when they could be put to work at once in an agriculture that yielded higher returns. Furthermore, funds used to purchase a labor force were not available for investment in capital goods. Those who had money to invest were evidently persuaded that the return to it, in prestige and social standing as well as in dollars and cents, would be greater if it were put into human chattels rather than in machines and business buildings.

There seems little question that slavery was profitable throughout the South. Extremely high net returns in parts of the Cotton Belt and rewards at least equal to those of alternative employments of capital in most areas of the Deep South were the rule. Continuing demand for labor in the cotton- and cane-growing country assured profitable breeding operations in the older states, and the post-bellum distress of southern agriculture in the sea- board and border regions is largely attributable to loss of income from slave breeding.[11] Nor were forces at work to make the slave economy self-destruc- tive. There is simply no evidence to support the contention that slave labor was overcapitalized, and clearly slaves did reproduce themselves sufficiently to maintain a growing work force. Finally, since maintenance of adequate income in the Old South depended upon the expansion of the plantation economy in the Cotton Belt, it is not hard to see why Virginians and Ken- tuckians were willing to join the rest of the South in fighting for the ex- tension of slavery into new territories.

The slave system must be judged, of course, in terms of its net advantages and disadvantages to the South. Although the evil concomitants of slavery, both social and political, are hard to evaluate, they were nonetheless real. The southern aristocracy was composed of a gifted, charming, and well- educated people. Yet these gracious Southerners constituted a political oligarchy, referred to by their contemporaries as the Slave Power, that was incompatible with the political and social development of the United States as a whole. Brought up to esteem a set of values that scorned work other than that in the professions, the southern leaders were unfitted to take over the responsibilities of a managerial class in the new environment that pre- vailed after the Civil War. One of the great tragedies of American history was the fall from eminence of the Southerner as a leader.

Thus we may explain the economic prostration of the South after the War. In terms of the traditional classification of the factors of production— land, labor, capital, and entrepreneurial ability—the South suffered from grave deficiencies. So long as these deficiencies could be offset by the exploita- tion of slaves, the southern economy performed well enough—at least from the standpoint of those in charge of directing resource allocation. When it became necessary to adapt to the mechanism of a normal capitalist system, a feeble managerial class was unable to bring an incompetent labor force and inadequate capital into an effective productive combination. Entre- preneurship had not taken root in the South in the face of easy profits to be made in cotton growing. Since a foolish and cruel public policy decreed an emancipation without land for the freedmen or remuneration to their former owners, the South was doomed to a century of lagging development.

---

[11] Conrad and Meyer, p. 121.

Transportation and
Economic Unification

Once more upon the waters! yet once more!
And the waves bound beneath me as a steed
That knows his rider. Welcome to their roar!
Swift be their guidance, wheresoe'er it lead!

LORD BYRON

The ratification of the Constitution in 1789 joined the thirteen states into a nation. The impact of political unification would be felt in the economic life of the nation and, in turn, the new country would be truly welded together only as it developed a unified economy. Of first importance were the new relationships among the states in matters of commerce and transportation. Establishment of tariff barriers by the states was forbidden, and regulation of commerce among the states and with foreign nations was vested in the federal government. In 1789 trade among the colonies was of much less consequence than trade with western Europe, but the uneasy bonds among the isolated settlements of America would soon strengthen. The commercial stirrings of the United States impelled extensions of colonial transportation routes and facilities.

Trails, Turnpikes, and Tow Paths

Although the favored means of travel in the New World was by water, not every place could be reached by boat. As the growing colonies spread back from the coastal area, transportation to settlements not on waterways was perforce by pack train, a lucrative business employing thousands of people. Carrying goods by horseback was prohibitively expensive except for commodities of high value relative to their weight, such as fur and whiskey. The exorbitant cost of pack-horse transportation led to the improvement of trails so that wagons might be used where distances were not too great. Usually little more than improved paths with trees, underbrush, and large obstructions removed, the roads were of two broad functional types.

There were first of all the country roads leading from farm to village and, if the village were not on a waterway, on to another village that was. Country roads were the basis of the early transportation net. Unbelievably bad, they were primarily for farm-to-market use. Since the time for travel over them could be selected, ordinarily after the growing season, farmers carefully balanced the savings of less expenditure on their construction against any gains to be had from speedier movement of crops to market.

Longer roads connected the larger centers of the East with each other and with the growing settlements of the West (see map, p. 127). By 1816 Maine and Georgia were joined by a single route. To the west, crossing the mountains, ran other through roads and trails. These highways of emigration, settlement, and commerce usually followed the old Indian hunting and war paths, which in turn had followed the stream valleys providing the easiest lines of travel. One of the most important was the Wilderness Road pioneered by Daniel Boone. Penetrating the mountain barrier at Cumberland Gap, near present-day Middlesboro, Kentucky, it then went north and westward into the Ohio Territory. Over this road, in many places only a marked track, poured thousands of emigrants.[1] Other trails west of the mountains followed the Holston and the Watauga rivers as they flowed from their Appalachian sources into the Tennessee; thus, geography directed part of the flow of emigration to the southwest. Although most of the overland roads turned into quagmires in the rainy season and into billowing dust clouds in the dry season, some of them were well constructed and well maintained through portions of their length.

Most notable of the surfaced highways was the Cumberland Road or "National Pike," built by the federal government after much controversy. Begun at Cumberland, Maryland, in 1811, the road was opened to Wheeling on the Ohio River in 1818 and was later completed to Vandalia, Illinois. At a cost of from $10,000 to $13,000 per mile, quite high for the time, the road was constructed with a foundation of crushed stone fifteen inches thick and a 30-foot macadamized strip in the center. How well the work was done is attested by the fact that the stone bridges of the road, built more than a century ago, are still adequate for modern auto traffic over Highway No. 40.

---

[1] This same type of road or marked track appeared during the overland migration to the West Coast. The Oregon Trail, over which travel began in the early 1840s, was 2,000 miles long and carried settlers to the Pacific Northwest and to California. The Mormon Trail, broken by Brigham Young in the late 1840s, paralleled the Oregon Trail along the Platte for some distance. Earlier trails marked by the Spaniards, such as the Santa Fe Trail, into present-day New Mexico and Arizona, and *El Camino Real*, or King's Highway, were valuable to early explorers and traders.

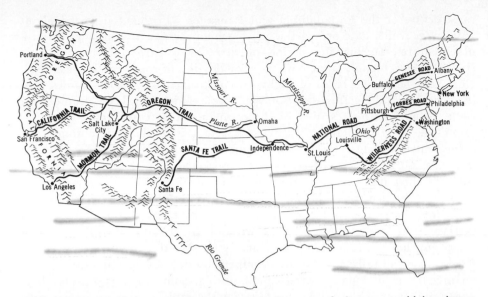

Westward Travel: Massive physical barriers in the way of pioneers could be circumvented by following famous routes such as the Oregon Trail (through the Rockies) and the Sante Fe Trail ("across the wide Missouri").

The national government did not repeat its success with the Cumberland Road. As early as 1808 Albert Gallatin had put forward a plan for a system of federal roads, and progressive, enlightened people generally urged a comprehensive program of internal improvements. Opposition was ostensibly based on the assertion, repeated endlessly, that federal participation in such activity was unconstitutional. Actually, sectional rivalries prevented much needed construction. The West persistently and loudly called for a national road system. At first the middle states were inclined to go along, but after New York and Pennsylvania had developed their own routes to the West they did not wish to promote federally financed competition. New Englanders, with fairly good roads of their own, were even more disinclined to encourage further drains of population or to improve the commercial positions of Boston's rivals. The South, mired in the mud, was bitterly antagonistic to any program that would add to the government's financial needs or make access to nonslave portions of the West easier. In spite of all the opposition, Congress could not avoid appropriating increasing sums for post and military roads; nevertheless, great opportunities went ungrasped.

TURNPIKE COMPANIES

When for one reason or another a unit of government would not undertake the construction, roads were often built by private turnpike companies, which collected tolls for the use of privately built thoroughfares. Gates consisting of pikes or spears were turned or lifted to let the tollpayer pass to and from the road at selected points. The turnpike era began in 1789 with the construction of the Philadelphia and Lancaster Turnpike; it ended about 1830, after which date only a few private highways were attempted as business ventures. During the period of turnpike construction Pennsylvania chartered 86 companies that built over 2,000 miles of road. By the year 1811, New York had 1,500 miles of highways constructed by 135 companies, and in New England by this date some 180 companies had been granted the right to build turnpikes. Few of the companies that constructed roads for public use were profitable ventures; in fact, it is doubtful if a single one earned anything close to the going rate of return. Teamsters avoided the tolls if at all possible, and receipts were pocketed by dishonest gatekeepers. But the chief difficulty, one unforeseen by most promoters, was that the only long-distance trade the roads got was from stagecoach passengers and emigrants. Freight would not, for the most part, stand the cost of land carriage over great distances, and without freight the turnpikes simply could not show a profit. They were finally faced with extensive competition from canals and railroads, but this competition did not appear until returns on invested capital had proved disappointing. Some turnpikes were abandoned and later acquired by the states for the rapidly growing public road system; others were purchased by local governments and made free highways.[2]

PLANK ROADS

Another kind of toll road, the plank road or "farmer's railroad," developed shortly after the decline in turnpike construction. Plank roads were built by laying wide, heavy planks or "rails" on stringers or ties placed at right angles to the direction of travel. The first plank road in the United States was built at Syracuse in 1837; within the next twenty years or so several thousand miles of them were in use throughout the country, the heaviest concentration being in the middle Atlantic states. So important did they seem that some were subsidized by the states, although most were privately financed.

There were several reasons for the widespread construction of plank roads. Their cost was far less than that of a macadamized highway or turnpike. A team of horses could draw much heavier loads on the smooth plank roads than it could draw on a highway. They were ideal for the short-haul, farm-to-market travel. Finally, investors preferred the plank road to the new-fangled steam railroad on which cars were pulled at frightening speeds by an engine that was expected to explode at any minute or to leave the track on the first curve.

Financially, few plank roads were successful, for upkeep was high. The stringers and planks were exposed to the elements at all times, and pre-

[2] A few private roads continued into the twentieth century, but all that now remains of them is the name *turnpike* given to some important arteries of the highway system. These throughways differ from the older turnpike in that the modern enterprises are owned by public corporations. As we shall see in Chapter 19, toll roads are once again disappearing as they are absorbed into the Interstate and Defense Highway Systems.

Plank roadways proved essential wherever heavy military or commercial traffic was concentrated.

servatives such as creosote were not available to prevent deterioration. Estimates made in Ohio showed that with the best hardwood (hemlock) available the life span of the road was about seven years.

In some instances the plank road retarded the construction of railroads. In Alabama a plank-road company replaced an unsuccessful railroad company, and no effort was made to construct railroads in that area for some years. On the other hand, plank roads served as feeder lines to certain railroads and gave them profitable traffic not obtainable as cheaply by steam railroad feeders. The Michigan Central mentioned in its *Annual Report* for 1850 the contributions of the plank road in concentrating freight for its operations. The plank road, although superseded by the railroad, played a significant part in the development of freight carriage in the United States. Like the private turnpike it was forced to give way to a means of transportation that could offer a cheaper and faster method of moving goods.

From Portland, Maine, to Charleston, South Carolina, and on almost every watercourse in between, there was talk of, if not activity in, improvement of waterways. As early as 1792, a stock company began the construction of the Santee Canal, connecting the port of Charleston with the interior via the Cooper and Santee rivers, and by 1795 a canal had been built in Maine from the Kennebec River to Casco Bay. Several other short canals were constructed at an early date, mostly to afford passage around rapids and other obstructions in rivers.

Before 1817, however, only minor ventures were undertaken. In that year the legislature of the State of New York authorized the construction of the Erie and the Champlain canals, and work was begun shortly thereafter. With the powerful DeWitt Clinton as guiding spirit, the Erie was promoted with enthusiasm, and sections were opened to traffic as they were completed. It became quickly apparent that the canal would have a great success, and even before its completion in 1825 a "canal fever" seized promoters throughout the country. In the tremendous building boom that followed, canals were constructed to link three kinds of areas. Some ran from "back country" to tidewater; some traversed, or attempted to traverse, the area between the older states and the Ohio Valley; and some, the western canals, linked the Great Lakes and the waterways running to the East.

The most important of the early canals, though not the only profitable one, was the Erie.[3] It was a massive undertaking. Beginning at Albany on the Hudson River, it traversed the State of New York westward to Buffalo on Lake Erie for a distance of 364 miles. The work cost approximately $7 million and took some nine years to complete. The constructors overcame countless difficulties, not the least of which was their own ignorance. Almost none of the engineers had ever had a hand in canal construction, and much experimentation was necessary in the process. Some sections of the canal did not at first hold water and had to be lined with clay after work had been completed. The locks presented a special difficulty, but ingenuity and the timely discovery of water-resistant or hydraulic cement led to the solution of problems of lock construction.

The Erie system, in its final form, reached a fair portion of New York State. The Cayuga and Seneca, the Chemung, and the Genesee extensions connected important territory to the south with the canal. A branch to Oswego provided access to Lake Ontario, and the Champlain Canal gave access to the north. The system not only furnished transportation to much of the state but also tapped the Great Lakes area and the vast Ohio Territory. Beginning about 1835 a large part of the traffic that had formerly gone from the West down the Ohio and Mississippi rivers was diverted over the Erie to the port of New York. Lumber, grain, and meat products were the chief commodities to move eastward, while textiles, leather goods, ma-

---

[3] This system still exists in an expanded and improved form as the New York Barge Canal.

chinery, hardware, and imported foods and drugs went west in exchange. Passengers, too, rode the horse-drawn packet boats in great numbers, speeds of one hundred miles in a twenty-four–hour day compensating in part for the discomfort of cramped and poorly ventilated cabins.

Pennsylvania's answer to the competition of the Erie Canal was the Main Line of the Pennsylvania Public Works, a system of railroads *and* canals chartered in 1826 by the state legislature. The terrain traversed by the Erie to reach the western frontier was difficult enough for canal building, though at its highest point it rose only 650 feet above the Hudson at Albany, but the terrain of western Pennsylvania proved insurmountable by canal. The Main Line crossed the mountains, lifted passengers and freight to an altitude of over 2,000 feet, and deposited the traveler, westbound from Philadelphia, at Pittsburgh some four hundred miles away. All this was done by as fantastic a combination of transport as the country had ever seen. From Philadelphia, at tidewater, to Columbia, eighty-one miles westward on the Susquehanna River, a horse-drawn railroad carried both passengers and freight.[4] At Columbia the railroad joined the Juniata, or Eastern Division of the Pennsylvania Canal, whence passengers and freight were carried up a river valley by canal 173 miles to the Portage Railroad at Holidaysburg. Here the intrepid passenger saw his boat separated into a front and rear section and mounted on cars run on underwater rails into the canal. A thirty-six–mile trip on the Portage Railroad then began. The inclined tracks, over which cars were pulled by stationary steam engines winding cables on drums, accomplished a lift of 1,399 feet on the eastern slope to the summit and a descent of 1,172 feet on the western slope to another canal at Johnstown. From Johnstown to Pittsburgh, a distance of 105 miles, the water journey was comparatively easy.

The completion of this colossal work in 1834 was heralded by a celebration at Liberty Hall in Philadelphia. An old print depicts one of the half-boats decked with bunting and flags being drawn away from the hall by teams of prancing horses. In the sense that it carried all the traffic that it could carry, the Main Line was successful, but the bottleneck of the Portage Railroad plus the fact that it had twice as many locks as the Erie kept it from being a serious competitor for the western business. Over the years the Main Line carried between 5 and 10 per cent of the traffic volume of the Erie Canal, to the great disappointment of the people of a state that spent more on waterways than any other.

Other states expended large sums of money on canals to draw the trade of the new West. The Chesapeake and Ohio Canal was projected up the valley of the Potomac to Cumberland, Maryland, and on to the Ohio River. The canal company was chartered by the State of Virginia with the assent of the Maryland legislature, and the federal government contributed heavily

---

[4] Although the steam locomotive was not employed in the United States until 1829, rails to permit smooth haulage had been used in America and in Europe for some years.

Lockport, in Niagara County, New York, was a busy canal town in the early 1800s, an important point in the route that became the pre-eminent link between the Midwest and East Coast urban centers.

to the venture. But in spite of the political blessings of two states and the federal government, the generous financial backing of all three, and the aid of some local governments, the project was completed only to Cumberland because of technical difficulties.

The financially successful canals in the East were those that facilitated the carriage of anthracite coal from the fields to tidewater. In the West the most important canals were two that contributed to the development of Ohio: the Miami and Erie Canal, which connected Cincinnati on the Ohio River with Toledo on Lake Erie, and the Ohio and Erie Canal between Portsmouth on the Ohio River and Cleveland on Lake Erie. These canals traversed from north to south the western and central sections of the state and gave access both to the Great Lakes for eastbound traffic and to the Ohio-Mississippi river system for westbound and southbound traffic. The Miami and Erie and the Ohio and Erie, both well built and soundly financed, did a good business and unquestionably helped to start the great flow of agricultural products to the East via the Erie Canal. On the other hand, Indiana's experience with the Wabash and Erie was a sad one. The longest canal in the United States, it was completed too late to have more than a few years of operation free of rail competition. Despite the financial failure of the venture, the Wabash and Erie may have been worth more than it cost the people of the state in the assistance it provided in opening Indiana.

Many other canals, financially unrewarding, hastened the growth of the country. Before the advent of the railroads the United States was well served by them in the opening of the West. Some that have been considered preposterous mistakes might have turned out to be monuments to man's inventiveness had not the railroad come at almost the same time. But the limitations on horse-drawn vehicles are great except for a few commodities. Canals were supposed to provide a *system* of waterways, but as often as not boats of the larger canals could not get through the smaller ones. Floods and droughts often made the movement of the barges uncertain. Yet the chief reason for the eventual failure of canals was the railroad, which made possible the carriage of a wide variety of commodities at great speed. Speed was requisite to a genuine transportation revolution.

The Beginnings of a Modern Transportation System

The genesis of the railroad illustrates technical innovation by small steps. The two main elements of the railway—rails and locomotives—developed separately in England over many years. In the coal fields of Durham and Newcastle, as early as the last quarter of the seventeenth century, a roadbed of planks was laid down over which were drawn wagons with unflanged wheels. In the middle of the eighteenth century, flanged rails of cast iron were introduced to hold "flat" wheels more securely, and shortly afterwards experiments were begun with flanged wheels and a dumbbell-shaped rail. Cast-iron wheels and rails were so brittle that they broke easily, especially in cold weather, and early in the nineteenth century malleable wrought-iron rails came into use. By 1820, or thereabouts, a rather advanced type of rail was employed by the horse-drawn tramways.

The initial contribution of the steam engine to transportation was in supplying power for tramways, which consisted of rails on which cars were drawn by a cable wound on a drum.[5] But for the steam engine to add significantly to the improvement of transportation, it had to be mounted so that motive power could be transmitted to the wheels. Then the vehicle would be locomotive or self-propelled. As early as 1769 attempts to combine the steam engine with a wheeled carriage had been made by the Frenchman Cugnot, who designed a vehicle to travel over the ordinary roads of that day. What with the quality of the roads and the cumbersome character of the steam-propelled wagon, the venture was hardly a success. Others who tried a like combination achieved no more than Cugnot.

---

[5] The inclined planes of the Main Line of the Pennsylvania Public Works might be regarded as a sort of tramway, though tramways are generally associated with mines or quarries.

The first use of a steam locomotive to pull carriages on rails is attributed to Richard Trevithick, who, in 1801, used his invention in a Cornish mine. For the next quarter-century or so a number of men brought out heavy-duty locomotives for work in coal fields and mines, but none had enough power to be serviceable. Success waited on two key inventions—the increase of boiler surface to secure a greater volume of steam and the use of exhaust steam so that heat could be intensified in the firebox.

It remained for the Stockton and Darlington Railway Company, the first public railway company in England, to operate, in 1825, the first steam-powered vehicle manufactured for public use. George Stephenson, designer and builder of the locomotive, was also the engineer.[6] Four years later Stephenson won the prize of £500 sterling offered by the directors of the Liverpool and Manchester Railway for a locomotive engine that would cost a maximum price of £500 and would run at a minimum speed of ten miles per hour. The *Rocket*, built by George Stephenson and his son Robert for the Liverpool and Manchester competition, is generally recognized as the earliest practical steam locomotive. Weighing approximately five tons, it was able to draw a load three times its weight at a speed of twelve and a half miles per hour; with only a carriage and passengers its speed could be increased to twenty-four miles per hour.[7]

The interest shown in England and on the Continent in the use of steam engines for propulsion was not without its counterpart in America. As early as 1786, Oliver Evans had unsuccessfully petitioned the legislature of Pennsylvania for a monopoly to operate steam wagons on the highways. In 1820, John Stevens, a New Jerseyite who had previously built a steamboat called the *Phoenix,* demonstrated a narrow-gauge steam railway near Hoboken. Yet it was an English locomotive, the *Stourbridge Lion,* which in 1829 made the first trial run on the tracks of an established American company. One of three ordered from Foster, Rastrick and Company of Stourbridge, England, the locomotive was tested over the gravity railway of the Delaware and Hudson Canal Company. The test was considered a failure because the engine was too heavy for rails and trestles designed only to support loaded cars.

The *Tom Thumb* was the first American-built steam locomotive. Manufactured to demonstrate the feasibility of steam power, it had a short trial

---

[6] George Stephenson (1781–1848) began his career in the mines of Scotland. Carefully studying the crude pumping engines used at the mines, he taught himself the principles of steam power and mechanics. His observations led to improvements on stationary engines and locomotives, and experience with tramways and rails brought him employment by various railway companies in England. He was an ardent advocate of flat grades and curves of long radius. Many engineers were opposed to these theories, but Stephenson's methods are the present practices of railroads here and abroad. It is the modern view that George Stephenson's chief claim to fame lies in his contribution as a civil engineer.

[7] In 1837 the Rocket carried the results of a political contest a distance of four miles in four and a half minutes. See Samuel Smiles, *Life of George Stephenson* (New York: Harper, 1868), p. 327.

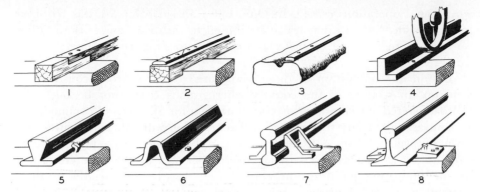

The evolution of rails: (1) wood; (2) strap on wood; (3) strap rail on grooved granite; (4) tramway or plate rail, unflanged wheel; (5) flat-foot rail; (6) "U" or bridge rail; (7) double-headed rail; and (8) "T" rail, first used in 1831.

run in 1830 but was never used in commercial service. The *Peter Cooper*, named after the designer of the *Tom Thumb*, the *York* of the Baltimore and Ohio, and the *Best Friend of Charleston* of the Charleston and Hamburg were the best known of the early steam locomotives. After the practicability of steam locomotion had been proved by these vehicles in America, others were built and put into regular service, for the speed and tractive power of the new means of hauling freight and passengers far surpassed any other then known. Yet for some twenty years after the opening of the two pioneer railroads, canals remained the primary means of transportation. Possibly the most important hindrance to railroad development was public antipathy, which had its roots in ignorance, conservatism, or vested interest. People thought that speeds of twenty to thirty miles per hour would be physically harmful to the passenger. At least one city in Massachusetts directed its representatives in the state legislature to prevent ". . . so great a calamity to our town as must be the location of any railroad through it." Many honestly believed that the railroad would prove to be impractical and uneconomical and would not provide service as dependable as that of the waterways.

RAILROAD CONSTRUCTION, 1830–1860

The most vigorous opposition to railroads came from groups whose economic interests suffered from the competition of the new industry. Millions of dollars had been spent on canals, highways, and plank roads. Thousands of people were dependent upon these transportation enterprises for a livelihood. Tavern keepers envisioned their businesses ruined, and farmers imagined the market for hay and grain gone when the "iron horse" replaced the flesh and blood animal that drew the canal boat and pulled the wagon over turnpike and plank road. Vested interests joined to embarrass and hinder the railroads, causing several states to limit the traffic on them to passengers and their baggage or to freight hauled only during the months when canal operations ceased. In Ohio one railroad company was required to pay for any loss in canal traffic attributed to railroad competition. Other railroads were required to pay a tonnage tax to support the operation of canals.

Despite the opposition of those who feared them, railroad construction went on. In sections of the country where canals could not be built the railroad offered a means of cheap transportation for all kinds of commodities. In contrast to the city that wished to exclude the railroad, many cities and towns, as well as their state governments, did much to encourage the construction of railroads. The federal government was at the time restrained by the prevailing political philosophy from assisting financially in their promotion. It did, however, make surveys for rights-of-way and provided tariff exemptions on railroad iron.

Baltimore, Charleston, Philadelphia, and Boston, great seaports without important connections with the interior, were each seeking to increase their trade areas. New York was draining the West of its products by way of the Erie Canal and the Hudson River, and the railroad appeared the best hope of challenging the threatened dominance of the new metropolis. Businessmen in Baltimore built and operated the first important railroad in America. The Baltimore and Ohio Railroad, designed to extend to the Ohio River, received a charter in 1827 and in May, 1830, put thirteen miles of track into operation. In Charleston, a desire to secure the trade of inland South Carolina and Georgia impelled a wide-awake Chamber of Commerce to build the Charleston and Hamburg Railroad, which successfully intercepted commerce between the rich cotton region of the piedmont and Savannah at the mouth of the river. Opened for passenger traffic over part of the route in 1831 and completed to a length of 136 miles in 1833, the road was the longest in the world at the time.[8] In the North, railroads projected westward from Boston, Lowell, Worcester, and Providence were in operation by 1835, but connection with the Hudson River was not accomplished until 1841.

New York State was a laggard in the very early railroad construction because of the successful system of waterways within her boundaries. Only short lines were built in the decade 1830–40, principally because of commercial rivalry of the larger cities. Committed like New York to heavy expenditures on canals, Pennsylvania likewise held back on extensive railroad ventures. In 1834 the state completed the Philadelphia and Columbia as a steam road to connect the seaport with the system of canals. Feeder rail lines connected coal fields with rivers and canals, and the Philadelphia and Reading transported coal from mine to tidewater. But the great undertakings were to come later as both New York and Pennsylvania would strive heroically to catch up.

By 1840 railroad mileage in the United States totaled 2,818, about equal

---

[8] Hamburg, the western terminus of the railroad, was located on the east bank of the Savannah River opposite Augusta, Georgia.

Transportation: Vastly improved canal and river systems plus better roads made transportation in the 1840s better than most Americans had ever known, better, some said, than transportation anywhere since the breakup of the Roman Empire.

to the total length of all canals, but the volume of goods carried by water still far exceeded that of the rails. (See map above.) Furthermore, rail construction was pretty much restricted to the middle and New England states.[9] The decade of the 1840s was one of expansion, and by 1850 over 9,000 miles of railroads had been built. The Western and Atlantic was completed by the State of Georgia to provide better transportation for the towns of the

[9] The success of the Charleston and Hamburg had prompted the building by Savannah citizens of the competing—and equally successful—Central of Georgia. But early venturing in railroads was not typical of the South.

Georgia piedmont, the Georgia Railroad connected Atlanta with the Charleston and Hamburg at Augusta, and Chattanooga was linked with both Savannah and Charleston. In Ohio a through line was completed from the Ohio River to Lake Erie. By 1850 the eastern net was well on its way to taking shape. Through routes were established from Boston to Albany and from Boston to New York, and Baltimore was nearly linked with Wheeling. The Erie Railroad, which for more than a decade had been extending a line westward from New York City across the southern counties of New York, would reach Dunkirk on Lake Erie in another year, and Philadelphia capitalists were working to overcome the difficulties of reaching Pittsburgh by rail.

Between 1850 and 1860, over 20,000 miles of rails were added to the transportation system. Total trackage approached 30,000 miles at the end of the decade, and the volume of traffic equaled that of the canals.[10] All of the states east of the Mississippi were connected during this decade. The eastern seaboard was linked with the Mississippi River system, and the Gulf and south Atlantic states could interchange traffic with the Great Lakes. Growing trunk lines like the Erie, the Pennsylvania, and the Baltimore and Ohio completed construction of projects that had been started in the forties, and combinations of short lines provided new through routes. By the beginning of the Civil War the eastern framework of the present rail-transportation system had been erected; it was then possible to travel by rail the entire distance from New York to Chicago to Memphis and back to New York.

The outbreak of the Civil War drastically reduced railroad building in the North and temporarily halted it in the South as the efforts of both sections were diverted from internal improvements to internal destruction. Not until the question of secession had been settled could promoters continue their efforts to complete the railway net.

FINANCING RAILROADS, 1830–1860

Both private and public capital were contributed to the construction of railroads in the first thirty years of development. Private capital, however, was both scarce and timid, and railroads were not its only haven. The new nation was expanding economically in all directions at a rapid rate, and safer, or at least more familiar, lines of business attracted the investor's dollar. In areas of sparse population, where revenues sufficient to cover all costs might not be forthcoming for years, states and municipalities contributed heavily. Before 1860 public funds accounted for perhaps 40 per cent of construction in the North and more than 50 per cent of construction in the South.

---

[10] Railroads had won from canals almost all the passenger business, except that of poor immigrants coming across New York State, and the carriage of nearly all light, high-value goods.

Despite the massive investment of public money, most railroads were considered private enterprises. They were chartered by the several states and their corporate structures and privileges were much like those of the turnpike companies. To obtain funds for construction the railroads were pioneers in devising new types of securities. Most corporations of that day were financed almost exclusively through the issuance of common stock, but promoters devised ways of keeping the voting rights of the common in their own hands. One innovation, for example, was the issue of a new certificate called preferred stock, with no voting rights, a prior claim on dividends, and a fixed rate of return. Short-term notes were converted into long-term bonds, and where the promoters of the company had to use their own credit, a new form of financial organization—the "construction company"—was used.

After 1850 much capital from European sources was invested in American railroad ventures. Before this time, capital from abroad, especially from England, had been put into various other types of enterprise, especially into the canal companies. The failure of the canals and the panic of 1837 ruined the European market for securities of American companies until the early 1850s. Some railroads, such as the Illinois Central, then drew heavily on foreign capital.[11] Other roads with large capital contributions from abroad were the Louisville and Nashville, Chicago and Northwestern, the Reading, and the Pennsylvania.

Financial assistance from governmental units took many forms. Fear of federal interference in local affairs, as well as bitter sectional antagonisms, precluded direct participation of the federal government in railroad and other transportation financing. However, in 1824 Congress authorized government survey of roads and canals, and before the act was repealed in 1838 some sixty railroad surveys had been made. An act of 1832, repealed eleven years later at the insistence of domestic iron manufacturers, remitted duties on railroad iron, most of which was imported from England. And future assistance of the federal government was adumbrated in 1850 when a land grant of several million acres was made to the Illinois Central. Before the Civil War substantial amounts of public land were given to more than forty companies, but as we shall see in Chapter 12 the really big land grants went to the transcontinentals after 1865.

Counties and municipal governments gave varied and extensive aid to railroads. They subscribed to railroad stock, made loans to railroads by purchasing their bonds, and guaranteed the bonds of railroads passing through their confines. Such assistance usually meant the creation of debt, and many municipalities obligated their citizens for startling amounts. So burdensome became some of the obligations of local governments that a number of states restricted financial aid to railroads by municipalities.

---

[11] A majority of this railroad's stock was held abroad from its inception in 1851. Significant portions of other railroad stocks were held abroad until about 1898, after which large quantities of foreign-owned securities were purchased by Americans.

The states themselves were not innocent of granting largess to railroads. Such privileges as power of eminent domain, monopoly rights between distant points, and freedom from taxation for stipulated periods or in perpetuity were frequently given. Some states also assisted railroads by permitting them to engage in banking. Acting as a bank, a company could issue paper money to pay for purchases made in its capacity as a railroad. In 1836 Vermont granted this privilege to the Rutland and Whitehall Railroad; later Georgia and other states gave similar permissions. More important than special and unusual privileges was direct financial aid, which paralleled in part the assistance given by counties and cities. Although the states had greater credit resources than local governmental units, state contributions were probably less. The subsidies usually took the form of loans that often turned out to be gifts, states purchasing the bonds of the companies with funds raised by the sale of state obligations. Actual subscriptions to common stock were not infrequent.

Government aid to railroad construction was prompted by the desire of ambitious states and municipalities to obtain transportation facilities sooner than the unassisted price mechanism would have provided them. Unwise investments resulted in overbuilding and uneconomic routes, but the first part of the railroad network was laid far more rapidly than would have been possible on a private basis. Dollar losses by private investors and governmental bodies considered as a whole were probably recouped in the hastened expansion of the new nation into the undeveloped areas of the mid-continent.

STEAMBOAT ON THE RIVER

Early attempts at mechanical propulsion of boats failed to achieve commercial success until Robert Fulton, with the assistance of Robert R. Livingston, made the steamboat *Clermont*. In 1807 the *Clermont* completed a historic voyage up the Hudson River from New York to Albany, a distance of 150 miles, in thirty-two hours. Following the initial trip, regular passenger service from New York to Albany was inaugurated, and the dependability of the steamboat was quickly demonstrated. A new era of transportation on the rivers of America had begun.

Fulton's experiment took place on a river that emptied into the Atlantic Ocean and provided the most favorable conditions for both navigation and traffic. Trials of other vessels on other coastal rivers convinced skeptics that the steamboat would find a permanent place in inland navigation. But not until the steamboat was put into service on the "western waters"—the Mississippi River and its tributaries—could its full potentialities be judged.

Immigrants settling in the West before 1825 found the transportation of their products confined to rude roads and trails that led back to the eastern seaboard or to downstream traffic on the Ohio or Tennessee to the Mississippi. The great river system was in use by settlers soon after the Revolution, but the Spaniards, and subsequently the French, imposed onerous restrictions and taxes on the movement of goods until 1803. After the Louisiana Purchase Americans were free to exploit the great waterways.

Travel downstream was difficult and hazardous in the extreme. The simplest sort of craft was a raft of logs with a shed for the protection of crew and cargo and with steerage provided by huge sweeps or oars. An improvement on the raft was the barge or bateau or "ark," a boxlike, flat-bottomed affair built of planks with a cabin or house covering part of the deck. Both the raft and the ark were broken up and sold for lumber at the destination, usually New Orleans, and the crews, ordinarily the owners of boat and cargo, made their way home overland on foot and horseback. The keelboat, with its finer lines and keel, was such an improvement over the flatboats that journeys upstream were possible. Keelboats were operated by ten or twelve crewmen who pulled the oars, manned push poles in shallow water, and on occasion went ashore to drag the boat through swift currents in the manner of a canal boat. The physical prowess and reckless attitude of the keelboat men brought forth the description, "half-horse, half-alligator." Dangerous currents and floods, attacks from Indians who still lurked in the river-bank forests, and the depredations of river pirates caused losses in men, vessels, and cargo. Obviously raft, ark, and keelboat freight charges were high, but the demand for service kept them plying their hazardous trade.

Through traffic originated at numerous points along the river system. Pittsburgh, situated where the junction of the Allegheny and the Monongahela forms the Ohio River, early became a leading river port. Plentiful supplies of timber and the local iron industry were the basis for a flourishing shipbuilding industry there. It was at Pittsburgh that the first steamboat to ply the inland waters was constructed by Nicholas Roosevelt under the Fulton-Livingston patents. Named the *New Orleans,* she left Pittsburgh on October 20, 1811, and completed her voyage to the Gulf, despite an earthquake at New Madrid, Missouri, in a little over two and a half months. Some six years passed before regular service, both upstream and downstream, was established. From 1820 on, steamboating developed rapidly on the Ohio and Mississippi and to a considerable extent on tributaries like the Wabash and the Cumberland. In the year 1826 alone, fifty-six vessels were built on the Ohio River. By the decade of the 1850s perhaps 750 steamboats sailed the western waters.

Variations in the height of the rivers made for uncertainty and even danger of navigation. Ice in the spring and sand bars in the summer were ever-present hazards, and snags, rocks, and sunken vessels continually damaged and wrecked the steamboats. The high-pressure boilers frequently exploded, such accidents killing thousands over the decades.

Designs were improved to reduce these hazards. Better boilers and engines at last led to safer vessels, and broad hulls and stern wheels produced boats with drafts of less than three feet. These were the sumptuously furnished Mississippi River packets of television and the movies, patronized by the plantation owner, his many-petticoated wife, and pantalooned daughters.

There is little doubt that this romantic means of transportation was a major influence in the growth of the West. It is hard to realize that vessels moving only ten to fifteen miles an hour downstream could revolutionize transportation, but the steamboat did precisely this for Westerners. For one thing, they made possible comfortable travel; for another, the time of arrival of freight could be estimated within reasonable limits. Paradoxically, the steamboats also stimulated the business of the flatboats, largely because those who operated the slower vessels could more readily get back upstream to bring down a new load. But by 1850 the railroad had begun to encroach on all river traffic.

If the speed of the steamboat led to its success, the greater speed and certainty of the railroad meant the ultimate victory of land travel over water travel. The slowest freight trains covered distances much faster than the best steamboats. Railroad routes were more direct, distances between key points sometimes being half as great as they were by a meandering stream. Nor was distance the whole story. Railroads could set up and maintain schedules, whereas steamboat departures and arrivals, even though more reliable than those of the flatboats, were still dependent upon the vagaries of the weather and of stream flow. Even before the Civil War cast its pall over the land, railroads had made serious inroads upon river traffic.

On the waterways of the East and on the Great Lakes the steamboat never attained the importance that it did in the Midwest. Canals and turn-pikes furnished alternative means of transportation, and the rail net had

Steam-powered boats, beginning with ships like the Clermont (above), shortened ship-ping times, increased returns to commerce and trade, and acted as stimuli to economic growth.

Bustling inland shipping points like Cincinnati early became major markets for an increasing variety of goods and services.

an early competitive start. The steamboat in the East was primarily a passenger carrier, great side-wheelers furnishing luxurious accommodations for those who traveled between major cities. On the Great Lakes, contrary perhaps to what might be expected, sailing ships successfully competed for freight throughout the ante-bellum years. Where human comfort was a factor, however, the steamship gradually won out. Even so, the number and tonnage of sailing vessels on the lakes in 1860 was far greater than those of steamboats; but here, as on the rivers, the train was rapidly winning over all the customers except those who simply wished to go for a boat ride.

THE MERCHANT MARINE

During the Revolution the American seaman distinguished himself in battle against the paramount sea power of the world. Though his ships and armament were not the best, his seamanship and daring won him many victories and the respect of seafaring nations. Commodore Whipple and his fishermen, turned fighting men, annoyed the British in New England waters, and John Paul Jones in the *Bonhomme Richard* demonstrated to the world the skill of the new nation's sailors. The seamanship that had been decisive in battle helped win in the commercial rivalry that arose after the Revolution. Yet the abilities of the men who manned the ships accounted only in part for the continuing advantage of the American merchant marine after the colonial period. Supplies of timber in the eastern part of the United

States remained sufficient to permit continuing cheap construction of wooden vessels. And if American designers were not men of great originality, they were highly successful adapters. From 1820 to the Civil War the United States was the leading maritime nation.

After a decade or so of indifferent business following the Revolution, American shipping was stimulated by the Napoleonic wars. Two types of vessels engaged in the lucrative foreign trade. The tramp, or transient, sailed on no fixed itinerary, picked up cargo wherever it could, and often remained away from its home port for many months or even years. The regular traders, owned by a substantial merchant or by a group of merchants, did not operate on a schedule but did have a pattern of port calls that was followed unless some tempting bit of business interrupted it. Although the merchants who owned regular traders shipped their own cargoes, they also handled goods for other shippers, nor did they object to carrying passengers.

Regularly scheduled sailings were instituted in 1818 by the Black Ball Line of New York. This, the first of the packet lines, owned four ships. In the first week of each month a vessel sailed from New York bound for Liverpool, and at the same time a ship began the Liverpool–New York passage. In the 1820s the Black Ball Line increased its trips to two a month each way, and other packet lines between New York and European ports were soon established. Henceforth, passengers could count on sailing at a particular hour on a given day, and merchants could book freight with something more than a vague hope that it would arrive in time to permit a profitable transaction.

Between 1820 and 1860 there were remarkable changes in design of sailing ships that led to increases in tonnage and efficiency. From an average of 300 tons in the 1820s, American sailing ships increased in size to 1,000 tons in the 1850s, and vessels of 1,500-tons burden were not uncommon. There was a marked increase in length-to-beam ratios and spread of sail for the ordinary packet ship, and the centuries-old practice of making the widest part of the vessel forward of the center was abandoned. Borrowing from French designers, Yankee shipbuilders produced a special type that was to dominate the seas for the three decades before the Civil War. This was the famed clipper ship, which, at some sacrifice of carrying capacity, attained unheard-of-speeds. The clipper was a graceful ship of three masts, square-rigged but equipped with abundant fore-and-aft sails that gave it a great advantage going into the wind and thus increased its speed. Manned by fewer hands than vessels of foreign register, a clipper was to be driven twenty-four hours a day, not put to bed for seven or eight hours at night.

The first American or "Baltimore" clipper was the *Ann McKim,* launched in 1832. Her builder, Donald McKay, became a legendary figure, and some of the ships of his design bore names that are even now remembered: The *Flying Cloud,* the *Sovereign of the Seas,* the *Great Republic,* and the *Lightning* were spectacularly beautiful—with concave sides and bow and sail towering two hundred feet above the deck. On her maiden voyage across

Transatlantic steamship service like that provided by the U.S.S. Baltic shortened the time it took to convey merchandise and business documents like drafts and letters of credit from New York to Liverpool. Equally important was the ability of steamships to adhere to roughly predictable schedules.

the Atlantic the *Lightning* logged a record 436 miles in one day for an average of eighteen miles an hour. Even today many ocean-going vessels do not approach this speed.

Clippers were designed for the express purpose of carrying passengers and high-value cargo long distances. On the Atlantic runs they did not pay because of their limited capacity. But they dominated the China trade, and after '49 they made fortunes for their owners carrying passengers and freight in the gold rushes to California and Australia. On the New York–San Francisco trip around Cape Horn, a distance of 16,000 miles, the *Flying Cloud* set a record of just over eighty-nine days, and a little over one hundred days was about par for the clipper voyage. Thus a time saving over ordinary ocean travel of up to three months was effected, for which some merchants and travelers would pay a good price.

Clippers, however, were not the only vessels in the American merchant fleet. Broad-beamed and full-bowed freighting ships, much slower than the clipper, were the backbone of the nation's merchant marine. Officered by men to whom seafaring was a tradition and a career of considerable social prestige, manned by crews of Americans bred to the sea, and owned by merchants of vision and daring like Stephen Girard of Philadelphia, the cheaply and expertly built ships from the marine ways of New York, Boston, and the Maine coast were the great ocean-freight carriers until the Civil War.

In the meantime, the British were making technical advances that enabled them to challenge American maritime supremacy and finally to overcome it. The major British innovation was the adaptation of the steamboat, invented for use on rivers and protected waters, to navigation on the open sea. Principal changes made by the British were, first, the use of iron instead of wood for the hull and, second, the employment for propulsion of the Archimedean screw principle instead of paddles. Iron hulls were necessary to carry safely the heavy machinery of the early steam era, but they also had greater strength, buoyancy, and durability than wood. From the 1830s on, the British rapidly solved the problems of iron-ship construction. The composite ship—with frame of iron and hull of wood—was tried for a while, but the acid in the oak timber corroded the iron. When the British perfected techniques of riveting and working with sheet iron and steel, they had an absolute advantage in making iron ships as great as the advantage the United States had enjoyed in the making of wooden ones.

The inefficiency and slow speeds of the early steam engines were a source of unending difficulty. For a long time steamships had to carry a greater weight of coal than of cargo, and low engine speeds made the inefficient paddle wheel necessary despite its theoretical inferiority. By 1848 steam engines were designed that could maintain higher speeds; the screw propeller was then rapidly adopted, and fuel consumption was cut greatly. During the 1850s both numbers and registered tonnage of steamships increased by leaps and bounds, and the passenger and high-value freight business was almost entirely captured.

In 1860 sailing ships still carried the greater part of the world's international freight. Yet the shape of the future was by this time clear to all except diehard American entrepreneurs who, unable to comprehend the rapid obsolescence of their beautiful wooden ships, failed to take vigorous steps to compete with Britain. Although government subsidies to American steamship builders began as early as 1845, they were both insufficient and poorly administered. Under the most favorable circumstances, however, builders in the United States could scarcely have competed on a cost basis with the vastly superior British iron industry. The signs were there for those who chose to read them. During the 1820s American ships had carried close to 90 per cent of the foreign trade of the United States; by the 1850s the figure was down to about 70 per cent. The times had changed and Fortune's hand was laid on other shoulders.

Money and Banks
in a Young Economy

Hamilton was, indeed, a singular character. Of acute understanding, disinterested, honest, and honorable in all private transactions, amiable in society, and duly valuing virtue in private life, yet so bewitched and perverted by the British example as to be under thorough conviction that corruption was essential to the government of a nation. . . .

THOMAS JEFFERSON

 Less spectacular than the opening of the West and the building of railroads, but scarcely less important to American economic growth before 1860, was the creation of a banking system and an adequate money supply. No other set of problems so perplexed our forebears, and on no other score is it so easy to criticize them adversely. Yet we must remember that there had been no comparable experience to serve as a guide. Haltingly, more often than not doing things the hard way, bankers and politicians together devised ways and means of furnishing an adequate, if heterogeneous, medium of exchange. The paradoxical result was to place control of the money supply in the hands of two categories of entrepreneurs who lived dangerously—early American bankers and their crap-shooting customers.

The Adoption of the American Monetary Unit

At the outset we may inquire how it came about that the monetary unit in the United States is the dollar rather than the pound. Remember that the early flow of international trade was such that the

Spanish dollar and its subdivisions became, for the seaboard as a whole, more plentiful than any other coins. Colonial trade with countries other than Great Britain left the colonies, all items considered, with a "favorable" balance of payments. But trade with Great Britain left them with a balance of payments in favor of the British, which meant that English coins tended to move, year in and year out, to the mother country.[1] In the two decades preceding the Revolution this tendency was especially marked, so that it became common to reckon accounts in terms of dollars. Even so, custom exerted a strong pull in favor of retaining the English monetary unit.

COINS AND COINAGE

Three men—Robert Morris, Thomas Jefferson, and Alexander Hamilton—were responsible for the decisions that established the American monetary unit. Morris, an able financier, had in 1778 been appointed by the Continental Congress to the chairmanship of a committee on monetary and financial matters. Four years later, as Superintendent of Finance, Morris submitted a report containing his recommendations concerning the coinage. He suggested that the Congress adopt as the basic monetary unit one 1,440th of the Spanish silver dollar, a weight of one-quarter of a grain of silver.[2] He proposed that the smallest silver coin, to be called a cent, contain one hundred of these basic units, and that there be coined in addition a quint equal to five cents and a mark equal to ten cents. He further recommended the establishment of a mint to coin the pieces. Congress adopted his report and requested Morris to prepare detailed plans.

In the meantime Thomas Jefferson submitted a report in which he took issue with Morris on several points. He objected to the adoption of so small a basic unit, although he agreed that some form of decimal system should be used. Insight into the problem of coinage can be gained from the opening paragraphs of the notes Jefferson prepared for congressional consideration.

> In fixing the unit of money, these circumstances are of principal importance.
>
> 1. That it be of a *convenient* size to be applied as a measure to the common money transactions of life.
>
> 2. That its parts and multiples be in *an easy proportion* to each other, so as to facilitate the Money Arithmetic.
>
> 3. That the Unit and its parts, or divisions, be *so nearly of the value of some of the known coins*, as that they may be of easy adoption for the people.

---

[1] The southern colonies, which produced the staples so much in demand in England, often had a favorable balance of payments on English account; British coins were for that reason more common in the South than in the middle and northern colonies.

[2] He was led to adopt this strange unit, as Thomas Jefferson put it, ". . . by a mathematical attention to our old currencies, all of which this unit will measure without leaving a fraction."

The Spanish Dollar seems to fulfill all these conditions.

1. Taking into our view all money transactions, great and small, I question if a common measure of more *convenient size* than the Dollar could be proposed. The value of 100, 1,000, 10,000 dollars is well estimated by the mind; so is that of the tenth or the hundredth of a dollar. Few transactions are above or below these limits. The expediency of attending to the size of the money Unit will be evident, to anyone who will consider how inconvenient it would be to a manufacturer or merchant, if, instead of the yard for measuring cloth, either the inch or the mile had been made the Unit of Measure.

2. The most *easy ratio* of multiplication and division, is that by ten. Everyone knows the facility of Decimal Arithmetic. Everyone remembers, that, when learning Money-Arithmetic, he used to be puzzled with adding the farthings, taking out the fours and carrying them on; adding the pence, taking out the twelves and carrying them on; adding the shillings, taking out the twenties and carrying them on; but when he came to the pounds, where he had only tens to carry forward, it was easy and free from error. The bulk of mankind are schoolboys through life. These little perplexities are always great to them. And even mathematical heads feel the relief of an easier, substituted for a more difficult process. Foreigners, too, who trade and travel among us, will find a great facility in understanding our coins and accounts from this ratio of subdivision. Those who have had occasion to convert the livres, sols, and deniers of the French; the gilders, stivers and frenings of the Dutch, the pounds, shillings, pence, and farthings of these several States, into each other, can judge how much they would have been aided, had their several subdivisions been in a decimal ratio. Certainly, in all cases, where we are free to choose between easy and difficult modes of operation, it is most rational to choose the easy.[3]

Jefferson then went on to point out that the dollar was in fact in general use in the states and that people everywhere would readily accept it as the monetary unit. The only difficulty, he said, was that the Spanish dollars varied in their content of pure silver. He suggested that proper persons be appointed "to assay and examine with the utmost accuracy possible the Spanish milled dollars of different states in circulation with us." Assaying and examination would determine the *average* number of grains in circulating Spanish dollars, and Jefferson suggested that this average be the number of grains of silver in the new United States dollar. Jefferson felt that silver ought to be accepted at the mint at the rate of fifteen ounces of silver for one of gold. Finally, he recommended the striking of a ten-dollar gold piece, a one-dollar silver piece (this piece to be the basic unit of account), a ten-cent piece, and two copper pieces—one a cent, the other a half-cent. With

[3] Paul Leicester Ford, ed., *The Writings of Thomas Jefferson* (New York and London: Putnam's, 1894), pp. 446–47.

Spanish milled dollars, their edges designed to discourage the age-old custom of clipping or shaving minute slivers of precious metal, became a standard form of money in the colonial period.

modifications, Jefferson's proposals were adopted by the Confederation Congress and incorporated in the Mint Act of 1786.

No coins except a small quantity of coppers were struck under the authority of this act, and there was American coinage in significant amounts only several years after the Constitution went into effect on March 4, 1789. So it was left to the first Secretary of the Treasury, Alexander Hamilton, to make the decisions leading to the determination of an American monetary unit. Hamilton was so preoccupied with the public debt and the establishment of a banking system that he did not get around to a consideration of coinage until 1791, when he made a report to Congress that contained most of Jefferson's proposals. Congress dallied for over a year before passing, upon the insistence of President Washington, the Coinage Act of 1792.[4] This statute, with one or two exceptions, enacted the language of Hamilton's report into law. Certain provisions ought to be remembered.

1. The dollar was officially adopted as the American unit of account, and it was defined in terms of both silver and gold. The silver dollar was to contain 371.25 grains of pure silver. While no provision was made for the coinage of a gold dollar (contrary to Hamilton's recommendation), the gold eagle or ten-dollar gold piece was to contain 247.5 grains of pure gold and the gold in a dollar, had it been coined, would thus have amounted to 24.75 grains. The silver dollar, then, was to contain fifteen times as much metal, by weight, as the gold dollar.

2. Three gold coins—eagles, half eagles, and quarter eagles—were to be struck in addition to five silver coins—the dollar, half-dollar, quarter-dollar, dime, and half-dime. A copper cent and half-cent were also authorized.

---

[4] It is of passing interest that the first building the United States ever erected was the mint at Philadelphia.

Early in the nineteenth century the variety of American coinage already included (from left to right and top to bottom) a quarter, a five-dollar gold piece, a silver dollar, and a copper cent (obverse and reverse).

3. A mint was established, and free and unlimited coinage of both gold and silver was authorized. Gold and silver were both made full legal tender, and since the right to unrestricted ownership and use of the precious metals was unquestioned in those days, the United States was on a bimetallic standard.
4. Coinage was to be gratuitous—i.e., without "seigniorage," the charge exacted from persons for coining their bullion at the mint.[5]

THE START OF A BIMETALLIC STANDARD

For nearly three-quarters of a century the United States was legally a bimetallic country. But it is one thing to adopt bimetallism formally and

---

[5] "Gratuitous" coinage is not to be confused with "free" coinage, which means that any private person has the right to have bullion coined at legal rates.

an altogether different thing to maintain it as a standard. As we have just seen, the weight of silver contained in the dollar, as defined in 1792, was 15 times that of gold. The ratio of 15 to 1 is called the *mint ratio*. Now if the mint ratio always corresponded to the valuation placed on the two metals by those who trade in them, there would be no difficulty in maintaining a bimetallic standard. The mint ratio has never prevailed in the open market for long, however, and the experience of the United States and other countries furnishes plentiful evidence of the futility of trying to keep mint ratios and market ratios in correspondence. Thus, even though a *mint ratio* of 15 to 1 closely approximated the prevailing *market ratio* in 1792, world conditions of the supply of gold and the demand for gold were such that the ratio in the market rose gradually during the 1790s to about 15.5 to 1.

When a government adopts a mint ratio of 15 to 1, it in effect agrees to exchange 1 ounce of gold for 15 ounces of silver and vice versa. If those who make a business of dealing in the precious metals are willing to exchange 1 ounce of gold for 16 ounces of silver, it would pay anyone who can put his hands on 15 ounces of silver to take it to the mint, exchange it for an ounce of gold, take the ounce of gold to a broker, and exchange the ounce of gold for 16 ounces of silver. Needless to say, those who are aware of such possibilities of gain will take silver to the mint in quantities in order to buy gold; if they wish to continue the process by exchanging gold for silver in the market and delivering the silver to the mint in exchange for gold, they may do so.[6] The end result of such transactions is to drain the mint of gold and furnish it with silver for coinage.

In the example we have assumed a *market ratio* of 16 to 1 and a *mint ratio* of 15 to 1. Technically, this relationship is one in which *silver is overvalued at the mint*, for under such circumstances people can get more for silver at the mint than they can by taking their silver "to market." If the *market ratio* were below *mint ratio* at, say, 14 to 1, we should say that *gold is overvalued at the mint*. A little reflection will enable the student to see that if the mint will give 15 ounces of silver for an ounce of gold, whereas brokers will give only 14 ounces, those who want to exchange gold for silver will profit by going to the mint. In fact, a profit can be made under such circumstances by taking gold to the mint, converting it into silver, taking the silver "to market," and converting it into gold again.[7]

---

[6] It should be emphasized that only experts—money-brokers and dealers in gold and silver as *commodities*—were actually aware of the profits to be made by such transactions. As Prof. Laughlin has pointed out, ". . . the general public know little about such things, and if they did, a little arithmetic would deter them." For an interesting and readable account of the history of silver as money in America, see J. L. Laughlin, *The History of Bimetallism in the United States* (New York: Appleton, 1900).

[7] All this may seem unnecessarily involved and technical; yet an understanding of the principles involved is absolutely necessary for a comprehension of United States monetary history, especially in the late nineteenth century.

For centuries observers had noted that debased coins tended to remain in circulation while full-bodied coins were either hoarded or exported to pay for imported goods. One naturally paid out debased coins whenever it was possible to pass them off at their nominal value. Popular saying to the effect that "bad money drives out good money" or "cheap money will replace dear" thus came into various languages. Sir Thomas Gresham, Queen Elizabeth's master of the mint, made a formal statement of this economic tendency, which has become known as Gresham's law. For our purposes we may best state the law as follows: *Money overvalued at the mint tends to drive out of circulation money undervalued at the mint.*

Only a little while after the new republic set an official rate for the coinage of gold and silver, Gresham's law became operative. The ratio of 15 to 1 probably overvalued silver in terms of gold from the beginning; during the 1790s the overvaluation became greater, and in 1808 it reached 16 to 1.[8] Through ignorance, gold was brought to the mint in some quantity, but American gold coins were for the most part either exported or kept in private hoards so that silver constituted the chief part of the circulation. The French coinage law of 1803, which set the ratio in France at 15.5 to 1, gave impetus to the drain of gold from this country, and the minting of English subsidiary coins at a ratio of 16 to 1, beginning in 1816, brought about the almost complete disappearance of gold. American authorities were well aware of what was going on, of course, and during the 1820s there was much discussion in Congress concerning the advisability of changing the official ratio.

There was general agreement among those informed in such matters that gold was *undervalued* at the mint and that silver, which was *overvalued,* tended always to drive gold out of circulation. The question that could not be settled, even after interminable argument, was what ought to be the *mint ratio* that would correspond to the *market ratio.* At long last, in June of 1834, two acts were passed changing the mint ratio to just a fraction over 16 to 1. Now gold was overvalued at the mint, and even though American coinage of silver had never been so high as it was in the years immediately after 1834, gold slowly began to replace silver, which was either hoarded or exported.

The tendency of first gold and then silver to disappear from circulation was not the only monetary problem confronting the government in the early years. Although from the start some silver was brought to the mint, it was soon evident that the United States would for a while have to depend on foreign coins for a part of its circulating medium. An act of 1793 made foreign metallic money legal tender for three years, and later statutes were passed from time to time making designated foreign coins either legal tender or acceptable in payment of certain obligations to the United States. Not until 1857 was a law finally passed repealing ". . . all former acts authoriz-

---

[8] Annual averages of market ratios show considerable fluctuation during these years, but the trend was upward until 1813.

Robert Morris (as painted by the distinguished artist and scientist Charles Willson Peale) was a prominent American who helped establish the Bank of North America in 1781 and almost singlehandedly directed the financing of the American Revolution. Unfortunately, his speculation in land brought him to ruin.

ing the currency of foreign gold or silver coins, and declaring the same a legal tender in payment for debts. . . ."

Thus coins of all Western countries passed current. Oddly, it was hard to keep American silver coins in circulation even when silver was overvalued at the mint. Merchants engaged in the West Indian trade soon discovered that shiny, new American dollars and subsidiary coins could be exchanged abroad for dull Spanish pieces containing a somewhat greater amount of silver. The Spanish money was even presented at the United States mint to be recoined into American pieces which were then exported. The problem became so bad that in 1806 coinage of the silver dollar was suspended by direction of President Jefferson; not until after the legislation of 1834 was it again struck at the mint. Thus Spanish silver coins and, subsequently, the French five-franc silver piece served as the chief "hard money" in circulation before 1834.

The First American Banks

We must now turn our attention to the first commercial banks in the United States. After we have inquired briefly into their functions, we shall be better able to understand the workings of the first Bank of the United States, an institution that very nearly became our permanent central bank.

Bills of Exchange, like this one signed by Robert Morris, provided an early and easy way to avoid the cumbersome and expensive shipment of eight hundred pounds sterling to London from America.

COMMERCIAL BANKS

The severing of relationships with the English during the Revolution, together with the relinquishment by the states of the right to issue bills of credit, made the establishment of modern credit-granting banks inevitable.

In 1781 Robert Morris and a few associates founded the Bank of Pennsylvania to assist in financing the Revolution. This bank so helped the harried Continental Congress by facilitating the payment of troops and the purchase of provisions that after three years Morris was able to persuade Congress to grant a national charter to a new institution—the Bank of North America. The Bank of Pennsylvania soon went out of business, but many of those interested in it bought shares in the new venture. It was fitting that the first chartered bank should be established in Philadelphia, which for several decades was to be the financial center of the country. Two other banks were chartered in 1784—the Bank of New York in New York City and the Massachusetts Bank in Boston. These were the only three commercial banks in the country before 1790, when the Bank of Maryland was chartered.[9]

The first three banks were "founded on specie." Their capitals were subscribed for the most part in gold and silver, a large part of the capital of the Bank of North America being furnished by the government. All three received deposits and made loans and in general functioned just as commercial banks do today. Although checks were drawn against deposits

---

[9] The first three banks have had a continuous existence since their incorporation, although the names have changed because of subsequent mergers.

from the beginning, it was more common for people to make payments by bank notes manufactured to each bank's order by a private engraver. When a bank officer made a loan, he could credit the borrower's checking account with the amount, but more commonly he handed over the proceeds of the loan in bank notes, which the borrower then put in circulation as money. In effect, the bank exchanged its more acceptable evidences of debt for businessmen's less acceptable promissory notes.

Loans, or discounts as they were more properly and more commonly called, were for thirty days only and at first were not renewable.[10] For a while the minimum amount that could be deposited with the Massachusetts Bank was $300, and the smallest check that could be written (except when closing out an account) was $100. These restrictions were designed to keep out small depositors and to get accounts from the wealthy, who would keep stable and sizable balances.

A number of commercial banks were chartered in the 1790s. By 1800 there were twenty-eight, and by 1811, eighty-eight. All save two of these banks were incorporated by special charter upon passage of a bill by a state legislature. Early charters contained few provisions restricting a bank's activity, though not infrequently they required that circulation be limited to two or three times the amount of a bank's capital and occasionally regulated the ratio of notes in circulation to specie reserve. The charter bills were passed only after "politicking" and, on occasion, actual bribery of legislators. The Federalists, generally in power before 1800, granted charters to their supporters; after 1800 the friends of Democrats were more often given the valuable privilege of starting a bank.

On the whole, banks before 1811 were sound. Banking was carried on in an orderly way, considering the lack of experience of officers, but the beginnings of bad practices could be discerned. For example, the legislature of North Carolina in 1804 chartered a bank at Cape Fear and one at Newbern, each to have a capital of $800,000 payable in specie. Only a small part of the capital was ever paid; but the two banks issued over $3 million of their notes in making loans that drew interest at a rate of 6 per cent, the promoters of the project receiving about $200,000 per annum with practically no investment. This is an especially bad example for the years before 1811, but the charter laws in many states, which required only a partial payment by shareholders at the start of a bank's operations, made similar abuses possible. Frequently the time of payment of the remainder of the capital subscription was left to the discretion of the directors of the bank. What we are describing here, however, is only laxness; actual fraud, a not uncommon characteristic of American banking later in the century, was unusual before 1811.

---

[10] A note or bill is said to be "discounted" when the bank deducts the interest from the proceeds of the loan at the beginning of the lending period. The word *discount* is more common in the literature of early banking than the word *loan*.

Architect of the new nation's financial superstructure, Alexander Hamilton (as shown here in the John Trumbull portrait) contended with agricultural interests to promote manufacturing self-sufficiency.

THE FIRST BANK OF THE UNITED STATES

Shortly after becoming Secretary of the Treasury, Alexander Hamilton proposed the establishment of a semipublic banking institution, which was to become the first Bank of the United States. Although the idea was opposed by Thomas Jefferson and Edmund Randolph, respectively the Secretary of State and Attorney General in the first cabinet, Hamilton won Washington to his side, and approval of the bank was assured.

Hamilton's *Report on a National Bank*, in which he argued for a Bank of the United States, shows remarkable insight into both the financial problems of the young country and the economic implications of banking. Hamilton asserted that a "National Bank" would augment ". . . the active or productive capital of a country." By this he meant that it would increase the convertible paper money, possibly by as much as two or three times the specie base, because specie withdrawals from a bank were under normal circumstances approximately offset by specie deposits. Notes remained in circulation because of public confidence in them, and furthermore a

> . . . borrower frequently, by a check or order, transfers his credit to some other person, to whom he has a payment to make; who, in his turn, is as often content with a similar credit, because he is satisfied that he can, whenever he pleases, either convert it into cash, or pass it to some other hand, as equivalent for it.

As important to Hamilton as the salutary effects of the proposed bank on the economy of a country was the assistance it could give the government by lending money to the treasury in times of stress. Moreover, the institution could serve as fiscal agent for the government, acting as a depository of government funds, making transfers of funds from one part of the country to another, and (Hamilton hoped) serving as a tax-collection agency.

The bill creating the bank followed Hamilton's report closely. There was substantial opposition to it even in the predominantly Federalist Congress, on the grounds that (1) it was unconstitutional, (2) it would create a "money-monopoly" that would endanger the rights and liberties of the people, and (3) it would be of value to the northern states but not to the agricultural South. Although the arguments of the opposition were eventually to prevail, they were unsuccessful at this time. The bill carried on a sectional vote, and Washington signed it on St. Valentine's Day in 1791.

The Bank had a capital of $10 million, a sizable sum in those days and considerably greater than the capitals of any existing American bank.[11] So large an amount was made possible by having three-fourths of the private subscription of $8 million payable in bonds of the United States, and only one-fourth in specie, subscriptions to be paid in four installments.[12] The United States bought one-fifth of the capital stock. Apparently the desire of the Bank's founders to have the government share in the profits of the enterprise overcame any possible concern about the control the government might exercise through its five appointed directors. The government paid for its shares with the proceeds of a $2,000,000 loan made by the Bank on the security of its *own* stock, the loan to be repaid in ten equal annual installments. At the start of operations, then, the United States participated in the earnings of a privately financed venture without contributing a penny to the original capital.

The first Bank of the United States was clearly intended to earn the greater part of its income by carrying on a regular commercial-banking business. It was run ". . . in the main with an eye single to business and profit . . ." and returned substantial dividends to its owners. Its earning assets consisted for the most part of short-term loans to businessmen, discounts ordinarily being made for sixty days. Loans to the government were also a lucrative source of income, especially at the beginning and toward the end of the Bank's existence.

Although the Bank was essentially a private one, operated for the profit of its stockholders, it performed invaluable services for the treasury—just as Hamilton had said it would. While it was not a central bank in a formal sense, it performed central banking functions, especially in its capacity as

---

[11] The Bank of North America, for example, started with a capital of $300,000, over half of which had been contributed by the government.

[12] It would have been impossible to obtain the whole $10 million in specie, and the requirement that United States securities be used for such a purpose strengthened the market for them. Most of the Bank stock was in fact paid for in U.S. bonds. According to Hammond, "The Bank was permitted to organize as soon as $400,000 had been received from the subscribers. Whether much more was ever got from them is doubtful, though the Bank subsequently accumulated a treasure much in excess of what the stockholders were supposed to pay." See Bray Hammond, *Banks and Politics in America from the Revolution to the Civil War* (Princeton: Princeton University Press, 1957), p. 123.

The first Bank of the United States issued these ten-dollar notes, canceled after they had become worn with three or four x's inked on their faces.

fiscal agent for the government. The treasury kept most of its deposits with the Bank, and in return the Bank transmitted government funds from one part of the country to another without charge. After 1800 the Bank helped collect customs bonds in cities where it had branches.[13] It further facilitated government business by effecting payments of interest on the public debt, carrying on foreign-exchange operations for the treasury, and supplying bullion and foreign coins to the mint.

The relationships between the Bank of the United States and the commercial banks are not altogether clear. It is evident that it exercised *some* measure of control over them, particularly in restraining their note issues. The conservative lending policy of the first Bank made it on balance a creditor of the state banks, and it continually received a greater dollar volume of state bank notes than state banks received of its obligations. It was thus in a position to present regularly the notes of the state banks for payment in specie, assuring a moderate note issue for the country as a whole.[14] Notes of the United States Bank and its branches circulated at, or very close to, par throughout the country. The Bank had at all times a considerable portion of the gold and silver in the country, its holdings during the last three years of its existence probably standing at or near $15 million, about the amount held by all the state banks. That it came to the aid of other banks with specie loans seems certain.[15] Although there was no established custom of using deposits with the Bank of the United States as reserves and

---

[13] By 1800 the Bank had branches in Boston, New York, Baltimore, and Charleston. Branches were added in Washington and Savannah in 1802 and in New Orleans in 1805.
[14] Students of the period speak of the "friendly co-operation" of the large institution; it apparently refrained from embarrassing banks that seemed to be operating legitimately.
[15] In the second petition for renewal of the charter it was asserted that the commercial banks generally had the use of not less than a tenth of the Bank's capital.

no obligation on its part, legal or customary, to assist other banks in need, it in practice became a lender of last resort. Thus the Bank was clearly on its way to being a recognized central bank when Congress refused to recharter it.

In retrospect the reasons for the continued operation of the United States Bank seem compelling. During the two decades of its existence there was a well-ordered expansion of credit and general stability of the currency; compared to the difficulties before 1791, the money problems of the 1790s and early 1800s were insignificant. The first Bank of the United States went a long way toward giving the nation a better monetary system than it had any reason to hope for in 1791.

But arguments based on cold economic facts are rarely as effective as arguments based on appeals to human emotions and prejudices. Those who opposed the recharter of the Bank made the points advanced when the matter was being debated nearly twenty years before. The Bank was unconstitutional. It was a financial monster so powerful that it would eventually control the nation's economic life and deprive the people of their liberties. To these contentions was added a new objection: the Bank had fallen under the domination of foreigners, mostly Englishmen. Foreign ownership of stock was indeed something like $7 million, or 70 per cent of the shares, but the percentage of United States bonds owned by foreigners was about the same. Only shareholding American citizens could be directors, and foreign nationals could not vote by proxy; nevertheless, many people felt that the influence of English owners was bound to make itself felt through those American directors with whom they had close business contacts.

The debates were not so important as the opposition of some bankers, the tactless lobbying of the Bank's supporters, and political expedients of the moment, including the pacification of frontiersmen and agrarians who were against anything called a bank. It has often been remarked that business interests, and particularly the state banks in competition with it, did not oppose the Bank. This statement is only partly true. In areas outside the well-established financial centers there was opposition by the state banks, which were certain to acquire new business if the big Bank were destroyed. Managers and directors who anticipated an increased volume of business and who were not impressed with the importance of the United States Bank as a stabilizing institution very definitely opposed it. The power of the Bank with respect to the state institutions was a major force creating enmity toward the Bank.

The outcome of the showdown on the issue of recharter was determined by purely political considerations. In order to reduce its indebtedness to the institution, which by 1796 was in excess of $6 million, the government began to sell its shares, then much appreciated in value. In 1802 the government disposed of its remaining ownership interest. Even so, the old bugaboo of unconstitutionality loomed large. On a number of occasions Thomas Jefferson had stated his abiding conviction that the Bank was unconstitutional and a menace to the liberties of the people. Although he was no longer President when the issue of recharter came up, his influence was tremendous in Congress. Many of his followers doubtless were swayed by his view. But the decisive votes were turned against the Bank by personal antagonism toward Albert Gallatin, champion of the Bank though a member of Jefferson's party. In the House consideration of the bill for renewal of the charter was postponed indefinitely by a vote of 65 to 64. In the Senate, Vice-President George Clinton, enemy of both Madison and Gallatin, broke a 17–17 tie with a vote of nay.

General Characteristics of State Banks, 1811–1834

During the half-century that lay between the failure to renew the charter of the first Bank of the United States and the outbreak of the Civil War, the American banking system took on many permanent characteristics. This period of banking was characterized on the one hand by unsound and fraudulent practices and on the other hand by a growing awareness on the part of practical bankers and academic observers of the essential functions of a commercial bank. It was further distinguished by efforts of legislatures to achieve safety through reform. Because of the complexity of the changes, it will be convenient to divide the half-century under consideration into two periods, 1811–34 and 1835–61.

Following the failure to recharter the first Bank of the United States, the number of state banks increased rapidly, from 89 in 1811 to nearly 250 in 1816. This threefold increase was not unexpected. There was opportunity to take over the business of the big Bank, and investors felt that without its controls bank profits would increase. The rise in the level of manufacturing activity brought about by the War of 1812 made possible the fulfillment of bank promoters' hopes for high earnings. The sharp increase in note issues, together with deficit financing by the government, led to an inflation that was stimulating to business ventures. All banks except the more conservative ones in New England and New York were forced to suspend specie payments in 1814, but suspension was considered a blessing by most bankers, for there was then no need to worry about the ratio of gold and silver reserves to liabilities. The onset of depression in 1818, which remained severe through 1819, brought about mass failures of banks in the West and South, but even so 300 banks still existed in 1820. During the next decade new charters exceeded failures, and in 1830 there were 330 state banks. Four years later more than 500 commercial banks were doing business.

BANK CAPITALS

Bank charters in the 1790s and 1800s commonly contained a provision giving the incorporating state an opportunity to contribute to a bank's capital, enabling the state to share in the profits of the venture, to have a direct part in management, and to obtain loans easily. Nearly all the older states at one time owned bank stock, but after 1812 they gradually disposed of it. In the East banks were ordinarily established by individuals, but in the South and West, where sufficient private capital was often difficult to raise, state governments actually promoted the establishment of banks and state ownership of bank stock was common. Some states subscribed the entire capital of a bank, as was the case with the first State Bank of Illinois chartered in 1821, but in most instances the states contributed less than half the total.

Early methods of subscribing to bank capital would shock a twentieth-century bank examiner. The capital of a bank presumably constitutes a margin of safety for all creditors, since it serves as a source of funds should depositors' money be lost through unwise selection of assets by the bank management. In the years under consideration charters usually provided for the payment of stock in installments, the entire subscription frequently not being required for several years. In many instances the entire capital never was paid in. Since banks were presumably on a specie basis, one would suppose that the capital would be paid in gold and silver. In reality, often only the first installment was paid in specie, and the remaining installments were met by borrowing the money on "stock notes." A shareholder would put his bank stock up as collateral for a loan and use the proceeds to pay the bank for amounts due on his capital subscription. This way of paying in capital was sanctioned by the very strongest banks. One of the most able, if violently biased, contemporary observers of the period, William Gouge, described this procedure.

> The first instalment, which we will suppose to be $5 on a share, enables the banks to purchase desk and a counter and to pay for engraving and printing its notes. It has then the necessary apparatus for commencing its operations, and has, perhaps, a specie fund in reserve, of three or four dollars for each share of stock, to meet contingencies. It then begins to discount notes and circulate paper. . . . As the Bank notes will serve the purpose of trade in the neighborhood, the specie is sent to distant places to procure commodities. . . . Then comes the time for paying the second, third, or fourth instalment. The Bank makes a call on the stockholders. Some of them hypothecate their stock, that is, pledge it to the Bank and with the means obtained from the Bank itself pay in their proportion. Others have obtained the means by discounts of accommodation notes, without any hypothecation of stock. Some few pay in real money: but they generally pay in the notes of the Bank itself, or of similar institutions. It is by this kind of hocus-pocus that Bank capitals are formed. After the first instalment is paid, the Bank by its own operations, facilitates the paying of the others. . . . Thus, Bank capitals are formed by exchanging one kind of promises to pay for another kind of

promises to pay. This mode of forming Bank capitals, with the stock notes of the subscribers, is not peculiar to banks of the second and third order. The Banks of the most approved standing have formed their capitals in the same way.[16]

BANK NOTES

Fundamentally there was no difference between a bank note as money and a bank deposit as money. When a bank made a loan to a customer, it gave him the proceeds in the form of its own (bank) notes, which then circulated as cash, or as a deposit credit against which he could draw checks. Nowadays, of course, banks no longer issue notes, and the paper money that passes from hand to hand is issued by Federal Reserve or the treasury; moreover, whenever a firm borrows money today it takes the proceeds as a credit to its account. But during the years before the Civil War, and even for some time after that in rural areas, a bank issued notes much more frequently than it made credits to a customer's account.

Although bank notes were more important than checks, checks were used, particularly by urban businessmen. Even before the end of the eighteenth century they were no longer rare in cities, and during the first three decades of the nineteenth century, city businessmen came to make nearly all their payments, except wage payments, by check. But retail trade was carried on in cash, and tradesmen remitted to suppliers in cash. In the South and West, particularly in frontier communities, checks were a sophisticated and unusual means of payment until well past mid-century.

Until the late 1820s notes were issued against the "general assets" of a bank. Limitations placed on note issue by charters were not highly restrictive, the usual requirement being that the total amount should not exceed a certain multiple of a bank's capital. A stipulation that the "circulation" of a bank should not be more than twice or three times its capital was usual, and limitations of one and a half times or of four times the capital were not infrequent. At an early date it was seen that a better way to prevent overissue would be to require bankers to keep in their vaults a certain percentage of specie against their note liabilities. There was no agreement on an ideal required reserve ratio, but amounts between 20 per cent and $33\frac{1}{3}$ per cent were suggested. From 1820 on there was awareness of the fact that deposits, as well as notes, were liabilities, and in the 1840s the idea of requiring a *legal* reserve began to take hold.[17]

---

[16] William M. Gouge, *An Inquiry into the Principles of the American Banking System* (New York: *The Evening Post,* 1840), p. 25. If shareholders were rich, their debts were a good guarantee of eventual repayment; creditors were endangered only to the extent that their promissory notes might be illiquid in periods of deflation and precipitate liquidation.
[17] Actually, the idea of a bank "based on specie" implies some notion of a maximum issue relative to gold and silver in the vaults. In the early days, however, the proportion of specie to notes varied widely; not until the middle of the century was there fairly general agreement as to what was a "safe" fractional reserve.

Meanwhile, banks aimed at maintaining convertibility into specie. At infrequent intervals general "suspensions" occurred, but there was ordinarily at least a pretense of redeeming notes. Bankers soon learned stratagems for avoiding the embarrassment of too much note redemption; some made loans only on condition that the borrower keep the notes in circulation for a minimum period, while others required borrowers to spend the proceeds of a loan only at stipulated distances from the home office. And all but the very largest banks liked to put out bills in small denominations because there was less pressure for redemption of them. There was controversy over what were desirable minimum denominations. A plethora of small notes made counterfeiting as well as excessive issue too easy, and laws setting $3, $5, or $10 minimums were passed by some states.[18] People wanted small notes, however, because they were convenient and because they knew issue tended to be greater on that basis. And people got what they wanted because their interests and the interests of those with power in state legislatures coincided.

The bank notes issued by different institutions came to be accepted at widely varying rates. Notes of established, reputable, "specie-paying" banks were taken at their face value—i.e., at par—over wide areas. Bills of other banks were received at discounts from 1 or 2 per cent up to 50 per cent or more. Distance from the city where the issuing bank was located affected the acceptability of notes. For example, the paper of Baltimore banks circulated at 1 to 2 per cent discount in Washington, some forty miles away, when Washington bills were at 1 to 2 per cent discount in Baltimore. However, a bank that did not redeem in gold or silver in a period when specie payments were not generally suspended would find its bills circulating at a discount even in the immediate vicinity.

In nearly every city there were dealers or brokers who bought and sold bank notes. These note-brokers or "shavers" made profits by exchanging paper that did not circulate at par in a given area for paper that did. Notwithstanding the castigation of their activities by prominent citizens, their business flourished from the beginning of the nineteenth century. We shall presently consider the difficulties caused by the heterogeneous currency that existed from the War of 1812 to the Civil War.

Three Pre–1834 Developments in Control

Before 1834 some successful attempts were made to provide a homogeneous currency, to prevent serious losses to bank creditors, and to keep the money supply within reasonable bounds. We now have to consider three institu-

---

[18] In 1830 three states effectively prohibited notes under $5—Pennsylvania, Maryland, and Virginia. In the Carolinas at that time the circulation contained notes for fractions of a dollar—some as low as six and a half cents. There was recurring agitation for minimum restrictions right up to the time of the Civil War, but restrictive legislation was often repealed during periods of specie suspension.

tions that served as early experiments in the social control of banking in the United States.

THE SUFFOLK BANK SYSTEM

From about 1800 on, banks in Boston were confronted with the problem of competing with the circulation of the currency of country banks.[19] Bills issued by banks located at varying distances from the city, but within the Boston trade area, were used by small traders to pay for goods bought from the big-city merchants. This "foreign" money circulated at discounts of from 1 to 5 per cent, because of the costs involved in redeeming over bank counters miles away and because of general suspicion of the country banks' ability to redeem in specie. Boston banks refused to accept country bills and as a consequence found their own notes continually returning, either in payment of obligations to them or as demands for specie payment. Gresham's law operated, and "foreign" money, because it was overvalued relative to Boston money, became the commonly used medium in the city. As a further inroad on the business of the city institutions, country banks established agents in Boston to lend bills of the country banks in the form of call loans at interest rates lower than those charged by Boston banks.

In 1819 the Suffolk Bank, established but the year previously, decided to try a different way of handling the problem of country bank notes. The plan was copied from an operation the New England Bank of Boston had been carrying on for five years. On the condition that the country bank keep Boston deposits only with the Suffolk or else keep with it a permanent deposit of $5,000, plus a further sum sufficient to cover bills redeemed, the Suffolk Bank offered to allow the country bank to receive back its own bills at the discount at which they had been redeemed. Banks refusing to take advantage of the offer had to contend with presentation of their notes for payment at par in specie and in amounts that were often embarrassing.

In 1824, the directors of the Suffolk prevailed upon six other Boston banks to co-operate in the venture. A fund of $300,000 was established, and the Suffolk was made the agent of the six city banks for the collection of country notes. Competition between the New England Bank and the Suffolk had by this time brought the discount on "foreign" money to as low as one-fourth of 1 per cent. With seven city banks redeeming country bills, the discount on them fell to zero, and in 1825 the Suffolk System began both to receive and to collect country notes *at par*. This meant that banks all over New England could send in for deposit notes received from any other bank; the Suffolk Bank was, in effect, a *clearing* agency.[20] Notes of

---

[19] The same problem was met by bankers in New York and Philadelphia, who took similar, though less successful, measures to solve it.

[20] Thus the Suffolk "collected" notes when it presented them to issuing banks for payment. It served as a "clearing" agency by receiving notes from all banks, sorting them, and making charges and credits to the accounts of the banks maintaining deposits with Suffolk.

both Boston and country banks then circulated at par even outside New England. Some banks, particularly those in Maine and Vermont, protested vigorously against the plan and tried to take concerted action against the system. Most New England banks were forced to contract their note issues, because if their circulation were too great they would be continually faced with adverse balances in the clearing process at the Suffolk. Nevertheless, the advantages of a uniform currency were so obvious to banks and merchants that by 1830 the Suffolk System was firmly established. Not even the panic of 1837, with its accompanying suspension of specie payments and consequent temporary loss of coercive power by Boston banks, caused the country banks to pull out of the system. The Suffolk Bank continued as the agency for the clearing of New England notes until 1858, when a rival institution was organized by some new Boston banks and by country banks that resented the dictatorial policies of the Suffolk. Shortly afterward, national banking legislation did away with state bank notes and with the need for such regional systems.

The Suffolk Bank was not motivated by the altruism of its directors, nor did the other Boston banks co-operate because they wanted to do something nice for people. The Suffolk had originally wanted to handle "foreign" money because the business meant substantial deposits, and the other banks agreed to go along in 1824 because they hoped, by reducing the discount at which country money circulated, to make more room in Boston for their own notes. If in the process country issues were restricted and some banks were forced out of business, city bankers deemed this result all to the good.[21] The fact to remember is that a purely private venture in banking, undertaken solely with a view to making profits, resulted in lasting social gains and in a monetary system that would benefit the New England economy for decades.

THE SAFETY-FUND SYSTEM

The Safety-Fund System, established by the New York legislature in 1829, was suggested by Joshua Forman, leading businessman of the state and one of the chief promoters of the Erie Canal. He sold the safety-fund idea to Martin Van Buren, then governor of New York, and despite the vigorous opposition of the banks in New York City, the plan passed the legislature. At so early a date we see the first attempt of a governmental unit (as distinguished from the managers of banks under the Suffolk plan) at systematic regulation of banking. This first bit of intervention was a forerunner of modern plans of deposit insurance.

The Safety-Fund Act provided that, as bank charters came up for renewal by the legislature, a condition of recharter would be participation in the Safety-Fund System. Over a period of years the banks in New York,

---

[21] The circulation of Boston banks did not increase much, even after the system was in successful operation, largely because of the considerable use of "deposit currency" by city firms.

with the exception of two with perpetual charters, would thus become members of an organized system, the chief aims of the system being (1) protected note issues of all banks and (2) closer supervision of individual institutions.

Protection of note issues was to be achieved through the creation of a contributory fund. Each member bank was to pay annually into the safety fund an amount equal to one-half of 1 per cent of its capital until its total contribution had reached a maximum of 3 per cent of its capital. No further payments would then be required unless the fund should be depleted, and in no case was a yearly assessment to exceed one-half of 1 per cent of a bank's capital. All monies were to be invested, and if the earnings of the fund exceeded expenses of administration, the income was to be returned to the banks as dividends. If a member bank failed, its debts, after its assets were exhausted, were to be paid out of the safety fund. Although the emphasis was on protecting persons caught with the notes of a broken bank, the bill protected depositors as well.

The Safety-Fund Act also provided for periodic and rigorous bank examinations. Inspections were to be made every four months under the supervision of three commissioners, and examination of any bank could be requested by any three member banks. Irregular cursory examinations had in the past been required under occasional state charters, but this law provided for thorough investigation of banks at frequent intervals.

In such fashion one state recognized the responsibility of government to regulate institutions affecting the public interest. Needless to say, the law did not get on the books without opposition. Directors of New York City banks insisted that the legislation was unjust because, having relatively large capitals, city banks would have to pay disproportionately large amounts into the fund. It was further argued that well-managed banks would have to pay for the mistakes of poorly managed ones. Even after the system was in operation, there was continual complaint that the law had not done away with the favoritism of individual charters.

More than one hundred charters were granted under the Safety-Fund Act. The law's limitations became apparent in the depression years following 1837, when contributions to the fund were not sufficient to cover losses to noteholders and depositors of failed banks and the State of New York had to make up losses to the extent of nearly $1 million. Nevertheless, the safety fund was continued under the free-banking act of 1838.

THE SECOND BANK OF THE UNITED STATES

A modern central bank, like the Bank of England or the Federal Reserve System, has two jobs. First, it tries to control the quantity of money in the economy, thereby affecting business activity and (hopefully) the level of prices. Second, it renders the government and commercial banks a number of routine, mechanical services. To grasp the historical significance of the second Bank of the United States, it is a good exercise to inquire

President of the second Bank of the United States, archfoe of Andrew Jackson, and advocate of central-bank controls was Philadelphia aristocrat Nicholas Biddle. Some argued that his hauteur cost the Bank its charter; others felt that Wall Street would have done Chestnut Street in anyway.

how many of the control and service functions were performed by the Bank.

Difficulties of financing the War of 1812, monetary confusion resulting from the rapid increase in the number of state banks, and the sharp inflation that occurred after the suspension of specie payments in 1814 convinced people of the need for a second national bank. It took two years of Congressional wrangling and consideration of no less than six separate proposals before a bill to charter a second national bank was passed. Alexander Dallas and John C. Calhoun played the chief political roles in the establishment of the new bank, Dallas being especially useful in winning President Monroe's approval. Pressure from three wealthy proponents of the Bank—Stephen Girard, John Jacob Astor, and David Parish—helped secure final passage of the act. Knowledgeable people were sure there would be a great demand for the bank stock and, consequently, for government bonds with which to pay for stock subscriptions. Since these men owned large amounts of United States securities, they were vitally interested in a charter plan that would stimulate the market for them.

The charter of the second Bank of the United States resembled that of its predecessor. The capital was set at $35 million, four-fifths of it to be subscribed by individuals, firms, or states and the remaining one-fifth by the federal government. Most of the capital was to consist of government bonds, but one-fourth of the private subscription ($7 million) was to be paid in gold or silver coin. There were to be twenty-five directors, twenty elected by private stockholders and five appointed by the President. The main office of the Bank was to be located in Philadelphia, and branch offices were to be established on the initiative either of the directors or of Congress.

The first president of the Bank was William Jones, an ex-merchant and an undistinguished member of the cabinets of both Jefferson and Madison. Jones was simply not competent to manage the Bank. Under him branches in the West overextended loans, and outright fraud, particularly in Baltimore, led to substantial losses. In 1819, Langdon Cheves succeeded Jones to the presidency. To Cheves must be given credit for taking full and complete charge of the Bank and its affairs and getting rid of the incompetent and even dishonest officers who had gotten the branches into trouble.[22]

In 1823 there came from the Bank's board of directors to its presidency one of the notable figures in American history—Nicholas Biddle. Sophisticated, widely traveled, and well educated, Biddle typified the early American aristocrat. He had everything that a man could wish—wealth, power, and a mind that enabled him to become not only a master of the business of banking, but an economist as good as any in America in the first half of the nineteenth century.

It was in developing the control functions of the Bank, as distinguished from the service functions, that Biddle made his great contribution. The service functions were nonetheless important. As an agent of the government, the Bank (1) received and kept all funds of the United States, (2) transferred funds on government account from one part of the country to another without compensation, and (3) made payments to owners of government bonds and to government pensioners. On several occasions the Bank lent money to the government on terms better than could otherwise have been obtained, although it was never put to the ultimate test in this regard because it never had to do any war financing.

The Bank acted as fiscal agent for the government from its beginning and exercised limited control functions under Jones and Cheves. Because of its size it could not help but affect other banks and consequently the monetary medium of the country. Under Biddle, however, there was both a full realization of the potential power of the Bank and a conscious attempt to regulate the banking system according to certain preconceived notions of what *ought* to be done.

In the first place, the Bank under Biddle soon came to be the lender of last resort to the state banks. State banks did not keep their reserves as deposits with the Bank of the United States, but they did come to depend on the second Bank in times of crisis, borrowing specie from it to meet their obligations. *The second Bank was able to meet such demands because*

---

[22] See Fritz Redlich, *The Molding of American Banking—Men and Ideas*, Pt. I (New York: Hafner, 1947), p. 109.

it kept a much larger proportion of specie reserve against its circulation than did other banks. Another way it assisted in times of stress was by lending to business firms when the other banks could not or would not, thus furnishing indirect assistance in the same fashion as the Bank of England. While, because of these functions, many came to regard the big Bank as *the holder of ultimate reserves,* probably only Biddle actually realized what its power was in this respect.

In the second place, and even more important as a means of control, the Bank under Biddle developed a policy of presenting regularly the notes of state banks for payment. In the course of business over the years the Bank always took in more state-bank notes than state banks received of its notes. This net redemption against the state banks was no accident. The Bank had to take care to keep its own note issues (including that of its branches) within bounds, so that state banks had a reciprocal influence on the institution that was presumably doing the controlling. Nevertheless, the Bank of the United States was definitely in the driver's seat, and by presenting the notes of state banks for payment in specie it kept their issues moderate. The Bank not only furnished a currency of its own of uniform value over the entire country, but it reduced to a nominal figure the discount at which state-bank notes circulated. By the late 1820s the paper money of the country was for the time being in a satisfactory state.

Biddle did not use the interest rate as an instrument of control largely because the maximum rate of interest the second Bank could charge was 6 per cent, in those days a rate so low that it was both maximum and minimum except in unusual cases. At the beginning of a period of economic recession, Biddle would *sell* government bonds in order to strengthen the Bank's position, an action exactly the opposite of what a modern central bank, with full responsibility for the whole banking system, would take.[23]

Nicholas Biddle tried to affect the general economic climate of the United States by alternate expansion and contraction of the Bank's loans. Furthermore, he made the Bank the largest American dealer in foreign exchange and was able to protect the country from severe specie drain when a drain would have meant harmful contraction of monetary reserves. It might also be noted that in those days the problem of making payments over considerable distances *within the country* was not much different from the problem of effecting remittances *between countries.* There was a flourishing business in "domestic exchange," and the Bank obtained a large portion of it.

By 1829 the position of the second Bank of the United States seemed secure. It had grown and prospered. It had attained a shining reputation abroad, so much so that when the Bank of Spain was reorganized in 1829 the Bank of the United States was explicitly copied. Although it had made

---

[23] A selling operation lowered deposits and reserves of the state banks and improved the cash position of the Bank of the United States. Thus Biddle was looking out for the Bank's interests in the first instance but stood ready to come to the aid of the state banks as long as such action did not jeopardize those interests.

enemies, there was a wide acceptance of the idea of a "national institution," and there was grudging admittance by those who persistently opposed "the monster" that it had been a good thing for business. Congress had made sporadic attacks on the Bank, but these had been ineffective. Yet the apparent permanence of the Bank was illusory. Its fate had already been sealed.

In 1828 Andrew Jackson had been elected to the Presidency. Beloved by the masses, Jackson had the overwhelming support of the people during two terms in office. And Jackson had long since decided against banks in general and the big Bank in particular. A student of early Tennessee history has called attention to some of Jackson's unfortunate personal experiences with banks and bankers. As a young man he had taken in payment for 6,000 acres of land the notes of a Philadelphia merchant that passed as currency. When he gave these notes in payment of goods for his store, he found that they were worthless because the merchant had failed. Jackson had to make them good and as a consequence suffered years of financial difficulty in addition to the loss of his land. Later he and his business partners often found themselves victims of exorbitant charges by bankers and bill-brokers in both New Orleans and the eastern cities.[24] On one occasion Jackson bitterly opposed the establishment of a state bank in Tennessee, and as late as 1826 he worked against repeal of a law prohibiting the establishment of a branch of the Bank of the United States in his home state.

In his first annual message to Congress, some seven years before the charter of the Bank was to expire, Jackson called attention to the date of expiration, stated that "both the constitutionality and the expediency of the law creating this bank are well questioned by a large portion of our fellow-citizens," and speculated that ". . . if such an institution is deemed essential to the fiscal operations of the Government, I submit to the wisdom of the Legislature whether a national one, founded upon credit of the Government and its revenues, might not be devised which would avoid all constitutional difficulties and at the same time secure all the advantages to the Government and country that were expected to result from the present bank." We have the great Democrat's word for it that his statement was toned down by his advisers. It was the beginning of the "Bank War."

The detailed story of that war we shall have to omit. It must be said for Biddle that he tried to win Jackson over, but his efforts were without success. Henry Clay, charming and popular Presidential candidate of the National Republicans (Whigs), finally persuaded Biddle to let him make the question of recharter a campaign issue in the election of 1832. In the summer of that year there was enough pro-Bank power in the Congress to secure passage of a bill for recharter, a bill Jackson returned, as expected, with a sharp veto message prepared by Presidential advisers Amos

---

[24] Claude A. Campbell, *The Development of Banking in Tennessee* (published by the author, 1932), pp. 27–29.

In this cartoon Jackson (left) attacks the many-headed serpent (the second Bank of the United States) with his walking stick (his veto). The largest head is Nicholas Biddle, the Bank's president. The other heads represent other officials of the Bank and its branches. Jackson is assisted by Martin Van Buren (center).

Kendall and Roger Taney. In that political document the President contended that (1) the Bank was unconstitutional, (2) there was too much foreign ownership of its shares, and (3) domestic ownership was too heavily concentrated in the East. A central theme ran through the message: the Bank was an instrument of the rich to oppress the poor; an institution of such power and so little responsibility to the people could undo the democracy itself and should be put down. Agrarians of the West and South, moistly devotional, needed no assurance of their leader's sincerity. But wily Martin Van Buren, whose banker friends in New York had so desperately sought his aid in getting the money center moved from Chestnut Street to Wall Street, must have enjoyed an ironic smile at the President's tender concern for the poor.

After a furious campaign Jackson emerged the victor by a substantial margin. He considered his triumph a mandate from the electorate on the bank question, and the acclaim he was receiving consequent upon his masterful handling of the problem of nullification [25] strengthened his resolve to do the Bank in at once. In the fall of 1833, the government discontinued making deposits with the Bank, and Editor Greene of the Boston *Post* was moved to write its epitaph: "Biddled, Diddled and Undone." [26]

Biddle was not through. Beginning in August of 1833 and continuing into fall of the next year, the Bank contracted its loans sharply and continued its policy of presenting the notes of state banks for payment in specie. Biddle maintained that his actions were necessary to prepare the Bank for liquidation, though doubtless there was a punitive motive in the vigor of his actions.

The administration held firm in its resolve to end the Bank, which in 1836 became a state bank chartered under the laws of Pennsylvania. Even though stripped of official status, the United States Bank of Pennsylvania remained for a few years the most powerful financial institution in America. With its resources alone Nicholas Biddle could still engineer a grandiose scheme to support prices of cotton and other agricultural staples in a heroic effort to cure the nation's economic troubles of 1837 and 1838. But this last convulsive effort started a chain of events that led to the Bank's failure in 1841, not two years after Biddle's retirement in 1839.

Banks and the Money Supply, 1834–1860

When it became certain that the second Bank would not be rechartered, there was a sharp increase in the number of state banks and in the total amount of state-bank capitalization and note issue. It had become apparent that the banking business returned handsome rewards to investors, particularly during times as good as those of the early 1830s. New banks were chartered in great numbers in the economically advanced East as well as in the South and West, and state legislatures were besieged with requests for charters.

FREE BANKING

The rapid increase in the number of state banks did not go unopposed. There was strong support for the "hard-money" position of Jackson and his advisers, notably by the Loco-Foco or Equal Rights Party, a workingman's organization especially strong in New York City. Over the whole

---

[25] The principle of nullification, first enunciated by John C. Calhoun in 1828, was that any state could refuse to be bound by a federal statute it considered unjust until three-quarters of the states had agreed to the statute. South Carolina tried to apply the principle in 1832–33 during a dispute over a tariff bill. Jackson's strong stand defeated the attempt.

[26] For a racy, pro-Jackson account of the "Bank War" see Arthur M. Schlesinger, Jr., *The Age of Jackson* (Boston: Little, Brown, 1945), pp. 74–114. The Bank's side is equally well presented by Bray Hammond, *Banks and Politics in America from the Revolution to the Civil War* (Princeton: Princeton University Press, 1957), pp. 326–450.

country, however, hard-money doctrine, which urged the replacement of paper money by gold and silver coin, was received with slowly declining enthusiasm. A compromise of sorts lay in the idea of free banking, for here was to be found something to suit both the proponents of hard money and those who held the democratic position that everyone should have a chance to enter the profitable business of banking.

The first important free-bank law, drafted by Abijah Mann, author of the Safety-Fund legislation of 1829, passed the New York Assembly in 1838. Actually, between the time of beginning agitation for the New York system and final passage of the act establishing it, a Michigan statute provided for a similar plan, but the chief influence on American banking was to come from New York. The adjective "free" indicates the most important provision of the law. Under it, any individual or group of individuals, upon compliance with certain regulations, could start a bank in the State of New York.[27]

The state Comptroller of the Currency was to issue bank notes to promoters of a bank *upon deposit with that officer of an equal dollar amount of bonds of the United States, of the State of New York, and of certain other states approved by the Comptroller.* In addition, mortgages on New York land worth at least twice the face amount of a mortgage could be used as security to obtain notes, but not more than half the value of the notes issued to any bank could be so secured. Banks organizing under the law *were required to keep a specie reserve in their vaults of at least 12½ per cent of their outstanding notes.* Should a bank fail to redeem on demand a note under $1,000, the Comptroller could, after protest, sell the securities deposited with him to redeem the note. Meanwhile, noteholders on which payment had been suspended were entitled to annual interest of 14 per cent on the amount due them.

In 1840 the requirement of a specie reserve was repealed, just at the time when required reserves were being urged in most states. The law was strengthened in other respects, however, and average annual losses to noteholders over the entire experience of the New York free-bank system amounted to only one-tenth of 1 per cent. The system was adopted by other states, where it was not very successful because of the poor quality of the securities pledged with state officers. Nevertheless, faith in bond-secured note issues persisted, and this basic idea would be incorporated in the first national law to regulate banking.

THE SURGE OF STATE BANKING

Pre–Civil War economic statistics are notoriously inaccurate, but they serve to indicate trends. Toward the end of the depression years 1837–42 there was a marked reduction both in the number of banks and in their note and deposit liabilities. From 1843 on there was a steady movement

---

[27] Under this law any person or group had a *right* to start a bank. Under the old rule, the *privilege* of starting a bank had to be granted by special legislative act.

Table 7-1

Number of State Banks, 1819–1862

Year	Number	Year	Number	Year	Number
1819	274	1841	784	1852	913
1820	307	1842	692	1853	750
1829	329	1843	691	1854	1,208
1830	330	1844	696	1855	1,307
1834	506	1845	707	1856	1,398
1835	704	1846	707	1857	1,416
1836	713	1847	715	1858	1,422
1837	788	1848	751	1859	1,476
1838	829	1849	782	1860	1,562
1839	840	1850	824	1861	1,601
1840	901	1851	879	1862	1,492

SOURCE: *Historical Statistics of the United States, Colonial Times to 1957.*

upward, and the decade of the 1850s was one of remarkable expansion, as Table 7-1 shows.

It will be recalled that, from the first, state governments participated in the ownership of banks. The eastern states began to divest themselves of bank stock after 1812, just as states in the South and West were starting to promote banks. After 1834 the partially state-owned banks of Alabama, Mississippi, Kentucky, Florida, Michigan, Illinois, and others brought losses to private stockholders, to creditors, and to the states themselves; but a few like the Bank of Missouri, the Bank of Indiana, and the Bank of Ohio were towers of strength and models of successful banking.

The "little monsters" (as the state-owned banks were called) were spectacular, but the banks chartered by individual promoters were more important. The classic examples of "wildcat" banks were furnished by the State of Michigan in the late 1830s. Michigan's free-bank act of 1837 provided that ". . . any person or persons resident in the State . . . desirous of establishing a bank . . ." might go into the business. Despite apparent safeguards, including a safety fund, the law permitted the poorest securities to be put up as a guarantee of note redemption. And enterprising bankers showed an amazing ingenuity in outwitting examiners. For example, two commissioners noted a remarkable similarity in the packages of specie in the vaults of several banks on their examination list and later discovered that a sleigh drawn by fast horses preceded them as they went from place to place. In at least one instance a bank filled its specie kegs with glass, lead, and ten-penny nails, topping these materials off with a layer of silver. Nearly all banks operating on such a basis failed and disappeared by 1840, but not before a victimized public had been stuck with their worthless notes.

Banking reform took hold in most states after 1842. Irresponsible "wild-catters" had not yet disappeared, and shaky or fraudulent frontier banks with their issues of "red dog," "blue monkey," and "sick Indian" notes [28] were a source of difficulty until after the Civil War. But states with unsound state-owned banks began to liquidate them; after 1850 only Missouri, Ohio, and South Carolina (all with well-managed institutions) had not divested themselves of their banking interests. During the forties and early fifties, by legislative act or constitutional amendment, no less than nine states made all banking illegal, but such severe restrictions did not long remain. Free-banking laws modeled on that of New York were enacted before 1860 by approximately half of the state legislatures. Although in many cases the securities pledged against notes failed to secure the paper money adequately, bond-secured note issues made for more responsible management than did the older practice of issuing against general assets.

Reasonably sound banking systems developed as states achieved a degree of economic maturity. It was not by chance that the Louisiana law of 1842 set up a system that became a model of sound and conservative banking. With a port second only to that of New York, Louisiana had economic ties with both a great productive hinterland and the rest of the world. Legislators drafting the banking statute knew that any temporary gains resulting to some entrepreneurs from reckless creation of command over capital could not possibly equal the profits to be made by merchants *and* bankers through a soundly financed trade.

The Louisiana law required banks chartered under it to keep a specie reserve equal to one-third of their *combined note and deposit liabilities.* Before 1863, several states came to require specie reserves against notes, ranging variously from 5 per cent to $33\frac{1}{3}$ per cent, but except for Louisiana and Massachusetts they did not require reserves against *deposit liabilities* as well. Some banks everywhere, simply as matter of prudence, maintained reserves larger than those required by law.

A second important provision of the Louisiana act evidenced growing emphasis on the need for liquidity. The two-thirds of all liabilities not covered by specie reserves were to be backed by nonrenewable commercial paper with no more than ninety days to run. Enlightened bankers had long since realized that, although a bank's securities might be sound and the signers of its promissory notes reliable, it could still have difficulty in meeting its specie obligations. These difficulties were not so serious when loans made at short-term were regularly maturing, for the directors had only to cut down on new lending to improve the liquid—i.e., cash—holdings of the bank. On the other hand, if a bank's resources were tied up in loans against real estate or in long-term securities, as was common in the West and South, insolvency might quickly become a reality.

Pre–Civil War lending practices varied from one area of the country to another. In cities, particularly in the East, notes usually ran for short periods and advances financed specific, short-term business transactions. The

[28] Bills acquired such names because of the figures engraved on them and the color of the ink used.

"accommodation" note, made to finance long-term commitments and re-newed time after time, persisted everywhere.

After 1830 loans against stocks, particularly against bank stocks, were regulated. In New York City the practice of lending "at call"—i.e., of making loans repayable on demand against the security of stocks and bonds—was growing all the while. Finally, loans on the security of real estate remained important in the South and West until the close of this period; in fact, some banks were formed for the very purpose of making real-estate loans.

THE STATE OF THE PAPER MONEY

In many states, then, both practice and legislation were bringing about improved banking. In one respect matters were worse than ever. In the two decades before the Civil War, the state of the paper currency was nothing less than chaotic. If we may believe contemporary descriptions, it is a wonder that business was carried on at all. A heterogeneous paper currency was the price paid for state control of banks.

By 1860 each of the more than 1,500 state banks was issuing, on an average, six denominations of notes, so that not fewer than 9,000 different types of notes were being passed. Some were as good as gold; but most were acceptable only at a discount, and anyone ignorant of the actual worth of a note was open to loss. Notes of broken or liquidated banks often remained in circulation for long periods, and the country was continually flooded with counterfeits. Some gangs issued obviously spurious counterfeits that imitated the notes of no particular bank, while others concentrated on care-ful imitations of genuine bills. Perhaps the most successful way of counter-feiting was to alter the notes of a broken bank to make them appear the issue of a solvent bank, or to change bills from lower to higher denomina-tions. Some counterfeiters specialized in the *manufacturing* end of the busi-ness, while others, called "utterers," were adept at *passing* the bogus money. To combat counterfeiters, banks formed anticounterfeiting associations, hiring men called "snaggers" to ferret out makers of spurious bills.

In the struggle to determine the genuineness of a bill and the discount at which a valid note should be accepted, it was every man for himself. If a bill were much worn, or if it were perforated many times by the bank teller's needle-like staple, one might presume it to be genuine. Anyone who regularly took in paper money had to have more assistance, however, usually in the form of a "bank-note reporter" or a "counterfeit detector."

From the beginning of the nineteenth century there were efforts to pro-vide currency information to businessmen. In the first decades the infor-mation was made available in newspapers, which carried "bank-note tables." With the coming of regular, inexpensive "reporter" service, tradesmen and bankers had a greater degree of protection. *Thompson's Bank Note and Commercial Reporter,* a weekly, contained alphabetical listings, by states, of the notes of banks and of the discounts at which they should be received, together with descriptions of all known counterfeited bills. *Thompson's*

Bank Note Descriptive List, published at irregular intervals, contained word descriptions of genuine bills of banks in the United States and Canada, while the *Coin Chart Manual* of the same firm furnished facsimile drawings of the most common gold and silver coins, both foreign and domestic, current in the United States.

Some of the services, like *Bicknall's Counterfeit Detector and Bank Note List,* specialized in counterfeit detection. *Nicholas' Bank Note Reporter* at one time listed 5,400 counterfeits known to be in circulation, and *Hodges' Bank Note Safeguard* contained 360 pages of facsimile reproductions of genuine notes. *Thompson's Bank Note and Commercial Reporter* used facsimiles only for certain bogus bills, and most of the others relied on word descriptions. None of the services achieved complete coverage, but some of them did a remarkably good job. For example, in 1859 *Hodges' Genuine Bank Notes of America* carried a listing of 9,916 notes of 1,365 banks, omitting the issues of fewer than 200 banks.

However helpful the reporters and lists may have been, they are a re-markable commentary on the money supply of the United States in the years preceding federal legislation. The student can best keep in mind the weak-ness of the pre–Civil War money and banking system by recalling the plight of the merchant who, many times in the course of a day's business, had to take his reporter from the hook to see what the bill being proffered was really worth—if, indeed, it was worth anything at all.

THE STATE OF THE COINAGE

We learned earlier that Congress in 1834 defined the dollar in terms of gold in such a way that the American *mint ratio* was just a little over 16 to 1. A Congressional act of 1837 changed the gold content of the dollar to 23.22 grains but let the silver content remain at 371.25 grains.[29] Now 371.25 divided by 23.22 equals 15.988, a figure so close to 16 that it became customary to refer to the official mint ratio as 16 to 1. In 1837 the average market ratio of silver to gold was 15.83 or just under the mint ratio. To put the matter in a different way, the average bullion value of the silver contained in the official dollar (371.25 grains) was slightly under $1.01 in terms of gold. In the language used in discussing bimetallism, silver was now *under-valued* at the mint, or what is the same thing, gold was *overvalued* at the mint. In succeeding years the market (commercial) ratio of silver to gold fluctuated, but by 1851 it had dropped below 15.5. Two years later the bullion value of the silver in an official dollar rose to over $1.04.

By the early 1850s it was thus profitable to melt down even minor coins in order to sell the pure silver in the market. Coins used for making change had almost completely disappeared, causing inconvenience to everyone. To provide a fractional currency some banks began to issue paper money in denominations of less than $1. By 1853 the shortage of coins was so acute

---

[29] The gold content of the dollar then remained unchanged for almost a century. The silver content of the dollar is the same today as it has always been.

that Congress reduced by about 7 per cent the amount of silver contained in half-dollars, quarters, dimes, and half-dimes, making the mint ratio less than 15 to 1. Had the mint been willing to take an unlimited amount of silver for coinage at this rate, silver would have again tended to replace gold at the mint. The law provided, however, *that the mint need take only such amounts of silver as were necessary for making small change.* Since it no longer paid to melt down these devalued coins, a supply of them quickly came into use and the problem was solved.[30]

During the years from 1834 to 1849, and particularly from 1843 on, gold coinage increased somewhat because of the Coinage Acts of 1834 and 1837, rising output of American domestic gold mines, and a net inflow of gold from abroad. Despite an unfavorable balance of *trade* the United States had a favorable balance of payments. We were able to import gold because of the good business of our merchant marine and because of continuing European investment in our country. The total coinage of gold in these years was small, however, compared to the amounts coined after the Gold Rush of 1849. From 1850 to 1860, largely because of good times and a growing propensity to import, the United States had a persistent unfavorable balance of *payments* as well as an unfavorable balance of trade. Despite a consequent gold outflow during this period, $400 million of gold coins were struck by the mint. By 1850 the complaints about an insufficient amount of specie, so loud for the first sixty years of the republic, almost ceased. This fortunate increase in the monetary base had a lot to do with the sharp upturn in American business activity in the decade of the fifties.

THE CONCEPT OF AN INDEPENDENT TREASURY

One major question remains to be considered in our treatment of monetary and banking developments before the Civil War. After the demise of the second Bank of the United States, which had served both as regulator of the currency and fiscal agent for the government, what was the relationship of the government to the commercial banking system?

When Andrew Jackson and the Democrats were fighting the recharter of the second Bank of the United States, they seemed unconcerned about the prospect of keeping government funds in state banks. In fact, Jackson began to place these funds in certain state institutions—his "pets," to use the opprobrious term coined by the President's critics—beginning in September and October 1833.[31] Nevertheless, Jackson and his advisers gave evi-

---

[30] The figures on the market value of bullion are taken from the *Annual Report of the Director of the Mint* for the fiscal year ended June 30, 1947. Advanced students will probably find this a handy reference. Anyone wishing to obtain ratios for years before 1837 should refer to the *Annual Report* for 1934.

[31] Although Secretary of the Treasury Taney at first selected banks run by party faithfuls, it became progressively more difficult to find ably managed banks without Whigs on their boards of directors. Congress had prescribed no regulations for selection of depositaries and both Taney and his successor, Levi Woodbury, were constrained to put safety of Treasury funds ahead of political considerations.

dence of their latent distrust of banks in general when, in the Specie Circular of July 1836, the administration required that payment for all public land be made in specie or in obligations of the United States. Before the end of Jackson's second term agitation arose to put the federal government entirely on a hard-money basis, and the movement continued during Van Buren's administration.

Those in favor of separating the federal treasury from the banking system contended that, if the government were to receive only gold and silver in payment of obligations, it would never again incur losses from the depreciated notes of suspended banks as it had during and after the panic of 1837. Whigs and some eastern Democrats (notably Albert Gallatin) held that separation would be utterly impossible in practice. Because, they argued, treasury receipts and disbursements are rarely (or never) in balance, gold and silver would sometimes pile up in treasury vaults and at other times would be expended in such concentrated amounts as to disrupt the money market. In the former case specie reserves of banks would be depleted, the money to lie idle in the treasury; in the latter case bank reserves would suddenly swell, with a tendency for credit to expand rapidly.

The opposition of the Whigs and eastern Democrats was so strong that an act establishing an independent treasury was not passed until the latter part of Van Buren's term of office, and it did not go into effect until the middle of 1840. The Whigs won the elections of that year and repealed the independent treasury law in 1841. They wished to go further and create a new national bank along the lines of the second Bank of the United States. Bills that would have established such an institution twice passed both houses of Congress only to be vetoed by President Tyler. With the return of the Democrats to power in the next election the old battle over the establishment of an independent treasury was renewed. Again, the proponents of the plan won out, and in 1846 the independent treasury was re-established.

Henceforth, government officials were "to keep safely, without loaning, using, depositing in banks, or exchanging for other funds than as allowed by this act, all the public money collected by them, or otherwise at any time placed in their possession and custody, till the same is ordered . . . to be transferred or paid out." The federal government was to accept only gold and silver in payment of sums due it. Government funds were to be kept only in the vaults of the treasury at Washington or in those of subtreasuries in various cities.

The difficulties foreseen by the opponents of this method of fiscal separation quickly materialized. During the seventy-five years or so in which the legislation was in effect, secretaries of the treasury rarely followed either the spirit or the letter of the law; violations began almost as soon as the law was in force. Frequently, treasury officials sought the aid of the banks in transferring funds about the country in order to avoid expensive and dangerous shipments of coin. The transfer of funds was a small problem, however, compared with that occasioned by treasury surpluses, which became usual during the 1850s. As the treasury year after year took in more than it expended, there was a withdrawal from the banks of the gold and silver that constituted their reserves. On occasion the Secretary of the Treasury would get coin back into the banking system by purchasing obligations of the federal government in the open market, though some restriction was placed on such action by the law preventing repurchase of government "stock" at a figure above par. During the financial stringencies of 1853 and 1857 the Secretary had to take vigorous action to assist the banks; these open-market operations were only the beginning of varied kinds of manipulation to be required of secretaries in the next half century. Within a few years of the passage of the law establishing an independent treasury it became quite apparent that independence could *not* be maintained.

Our description of banking activity during the first three-quarters of a century of the republic's history should not leave readers with the impression that banks were operated by unprincipled men for selfish ends and that the unsound and fraudulent practices of the period had only harmful results on the economy as a whole. This was the view of a group of historians who wrote on the subject some forty or fifty years ago, and their judgments have largely persisted into the present. Two points should be borne in mind. First, those who directed the destinies of banks were operating in a new field and for the most part did not clearly understand the social implications of banking. Given the business ethics of the time, directors and officers of banks were probably neither better nor worse than businessmen in general.

A second, and more important, consideration is that early banks brought about a steady and rapid development of the American economy that would have been impossible without them. Despite the hardships imposed on large numbers of people from time to time, the net effect of early commercial-bank activity was to reduce the cost of finance and assure the most aggressive entrepreneurs of a steady source of funds. As canals and railroads were built, as American manufacturers developed, and as wholesale and retail trade expanded, there was a growing demand for money. As Professor Hansen has put it:

> Credit provided access to productive resources, and it promoted technological developments. It was not enough that rich natural resources were available to be exploited by a rapidly growing and energetic population equipped with the necessary skills and techniques. New undertakings had to be established and new production had to be set going. And this required money. This money could not be drawn from the older and settled parts of the economy. *New* money was needed to set up a *new* circuit of production and to circulate the ever-growing volume of trade.[32]

---

[32] By permission from *Monetary Theory and Fiscal Policy* by Alvin H. Hansen, p. 17. Copyright 1949. McGraw-Hill Book Co., Inc.

Banks were willing and able to meet the demand for money by the simple process of exchanging the notes (and to some extent the deposit credits) of a *bank* for the promissory note or bill of exchange of a firm or individual, i.e., by exchanging one kind of debt for another. The evidence of a bank's debt had general acceptability as a medium of exchange; the evidence of a firm's or individual's debt did not. Thus, by *monetizing private debt*,[33] the growing demand for money was met. To have restricted the money supply in the early years to the amount of specie in existence would have been unthinkable. The issue of paper money could, of course, have been left exclusively to a "national" or central bank. Either the first or the second Bank of the United States could have done the job satisfactorily, but a strong central bank was not politically acceptable. Thus, toward the end of the period the money supply depended upon (1) net additions to the quantity of specie in the country resulting from the importation of the metals and from mining and (2) the amount of paper money and deposits created by the commercial banks within the limits prescribed by state laws. In a later chapter we shall see to what extent the federal government modified this arrangement.

---

[33] Some writers speak of "monetizing private *credit*." This way of putting the matter does just as well. Why?

Industry

in First Transition

One must recognize that if machines are at the beginning optional, they finish by being obligatory; the better informed hasten to adopt them in order to make profits; the tardy ones decide to employ them in order not to be ruined.

P. E. LEVASSEUR

In the years between the American Revolution and the Civil War a fundamental change took place in the structure of the American economy. These were the years in which the groundwork was laid for the ultimate leadership of the United States as an economic power. In 1860 the United States was still an agricultural country, and the size of the industrial firm was, by modern standards, still small. But changes had taken place in the economy which, though halting and uneven, marked the advent of the industrial state. The most significant change was the evolution of a new way of combining the factors of production. Having familiarized ourselves with the beginnings of the westward movement, the rapid changes in transportation, and the characteristics of the early money supply, we are now ready to understand the growth of manufacturing activity and the crucial changes in the organization of the industrial firm.

The Revolutionary War boosted productive activity and encouraged that romantic form of legalized piracy known as privateering. For a year or two after the outbreak of hostilities there were goods shortages, but beginning in 1777 the ingenuity of the privateers asserted itself. From continental Europe came luxuries and necessaries that war-expanded incomes could afford. One way or another, even the highly esteemed products of England found their way into old channels. Yet domestic household production also was stimulated by the war, and of course munitions output increased greatly.

For at least twenty-five years after the first inauguration of Washington people made things in almost the same way and with much the same tools they had employed before the Revolution. The extractive industries remained in first place, and manufacturing output, despite its steady growth, no more than kept pace with the increase in population. Finished goods aggressively competed with domestic products, cutting seriously into the markets of domestic producers in the brief interludes when unhindered international trade was possible.

The colonial economy extended, in its main outlines, into the 1800s. Americans continued to look to the land as the source whence most material blessings flowed. Men who did not farm land took raw materials from it, but the firms that processed raw materials remained small-scale and dispersed. The shortest way to fortune still lay in a career as a merchant.

Fortunately for the young United States war broke out between England and France in 1793, none too soon to revive the carrying and re-export trades so dreadfully injured by the Revolution. The expansion of trade was largely the consequence of the disappearance from the seas of the ships of every belligerent except England. Holland, France, and Spain had all been important carriers; when they were drawn into the conflict neutrals, especially the United States, quickly filled the void. In order to qualify as the exports of a neutral and thus avoid interception en route, tropical products were first imported into the United States, and duties were paid on them. The products were then re-exported, whereupon the importer could obtain in the form of a "drawback" most of the duties paid. In the same way, European manufactures were brought to American warehouses before being re-exported to the non-European cities of the world.[1]

Following the Treaty of Amiens in 1801, United States trade dropped sharply, only to shoot back up as France and England resumed hostilities in 1803. Yet the very vigor of the trade led to its undoing and finally to a second war with England. A succession of British Orders in Council and French decrees, by which each of the two belligerents attempted to blockade the other, would have increased the already substantial seizures of American ships by the British and French. In 1807, at the insistence of Jefferson, Congress passed the Embargo Act, which so effectually reduced the volume of exports of raw materials and imports of finished goods that it furnished a pronounced stimulus to American manufactures. By completely prohibiting the export of American products, the Embargo Act was calculated to force England and France to cease their depredations upon American shipping.

---

[1] For further detail see Douglass C. North, *The Economic Growth of the United States, 1790 to 1860* (Englewood Cliffs, N.J.: Prentice-Hall, 1961), pp. 36–45. In Chapter 10 we return to the subject of American foreign trade in the early nineteenth century.

It resulted in the loss of foreign markets for agricultural products and in the prostration of industries, such as shipbuilding, that were dependent on international trade for their well-being. The resulting economic distress led to repeal of the Embargo Act and passage of the Non-Intercourse Act of March 1, 1809, by which commerce with all countries except France and England was permitted. But nonintercourse was accompanied by harassment and seizure, and after double-dealing on the part of the two European powers, the United States drifted into a second war with England. Not until the early days of 1815 was peace restored.

At the end of seven years of economic and shooting war the economy of the country had ceased to be colonial. Although merchants dependent upon foreign commerce were in some instances brought to ruin, output in the home and in the craft shop increased greatly. The putting-out, or domestic, system began to achieve new importance as a form of organizing production. Not least of all, in these years true factory manufacture obtained a foothold. Factory organization, however, did not quickly replace ways of manufacture typical of the colonial era. To get a proper perspective, let us consider the status of household manufacture in 1815 and note its trends from 1815 to 1860. Then we shall see how manufacture for expanding markets during three decades relied upon craftsmen working both singly and in groups. Finally we shall examine the development known as the "rise of the factory system."

Primitive Methods of Organizing Production

HOUSEHOLD MANUFACTURE

Household manufacture, after a decline in the two post-Revolutionary decades, revived in the years of international upheaval between 1805 and 1815. At the latter date products made in the home probably reached a peak in both volume and total value. Various estimates indicate that as late as 1820 two-thirds of the textiles used in American homes were made by American families. Doubtless an even greater proportion of food processing was done at home. Although home production was carried on primarily for home consumption, much of it was for general sale.

By 1830 there was a marked decline in household manufacture in the East, a decline that was just about offset by an increase in such production on the frontier. From 1830 on, however, household manufacture tended to disappear in all but the most inaccessible places, exceptions being that food processing and garment-making in the home were common everywhere until the Civil War. The major cause of the decline of household manufacture was the development of industrial organization and modern means of transportation. Wherever steamboats ran or canals, highways, and railroads were built, home manufacture fell off quickly. Even on the frontier after the middle of the nineteenth century most households had access to the products of domestic or European factories. How important transportation was is

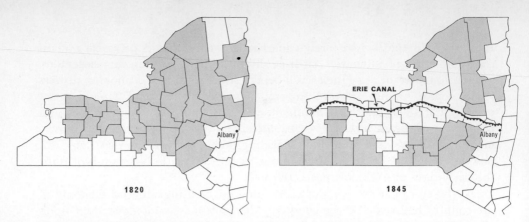

1820

1845

Arthur A. Cole, *The American Wool Manufacture*, Vol. I (Cambridge: Harvard University Press, 1926).

Canal Impact: Household manufacture of woolen cloth (an index of isolation from commercial routes) underwent a drastic change between 1820 and 1845 along the Erie Canal.

illustrated by the maps above. The shaded areas on the two maps of New York show the third of the counties in the state having the highest per-capita output of woolen goods made in homes in two different years—1820 and 1845. Note that in 1820 no county lying along the Hudson below Albany was in the top third of the counties. In 1845 the counties lying along the Erie Canal had similarly dropped in amount of home manufacture. But V. S. Clark reports that as late as 1865 nearly all of the country people of Tennessee, especially those living in the mountain areas, wore clothing made at home.

THE CRAFT SHOP AND THE PUTTING-OUT SYSTEM

Until approximately 1850 the substantial increases in manufacturing output were effected by craftsmen operating independently or in a craft shop. The former did "bespoke" work, making commodities only to order, maintaining the highest standards of quality, and selling through their own little retail outlets. But the production of independent craftsmen declined rapidly after 1815. More important at that date and for some time afterward was the craft shop run by a master who employed several journeymen and apprentices. Sometimes, as in the case of the hatters of Danbury, Connecticut, there was an agglomeration of craft shops selling a quantity output to merchant wholesalers for distribution over wide market areas.

The putting-out, or domestic, system does not fit readily into a classification. In some ways it is a unique form of organization, and yet it cuts across the categories of both household and craft production. For example, before 1830 the enterprising merchant frequently distributed cotton yarn among families for hand-looming, but for the finer fabrics he employed skilled craftsmen to loom the yarn in their shops. Until somewhat later woolen yarn might be spun in a mill and put out to households for hand-looming, the finishing processes of bleaching and dyeing to be finally carried out by workmen assembled under one roof. In the boot and shoe industry the leather might be cut under the supervision of a merchant, the pieces distributed to craft shops for sewing, and the nearly finished shoes returned for final processing. As people who bought ready-made shoes became more exacting in their demand for quality and fit and as machinery was developed for making a better product in quantity, the industry slipped easily into factory methods. Straw hats and galluses, on the other hand, were made by women and children in the home and sold by enterprising merchant employers in a wide market up to 1860.

MILL INDUSTRIES

As in colonial days, the small mill was to be found everywhere during the years 1815 to 1860. In nearly all localities a restricted but profitable market existed for the processed products of agriculture, forest, and mine. The Census of 1860 reported nearly 20,000 sawmills and 14,000 flour mills in the country. With few exceptions tanneries, distilleries, breweries, and iron forges likewise produced for a local market. The decentralization of American industry before 1860, favored by high transportation costs and the use of water power, made for small firms that often constituted effective local monopolies.

Before 1860 some mills had achieved large-scale production, using methods of manufacture typical of the "factory." Furthermore, large mills in two industries tended to centralize in certain rather well-defined areas. The flour-milling industry, which even in colonial days had been attracted to the Chesapeake area, continued to cluster there as farmers in Maryland and Virginia substituted wheat for tobacco. As cities grew larger and the demand for building materials increased, it became profitable for large lumbering firms to exploit timber areas located at some distance from markets; typical were those situated by 1850 on the upper reaches of streams flowing through New England, New York, and Pennsylvania.

The Development of Factory Production

Not until after 1845 did it become clear that the methods of production just described would be outmoded. At mid-century no one could have foreseen that tragedy, in the form of civil strife, would hasten the process of change. Yet the developments of the 1850s were such that even the most casual contemporary observer could not fail to be impressed. We must now trace the evolution of the "factory system." As an introduction, it will be helpful to consider a subject familiar to anyone who has studied the history of England.

THE INDUSTRIAL REVOLUTION

"The outstanding feature . . . which distinguishes the period since the 'industrial revolution' from the ages which preceded it is the extent of the use of machines as substitutes for manual labor." Professor A. P. Usher thus calls attention to the difference between the old way of making things and the new. Is Usher justified in using the word "revolution" in this context? The point is a perplexing one. Many historians and economists maintain that the transition from hand to machine manufacture has happened over centuries and still goes on apace. They contend that revolution implies an abruptness of change that is simply not characteristic of technological development.

Professor Usher would insist that "revolution" is a helpful and descriptive word and that its use can be defended. He has remarked that there are three stages in a revolution. First, there is a process of change or adaptation in cultural, political, or economic institutions. Second, an obstacle persistently obstructs the process of change or adaptation. Third, there is an abrupt removal of the obstacle to change, often accompanied by violent repercussions. If we accept this notion of revolution, Usher would argue, we are justified in using the term to describe the remarkable events that occurred in the economic life of late eighteenth-century England. From the late Middle Ages the economy of that country, and to a lesser extent the other economies of western Europe, had gradually changed from a loose agglomeration of primitive, localized, self-sufficient units to elaborate economic organizations in which people were more and more dependent on each other for goods that were increasing in richness and variety. While becoming a nation-state, England developed a great colonial empire, finding everywhere opportunities for profitable commerce. Wealthy merchants strove to increase their trade, but one serious obstacle stood in the way of expansion: old methods of producing and transporting things were woefully inadequate to supply a growing demand both at home and abroad. Where they were least adequate, special inducements in the form of prizes were offered to encourage innovation, and the great interest thereby aroused led to a few major breakthroughs within half a century—roughly between 1750 and 1800. Thus was removed the obstacle to progress, with an abruptness that seemed remarkable to contemporaries. There followed changes in both business organization and the social structure that were scarcely less sudden.

Now all this sounds too pat. Brief, general statements about history frequently do. The skeptical reader may raise two fundamental objections. First, he may complain that we make it appear as though the English, in a crucial period, were able to raise themselves by their own bootstraps. We might reply, "Necessity is the mother of invention," for there is truth in the adage. But the fact remains that the English made practical applications of scientific discoveries sooner than other countries.

Second, the student may say that English inventions of the late eighteenth century were the culmination of age-old inquiries and that many decades would pass before the inventions were perfected. It is characteristic of innovation in general that much groundwork must be laid before some person makes the decisive invention, the one that is commercially successful, the one that can be put to practical use. Once it is in use other men will improve upon it. Improvements may lead eventually to an even more striking synthesis, which may in turn be the basis for more "new" ideas. Such considerations notwithstanding, the decisive invention may be an achievement of the highest order. By way of illustration we may trace the developments that led to (1) the successful use of steam power and (2) the application of power to basic processes in the textile industry.[2]

As we shall see, much of the machinery that so greatly changed the textile industry was first run by water power, but water power restricted location to streams. Essential to freedom of location as well as to improvement in transportation facilities was the introduction of power in a *generalized* form. This was the great contribution of the steam engine to modern industry. Steam power could be used whenever and wherever an operator wished to employ it.

As early as 1690 a French physicist, Denis Papin, devised a working model of a steam engine, but his engine could never be put to practical use because it combined the boiler and cylinder in one vessel.[3] The first engine to do any work was that of Thomas Savery, who, in 1698, received a patent for a "water-raising" engine, a machine both dangerous and inefficient. About 1702 Thomas Newcomen invented an engine with a piston and cylinder, a separate boiler, and hand-operated valves, and within a few years this device was employed to pump water out of mines. Not as dangerous as Savery's engine, but almost as wasteful of fuel, the Newcomen engine could be used only where coal was very cheap. During the next fifty years Newcomen's engine was improved in efficiency, notably by John Smeaton, famous as the constructor of the Eddystone lighthouse. Yet even the Smeaton engine achieved a thermal efficiency of only about 1 per cent and because of excessive fuel consumption was still restricted to use near coal mines. Despite the fact that the Newcomen engine was useful for more than sixty years, laying the foundations of British industrial development by facilitating exploitation of her minerals, it was no more a general source of power than streams.

Ordinarily we reluctantly assign to any one man a major part of the credit for the invention of anything. In the case of James Watt it is possible to give credit with more confidence than usual. In 1757 Watt was appointed mathematical-instrument maker to the University of Glasgow and a few years later was assigned the task of repairing a Newcomen engine. Impressed with the waste of fuel resulting from condensation of steam in the cylinder, Watt developed the idea of a separate condensing chamber, and a patent on this improvement was applied for in 1769. Watt's first engine, like all the engines that had preceded it, had the grave defect of being "single-acting,"

---

[2] The foregoing is intended only as an introduction to the perplexing subject of the social and economic conditions that encourage industrial inventions. We shall return to this topic, notably in Chapters 14 and 21.

[3] Papin was nonetheless well known for his inventions of the steam pressure-cooker or "digester," as it was known then, and of the safety valve.

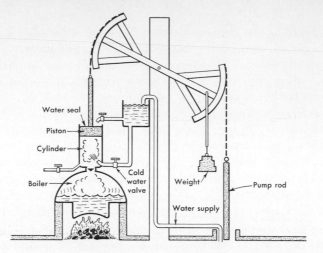

The Newcomen engine (above) wasted energy because its piston cylinder had to be heated anew for each movement of the piston. The Watt engine (below) was far more efficient. Its cylinder remained hot because the steam passed off and was condensed in a separate chamber.

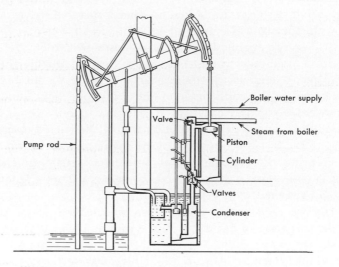

i.e., of having the piston forced through the cylinder in one direction only by steam with the return movement being made by the weight of a counterpoise.[4] Watt later solved this problem with his "double-acting" engine, which used steam alternately on both sides of the piston head. In addition, he invented, or co-operated in the invention of, a number of devices that made great strides in this area of technology. Among these were a special

---

[4] Modern internal-combustion engines are single-acting but because of multiple cylinders are efficient enough to be economical. Steam pioneers concentrated on single-cylinder engines.

valve for regulating the rate at which steam was admitted to the cylinder and a governor for controlling steam pressures. Although Savery was probably the first man to use the term *horsepower* as a way of measuring work performed, it was Watt who defined it numerically as the raising of 33,000 pounds a distance of one foot in one minute.

All this is impressive. Watt was a genius in the history of technical change, although he did not work alone. He had a number of gifted associates, among them his assistant, John Southern. Moreover, Watt's experimentation was quite beyond his own means, and without the financial help of the noted English industrialist Matthew Boulton, he would not have gotten much past the stage of his single-acting engine of 1769. Watt also had assistance from allied fields of technological endeavor. He depended for his most advanced engines upon the boring machine of John Wilkinson; without the precision of cylinder manufacture made possible by this device, the double-acting engine would not have passed the experimental stage. Finally, the perfecting of Watt's engines and the ultimate achievement of the steam turbine had to await nineteenth-century progress in the construction of machine tools. Nevertheless, the Watt engine made the transition from the limited employment of pumping water out of mines to operating the machinery of factories. Industry was henceforth freed from the restriction of location alongside streams, and the emancipation was achieved within the short space of a quarter-century.

Equally impressive was the transformation that occurred in the cotton-textile industry.[5] Despite efforts of the woolen industry to prevent by statute the sale and use of pure cotton materials, comfort and fashion put calicoes, ginghams, and muslins in steady and growing demand. The result was unceasing effort to improve the four basic steps of textile manufacture: (1) the preparation of the fiber for spinning, (2) the spinning of the fiber into thread or yarn, (3) the weaving or knitting of the yarn into cloth, and (4) the finishing of the cloth for the manufacture of garments, household linens, and various commercial materials. The eighteenth century witnessed changes in all four processes for all kinds of fibers, but the most striking innovations were made in the application of power to the spinning and weaving of cotton goods.

Like the woolen manufacture before it, the English cotton industry was at first a cottage industry; in the humid country of Lancashire spinners and weavers worked in their own homes, utilizing the labor of their wives and children. The invention that started the removal of cotton manufacture from home to factory was a simple improvement on the old hand loom, an

---

[5] In tracing the economic history of Great Britain and the United States, it is hard to devote too much attention to the history of the cotton-textile industry. For a brief treatment with good illustrations, the student may consult *A History of Technology*, edited by Charles Singer *et al.* (London: Oxford University Press, 1958), pp. 277–307. My own favorite of the many works on the subject is Paul Mantoux, *The Industrial Revolution in the Eighteenth Century* (New York: Harcourt, Brace & World, 1927), especially pp. 193–276.

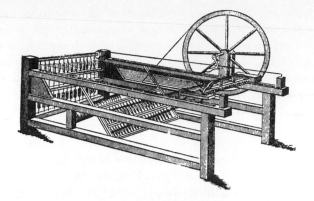

Hargreaves' spinning jenny (above) and Arkwright's water frame (below) were inventions of a high order freeing women from the age-old requirement that they spin one thread at a time, by hand.

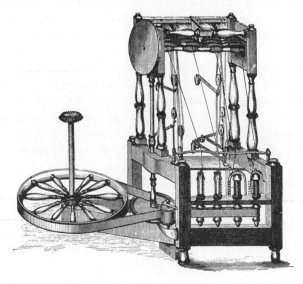

improvement designed originally to increase the width of cloth by more than a man's reach without employing two or more workmen. John Kay's invention of the flying shuttle in 1733 had immediate and disturbing consequences. By enabling one man, instead of two, to operate a hand loom, it almost doubled the output of weavers and put spinners to it to furnish enough yarn for making cloth. For several decades there was an unrelenting pressure to provide more yarn. At first the search for new techniques in spinning was not directed as much toward finding a substitute for manual power as it was toward enabling one person to spin more than one thread at a time. If we may believe a story, the invention of the machine that solved the problem was purely accidental. One day in 1765, the tale goes, James

Hargreaves so startled his wife that she overturned the spinning wheel at which she was working. Observing how the spindle continued to revolve while in a *vertical* position, Hargreaves bethought himself of a way in which a single operator could spin eight threads at a time with no serious danger of repeated breakage. The output of home spinners was thereby increased and the years-long imbalance between spinners and weavers corrected.

The first spinning jenny of Hargreaves was rapidly improved and soon from twenty to thirty threads could be produced with the labor formerly spent on spinning one.[6] Two difficulties remained. Human power was still necessary to operate the machine; and thread spun by the jenny was not firm and hard enough for warp (the vertical threads) though it could serve for weft (the horizontal threads). Both these difficulties were overcome by the invention of the water frame, so called to distinguish it from the jenny, a frame worked by hand. Water-frame (or throstle) spinning had as its basic principle the drawing out of rovings by rollers revolving at different speeds and the twisting of the threads by flyers and bobbins. Although many inventors tried to perfect roller spinning, the first commercially successful machine was installed and profitably operated by Richard Arkwright, the Barber of Bolton.[7] Throstle spinning could be powered by water wheels and produced a thread suitable for both weft and warp, but the product was too coarse for fine goods. In 1779 Samuel Crompton made known the principle of his spinning-mule. As the name suggests, it was a hybrid machine that combined the principles of the water frame and the jenny, borrowing the drawing rollers of the former and the moving carriage of the latter. Because of its final spinning at high tension, the mule made possible greatly increased production of fine, strong thread.

Once the problem of spinning was solved, attention was turned toward discovering a method of operating looms by power. In 1785 the Reverend Edmund Cartwright announced his invention of a power loom. The tricky operation of looming did not succumb readily, however, to the application of power. Threads broke easily, and it was to be many years before the power loom was to approach perfection. But the major impediments had been overcome. Within twenty-five years' time the cotton industry had surmounted the obstacles to rapidly increasing output.

PREREQUISITES TO FACTORY PRODUCTION

The classic Industrial Revolution by no means guaranteed the immediate establishment of the factory system in America. The English sought to pre-

---

[6] Within Hargreaves' lifetime jennies with eighty or more spindles were in use.

[7] In a suit attacking the terms of the Arkwright patent one Thomas Highs testified that he had made the original model of the water frame and shown it to John Kay of Warrington, an employee of Arkwright who actually built the first machine. The weight of evidence indicates that Arkwright knew little about spinning techniques. He nonetheless became the richest cotton spinner in England with large, well-managed factories. See Mantoux, pp. 232–39.

vent the dissemination abroad of the details of the new inventions, and their efforts possibly accounted for a time lag of some years in the introduction of the machines to the United States. On the other hand, the new techniques could be imported only as American entrepreneurs with sufficient capital became aware of the possibilities of employing them profitably.

Largely because of the relatively high cost of labor in the United States, American managers tended always to use the most nearly automatic machines available in a particular application. More important, they successfully innovated new ways of organizing production that saved labor expense per unit of output. Their chief contributions, the basic ideas that led to American pre-eminence in nineteenth-century manufacturing, were (1) interchangeable-parts manufacture and (2) continuous-process manufacture. Both advances were inevitably bound up with the development of machine tools and with changes in techniques of applying power.

The idea of standardizing a product and its various parts originated in Sweden in the early eighteenth century and before 1800 had been tried at least once in France, Switzerland, and England. Through standardization, the parts of one product could be interchanged for the parts of a like product, facilitating manufacture and repair. The first permanently successful application of the idea in a nontrivial use was made in the American armament industry. At the turn of the nineteenth century, Eli Whitney and Simeon North almost simultaneously obtained contracts from the government to manufacture firearms by the interchangeable parts method. The two men worked independently, making different contributions to the field, and it is hard to say which of these geniuses had the more important influence on the evolution of what Europeans came in time to call "the American System."

Manufacture by interchangeable parts involved recognition of the fact that the making of a product could be subdivided into a number of small jobs. In Whitney's factory a pattern was made for each metal part, and, after forging, the parts were filed down by hand to the shape and size of the pattern while the metal was yet soft. They were then annealed and hardened and worked down to an accuracy of $\frac{1}{32}$ of an inch. The ultimate tool of precision in those days was the hand file—"modern" production would have been unthinkable on such a basis.

Continuous-process manufacture—production with the plant so arranged that the manufacture is done with facility and as nearly in order as possible—probably had its first successful application in the mills; Oliver Evans' achievement in this direction, as early as 1785, has already been mentioned. But milling processes did not require assembly operations. Continuous-process manufacture in its most significant present-day form, with motor-driven moving assembly, was an outgrowth of the successful interchangeable-parts production of firearms, clocks and watches, sewing machines, and agricultural implements. Whitney's firearms company was small, employing little machinery and only sixty men. Yet division of labor within the plant was distinct, each worker specializing in making a particular part; and assembly of the entire piece was done by several workers, each one repeatedly performing the same action as the firearm passed down a "line." In the 1850s agricultural implement companies actually used conveyor belts to assemble in sequence the parts of major subassemblies.

Machine tools rather than hand tools were necessary to the manufacture of interchangeable parts within strict limits or "tolerances." Furthermore, ways of measuring the precision with which parts were machined had to be developed, and as the years passed it became imperative to make such tests with dispatch. The reader must not infer that machine tools are important only as an aid to making interchangeable parts. It is the function of machine tools to plane or grind, cut or bore, so that smooth, accurate surfaces may be obtained. Castings or forgings or rolled pieces nearly always have to have their surfaces finished to a certain size and smoothness if they are to fit as a part of a mechanism. Every kind of really intricate mechanism must be made with machine tools or with a machine constructed with their help. They are essential to all industrial production that has passed the hand stages.

Because of her head start in making machines and the more advanced stage of her iron-working industry, Great Britain long had an advantage in the manufacture of heavy machine tools. The United States either imported them or copied them from the English models. However, Americans independently developed light machine tools for the manufacture of small arms, clocks and watches, sewing machines, textile machinery, and agricultural implements.

It took more than a generation to make the essential innovations in the arms industry. Pattern turning was begun about 1817, reducing greatly the number of man-days needed to shape unsymmetrical wooden rifle stocks. Drop forging with dies was successfully introduced about 1827. By 1855, Samuel Colt, who had long since invented his six-shooter, could establish an armory in which machine work of a high degree of accuracy was carried on by skilled operatives.

Until it was possible to work *accurately* in metals, the inventions of the late eighteenth century could not be fully effective. After 1850 tools approaching modern standards were forthcoming. The *vernier caliper,* an inexpensive tool that permitted a workman to measure to thousandths of an inch, came from the shops of Brown and Sharpe in 1851. By 1854 the firm of Robbins and Lawrence was making turret lathes for general sale. From this date on, growth of the machine-tool industry was rapid, and its products steadily increased in complexity and precision.

Equally important were changes in techniques of applying power. During the period we are considering, chief reliance was placed on water, and until the 1840s water wheels furnished most of the motive power. Wheels were replaced soon after 1840 by water turbines, which gained favor during the next two decades. Despite a major reliance before 1860 upon water as a

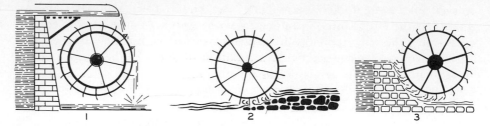

The types of waterwheel that powered textile and woodworking machinery were (1) an overshot wheel, (2) an undershot wheel with straight blades, and (3) a crooked-blade undershot wheel, the "breast type."

means of propelling machinery, it had become apparent by that year that the steam engine would shortly become a chief source of power.

A water wheel is always placed in a vertical position on a horizontal shaft and is moved at comparatively low speed by direct action of the water. Wheels are classified in accordance with the way in which water is applied to turn them. The kind used in colonial times, and for a while thereafter in frontier areas, was the *undershot* wheel, placed in the stream so that its blades were moved by the water passing underneath it. The undershot wheel, while easy to install, was inefficient, transmitting no more than 40 per cent of the power applied to it. The *overshot* wheel was moved by water running from a flume across the top of the wheel into buckets covering its surface; the weight of the water in the buckets moved the wheel in the direction of the stream flow. The overshot wheel was more efficient, easy to install, and satisfactory wherever there was a good head of water, but the power it developed was not great enough for heavy industrial purposes. Consequently, the big manufacturing concerns almost invariably used the *breast* wheel. This type, too, was equipped with buckets, but the water struck the wheel short of its highest point so that it rotated in an upstream direction; both the impulse of the water and its weight in the buckets enabled the wheel to utilize up to 75 per cent of the power applied to it. Installed in multiples, the breast wheel developed a sufficient horsepower to serve the largest early nineteenth-century industrial firms. The machinery of the Merrimack Manufacturing Company, for example, was run by eight breast wheels, each thirty feet in diameter with buckets twelve feet long. The illustration (see drawing) shows how the three types of wheels worked.

The slow-moving and cumbersome water wheels could develop several thousand horsepower, but they had marked disadvantages. Power from a wheel was transmitted by wooden shafts and cogwheels and was limited by the strength of the entire mechanism. Furthermore, industrial location was restricted to stream sites, and the problem of finding sites, especially in the industrialized areas, became a serious one. The first difficulty was partially overcome by making wheels and transmission parts of metal, the second by improved engineering of dams and canals. The water turbine, which revolved on a vertical shaft, was much more efficient than a wheel and by the 1850s was rapidly adding to the power potential of the country.

But what of the steam engine as a source of industrial power? Why did the steam engine not win as ready acceptance in industry before 1860 as in transportation? The reasons are not hard to find. The steam engine had an extremely high first cost. Breakdowns were frequent and technicians expert in their repair were few and far between. In transportation the steam engine could pull loads so much heavier at such increased speeds that these disadvantages were more than offset, but in industry water power was for a long time cheaper than steam power. It has been estimated that in 1812 only eleven engines of the high-pressure type developed by Oliver Evans were in use in this country.[8] During the next two decades steam engines became more common in the South and West, most of them being used in ironworks and glass factories requiring fuel for other purposes or in mills that could not be conveniently located near water. Around 1840 manufacturers in New England and the middle Atlantic states estimated the annual cost per horsepower for steam to be five or six times that of water. With the improvement of technology in the metal-working trades that came within the next twenty years, the first cost of steam engines was lowered and both efficiency and reliability were improved. By the 1850s steam engines were replacing water wheels in the heat-using industries and wherever, as along the Ohio River, stream flows were highly variable. In New England steam engines were being installed to power textile mills because of the serious lack of adequate power sites. As of 1860 water was still the chief source of power, but the years of the water wheel were clearly numbered.

One further question suggests itself regarding technological change leading to the rise of factory methods. How were the revolutionary improvements in manufacturing processes, largely brought over from England, applied in this country?

1. *The American textile industry was almost completely mechanized by 1860.* As might be surmised, the most rapid change occurred in the manufacture of cotton goods. By 1815 the Boston Manufacturing Company had installed in its Waltham plant power looms that performed satisfactorily. Between 1815 and 1860 the inventions of the earlier years were improved, chiefly in the direction of attaining increased automaticity and greater speeds. The woolen industry lagged as it had done in England, largely because of the greater technical difficulties involved in each of the four stages of textile manufacture. (It was a problem, for example, to get woolen warps strong enough to stand the strain of power looming.) After 1840 the innovations necessary to complete mechanization of the woolen industry were introduced. Home manufacture of woolens lingered on the frontier, however, as did the carding and fulling mills of olden times, and fine woolens were

---

[8] Victor S. Clark, *History of Manufactures in the United States, 1607–1860* (Washington, D.C.: Carnegie Institution, 1916), p. 409.

imported from England. For making coarse materials, including flannels and carpets, the American industry was adequately equipped by Civil War times.

2. *While discussing the iron industry of colonial days, we noted the two major stages of smelting and refining.* Pig iron from the small blast furnaces was further refined in forges, usually under the weight of water-driven hammers. The resulting wrought-iron "merchant" bar or plate was then ready to be worked up into finished products—by the village blacksmith at one end of the scale and by the manufacturer of steam engines and iron rails at the other. The domestic demand for iron was mostly for agricultural equipment, and it remained so during the first half of the nineteenth century. There was also a demand for cast-iron articles—kettles and pots, great pans and skillets, fireplace hardware, and the like, which were often produced in connection with the original smelting process. Not until the decade of the 1850s, however, did industrial demand assume proportions that would determine the size and character of the industry.

Between 1815 and 1850 three British innovations were introduced into the United States. In 1817 the rolling of bars and plates began to replace the ancient method of hammering. Shortly thereafter ironmasters began to refine pig iron by "puddling" it in a furnace that kept molten metal from contact with the fuel. More metal could then be worked at one time, and coal, which left impurities in the iron when burned with it in refining, could be used instead of charcoal. Probably the most important improvement was the gradual introduction of coal into the smelting stage, a change that the English had long since made because of their growing scarcity of timber. Even in America, where wood was plentiful, charcoal was more expensive than coal, but charcoal-iron was more malleable and more easily welded and thus suited the small operators who served the agricultural market. Industrial requirements, which first made themselves seriously felt in the 1840s, led to the use of first anthracite and then bituminous coal and coke as the reduction fuel.

3. *During the first two decades of the existence of the Patent Office an average of 77 patents was issued annually.* During the 1850s the number exceeded 2,500 annually. With allowance for the eccentric nature of many of the patents, the figure indicates the growing inventiveness of Americans. The sewing machine, patented first by Elias Howe in 1846, is a good example. With improvements by Isaac Singer and Allen B. Wilson, quantity output of these machines was possible in the early fifties, and they became the first household appliance to gain wide acceptance. More important, they enabled both the shoe and garment industries to become mechanized and to increase the attractiveness of their products. By the late 1840s the rubber industry, capitalizing on Charles Goodyear's invention of the vulcanization of rubber in 1839, was turning out its first crude but wondrous product—overshoes, buskins, and sandals. In food processing Americans, importing French and English ideas, "put up" items ranging from vegetables to seafood. Glass jars

were used at first, handmade tin cans making their appearance about 1820. Modern canning factories were not established until well after the Civil War, but the principles of sterilization and handling were generally known by 1860. Gail Borden's method of canning evaporated milk, for which a patent was sought in 1853, was another step toward emancipating housewives from dependence on fresh food.

Developments like these were inextricably linked with the emergence of the factory, as the following section will show.

THE EMERGENCE OF FACTORIES

The word *factory* has been customarily used to designate manufacturing units with the following characteristics:

1. A substantial output of a standardized product made for sale in a wide, more-than-local market.
2. Complex operations carried on in one building or a group of juxtaposed buildings. Implied is a considerable investment in fixed plant, mechanization of processes, and the use of power.
3. An assembly of workers under a definite organizational discipline. All the factors in the combination except the workers—plant, machinery, tools, and land—are owned by the "capitalist" who has, for this reason, always felt that he is the boss. The factory system is unique for the kind of personal relationships it sets up between employer and employee.

Even if we agree that these are the essential characteristics of factory organization, we may have some difficulty in concluding whether a particular firm of the pre–Civil War period fell in the category of "mill industry" or factory. Perhaps the distinction is not important as long as we are aware that an evolution did take place. Certainly it did not take place evenly in any one industry nor at approximately the same time in different industries. Let us take an example or two.

The factory developed first in the cotton textile industry. Because of the unusual nature of its founding we think of the mill of Almy, Brown, and Slater, in operation by 1793, as the first American factory. Moses Brown and William Almy were men of wealth in the New England mercantile tradition. Like many another American enterpriser, they had tried and failed to duplicate English spinning machinery. In 1790 there came to Rhode Island a young mechanical wizard, Samuel Slater, who had worked for years in the firm of Arkwright and Strutt at Milford, England. Having memorized the minutest details of the water frames, Slater emigrated to the United States, where he hoped to obtain a fortune for his information. Getting in touch with Almy and Brown, Slater agreed with them to reproduce the equipment for a mechanized spinning mill. Though small, the enterprise served as a training place for operatives and as a pilot operation for managers.

Located on the Blackstone River in Pawtucket, Rhode Island, the Almy, Brown, and Slater mill was in yarn production by late 1790. By 1793 carding, roving, and spinning operations were all mechanized, and workers were assembled in a single "factory house" under central supervision. Almy and Brown began pushing their markets northward from Providence into Connecticut, Massachusetts, and Maine, and by 1801 they were shipping yarn into New York City, Philadelphia, Baltimore, and even further south to meet a burgeoning demand.

A number of small mills like the Slater mill were started, but most of them failed by the turn of the century because their promoters had not learned the trick of shooting for a wide market. Not until the Embargo Act of 1807 and the consequent scarcity of English textiles stimulated demand for domestic manufactures did spinning mills become numerous. Between 1805 and 1815 a total of ninety-four new cotton mills were built in New England, the mounting competition leading Almy and Brown to push their markets south and west so that by 1814 70 per cent of all consignments were to the Middle West via Philadelphia. Only two decades after Arkwright machinery was introduced into this country, the market for yarn was on its way to being a national market, and the spinning process was becoming a true factory operation as it was in England.

Before the change could be accomplished two events forestalled it. One was the successful introduction of the power loom into American manufacture; the other was the organization of production with *all four* stages of the manufacture of cotton cloth brought within one establishment. After close observation of the working of textile machinery in Great Britain, Francis Cabot Lowell, a New England merchant, gained sufficient knowledge of the secrets of mechanized weaving to enable him, with the help of a gifted technician, to construct a power loom superior to any that had hitherto been made. It was as an enterpriser, however, that Francis Lowell made a more significant contribution, for he persuaded other men of means to participate with him in establishing at Waltham a firm that had all the essential characteristics of factory production. This was the famed Boston Manufacturing Company, forerunner of several similar firms in which the so-called Boston Associates were interested. Specializing in coarse sheetings, the Waltham factory sold its product all over America. Bringing all four steps of textile manufacture into a single plant lowered costs. A large number of specialized workers were organized into departments and directed by executives who were not necessarily technical supervisors. The factory, by using power-driven machinery, produced standardized commodities in quantity.

At Lowell, where the Merrimack Manufacturing Company followed the Waltham pattern, and at Manchester and Lawrence, the factory system gained a permanent foothold. In the other great center of New England textile manufacture—the Providence-Pawtucket region—there was a similar trend, though the factories there were fewer and smaller. The third great

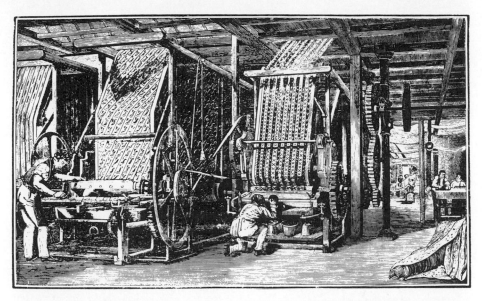

Calico printing (above) and power-loom weaving (below) as demonstrated in these prints from the *Memoirs of Samuel Slater* illustrated anew the complexity of mechanized factories and the substantial economies of scale that came with them.

district, located about Paterson and Philadelphia, had mainly small mills that performed a single major process and turned out finer weaves. But by 1860 New England's industry had nearly four times as many spindles as the middle Atlantic industry and accounted for nearly three-fourths of the country's output of cotton goods. The factory had demonstrated its superiority in the textile field.

It was simply a matter of time until other industries should adopt the same organization. For the reasons given above the production of woolen cloth tended to remain in the small mill longer than cotton production did, but after 1830 woolen factories began to adopt the characteristics of the Waltham system; by 1860 the largest textile factories in the United States were woolen factories.[9] Again, New Englanders far surpassed the rest of the country in combining the factors of production in large units; two-thirds of American woolen output was made in New England in 1860.

In most other industries the decade of the 1830s was one of expansion and experimentation with new methods. In the primary iron industry there were, by the 1840s, establishments that dwarfed the ones of a quarter-century before, and even in the pre-steel era some of them had gotten far beyond what we have called the mill stage. By 1845 the Brady's Bend Iron Company in western Pennsylvania owned

> . . . nearly 6,000 acres of mineral land and 5 miles of river front upon the Allegheny. It mined its own coal, ore, limestone, fire-clay, and fire-stone, made its own coke, and owned 14 miles of railway to serve its works. The plant itself consisted of 4 blast furnaces, a foundry, and rolling mills. It was equipped to perform all the processes, from getting raw materials out of the ground to delivering finished rails and metal shapes to consumers, and could produce annually between 10,000 and 15,000 tons of rails. It housed in its own tenements 538 laboring families. This company, with an actual investment of $1,000,000 was among the largest in America before the Civil War, though there were rival works of approximately equal capacity and similar organization.[10]

In the anthracite region to the east, factory operation of furnaces and rolling mills had been achieved by 1850.

By the 1850s factories were manufacturing arms, clocks and watches, and sewing machines. How one industry could adopt new methods as a consequence of progress in another is shown by the fact that, as the sewing machine was produced on a quantity basis, the boot and shoe industry developed factory characteristics. Carriages, wagons, and even farm implements came to be produced in large numbers, although the term *mass production* was not yet applicable to them. And finally, where markets were more than local, where there was a substantial investment in fixed plant, and where the work force was subjected to formal discipline, some firms in the traditional mill industries other than the textile and iron industries achieved factory status. The great merchant flour mills of Baltimore and Rochester fell in this category, as did some of the large packing plants of New York, Philadelphia, Baltimore, and, after 1840, Cincinnati.

[9] Cf. Clark, p. 453.
[10] Clark, p. 446.

The Status of Manufacture in 1860

What were the leading industries of the country in 1860 and how did they rank? To answer this question we must accept the figures of the *Eighth Census of the United States: Manufactures,* remembering that both the techniques of census-taking and the concepts of the census-takers were far from refined.

First, let us look at Table 8-1 in which the leading industries are ranked by *value added by manufacture.* There is a close correspondence between that ranking and the one by *value of product,* but note that flour and meal, fourth in value added, accounted for the greatest value of product. However, we are interested primarily in showing the importance of actual processing as measured in money terms. Cotton manufacture, with New England leading the way, ranked number one, having grown from infancy in fifty years. Lumbering was a close second; moving from its old seat in the New England and middle Atlantic states to the West and the South, it constituted the most important processing activity for these new areas. Of the first ten industries the milling of flour and meal was the only other one in the West and South with a significant output; remembering the economy of colonial America, the student should readily grasp the reason why. Iron manufactures were underrated because of narrow census definitions; had all iron products and machinery been combined in a single category, it would have been the most important group of all. Between 1850 and 1860 the doubling of

Table 8-1

United States Manufactures, 1860

Item	Cost of raw material	Number of employees	Value of product	Value added by manufacture	Rank by value added
Cotton goods	$ 52,666,701	114,955	$107,337,783	$54,671,082	1
Lumber	51,358,400	75,595	104,928,342	53,569,942	2
Boots and shoes	42,728,174	123,026	91,889,298	49,161,124	3
Flour and meal	208,497,309	27,682	248,580,365	40,083,056	4
Men's clothing	44,149,752	114,800	80,830,555	36,680,803	5
Iron (cast, forged, rolled, and wrought)	37,486,056	48,975	73,175,332	35,689,276	6
Machinery	19,444,533	41,223	52,010,376	32,565,843	7
Woolen goods	35,652,701	40,597	60,685,190	25,032,489	8
Carriages, wagons, and carts	11,898,282	37,102	35,552,842	23,654,560	9
Leather	44,520,737	22,679	67,306,452	22,785,715	10

SOURCE: *Eighth Census of the United States: Manufactures.*

output of primary iron products and machinery forecast the shape of America's industrial future.

The sectional figures in Table 8-2 testify to the primacy of the East in early manufacturing. Because the Census counted the smallest sawmills and gristmills as "manufacturing establishments," the West and South showed a large number of establishments. By any other criterion New England and the middle Atlantic states were the leading sections, their importance as employers of labor and producers of high value-added products being unmistakable. The figures for the western states reflect in part the rapid ante-bellum industrial growth of the Ohio Valley and the burgeoning of the Chicago area.

Table 8-2

Manufacturing, by Sections, Census of 1860

Section	Number of establishments	Capital invested	Employment		Annual value of products	Value added by manufacture
			Male	Female		
New England	20,671	$257,477,783	262,834	129,002	$468,599,287	$223,076,180
Middle	53,287	435,061,964	432,424	113,819	802,338,392	358,211,423
Western	36,785	194,212,543	194,081	15,828	384,606,530	158,987,717
Southern	20,631	95,975,185	98,583	12,138	155,531,281	68,988,129
Pacific	8,777	23,380,334	50,137	67	71,229,989	42,746,363
Territories	282	3,747,906	2,290	43	3,556,197	2,246,772
TOTALS	140,433	$1,009,855,715	1,040,349	270,897	$1,885,861,676	$854,256,584

SOURCE: *Eighth Census of the United States: Manufactures.*

During the period 1810–60 total value of products increased from about $200 million to just under $2 billion, or roughly tenfold. Capital invested increased from perhaps $50 million to $1 billion, or twentyfold. These figures are expressed in dollars current then and are less reliable than the ones available from 1870 on. Yet it is obvious that manufacturing had made tremendous gains in the decade and a half before the Civil War. Farming was still in first place as a means of earning a livelihood, for value added by manufacture in 1860 was markedly less than the value of three major crops—corn, wheat, and hay—and total capital investment in industry was equal to less than one-sixth the value of farm land and buildings. But the United States was even then second only to Great Britain in manufacturing and would soon be the industrial leader of the world.[11]

---

[11] The *Twelfth Census of the United States,* quoting Mulhall's *Industries and Wealth of Nations,* placed the United States in fourth place after Great Britain, France, and Germany. But see Douglass C. North, *The Economic Growth of the United States, 1790 to 1860* (Englewood Cliffs, N.J.: Prentice-Hall, 1961), p. v.

The Laborer
and His Employer

Do ye hear the children weeping, O my brothers,
  Ere the sorrow comes with years?
They are leaning their young heads against their mothers,
  And *that* cannot stop their tears.

ELIZABETH BARRETT BROWNING

Ideally we should pause here to reflect on the kind of man the ante-bellum American was. We ought to inquire what he ate and drank, what he wore, and how he housed himself. And we should like to know more. What were his aspirations? What were his politics? What were his special abilities? What did he achieve in science, in literature, and in the arts? The more we know of man and his society, the better we understand economics.

To a general history of the United States we must leave this broader inquiry; for our subject is *economic* history, and we must confine ourselves to the study of the American and his economic life. In this chapter we shall study him at work. Although before 1860 the greater part of the population was rural and self-employed (on farms and in shops), the rapid industrialization and urbanization of the 1850s foreshadowed a massive transformation of the ways of earning a living. The change to working for an employer had serious consequences, for the depersonalization of relations between employer and employee led to tensions that would one day become seriously disruptive. But before the Civil War the working man was disposed to know and keep his place, even while his more venturesome fellows stirred the beginnings of the "labor movement."

The Emergence of a Laboring Class

As we have seen, wages of American workers during colonial days were remarkably higher than those of contemporary English workers. When American industry started to develop at the turn of the nineteenth century, money
wages of unskilled adult labor were still much higher than they were in
England, perhaps by as much as a third to a half higher.[1] The differential
was attributable to the fact that a floor to the remuneration of labor in industry was set by rewards in agriculture. Well into the 1800s there were no
insuperable obstacles, either of distance or expense, to obtaining a fertile
farm. Output per man in agriculture was relatively high, and the course of
agricultural technology in the early nineteenth century tended to increase
output per man rather than output per acre, as was the case in England.
Moreover, the farmer in America, ordinarily the owner of his land, received
in addition to the wages of himself and his family elements of rent and profits, which in England went to the landlord and the tenant farmer, as distinguished from the agricultural laborer. Finally, American farmers stood
always to gain from appreciation in land values as population moved westward.

In Chapter 10 we shall see how the relative dearness of labor in America
encouraged technological innovation that determined the evolution of the
American system of manufacture. Presently we need only observe that,
however hard the lot of ante-bellum laborers may seem by today's standards, workers in the United States were well off by comparison with those
of England. Sharp increases in immigration during the 1830s and 1840s,
along with the removal of settlement opportunities farther and farther from
the urban East led to a narrowing of the wage differential between British
and American labor; even so, the floor set to industrial wages was, by consensus of voluminous testimony, relatively high up to 1860. During the first
decades of the nineteenth century, as in the colonial period, premiums paid
for artisan skills in America were apparently less than those paid in England, but the difference in premium declined as the century wore on.[2]

The craftsman—i.e., the artisan or "mechanic"—was not seriously affected
by machine techniques until at least the middle of the nineteenth century.
In a few trades, like shoemaking, his position was weakened as the demand
for his product increased, for he found himself making standardized products for general sale. First in craft shops and then perhaps in factories output

---

[1] See H. J. Habakkuk, *American and British Technology in the Nineteenth Century* (Cambridge: Cambridge University Press, 1962), p. 11. The following passage draws heavily from
Professor Habakkuk's splendidly useful book.
[2] It seems to be a general rule that in times of a persistent surplus of labor those without
skill have the hardest time finding employment; on the contrary, a shortage of labor is
usually felt most acutely in the unskilled ranks. But the lower premium paid for skill
in early nineteenth-century America resulted particularly from such causes as the greater
pulling power of agricultural expansion on unskilled labor and the higher proportion of
skilled migrants from England to the United States before mass migration began. For
other reasons see Habakkuk, pp. 23–24.

was for sale in ever larger markets, and pressures were great to achieve volume at the expense of artistry. In this way skilled workers in a few industries might be replaced and the status of some craftsmen reduced.[3] On the whole, though, the services of skilled workers were scarce in ante-bellum America, and only during severe business slumps was the artisan in danger of unemployment.

THE FACTORY AND THE WAGE EARNER

In the industries affected the change from craft-shop artisan to factory worker was made gradually. Specialized operatives were needed to do some of the work of the factory, and men as highly skilled as artisans were required to repair machines and devise and construct machine tools. But much factory work consisted of machine-tending, making simple adjustments, carrying materials, starting materials in the machines, and taking finished goods out of the machines and required no great physical strength, no specialization, and simple skills. Yet it was difficult for employers to hire even unskilled male laborers. There had been no enclosure movement in the United States comparable to that of Great Britain, and such a movement as did take place in New England threw no great numbers of agrarians off the land to shift for themselves. Unlike English entrepreneurs, Americans had to *attract* a labor supply from farms and shops, a hard task because mills and factories stood beside streams often removed from centers of population.

Mill and factory owners in the textile industry solved employment problems in two ways. Under one system, called the Rhode Island system, they hired whole families, put father, mother, and children each to tasks suitable to his strength and maturity, and housed the families in company-constructed, cheerless tenements. The Rhode Island system was used almost exclusively south of Boston, partly because child labor was first introduced there in imitation of English methods, and partly because the mule spinning typical of the area required both heavy and light work. Francis Cabot Lowell and the Boston Associates introduced the Waltham system, under which women in their late teens and early twenties were brought together to form the nucleus of a labor force for large factories. Housed in dormitories—or boarding houses—they remained under the careful supervision of matrons who kept any taint of disreputability from touching the girls.

What of the conditions under which these early factory people worked? Hours of work were unbelievably long. A twelve-hour day was thought not at all unreasonable, and half an hour off for meals was standard. From sunrise to sunset it was possible to operate machinery without artificial light, and in wintertime candles furnished enough illumination to permit operation on into the evening. Because of the slow speeds of early machines the

---

[3] John R. Commons, "American Shoemakers," *Quarterly Journal of Economics,* XXIV (November 1909), 39–81.

Factory labor, as this Winslow Homer drawing suggests, was in significant part made up of women and children, and (judging from the expressions on their faces) the prospect of such work was no cause for rejoicing.

work pace was not great; for this reason women and children could work a seventy-two–hour week without physical breakdown. By mid-twentieth century standards wages were pitifully low, but a family under the Rhode Island system earned enough to keep it alive and in such creature comforts as the nineteenth-century working class presumably merited. Girls under the Waltham system were better off; they spent half their weekly wage of $2.50 to $3.00 on room and board and were able to save some money. Both families and single people worked under a paternalistic regime, the concern of employers being largely for the morals and behavior of the workers. So long as the level of living kept workers reasonably efficient, it was thought proper, in the interests of strengthening character, to keep luxuries and leisure time at a minimum.

The life of a New England textile worker was tiresome and drab, though no worse than the life of a poor New England farmer, whose dawn to dusk regimen left little time for the pleasure or intellectual growth of the household. The girls might find escape from the boredom and isolation of farm life, and possibly a husband, by going to work in a factory; or they might join their mothers in handweaving or making straw hats, palm-leaf hats, and shoes. The domestic system provided much part-time or even full-time work for both villagers and farmers of the Northeast right up to the end of the 1850s. Pay was low, sometimes only twenty-five cents a day or less, but the work was leisurely and the income kept many a family from penury. Too, work was done at home so that the sociological strains of taking the young out of the home were avoided.

The New England factory worker escaped the Stygian horrors to which his English counterpart was subjected during the first decades of the factory system. He was better off because American manufacturers were compelled to a certain standard of decency by the necessity of attracting and holding labor. Nor does evidence show that American factory owners were cruel to children as the English were, a fact that may be accounted for by the respect for human rights and feelings already developed by the people of the New World.

Yet after the early 1840s there appeared the first definite signs of an ugly urban society to come. City workers, who led impoverished lives, bore the brunt of early industrialization. Under the domestic system city employees fared less well than country people; unable to eke out an existence by farming or fishing, they were subject to the artful exploitation of merchant employers.[4] "Sweated" workers slaved from fourteen to sixteen hours a day in the garment industry in New York, Philadelphia, and Boston, and common laborers sold their services for a pittance to transportation companies and urban building contractors. Factory and mill workers found themselves in an unenviable position as competition from immigrant labor retarded the growth in real wages.[5] Whatever the long-run benefits of immigration, the immediate effect was to dilute the gains the American laborer would otherwise have obtained from rapidly increasing industrial productivity.

POPULATION CHANGES AND IMMIGRATION, 1790–1860

Between 1790 and 1820 the population of the United States increased from nearly 4,000,000 to 10,000,000 people. Nearly the whole of this increase resulted from the remarkable birth rate of Americans, for not more than

---

[4] The word exploitation is one we shall have to use from time to time, and there is some point in making its technical, economic meaning clear at the outset. A worker is said to be "exploited" when he does not receive, in any time period, an amount equal to the "value of his marginal product"; i.e., a worker is exploited when he does not receive an amount equal to what he, in combination with the other agents of production, contributes to the value of output. This contribution can be determined by holding all the conditions of employment constant, removing the worker from the combination, and observing how much output (and, consequently its value) falls. To the Marxians, of course, the word is more sinister, meaning the failure of labor to receive the combined product of all the factors.

[5] Necessarily rough estimates indicate that real hourly earnings grew at an average rate of less than 0.5 per cent per annum in the two decades before the Civil War. See W. S. Woytinsky and associates, Employment and Wages in the United States (New York: Twentieth Century Fund, 1953), p. 46.

250,000 new settlers came from abroad during these thirty years, and half of them came after the War of 1812. During the decade of the 1820s the influx of foreigners was less than 150,000. As the chart below shows, immigration grew substantially in the 1830s and early 1840s, the great movement beginning about 1845.

Nationals of three countries constituted the overwhelming majority of the newcomers. A steady stream of immigrants from England flowed into the United States until a decade after the Civil War. After 1830 Irish and Germans came in ever increasing numbers, repelled by conditions at home and attracted by economic opportunities in a new land. The tragic potato famine of 1845–47 precipitated the heavy Irish emigration that lasted well into the 1850s. Fleeing starvation and the oppression of hated absentee landlords, the Irish found employment as common laborers and factory hands. The Census of 1850 reported nearly a million Irish in the United States, 40 per cent of whom had settled in large cities where their "shanty towns" became the notorious slums of the era. Only a little later came the Germans, following the failure of the democratic and nationalistic revolutions of 1848. Within fifteen years 1,300,000 had arrived. Most Germans, having a little capital, settled on farms in the Middle West, but almost one-third of them swelled the populations of booming cities like Cincinnati, Chicago, Milwaukee, and St. Louis.

Labor Force: To a nation rich in land and rapidly increasing its stock of capital, laborers (a third principal factor of production) at last came in huge numbers during the post-1848 period, when famine in Ireland and domestic unrest in Germany sent millions across the ocean to America.

In Thousands

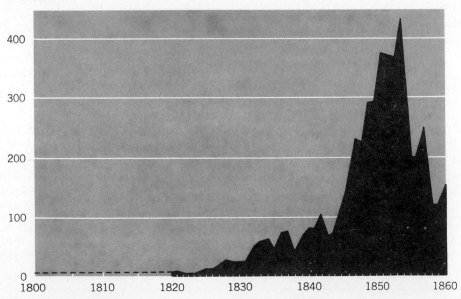

Between 1820 and 1860 the population of the country trebled to 31,500,000. Density of population, only four and a half persons per square mile in 1790, was almost eight per square mile in 1850. Population density was much greater than the average in older areas, but America was still far from crowded.

It is impossible to glean data from the early censuses comparable to any of the modern series of the Bureau of Labor Statistics. Concepts and definitions were crude. The Superintendent of the Census, as he was then called, took more pains with his rhetoric than with his figures, placing undue emphasis on counting the lame and the halt, the deaf and the blind, the insane and the idiotic. But if we remember that in both 1850 and 1860 the census of manufactures included every establishment "producing . . . of any kind of manufactured article the amount annually of five hundred dollars," we can extract some informative labor statistics. The Census excluded "the very large aggregate of mechanical productions below the annual value of five hundred dollars," as well as "carpenters, bricklayers, painters, and the members of other mechanical trades not classed as manufacturers." People employed in trade, commerce, and the transportation industries were likewise excluded. With these exceptions there were by 1850 just under 950,000 people of all ages employed in manufacturing industries, approximately one-fourth of whom were females. How many children were employed we have no way of knowing. In the early thirties as many as one-half the operatives in some cotton textile factories were children. In the next two decades the percentage of children employed in the industry fell while the absolute number rose. At mid-century women were dominant in textile manufacture; about twice as many females as males worked at making cotton fabrics, though males exceeded females in woolen manufacture. About one-third of the 225,000 females who had jobs in industry worked in textile factories. The rest were for the most part home workers under the domestic system.

By 1860 the number of "hands" in industry had risen to 1,385,000. Women now constituted only one-fifth of the manufacturing labor force, indicating the lessening *relative* importance of textile manufacture. The cotton-textile industry still employed the most females (many of whom were children), and the clothing and boot and shoe industries were second and third in this respect, ahead of woolen textiles. The Superintendent of the Census estimated that each person employed in manufacturing maintained, on an average, two and one-half other persons; thus nearly one-sixth of the population was directly supported by manufactures.[6] Another one-sixth of the population may have been supported by other nonagricultural pursuits. These figures remind us that in 1860 the people of the United States were predominantly agrarians, two-thirds of them gaining their livelihood directly from the land. But urban workers had achieved a numerical importance

---

[6] *Preliminary Report on the Eighth Census*, p. 59.

that made them a force to be reckoned with. Let us see how they acquired a unifying sense of class consciousness.

The Early Labor Movement

Economists like to say that the modern labor problem springs from "the separation of the worker from his tools." [7] Like most generalizations this one has its uses, but it may lead the unwary to false inferences. The Industrial Revolution placed great numbers of laborers in a position of uncertainty and insecurity—dependent upon the vagaries of economic fluctuations and the mercies of employers. Yet the first impetus to a genuine labor movement was furnished by craftsmen who were by no means separated from their tools. The ever increasing numbers of factory workers became articulate and powerful only with the passage of time. At first factory workers were little more adept at organizing than were day laborers, and their bargaining strength was slight. In the first half of the nineteenth century, factory operatives, except for the influence they could exert at the polls, served labor's cause chiefly by demonstrating how rising industrialism might create permanent class distinctions.

ORGANIZATION: ECONOMIC MOTIVATION

In colonial days craftsmen of the same trade banded together in benevolent and protective associations, but until just before the Revolution there seem to have been no organizations that could be called unions. Beginning in the 1790s craftsmen in Philadelphia, New York, and Boston founded the prototypes of modern unions. Most of the societies were established in the vain hope of securing increases in real wages (i.e., of pushing up money wages faster than prices of consumer goods), though attempts were made to gain shorter working hours, to establish and maintain a closed shop, and to regulate the conditions of apprenticeship. Invariably there was some fraternal motivation; men who made a living in the same way forged an easy social bond. In nearly all the major cities shoemakers (cordwainers) and printers were among the very first to form "workingmen's societies," and carpenters, masons, hatters, riggers, and tailors likewise thought it worthwhile to organize.

The early craft societies were transitory. Many of the unions of the 1790s were begun for particular objectives and, succeeding or failing, passed quickly out of existence. Apparently the Philadelphia cordwainers, who maintained a union from 1794 to 1806, were the first to keep their organization going more than a very few years.

Two influences worked against permanence. One was the cyclical nature of economic activity. The other was the unfavorable attitude of the courts, which before 1850 were uniformly hostile toward union activity. Member-

---

[7] The artisan, no matter how inexperienced, had always owned the customary implements of his trade. When he became a factory worker, the capitalist furnished his equipment.

ship of the unions always rose rapidly during prosperous periods and fell just as rapidly with the onset of depression. On the economic upswing everything was favorable to organizing endeavors. Price rises in commodities, both retail and wholesale, preceded increases in rents and wages, and real incomes fell at a rate that frightened workers into collective action. Nor did they fear the wrath of employers because of union activity, for jobs were plentiful. Furthermore, employers were less likely to resist efforts to form societies, for they could always pass on to their customers such wage-rate increases as might be extracted from them. On the downswing labor's advantage was undone. As general unemployment came on, those fortunate enough to have jobs accepted wage cuts rather than go hungry. Attempts by unions to resist wage reductions were met by counterefforts of belligerent employers, themselves frequently banded together. Union members, when called upon to strike rather than take lower wages, withdrew from the society, for they knew the employer could hire nonunion labor to break the strike.

In good times and bad there was always the threat and sometimes the actuality of court action to hinder and thwart organizational efforts. Conservative judges, in their instructions to juries, contended that union action *per se* was illegal. Societies of workmen were held to be conspiracies under the English common law, a conspiracy being defined as ". . . a confederacy of two or more, by indirect means to injure an individual or to do any act, which is unlawful or prejudicial to the community." A doctrine developed in England during the late Middle Ages was thus applied some five hundred years later to restrict the unionization of craftsmen. In the famous case of the Pittsburgh Cordwainers in 1815, the judge contended that both the master shoemakers *and* the journeymen were coerced. "No shoemaker dare receive one who worked under price; or who was not a member of the society. No master workman must give him any employment, under the penalty of losing all his workmen." Moreover, ". . . a conspiracy to prevent a man from freely exercising his trade, or particular profession, in a particular place, is endictable. Also, it is an endictable offense, to conspire to compel men to become members of a particular association, or to contribute towards it." [8] The jury in this case agreed that the master shoemakers, the journeymen, and the public were endangered by the association of journeymen and returned a verdict of guilty of conspiracy, though the court fined the defendants only one dollar each and the costs of prosecution. Judgments against unions were not severe, and times remained good until 1818. It took the depression of 1819–20 to wipe out most of the societies.

From 1824 until 1837 there was a gradual resurgence of craft unions. Gathering momentum from 1834 on, the movement reached substantial proportions, and had it not been for the devastating severity of the Panic

---

[8] Reprinted by permission of the publishers, The Arthur H. Clark Co., from Commons' *A Documentary History of American Industrial Society*, Vol. 4, pp. 82, 83.

of 1837, American labor might have attained a position at mid-century which, in fact, it was not to reach until around 1900. Aside from the political gains made in these years, unions progressed in two directions.

1. *The technique of bargaining collectively was learned, and fighting unions began to use the weapons of the strike and boycott with skill and daring.* The closed shop, an agreement whereby membership in a recognized union is made a condition of employment, was soon tested as an instrument for maintaining union security. The benevolent and protective aims of labor organizations tended to disappear, and militancy replaced early hesitance and reluctance to act.

2. *The rapidly increasing number of individual societies began to coalesce.* Local federations appeared and then national organizations. In 1827 unions of different crafts in Philadelphia federated to form a "city central" or "trades' union"—the Mechanics' Union of Trade Associations. Six years later the societies in New York established a General Trades' Union. In the next three years city centrals were formed in several major cities, not, as might be supposed from the modern functions of such organizations, to exchange information or engage in political activities, but for the more pressing purpose of aiding individual unions engaged in battle with employers. Attempts at organization on a national scale followed. In 1834 the General Trades' Union, New York's city central, called a national convention of these city federations, with the result that a National Trades' Union was founded. At the same time some of the craft societies began to see advantages in a national organization along strict craft lines, and in 1835 and 1836 no less than five national unions of this type were established. Strongest of these were the shoemakers and printers.

However remarkable these early gains, labor's élite, the craftsmen, benefited primarily. Factory workers and home workers under the domestic system were almost completely outside the union movement. There are records of occasional organizations of factory hands in the textile industry, but the embryo unions were unstable. Spontaneous strikes occurred from time to time, even in the absence of formal organization, but they were easily broken. It went hard with a factory girl or with a laborer and his family if the wrath of an employer were incurred. The "blacklist," which was to have a long and dishonorable future, contained the names of those known to be disruptive influences, and its circulation in an area precluded their employment.

The shock of the long depression that began in 1837 brought to an abrupt end the trend toward unionism of the preceding ten years. As unemployment spread, the city centrals and the national organizations disappeared. So did all but the hardiest locals. For several years there were only sporadic efforts to revive unions, and activity was confined to the urban centers of the East. By the early 1840s it looked as though the energies spent in bringing American trade unionism to some degree of maturity had been wasted.

As unions gathered strength toward the mid-thirties, people of property and their natural allies in the professional classes looked with alarm upon what seemed to them a dangerous growth of labor power. The courts were in agreement with this view. Two cases reminiscent of the older conspiracy trials were important in checking the union movement. The first was that of the Geneva Shoemakers. The journeymen shoemakers of Geneva, New York, had agreed not to work for any master who did not hire union men. One master hired a nonunion member at below union rates, and the other workers in the shop promptly struck. For refusing to work the journeymen were indicted and convicted for criminal conspiracy. The case was appealed to the State Supreme Court, and Chief Justice Savage upheld the conviction on the grounds that such union action was harmful to trade. "It is important to the best interests of society," he said, "that the price of labor be left to regulate itself. . . . Competition is the life of trade." Meantime, in New York City the Society of Journeyman Tailors had secured an increase in wage rates for its members only to have them later reduced by a combination of master tailors. A strike, accompanied by much strife, ensued. "Dungs," as scabs were then called, were hired by the masters to break the strike, with resulting violence. After Justice Savage handed down his decision in the Geneva Shoemakers case, the master tailors charged twenty of the journeymen with conspiracy. Again, the strike was the offense. The judge followed Justice Savage in his charge to the jury, and the tailors were convicted and fined heavily. Because of the trial judge's contention that American "trades and tradesmen" had hitherto flourished without the aid of combinations and that the unions must therefore have been "of foreign origin . . . and upheld by foreigners," there was much indignation among labor supporters over the outcome of the trial. In two similar cases union members were acquitted, but the legality of union activity was still very much in question.

A definite turning point came in the now famous case of *Commonwealth* v. *Hunt.* In the fall of 1840 Hunt and other members of the Boston Bootmakers' Society were haled into municipal court for attempting to enforce a closed shop. Again, after a strict charge from a judge who felt that such union activities could lead only to a "frightful despotism," the accused were convicted. The case was appealed to the Supreme Court of the Commonwealth of Massachusetts, and in 1842 Chief Justice Lemuel Shaw gave a monumental decision that set a precedent on one point and opened the way to more liberal decisions on another. First, he held that a combination of union members was not criminal unless the object of the combination were criminal; the mere fact of organization implied no illegal conspiracy. Second, he asserted the doctrine that union members were within their rights in pressing for a closed shop and in striking to maintain union security. Justice Shaw was no radical and was not particularly sympathetic with labor's cause, but he was well aware of the economic realities that made it necessary for labor to act collectively. This decision did not mean that trade unions were done with the courts; but there were no more serious efforts to make the mere fact of organization a criminal offense, and there would henceforth be some reticence about presuming the use of any and all weapons of trade unions to be socially harmful.

After a tentative revival in the mid-forties, workingmen's societies made a strong comeback during the 1850s. From 1850 to 1854 the rapidity of organization of craft unions was comparable to that of twenty years before, with inevitable retardation accompanying the depression of 1854. Another setback came with bad times in 1857, but the end of the period saw definite progress. City centrals were back on the scene, as were national craft unions, and there were signs that the federations could do more than discuss matters of "mutual interest." Individual unions acquired memberships disposed to greater militance. Funds were accumulated for assisting the successful prosecution of strikes, and serious attempts were made by the stronger crafts to bargain with *all* employers in a particular locality.

Leaders who viewed the labor movement as a whole still had to face the problem of the growing masses of workmen who had no particular skills. People who worked in factories had always been hard to organize. As the uneducated Irish, largely with an agricultural background, swelled the ranks of industrial workers, the problem became increasingly difficult to solve. Yet the English and Germans were not without a tradition of labor solidarity, and they would be a source of strength in years to come. Such matters will be better considered in a later chapter; at the moment we must review briefly the political manifestations of the labor movement.

ORGANIZATION: POLITICAL MOTIVATION

Anyone concerned with modern labor problems must be aware of a certain artificiality in distinguishing between the economic and political aspirations of labor. The two classes of ends merge and blend into one another so as to be at times indistinguishable. Yet there have always been certain goals to be reached through the collective action of men who make their living in the same way, and there have been others that could only be achieved through political processes. A hundred years ago many of labor's demands were for rights that today are matters of common decency. But these same rights were then objects of desperate striving, and the struggle for them was carried on in an atmosphere of hostility and vindictiveness hardly imaginable today.

Labor's political awakening did not come until toward the end of the 1820s. It was not by mere chance that this was so. We do not disparage the Founding Fathers when we remark that most of them were not democrats. The Constitution was not designed to give great power to the masses, and the state governments favored people of wealth and property. During the first decades of our history as a republic there was a persistent demand on the part of the people for more voice in political affairs. The most significant gain in this regard was the broadening of suffrage. The requirements that a person own a minimum amount of real property or pay a certain amount of taxes were modified. The struggle for voting privileges took place in the original thirteen states, for of the new states entering the Union only four placed property or tax-payment qualifications on the right to vote. By the late 1820s the suffrage had been extended sufficiently to enable working people to participate in the elections of the populous states. First to disappear was the property-owning requirement; by 1821 only five states retained it. Thirty years later five states still had a tax-paying restriction, but it was purely nominal.[9] Generally speaking, by 1860 white male citizens of the United States could vote, Negro males could vote in New York and New England, and aliens could vote in the agricultural Northwest.

In the 1820s there came into prominence leaders of persuasive powers and genuine conviction who were able to stir laboring people to a sense of political destiny. Robert Owen, a Scot, was too impractical to gain a widely enthusiastic reception, but his countrywoman and disciple, Frances Wright, got a firm hold on the imaginations and passions of a large segment of the laboring population. She cried out against the reactionaries on the bench and among clergy of all denominations and insisted upon a rational program for improving material welfare. Fanny Wright and other ardent leaders of the workingmen's movement strove hardest for reforms in education. Except in New England the children of the poor received little or no education, and in New England the early training was of poor quality, having also a religious slant obnoxious to equalitarians. Fanny Wright and her followers proposed that the state establish boarding schools for the education of rich and poor children alike, where class distinction would be eliminated.

Other proposals of the workingmen's movement were less radical than this state-guardianship system of education; indeed many supporters of Fanny Wright broke with her when they proposed a simple plan of free public schools. Some of the movement's intellectuals believed that hard money (literally, a money supply made up of gold and silver coins) was necessary to the economic salvation of the worker, for they were convinced that ruin for the little man must result from giving the money-creating power to the state banks. In the minds of working people the most needed reform, next to that of the educational system, was the abolition of imprisonment for debt. Thousands of citizens were jailed annually for failure to meet obligations of a few dollars, and against this injustice there was understandably fierce resentment. The unfairness of the militia systems of the several states, which favored the rich, rankled in the hearts of poor men faced with the alternatives of a term in the service or a term in jail. These and other objectives—removal of the competition of convict labor and obtaining the right to file liens on the property of employers for back wages—

---

[9] Comparing votes for President with total population, we find that there were two big jumps in the electorate: from 1824 to 1828 (3.2 per cent to 9.3 per cent) and from 1836 to 1840 (9.6 per cent to 13.6 per cent).

inflamed the spirits of great numbers of laborers, small businessmen, and professional people with a high degree of social consciousness.

But flaming spirits accomplish little unless they have organizations through which to work. In Philadelphia in 1827, and shortly thereafter in New York City, independent workingmen's parties were formed to do battle at the polls. Similar political groups sprang up in most of the northern states and were more or less successful in their own localities. Supported by about fifty newspapers and by a voluminous pamphlet literature, tickets of workingmen's parties frequently ran well in local elections. But these independent labor parties were short-lived; they tended to be absorbed into the Democratic party, where they formed a radical wing, sympathetic with Jacksonian principles. The heated national election of 1832 hastened this process, for American labor early learned that it must take on the aura of respectability and orthodoxy of a major party if more than local success were to be gained at the polls.

The first political movement had borne fruit. Some progress had been made in the educational field. The militia system became less onerous, mechanics' "lien laws" were passed in many states, and imprisonment for debt was outlawed in most jurisdictions. But this first movement lost momentum after 1832 as labor turned its energies during the ensuing period of prosperity to advancing the cause of unionization. The onset of depression in 1837 dashed the hopes of those who looked for victory in the economic sphere, and more than a decade passed without a return to sustained high levels of business activity. Out of the frustration and disillusionment that accompanied the breakdown of the economic mechanism came a second wave of political activity, this time with vaguer goals and an even greater participation by intellectuals and reformers.

The 1840s were characterized by the Utopian schemes of idealists and the mundane agitation of men who looked to specific movements for relief. Of the Utopian notions, the associationism of Charles Fourier and the land reform of George Henry Evans vied chiefly for the interest of workers. Fourierism (associationism) advocated the division of society into "phalanxes"—communities of 1,600 producing members. Residing in a common building (phalanstery), members of the community would occupy themselves primarily in agriculture, but they were divided into a sufficient number of groups to permit a wide variety of pursuits, including menial domestic service. To avoid monotony, people could change jobs, but division of the total product was to be made according to a formula that took into account each individual's contribution of labor, "talent," and capital. No matter what his contribution, however, each person was assured a certain minimum livelihood, and it was hoped that everyone would live together in peace and classless harmony. Between 1840 and 1850 perhaps forty phalanxes were established in the United States. Of these, Brook Farm, near Boston, was the most famous because of the association with it of well-known New England literary figures. Differing somewhat from Robert

Owen's earlier socialist experiment at New Harmony, Indiana, the phalanxes nevertheless came to the same quick end. The chief trouble was
that Fourierism did not accept the growing industrialism of the nineteenth
century as an inescapable fact of human existence. Instead, the doctrine
suggested a withdrawal of uneconomically small groups into the agricultural and craft society from which the nations of the Western world were
emerging.

The Agrarianism of George Henry Evans looked backward, too. Evans
found the root of the worker's plight in technological change. Machines,
he felt, would continue to displace human labor, with chronic unemployment and low wages as a consequence. The remedy lay in free grants of land
from the public domain to groups of farmers and craftsmen who would
form self-sufficient townships on the frontier. After a flurry of acceptance
by isolated groups, Evans' land-reform effort faded. It had no lasting results
and little influence except as it added to the clamor for a homestead law
and strengthened the arguments of those who demanded free land for any
worker who wanted it.

The laboring man's selfish interest was for a time captured by proposals
for co-operation. Both producers' and consumers' co-operatives were advocated, the latter gaining a rather impressive acceptance. Co-ops of both
kinds had been started in the 1830s and had failed in the depression years.
Revived in the mid-forties, they reached a peak during the early fifties
and declined almost as suddenly. Producers' co-ops were started by craftsmen
in many cities as attempts to provide steady and permanent employment
for those who combined to set up the co-operative shop. Sharing the expenses of a retail establishment, workers hoped to provide a marketing outlet that would enable them to *share* profits instead of allowing a capitalist to
take them. Consumers' co-ops aimed to reduce the living costs of the worker
by rebating to him a share of the profits of a store on the basis of his
patronage. Some success was attained in New England, where member stores
of the New England Protective Union did a retail business of $4 million in
one year. The success of consumer co-operatives in America has always
been limited by the necessity of operating on a shoestring capital, meager
managerial talent, and the lack of loyalty of members. Co-ops temporarily
vanished before 1860.

Only one movement of the period gained quick relief for workers—the
struggle for the ten-hour day. Why a ten-hour day should have become
a goal is not entirely clear; perhaps because to the people of the time it
seemed a great improvement and one possible of eventual attainment. The
goal was set as early as 1835, but there was then no serious prospect of
reaching it. Hope rose in 1840 when Martin Van Buren set a ten-hour day
for federal employees. Craftsmen in some trades already worked no longer
than ten hours, but factory operatives still labored from twelve to fourteen
hours daily. In the mid-forties New England factory workers added to the
agitation for shorter hours. In 1847 the New Hampshire legislature passed

Labor organization, as always, proceeded with heartbreak and acrimony. Here, striking Pennsylvania coal miners and their wives taunt nonstriking miners.

the first regulatory law setting a ten-hour upper limit for a day's work, but there was a loophole in it. The law provided that if workers *agreed* to work longer hours the ten-hour limit might be exceeded. Threatened with discharge if they did not agree, factory hands found themselves no better off. Statutes passed by other state legislatures followed the same pattern, with the significant exception that statutes limiting the work day of children to ten hours did not contain the hated "contract" clause. Perhaps the most important effect of the agitation for regulatory acts was the pressure of public opinion thereby exerted on employers. Many large factories voluntarily established eleven-hour days. By 1860 a ten-hour day was standard in all the craft trades, and already a new standard of eight hours was being timorously suggested.

When we reflect on the temper of the era, this shortening of the work week seems a notable advance. Labor had argued that acceleration of the working pace made a reduction in hours mandatory and that a shorter work day would result in improved health and efficiency of those who toiled. But it was hard to marshal evidence in support of the contention that *employers* would benefit from a sixty-hour week. What won the day was insistence upon the right of the workingman, in a free and democratic society, to have some time for himself—for improvement of his mind and soul or for relaxation. It is to the credit of Americans of a century ago that this argument made sense.

This brief sketch has left unanswered some questions about the status of labor after nearly seventy-five years of our national history. In many respects the results were disappointing. Craft unions were stronger in 1860 than they had ever been. A certain realism, in the best sense of the word, had crept into their endeavor. Objectives were clearer, and the techniques of attaining them had been learned. Yet employees of the factory and domestic systems remained for the most part outside the union movement. On balance immigrants weakened the position of labor and prevented solid and unquestioned gains. It was impossible to strike effectively against an employer who could turn for his unskilled and unspecialized help to an endless supply of job-hungry foreigners.

There were impelling reasons for a struggle to secure union privileges and protection for the whole labor force. The worker's relation to his employer was being depersonalized; consequent upon separation of private morality and business morality, most laborers no longer had the protection of warm, friendly, *personal* relations with the boss. What the owner of a craft shop or small mill would never have countenanced, because of scruples of conscience, the manager of an urban factory thought nothing of. Nor was the increasing use of the corporate form (to be discussed in the next chapter), with increasing divorcement of ownership and control, likely to mitigate the workers' plight. Protection could come from government, but government would be slow to guarantee a climate wherein the toiler could earn his daily bread and a little more without having to pour out the whole of his life doing it. Meantime, labor had to rely on its own efforts.

One series of Congressional acts had already helped labor's cause. The victory of the liberal land forces provided occupational alternatives for some. As we have seen, during the first half century of our history under the Constitution, opportunities in agriculture set a floor to industrial wages. If land for settlement had not been available, many immigrants who came directly to the West would have looked for work in the cities of the East and worsened labor conditions. Those who would escape the hopelessness of life at a bare level of subsistence on an unproductive farm in New England, New York, or Pennsylvania could move to the frontier; or if they could not stand the rigors of pioneering they could settle on improved land short of the frontier. At least they could until about 1840.

After 1840 the "safety-valve of the system" was an unreliable mechanism, as factory workers and common laborers began to constitute a larger proportion of the work force. Factory workers who lived in a manufacturing town were not fitted for agricultural pursuits even if they preferred a sod house to a tenement; and unlike the craftsmen they could not make a living at a trade. Financing a trip to the frontier for self and family became more expensive as the frontier moved further away, and once there an ever more substantial outlay of cash had to be made for land and expenses of initial settlement. That the frontier itself did not attract many working people directly has been conclusively demonstrated; laborers, when they did migrate, went only a short way west to jobs of much the same sort that they had previously held. All this notwithstanding, the West did drain off failing eastern farmers who might have swelled the industrial labor supply and forced wages down, a fact attested to by the vigor with which manufacturers in the old states opposed liberal land laws.

From the end of this period it would be but thirty years until the frontier officially disappeared. Even in 1860 wise leaders foresaw that remaining vestiges of the refuge of space must one day be taken from the laborer. What then would he do to relieve his woe?

Commerce
and Growth

The greatest improvement in the productive powers of labour, and the greater part of the skill, dexterity, and judgment with which it is any where directed, or applied, seem to have been the effects of the division of labour.

ADAM SMITH

The United States in 1790 was in one sense an underdeveloped country. Its population of 3,900,000, of which 700,000 were slaves, was about evenly divided between North and South. Approximately 200,000 people lived west of the Allegheny Mountains, nearly the same number that resided in the twenty-four places listed as urban—i.e., having a population of 2,500 or more. Two cities with a total population of 61,653 fell in the 25,000–50,000 category, and three cities with a total population of 48,182 were in the 10,000–25,000 bracket. An overwhelming 95 per cent of the population was rural.

There were no prospects that the size of the domestic market would soon increase. Although not all urban dwellers were necessarily engaged in market production and not all rural inhabitants were self-sufficient farmers, the preponderantly rural population meant that the domestic market was small and diffused.[1] Moreover, there was little likelihood in 1790 that the foreign market would expand rapidly. Trade with Great Britain in that year was less by a third than it had averaged in the six years before 1774, and commercial policies of other western

---

[1] Cf. Douglass C. North, *The Economic Growth of the United States, 1790 to 1860* (Englewood Cliffs, N.J.: Prentice-Hall, 1961), pp. 17–18.

European countries did not make them exciting prospective customers. What forces could possibly work to get the American economy off dead center?

The growth of the United States would have been slow and painful indeed if the economy had been a closed system. But it was not, of course, and with a little bit of luck, tremendous natural resources, substantial generation of income on foreign account, and rapid .regional specialization the domestic market began to expand. We must now return to a subject touched on ever so briefly in Chapter 8.

Foreign and Domestic Commerce, 1783–1860

THE PATTERN OF FOREIGN TRADE

Risky though the overseas trade had been during the American Revolution, it nevertheless went on briskly and to the great profit of merchants who were not under surveillance by British troops. With the coming of peace in 1783 commerce declined; all foreign traders, but especially the ones with little capital, were adversely affected.

The reason for the dislocation of American foreign trade, particularly during the decade after the Revolution, is not hard to find. Americans, who for so long before the war had operated in the comfortable warmth of the British Empire, now found themselves on the outside looking in. England debated the question of future trade relationships between the new and independent nation and British possessions. Certain English leaders, foreseeing the eventual English decision in favor of free trade, argued that the United States should be allowed to trade with the mother country *and* with the colonies on the old basis of equality. Sterner views prevailed, however, and it was decided that the Navigation Laws should apply to the United States. A few tariff concessions were made on the direct importation into England of goods essential to the welfare of British businessmen, but agricultural products were nearly excluded by high duties. More harmful than these restrictions were the prohibitions placed on United States trade with the colonies, particularly with the British West Indies. To the injury of both the American merchant and the British West Indian planter, England attempted to make Canada the chief source of provisions for the islands. Furthermore, American shipping was excluded from practically all except the direct trade with England. The British merchant marine was to carry goods between the British colonies and England, among the colonies, and between the colonies and the other parts of the world, including the United States.

For a decade the future of American foreign commerce was uncertain. During the 1780s enterprising merchants and sea captains moved to free themselves, at least partially, from English restriction. Time-honored methods of evading laws proscribing American trade with the West Indies were invoked. French, Dutch, and Danish ports in the West Indies were open to the Yankees, and it was easy to re-export goods for sale to the British plantation owners. Haiti and Cuba quickly developed into thriving markets and good sources for sugar. But the "long haul" from the islands to Europe was effectively closed to Americans, and this leg of the triangular trade had been highly profitable. The opening of lucrative new trade with the Far East did not offset, except for big merchants, the loss of commerce within the Empire.

The outbreak of conflict between England and France in 1793 was good news to American merchants and shipbuilders, who, as nationals of the most important neutral nation in the world, would find their goods in great demand. The dollar value of exports and imports surged upward, the tonnage of the merchant marine increasing eightfold in fifteen years. With embargo, nonintercourse, and finally the War of 1812, foreign commerce fell off to practically nothing, only to bound back for three years with the coming of peace in 1815. Americans were especially eager for the manufactures of Europe, and foreigners were just as eager to have our cotton, tobacco, and foodstuffs at fancy prices. But when war-postponed demands had been met, the postwar boom faded.

What happened to the foreign trade of the United States with the return of "normalcy" in 1818? Let us characterize the period 1818–60 with respect to the aggregate of merchandise exports and imports. Then we shall see what commodities entered into the merchandise account and examine the composition of the international balance-of-payments statement.

The growth of foreign trade. A glance at the dollar figures would lead to the inference that merchandise exports and imports went into a decline from late 1818 to about 1829. But these were years of a falling general price level; actually, the physical volume of trade increased a little while the dollar volume was falling. Cotton exports more than doubled in the decade of the 1820s to begin the remarkable upward thrust that was to give this commodity first place among American exports. The prosperity of the early and middle thirties was reflected in large volume and dollar gains in foreign commerce, but the panic of 1837 and the years of uncertainty until 1845 brought reversals. After the mid-forties total foreign trade increased handsomely, especially during the 1850s. In 1860 the total value of merchandise exports and imports neared the $700 million mark, and average yearly figures for 1856–60 were more than three times those for 1815–20. Over this period the percentage gain in merchandise exports and imports of the United States was somewhat greater than that of the United Kingdom, although in 1860 American foreign commerce had a money value scarcely more than a third that of the British.

Commodities dealt in. In our previous discussion of commodities entering into foreign trade we observed that items imported for the express purpose of re-exporting them fall in the broad category of the "re-export" trade. Goods imported for home consumption and those produced at home for export are referred to as "domestic" imports and exports.

From 1807 to 1860 the re-export trade steadily declined in importance. During the Napoleonic Wars re-exports exceeded domestic exports in dollar value, and as long as communication and transportation facilities remained primitive they continued important. Re-exporting consisted largely in bringing to America the products of tropical and subtropical lands and the Far East and re-exporting them to western Europe. There was then a return flow of European manufactured goods, mostly textiles and iron articles, that were passed on to the countries of Latin America and the Far East. After the 1830s the United Kingdom encroached heavily on this indirect trade, as the United States merchant marine handled an ever smaller portion of American commerce. Too, the growing textile output of the United States began to supplant English goods that had once been re-exported. Beginning with the 1840s re-exports to Canada grew to substantial proportions, as Canadian merchants, after overland transportation became cheaper, ordered increasing amounts of goods from merchants in the northeastern United States rather than from overseas. But this increase in Canadian trade did not offset the general decline, and by 1860 re-exports constituted less than 5 per cent of total exports.

What were the major items that Americans bought from foreigners? Clearly the economy at mid-century was still agricultural, for imports were much the same in the 1850s as they had been seventy-five years earlier. Manufactures in finished form constituted from one-half to three-fourths of total imports over the years, amounting to something over a half at the end of the period. The finer textiles—wool, silk, and cotton—made up the biggest single import category, and iron products were about as important as any one of the three leading textiles. Foodstuffs that could not be produced in the United States except at great cost varied from one-fourth to less than a third of the total; then, as now, coffee, tea, sugar, and some alcoholic beverages had to come from exotic lands. It was significant of increasing industrialization that toward 1860 raw materials and semimanufactured goods brought in to be worked up into finished products comprised one-eighth of the imports of the United States.

Products of the land were the leading American exports. We have previously remarked that the South had a tremendous comparative advantage in cotton-growing. About 1815 cotton replaced tobacco as the number one export. It constituted 39 per cent of the value of exports from 1816 to 1820 and reached the astonishing proportion of 63 per cent of total export value in the years 1836–40. The proportion dropped slowly from the early 1840s on but remained well over half until 1860, when it soared to two-thirds as foreign users began to stockpile supplies. As a category, foodstuffs were in second place. Wheat and wheat flour, after the mid-forties, made up more than 10 per cent of our exports, and pork products were next among the foodstuffs. Between 1820 and 1860 manufactures furnished from 10 to 12 per cent of all exports.

As an importer of finished goods and as an exporter of the agricultural

Table 10-1

Balance of International Payments, United States, Any Year

Items	Exports (credits)	Imports (debits)
I. Current account		
A. Merchandise		
B. Invisible items		
1. Shipping services		
2. Travel expenditures		
3. Interest and dividends		
4. Private gifts or public grants		
II. Gold and silver account		
A. Gold and silver movements		
III. Securities account		
A. Long-term corporate and government securities		
B. Short-term securities and bank funds		

products of a temperate zone, the United States found western European countries its chief source of supply and its best customers.[2] Three-fourths of our exports went to Europe; two-thirds of our imports came from there. The United Kingdom dominated the trade, but France grew to be a strong competitor of the United Kingdom by 1860. After 1830 the old British West Indian trade declined because the planters there had exhausted their land, were forced to free their slaves, and were faced with competition from the rest of the West Indies. Increased trade with Canada, Cuba, and the Latin American countries made up for the slackened West Indian trade, and by 1860 these countries were developing even closer relationships with the United States.

The international balance of payments. Like all countries, the United States from its very beginnings found it convenient and necessary to exchange its goods and services for those of other countries. Generally speaking, goods and services bought abroad were paid for with goods and services sold to foreigners. Yet the export-import figures for the years 1815–60 reveal an excess of imports over exports in *most* years.

To explain, it will be helpful to draw up a sample of an international balance-of-payments statement between one country—the United States—and the rest of the world. It is customary to make a three-column form (see above); in one column we put the headings of the three main "accounts"—the

---

[2] England more than any other country drew the United States into the Atlantic Economy. After 1840 the United Kingdom consistently imported 25 per cent of her total imports from the United States and for nearly forty years depended upon the United States for over three-quarters of her cotton supplies. During the first half of the nineteenth century the United Kingdom supplied about 40 per cent of American imports and took between one-third and one-half by value of American exports. See J. Potter, "Atlantic Economy, 1815–1860: The U.S.A. and the Industrial Revolution in Britain," *Studies in the Industrial Revolution* (London: Athlone Press, 1960), pp. 240–41.

current account, the gold and silver account, and the securities account. Under the three headings we classify all "items" that cross international boundaries. In the second column are listed the export figures, and in the third column are listed the import figures. The following characteristics of the international balance-of-payments statement are worth noting.

1. *The total of export (credit) items must equal the total of import (debit) items for any period of time.* Goods and services must be exchanged for goods and services, *or,* if these items do not offset each other, the balance must be made up by gold payments or by borrowing.

2. *Any one "account" may be out of balance as may groups of items within an account.* Centuries ago, trade in goods was preponderantly important, so that attention was focused on the merchandise account. Because the mercantilists felt it desirable to have an excess of merchandise exports over merchandise imports, it became customary to speak of a "favorable balance of trade" when the value of exports exceeded the value of imports. This expression persists in common usage. Whenever we refer to a *balance of trade* we mean only the *merchandise* items, whether capital goods or consumer goods. Whenever we refer to *all* the items in the current account,

Table 10-2

Merchandise Trade: Exports and Imports, 1790–1819 (millions of dollars)

Fiscal year [a]	Exports	Imports	Fiscal year	Exports	Imports
1790	20	24	1805	96	126
1791	19	31	1806	102	137
1792	21	33	1807	108	145
1793	26	33	1808	22	58
1794	33	36	1809	52	61
1795	48	71	1810	67	89
1796	67	83	1811	61	58
1797	57	77	1812	39	79
1798	62	71	1813	28	22
1799	79	81	1814	7	13
1800	71	93	1815	53	85
1801	94	113	1816	82	151
1802	73	78	1817	88	102
1803	56	67	1818	93	127
1804	78	87	1819	70	94

SOURCE: Douglass C. North, "The United States Balance of Payments, 1790–1860," *Trends in the American Economy in the Nineteenth Century* (Princeton: Princeton University Press, 1960), p. 577.

[a] Year beginning October 1 to September 30.

Table 10-3

Calculation of the Balance of Payments, Yearly, 1820–1860 (millions of dollars)

Fiscal year	Merchan-dise trade balance	Specie balance	Service and current items	Interest and dividends	Annual net balance	Capital accounts	Aggre-gate indebted-ness
1820	−4.7		10.2	−4.8	0.7		86.7
1821	0.1	2.4	7.3	−4.8	5.0		81.7
1822	−18.5	7.4	7.2	−4.5	−8.3		90.1
1823	−4.2	1.3	9.8	−5.0	2.0		88.1
1824	−3.2	−1.4	10.4	−4.8	1.0		87.1
1825	0.5	2.6	8.4	−4.8	6.8		80.3
1826	−5.2	−2.2	9.2	−4.5	−2.6		82.9
1827	3.0	−0.1	11.7	−4.6	10.0		72.9
1828	−17.0	0.8	8.9	−4.0	−11.4		84.3
1829	0.3	−2.5	8.2	−4.6	1.5		82.3
1830	9.0	−6.0	9.5	−4.6	7.9		74.9
1831	−23.6	1.7	11.9	−4.1	−14.1		89.0
1832	−15.5	−0.3	13.9	−4.9	−6.8		-95.7
1833	−15.5	−4.5	11.8	−5.3	−13.5		109.2
1834	−8.5	−15.8	11.6	−6.0	−18.0		128.0
1835	−24.3	−6.7	8.0	−7.0	−30.0		158.1
1836	−55.8	−9.1	11.3	−8.7	−62.2		220.3
1837	−21.6	−4.5	12.4	−8.8	−22.6		242.9
1838	6.1	−14.2	12.6	−9.7	−5.3		248.1
1839	−47.4	3.2	8.8	−13.6	−49.1		297.2
1840	23.4	−0.5	19.7	−11.9	30.8		266.4
1841	−13.6	5.0	9.0	−8.0	−7.6	12.0	262.0
1842	1.9	0.7	11.5	−7.9	6.2	12.0	243.8
1843	39.6	−20.8	10.8	−7.3	22.2		221.6
1844	1.1	0.4	9.9	−6.6	4.7		216.8
1845	−9.4	4.5	17.4	−8.7	3.8		213.0
1846	−13.0	0.1	22.2	−8.5	0.8		212.2
1847	29.4	−22.2	27.9	−8.5	26.6	−8.0	193.7
1848	−16.4	9.5	24.2	−11.6	5.7	−8.0	196.0
1849	−6.5	−1.2	27.8	−11.8	8.3	−5.5	193.2
1850	−36.1	2.9	20.2	−11.6	−24.6	−4.3	222.1
1851	−30.3	24.0	15.5	−13.3	−4.1	−3.4	229.6
1852	−48.8	37.2	13.5	−14.9	−13.0	−3.2	245.8
1853	−70.8	23.3	8.0	−16.0	−55.6		301.3
1854	−72.7	34.4	22.7	−19.6	−35.1	−7.0	343.4
1855	−49.2	52.6	6.1	−22.3	−12.9		356.3
1856	−41.6	41.5	12.5	−23.2	−10.7		366.9
1857	−68.5	56.7	10.1	−14.7	−16.4		383.3
1858	−1.9	33.4	6.9	−15.3	23.1		360.2
1859	−51.7	56.5	−7.6	−23.4	−26.2		386.5
1860	−34.2	58.0	8.6	−25.1	7.3		379.2

SOURCE: North, "The United States Balance of Payments, 1790–1860," p. 581.

including both merchandise and the invisible (or service) items, we speak of a favorable or unfavorable *balance on current account.*

In no year of the period 1790–1819 and in only eleven of the forty-one years between 1820 and 1860 did the United States have a favorable balance of *trade.* Usually the years of favorable balance fell in periods of business contraction, when because of falling incomes imports were low and because of deflated prices exports were high.

In drawing conclusions from the treasury figures, we must take into account the likelihood that, especially for the early years, they undervalued the volume of imports and exports. Although there was no special reason to state the value of exports incorrectly, they were not subject to check, as were imports, for duty purposes. But import figures were liable to understatement because of smuggling and undervaluation of merchandise upon declaration. Statistics for the entire period have recently been refined and corrected, but even Professor North's careful estimates of the composition of the international balance of payments involve some errors.[3]

We should remark three different trends in international trade during the period 1812–60.

1. *From 1790 until 1820 the relatively high level of imports was made possible by receipts from shipping services, more than half the excess of imports over exports being made up by the earnings of the American merchant marine.* The rest was made up by mercantile credits, extended to Americans by Europeans, upon which many Americans defaulted during the crisis of 1818–20.

2. *In the period from 1820 to 1849 the balance of trade was unfavorable by more than $200 million.* A slightly larger debit item was interest and dividend payments to foreigners, but this item was largely offset by sums invested by Englishmen, chiefly in American canal and railway ventures. Immigrants, arriving in ever greater numbers in the forties, had to exchange their home currencies for dollars, but Americans traveling abroad spent sufficient money to balance the immigrant currency credit. American shipping came to the rescue with a credit balance so substantial that over $70 million of gold and silver flowed to the United States in the thirty-year period.

3. *The decade of the 1850s was a good one for United States trade.* Economic expansion was phenomenal, and as the incomes of Americans increased they bought more goods from foreigners. Imports exceeded exports by nearly $475 million, and the return to foreign investments was nearly two-fifths this amount. Furthermore, it was fashionable then for Americans to go abroad, their expenditures creating a debit greater than the total of interest and dividend payments made to Europeans. How was the balance made up? Europeans invested heavily in American enterprise during the decade, buying a greater dollar amount of securities than they had in the

---

[3] For the problems encountered in this estimation see North, "The United States Balance of Payments, 1790–1860," pp. 573–627. See also *Historical Statistics of the United States,* pp. 529–66.

quarter-century before. In a final burst of glory the merchant marine earned $108 million. Immigrants converted the currency of their homelands into dollars to the extent of $100 million. But it was gold, coming from the mines of California, that was at once a major force in creating the prosperity of the 1850s and the means of making up the balance of international payments; over $360 million in gold flowed outward during the decade.

To sum up, the United States during the first sixty years of the nineteenth century had a generally unfavorable balance of trade. Exports showed persistent and substantial gains over the period, to be sure, but it was the earnings from shipping and the unilateral transfers of immigrants that tended to balance the *current account* items. Specie tended to flow in until the last ten years, when there was a remarkable outflow. Finally, Europeans made substantial loans to American industrialists, foreign holdings of American securities amounting in 1860 to an estimated $400 million or perhaps one-fifth of total investment in manufacturing and transportation industries.

THE PATTERN OF DOMESTIC TRADE

By 1860 the East or, more specifically, the New England and middle Atlantic states, had achieved about the same relationship to the rest of the United States that England had borne to the colonies a century before. As the nineteenth century went on, eastern manufacturers turned out a growing list of goods to meet the needs of the West and South, and the finer wares still imported into the United States passed through the ports of New York, Boston, Philadelphia, and Baltimore. Meantime, towns located at key points on the western lake and river system became commercial cities. Pittsburgh, Cincinnati, and Louisville were the great ports on the Ohio, and Cleveland, Toledo, and Detroit became major distributing centers on the Lakes. Between 1820 and 1850 Cincinnati had no equal in the western trade, but as the westward movement progressed it appeared that St. Louis and Chicago would be the final rivals for midwestern supremacy.

A century ago her citizens did not doubt that St. Louis, located near the confluence of the Missouri and the Mississippi, would be the principal city of the Midwest, if not of the country. Providentially situated where the trade of the upper Mississippi River terminated and that of the lower river began, St. Louis held a strategic economic position. It was the northern terminus for the large steamboats of the lower river and the southern terminus for the smaller steamboats of the upper river, and it was here that cargoes were unloaded and reloaded for further shipment. There seemed little doubt that the commerce of the Mississippi Valley would continue in a predominantly north-south direction and that it would hinge on St. Louis. Moreover, it appeared that the future physical expansion of the United States would take place with St. Louis, a natural gateway to the West and Southwest, as a base of operations.

St. Louis's hope of primacy disappeared as technological change removed the great obstacle to the development of Chicago. Possessed of facilities for water transportation eastward, Chicago had the problem of tapping the rich territory to the west. The advent of the railroad meant that Chicago, with its more favorable location for east-west rail traffic, would one day break the commercial hold of St. Louis on the upper Mississippi Valley.[4] And as early as 1850, though St. Louisans did not realize it, trade from east to west had surpassed the trade from north to south in volume.

The great east-west intersectional trade was made possible by the opening of the western section of the Erie Canal in 1825, but not until 1832, when the Ohio Canal was completed, did it begin in earnest. After 1835 lumber, grain, and livestock products flowed in an ever increasing stream through Buffalo to the East, where they were consumed or passed on for export. Low ton-mile rates on Mississippi River freight for a time kept western products moving in unabated volume to New Orleans. By 1846, however, Buffalo was handling more wheat and wheat flour than New Orleans. A few years later the Ohio Valley was sending nearly all its grain via the canals, though whiskey and meat products still went preponderantly south. During the 1850s the volume of western products funneling through St. Louis was stable at a high level, but the relative importance of this commerce declined steadily as New Orleans more and more relied on the southern staples for her trade.

---

[4] Cf. Wyatt Winton Belcher, *The Economic Rivalry Between St. Louis and Chicago* (New York: Columbia University Press, 1947).

Life on the Mississippi, so long as the current was with you, seemed idyllic and easy. With horses and cattle for ballast, all you had to do was steer.

Picturesque paddle-wheel river boats made the upstream run possible, increasing the volume of domestic trade in the Midwest.

As late as 1860 New Orleans was the leading export city of the country. New York was second, and the southern ports of Mobile, Charleston, and Savannah followed in that order. The high rank of these southern cities as export centers reflected the economic dependence of the South upon the sale of cotton to foreign countries. But the South also provided, through the great coasting trade, raw materials and food for the industrial Northeast. Cotton for the flourishing textile industry of New England led the list of commodities, but sugar and molasses, naval stores, timber, rice, and tobacco were exchanged in quantity for the manufactured articles of the North. Traffic from the South to the Northwest and West, never as great as the downstream flow, became insignificant in the decade before the Civil War.

Trade between the East and Far West hardly existed before 1848. After the discovery of gold in California the overland commerce swelled, but the difficulties of travel were so fearful that bulky items were shipped by way of Cape Horn; passengers and freight of great value might go via Panama or Nicaragua, but there was no easy route to California. The gold that came back, however, had effects on commerce out of proportion to its value, for by increasing the money supply of the country it stimulated all economic activity, including the great regional exchanges.

THE CHARACTER OF RAW MATERIALS AND THE CURRENTS OF TRADE

In our discussion of early American commerce we have rightly emphasized transportation and the direction of settlement as determinants of both the magnitude and direction of trade. But why was it not possible to eliminate or shorten some of the distances over which goods were carried?

Cotton comes to mind as an example. Since cotton had to be worked up into finished products *somewhere,* why did economic forces not ensure the work be done where the raw materials were grown? How was it possible for New England to lead the way in the manufacture of cotton textiles when it was necessary to transport the raw fiber such long distances?

In answer, let us first set up two classes of raw materials—"pure" and "weight-losing" raw materials. Pure raw materials like fibers and metals lose little weight in the manufacturing process; cotton, for example, loses only 1 or 2 per cent of its weight in most manufacturing. The industry that processes the cotton need not be located near the source of the material; it is as economical to send baled cotton from Memphis to Boston as it is to send finished goods.[5] If Boston has access to capital for investment in manufacturing enterprises and is close to major markets for final products, raw cotton will move from Memphis to Boston for spinning and looming.

Let us consider an example of a "weight-losing" raw material. As the term implies, weight-losing materials lose a large percentage of their weight during manufacture. Fuels for the reduction of ores and for developing power are weight-losing raw materials. It is advantageous for an industry to locate near the source of weight-losing materials, and if several are used in one process an optimum point will be selected.

And now another classification must be considered—"ubiquitous" and "local" materials. The meanings of the terms *ubiquitous* and *local* are self-evident—materials classified as ubiquitous are found everywhere and local materials are found only in particular places. Coal, if we disregard differences among types and qualities, is a ubiquitous material, but anthracite coal and bituminous coal of coking quality are local materials. Therefore, it is not astonishing that the iron industry, until later in the nineteenth century, showed little tendency to concentrate. Satisfactory bog iron and rock ores were found everywhere, and so was weight-losing charcoal for processing ores. Weight-losing and local raw materials strongly influence the location of any industry; industries using pure and ubiquitous materials can locate anywhere. (Occasionally the degree of perishability of materials may be decisive.)

The foregoing is by no means an account of all the influences affecting the location of industry. We shall later consider the influence of the supply of labor and entrepreneurial ability, markets for finished products, "style" considerations in selling the finished product, and so on. We have only shown why it was possible for New England to bring cotton long distances, manufacture it, and sell it profitably without fear of competition from southern mills. Similarly, we have given a reason for the concentration of the iron industry observable by the 1840s—first in eastern Pennsylvania around the anthracite deposits and later in western Pennsylvania about the supplies of coking coal.

Growth and Instability

Our narrative of industrial and commercial development has taken only indirect account of national economic growth and changes in the pace of

---

[5] Under modern conditions of setting rates by classes of commodities it might be more economical, for finished goods are generally subject to higher rates than raw materials.

economic activity. At the risk of redounding previous passages, let us refresh our thinking about the growth of the economy between 1789 and 1860 and then turn to one of the stickiest questions in American economic history: Can we *measure* the performance of the economy from 1789 to 1860?

Our narrative can now be recast in the following simplified outline:

1. The United States of 1789, with its small domestic market and shriveled foreign trade, seemed a poor prospect for satisfactory economic growth.

2. Fortuitously, the outbreak of war between England and France swelled the re-export trade of the United States, at the same time opening a thriving business for American merchant carriers.

3. With the income thus earned, American merchants and shippers increased their demands for certain subsidiary or complementary services such as brokerage, marine insurance, financing, warehousing, and docking. Directly and indirectly shipping and the re-export trade encouraged the urbanization of the Northeast. Between 1790 and 1810 the urban population grew from 5.1 per cent to 7.3 per cent of the total population, most of the increase occurring in the four major ports of New York, Philadelphia, Boston, and Baltimore. As the urban population grew, there was in turn an increased demand for consumer goods, especially food.

4. After 1815 the major independent variable of American development was the cotton trade.[6] With income earned from cotton (and the other traditional staples) southern planters imported luxury goods, purchased the services necessary for marketing their exports, and bought much of the food necessary for the sustenance of themselves and their slaves. Southerners with money to invest were inclined to put their funds into land and the slaves and equipment to work the land, partly because more mundane work had the curse of Cain on it but primarily because the return to investment in plantations was better than the return to alternative employments.

5. Cotton linked the United States to the Atlantic economy, strengthening economic bonds with the United Kingdom in particular. More important, by importing from the Northeast the services necessary for transporting, financing, insuring, and marketing cotton, the South stimulated the further urbanization of the New England and Middle Atlantic states, which increasingly provided the South with manufactured goods. Moreover, the South imported food from the West in increasing amounts, and with the income received the West in turn bought manufactured goods from the Northeast. Thus was established a regional specialization that quickly made the United States a great common market.

6. The industrialization of the Northeast was favorably influenced by a number of circumstances, not the least of which were the substantial accumulated capitals of a wealthy merchant class and the heritage of the English Industrial Revolution. Yet American entrepreneurs were stimulated

---

[6] See Douglass C. North, *The Economic Growth of the United States, 1790 to 1860* (Englewood Cliffs, N.J.: Prentice-Hall, 1961), pp. 66–100.

to technological innovation by the relative dearness and inelasticity of supply of labor.[7]

7. In the early nineteenth century the money wages of unskilled labor in America were from a half to a third higher than they were in England. Good, cheap land, available after 1820 at minimum auction prices of $1.25 per acre, set a floor to money wages. The minimum amount of eighty acres could be bought for $100 and necessary equipment for perhaps another $100. Farmers could have the whole return to the enterprise—rent and profits as well as wages—and as long as the frontier was accessible (at least until the early 1840s), the alternative of movement to the West was open to a large part of the eastern work force.

8. Wage *rates* do not necessarily determine wage *costs*, for labor that is paid high wages may be so productive that its actual cost is lower than that of low-paid labor. But wage costs in America were certainly higher than those in England for the following reasons: (a) the ablest people struck out on their own and moved to the land; (b) American employers often had to incur housing costs by providing dormitories for single girls and tenements for families; (c) the rate of turnover of labor was higher in the United States than in England. Moreover, until past mid-century England was technically superior to the United States in the production of two main products, textiles and metals, so that English labor productivity was probably higher in these industries.

9. Wage differences between America and England were less for skilled than for unskilled occupations. As noted above, the difference in wages for nonskilled labor ranged from a half to a third; skilled labor probably commanded a premium in America of from 15 to 20 per cent.

10. One of the consequences of relatively high-cost American labor was to cause entrepreneurs to move along the technological spectrum from labor-intensive to capital-intensive methods. That is, where American managers thought that a new method promised a reduction in the use of labor, even though it meant some increase in capital, they were encouraged to experiment with the innovation. Some methods, like the new spinning machines, were so much more productive for all the factor inputs that they would have been introduced without regard to wage levels. But the power loom was not so obviously superior for many years after its invention, and its rapid introduction in American manufacture was unquestionably motivated by the saving of labor thus made possible.

11. Relatively high-cost labor not only encouraged the introduction of labor-saving machines but also induced manufacturers in the United States to organize their labor more efficiently. So continuous-process and inter-changeable-parts manufacture was doubtless attempted by a few gifted

---

[7] See H. J. Habakkuk, *American and British Technology in the Nineteenth Century* (Cambridge: Cambridge University Press, 1962), pp. 11–29. Although I have relied heavily on Professor Habakkuk for substantiation of the following argument, some of my conclusions are at variance with his and should not be attributed to him.

entrepreneurs, and once the more perceptive innovators had proved the new methods, others were forced by the competition to adopt them.

12. By the 1820s American manufacturing was highly competitive with European industry in some lines of manufacture; at the same time investment in canal building reached significant proportions, to be followed in a few years by the beginning of railroad investment.

13. Throughout the first fifty years of American history under the Constitution, financing presented few problems. Merchant fortunes were supplemented by long-term loans from England at rates ordinarily not more than 1 per cent higher than rates in England. Short-term loans were readily available from a commercial banking system that was subject only to constraints imposed on it by the first and second Banks of the United States. And as we shall see shortly, manufacturing was further aided and abetted by a tariff of protective significance and by the emergence of benign legal attitudes toward the corporation as a form of business organization.

It is one problem to explain *how* the growth of the economy occurred in the pre–Civil War period. It is another problem altogether to measure this growth, because the economic statistics for these years, at least up to 1840, are almost hopelessly thin. There is a temptation to skip over these difficulties, leaving the student content with a qualitative rather than a quantitative description. Yet here is a good opportunity to demonstrate, by actual example, how the economic historian is compelled to wrestle with a problem that may turn out to be impossible of solution.

The only estimates of national income for the period 1799–1839 are those of Robert F. Martin prepared while he was with the National Industrial Conference Board. The relevant part of Martin's data for these census years

Table 10-4

Realized National Income, Total and per Capita, in Current and Constant Dollars of 1926 Purchasing Power, 1799–1859

Year	Total realized national income, millions of dollars		Per-capita realized national income, dollars	
	Current income	Income adjusted by the cost of living	Current income	Income adjusted by the cost of living
1799	677	1,115	131	216
1809	915	1,441	130	204
1819	876	1,625	93	173
1829	975	2,057	78	164
1839	1,631	3,295	98	198
1849	2,420	5,319	107	235
1859	4,311	9,095	140	296

SOURCE: Robert F. Martin, *National Income in the United States, 1799–1938* (New York: National Industrial Conference Board, 1939).

is shown in Table 10-4. Note that the second column lists income in dollars current in the year cited. But to form a judgment about changes in the welfare of people, we must adjust the national income figures for variations in prices and for increases in population. Thus in the third column income figures are adjusted upward to allow for a falling cost of living, and in the fourth column income for the selected years is divided by the population figures for those years. In the fifth column per-capita income is adjusted for cost-of-living changes.

When these estimates were first published, economic historians were startled by their implications. Even making allowance for possible errors and for the fact that some of the census years were years of depression and others years of prosperity, it appeared that per-capita income of Americans declined steadily between 1799 and 1829. In fact, if we convert Martin's series of private production income per capita to an index (1799 = 100), we have the following result:

	1799	1809	1819	1829	1839
Current dollar series	100	99	71	58	74
Cost-of-living series	100	96	79	77	92

From these data it can only be concluded that for these fifty years (1) output did not increase as rapidly as population, and (2) growth of output was particularly slow during the 1810s and 1820s.

As early as 1952, Simon Kuznets suggested that the Martin series should be discarded.[8] Kuznets, however, did not directly examine Martin's methods but inferred from other evidence that a falling per-capita real income was improbable for the years 1800–40. More recently, Professor William N. Parker and an associate have examined the Martin series in detail, concluding that the Martin estimates are faulty but not going so far as to concur in the Kuznets inference that per-capita real income followed a rising trend from 1800 to 1840.[9]

What in fact was the trend of per-capita income in the United States before 1840? Because the evidence is conflicting no final or positive answer can be given until a more reliable income series is constructed. The orthodox view, while not concurring in the Martin judgment of a decline in income per person, holds that increases in income per head were quite small until

---

[8] Simon Kuznets, "National Income Estimates for the United States Prior to 1870," *Journal of Economic History* (Spring 1952), pp. 115–30.

[9] William N. Parker and Franklee Whartenby, "The Growth of Output Before 1840," in *Trends in the American Economy in the Nineteenth Century* (Princeton: Princeton University Press, 1960), pp. 191–212. Serious students should read this article and the comment by Professor Samuel Rezneck that follows it. Although Parker and Whartenby pretty conclusively demonstrate the statistical deficiencies of the Martin series, the Martin estimates will prove useful as a starting point for the calculations that must one day be done. The first person to undertake a venture often makes mistakes that have to be corrected by those who follow in his footsteps, but those who follow have an easier path because of his pioneering.

the mid-1840s. Professor W. W. Rostow argues that the "take-off" of the American economy began in 1845 and ended in 1860, when the "sustained drive to maturity" began.[10] But Rostow bases his propositions about the stages of economic growth largely on statistical evidence compiled from twentieth-century rather than nineteenth-century experience.

I am inclined to give substantial weight to the calculations of Professor Robert E. Gallman. After reckoning the value of commodity output for the period 1839–99, Gallman infers the magnitude of the gross national product for these years.[11] In the period 1839–59 the average decennial increase in the value of commodity output was a whopping 57 per cent, compared with a low rate of advance (23 per cent) during the Civil War decade (1859–69) and an average rate of increase of 54 per cent per decade over the period 1869–99.[12] If as seems likely, the gross national product grew at a rate not much higher than commodity output, there was probably some acceleration of the rate of growth of per-capita GNP between 1839 and 1899. Nevertheless, the rate of growth in the twenty years preceding the Civil War was astonishingly high. The fact that it was so high in the decade of the 1840s, when industrialization is traditionally supposed to have begun, suggests that growth rates between 1789 and 1839 were possibly greater than have been generally supposed. Indeed, income per capita may have increased by as much as two-thirds over this fifty-year period. Further evidence of rapid growth during the first half century of our national history is furnished by Gallman's estimate that American real gross national product per head in 1839 was only slightly less than one-fifth of what it was in the late 1950s. This ratio is probably larger than the ratio of per-capita world income to per-capita U.S. income in the late 1950s.

The fact that Americans got started on interchangeable-parts and continuous-process manufacture by 1800, plus the fact that the factory system was instituted in the textile industry before 1815, adds credence to the view that American growth was steady at a fairly high rate since the country's beginning under the Constitution. Moreover, there has probably been a tendency to underestimate the effects of canal building during the 1810s and 1820s and railroad construction in the 1830s.[13] The hypothesis that the

---

[10] W. W. Rostow, *The Stages of Economic Growth* (Cambridge: Cambridge University Press, 1961), esp. pp. 7–10 and pp. 36–58.

[11] Robert E. Gallman, "Commodity Output, 1839–1899," *Trends in the American Economy in the Nineteenth Century* (Princeton: Princeton University Press, 1960), pp. 13–67. Gallman takes "commodity output" to be "the sum of value added by agriculture, mining, manufacturing, and construction," and "value added" is "the value of output, at producers' prices, less the value of materials and fuels directly consumed in production, at delivered prices." Estimates do not account for "value added by fishing, forestry, precious-metals mining, nonfarm home manufacturing, and the independent hand trades . . ." Professor Gallman thinks that commodity output may have run 80 per cent (or less) of the gross national product in 1839.

[12] Gallman, p. 16.

[13] There has probably been a contrary tendency to overestimate the consequences of railroad investment in the 1840s.

rate of growth did not jump suddenly in the 1840s, but rather accelerated only slightly between 1790 and 1860, certainly requires verification or refutation. Nevertheless, it is a tenable hypothesis, and if it can be substantiated, there may have to be some revision of the theory of the way growth took place in the United States.

Whatever the rate of growth of the American economy before 1860, it experienced wide oscillations in the pace of activity. There were protracted periods, covering several smaller cycles, of rising and falling prices with consequent effects on business and agricultural activity and upon income distribution among sectors of the economy. From the end of the Revolution until 1815, prices were generally rising and times were good. Between 1816 and 1847 the trend of prices was down, periods of prosperity (except for a nice stretch in the 1830s) were brief, and agriculture suffered. The year 1848 saw the beginning of another upward secular trend of prices that did not culminate until 1873.

Sometimes reinforcing the secular trends and sometimes running counter to them were cyclical fluctuations ranging in duration from several months to several years. In the period from the end of the Revolution to the end of the War of 1812 oscillations were frequent and wide, reflecting the changing fortunes of the European belligerents and the vagaries of international politics. The 1816–47 period contained two crises of great severity, the panics of 1818 and 1837. Each crisis was followed by years of deflation and distress typical of these three decades.[14] Yet the boom of 1834–37, with its rapidly rising incomes, full employment, inflation, and speculation (in land rather than in securities), foreshadowed the recurrent upward surges of activity that would characterize the growth of the economy. In 1843 a long period of prosperity began, marred by a brief crisis in 1854 and a short, nasty depression from 1857 to 1858. These years just preceding the Civil War nevertheless gave evidence of the kind of sustained forward movement of which the economy was capable.

How shall we account for such pronounced swings in output, employment, and prices? Under capitalism, opportunities for profitable investment confront entrepreneurs in clusters. Wars, industrial innovations, and the opening of new agricultural lands and mineral sources recurrently offer such tempting possibilities of pecuniary reward that they lead to capital commitments in excess of immediate demand for finished products. Unless, fortuitously, demand is stimulated, the resulting flow of consumer goods may find takers only at prices yielding returns well below anticipations. The result is a falling off of investment, declining incomes, and unemployment in industry as firms retrench. Before 1860, investment in the transportation industries, and to a lesser extent in housing and manufacturing, repeatedly overshot the mark of profitable demand. Swings in the money supply through creation and destruction of credit by the banking system

---

14 After the contraction of 1837–38 there was a substantial recovery that peaked in 1839 and then disappointingly vanished.

and, after 1848, the stimulus provided by newly mined gold only amplified the fluctuations induced by more fundamental changes.

Pre–Civil War economic statistics are inadequate for detailed elementary analysis. As preparation for further examination, however, we may describe two man-made influences that hastened the economic growth of the United States between 1815 and 1860 and left a permanent mark on the economy.

The Question of Protection

After the peace of 1814 imports of English manufactured goods reached what were from the viewpoint of American businessmen alarming proportions. Before 1814 duties on foreign goods had been set at rates that, although originally intended to protect, in hit-or-miss fashion maximized governmental revenues. Growing protectionist sentiment in the Northeast gained enough support from the West and South to secure passage of the Tariff Act of 1816, which established the philosophy that was to guide framers of the tariff acts of 1824, 1828, 1832–33, 1842, 1846, and 1857.

Ironically, John C. Calhoun was a leading advocate of passage of the tariff of 1816, which levied *ad valorem* duties of from 20 to 25 per cent on most manufactured goods and from 15 to 20 per cent on raw materials. In general the level of duties on manufactures did not at that time prevent the entry of many goods, though cheap cottons were shut out of the home market by specific duties—i.e., duties of so much per yard. Moreover, the tax on raw materials, particularly raw wool, lowered the expansion potential of some domestic industries.

From 1816 until 1832 the protectionist tide rose; cottons, woolens, glass, and iron products received the greatest favors, with raw wool and hemp coming in for their share. Shortly, however, the tariff enthusiasm of Southerners began to abate. They saw that the American market for southern staples, especially cotton, would not soon replace the European market; industrialization simply could not take place fast enough. Meanwhile the "terms of exchange" would run heavily against the South—they would buy dear and sell cheap. Offsetting the defection of the South, however, was the growing tendency of the New England merchant class to align itself with the manufacturers in favor of taxes on imports.

The political shenanigans leading to the high tariff of 1828—The Tariff of Abominations—precipitated agitation in the South and necessitated a compromise but a few years later. In Chapter 7 we mentioned the threat to the Union of the Nullification Ordinance of the South Carolina legislature, passed even after downward revisions in imports had been made in 1832. The Compromise Tariff of 1833 provided that all duties would be reduced to a maximum of 20 per cent *ad valorem* within a decade. But only two months after the 20 per cent maximum level was reached in 1842, the Whigs passed a bill putting rates back to about the protective level of ten years before, and President Tyler, a Southerner, accepted it because he felt it would provide more revenue for the government. With the return of the Democrats to power more moderate tariffs were speedily secured, and the Walker Tariff of 1846 set a precedent to be followed until 1861. The principle of protection of domestic industry was maintained, but the classification of commodities, the removal of specific prohibitive duties, and the introduction of a system of warehousing of imports until duties were paid bespoke a more enlightened and liberal attitude toward tariffs by the United States.[15] The good times of the 1850s and the consequent increase in imports so swelled the revenues from tariffs that the government ran great surpluses. The piling up of cash in treasury vaults led to a general reduction in rates and the placing of many items on the free list. Just before the Civil War it appeared that the United States might join the United Kingdom as a free-trade country. In 1860 tariffs averaged less than 20 per cent of the value of dutiable imports and 15 per cent of the value of all imports, levels that had only moderate protective significance.

It is hard to estimate the effects of tariff legislation on the economy of a country, for strands of causality cannot be separated. All writers on the period are agreed, however, on certain points. First, during the years 1816–32, when the protectionist sentiment was waxing, duties on cheap cottons and woolens reserved the American market to Americans. But finer textiles continued to come in from England, and after 1825, instead of selling coarse textiles to American consumers, England sold textile machinery to United States manufacturers. After 1833 the reduction of import duties lightened the burden on importers and in turn on the American consumer. In the depressed 1840s, as in the twenties, tariffs probably kept industrial output and employment from falling as much as would have been the case in a free market. On the other hand, the high tax on imported raw wool, together with the inferiority of the American product, accounts in large part for the failure of American woolen manufacturing to develop before 1860. In sum, though, American manufactures were stimulated and the dollar value of foreign commerce was reduced by tariffs. Second, the South suffered insofar as tariffs cut American imports and thus the amount of American exports that foreigners, particularly the English, could buy. Southerners were probably bothered also by higher prices of imported implements, hardware, housewares, and cheap clothing for the slaves. But when all is said and done the southern planters were prosperous during the period despite protective tariffs. What people *think* is bad, though, may frequently lead

---

[15] By classifying dutiable articles into a number of schedules, Secretary of the Treasury Walker wished to discriminate among imports according to luxuries, semi-luxuries, necessities, etc. Brandy, for example, was placed in a schedule carrying a 100 per cent duty, whereas most raw materials were in a schedule carrying a 5 per cent duty. Schedule C, the main category, levied an *ad valorem* tax of 30 per cent on iron and other metals, metal manufactures, wool and woolens, and manufactures of leather, paper, glass, and wood. Cotton manufactures, in Schedule D, were taxed at 25 per cent. The warehousing provision enabled importers to keep goods in a government warehouse up to one year without having to pay duties until goods were withdrawn for sale.

to trouble, and the question of the tariff was one of the causes of eventual civil strife.

Of one thing we may be sure: receipts from customs constituted by all odds the most lucrative source of income for the federal government before the Civil War. But to the question "Did tariffs alter the course of early industrial and commercial development?" our reply should be, "Not much," for there is no evidence that tariffs seriously changed the direction of investment. Some industries, like the iron industry, refused to grow up, remaining inefficient infants for a long time. But the *rate* of growth of manufacturing industry was stimulated by tariffs, and the economic progress of the country was thereby hastened.

THE RISE OF CORPORATE ORGANIZATION

We must finally consider the change that was taking place in the legal concept of the business firm—i.e., the change from sole proprietorship and partnership organization to corporate organization. The corporation grew to prominence chiefly because some businesses required more capital than one man or a few men could provide. By 1810 the corporate form was usual for banks, insurance companies, and turnpike companies. We have seen how, in the ensuing decades, canals and railroads could be financed only by tapping various sources of funds, for such projects were far beyond the means of one man or several. It was necessary to attract funds for the transportation companies from small merchants and professional men along proposed routes and from English capitalists thousands of miles away. Indeed, to promote building at a politically acceptable rate, governmental units before 1869 contributed more capital for canal and railroad construction than did private interests.

The corporation, a legal entity with privileges distinct from the people associated with it, evolved over the centuries of the growth of Western civilization. In England it had two major lines of development. Municipalities and universities were established under corporate charters granted by the sovereign, and the great trading companies, formed for the purpose of exploiting foreign lands, were organized as "joint-stock" associations that borrowed many of the features of the corporation.

So the development of the corporation was in reality the transformation of an instrument of communal service to accommodate the demands of a new industrial age. It is almost a convention of economic historiography to begin the corporate cycle with Chief Justice Marshall's *Dartmouth College* opinion, reading into it the legal foundation of modern capitalism. It is true that Marshall implied as much when he made Dartmouth's royal charter a contract between the college and New Hampshire and, as such, beyond the constitutional power of that state to repeal or amend. Nevertheless, he only implied it; his explicit references concerned only municipal bodies and private charities. It is in Justice Joseph Story's concurring opinion that we find the principle extended to business enterprises. Contemporary opin-

The Wall Street panic of 1857 drove alarmed speculators into heated sidewalk conversations, fed by roving newsboys and by word of mouth with news of fresh disasters.

ion, both friendly and hostile, recognized Story's analysis as novel and significant.

This creative revisionism, as a few historians have noted, made a radical change in traditional analysis. The mere fact that public authority granted a charter meant the corporation had, in some sense, a "public" purpose; taken on its face, this characteristic suggested ability of the chartering authority to regulate, revise, or even revoke the privilege it had granted. But Story discarded any purpose and substituted property as a starting point, achieving a twofold division in result—on the one hand, private corporations holding private property and, on the other, public corporations charged with government or administration. One group the state could regulate without restraint; the other it could approach only with the deference required by vested right and private interest.

An equally significant development was Story's engrafting the ancient law of trusts on the emerging form of the business enterprise. Here the consequence was a separation of ownership and control. Under this division the capital of a corporation became a trust fund for the successive benefit of creditors and stockholders, the directors became trustees, and the corporation itself increasingly assumed a character and personality distinct from the persons who had provided its resources. The end result was an ideal apparatus of capital formation involving at one and the same time permanent contributions of resources and transferable, judicially protected claims.

As it first appeared in the United States, the corporation lacked many of its present-day characteristics. Charters were granted by special acts of legislatures, and the question of the liability of stockholders was far from settled. The corporation nevertheless had a number of advantages over the sole proprietorship and the partnership, and its legal status came to be more definite than that of the joint-stock company. Of its unquestioned advantages the most notable, in addition to the obvious one of attracting greater numbers of investors, were permanence and flexibility. The partnership and sole proprietorship have one inescapable drawback: if one partner or the proprietor dies, the business is dissolved. The business can go on, of course, under a new partnership or proprietorship, but continuity of operation is contingent upon the lives of particular individuals. Furthermore, a partnership is dissolved when a partner sells his interest. But the shares of a corporation can be transferred, and investors, big and little, can enter and leave the business without destroying the structure of the corporation, all the while fitting their investment contribution to their means.

Early corporations did not have certain advantages that corporations have today. Take the question of liability, for example. What the liability of the shareholders for the debts of the corporation should be was a matter not easily determined. Stockholders of the English joint-stock companies had finally come to assume "double liability"—i.e., the stockholder was liable to the extent of his investment plus a like amount—and some states experimented with charters specifying either double liability or unlimited liability. After 1830, however, statutes were passed in the various states providing for limited liability, and by 1860 this principle was generally accepted. Under limited liability stockholders could lose, upon failure of a corporation, only the money they had put into a venture and nothing besides.

The early requirement that incorporators of banks, insurance companies, canals, and railroads obtain their charters by special act of a state legislature was not always a disadvantage. For those with political connections it involved little uncertainty and expense, and there was always the possibility of getting a charter with exceptionally liberal provisions. However, the politically unfavored could spend years futilely lobbying for corporate charters. As early as 1800 there was agitation on the part of those who looked on incorporation by special act as "undemocratic" to secure "general" acts of incorporation—i.e., laws making it possible for any group, provided it observed and met prescribed regulations and requirements, to obtain a charter. Others, fearful of the too rapid spread of the corporation if their elected representatives did not pass on *each* application for charter, opposed general acts. In 1837 Connecticut passed the first general act that made incorporation a right of anyone.[16] From that date on, *permissive* general acts were gradually put on the statute books of most of the chief manufacturing states, and before 1861 the constitutions of thirteen states *required* incorporation under general laws. In those states where permissive legislation had been enacted, incorporators continued to obtain special charters because they could thereby secure more liberal provisions than they could get under general laws.

After 1837 mercantile and manufacturing firms organized as corporations with growing frequency. Especially during the 1850s was there a rapid increase in the number of manufacturing corporations. *Yet in 1860 the greater part of resources devoted to manufacturing was under the control of proprietorships and partnerships.* A rolling mill of the most modern design could then be built for $150,000, and the largest textile factory did not require an investment beyond the means of a single very wealthy man. The course of commerce and industry would not have been much changed before 1860 if the privilege of incorporation had been given only to financial and transportation firms. Contemporary observers were nonetheless aware that the corporate form would be inseparable from the enterprise of the future, for bigness obviously lay in the future. For technical reasons, if for no other, the size of the firm had to become larger, and, as the railroad companies had already demonstrated, enterprisers had to choose the corporate type of business organization when huge capital outlays were required.

---

[16] In 1811 New York had passed a law that permitted incorporation, without special act, of certain manufacturing concerns with capitalizations of under $100,000.

Part Three:

1861–1920

The Civil War was the great American tragedy. As in any tragedy, the players were enmeshed in a web spun of fortuitous circumstance and human weakness; but transcending coincidence and foible were the inexorable forces of doom that had been gathering more than a hundred years. For the conflict between North and South began before the American Revolution (some say it began with the *English* Civil War) and was forebodingly apparent in the Constitutional Convention that met in 1787. In one sense the constitutional crisis that led to Civil War was simply a final terrible outcome of the divisions that separated American leaders during the days of the Confederation.

The Civil War settled only a constitutional question—the power of the federal government to coerce the states. The haunting tragedy of the war lay not so much in the death and disfigurement of more than a million Americans as in the legacy of injustice it bequeathed. Landless emancipation, which left Negroes without an independent source of livelihood and planters without compensation for the loss of their chattels (the chief form of capital in southern agriculture), was a stupid bit of business. Reconstruction perpetuated the cruelty and stupidity; for as we have observed, the institution of slavery was by no means about "to fall of its own weight," and the vindictive horrors perpetrated on the South only made desperate problems insoluble.

Except for those with a particular interest in the economics of war, the four-year period of conflict has had little attraction for economic historians. The outcome of the war was what knowledgeable observers would have predicted. The North was clearly superior to the South in every major category of economic resource. In 1860 the population of the North was twenty-two million compared with nine million, more than a third of them slaves, in the South. Perhaps 90 per cent of the country's manufacturing capacity was located in the North, and a similar percentage of the skilled work force lived there. Moreover, in the specific business of providing armaments, the South was hopelessly outweighed; V. S. Clark has remarked that in 1861 the only important engineering works in the Confederacy were at Richmond, and southern emergency efforts to produce war materiel were limited and all too quickly undone by invading troops. The northern railway net was not only substantially larger but much better designed for direct connection of major centers. Only in the number of farm units was the South comparable to the North, but southern agriculture was not nearly as productive of food as northern agriculture.

It has long been widely accepted that the Civil War provided little stimulus to innovation, North *or* South, in manufacturing processes. In some industries northern production was of course accelerated by surging demand for war materials, and some manufactures, notably machine tools, steam engines, photographic equipment, and glass, benefited from technological improvement. But no epoch-making innovations occurred during the war, and even among the military only United States naval officers showed any disposition to try new weapons and introduce new devices.

The question still remains whether the Civil War accelerated the industrialization of the United States. The weight of opinion among American historians is that it did. The fact remains, as Professor Thomas C. Cochran has recently been at pains to show, that the rate of growth of the American economy slowed perceptibly during the decade of the 1860s.[1] The evidence is clear that the rate of increase of manufacturing production was lower between 1859 and 1869 than in either of the two decades that preceded these years or the two decades that followed them, and most of the other economic indicators moved sympathetically. Yet as Stephen Salsbury has argued, it is by no means clear that the postwar performance of the American economy, characterized by spectacular growth in some industries, was not stimulated by changes brought by the Civil War.[2]

There is much to be said for both points of view. During the Civil War the northern states certainly experienced an economic euphoria in sharp contrast to the dreary lot of the Confederacy. Northern farmers, who replaced hands gone to war with new-fangled machinery long since proved in practical application, increased their own productivity tremendously. After the first shock of disrupted trade with the South had passed, northern merchants and tradesmen prospered directly and indirectly in the business of provisioning and outfitting troops. Nor is there any question that for four years some kinds of

---

[1] Thomas C. Cochran, "Did the Civil War Retard Industrialization?" *Mississippi Valley Historical Review*, XLVIII (September 1961), 197–210.
[2] Stephen Salsbury, "The Effect of the Civil War on American Industrial Development," *The Economic Impact of the American Civil War*, Ralph Andreano, ed. (Cambridge: Schenkman, 1962), pp. 161–70. Professor Cochran's article is reprinted in this volume, and a statistical supplement makes relevant data available to those interested in this controversy.

industrial output increased rapidly and with it the real incomes of entrepreneurs who were smart enough and unscrupulous enough to seize the opportunities for profits. Many of the élite of late nineteenth-century businessmen made their fortunes in the Civil War.

It is probably true, though, that 1860 approximately marked the dividing line between a long swing of exuberant economic activity and another long swing of dampened economic activity, postponed somewhat by the advent of war. At least two impellents to economic growth, railroad construction and cotton-textile manufacture, were severely restricted by the war. Wage earners suffered a drop in real income, as prices rose by nearly 75 per cent while wages rose by less than half that amount. And of course the South ceased to be a part of the American common market during the war and only slowly made its way back into something like full participation afterward.

Natura non facit saltum reads the motto on the title page of Alfred Marshall's famed *Principles of Economics*. Nature does not move by leaps and bounds! Nor do economies, much as we'd like to think they do. In the fifteen years before the Civil War the American economic machine did not "take off," to use Professor Rostow's colorful figure, any more than it had been taking off during the preceding half century. Nor did the war seriously increase or retard industrialization and growth. Variance in annual rates of growth of the nineteenth-century economy was not nearly as great as we were once led to believe. Persistent, fundamental forces were at work to forge the economic system, to give it size and vitality, and not even the catastrophe of internecine strife could greatly affect the outcome.

Agriculture

Comes of Age

. . . Any person who is the head of a family, or who has arrived at the age of twenty-one years, and is a citizen of the United States, or who shall have filed his declaration of intention to become such . . . and who has never borne arms against the United States Government or given aid and comfort to its enemies, shall, from and after the first January, eighteen hundred and sixty-three, be entitled to enter one quarter section or a less quantity of unappropriated public lands . . .

THE HOMESTEAD ACT OF MAY 20, 1862

The Second Phase
of the Westward Movement

LAND POLICY TO 1920

Congress passed the Homestead Act of 1862 as the frontier line approached the hundredth meridian. First-class land still remained in western Iowa and western Minnesota and in the eastern parts of Kansas, Nebraska, and the Dakotas, but it was soon taken up. Most of the unclaimed land then lay west of the hundredth meridian, either in the Great Plains, an area of light annual precipitation, or in the vast mountain regions.

In both the plains and the mountains the 160-acre homestead of the act was impractical economically, for the land was only suitable for the production of livestock, which require much larger acreages. Moreover, mining companies and land speculators wanted to expand their holdings with as little outlay as possible. At the behest of special-interest groups in the West, Congress passed four principal land acts.

1. *The Timber-Culture Act of 1873.* This law, ostensibly passed to encourage the growth of timber in arid regions, made available 160 acres of free land to anyone who would agree to plant trees on 40 acres of it.
2. *The Desert Land Act of 1877.* By the terms of this law 640 acres at $1.25 an acre could be purchased by anyone who would agree to irrigate the land within three years. (The serious defect of the act was that there were no clearly defined stipulations as to what constituted irrigation.)
3. *The Timber and Stone Act of 1878.* This statute provided for the sale at $2.50 an acre of valuable timber and stone lands in Nevada, California, Oregon, and Washington.
4. *The Timber Cutting Act of 1878.* This law authorized the citizens of certain specified areas to cut trees on government lands without charge. There was a stipulation that the timber should be used for agricultural, mining, and domestic building purposes.

There were other ways of transferring public lands into private hands, including purchase at public auction under the Pre-emption Act, which continued in force until 1891. Furthermore, huge acreages granted by the government as subsidies to the western railroads and to the states for various purposes were in turn sold to settlers.[1] Nearly 100,000,000 acres from the Indian territories were opened for purchase by the Dawes Act of 1887 and by subsequent measures.

Under the administration of Grover Cleveland, the first steps were taken to tighten up on the disposition of public lands. In a single bill, the General Revision Act of 1891, several loopholes were closed. The Pre-emption Act was repealed, and the Desert Land Act of 1877 was amended by inserting definite provisions regarding the irrigation of land secured under this law. The Timber Cutting Act of 1878 was repealed, removing from the books one of the most flagrantly abused of all the land laws. Finally, the President was authorized by the 1891 act to set aside forest preserves, the first step in the conservation movement that was shortly to gain general support.

The Homestead Act was modified after the turn of the century to enable settlers to obtain farms of economic size. After 1904 a whole section could be homesteaded in western Nebraska. The Enlarged Homestead Act of a few years later made it possible to obtain, free, a half-section in many areas. Still later, residence requirements were reduced to three years, and in 1916 the Stock-Raising Homestead Act allowed the homesteading of 640 acres of land suitable only for grazing purposes.

From the findings of a commission that reported to President Theodore Roosevelt on the pre-1904 disposition of public lands, we may take data for a recapitulation of United States land policy. The total public domain

---

[1] As late as 1891 an individual could buy, at one time, a maximum of 1,120 acres under the public land acts. Unlimited amounts of land could be purchased from railroad companies and from states at higher, though still nominal, prices.

in the United States from 1789 to 1904 contained 1,441,000,000 acres. Of this total 278,000,000 acres were acquired by individuals through cash purchase and 273,000,000 acres were granted to states and railroads. Lands acquired by or available to individuals free (mostly via the Homestead Act) amounted to 147,000,000 acres. The rest of the public domain, aside from miscellaneous grants, was either reserved to the government (209,000,000 acres) or unappropriated (474,000,000 acres). Between 1862 and 1904, acres homesteaded exceeded cash sales by the government to individuals. If, however, we count purchases from railroads and states, ultimate holders of land bought twice as much between 1862 and 1904 as they obtained free.

After 1904 United States land policy became more prudent, but by that time nearly all the good agricultural land, most of the first-rate mineral land, and much of the timberland close to markets had been disposed of. Between 1904 and 1920 about 100,000,000 acres of land was homesteaded in the dry and mountainous country. During this same short period the government reserved about 175,000,000 acres. Of the original public domain, 200,000,000 acres of land yet to be disposed of were "vacant" in 1920.

The outstanding feature of American land policy was the rapidity with which the valuable agricultural, mineral, and timberlands were put into private hands. During the nineteenth century the goal of making a piece of ground available to anyone who wanted it was largely fulfilled. In the process of achieving this goal great tracts of land fell into the hands of corporations and wealthy individuals. In the case of railroad grants, disposal of land to powerful business interests was the consequence of a considered public policy. Large grants to the states for educational purposes could be justified, even though the politically favored often purchased them advantageously. But much good land was obtained fraudulently—by mining and lumber companies and by speculators. Aided by lax administration of the land laws, large operators could persuade individuals to make a homestead entry or a purchase at minimum prices and then transfer title for a song. With the connivance of bribed land officials, entries were made for people who did not exist. Some chiseling was inevitable, however, and though the injustice of it rankles, it is not on a basis of fairness to individuals that we can decide whether American land policy was good or bad.

The great and lasting evil resulting from rapid distribution of the public domain was that this policy laid the groundwork for the modern agricultural problem. All sorts and conditions of men settled on the land. The less capable ran into difficulties, lost their holdings, and became either tenants or agricultural laborers. The new West early began to spew forth its commercial crops at such a rate that they could not be taken from the market at prices that covered the costs of most producers. Finally, the apparent inexhaustibility of the land supply led to farm practices that permanently damaged the soils of certain well-defined areas.

It is easy, in the 1960s, to look back on bad practices and view them with righteous indignation. Yet we must never forget, either in this connection or in others, that a chief cause of America's present greatness has been its rapid, vigorous growth. If at times this expansion has been carried out too quickly, it has probably been the price that had to be paid for progress at a rate acceptable to Americans.

Within thirty years after 1860, the area that lay between the frontier line of that year and the West coast was completely overrun, and a clearly marked frontier no longer existed. The region was not completely settled by 1890; there were great islands of land as yet unclaimed, and not until the eve of World War I was all the good land gone. But after 1890 westward settlement was essentially a filling in.

The final major thrust to the West was spearheaded by two occupational groups, the miners and the cattlemen, who gave direction and pace to the movement. For more than ten years after the discovery of gold in California, the Great Plains and the western mountains were only barriers to be crossed by those who sought their fortune in California or Oregon. In 1859 gold was discovered near Pikes Peak in Colorado, and a rush to this area followed at once. Simultaneously the famed Comstock Lode of silver was discovered in western Nevada. The gold boom in Colorado tapered off shortly only to be renewed with the finding of rich silver deposits there.[2] These fabulously successful operations stimulated prospecting all over the West. Into the territory from which Idaho, Arizona, and New Mexico were later carved and into western Montana flocked men who hoped to strike it rich. The last great rush was to the Black Hills of South Dakota, where Indian troubles flared as white men overran the reservations.

These sharp, quick moves into widely separated districts gave impetus to the settlement of the last frontier. In the wake of the miners came the first businessmen, artisans, and early-day professional men to furnish goods and services; not far behind came small numbers of farmers and ranchers to grow food and livestock in the limited valley areas that surrounded the mining towns. The opening-up process was overlaid with a spirit of adventure and a novel standard of moral values that helped make the West a genuinely new area in America.

After the Civil War there developed in the Great Plains the range-cattle industry, as important to this region as mining was to the territory just west of it. Even before the war some Texas cattle had been sent to northern markets, but from the middle sixties on, in response to high prices, beef animals moved in ever increasing numbers to the northeast. Since there were no transportation facilities, the cattle were driven overland in great herds from Texas to the nearest railway point from which shipment could

---

[2] The output of silver was so great in the next few years that by the middle seventies the world price of silver began to fall rapidly, a fact that was to have important economic and political repercussions.

be made to the urban centers. At first the terminal point of the drives was Sedalia, Missouri, but as soon as the rails reached into Kansas a much easier journey was possible to Abilene and Dodge City. Near these towns in Kansas and to the northwest cattle were fattened on the natural grasslands and sent to Kansas City, Omaha, and Chicago.

For twenty years after the Civil War the range-cattle industry flourished. It reached its peak around 1885 and fell off rapidly in the late eighties, but not before it created cattle kings from Texas to Montana whose wealth would dominate the West for generations.[3] The railroads made possible the growth of this business, and they were also instrumental in putting an end to it; for they enabled the land-seekers from the East to move with little difficulty into the open range and by increasing the number of shipping points decentralize cattle operations. Newly invented barbed wire made it possible for the farmer to fence off his property, and eventually the long drives were effectively disrupted. Cattle-raising was henceforth to be done on ranches, and other ways of getting the animals to market would be used.

Whatever the importance of miner and cattleman as path-breakers, the abiding economic pattern of the West was set by the family that grabbed a piece of ground. Most of the participants in the final opening of new land came from places that but a few years before had been the object of settlement. People who moved into Kansas, Nebraska, and the Dakotas, and later into Montana and Colorado, more often than not came but a little way. They might have settled previously in Missouri or Iowa, Minnesota or Wisconsin, Indiana or Illinois. Or they might have been the sons and daughters of the pioneers of a previous generation. It was not uncommon for settlers to move from place to place within one of the new states. No matter how bitter previous pioneer experiences had been nor how drab and unrewarding the life on virgin land, there persisted always the hope of better times if only new soil could be broken farther west. Joining the restless movement of people already in the West was a continuing stream of migrants from the old East and from abroad, but these newcomers were usually content to cultivate more intensively land already broken and let experienced pioneers serve as a vanguard.

PRINCIPAL NEW AGRICULTURAL AREAS

During the period under consideration areas of major crops were marked off. The Midwest became the center of food and feed production, though an ever extending agriculture knew no sectional bounds. (See map, p. 256.)

The wheat and corn belts. To the north, in western Minnesota and the Dakotas, spring wheat gained an early lead as the chief bread grain.

---

[3] See Lewis Atherton, *The Cattle Kings* (Bloomington: Indiana University Press, 1961). Scions of wealthy eastern families like Richard Trimble and Teddy Roosevelt could not resist the West, but the men who, starting from scratch, made fabulous successes were for the most part flat-headed country boys from the Midwest and South or cowboys only a few years away from the hard-drinking, roistering life of Newton or Dodge City.

Wheat-harvesting in South Dakota as shown in this old drawing (1887) suggests the scale to which American commercial agriculture had grown and the kind of innovation that was raising productivity on the farm.

Winter wheat cultivation spread from southern Illinois across southern Iowa and Missouri into southern Nebraska, Kansas, and Oklahoma. Sandwiched between the spring wheat belt to the north and the winter wheat belt to the south was the corn belt of Indiana, Illinois, Iowa, and eastern Nebraska. Other grains—oats, barley, and rye—were grown, but their production could not compare with that of wheat and corn. Between 1860 and 1915 annual corn production increased from 800,000,000 to nearly 3,000,000,000 bushels. In the same period the yearly output of wheat increased from 173,000,000 to a little over 1,000,000,000 bushels.[4]

Cotton. From 1860 to 1914 cotton production, with large annual variations in output, approximately quadrupled. By 1870 cotton had recovered from the disruption of the Civil War, and the trend from then on was persistently upward. The 1914 crop reached a new high of over 16,000,000 bales, total acreage harvested exceeding 35,500,000 acres. During the period the pre-eminence of the cotton states east of the Mississippi River was beginning to disappear. By 1900 Texas was first in cotton production, harvesting in that year a crop equal in size to the production of the entire South just before the Civil War.

---

[4] For detailed production statistics see *Historical Statistics of the United States, Colonial Times to 1957.* For figures on corn and wheat production, see pp. 296–97 of this publication.

Tobacco. While cotton was moving westward, tobacco firmly established itself as the second crop of the old South. Like cotton, tobacco was hard hit during the 1860s. By 1880 total annual production recovered to something less than half a billion pounds, and by 1910 output doubled to a billion pounds. The old tobacco states of Maryland and Virginia gave way to Kentucky, Tennessee, and North Carolina, with Kentucky the chief producer to the end of World War I. Even the smallest operators in the border states cultivated some tobacco, and in the mid-South it increasingly became the important cash crop.

Milk and milk products. Dairying, too, moved westward to form a "belt." Farmers in New England and New York had specialized in dairy products for urban markets as western competition forced down prices of cereal grains. Similarly, as the wheat and corn belts began to take shape, farmers in states around the Great Lakes found it profitable to produce less cereals and more milk products for the growing cities nearby. The soil and climate of central and southern Michigan, Wisconsin, northeastern Iowa, and large parts of Minnesota were ideal for the growth of hay and forage, and the Scandinavians, Germans, and eastern Europeans who settled there were disposed to carry on a type of agriculture with which they were familiar.

Fruits and vegetables. Farmers strategically located with respect to the cities of the northeast specialized early in the production of fruits and vege-

Farming: Major sections for cash crops follow these approximate specializations (although boundaries between one section and the next do change and many crops are grown within various belts).

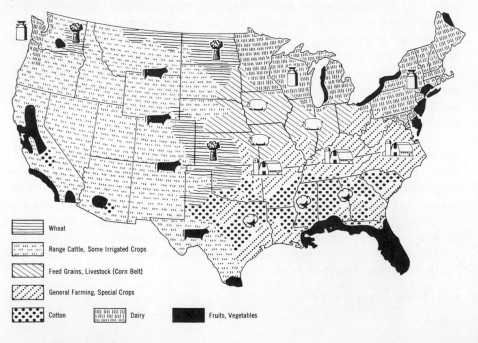

Wheat

Range Cattle, Some Irrigated Crops

Feed Grains, Livestock (Corn Belt)

General Farming, Special Crops

Cotton Dairy Fruits, Vegetables

tables. As the center of population shifted westward, this kind of specialization spread. Specific local advantages of soil, climate, and market helped innumerable small areas become famous for a particular product. In places favored with fertile soil and warm climate it was possible to produce for year-round consumption for people who lived in the North. With the introduction of the refrigerated railroad car in the late 1880s, California began a rise to a position of importance in American agriculture. Florida and the warmer states of the South entered somewhat later into cultivation of fruits and vegetables and by 1920 were established as competitors of California for the eastern markets.

Growth and Instability in American Agriculture

TECHNOLOGICAL CHANGE IN AGRICULTURE

Technological change in agriculture comes about in two ways, through mechanization and through the application of the discoveries of pure science. Mechanization and scientific applications are not entirely independent of each other; scientific discovery may affect the invention of machines, and a certain level of mechanical development must be attained before some scientific applications can be made. Nevertheless, the classification is useful in helping us to analyze the troubles that have lately beset the American farmer.

In the world history of agriculture, machines have ordinarily been introduced where population is thin and labor scarce, for machines are generally labor-saving; they enable a man to cultivate more ground, to work more extensively. Scientific applications are more likely where population is heavy and land relatively scarce, because they permit more intensive cultivation and help a given amount of land to higher production.

Machines may have both a direct and an indirect effect upon farm output. They enable the farmer to do some things better and faster than he could do them without their aid. They also enable him to do some things he could not otherwise do at all. These are direct effects. Indirectly, machines provide rapid and dependable means of transporting products to market and refrigeration facilities that make possible long-distance marketing. A secondary, though not unimportant, indirect effect of machine innovation may be the transfer of processing from the farm to a separate business establishment as, for example, in butter and cheese manufacture.

The physical and biological sciences can aid the farmer in three ways—by improving the soil, by developing better plants and animals, and by destroying the natural enemies of crops and livestock. It is possible to restore or even increase soil fertility by the use of fertilizers and by the introduction of restorative crops. Moreover, the scientist has discovered new crops more suitable to particular soils than the crops previously grown. He has also developed varieties and breeds of plants and animals especially suited to particular soils and climates and, through the application of genetic principles, has greatly increased the productivity of nearly everything that grows. By the elimination or control of diseases and insect pests, much of the uncertainty that was formerly an inescapable part of farming has been removed.

Mechanization and the application of scientific discovery are simply ways of applying capital to land, increasing the productivity of the land and of him who tends it. It is interesting to observe that machines, when first introduced, may increase output per man without increasing output per acre or per plant or per animal. This is simply a way of saying that machinery may have the first effect of bringing about a more *extensive* cultivation of available land. But machines eventually raise the amount of product per acre. For example, they enable work to be done more quickly at the crucial harvest time and thus help to avoid loss through damage from the elements. It goes without saying that the development of bigger, better, and healthier plants and animals adds to output per unit of land.

Mechanization. As regards mechanization there have been three more or less clearly distinguishable periods overlapping each other. The first was one of basic invention running from about 1830 to 1880. The second, covering the half-century from 1860 to 1910, was the period of extensive use of machines dependent upon animal power. The third was the period beginning about 1900 and continuing into the present, the period of innovation of power-driven machinery, typified by the rapid introduction of the gasoline engine.

Until the 1830s grains were invariably harvested with hand tools. The sickle and, in some areas, the cradle were employed in harvesting small grains. The most significant of the many agricultural inventions in the years before the Civil War was the mechanical reaper. By 1830 Cyrus McCormick had built a working reaper, but Obed Hussey secured the first reaper patent on December 31, 1833. Moving his main implement plant to Chicago in 1848, McCormick was strategically located to capture a large share of the reaper market, though not without competition from other smart innovators. Scarcely less important, if less impressive, were improvements in that prosaic instrument, the plow. Beginning in 1819 with Jethro Woods's perfecting of a cast-iron plow with replaceable parts, new types and patterns developed by 1850. But cast-iron plows generated too much friction in the tough prairie soils of the Midwest, nor would they polish or scour. A solution to the problem lay in the invention of a steel plow; by 1857 John Deere was producing 10,000 steel plows annually at his plant in Moline, Illinois. Seed drills, cultivators, mowers, rakes, and threshing machines were in common use before 1860.

These newly invented farm implements effected a surprisingly small saving of labor, reapers of the 1850s reducing by only about one-third the number of men required for harvesting. But wheat prices were good from 1853 on and harvest hands cost a dollar a day; by 1860 80,000 reapers had

High horsepower almost became a logistical problem before the advent of steam- and gasoline-powered tractors, as this scene indicates. Here a California family gathers proudly around, on, and in its precious possession, a combine.

been sold,[5] and further impetus was given their adoption by the manpower shortages of the Civil War. Also, steady improvements in machinery, as, for example, the various attachments and gadgets devised for harvesting machinery, increased their usefulness. Thus, early reapers threw the cut grain onto a platform from which it was raked by hand. An improvement was the addition to the machine of a mechanical raker that raked the grain from the platform and dropped it to the ground in sheaves that were then bound by hand. In a further improvement, the Marsh harvester, which came into use in the middle sixties, enabled two or three men to ride on the platform and bind grain as it was raked.

Finally came the binding mechanisms. The first binders, manufactured in the seventies, used wire that was dangerous to the harvest hands; moreover, it often broke into small pieces that sometimes became mixed with the threshed grain. A Marsh-type harvester, with the attachment of John Appleby's twine binder, was sold in the 1880s as the Deering harvester and quickly outstripped its rivals. The combined harvester-thresher or "combine," which had developed over many decades, came into use in the 1880s

[5] Paul W. Gates, *The Farmer's Age: Agriculture, 1815–1860* (New York: Holt, Rinehart and Winston, 1960), p. 287.

in dry, level wheat-growing regions. Late-century combines used a steam engine to power the thresher, but 30 or 40 horses had to pull the huge outfits.

By 1900 the list of farm implements was almost as various as it is today; the gang plow, the spring-tooth harrow, the disc harrow, and the lister were well known. Specialized equipment, from corn binders to fertilizer spreaders, was on the market. Total animal power available on farms in the United States had reached something over 18,500,000 horsepower, roughly three times what it had been in 1850. Steam engines accounted for about 3,500,000 additional available horsepower. It is a curious fact, however, that horsepower available *per agricultural worker* in 1900 was only 2.2 compared with 1.8 per worker in 1850; both the number of workers and animal power had about trebled in the half-century.[6]

About 1905 the gasoline tractor was introduced, and by the outbreak of World War I it was apparent that tractors would one day supersede draft horses. In 1920 there were only a quarter of a million tractors on farms, but the number was to increase phenomenally from then on. In addition, "power on the farm" would include trucks and automobiles, and, with electrification, fractional horsepower motors.

Applications of science. Before 1920 mechanization was more important in the development of agriculture than applications of pure science. Not until 1890 or thereabouts was there a general awareness of the importance of the contributions of the sciences. "Book farming" was derided by the rank and file throughout the nineteenth century, and only the well-to-do and those pressed by rapidly deteriorating soils were serious about it.

Despite the general lack of interest in scientific developments, scientific improvements were made during the nineteenth century. Many modern animal breeds had been imported before 1860, and after the Civil War the improvement of these breeds went on apace. Plant importations, mutations, and natural hybridizations were continually changing the characteristics of plants, and farmers began to select their seed carefully. Standard fungicides and insecticides were developed and came slowly into general use. By 1890 much was known about the chemistry of soils, and the combination of essential plant foods in artificial fertilizers enabled producers in older regions to compete with farmers in newer regions. The "miracles" of modern science were yet to be worked, but a firm groundwork had been laid by the time of World War I. Methods of disseminating information had only to become efficient; then scientific applications and mechanization could move forward together.

BAD TIMES ON THE FARM, 1864–1896

The years from the close of the Civil War to the end of World War I comprise two major periods in agricultural history. The first of these runs

---

[6] See Erich W. Zimmermann, *World Resources and Industries,* rev. ed. (New York: Harper, 1951), p. 160, for a convenient table of data on agricultural power compiled from Department of Agriculture materials.

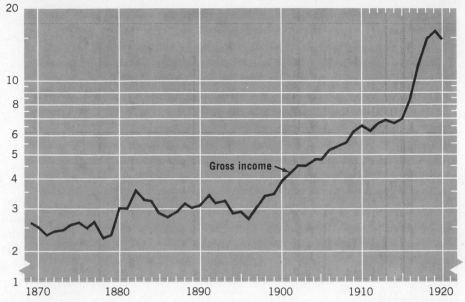

Billions of Dollars

Gross income

Strauss and Bean, *Gross Farm Income and Indices of Farm Production and Prices in the United States, 1869–1937.*

Farm Income: Like a fever chart, figures on agricultural revenues tell much about political realities in the United States. During the decade and a half preceding the election of 1896, farm income languished. During the next two decades, it rebounded sharply, rising dramatically during World War I only to fall off in the postwar recession.

from 1864 to 1896, the second from 1896 to 1920. The former period was characterized on the whole by great hardship in agriculture, whereas the second was remarkable for sustained improvement in the lot of the farm population generally.

Let us begin our analysis of the two periods by looking at a chart of gross farm income for the years 1869 to 1920. Although changes in income levels are by no means the only indicators of welfare trends for a particular economic group, they give us perhaps the best single measure we can find. The chart above shows that from 1869 to 1896 gross farm income rose little; since, as the years went by, this income was divided among a rapidly growing farm population, income per farm unit was decreasing. From 1896 on, the upward thrust of the income curve is very sharp indeed, in years of peace and war. Since the rate of increase of the farm population had slackened by 1896, income per farm family rose rapidly.

From the middle 1860s to the middle 1890s, the American farmer knew, without being shown data to prove it, that his was a hard lot. Farm people were living under frontier conditions, and the utter drabness of their surroundings combined with physical hardship was not conducive to a cheerful acceptance of the difficulties of economic life, which included falling prices and income, indebtedness, and the necessity of purchasing many goods and services from industries in which there was growing concentration of economic power. Following a normal postwar deflation, prices of commodities continued to drop. Farm prices, except for the early years of the seventies, fell precipitously until 1878. The figure on p. 263, on which is charted an index of total farm prices and an index of total farm production, shows the downward drift of the price curve. The curve of total farm production, on the contrary, moved sharply upward, though the annual rate of increase fell from 6 per cent in the seventies to about 2 per cent in the eighties and nineties.

We may now summarize the causes of the farmer's plight during the period. The supply of farm products was increasing at a rate much greater than the demand for them at prices that would cover the costs of most farm units. All over the world—in Canada, Australia, New Zealand, and the Argentine—fertile new lands were coming into production. In the United States the number of farms nearly trebled between 1860 and 1900 (Table 11-1). Reinforcing this trend was the increased productivity per farm worker consequent upon mechanization and the application of scientific discoveries.

Now if the demand for farm products had been increasing at a rate equal to the rate of increase in supply, there would have been no difficulty. A favorable influence on the domestic demand for food, feed, and fiber was the rapid increase in the population. After 1870 the *rate* of population growth in the United States fell, but until 1900 it was still large. In the decades of the seventies and eighties the increase was just over 25 per cent, and in the nineties it was more than 20 per cent, a substantial growth in the number of mouths to feed. But there was an offsetting factor. In 1870 the people of the United States spent a third of their current per-capita incomes on farm products. By 1890 they were spending just over one-fifth

Table 11-1

**Increase in Number of Farms,
1860–1920**

Year	Number of farms
1860	2,044,000
1870	2,660,000
1880	4,009,000
1890	4,565,000
1900	5,737,000
1910	6,406,000
1920	6,518,000

SOURCE: *Historical Statistics of the United States, Colonial Times to 1957*, p. 278.

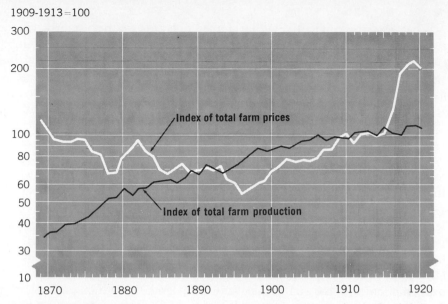

1909-1913=100

Strauss and Bean, *Gross Farm Income and Indices of Farm Production and Prices in the United States, 1869–1973.*

Production and Prices: From 1870 on, steadily improving levels of output per acre and per man reflected great advances in technology. After more than a quarter-century of downtrending prices, there followed a quarter-century of generally rising prices. The period from 1896 to 1920 is often called the "Golden Age of American Agriculture."

of their current incomes per person on farm products, and in the next few years this proportion tended to drop a little farther. Thus while both the money and real incomes of the American population rose during the period, the proportion of those incomes going to farm people fell off rather rapidly.

Export demand for farm products increased steadily until the turn of the century, when there began a drift downward until the eve of World War I. Wheat and flour exports reached their peak in 1901, at which time nearly a third of domestic wheat production was sold abroad. Meat and meat products likewise were exported in larger and larger quantities until 1900, when these exports fell off. The dollar value of exports from the end of the Civil War to 1896 fluctuated, and the fall in world prices during the period meant that the dollar value of farm exports did not rise in proportion to the increase in physical units sent abroad. To take a single example, the export value of crude foodstuffs (largely grains, fruits, and vegetables) was $12 million in 1860 and just under $130 million in 1896, yet in 1880 it had been as high as $266 million. Nevertheless, the value of agricultural exports rose from $297 million in 1870 to over $840 million in 1900. Exports of farm products during nearly three decades of bad times for agriculture alleviated the agricultural problem, but they were far from sufficient to correct the deep-seated difficulty.

What was this difficulty? What forces operated so persistently to the detriment of agriculture when some demand variables were reasonably favorable? Our tentative answer is this. *The rate of increase of industrial production in the United States from 1865 to 1896 was not sufficient to offset the extremely rapid rate of increase of agricultural production within the period.* One basic requirement for a healthy American agriculture is a rate of increase of industrial output much greater than the rate of increase of agricultural output. This is not the only requirement, but it is an *essential* one. Rising output in the nonagricultural sector of the economy, accompanied as it always is by rising employment and incomes, has traditionally meant growing demand for farm products. The rapid increase in the supply of farm products after the Civil War meant that output in the nonagricultural sector of the economy had to rise at a much greater rate than agricultural output if agriculture was to remain on an even keel.

Look now at the figure that follows. Here, on a semilogarithmic or "ratio" chart are spread data compiled by Professor E. R. Frickey for both farm crop output and industrial and commercial production beginning about 1865 and running to 1914.[7] Since these are semilog graphs, the curves show percentage changes, and we can compare the rates of growth of the two kinds of output at a glance. The upward drift of the two curves is about the same until 1885; then the rate of increase of industrial and commercial production exceeds that of crop output. In the decade of the seventies when the farmer was in straits, the agricultural curve shoots up even faster than the industrial one. There were year-to-year variations in the two kinds of output. For example, farm production was at a peak in 1875, a year of industrial depression. Farm prices slumped severely in the industrial depression of the seventies and recovered as industry went into the relatively good times of the early eighties. We must not, however, let attention to details cloud our understanding of the main point—that industry after the Civil War did not grow fast enough to take farm output from the market at profitable prices.

AGRICULTURE'S GOLDEN ERA, 1896–1915

The 1896–1915 period was one of rapid improvement in the economic position of the American farmer. (The reader should turn to the charts on pp. 261 and 263.) Farm production slackened its rate of increase, approximating one-half of 1 per cent per annum over these years. Farm prices and gross farm income rose steadily. The agricultural population remained constant at 32,000,000, as the natural rate of increase of farm people (650,000 per year toward the close of the period) was offset by the movement of farmers to city occupations. Consequently, from 1911 to 1915 income per person employed in agriculture was $370 compared with $595 per person

---

[7] The agricultural data are for farm crops alone, but available studies show that we do not go far wrong when we take crop output changes as about equal to changes in agricultural output as a whole.

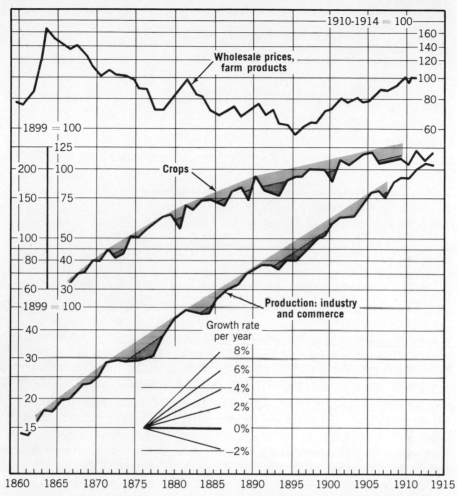

Reprinted by permission of the publisher from Edwin Frickey, *Economic Fluctuations in the United States,* Cambridge: Harvard University Press, copyright 1942, by the President and Fellows of Harvard College. Adapted by A. G. Hart, *Money, Debt, and Economic Activity,* 1st ed. (Englewood Cliffs, N.J. Prentice-Hall, 1948).

Agriculture, Industry, and Prices: A major reason for the improvement of agricultural prices after 1896 was that crop output did not rise nearly as fast as industrial production.

employed in industry, a remarkably favorable ratio not achieved again until the World War II years. Moreover, farmers' assets—land, buildings, and livestock—continually appreciated in value.[8] Many people on the land were still abysmally poor, but the economic position of major producers was much improved.

[8] These figures are taken from Theodore W. Schultz, *Agriculture in an Unstable Economy* (New York: McGraw-Hill, 1945), pp. 114–16. The analysis of this chapter is cast in the form set by Professor Schultz in this work.

Table 11-2

Indexes of Industrial and Agricultural Production and Agricultural Terms of Exchange (1895 = 100)

Year	Industrial production	Agricultural production	Agricultural terms of exchange
1895	100	100	100
1900	120	119	98
1905	174	130	105
1910	198	132	124
1915	256	150	115

SOURCE: By permission from Theodore W. Schultz, *Agriculture in an Unstable Economy*, p. 115. Copyright, 1945, McGraw-Hill Book Company, Inc.

Table 11-2 reveals that between 1895 and 1915, industrial production rose 156 per cent as agricultural production increased 50 per cent. Because the rate of industrial expansion was as high as three times that of agriculture, industrial income was able to purchase the 50 per cent increase in farm products and simultaneously to absorb the normal increase in farm population. Moreover, the terms of exchange moved in favor of agriculture—another way of saying that the prices of things the farmer sold rose relative to the things he had to buy.[9] The volume of agricultural exports fell off between 1896 and 1915, but the effects of the fall in volume were just about offset by a rise in the prices of export commodities. Because farm exports were not a strongly stimulating influence, the prosperity of these years can largely be accounted for by the rapid domestic industrial expansion.

THE EFFECTS OF WORLD WAR I ON AGRICULTURAL PRODUCTION

The effects of World War I on agricultural production have often been exaggerated. Only in the case of wheat was there a wartime increase in both output and acreage harvested sufficient to contribute to future difficulties. Following a record crop in 1915—the first billion-bushel crop in history—

---

[9] A word of explanation may be necessary about the computation of this terms-of-exchange index. On the basis of the Bean and Strauss series of farm prices used earlier in the chapter and on the basis of United States Department of Labor data on all wholesale prices, the 1895 index of farm prices was 60.4 and the index of industrial prices was 72.5. Now 60.4 divided by 72.5 equals 83. For our index of the terms of exchange, we set the ratio 83 equal to 100. Column 3 of Table 11-2 shows that the index numbers indicating changes in the agricultural terms of exchange rose during the twenty-year period. A rise in the terms-of-exchange index means that the numerator of the fraction, the index of farm prices, was rising faster than the denominator of the fraction, the index of industrial prices. The idea may seem complicated, but the reader is urged to master it because farm people were later to complain bitterly about adverse terms of exchange.

there were two poor years and two very good ones. Wheat acreage harvested in 1919 was 74,000,000 compared with 47,000,000 for the period 1909–13, an increase of over half. The acreage increase was achieved at the expense of other grains and by plowing up meadows and wild grassland in the Great Plains states and in Minnesota and Montana. World War I wheat production was consequently 38 per cent greater than the 1909–13 average.

Corn acreage remained stable through the World War I period at around 100,000,000. Taking all grains together—wheat, corn, oats, barley, rye, buckwheat, and rice—acreage increased from 203,000,000 in 1914 to only 227,000,000 in 1919, or 12 per cent. Production of all grains during the war was up only 5 per cent, and on a per-capita basis not at all. Hog production was up sharply relative to other meat animals, and meat production rose about 23 per cent during the period. Livestock on farms, including poultry, rose 16 per cent. In no single war year did cotton acreage harvested reach the 36,000,000 figure of 1914. Tobacco acreage was up 60 per cent by 1920, but as it turned out the increase was a permanent consequence of war-induced changes in tobacco consumption.

These statistics indicate only moderate increases in acreage and output for American agriculture during World War I. There were distortions of significance only in wheat and hogs, and these were not great enough to be root causes of the farm troubles that began in the 1920s. Table 11-3 gives data for the period 1915–20 similar to that contained in Table 11-2. Taking 1915 as the base year in order to show changes for the war period, we observe that industrial production rose greatly and then dropped. Agriculture was well off during these years, partly because of the sudden jump in United States industrial production, and partly because of sustained high demand for American farm products by the Allies.

Table 11-3

Indexes of Industrial and Agricultural Production
and Agricultural Terms of Exchange
(1915 = 100)

Year	Industrial production	Agricultural production	Agricultural terms of exchange
1915	100	100	100
1916	119	96	110
1917	118	99	138
1918	117	105	136
1919	102	106	134
1920	111	107	87

SOURCE: By permission from Theodore W. Schultz, *Agriculture in an Unstable Economy*, p. 121. Copyright, 1945, McGraw-Hill Book Company, Inc.

Agrarian Movements and Federal Intercession

HARDSHIP ON THE FARM AND AGRARIAN AGITATION

The farmer of the late nineteenth century was painfully aware of the *symptoms* of his distress. Like people of any age and time who have symptoms, he reasoned back to *particular* causes; having discovered these causes, he wanted to remove them, one by one, by any means available.

The rapid movement to the West that followed the Civil War was accompanied, as we have seen, by persistently falling prices. Although land could be had for nothing, many found it necessary to lay out money for the purchase of a farm in the better locations. Even if land were obtained free, it was becoming necessary to make bigger capital outlays for equipment. Typically, the westerner obtained funds by mortgaging his place, and more often than not he found himself in the squeeze suffered by debtors in times of falling prices. Amounts owing banks or eastern mortgage companies had to be repaid in continually appreciating dollars. If the farmer lost his health, or if he had some bad crop years, he often lost his land through foreclosure. Even if he were not forced off his farm, he might find it psychologically easier to escape his indebtedness by moving farther west or becoming a tenant on his former land. Such insecurity led to deep-seated frustration and bitterness. The remedy, too, was plain. What the country needed was more money. Or at least so the farmer thought, and he could bring forth some good arguments to prove his point.

There was another major complaint. Farmers felt that the business sector of the economy was getting more than favorable treatment under the law. For generations there had been a strong "anti-monopoly" sentiment among country people, and after the Civil War they were strongly convinced that centralized economic power was a great evil. The agrarian wanted to take especially vigorous action against his "oppressors"—bankers, railroads, and great landholders. But there were other oppressors. Processors of farm products, like the meat packers, appeared to charge monopoly prices for their products while beating down the prices of commodities bought from the farmer. There was also a hated class of "middlemen"—commission merchants, wholesalers, and speculators on the recently organized commodity exchanges. Again, the solution to the broad problem was clear enough. Regulatory action on the part of government was necessary.

In what has been called the "Thirty Years' War" against the princes of privilege, a number of organizations, large and small, were formed to do battle for farmers. Some organizations were influenced by industrial urban labor, and many of the ideas of the agrarians originated in the urban radicalism of the East.[10] The so-called agrarian revolt was not a purely agrarian agitation. It was neither closely knit nor well organized. There

---

10 For a readable treatment of this matter, see Chester McArthur Destler, "Western Radicalism, 1865–1901: Concepts and Origins," *Mississippi Valley Historical Review*, XXXI (December 1944), pp. 335–68.

Granger Movement meetings like this one in Scott County, Illinois, found their discontentments focusing on big-city ways, monopoly, the tariff, and low prices for agricultural products. From such roots grew pressures "to do something" for agriculture.

were four separate and rather clearly distinguishable movements, dominated, if not entirely motivated, by farmers of the West and South.

The Grangers. The first farm organization of importance was the National Grange of the Patrons of Husbandry. Formally organized in 1867, the order had a rapid growth. By 1874 the National Grange had 20,000 local branches and a membership of around 1,500,000. After seven years of ascendancy a decline set in, and by 1880 membership had largely disappeared except in a few strongholds such as the upper Mississippi Valley and the Northeast.

Although formal political action by the Granges was strictly forbidden by organization by-laws, members held informal political meetings and worked through reform parties for passage of regulatory legislation. In several western states the Grangers were successful (1) in obtaining laws that set an upper limit to the charges of railroads and of warehouse and elevator companies, and (2) in establishing regulation of such companies by commission, a new concept in American politics. The Grangers developed a new weapon for fighting unfair business practices. If prices charged by businessmen were too high, then, it was argued, farmers ought to go into business themselves. The most successful type of business organization established by Granges was the co-operative, formed for the sale of general merchandise and farm implements to Grange members. Co-operatives and stock companies were set up for processing farm products, and the first large mail-order house, Montgomery Ward and Company, was established to sell to Granges.

The Greenback movement. Farmers disappointed in the Grange joined forces with a labor element to form an Independent National Party, which entered candidates in the election of 1876. This group was hopelessly unsuccessful, but a "Greenback Labor" party, formed by the same people, made headway in the election of 1878. To finance the Civil War the government had resorted to issue of fiat paper popularly known as "greenbacks," and the suggestion that a similar issue be made in the late seventies appealed to poor farmers. The "Greenback Labor" platform centered more than any other political party on demands for inflationary (they would have said "reflationary") action.

Although Greenback Labor candidates were entered in the presidential campaign of 1880, they received a very small popular vote because labor failed to participate effectively. Greenback agitators continued their efforts through the election of 1888, but with continuing indifferent success. The movement is worth remembering for two reasons. First, Greenback agitation constituted the first attempt of farmers to act politically on a national scale. Second, the central tenets of the group were taken over by the later Populists as the most important part of their appeal to the electorate in the nineties.

The Alliances. At the same time that the Granges were multiplying, independent farmers' clubs were being formed in the West and South. Independent clubs tended to coalesce into state "alliances," which in turn were brought into two principal groups—the Northwestern Alliance and the Southern Alliance. In 1889 an attempt at merger of the Alliances failed, despite the similarity of their aims. The Alliances advocated money reforms like those urged by the Greenback parties, and, like the Grangers, were in favor of government regulation and co-operative business ventures. Alliance memberships favored actual government ownership of transportation and communication facilities. Each Alliance proposed a scheme that has a highly modern ring. The Southern Alliance recommended that the federal government establish a system of warehouses for the storage of nonperishable commodities in order that farmers might obtain low-interest loans up to 80 per cent of the value of products stored. The Northwestern Alliance proposed that the federal government make long-term loans in greenbacks up to 50 per cent of the value of a farm. Because of their dangerously revolutionary nature such ideas received little support from voters.

The Populists. After the mild prosperity of the early and middle eighties, there was a further downturn in economic activity, and the hardships of the farmer and laborer again became unbearable. In 1891 elements of the Alliances met in Cincinnati with the Knights of Labor to form the People's Party. At the convention of 1892, held in Omaha, the famed agrarian and formidable orator, General James Weaver, was nominated for the Presidency. Weaver, an old Greenbacker, won twenty-two electoral votes in the election of 1892. Two years later the party won a number of congressional seats, and it appeared that greater success might be forthcoming.

Populism thus emerged from thirty years of unrest, unrest that was chiefly agricultural but with urban connections. To its supporters Populism was something more than an agitation for economic betterment: it was a faith. The overtones of political and social reform were part of the faith because they would help to further economic aims. The old ferment against monopoly control, against the oppression of corporations, banks, and capitalists, had come to a head. Along with the key principle of antimonopolism there was accepted a strongly collectivist doctrine, for Populists felt that only through government ownership of banks, railroads, and the means of communication and through government control of the monetary system could the evils of monopoly be put down. In fact, "yardstick" operation of firms in basic industries was advocated by some Populists so that the government could determine whether or not monopolistic prices were being charged.

The extreme radicalism of the People's Party alienated the support of established farmers in the older areas, for the established landowners had a definite conservative bias. Had the leaders of the 1896 coalition of Populists and Democrats not chosen to stand or fall on the issue of free coinage of silver, there is no telling what the future of the coalition might have been. But inflation was anathema to the property owner, and when the chips were down property owners, rural as well as urban, supported "sound" money.

Attempts of the farmer to improve his condition through organization were not successful as far as immediate goals were concerned. But the way had been opened to legislation that would ultimately help him. We now turn to a review of the first laws passed for the benefit of agriculture.

THE BEGINNINGS OF FEDERAL ASSISTANCE TO AGRICULTURE

The land acts of the nineteenth century worked to the advantage of farmers, but they can scarcely be thought of as part of an agricultural "program." Similarly, much regulatory legislation passed late in the nineteenth and early in the twentieth century, while originating in agrarian organizations, had effects not restricted to agriculture. In speaking of federal assistance to agriculture before 1920, we refer to attempts to compile and disseminate information of help to the individual farmer. Such efforts were calculated, however, to increase productivity; they were not designed to alleviate distress as New Deal legislation was.

The Department of Agriculture. As early as 1839 an Agricultural Division had been set up in the Patent Office. In 1862 Congress created a Department of Agriculture, but its head, who was designated the Commissioner of Agriculture, did not have Cabinet rank. Not until 1889 was the department given Cabinet status.

Until 1920 the Department of Agriculture performed three principal functions. These were (1) research and experimentation in plant exploration, plant and animal breeding, and insect and disease control; (2) distribution of agricultural information through publications, agricultural experiment stations, and county demonstration work; and (3) regulation of the quality of products consumed by human beings through authority to condemn diseased animals, to prohibit the shipment in interstate commerce of adulterated or misbranded foods and drugs, and to inspect and certify meats and dairy products in interstate trade. There was always pressure on the Department to give "practical" help to farmers, evidenced by the fact that throughout this period free seeds were distributed regularly by the Department. In retrospect it seems that the chief contribution of the Department of Agriculture in earlier years lay in its ability to sell dirt farmers on the value of "scientific" farming.

Agricultural education. Attempts to incorporate the teaching of agricultural subjects into the educational system began locally, but federal assistance was necessary for adequate programs. By 1860 colleges of agriculture had been established in several states, but it was the Morrill Act of 1862 that gave impetus to agricultural training at university levels. The Morrill Act established in the several states "land-grant" colleges, which gradually came to take over state-wide leadership in agricultural research. The Hatch Act of 1887 provided federal assistance to state agricultural experiment stations, many of which had already been established with state funds. The Hatch Act also provided for an Office of Experiment Stations in the Department of Agriculture in order to tie in the work of the department with that of the states. After 1900, as the quality of work done by the agricultural colleges reached university level, interest began to develop in secondary school work. The Smith-Hughes Vocational Education Act of 1917 provided funds to states undertaking to expand vocational training at the high-school level in agriculture, trades, and home economics.

Conservation of Natural Resources: The First Stage

Because of the rapid rise of the conservation movement at the turn of the present century, there is a tendency to think of it as the result of a sudden awakening—an awakening to the realization that private exploitation of the land is not necessarily consistent with the public good. The political charm of one man—Theodore Roosevelt—was the chief influence in convincing the nation of the necessity for conservation. Yet from the very beginning of the country some citizens had urged a prudent land policy because it seemed like good business and because posterity deserved some consideration. And as early as the 1880s there were strong pressures for reform from scientific organizations and major periodicals.

The first major step toward reform of the land system—the General Revision Act of 1891—has been mentioned. This law repealed measures that had been an open invitation to fraud and made it more difficult for corporations and wealthy individuals to steal timber and minerals. Prevention of theft scarcely constitutes conservation, but one section of the 1891 act, which empowered the President to set aside forest reserves, was genuinely a conservation measure. Between 1891 and 1900 50,000,000 acres of valuable timberland were withdrawn from private entry in spite of strong and growing opposition from the western states. Inadequate appropriations made it impossible for the Division of Forestry to protect the reserves from forest fires and from depredations of timber thieves, but a start had been made.

When Theodore Roosevelt succeeded to the Presidency in 1901 there was widespread concern, both in Congress and throughout the nation, over the problem of conservation. During both his terms, Roosevelt, with imagination and fervor, sought legislation to provide a consistent and thoroughgoing program. By 1907 he could point to certain major achievements.

1. National forests comprised 150,000,000 acres, of which 75,000,000 acres contained merchantable timber. In 1901 a Bureau of Forestry was created, and in 1905 the Bureau became the United States Forest Service. Under able Gifford Pinchot, Roosevelt's chief adviser in all matters pertaining to conservation, a program of scientific forestry was initiated. The national forests were to be more than just locked-up preserves; the "crop" of trees was to be continually harvested and sold and ever larger future crops assured.

2. Seventy-five million acres of lands containing mineral wealth were reserved from sale and settlement. Most of the lands containing metals had already passed into private ownership, but the government was able to retain large deposits of coal, phosphates, and oil.

3. There was explicit recognition of the future importance of water-power sites. A policy was established of leasing government-owned sites to private firms for a stipulated period of years; actual ownership was reserved to the government.

4. The principle was accepted that it was a proper function of the federal government to carry out a program of public works for the purpose of controlling stream flows. Specifically, storage dams and irrigation works were to be constructed for the benefit of western settlers. The Newlands Act of 1902 provided for the use of receipts from land sales in the arid states to finance the construction of reservoirs and irrigation works, with repayment to be made by settlers over a period of years. In this way the idea of "reclamation" entered into the broader concept of conservation.

To the modern student such achievements seem modest enough. But in the first decade of the twentieth century there were men who bitterly opposed any interference with private exploitation of the remaining public domain. The controversy became a matter of the East versus the new West. Westerners argued that settlers in the older parts of the country had once

The idea of conservation got a powerful boost from President Theodore Roosevelt, shown here at Yellowstone National Park.

had *their* feet in the trough and that the same principles should apply in the West until settlement was complete. Easterners rejoined that the West was full of wicked men who would not rest until they had despoiled the land. Westerners contended that without free access to natural resources the development of the new states would come to an end; Easterners had hard things to say about the harm that was being done to generations yet unborn. And there were divisions within the sections. The large western timber interests, for example, were in favor of conservation. The withdrawal by the government of supplies of timber from the market meant higher lumber prices, and big companies were in a favored position to buy ripe trees from the national forests. In the East, on the other hand, some people had misgivings about government ownership of reclamation projects, for such doctrines might some day be applicable to easterners.

Theodore Roosevelt was aware of these deep-seated differences. As he neared the end of his second term, he feared that without stronger popular support his conservation program might eventually fall apart. For this reason he called a conference of state governors, to be held in Washington in May of 1908. "The object of the meeting was to create a uniform public sentiment looking to the conservation of all natural resources and their ultimate complete utilization in the manner which would yield the most profit with the least waste, so that these resources might be passed down to future generations unimpaired save by unavoidable wear and tear." [11] The conference received wide publicity and led to the creation of the National Conservation Commission, with Gifford Pinchot as chairman. Early in 1909 the findings of the commission were published in three volumes, furnishing a wealth of material in support of the conservation cause. Roosevelt enlisted widespread voter support, even among Westerners, but, more important, he secured the active co-operation and assistance of leaders in many fields.

The achievements of the Roosevelt administration were not undone by the anticonservationists in the years that followed. In fact, halting steps forward were taken in the Taft and Wilson administrations. By the Withdrawal Act of 1910 all known coal, oil, gas, and phosphate lands remaining in the public domain were reserved, and in 1912 the practice of creating Naval Oil Reserves began. The Weeks Act of 1911 empowered the federal government to *purchase* forest lands in the Appalachian and White mountains, ostensibly for the purpose of protecting watersheds in order to maintain the navigability of streams. Henceforth, the East was to be included in conservation programs, and the power of the government to extend its conservation activities beyond the lands in the public domain was established. During the Wilson administrations the chief controversy centered about the disposition of public power sites. A Supreme Court decision of 1917 affirmed the right of the federal government to do with these sites as it saw fit, and the argument was temporarily concluded with the passage of the Federal Power Act of 1920. This law provided that private companies could lease land containing water power sites for a period not to exceed fifty years; at the end of the period the government could renew the lease or purchase any plant and equipment of the leasing company.

It seems sensible that the government should have taken steps to prevent unnecessary waste of its dwindling resources at the end of the nineteenth century. There is little question, though, that the early conservationists overstated their case. They failed to see that technological advances would enable the industrialist to use old materials more efficiently and new ones to the eventual exclusion of the old. They did not realize that estimated reserves of some minerals, especially petroleum, would be raised again and again. Nor did the conservationists of an earlier day direct sufficient attention to the most serious kind of resource depletion—soil erosion. A different emphasis would come with the inauguration of a second Roosevelt, but to comprehend the significance of the "new" conservation we shall have to wait until a later chapter where we trace recent developments in agriculture.

---

[11] Roy M. Robbins, *Our Landed Heritage* (Princeton: Princeton University Press, 1942), p. 355.

Spreading Transportation Networks

. . . The said corporation is hereby authorized and empowered to lay out, locate, construct, furnish, maintain, and enjoy a continuous railroad and telegraph, with the appurtenances, from a point on the one hundredth meridian of longitude west from Greenwich, between the south margin of the valley of the Republican River and the north margin of the valley of the Platte River, in the Territory of Nebraska, to the western boundary of Nevada Territory, upon the route and terms hereinafter provided. . . .

THE PACIFIC RAILWAY ACT OF JULY 1, 1862

Nineteenth-century Americans knew intuitively that a satisfactory growth rate depended upon rapid and dependable transportation. In small groups and large they were willing to make any sacrifice to secure a system that would link every community with any pretense to economic importance with every other.

Over the six decades 1860–1920 the railroads, taken together, had a monopoly of fast, efficient transit in this country. If ever a group of enterprises seemed likely to earn a fat return on invested capital, the railroads did. Yet throughout the period most companies were at one time or another in financial difficulties, and at the end of World War I there was a thoughtful and serious opinion that the system should be nationalized. Long before the advent of drastic (and largely subsidized) competition from airplanes, trucks, and privately owned automobiles, the railroads were in deep and persistent trouble. Why? A part of the answer will be found in the pages immediately following; the rest of the story must wait telling in Chapter 17, where we consider the railroad reorganizations of the 1890s.

Completing the Railway Net

Although the expansion of railroad systems was restricted during the Civil War, technological developments resulted in greater operational efficiency and increased capacities of engines and roadbeds. Most important was the introduction of the steel rail. Brought to this country from England shortly after 1860, steel rails were being rolled in American plants a few years later. Their first cost was high, but this disadvantage was offset by the fact that steel was far more durable than either wrought or cast iron. Steel also rapidly replaced iron in locomotives and rolling stock. Steel wheel rims, frames, and fittings were stronger than the iron materials that had been formerly used, and steel boilers permitted higher steam pressures with greater safety.

Not until the late 1860s was there progress toward overcoming the major safety problem of stopping heavy trains. In 1868 George Westinghouse patented his first air brake, which had the serious defect of stopping cars in order of front to rear—to the peril and discomfort of passengers at the end of the train. More than twenty years elapsed before satisfactory braking systems were developed. Meantime, after a decade of experimenting, George Pullman in 1865 produced the first really successful sleeping car, and within a few years the Pullman Palace Car Company was taking the torture out of long-distance travel with cars that were indeed palatial. As trains grew in size and durability, the cost of railroad carriage fell, and traffic was no longer limited by high rates to passengers and light freight.

Civil strife ended, the nation turned its eyes anew to the territory west of the Mississippi. The Gold Rush of 1849 had brought knowledge of the fabulous West Coast and exciting stories about the vast spaces that separated the East from the West. The hard routes to the land of opportunity were likewise described to the crowding populations of the East. Wagon trails to California and the Pacific Northwest were beset with the dangers of blizzards in winter, thirst in summer, and Indian attacks at all seasons of the year. The trip via the Isthmus of Panama, with an overland trek through malarial and pestiferous jungles to take ship on the other side, was a nightmare of suffering.[1] The third route, around "Cape Stiff," was no less dangerous and frightening; the long voyage in slow sailing ships to the Cape, the storms encountered there, and the final reach to the California coast deterred all but the bravest. Thus, when the Civil War was over and the rich goal of far western lands was contemplated, a safe rail connection with the new West was eagerly desired.

---

[1] The shorter sea route via the Isthmus could cut the six-to-eight month trip around Cape Horn to as little as six weeks. But from Chagres, squalid eastern port on the Isthmus, to Panama City was a five-day journey by native dugout and muleback, and at Panama travelers might have a long wait before securing passage north. For those who could afford it, the best way to California was by clipper ship, which made the passage in from 100 to 110 days.

Actually, the dream of spanning the continent by rail was almost as old as the railroad itself. The first concrete proposal has been attributed to Asa Whitney of New York, a merchant in the China trade, who in 1845 proposed to Congress the construction of a railroad from Lake Michigan to the mouth of the Columbia River. By 1853 Congress was convinced of the feasibility of a road to the West Coast and directed government engineers to survey the western areas for practical routes. The engineers described five possible routes. Years passed before construction began, the delay resulting from rivalry for the eastern terminus of the line. From Minneapolis to New Orleans cities on the Mississippi River vied for the position of gateway to the West and boasted of their advantages while belittling the claims of their rivals. The outbreak of the Civil War removed the proponents of the southern routes from Congress, and in 1862 a northern way through uninhabited country was selected. The Platte River route was picked because it was used by the pony express, stages, and freighters.

By the Pacific Railway Act of 1862 Congress granted a charter of incorporation to the Union Pacific Railroad, which was authorized to build a line from Omaha, Nebraska, to the western boundary of Nevada. The Central Pacific, incorporated under the laws of California in 1861, was at the same time given authority to construct the western part of the road from Sacramento to the Nevada border. Because of the uncertainty of revenues from the undertaking, it was necessary for the government to furnish financial assistance in two ways. Ten sections of public land (five alternate sections on each side of the right-of-way) were granted for each mile of track laid.[2] The government further agreed to lend the companies certain sums per mile of construction, the loans to be secured by first-mortgage bonds. Because the Act of 1862 failed to attract sufficient private capital, the law was amended in 1864 to double the amount of land grants and to provide for second-mortgage security on government loans, thus enabling the roads to sell first-mortgage bonds to the public. To encourage speed of construction, the Central Pacific was permitted to build one hundred and fifty miles beyond the Nevada line; later it was authorized to push eastward until a junction was made with the Union Pacific.

Both companies had to overcome enormous difficulties. The terrain to be traversed contained both mountains and desert. From Omaha, the eastern terminus of the Union Pacific, rails were laid across the flat Great Plains. Grading problems were not severe, but obtaining ties and bridge timbers was difficult because the line traversed grasslands. In the initial stages of building, procurement of supplies was complicated by lack of a railroad connection from the east with the jumping-off spot at Omaha. Materials and

---

[2] The land had little or no value without means of access to it, but everyone knew that it would increase in value after the railroad was built. The fact that the companies had assets that would appreciate, in addition to the prospect of growing revenues, made private investment more attractive.

The Victorian splendor of overdecorated Pullman cars appealed to the passengers who flocked to travel in this Illinois Central "Palace" Pullman. Each millionaire of the first rank had his own plush car as well.

supplies were freighted to the rail terminus by wagon at a considerable cost.

The recruiting of a labor force for work on the Union Pacific did not prove easy. The expanding war economy in the urban East kept workers close at home; with jobs plentiful few wished to endure the hardships of railroad construction in the wilds of the West. The labor problem was partly solved by hiring demobilized officers and soldiers from the Union and Confederate forces and partly by recruiting from the Irish who had settled on the eastern seaboard in the late forties and early fifties. The Irish found the adventure and good wages of western railroad building attractive, and many were lured from the Atlantic cities where, by and large, they had been poorly paid at manual labor or unskilled trades.

Procuring the necessary labor for the construction of the Central Pacific was not difficult. There was no local labor market to speak of, but thousands of Chinese were imported to prepare grades, build structures, and lay ties and rails. In the West, timber was readily available for ties and bridges, and stone for ballast and structures was abundant. But the Central Pacific was even farther away from supplies of iron and steel than was the Union Pacific. From the industrial cities and seaports of the East, around Cape Horn or by transshipment across the Isthmus of Panama, came the machinery and hardware that went into the building of the western part of the first transcontinental railroad. Some food and other supplies also had to be imported.

But the greatest difficulty confronting the builders of the Central Pacific was the terrain itself. The steeply rising slopes of the Sierra Nevada range presented serious problems of grading, cutting, tunneling, and bridging. Machine-driven tools were nonexistent. Horses and mules were used to move obstacles, but the dislodgment of earth and the breaking of rocks were largely effected by human exertion. Though blasting powder was used whenever possible, muscle and bone did most of the work of linking West and East.

The joining of the Union Pacific with the Central Pacific occurred amidst great fanfare and celebration on May 10, 1869, at Promontory Point, a few miles west of Ogden, Utah.[3] Two trains loaded to the running boards with dignitaries approached, one from the east and one from the west, the joining place of the rails. President Grant, by telegraph, gave the signal from Washington to drive in the last spikes. The hammer blows that drove the golden spikes home were echoed by Mr. Morse's telegraph to waiting throngs on both coasts. The hope was expressed that the fruits of the toil of farmer and laborer could now be transported swiftly and cheaply from coast to coast or from the interior to either coast. The continent had at last been spanned by rails; though transcontinental train travel was not without discomfort and even danger, the terrible trials of the overland and sea routes were gone.

Yet the thin rails that crossed half a continent could not carry all the traffic that the growing West demanded. New lines were quickly projected, but construction, although well under way, was halted by the Depression of 1873. In 1876 southern California was opened to transcontinental traffic by a road from San Francisco to Bakersfield, and thence to Los Angeles. Next the Southern Pacific lines reached eastward from California to El Paso. The Santa Fe and the Texas and Pacific soon provided connections from St. Louis and Kansas City to the Los Angeles area, and only a little later the Southern Pacific thrust on east from El Paso. These southerly railroads provided the second of the three major transcontinental routes. The third route was the northern one from the Mississippi to the cities of Oregon and Washington. In 1883 the Northern Pacific, chartered nearly twenty years before, connected Portland with Chicago and Milwaukee and three years later reached Seattle.

EXPANSION IN THE SETTLED REGIONS

As the first transcontinentals were pushed to completion, railroad construction and integration elsewhere continued apace. The two decades following the Civil War witnessed the formation of the great trunk-line systems in the territory of the middle Atlantic and north central states—extending from the seaboard to Illinois and Wisconsin. Major lines strove continuously to free themselves of dependence upon competitors for connections with

---

[3] The last two years of construction were marked by a race between the two companies to lay the most track. With permission to build eastward to a junction with the Union Pacific, the directors of the Central Pacific wished to obtain as much per-mile subsidy as possible. The Union Pacific laid 1,086 miles of track, the Central Pacific 689 miles.

At Promontory Point, Utah, the "Rival Monarchs" nuzzled up to each other as hundreds cheered the completion of the transcontinental rail line. The date was May 10, 1869.

key traffic points; above all they tried to secure access to New York in the East and to Chicago and St. Louis in the West. By lease, purchase, and construction the Pennsylvania reached Chicago in 1869 and pushed westward to St. Louis. A chief competitor, the Baltimore and Ohio, entered Chicago in 1874 but for years encountered difficulties in obtaining a connection with New York. On the more northerly routes the New York Central achieved a through line from New York to Chicago by 1877, and the Erie did the same only a few years later. After the mid-eighties the trunk lines filled in gaps, gaining access to secondary railroad centers and building feeder lines in a north-south direction.

From 1864 to 1900 the greatest percentage of track, varying from one-third to nearly one-half of the country's total annual construction, was laid

Sherman Station, Wyoming Territory, looked like this six months after the completion of the coast-to-coast railroad line.

in the Great Plains states. Chicago became the chief terminus of roads extending to the north, west, and south, but a web of rails also surrounded cities like St. Louis, Kansas City, Minneapolis, Omaha, and Denver. Many systems—the Burlington and the Rock Island are examples—built main lines across the prairies from Chicago to Denver, and then proceeded to extend branches into small towns in the rich farm country. A few roads, like the Chicago, Milwaukee, and St. Paul, began as regional systems and became at last transcontinentals. Throughout the midlands competition for business led to the entry into small towns of two and sometimes even three or four roads where one could scarcely have done a profitable business.

The Southeast and the Southwest lagged both in construction and in the combination of local lines into through systems. Sparseness of population and war-induced poverty accounted in part for the backwardness of the Southeast, but competition of coastwise ships was also a deterrent to railroad growth. The only southern pass utilized before 1880 for a trans-mountain crossing was that of the Chesapeake and Ohio, and, except for the Southern, no main north-and-south line was completed until the 1890s. In the early 1900s competitive building was still going on in Florida. Meantime, although the Southwest had been tapped as early as 1873 by lines running from St. Louis and Kansas City, construction of a closely knit network did not begin until the 1890s and this activity was flourishing until the eve of World War I.

Because the rate of growth of the railway net varied so in different regions, investment was extended over time. Railroad investment proceeded in "towering waves," cycles varying in length from ten to twenty-three years. Annual investment in railroads rose to peaks in 1873, 1882, 1891, and 1911 and fell to troughs in 1876, 1886, 1897, and 1920.[4] Railroad construction contributed to economic instability and at the same time served as a powerful stimulus to economic growth, accounting for 20 per cent of United States

---

[4] Melville J. Ulmer, *Trends and Cycles in Capital Formation by United States Railroads, 1870–1950,* Occasional Paper 43 (New York: National Bureau of Economic Research, 1954), pp. 25–34.

gross capital formation in the 1870s, 15 per cent of the total in the 1880s, and 7.5 per cent of the total in each of the remaining decades to 1920.

FINANCING THE RAILROADS

An outstanding characteristic of the railroad industry is the indivisibility of much of the fixed plant required for operation. To provide any service at all between two points, large outlays must be made on roadbeds, tracks, bridges and other structures, and rolling stock. The capacity of a minimum amount of investment more often than not exceeded the actual demands of traffic during the early years of a road's operation. For this reason railroad builders had to augment capital obtained from private sources by subsidies from government units, even after the railroad had become an accepted means of transportation.

States and municipalities, set to competing with each other for lines that they thought would bring everlasting prosperity, continued to help railroads, though on a smaller scale than in the early days. They purchased or guaranteed railroad bonds, granted tax exemptions, and provided terminal facilities. Several states subscribed to the capital stock of the roads, hoping to participate in the profits of ventures. Michigan built three roads, and North Carolina controlled the majority of directors of three. North Carolina, Massachusetts, and Missouri took over failing railroads that had been liberally aided by state funds. Outright contributions of state and local units may have reached $250 million, a small sum in comparison with a value of road and equipment of $10 billion in 1880, the date by which assistance from local governments almost ceased.

Financial aid from the federal government exceeded that from states and municipalities, though by how much we cannot be sure. Perhaps $175 million in government bonds was lent to the Union Pacific, the Central Pacific, and four other transcontinentals, but after litigation most of this amount was repaid. Rights-of-way, normally two hundred feet wide, together with sites for depots and terminal facilities in the public domain and free timber and stone from government lands, constituted another form of assistance. But the most significant kind of federal subsidy was the grant of lands from the public domain.

Congress simply used the unsettled lands in the public domain in lieu of money or credit. Following the precedent set by a grant to the Illinois Central in 1850, alternate sections of land on either side of the road, varying in number from six to forty, were given outright for each mile of road constructed. The alternate-section provision was made in the expectation that the government would share in the increased land values resulting from the new transportation facilities. Land-grant subsidies were discontinued after 1871 because of public opposition to such profligate disposal of the public domain, but not before 323,000,000 acres (50,000,000 of which ultimately reverted to the government) had been given away. At one time or another the railroads were in possession of one-fourth of Minnesota and Washington, one-fifth of Wisconsin, Iowa, Kansas, North Dakota, and Montana, and significant portions of other midwestern and western states. Yet aid to the railroads was not freely given. Congress provided that roads receiving grants should transport mail, troops, and government property at reduced rates. In 1940 Congress relieved the railroads of land-grant rates for all but military traffic, and in 1945 military traffic was removed from the reduced-rate category. While land-grant rates were in effect, estimated reductions obtained by the government were over $500 million, a sum several times the value of the land grants when they were made and about equal to what the railroads have until now received from their sale.[5]

Subsidies doubtless added to profits and thus to incentives of builders until the early 1870s. But the great bulk of both new and replacement capital raised by the railroads came from private sources, domestic and foreign. Established merchants, especially in the East, sensed the opportunities for great gain from railroad investment, and the wealth of these men constituted a major reservoir of capital funds. A developing securities market enabled entrepreneurs to reach people of lesser means. The benefits of railroad transportation to farmers, small industrialists, and the general public along a proposed route were described in glowing terms by its promoters. Investors responded with enthusiasm and generosity, not to say with extravagance, their outlay of funds prompted in part by the realization that growth of their communities and increase in their personal wealth depended on the new transportation facility.

American capitalists were also successful in selling railroad securities to foreigners. European interests owned a majority of the stock in several railroads, and English, Dutch, and German stockholders constituted important minority groups in others. In 1876 European holdings amounted to 86 per cent of the common stock of the Illinois Central, and at one time two directorships of the Chicago and Northwestern were occupied by Dutch nationals. In 1914 Europeans, largely English, owned one-fifth of American railroad securities outstanding.

Most American and foreign investors were content to purchase securities and wait for legitimate returns in dividends and interest. Not so the more unscrupulous officers and directors of companies most active in post–Civil War construction. In a day when the issue of corporate securities was subject only to the cursory supervision of state authorities, promoters indulged in questionable and even fraudulent practices. Yet ways had to be devised of promoting private gain without running afoul of the law. The most common one was the organization of "construction companies," which stood between the railroad corporation itself and the contractor who actually did the building.

The construction company was originated to permit the sale of stock

---

[5] This comment is not intended to pass judgment on the wisdom of federal land grants to railroads but simply to suggest the magnitude of the sums involved. A reckoning of the total cost to the government would have to include interest.

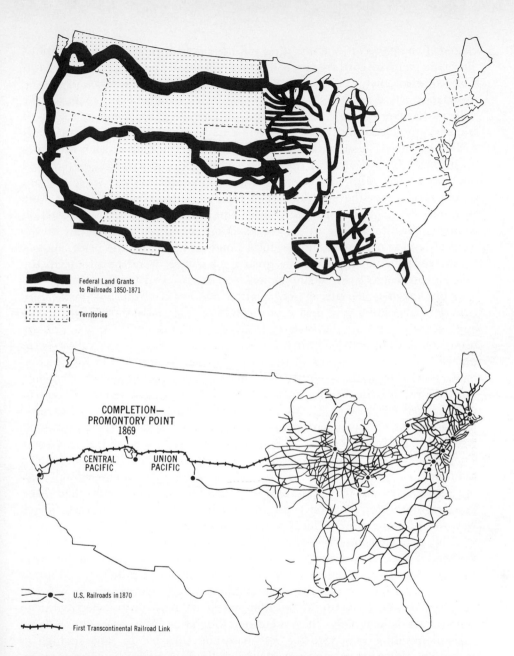

Federal Land Grants
to Railroads 1850-1871

Territories

COMPLETION—
PROMONTORY POINT
1869

CENTRAL
PACIFIC

UNION
PACIFIC

U.S. Railroads in 1870

First Transcontinental Railroad Link

Rail Impact: By 1870, huge tracts of lands had been taken over (for resale) by the railroads, while the coast-to-coast link had been made the year before in Utah. The Atlantic-Pacific trip was now a week's journey.

below par value, a practice prohibited by law in some states. The railroad contracted with a construction company to build a certain number of miles of road at so much per mile, payment to be made in stocks and bonds. The contract price was set high enough to permit the construction company to offer real "bargains" to the investing public and still come out with a profit.[6] Since the railroad corporation had issued the securities at par, no law was violated when they were sold at a discount by a second party, and by the transaction the construction company obtained enough money to build the road and make a profit. This method of financing, although smacking of trickery, provided funds that might not have been obtained otherwise. It was in the "inside" construction company that the real evils of such financing were found. The owners of the company were "insiders"—i.e., officers and directors of the railroad corporation. Common practice was to sell bonds of the railroad to the general public for cash. Costs of construction were then met by paying cash and issuing common stock to the construction company, besides passing to the construction company the subsidies in the form of land grants and state and local bonds. The higher the price charged by the construction company the greater, of course, were the profits to the railroad promoters made at the expense of the railroad company itself.

Although not all railroad construction was financed through inside construction companies, the device was common, especially during the sixties and seventies, and all the transcontinentals made use of it. It was not unusual for the proceeds of security issues, plus the value of the subsidies, to exceed twice the actual cost of the road. Most notorious of the inside companies was the Crédit Mobilier of America, chartered under Pennsylvania statutes, which built the Union Pacific. During the second term of President Grant, when Americans were far from squeamish about "conflict of interest," its operations caused a national scandal, for certain members of Congress were on the Union Pacific's directorate. By voting for land grants some Congressmen were indirectly voting themselves vast acreages in the western plains. Huge profits accrued to the Crédit Mobilier. A congressional committee reported in 1873 that over $23 million in cash profits had been realized by the company on a $10 million investment, and the cash "take" was over and above a $50 million profit in securities.

The managements of many railroads dissociated themselves from the welfare of their companies in a way that is unique in American business history. Officers and directors did not try to maximize railway earnings or net worth but instead endeavored to maximize their own wealth; as between keeping for the company $1 million worth of land or transferring it to a construction company, they preferred the latter. Moreover, the inflated costs of building went into the rate base and thus led to rates so high as to put the railroads later at a competitive disadvantage. Too often managements had no normal identification with their companies, and the result was to weaken the financial structures of most railroads for all time.

---

[6] Although the value of a company's assets, plus its current and potential earning power, might determine prices for more sophisticated investors, rank-and-file buyers quickly got used to getting $2,500 or more in stocks and bonds for every $1,000 laid out in cash. For fifty years or so after 1860, it was next to impossible to get individuals to buy common stock in a new venture without sweetening the deal with a bond or two.

Railroad Regulation

Before 1870 a railroad usually had some degree of monopoly power within its operating area, and the first serious manifestations of the monopoly problem thus made their appearance on the American scene. Monopoly privileges made it possible for operators in some areas to charge excessively high rates and to discriminate against shippers and localities. Service was rendered on schedules and at prices roughly calculated to maximize net revenues of the railroad, the attitude being that if a shipper did not want the service offered at the established rate he did not have to take it. Obviously, since the service offered was the only one available to the shipper, he had to use it or not move his goods to market.

As the trunk lines of the East and the transcontinentals of the West formed their "systems" and as the entire net grew, companies not favored with a monopoly position began to suffer the pangs of competition.[7] The result was a general fall in rates, beginning around 1865 and continuing through the 1870s. Simple general rate reductions, carried out in gentlemanly and orderly fashion, were hardly to be expected in a young and rugged industry. Rates were more readily lowered for favored firms—i.e., firms with real bargaining power. Shippers not favored by these discriminatory rates or outright rebates were naturally indignant at special treatment accorded their competitors. Railroads also discriminated among cities and towns, a practice especially resented by farmers and merchants of one locality who saw those of another enjoying lower rates for the same service. High costs and high prices of goods received in a community and low prices for goods shipped out were attributed, rightly or wrongly, to this form of discrimination. The resentment of shippers at discriminatory practices resulted in popular support of legislation directed toward social control of the railroad business.

The first attempts to regulate railroad practices were by the charters permitting incorporation. Some charters contained maximum charge schedules, and others provided for a reduction in rates if the return on investment exceeded certain percentages. Regulation by charter was not successful because the rates set were generally higher than the railroads would have charged anyway, and no provisions were made against discrimination. Another reason for the failure of regulation by charter was the difficulty in changing the provisions as conditions changed.[8] In some states, as in Massachusetts, charters expressly allowed alteration of the provisions by the state

---

[7] Not perfect competition, of course, in the sense of the norm of economic theory. Frequently only two lines would compete, and only in unusual instances would a shipper have more than half a dozen choices on long hauls. Nevertheless, *alternative* routings became more and more common.

[8] As we have seen, the decision of the Supreme Court in the Dartmouth College case had declared that a charter was a contract and could not be changed except by consent of both parties.

ILLINOIS CENTRAL RAILROAD COMPANY

OFFER FOR SALE

ONE MILLION ACRES OF SUPERIOR FARMING LANDS,

IN FARMS OF

40, 80 & 160 acres and upwards at from $8 to $12 per acre.

THESE LANDS ARE

NOT SURPASSED BY ANY IN THE WORLD.

THEY LIE ALONG

THE WHOLE LINE OF THE CENTRAL ILLINOIS RAILROAD,

For Sale on LONG CREDIT, SHORT CREDIT and for CASH, they are situated near TOWNS, VILLAGES, SCHOOLS and CHURCHES.

For all Purposes of Agriculture.

The lands offered for sale by the Illinois Central Railroad Company are equal to any in the world. A healthy climate, a rich soil, and railroads to convey to market the fullness of the earth—all combine to place in the hands of the enterprising workingman the means of independence.

Illinois.

Extending 380 miles from North to South, has all the diversity of climate to be found between Massachusetts and Virginia, and varieties of soil adapted to the products of New England and those of the Middle States. The black soil in the central portions of the State is the richest known, and produces the finest corn, wheat, sorghum and hay, which latter crop, during the past year, has been highly remunerative. The seeding of these prairie lands to tame grasses, for pasturage, offers to farmers with capital the most profitable results. The smaller prairies, interspersed with timber, in the more southern portion of the State, produce the best of winter wheat, tobacco, flax, hemp and fruit. The lands still further South are heavily timbered, and here the raising of fruit, tobacco, cotton and the manufacture of lumber yield large returns. The health of Illinois is hardly surpassed by any State in the Union.

Grain and Stock Raising.

In the list of corn and wheat producing States, Illinois stands pre-eminently first. Its advantages for raising cattle and hogs are too well known to require comment here. For sheep raising, the lands in every part of the State are well adapted, and Illinois can now boast of many of the largest flocks in the country. No branch in industry offers greater inducements for investment.

Hemp, Flax and Tobacco.

Hemp and flax canbe produced of as good quality as any grown in Europe. Tobacco of the finest quality is raised upon lands purchased of this Company, and it promises to be one of the most important crops of the State. Cotton, too, is raised, to a considerable extent, in the southern portion. The making of sugar from the beet is receiving considerable attention, and experiments upon a large scale have been made during the past season. The cultivation of sorghum is rapidly increasing, and there are numerous indications that ere many years Illinois will produce a large surplus of sugar and molasses for exportation.

Fruit.

The central and southern parts of the State are peculiarly adapted to fruit raising; and peaches, pears and strawberries, together with early vegetables, are sent to Chicago, St. Louis and Cincinnati, as well as other markets, and always command a ready sale.

Coal and Minerals.

The immense coal deposits of Illinois are worked at different points near the Railroad, and the great resources of the State in iron, lead, zinc, limestone, potters' clay, &c., &c., as yet barely touched, will eventually be the source of great wealth.

To Actual Settlers

the inducements offered are so great that the Company has already sold 1,500,000 acres, and the sales during the past year have been to a larger number of purchasers than ever before. The advantages to a man of small means, settling in Illinois, where his children may grow up with all the benefits of education and the best of public schools, can hardly be over-estimated. No State in the Union is increasing more rapidly in population, which has trebled in ten years along the line of this Railroad.

PRICES AND TERMS OF PAYMENT.

The price of land varies from $7 to $12 and upward per acre, and they are sold on long credit, on short credit, or for cash. A deduction of *ten per cent.* from the long credit price is made to those who make a payment of one-fourth of the principal down, and the balance in one, two, and three years. A deduction of **twenty per cent.** is made to those who purchase for cash. Never before have greater inducements been offered to cash purchasers.

EXAMPLE.

Forty acres at $10 per acre on long credit, interest at six per cent., payable annually in advance; the principal in four, five, six, and seven years.

	INTEREST.	PRINCIPAL.
Cash payment	$24.00	
Payment in one year	24.00	
" two years	24.00	
" three "	24.00	
" four "	18.00	$100.00
" five "	12.00	100.00
" six "	6.00	100.00
" seven "		100.00

Or the same farm, on short credit:

	INTEREST.	PRINCIPAL.
Cash payment	$16.20	$90.00
Payment in one year	10.80	90.00
" two years	5.40	90.00
" three "		90.00

The same farm may be purchased for $320 in cash.

Full information on all points, together with maps, showing the exact location of the lands, will be furnished on application in person or by letter to

LAND COMMISSIONER,

Illinois Central R. R. Co., Chicago. Ill.

Public land granted to the railroads as a subsidy and in turn sold to settlers was a continuing source of capital funds. Ads like this one appeared in city newspapers and lured hundreds of thousands of Americans westward.

legislature, but even in these instances it soon became apparent that some kind of quasi-administrative body would have to exercise authority.

In some New England states in the 1830s and 1840s commissions were created for regulating certain activities of railroads. Their powers were limited, however, and none could control rates. They were charged with the enforcement of laws relative to safety and had investigative powers to determine charter violations. They also collected accounting and statistical information from the railroads.

The first comprehensive railroad regulation came in the early 1870s, largely as a consequence of hardship in farming areas brought on by the depression that began in 1873. Agricultural prices, which had started to drop in the late sixties, declined more than prices of many things farmers had to buy, and the farmer in the Middle West attributed a large measure of his economic difficulty to the railroads. Many farmers had invested savings in railroad ventures on the basis of extravagant promises of prosperity that would result from better transportation facilities. When the opposite effect was apparent, agrarians, particularly in the Middle West, initiated a move for legislation to regulate rates. Prominent in the movement were members of the National Grange. Thus the demand for passage by the *states* of measures regulating railroads, grain elevators, and public warehouses came to be known as the "Granger movement," the legislation as the "Granger laws," and the review of the laws by the Supreme Court as the "Granger cases."

Between 1871 and 1874 regulatory railroad laws were passed by Illinois, Iowa, Wisconsin, and Minnesota. Because of the ill-feeling toward the railroads, some of the legislation was intemperate, but much of it was sound and set a pattern for future state and federal regulatory policies. The fixing of maximum schedules of rates by commission rather than by statute was a feature of the Illinois and Minnesota laws. One of the common practices that western farmers could not abide was that of charging more for carriage of goods over a short distance than over a longer distance in the same direction and by the same line. The "pro-rata" clause contained in the Granger laws, which prohibited railroads from charging short shippers more than their fair share of the costs, was intended to rectify this injustice and was the forerunner of the present-day *long-and-short-haul* clause of the Interstate Commerce Act. Both *personal* and *place* discrimination were generally outlawed. Finally, strong commissions were given power to investigate alleged violations and to institute suits against violators.

Almost as soon as the Granger laws were in the statute books, attempts were made to have them declared unconstitutional on grounds that they were repugnant to the "due process" clause of the Fourteenth Amendment to the Constitution. Pleadings in the courts were based on the premise that limitations on rates and charges restricted the earnings of companies and deprived properties of their value. Six suits were brought to test the laws. The principal one was *Munn* v. *Illinois,* an action involving grain elevators.

This case was taken to the United States Supreme Court after state courts in Illinois found that Munn and his partner Scott had in 1872 violated the state warehouse law by not obtaining a license to operate grain elevators in the City of Chicago and by charging prices in excess of those set by state law. Although the Munn case involved grain elevators, the Court held that the principles expounded applied to the five railroad cases then before it; in each instance the right of a state to regulate certain businesses was upheld. Justice Waite in the majority opinion stated that both in England and in the United States the activity of some firms had been regulated with respect to both services rendered and charges made. He remarked that while the Fourteenth Amendment was new to the Constitution of the United States, the principle (that a person could not be deprived of property without due process of law) was well established. Nevertheless, said the Court, when businesses are "clothed with a public interest" their regulation as public utilities is constitutional.[9] The Munn case settled the constitutionality of state regulation of railroads and certain other enterprises.

Between 1875 and 1878 the Granger laws were repealed or modified, and the active commissions were replaced with advisory ones having no control over rates and little control over services and discrimination. The reasons for the reversal in public attitudes were several. One was the vigorous campaign waged by the railroads that convinced people that the Granger legislation was a mistake and a burden on both business and agriculture. The obviously questionable provisions of the laws—the enforcing of competition by forbidding consolidations, the inflexible pro-rata clauses, and the legislative determination of maximum rates—were all emphasized. Furthermore, railroad building was brought to a halt by the panic of 1873, and economic difficulties were cited as evidence that capital was being driven away from railroad enterprises by the harsh and restrictive Granger laws. Swayed by such arguments, the legislatures of Illinois, Iowa, Wisconsin, and Minnesota took the teeth out of their laws. These four states kept some regulatory legislation, however, and by 1890 thirty other states passed laws affecting railroad operation.

The forces that brought about railroad legislation in the Middle West reached as far as Congress. While the first state laws were being passed, the Senate formed a select committee that made the famed Windom Report in 1874. Although the committee took cognizance of the problem of discrimination, it held that the chief troubles of the transportation system stemmed from insufficient facilities and extortionate charges. The committee recommended the construction, by state or federal governments, of lines from the Mississippi to the seaboard to compete with privately owned lines. Such competition it held, along with that of expanded waterway developments,

---

[9] Justice Field in the dissenting opinion objected to the vague language of the majority; he went on to say that the public is interested in many businesses and that to extend the reasoning of the majority might bring "calico gowns" and "city mansions" within the scope of such regulation.

would correct existing evils. No action was taken on the proposals in the Senate. The House passed bills in 1874, 1878, and 1884 that approached the problems of regulation from other points of view, but differences between the Senate and the House of Representatives prevented passage of legislation until 1887. There were three points of difference between the two bodies. The Senate wanted a commission to administer the law, whereas the House considered the machinery of the courts effective enough to enforce the law. The House wished to prohibit the practice of pooling freight and the revenues derived therefrom; the Senate's view was the opposite. The House favored a rigid application of the principle of the long-and-short-haul clause, but the Senate held that a flexible rule was justified.

A compromise might have been put off indefinitely had two pressures for action not exerted themselves. For one thing, discriminatory rate-making put so many firms at a competitive disadvantage that business joined agriculture in demands for reform. More important, perhaps, was a sharp change in attitude of the Supreme Court. In 1886 a decision in the case of *Wabash, St. Louis and Pacific Railway Company* v. *Illinois* made a critical delineation of the sphere of state control as distinguished from that of federal control. The state had found that the Wabash was charging more for a shorter haul from Gilman, Illinois, to New York City than for a longer one from Peoria to New York City and had ordered the rate adjusted because it violated the pro-rata clause in the regulatory statutes. The Supreme Court held that Illinois could not regulate rates on shipments in interstate commerce even in the absence of federal regulation, for such regulation would inevitably restrict freedom of commerce among the states. This view was an extension of the opinion of the Court in the Granger cases, where the contention of the railroads had been that the Granger laws were an interference with interstate commerce and thus an interference with the powers of the United States government. In the absence of federal legislation the Wabash case left a vast area without any control of carrier operation; there would have to be national regulation or hopelessly inadequate regulation. The public-policy answer was of more than passing importance, for it marked the first massive intervention of the federal government in the private economy.

Early in 1887 the Act to Regulate Commerce was passed by Congress and approved by the President. Its chief purpose was to bring under federal regulation all railroads engaged in interstate commerce. The Interstate Commerce Commission, consisting of five members to be appointed by the President with the advice and consent of the Senate, was created and its duties set forth. First, it was required to look into the business of the railroads; to this end it could subpoena witnesses and cause them to produce books, contracts, and other documents of the carriers. Second, the Commission was charged with hearing complaints arising out of violations of the Act and was empowered to issue "cease and desist" orders on findings of unlawful practices. The third duty of the Commission was to require railroads to submit annual reports based on a uniform system of accounts. Finally, the Commission was required to submit annual reports to Congress of its own operations.

The Act to Regulate Commerce seemingly prohibited all possible evil practices. Section 1 stated that railroad rates must be "just and reasonable." Section 2 prohibited personal discrimination; a lower charge could no longer be made in the form of a "special rate, rebate, drawback, or other device." Section 3 provided that no undue preference of any kind should be accorded by any railroad to any shipper, any place, or any special kind of traffic. Section 4 enacted, in less drastic form, the pro-rata clauses of the Granger legislation by prohibiting greater charges "for the transportation of passengers or of like kind of property, under substantially similar circumstances and conditions, for a shorter than for a longer distance, over the same line, in the same direction, the shorter being included in the longer distance."

Two other restraints on railroads were imposed by this pioneer regulatory effort. One was the prohibition of pooling agreements, by which railroads apportioned among themselves the available business between competitive points. The public concept of price regulation presupposed effective competition, and any attempt at collusion on the part of railroads was viewed with disfavor by shippers who feared the railroad monopoly. It was further provided that railroads should publish their fares or rates for the information of all concerned and that no increase in these charges should be made without ten days' notice.

The results of the 1887 act were temporarily encouraging if not altogether satisfactory. But the Commission soon encountered difficulty in enforcing its decisions. Although at first the roads usually complied with Commission orders, companies began to challenge certain powers delegated by Congress to the Commission, and compliance became spotty and uncertain. Moreover, Supreme Court decisions in the Social Circle case (1896) and the Maximum Freight Rate case (1897) affirmed only the right of the Commission to pass on the reasonableness of *existing* rates. If a rate were found to be unreasonable, a maximum *future* rate could not be prescribed. In effect these two cases deprived the Commission of the power to regulate maximum rates and destroyed its effectiveness.

For the next few years uncertainty and confusion characterized attempts to control the railroad industry. As powerful systems vied with each other in unchecked rebating, it appeared that the whole decades-long movement was doomed to frustration and failure. But increasing freight rates and discrimination that put some shippers at great competitive disadvantage aroused anew the ire of large segments of the business community. Even some railroad executives began to argue for an "orderly" competitive environment. Still more important was the developing political climate, which became more and more hostile to "big business" and suspicious that it represented exploitation of small business and the public. Thus in the first decade of the twentieth century it became possible to get through Congress three major laws that closed most of the loopholes of earlier legislation and made control of the carriers solid and lasting.

The Elkins Act of 1903 dealt solely with the practice of personal discrimination. The law provided that the railroad corporation should be liable for unlawful violation of the discrimination provisions. Up to this time only officials and employees of a company had been liable for discriminatory actions; henceforth the corporation itself would be responsible too. A second provision made the *receiver* of rebates guilty of violating the law, even though the rebate was given voluntarily by the carrier. The most important provision dealt with the practice of departing from published rates. The courts had hitherto overruled the Commission in the enforcement of published tariffs by requiring that discrimination against, or injury to, *other* shippers of similar goods had to be shown. The Elkins Act made *any* departure from a published rate a misdemeanor and authorized the courts to enjoin railroads from (a) continuing to depart from published rates and (b) unlawful discriminations.

The Elkins Act corrected some of the more flagrant abuses, but something had to be done to restore to the Commission powers weakened by the Supreme Court decisions of 1896 and 1897. In 1904 and 1905 President Theodore Roosevelt recommended legislation that would give the I.C.C. firm control over rates and plug the remaining loopholes that still permitted discrimination by devious means. The Hepburn Act of 1906 extended the jurisdiction of the Interstate Commerce Commission to private-car companies operating joint express, tank, and sleeping cars. Services like storage, refrigeration, and ventilation, furnished by railroads in connection with transportation, were also made subject to the control of the Commission. The definition of a "railroad" was expanded to include spurs, switches, tracks, and terminal facilities. The extension of I.C.C. jurisdiction over these phases of railroad transportation was necessary because the management of the roads could use such services to discriminate among shippers in subtle fashion. Storage or refrigeration were normally charged for; if shippers were not charged for them, discrimination resulted. Another blow was struck at discrimination by the insertion in the act of a "commodities" clause, which aimed to keep railroads from engaging in business activities, such as coal mining, competitive with nonrailroad firms. The law prevented the railroads from moving over their own lines any commodity, except lumber, in which they had an interest. All these regulations were reinforced by giving the Commission strengthened authority to require regular reports and uniform systems of accounts and to inspect the books of any railroad at any time.

As we have seen, the original Act to Regulate Commerce required only that rates be just and reasonable and stated that all rates not meeting this test were unlawful. The Commission had assumed that if it found an unlawful rate it might prescribe the rate to be used in the future.

For nearly a decade after adverse Supreme Court decisions the Commission was powerless to give either shippers or the public adequate protection from unreasonable charges. It was the chief purpose of the Hepburn Act to remedy this defect. Under the doctrine of the Maximum Freight Rate case the Commission could condemn the wrong but could not provide the remedy. The Hepburn Act allowed the prescription of the remedy in that the regulatory body could henceforth set maximum rates for the future. Furthermore, where it was necessary for several roads to participate in carrying goods from one point to another, the Commission could henceforth establish through rates and joint rates and thus provide shippers and the public with full use of the transportation system.

The most significant portion of the Hepburn Act after the maximum-rate provision was the change in the procedure for enforcement of the Commission's orders. Congress thus took cognizance of the difficulty hitherto experienced by the Commission in getting court approval of its decisions. After the regulatory authority had made a decision, it frequently had to resort to the federal courts to make the ruling stick. In practice the courts reopened *de novo* most of the orders of the Commission appealed to them, allowing new evidence to be introduced into the appeals and so negating the authority of the Commission. The Commission—a representative of the government—had in effect to prove before the Court the case it had adjudicated under its authority set by Congress. The Hepburn Act put the burden of proof on the carriers. Disobedience of Commission orders carried a penalty of $5,000, and each day of violation constituted a separate offense. The right of judicial review was recognized, but the railroads, not the Commission, had to appeal, and the presumption was for, not against, the Commission. Procedural obstacles were removed in an effort to keep cases from dragging on for years in litigation.

Surely, it would seem, sufficient power to regulate in the public interest now lay in the hands of the government. One more piece of major legislation was necessary, though, before all the obvious avenues of escape from national authority were blocked. The Mann-Elkins Act of 1910 amended the long-and-short-haul clause incorporated in the original Act to Regulate Commerce in 1887. In the Alabama Midland case the decision of the Supreme Court had rendered the clause practically inoperative, for the Court held that the railroad—not the Interstate Commerce Commission—could determine the meaning of "under substantially similar circumstances and conditions." The effect of the Mann-Elkins Act was to return to the Commission the power to determine exceptions to the long-and-short-haul clause, for permission to charge less for a long than for a short haul had now to be obtained in advance. Perhaps as important in giving the Commission practical control over rates was a new power to suspend proposed changes in order to ascertain the effect of such changes on shippers and on the roads themselves. At last control over rates and discriminatory practices seemed satisfactory. Yet all was far from well with the railroad industry that, for all its great promise, had not achieved economic health even in the days when there were no seriously competing modes of transportation.

In retrospect it is not hard to see why most of the major companies, at one time or another, were in serious financial difficulties. During the first half-century of building, lines were persistently pushed ahead of profitable traffic. Except for roads that connected the already established commercial centers, there was at best a considerable lag between investment and fruition. In the zeal for expansion tracks were laid to isolated villages and hamlets that could not possibly provide enough business to make the capital investment profitable. An equally important cause of financial trouble was the overzealousness and greed of empire-builders, who either dishonestly milked the properties under their control or built far too many competing lines between major centers that promised a lucrative traffic.

Moreover, the regulatory authorities, however well intentioned, set some rates that were not fair and demanded practices that unreasonably reduced profits. Courts expressed concern over enforced competition with its consequent limitations on rates and earnings. In the landmark case of *Smyth* v. *Ames* the Supreme Court in 1898 called for the ambiguous goal of a "fair return on a fair value" of railroad property. If a ceiling were to be placed over earnings on the high side, then poetic justice called for a floor on the low.

So control followed a pattern that would become familiar. The first measure to regulate the industry contained flaws and loopholes. As these weaknesses were corrected, others appeared. Resentful of measures that limited their autonomy, railroad managers were endlessly resourceful in finding ways to avoid or evade the statute and then the statute as amended. A Newton's law of regulatory control was quickly operative—for each restrictive force imposed by government there was an equal and opposite reaction from the regulated industry. Soon the rules would become so complex that neither Commission experts nor private lawyers could discern the intent of Congress and the people.

Railroads During World War I

From the depression of the 1870s on, each major slump in business activity saw the receivership of major companies with vast mileages of track. During the last fifteen years of the nineteenth century, systems controlling over 60,000 miles of line became insolvent and passed through costly reorganizations aimed at safeguarding security values while corporate structures were revamped to fit earnings. Even in the good years from 1900 to 1915 any sudden sharp business contraction was sufficient to send major companies into receivership, for traffic fell off badly while high fixed charges went right on. It is hardly astonishing, then, that railroad managements found it difficult to obtain capital sufficient to keep roadbeds and equipment efficient and up to date. What was a merely unsatisfactory and unhealthy state of affairs became a dangerous crisis when the United States entered World War I.

With the declaration of war on Germany in April of 1917, the entire resources of the country were thrown into the conflict already raging in Europe. The railroads, as a part of these resources, were vital to the war effort, and the task that faced them was prodigious. Huge amounts of supplies and large numbers of troops had to be moved to Atlantic ports, and the job had to be done in spite of the loss of skilled men to the armed forces and to defense industries. Virtually all of the companies subscribed to a resolution that sought systematic co-operation under a Railroads' War Board composed of five railroad executives. The Board endeavored to meet war transportation needs by urging shippers to load cars more carefully and heavily and to load and unload cars more promptly. The railroads were requested to move cars more expeditiously and to reduce the percentages of cars and locomotives under repair at any one time. Passenger transportation was curtailed by limiting schedules and by eliminating excursions and luxury services. Under the Commission of Car Service, the Board pooled all the cars in the country and dispatched them where they were most needed.

But these measures were not sufficient. Toward the end of 1917 the Railroads' War Board, recognizing the imminence of a transportation breakdown, ordered the consolidation of the eastern railroads. A few days later the Interstate Commerce Commission made a special report to Congress, stating that unification of the railroads was urgently necessary to the prosecution of the war. Either the railroads should act as a unit, without restraints from the antitrust laws and the antipooling section of the Interstate Commerce Act and with loans from the United States treasury; or the President should operate the roads under the war powers granted by Congress, guaranteeing a suitable annual return to each company. The majority of the Commission made no recommendation as to the method to be used, although Commissioner McChord filed a separate report in which he pointed out that the Railroads' War Board was the fifth committee to deal with railroad problems since November 1916, and that the present Board had not accomplished its mission of securing adequate transportation.

During December the efficiency of the system declined to such an extent that President Wilson decided to act; on December 26, 1917, he took over the railroads by proclamation. He explained that the Railroads' War Board had done its utmost to effect a unified system, but he remarked that "only under government administration can the entire equipment of the several systems of transportation be fully and unreservedly thrown into a common service without injurious discrimination against particular properties." William Gibbs McAdoo, the Secretary of the Treasury, became Director-General of Railroads. By the Federal Control Act, effective March 21, 1918, the President was authorized to guarantee individual roads an annual sum not to exceed the average annual operating income for the three years previous to June 30, 1917. The Control Act allowed the railroads to issue such securities as were approved by the President and provided that loans for the purchase of equipment might be obtained from the government. Although the Interstate Commerce Commission remained the rate-making body, the Railroad Administration actually took over this power. The roads remained subject to the laws governing common carriers, and states continued to tax the roads and to enforce lawful police regulations as if they were privately operated. Federal control was to end within twenty-one months after the cessation of hostilities.

So far as the internal management of the roads was concerned, the transfer from private to government operation brought no remarkable changes. In the early days of federal control the firms' organizations remained intact, the president of each carrier acting under regional directors responsible to the Director-General. Later each president was replaced by a federal manager, in most cases the president himself or a senior vice-president, whose sole responsibility was to the government rather than to both the government *and* stockholders.

As soon as Mr. McAdoo assumed the duties of Director-General he advanced a number of policies to increase the efficiency of railroad operation. The first effort was directed to moving freight over the shortest route. Many savings resulted, though congestion in the East prevented some short routing. By General Order Number One, of December 29, 1917, unification of facilities was ordered, and joint use of both passenger and freight terminals that had hitherto served but one road followed. Reductions in passenger service, which had been started by the Railroads' War Board, continued as efforts were made to consolidate duplicate services. Measures to expedite car service included an increase in demurrage rates to discourage storage in cars. Store-door delivery and the sailing-day plan expedited the movement of freight away from terminals and made shippers bring goods to terminals on the day cars were to leave. Solid trainloads of particular commodities were made up and dispatched from origin to destination in one movement. Although these practices increased the volume of traffic handled, the Railroad Administration was not able to take all the freight that was offered and had to resort to permits for the shipment of freight. Most permits applied to goods destined for export, but traffic in congested domestic areas was controlled by permit to a limited extent. Another move toward efficiency was the Bituminous Coal Zone Plan whereby cross-hauling was kept to a minimum. A measure of lasting effect was the standardization of rolling stock. At the time the government assumed control over the roads it was estimated that there were nearly 2,000 types of freight cars; the Railroad Administration adopted twelve standard types of freight cars and six standard types of locomotives of two weights in each type.

The Federal Control Act expressly provided for the return of the railroads to private hands and contained assurances that temporary nationalization was in no way to be construed as prejudging future policy. Nevertheless, when the railroad system was released from the demands of a war economy, the question inevitably arose as to what policy should be. Great debates took place in Congress and in the press. In high-school and college debating societies the question "Should the federal government own and operate the railroads?" was the major topic of the day. The arguments invariably turned on the point of the relative "efficiency" of management under government versus private ownership. Whatever the merits of the evidence adduced by protagonists of either side, two facts were apparent. First, unification and the consequent provision of adequate wartime transportation were not achieved by individual railroad managements before the debacle of late 1917. Second, the government, by establishing an integrated, nationwide system, moved military and civilian traffic with reasonable dispatch and protected the investment in the roads. The American people did not conclude, on these grounds, that nationalization was desirable. The decision was to return the railroads to private operation; on what basis we shall see in Chapter 19.

Other Means of Transportation

DOMESTIC WATER TRANSPORT

Rivers and canals, which before mid-nineteenth century had furnished the chief ways for both goods and people, declined greatly in importance during the period from 1860 to 1920. Yet for a while after the Civil War some of the big arteries showed substantial absolute increases in commodity flows. Freight traffic on the Mississippi below St. Louis reached a high point around 1880. Peak tonnage on the Erie Canal was not achieved until 1889, seven years after toll charges for its use ceased. But even on these key waterways business had fallen off remarkably by the early 1900s. Along the Monongahela, the Allegheny, and the Ohio, where bulk cargoes related to steel production furnished most of the business, river traffic continued to flourish, but elsewhere it dropped to a small fraction of its former volume. By 1915 half of the country's canal mileage had fallen into disuse, though only the year before the Cape Cod Canal had been completed and the New York Barge Canal was not finished until 1918. Only one great nineteenth-century canal would be a vital part of the transportation system of the future. This was the Sault Ste. Marie Canal—the link that made Lake Superior an integral part of Great Lakes navigation, and in particular made its iron-ore deposits accessible for steel production on Lake Michigan and Lake Erie.

Modern industrial and commercial activity requires speed, punctuality, and dispatch. The railroads, for all their discrimination and relatively high ton-mile rates, usually met these requirements and thus furnished actually cheaper transportation than the waterways. However, some bulky commodities, such as iron ore, coal, and sand and gravel, continued to be shipped on slow vessels on a "pipeline" basis. Where annual requirements were stable and easily estimated, carriers could ply slowly back and forth in a continuous process of picking up cargo and discharging it.

The obvious economic justification of inland water carriage for this kind of traffic has made it easy for professional promoters to secure federal aid to improve and extend navigable channels, many of them useless but some of them so extensive and well designed as to secure an ultimate resurgence of traffic on the main rivers. The agitation first got results in 1907, when President Roosevelt appointed an Inland Waterways Commission to report on feasible projects. The first Congressional appropriation was made in 1911 for work on the channel of the Ohio River. World War I intervened to abate the enthusiasm of Chambers of Commerce and certain firms for this kind of subsidy, but large expenditures on river channels have been made since 1920.

While canal and river traffic was diminishing, the flow on the Great Lakes was growing phenomenally. When waterways in most sections reached their peak volumes in the 1880s, the Lakes System was just getting started. During the quarter-century after 1890, annual tonnage quintupled as the size of vessels increased and mechanical devices for loading and unloading cargoes were perfected. Iron ores from the great ranges of Minnesota and Wisconsin constituted the greater part of eastward shipments, though grain, flour, lumber, and copper moved in quantity. Coal was the chief commodity sent west to the lake ports, as various locational influences brought important units of the iron and steel industry into production there.

OTHER DOMESTIC TRANSPORTATION FACILITIES

It is easy to overlook the electric railway in an account of the development of the transportation system. The urban trolley car is rapidly being displaced. The "interurban," so familiar to the preceding generation, is almost extinct. Elevated railways, noisy manifestations of the need for speedy city transportation, are being torn down. Only the subway train is able to hold its own against the encroachments of motor vehicles.

Yet from 1865 to 1920 urban and interurban railways had an important economic and sociological impact. Pulled by horses or powered by steam before 1890, they were rapidly electrified after that date. By 1920 nearly 50,000 miles of track had been laid. Streetcars and interurban cars made possible the first movement of city people to suburban areas. By the same token, the trolley broadened the markets of city retailers and opened to country dwellers the pleasures and conveniences of the city. The great investment in these enterprises that took place between 1890 and 1914 provided a major boost to the economy in those years. As in the case of the railroads, great expectations led to overoptimistic expansion, and chicanery and fraud characterized much promotion. Nevertheless, even if we discount considerably the $5 billion of book value shown on the balance sheets of street railway companies by World War I years, there remains a remarkable amount of capital formation on this score.

At the time of street railway electrification the automobile was emerging from its status as an experimental gadget. Still a curiosity in 1900, fairly reliable cars were available in quantity by 1910. One hundred thousand autos were produced in 1910, well over 500,000 were made in 1914, and by 1917 annual output was almost 2,000,000 units. It was apparent, even to those with little feeling for the future, that the automobile would affect the basic structure of the economy.

Thus the highway, after an eclipse of nearly a century by the railroad, came back into its own. Before 1910 the small mileage of hard-surfaced roads adequate to support automobile traffic was confined almost entirely to the urban East. Beginning in 1891 efforts were made to move control of the roads from municipalities, where it had traditionally lain, to the state level. By 1914 state highway commissions could insist upon a certain minimum quality for key roads, supervise the raising of funds by bond issues, and experiment with new surfaces and types of road-building machinery. Concrete roads were laid as early as 1914, and only two years later the federal government made its first timorous financial contribution to a national system. Even with these improvements, as any motorist of those years can attest, major highways could be incredibly bad after inclement weather, and the estimated condition of the roads was a vital consideration when one contemplated a trip of any length. The firm establishment of the motor vehicle, especially as a freight carrier, was essentially a post–World War I development.

THE MERCHANT MARINE

The Civil War hastened the decline of the American Merchant Marine, for during the war ships were lost to privateers, and many owners took advantage of high prices offered by foreigners to rid themselves of their obsolete vessels. A slight revival of the shipping interests after the war was short-lived.

A partial exception to the decline was coastwise shipping. Protected by an old law limiting entry to vessels built in the United States and owned by her nationals, the coastwise and intercoastal trade increased in tonnage between 1860 and 1914. As might be expected, the railroads pre-empted the light and more valuable cargoes, leaving to ships such products as coal, iron, lumber, sand, and stone. By 1914 the railroads were carrying perhaps ten times as much freight by weight as the coastwise and intercoastal fleets.

The initial reason for the decline of the American merchant fleet was the unquestioned technical superiority in shipbuilding achieved by the British. Iron, and then steel, sailing vessels could be built more cheaply on English ways, and the British were probably ahead of Americans in steam-engine and propeller design until the 1880s. But the failure of the American merchant marine to make a comeback, long after technical differences had been evened out, must be attributed to other causes. One was lack of governmental subsidy. The United States granted nominal mail subsidies after the Civil War, but these did not compare favorably with the subsidies European shipowners received. After 1891 substantial mail subsidies were granted, but the investment required to be eligible for them was so great that their stimulating effect was negligible. Another cause was the regulation against purchase of foreign-made ships. Not until 1912 could cheaper, foreign-built ships be admitted to American registry, and then only under certain restrictions. Finally, largely because of the relatively high wages paid American seamen, profits from shipping were lower than what capital earned in the United States when put to internal pursuits.

By whatever criterion we measure the decline of the American merchant marine engaged in foreign commerce, the change was striking. Registered tonnage in foreign trade fell from about 2,500,000 in the 1860s to 750,000 in 1910. A more revealing indicator, perhaps, was the change in proportion of imports and exports carried by United States vessels. Two-thirds of the value of American foreign trade was carried by American ships in 1860. By 1900 the figure had fallen to one-tenth, and it remained at about this ratio until 1915. Surely the old glory had faded. And not even the opening of the Panama Canal in 1914 could bring the intercoastal trade into serious competition with the rails.

Between 1910 and 1915 there was a sharp rise in American tonnage in the foreign trade, brought about by increased exports to the European belligerents and by lowered costs consequent upon improved technical proficiency. Upon the entrance of the United States into World War I the foreign fleet, with the addition of German ships confiscated in American ports, may have totaled 3,000,000 tons. But 3,000,000 tons was so far from being adequate for war needs that the government had to get solidly into the shipping business. A shipping board was created in 1916 and provided with $50 million to obtain ships. Upon the United States' declaration of war, the shipping board organized the Emergency Fleet Corporation with $4 billion to spend on new construction. Over 2,000,000 tons were added to the foreign commerce fleet by the date of the armistice, and ships under construction in November of 1918 came off the ways for three years after the war. By 1921 tons registered in foreign trade had passed the 11,000,000 mark.

Because so much of this vast fleet was owned by the government, the question of ultimate disposition of the ships was scarcely less puzzling than the disposition of the railroads. A decision was reached in 1920 that determined government policy for the next two decades. The principle of "no subsidy" was discarded, the fleet was sold to private interests on favorable terms, tax concessions of all sorts were made, and the mercantilist doctrine of excluding foreigners from trade with colonies was continued. Whether or not this legislation promoted a vigorous and healthy merchant marine is a matter to be examined later.

Banking
and the Money Supply
(1861–1914)

You shall not press down upon the brow of labor this crown of thorns; you shall not crucify mankind upon a cross of gold.

WILLIAM JENNINGS BRYAN

As we observed in Chapter 7, free-wheeling pre–Civil War commercial banking arrangements were conducive to maximum economic growth. From the mid-1830s on there was no central bank to interfere with periods of business expansion, and within the rules of the Independent Treasury, succeeding Secretaries took steps to insulate the money markets from the effects of government transactions. Yet problems of seasonal fluctuations in bank reserves still remained, and technical difficulties of transferring funds and collecting checks were more and more vexatious as economic relationships became increasingly intricate. But the greatest pressure for "reform" came from advocates of a homogeneous paper currency. For more than a decade before the Civil War various plans had been suggested; war, as it so often does, made the prospect of greater economic efficiency more palatable to legislators. Yet it was not primarily on grounds of improved efficiency of the monetary mechanism that a federal banking law was passed.

The Banking Act of 1864

In 1861 Lincoln's Secretary of the Treasury, Salmon P. Chase, was faced with acute problems of war financing. Not yet convinced of the need for sharp boosts in tax receipts, he decided upon a policy of federal borrowing. His first experience in floating a large bond issue was disappointing. A way to strengthen the market for government bonds had to be found.

Secretary Chase had long been convinced of the need for a uniform national currency. Why not solve the financing problem and the currency problem at one stroke by adopting a plan of national-bank organization that would require banks to have a *bond-secured* note issue? The plan had worked well in New York under the Free Banking Act. It seemed obvious to treasury officials that if the bonds used to secure note issues were United States government bonds, demand for government securities would be stimulated and war loans would be easily obtained. At the same time state banks would be brought under federal control, and the country's hodge-podge note issue would be eliminated in favor of a homogeneous national currency.

Chase and his advisers were for these reasons receptive to proposals for federal chartering of commercial banks. There was not much support for the establishment of a central bank like the former second Bank of the United States, for the American electorate was still hostile to powerful financial institutions. Moreover, to achieve the twin objectives of an improved market for government securities and a uniform note issue, it was only necessary that individual banks be under the supervision of the United States rather than under the supervision of the several states.

Strong opposition to any measure that proposed to take banking from the easy control of the states was to be expected. There was much Congressional pulling and hauling over the question during 1862; early in the next year a bill called the Currency Act of 1863 was passed and signed by President Lincoln. So few banks were chartered under this law that it was necessary to secure a more comprehensive measure within another year. This new law, the Banking Act of 1864, left a permanent imprint on the economic system by providing the legal framework of a national bank system. We may summarize the provisions of the act under three headings.

Organization. Five or more persons could form an "association"—really a corporation—for the purpose of carrying on a banking business. Incorporators were to draw up articles of association and file them with the Comptroller of the Currency, who was to be the chief supervisor of all federally chartered banks. Associations in towns of less than 6,000 inhabitants had to have a minimum capital of $50,000, those in towns of more than 6,000 but less than 50,000 a capital of $100,000, and those in cities of 50,000 or more a capital of $200,000. Strict rules required capital subscriptions to be fully paid, and all the old abuses associated with raising bank capitals were effectively prohibited.

The basis of note issue. Each national bank was required to buy bonds of the United States government equal to one-third (later one-fourth) of the dollar amount of its capital stock, with the provision that no bank should have to buy more' than $50,000 worth. Each bank was to deposit its bonds with the Treasurer of the United States and was to receive notes, engraved in a standard design, in the amount of 90 per cent of the par value of the bonds deposited. A bank could own any amount of bonds it wished, but it could not have an amount of notes outstanding that exceeded its *capital* in dollar amount.

Reserves. By 1860 several state laws required banks to keep cash reserves against their deposit and note liabilities. In strict practice reserves were kept as gold and silver in bank vaults, but as time went on the custom developed of keeping deposits, known as correspondent accounts, with banks in other cities.[1] The National Bank Act recognized prevailing practice by permitting the new national institutions to keep their reserves in two forms —as cash in vault or as deposits with a national bank in one of seventeen "redemption" cities. Banks located in New York City (later called a "central reserve" city) were exceptions in that they had to keep *all* their reserves as cash in vault.[2] Banks in the sixteen other redemption cities (later called "reserve" cities) had to keep half their reserves as cash in vault but might keep the other half as deposits with national banks in New York. Banks in all other cities and towns (country banks) had to keep two-fifths of their reserves as cash in vault but might deposit the remaining three-fifths in a national bank in a redemption city. Reserves, in whatever form they were maintained, were set at 25 per cent for banks in redemption cities and at 15 per cent for country banks. *Reserves were originally to be calculated as a percentage of notes outstanding plus deposits.*

An important amendment affecting reserves was passed shortly after the panic of 1873. National banks were no longer required to keep reserves against *notes* but were to keep on deposit with the treasury a 5 per cent redemption fund that could also be counted as part of reserves against deposits. After 1874 national banks calculated their minimum legal reserves *only as a percentage of deposits.*

Growth of the National Banking System: The Resurgence of State Banks

It was felt that there would be a rush on the part of state banks to take out national charters, but at first most state banks kept their state charters. A state bank had nothing to gain by making the change except, perhaps,

---

[1] If a bank manager in Knoxville, Tennessee, knew that many checks drawn by depositors would be made payable to New York firms, he kept funds in New York to meet these foreseeable obligations. In case of emergency these deposits would serve him just as well as cash in his own vaults, for he could use them to meet obligations of his bank in New York or have the funds transferred for use at home.
[2] The law provided that the cash be "lawful money." In 1864, "lawful money" meant gold, silver, and greenbacks.

prestige and enhanced customer confidence, for the national law restricted traditional banking activities. The act made regular bank examinations mandatory, and each bank was required to submit financial statements upon the call of the Comptroller of the Currency. Real-estate loans were restricted, and loans could not be made on the security of a bank's own stock. Some banks refrained from taking out a national charter for a reason that seems trivial now: they did not want to give up an old, respected name, replacing it with a number (First National Bank of New York, Second National Bank of New York, etc.).[3]

Because the framers of the National Bank Act were determined to eliminate the heterogeneous note issue of state banks, it was necessary to make the issue of notes by state banks unprofitable. When the lack of enthusiasm for joining the national system became apparent, Congress passed a law in 1865 placing a prohibitive tax of 10 per cent per year on the circulation of state banks. Banks put their notes into circulation by lending money. If the interest on a loan were 7 per cent per annum and a bank were required to pay a tax of 10 per cent per annum on the amount of notes outstanding, the bank lost money on the transaction. As Table 13-1 indicates, the tax was effective. A majority of state banks immediately shifted over to federal jurisdiction. Banks retaining state charters were for the most part large city banks that were rapidly dropping the practice of issuing notes when they made loans. The reason becomes clear when we recall that during the middle 1850s bank deposits surpassed bank notes as the most convenient form of money. After the Civil War, deposits were far more important than notes in cities, and by the middle 1870s banks in all but backwoods areas could make their loans simply by crediting the account of the borrower. Within the next decade or so, some national banks even stopped availing themselves of the privilege of note issue.

Because they no longer found it necessary to issue notes and could operate under easier regulatory laws, state banks after 1875 began a steady increase. In 1892 they outnumbered national banks, and by 1914 there were more than twice as many state banks as national banks. But the total capital of state banks was less than that of national banks, and their deposits were only 50 per cent greater. State banks were smaller on the average than national banks, and in times of panic and depression they failed at a greater rate.

Indeed, a persistent source of weakness in American banking has been the large number of independent units under separate managements. Branch banking, which had shown signs of growth in the early nineteenth century, failed to gain a foothold even before the Civil War. The National Bank Act did not mention branch banking. It was assumed that national banks had no right to establish branches, though an amendment in 1865 permitted state banks to keep existing branches upon taking out a national

---

[3] This requirement was later removed.

Table 13-1

Commercial Banks in the United States, 1860–1914

Year [a]	State banks [b]	National banks	Year [a]	State banks [b]	National banks
1860	1,562		1890	2,250	3,484
1861	1,601		1891	2,743	3,652
1862	1,492		1892	3,773	3,759
1863	1,466	66	1893	4,188	3,807
1864	1,089	467	1894	4,188	3,770
1865	349	1,294	1895	4,369	3,715
1866	297	1,634	1896	4,279	3,689
1867	272	1,636	1897	4,420	3,610
1868	247	1,640	1898	4,486	3,581
1869	259	1,619	1899	4,738	3,582
1870	325	1,612	1900	5,007	3,731
1871	452	1,723	1901	5,651	4,163
1872	566	1,853	1902	6,171	4,532
1873	277	1,968	1903	6,890	4,935
1874	368	1,983	1904	7,970	5,327
1875	586	2,076	1905	9,018	5,664
1876	671	2,091	1906	10,220	6,046
1877	631	2,078	1907	11,469	6,422
1878	510	2,056	1908	12,803	6,817
1879	648	2,048	1909	13,421	6,886
1880	650	2,076	1910	14,348	7,138
1881	683	2,115	1911	15,322	7,270
1882	704	2,239	1912	16,037	7,366
1883	788	2,417	1913	16,841	7,467
1884	852	2,625	1914	17,498	7,518
1885	1,015	2,689			
1886	891	2,809			
1887	1,471	3,014			
1888	1,523	3,120			
1889	1,791	3,239			

SOURCE: *Banking Studies*, by members of the staff, Board of Governor of the Federal Reserve System (Baltimore: Waverly Press, 1941), pp. 422–23. See also *Historical Statistics of the United States, Colonial Times to 1957*, esp. pp. 623–32.

[a] All figures as of June 30, or nearest available date.

[b] Excludes unincorporated banks and mutual savings banks.

charter. In 1900 only eighty-seven banks operated branches, and most of them had state charters. During the first fifteen years of the twentieth century the number of banks with branches increased a little, but by 1914 only four hundred state banks and a handful of national banks operated branches. In part the antipathy toward branch banking originated in agrarian fear of domination by financial interests outside their own communities. But this sentiment was made effective in legislatures through lobbies led by small-town bankers, who feared competition from branches of city banks.

The banking system thus failed to achieve the strength that large banks, operating branches in different areas of diversified economic activity, would have provided. Borrowers probably lost through bank failures and higher rates of interest more than they gained by insisting on locally owned unit banks. And many a community failed to reach its economic potential because adequate financing of enterprises was not available from local institutions.

The Money Supply, 1863–1914

In the last quarter of the nineteenth century much economic hardship was imposed on Americans because leaders in politics and finance insisted upon "sound money." Following the inflation of the Civil War, prices in the United States began a decline that persisted, with brief interruptions, until a few years before the end of the century. During these years practically all groups in the economy suffered at one time or another from the protracted deflation. Farmers of the West and South were hardest hit and supported any measures that would reverse the long-time trend that began in the late 1860s. The reader will recall the three reasons for the farmer's attitude. First, as the general price level fell, farm prices fell more than nonfarm prices. Second, as farm prices fell, total farm income was reduced.[4] Third, the great majority of farmers had borrowed money to acquire their properties, and they were hard pressed to repay their indebtedness with dollars worth more than the ones they had originally borrowed. Merchants of the West and South, who depended directly on farm trade for their livelihood, were sympathetic to the farmer's view. Support came also from the laboring class, which suffered from unemployment during years of acute depression.

"Sound money" advocates could be found everywhere, but they were concentrated in the older, populous states of the North and East. Holders of assets in the form of money or fixed-income securities (bonds) are delighted when money increases in value—i.e., when the price level falls—provided the business contraction that usually accompanies the deflation does not lead to defaults on principal and interest. But propertied people are not ordinarily just creditors; they likewise own real estate and have interests in going businesses. Proprietors and owners of common stocks presumably desire a rising price level, which is invariably good for business. Nevertheless, businessmen of the North and East, almost without exception, bitterly resisted inflationary moves. The runaway inflation of Revolutionary times

---

[4] It is of course quite possible for total receipts from the sale of a good or service to *rise* as prices fall. Not so with many important farm products, including the cereal grains. We shall see why later.

had taught a lesson not yet forgotten. The business class felt that money ought to be tied to gold, which had become entrenched as the standard money metal. It is fruitless to contend (three generations later) that the business class would have been better advised to resist the strong deflationary pressures of the last quarter of the nineteenth century. The fact is that it did not, and it was able to muster sufficient political support to assure a government policy that today would be unthinkable.

At the outbreak of the Civil War the currency consisted of gold coins, subsidiary silver coins, and the notes of 1,500 state banks. By the end of the war, gold and silver had disappeared from circulation, and state bank notes were rapidly being withdrawn because of the prohibitive tax on them. In their place had come a national currency issue known as greenbacks, a queer fractional paper currency, and, of course, the new national bank notes.

GREENBACKS (UNITED STATES NOTES)

In 1861 the government of the United States was in financial straits. It had always depended for revenues on import duties, public-land sales and domestic excise taxes. After the war began, import revenues dried up rapidly. It soon became apparent that if sufficient money to finance the war were to be obtained by borrowing, interest charges would be exorbitant. A third alternative, printing paper money, was still open.

To meet its obligations the treasury issued a fiat currency. Officially designated a United States note, the paper was quickly nicknamed the *greenback* because of the coloring on the backs of the notes. People were bound to accept greenbacks in payment of all debts except interest on the public debt, and the government received them for all payments except customs duties. By 1863 three issues of greenbacks, totaling $450 million, had been authorized. It was an enormous issue for the time, almost half the amount of currency in circulation.

Had the government been able to nationalize gold and silver and put the country on a paper basis, problems of war financing would have diminished. But in the 1860s calling in gold and silver in exchange for bank deposits or greenbacks would have been an unthinkable violation of property rights. Greenbacks fell to a discount compared with gold and silver, two sets of prices soon being quoted for commodities and foreign exchange. On the gold market in New York, greenbacks at one time sold at a gold price as low as thirty-five cents on the dollar, but improving prospects of a northern victory brought them, by the close of the war, to over eighty cents. During the war state bank notes, which could be redeemed only in greenbacks, depreciated similarly; a serious element of instability was injected because the paper currency fluctuated violently below the gold par.[5]

---

[5] One of the effects of Civil War monetary difficulties is with us today. Merchants were so eager to have cash in hand for immediate use, thus avoiding the risk of further depreciation during a credit period, that they began to offer attractive discounts to anyone paying cash. The cash discount remains a customary business procedure.

At the end of the war there was agitation to have the greenbacks retired. Businessmen wanted to get back to a gold basis as quickly as possible, and most authorities agreed that gold redemption could come about only when the paper circulation was reduced. After the close of hostilities Congress authorized redemption of greenbacks at a rate of $10 million per month for six months and $4 million a month thereafter. Prices began to drop, however, and Congress stopped the retirement. Later a reissue of greenbacks was authorized; then for the second time a reduction was ordered. Finally, in 1878 the number of greenbacks authorized for circulation was left at an amount just under $347 million, the amount that remains outstanding today.

THE GOLD RESUMPTION ACT

Although agitation to increase the number of greenbacks in circulation was to continue for years, the question, as it turned out, had been finally settled. A second piece of legislation was to settle the problem of putting all money, including greenbacks, national bank notes, and bank deposits, on a par with gold.

A premium on gold meant that the price of a gold dollar in terms of all other money in the economy was above a dollar. During 1865 a gold dollar could be purchased, on an average, for a little more than $2 in, say, greenbacks or checks drawn on bank deposits. To bring about resumption of specie payments, this *premium* of more than a dollar had to fall to zero.

To achieve such a result, government policymakers had first to diagnose the problem, which was simple enough. Between 1860 and 1865 the money stock had trebled and the price level had approximately doubled. The market price of gold had moved with the general price level so that it was way above the mint price. Several alternative monetary policies were open to treasury officials, but for all practical purposes two courses were available:

1. The general price level could be forced down by contracting the supply of paper money. The price of gold would decline with the general fall in prices; when the mint price was reached, resumption could be proclaimed.
2. A slower, and probably less painful, decline in prices could be achieved by holding the money supply constant and allowing the growth of the economy to bring about a gradual decline in prices. Once again, the market price of gold would fall and ultimately reach the mint price.[6]

Actually, a severe policy of money contraction was initiated by Hugh

---

[6] Other alternatives included devaluation of metal dollars, abandoning the specie standard, and simply hoping and praying for a fortuitous increase in the supply of the money metals. See Richard H. Timberlake, Jr., "Ideological Factors in Specie Resumption and Treasury Policy," *Journal of Economic History*, XXIV, 1 (March 1964). See also James K. Kindahl, "Economic Factors in Specie Resumption: The United States, 1865–79," *Journal of Political Economy*, LXIX, 1 (February 1961), 30–48.

When gold fluctuated wildly in 1869, the Gold Room of the New York Stock Exchange was the nerve-center of speculation. In its center a bronze Cupid sprayed water quietly, while on the dais the secretary of the room cupped his ears to hear and record transactions.

McCulloch, Secretary of the Treasury in the Johnson Administration, and this strategy was approved by Congress in December 1865 by passage of the Contraction Act. But the deflationary medicine was too bitter, and Congress ended contraction in February 1868. Grant's Secretary of the Treasury, George S. Boutwell, followed a much easier policy, in general one of *easing* the money markets rather than tightening them.[7] Upon Boutwell's resignation in 1873, his Assistant Secretary, William Richardson, pursued a less vigorous policy but one nevertheless calculated to take the route of "growing into" resumption.

During the years from 1868 to 1874 the Republican Administration, while paying lip service to a return to gold, had taken the temperate and sensible course of not pressing for it through severe contraction of the money

---

[7] It was Boutwell who broke the dramatic corner on gold attempted by James Fisk and Jay Gould by selling $4 million of the money metal in the "Gold Room" of the New York Stock Exchange. A good exercise in the use of materials would be a trip to the Documents Department of the Library to read the official telling of this episode. See *Gold Panic Investigation,* Forty-first Congress, second session, House Report No. 31 by the Committee on Banking and Currency, James A. Garfield, Chairman, esp. pp. 1–4 and p. 463.

stock. But when the Democrats won control of the Congress in the election of 1874, lame-duck Republicans, fearful of the antipathy of western and southern legislators toward resumption, hastened to pass an act providing for a return to gold payments in four years. After January 1, 1879, the United States was to maintain strict interconvertibility between greenbacks and gold. Thanks to a favorable balance of trade in the latter years of the 1870s, gold stocks in this country increased at a rapid rate. The government removed the requirement that all customs duties be paid in gold so as to have no discrimination against greenbacks, and on the appointed day the United States began to maintain specie payments. For a technical reason to be discussed presently the United States was not finally and irrevocably committed to a gold standard. Not for twenty-one years were we to be *legally* on gold. Nevertheless, between 1879 and 1900 the government did *in fact* maintain parity of all other money forms with gold and during these years was on a *de facto* gold standard.

SILVER AND SILVER CERTIFICATES

During the Civil War, and for several years afterward, silver coins had gone out of circulation, having been replaced at first by ungummed postage stamps and later by fractional currency—paper notes issued by the government in denominations of 5, 10, 25, and 50 cents. It is not surprising, then, that when Congress came to simplify the coinage in 1873, the silver dollar was omitted from the list of coins to be minted. There was no serious agitation over the omission at the time, for at the mint ratio of approximately 16 to 1 silver was worth more in the market than at the mint, and little silver was brought to the mint for coinage. Yet scarcely three years later the failure to include the silver dollar in the Act of 1873 began a furor that lasted for a quarter of a century.

The reason for the subsequent agitation over the "demonetization" of silver lay in the fact that the price of silver was falling in the international markets. Increasing output of our western silver mines and a shift of the bimetallic countries of western Europe to the gold standard led to a growing surplus of silver. When the price of the silver contained in a dollar actually fell below the price (i.e., $1) that the government, under the Coinage Act of 1834, had *formerly* paid, silver producers took silver to the mint for coinage.[8] To their dismay they discovered that the government would take only as much silver as was needed for subsidiary coins. The cry that went up from the silver producers was horrendous.

Now a relatively small group like silver producers would not appear to have much power in a large country like the United States. During the seventies and eighties, however, a number of western states were coming into the Union, and silver men were influential politically. The "reflationist"

---

[8] It will be recalled that a dollar contained 371.25 grains of pure silver, or a little over three-fourths of an ounce. The *average* bullion value of that amount of silver in 1873 was $1.00368. The next year it dropped to $0.98909 and consistently fell from that year on.

Friends of silver saw in its monetization relief from depression, but continued grief and agony if gold continued its reign as the sole monetary metal in America.

element in the West and South joined the silver producers in a clamor for free and unlimited coinage of silver at the old mint ratio of 16 to 1. Silver advocates knew that at such a ratio silver would be brought to the mint in great quantities and that the monetary reserves of the country would consequently be increased. The cry of the opposition that gold would be driven out of circulation meant nothing to the unemployed, oppressed debtors, and others who wanted to raise the general price level. To the supporters of free coinage of silver, the act that had demonetized the metal became the "Crime of '73," even though the silver dollar was struck from the list of coins largely because no one thought the matter of any importance, and the slogan was a great help in stirring the emotions of the electorate.

Within two years the silver forces were able to push through Congress a compromise between the positions of the "sound-money" advocates and the free-coinage forces. This, the first of four major silver bills, was the Bland-Allison Act of 1878. The law provided for the coinage of silver in *limited* amounts. The Secretary of the Treasury was directed to purchase not less than $2 million and not more than $4 million worth of silver each month at the market price.[9] The conservative Secretaries in office during the next dozen years all purchased only the minimum amount, but by 1890

---

[9] By 1878, the market price of silver in New York averaged a little over $1.15 per ounce for the calendar year; the average market value of the silver contained in a dollar in that year was just over $.89. For the next dozen years silver prices consistently fell. Two points ought to be made in passing: the market price of silver was bolstered by government purchases, and the government made quite a profit (some $70 million) on its purchases under the act. The reader should see why this was so.

the treasury's monetary silver (not counting subsidiary coins) amounted to almost $380 million. According to the Bland-Allison Act and an amendment passed in 1886, the treasury could keep the actual silver in its vaults and issue silver certificates, dollar for dollar, instead. Because of the bulkiness of silver dollars, nearly everyone except Westerners preferred paper currency, and silver certificates circulated more than silver dollars.

But the silver question was by no means settled. After 1888 the Republicans were in control of both the Administration and Congress. In order to secure the passage of high-tariff legislation, it was necessary to have the votes of the silver senators. In exchange for their affirmative votes on the McKinley tariff bill, the Republican leadership agreed to further silver legislation. A new bill was carefully worked out so as to avoid the veto of President Harrison, and since Senator Sherman did the job, the resulting act is called the Sherman Silver Purchase Law of 1890.

The Secretary of the Treasury was directed to make a *monthly* purchase, at the market rate, of 4,500,000 *ounces* of silver. To pay for the bullion he was to issue a new type of paper to be known as treasury notes, the notes to be redeemable *in either gold or silver* at the discretion of the Secretary. At silver prices prevailing in 1890 the new law authorized the purchase of almost double the monthly amount of silver taken under the previous law. The market price of silver almost at once began a further sharp decline, and within three years the *dollar amount* being purchased was little more than it had been under the old act. In 1893, at the insistence of Democratic President Cleveland—a "sound-money" man at odds with his party on this issue—the Sherman Act was repealed. In over three years of purchasing under this law more than $150 million of the Treasury Notes of 1890 were issued. Between 1878 and 1893, $500 million was added to the circulating medium by silver purchases, a not inconsequential victory for the silver forces.

GOLD AND GOLD CERTIFICATES

Between 1860 and 1914 gold provided the largest single increase in the country's cash. (See chart, p. 314.) During the Civil War and for a decade thereafter, gold went into private hoards at home and abroad. After 1875, however, there was an almost uninterrupted increase in the monetary gold stock. In the 1880s monetary gold doubled in quantity, and between 1890 and 1914 the gold stock trebled.[10] American mines poured forth their treasure at a stable rate, and even in the years when the United States exported gold to make up adverse balances of payments, there were normally net additions to the total stock.

Although the silver acts of 1878 and 1890 made silver certificates redeema-

---

[10] Included in these figures are *gold certificates*. In 1865, Congress provided that gold certificates might be issued by the treasury in exchange for gold simply as a convenience to those who had to make certain payments, such as customs duties, in gold. After 1879 they circulated freely and were increasingly used. The backs of the gold certificates in use until 1928 were a bright yellow, and they were commonly referred to as "yellowbacks."

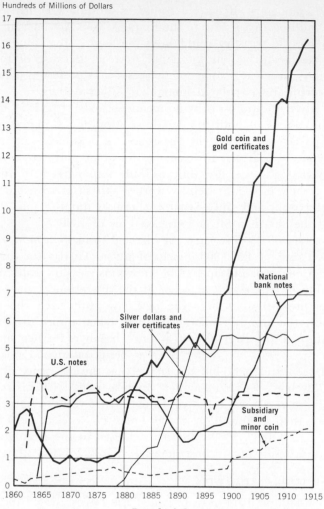

Hundreds of Millions of Dollars

Board of Governors of the Federal Reserve System.

Hard Cash: From the late 1870s to the early 1890s there were substantial additions to the country's monetary stocks of gold and silver, but the supply of paper money actually fell off during these years.

ble in *either* gold *or* silver, treasury authorities in practice redeemed them in gold if it were demanded. After 1879, treasury Secretaries felt that a minimum gold reserve of $100 million was necessary to back the paper circulation. Just at the time the Treasury Notes of 1890 were authorized, the government's gold reserve began falling toward the $100 million mark, as the public presented treasury notes and greenbacks for payment in gold. To meet current expenses the treasury had to pay the paper money out again almost as soon as it was received. By early 1893 the gold drain became serious, and toward the middle of the year the gold reserve actually dipped below the traditional minimum.

Several times during the next three years it appeared certain that the *de facto* gold standard would have to be abandoned. Two kinds of drains —"external" (foreign) and "internal" (domestic)—plagued the treasury from 1891 to 1896. Today abandonment of gold redemption hardly seems a fearful possibility, but in the middle 1890s conservatives considered going off gold the equivalent of national bankruptcy. The difficulty was that when the danger of leaving gold became apparent, people rushed to get gold and so made it even more likely that the treasury *would* go off gold. Chiefly by selling bonds for gold, the Administration replenished the government's reserves whenever it appeared that the standard was about to be lost. The repeal of the Sherman Act in 1893 cut down on the creation of treasury notes which, along with greenbacks, the public were presenting for redemption. Increasing exports at last brought an influx of gold from abroad in the summer of 1896, improving public confidence to the extent that the gold standard was saved.

The election of 1896 settled for nearly forty years the matter of a monetary standard. The money issue was clearly drawn. The Democrats, under the leadership of William Jennings Bryan, stood for free coinage of silver at a ratio of 16 to 1—even though the market ratio was then over 30 to 1. The Republicans, with McKinley as their candidate, stood solidly for the gold standard. The West and the South supported Bryan; the North and East supported McKinley. Any attempt to stop the long years of deflation was anathema to the conservative East, and industrial employers, aided and abetted by the professional class (including Protestant clergy), brought every possible pressure to bear on employee voters. Thus Bryan could not draw on the great urban vote, as Franklin Roosevelt was to do thirty-six years later, and when well-to-do farmers of the older agricultural states deserted him, the cause was lost. The Republican victory of 1896 was not followed immediately by legislation ending the controversy, for free silver advocates still had a majority in Congress. But the return of prosperity, encouraged by new gold discoveries, new methods of processing gold, and a rapid rate of investment, made Congress receptive to definitive gold legislation.

In 1900 the Gold Standard Act was passed. The dollar was defined solely in terms of gold, and all other forms of money were to be convertible into gold. The Secretary of the Treasury was directed to maintain a gold reserve of $150 million, which was not to be drawn upon to meet current expenses of the government. To prevent a recurrence of the difficulties of the nineties, provision was made for keeping redeemed silver certificates and greenbacks in the treasury during times of stress and for borrowing to meet deficits that might occur from time to time.[11] The United States had at last committed itself by law to the gold standard.

---

[11] The Treasury Notes of 1890 were retired by the Gold Standard Act.

This portrait of William Jennings Bryan as a young man shows the stately bearing and dignity that later served him so well on the political stump. Bryan was more than just a political leader; he also had a lively awareness of the need for economic and political reform. Although defeated on the money issue, his monetary prescriptions had a solid New Deal ring.

NATIONAL BANK NOTES

National bank notes became important by 1865, grew steadily in amount for a decade, and then began to fluctuate. (See chart, p. 314.) Originally the total issue was limited to $300 million, this sum having been allotted among the states in proportion to the population and the total of national bank capital within each state. Restrictions were removed by a clause in the Resumption Act of 1875, and from this year on national banks kept in circulation whatever amount of notes seemed profitable. The low point of notes outstanding was reached in the early 1890s. There followed a slow rise that in the early years of the century changed to a sharp increase, a record high of nearly $800 million being reached by 1915.

The decline of national bank-note circulation in the 1880s reflected the lessening importance of bank notes compared with bank deposits, the decrease in notes outstanding being greatest in the cities.[12] Too, as interest rates fell after 1873, prices of the bonds used to back national bank notes rose well above par, with the result that some banks found it did not pay to invest in these bonds while others sold their holdings to take a profit. On the other hand, as bond prices dropped in the late 1880s, banks again found it profitable to buy eligible government bonds, and in the 1890s they began to issue notes again. The Gold Standard Act of 1900 reduced the minimum capital requirements for national banks in small towns, making it more attractive for small banks (which would use the note issue privilege) to be-

---

[12] Some New York banks withdrew their circulation altogether.

come national banks. Finally, during the decade and a half before World War I, banks encountered an ever increasing demand for currency as the dollar volume of business increased.

SUMMARY OF CHANGES IN THE MONEY SUPPLY

In the chart on p. 318 are plotted the *absolute* changes in the total money supply and in the part of the money supply consisting of bank deposits. The chart on p. 314 shows the absolute changes in the different kinds of currency in use. First greenbacks, then silver, and finally gold provided marked increases in the supply of hand-to-hand money beginning at three successive points of time. These three types of currency provided, in order, the "dynamic" elements in the cash supply.

Yet, as the chart on p. 318 shows, the growth of bank deposits accounted for most of the increase in the total money supply. Cash, which (except for national bank notes) constituted the reserves of the banking system, was sufficient to permit a rate of increase in bank deposits about equal to the rate of increase in physical production. It follows that the causal role of coin and paper money in price level and income changes was probably overestimated by people who lived through the years between the Civil War and World War I. Other causes, as we shall see in Chapter 17, had much to do with bringing on the long years of sluggish business and intermittent depression that were followed by the prosperity characteristic of the first fifteen years of the twentieth century.

The Money Trust

In the 1860s and 1870s railroads and manufacturing firms increasingly turned to the corporate form of business organization, continuing to grow larger in volume of output, number of workers employed, and amounts of capital required. During the Civil War the United States Treasury also made unprecedented demands upon the capital markets, the national debt increasing from $59 million on December 31, 1859, to just short of $3 billion on September 1, 1865. The increasing demand for funds during and after the Civil War meant that previously untapped sources of funds had to be reached. It was the investment banker who devised new and more efficient methods of originating and marketing the securities necessary to finance the enhanced operations of government and business enterprise.

First of the investment bankers to achieve prominence and the outstanding figures in this field during and after the War were Junius Spencer Morgan (father of John Pierpont Morgan), Anthony Drexel, and Jay Cooke. Jay Cooke won fame in American investment banking by virtue of his sale of over a billion dollars worth of government bonds between 1861 and 1865. Cooke was the first investment banker to hit on the idea of selling government issues to the general public on a large scale, and the firm of Jay Cooke & Co. at one time had 2,500 salesmen aggressively promoting business.

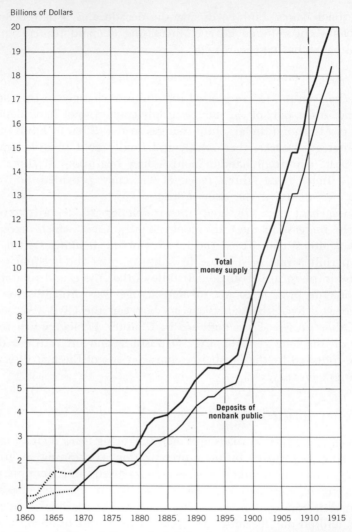

Billions of Dollars

Total money supply

Deposits of nonbank public

A. G. Hart, *Money, Debt, and Economic Activity,* 1st ed. (Englewood Cliffs, N.J.: Prentice-Hall, 1948).

Money Supply: Although the total money supply, like the metallic money stock, grew remarkably during the decade and a half after specie resumption, the increase was insufficient to correct a burdensome deflation.

Throughout the late 1860s and the early 1870s Jay Cooke & Co. was the leading firm in the field of government refunding operations. Unfortunately, the firm became overextended in the financing of the Northern Pacific Railroad and was forced to close its doors on September 18, 1873, accentuating the severity of the Panic of 1873.

With the failure of Jay Cooke & Co., the firm of Junius S. Morgan & Co. became the leading investment banking house in the United States. In 1871, during the Franco-Prussian War, Junius S. Morgan & Co. floated a risky French loan, the success of the venture putting the London firm among the leading investment banks in Europe. Until his death in 1890 Junius Morgan remained titular head of the Morgan interests, but young J. Pierpont was rapidly brought along as his father's ultimate replacement. In 1860, at the age of twenty-three, J. P. Morgan had established an office in New York, acting as the agent of George Peabody & Co., then perhaps the leading investment bankers in London. Four years later, on the advice of his father, young Morgan admitted a seasoned older man, Charles Dabney, as a partner. In 1871 Dabney, Morgan & Co. merged with the firm of Anthony Drexel to form the most prestigious investment banking house in America—Drexel, Morgan & Co.

Up to this time J. P. Morgan's apprenticeship had been spent learning the ins and outs of buying and selling gold, securities, and bills of exchange, usually on commission. During the 1870s he improved his skill as a trader by participating in the refunding of the public debt, a massive operation for the time. After successfully making his entrance into big-scale investment banking by means of government bonds, Morgan entered the field of railroad finance. His successful sale of a large part of William Vanderbilt's holdings in the New York Central Railroad brought him reputation, a strong foothold in railroad finance, and reportedly $3 million and a seat on the board of directors.

When Morgan became a director of the New York Central, thus becoming an "active" investment banker, he was merely following a principle suggested by the most sophisticated business experience of his time. Throughout his career Morgan continued to take an "active" role in the firms he served. A man of steadfast purpose, he aimed at making money for his clients and for his firm by introducing orderly and responsible administration within a "co-operative" system of interlocking interests.

Morgan used a specific procedure in his railroad (and other) reorganizations that came to be known as "Morganization," and an enterprise reorganized under his auspices was considered by the general public "Morganized." As we saw in Chapter 12, railroad promoters were careless about saddling their companies with an undue burden of interest expense, often throwing in a bond as a premium for buying a certain number of shares of common stock. As railroads (and manufacturing concerns with a high proportion of fixed to total assets) came on bad days, the problem was invariably one of reducing their fixed charges so that they could be met even in the depths of a depression. To achieve this end, Morgan and his partners would persuade bondholders of a firm in trouble to accept stock as payment for a large part of their bonds, at the same time assessing old and new stockholders for sums sufficient to provide adequate working capital for the reorganized company. Stockholders would then usually turn over their voting rights for a period of five or six years to a committee of financiers whom Morgan considered "sound"; this "voting trust" made sure that the company's direction would be prudently conservative and that outsiders would not "raid" it—i.e., gain control by buying up great chunks of the equity now in many hands. Needless to say, a Morgan man would almost certainly be on the board of directors after the voting trust was dissolved, and monkey business of any kind would be promptly reported to Mr. Morgan himself.

Free-handed issuance of stock in these reorganization proceedings led to charges of "stock watering"—i.e., creation of a common-share interest with a dollar value far in excess of the property values behind it. Moreover, there was a ruthlessness about the process that was bound to create enemies, particularly among erstwhile bondholders. But not until after the turn of the century were there anything like widespread complaints against the activities of the tight little investment-banking fraternity, and at first these were confined to the snide remarks of journalists, who objected primarily to the stock-watering that occurred when some of the great holding companies, such as United States Steel, were formed. A tide of protest swelled only a little when fraud was disclosed in the flotation of the securities of the International Mercantile Marine Company (the "Shipbuilding Trust") and when nearly forty of the new combinations failed in 1903.

Indeed, the resistance to old-style investment banking did not really become serious until there was a general realization of the degree of concentration in investment banking itself. It is an oversimplification to say that this crucial field of finance was controlled by Morgan interests on the one hand and Rockefeller interests on the other, for there was a curious overlapping of control that defies classification. It seems reasonable, though, to say that Morgan could depend upon the First National Bank of New York, headed by skilled, unscrupulous George Fisher Baker, as a major ally, along with the New York Life Insurance Company and the Mutual Life Insurance Company of New York. The Rockefeller millions were aided and abetted by Kuhn, Loeb & Co., headed by an investment banker second only to Morgan in influence, Jacob H. Schiff. The commercial-bank alliance of the Rockefeller camp was, if anything, stronger than that of Morgan, consisting of the National City Bank under James Stillman, which, like the First National Bank, owned substantial or controlling interests in other major commercial banks of New York City. Yet J. P. Morgan & Co. (the firm name was made more realistic in 1894) owned stock in the National City Bank, and Kuhn, Loeb & Co. certainly had interests in banks of the First National group. Furthermore, Boston firms did good business with both sides, the most important being Lee, Higginson & Co. and Kidder, Peabody & Co. and their three affiliated banks—the National Shawmut, the First National, and the Old Colony Trust Company. Connected with this "in" group, and sometimes acting as jobbers and distributors of securities while the dominant New York and Boston firms remained anonymous, were such companies as Kissel Kinnicut & Co., White, Weld & Co., and Harvey Fisk and Sons. Outside New York and Boston only the First National Bank of Chicago, the Illinois Trust and Savings Bank, and the Continental and Commercial

National Bank, largest financial institutions in Chicago, were really important as participants in the investment-banking business.

Not until official investigation disclosed the extent of the concentration could knowledgeable Americans be sure of the degree of financial control exercised by so few men. But long before evidence was spread on the record people who thought about such things were pretty sure there was a "money trust." The opinion was frequently expressed that the investment bankers had induced the Panic of 1907 in order to bring about a drastic fall in securities prices and so enable them to buy properties at bargain rates. It was well known that during the panic Morgan had headed a rescue committee that baled out some shaky institutions while allowing others to fail. And a sluggish recovery after the 1907–08 downturn convinced many middle-class leaders that the conservatives who dominated the money trust were inhibiting the economic growth of the country.

The final Congressional demand for an investigation was by no means separate from the vexing central-bank question. Yet it did result in part from a special insistence on the part of the electorate that the existence of a money trust be verified or denied. In 1912 a House subcommittee chaired by Arsène Pujo of Louisiana began lengthy hearings that brought the nation's leading financiers to Washington. Not the least of them was Morgan himself, who with marvelous aplomb blandly denied any influence in the companies he financed. The three volumes of testimony and exhibits make exciting reading even today, and the conclusion to which the evidence led was all too obvious. The subcommittee's answer to the question "Is there a money trust?" might seem equivocal at first reading, but in fact it was not.

> If by such a trust is meant a combination or arrangement created and existing pursuant to a definite agreement between designated persons with the avowed and accomplished object of concentrating unto themselves the control of money and credit, we are unable to say that the existence of a money trust has been established in that broad bald sense of the term, although the committee regrets to find that even adopting that extreme definition surprisingly many elements of such a combination exist.

But if by a money trust was meant "An established and well-defined identity and community of interest between a few leaders of finance which has been created and is held together through stock holdings, interlocking directorates, and other forms of domination over banks, trust companies, railroads, public-service and industrial corporations, and which has resulted in a vast and growing concentration of control of money and credit in the hands of a comparatively few men," there was no question about it. The committee had ". . . no hesitation in asserting as the result of its investigation up to this time that the condition thus described exists in this country today." [13]

---

[13] *Report of the Committee Appointed Pursuant to House Resolutions 429 and 504 to Investigate the Concentration of Control of Money and Credit* (Washington: Government Printing Office, 1913), pp. 129 and 130.

The Pujo Committee clearly pointed to J. P. Morgan as the leader of the "money trust." He and his close associates held 341 directorships in 112 corporations with assets totaling more than $22 billion. On February 28, 1913, the Pujo Committee submitted its report. On March 31, 1913, John Pierpont Morgan died. With the great man gone the committee report lost its bite, and besides the country thought it could solve the money problem by passing legislation creating an American central bank.

Central Bank Functions

The functions of a central bank fall into two categories.

1. *The Control Functions.* Central banks endeavor to regulate the money supply of an economy, together with credit conditions in general, so as to achieve certain economic aims. These aims have changed from time to time, but during the past fifty years or so the principal objective has been to aid other government officials in executing a total policy of stabilizing the economy through appropriate adjustment of the money supply and the rate of interest.[14]

2. *The Service Functions.* Central banks perform more or less routine, mechanical functions, such as furnishing coins and paper money to commercial banks for circulation, collecting checks, supervising bank managements, and acting as fiscal agent for the government.

Both kinds of activity, but the former more than the latter, presuppose the holding by the central bank of all, or nearly all, the reserves of the commercial banks of the system.

From 1836 until 1914 the United States had no central bank. (We might place the earlier date at 1832, when Andrew Jackson began to withdraw government deposits from the second Bank of the United States.) Americans generally were fearful of centralized control of the money supply, and until the early years of the twentieth century it was politically impossible to reestablish a central bank. Yet necessarily some central-bank functions were performed, for after 1850 the American economy was too complex to muddle along without any monetary guidance or assistance whatsoever. Such central bank control as there was developed by custom within the framework of the Independent Treasury Act of 1846 and the Banking Act of 1864, as amended.

THE TREASURY
AND THE BANKING SYSTEM

Ironically, monetary responsibilities were accepted by the United States treasury shortly after the passage of the law (see Chapter 7) that purported to make the treasury independent of the money market. The main purpose

---

[14] We later consider the criteria of an effective stabilization policy. At the moment we take it that governments will try to minimize swings of economic activity about a trend line of growth, at the same time engineering reasonably stable prices.

of the Independent Treasury Act was to put the government on a strictly cash basis. Under it banks periodically found their reserves reduced as people paid taxes and replenished as the government made disbursements from one of the subtreasuries. Even before the Civil War so much of the country's cash was at inopportune times locked up in treasury vaults that in order to replenish the reserves of banks the Secretary of the Treasury found it necessary to purchase government bonds in the open market and prepay interest on bonds outstanding. From the close of the Civil War until the establishment of the Federal Reserve System, relations between the treasury and the banks grew ever less tenuous. Policies varied with different secretaries, but with only a few exceptions there was a deep consciousness of the effect of treasury policy on the money market and of the responsibility the treasury had to the economy as a whole.

Treasury concern with central bank functions was stimulated by treasury surpluses, which were the rule from 1866 to 1915. The problem of getting back into circulation the cash taken in by the government reached such proportions that purchase of government securities and prepayment of interest on the public debt were not sufficient solutions. By liberalizing the interpretation of laws permitting deposits of treasury funds in national banks, successive secretaries developed a reliable technique of easing the money market. Leslie M. Shaw, who succeeded Lyman Gage as secretary in 1902, demonstrated particularly remarkable ingenuity in developing control instruments. He ruled that funds might be transferred from treasury vaults to depositary banks and back again, at the discretion of the secretary. Deliberately impounding funds during summer months, he released them, where needed, to relieve autumn stringencies.[15] When, in 1911, Congress finally authorized the treasury to accept certified checks drawn on commercial banks in payment of customs duties, the last hindrance to treasury influence on the money market was removed.

CORRESPONDENT RELATIONS
AND BANKING RESERVES

Even though the role of the treasury grew increasingly important, it was to the commercial banking system itself that bankers looked for most of the services ordinarily performed by a central bank. Since the early nineteenth century banks in small towns had kept deposits with banks in larger towns; in accordance with this practice the National Bank Act of 1864 enabled country banks to maintain part of their reserves as deposits with banks in seventeen major cities. As more and more banks secured national

---

[15] In his report of 1906, Shaw proposed that the secretary be authorized to vary required reserve ratios of national banks and that a fund of $100 million be made available for the sole purpose of easing and tightening bank reserves. However, Shaw argued against the establishment of a central bank on the grounds that government supervision of monetary operations would be thereby removed. *Annual Report of the Secretary of the Treasury*, 1906, pp. 41–50.

charters, city banks came to be major holders of the system's reserves, with a great concentration of reserves in New York City.[16] Moreover, country banks expected other services from the city banks in which they maintained correspondent accounts. They wanted loan accommodation, the large banks in turn acknowledging their obligation by rediscounting the paper of their correspondent customers. And all the so-called service functions of a central bank—providing cash, making collections, effecting large remittances, etc.— were carried out by the intricate correspondent network of commercial banks.

But the structure was faulty. New York banks, which held a large part of the reserves of the banking system, attracted accounts by offering interest on correspondent deposits and by rendering services at less than cost. Since they paid interest on the deposits, they had to put them to some profitable use. But the use to which they could be put was limited by the fact that country and reserve-city banks might at any time demand them. These deposits were therefore lent "at call" to dealers in securities, and they ended up financing, in varying degrees, stock-market speculation.

Moreover, banks in the interior, when pressed for funds, withdrew their deposits from the New York banks. Even in "normal" times there was a preference on the part of country and reserve city banks for reducing deposits with correspondents instead of their own cash holdings when they needed moderate sums for their customers. (Banks outside New York carried reserves over legal requirements, each bank considering these overages as "excess reserves" in the modern sense.) Also, when opportunities for profitable employment of funds at home presented themselves, country and reserve-city banks drew down their correspondent balances. Bank managers in New York could predict routine movements of funds to the interior with some degree of certainty and could prepare for these drains. But in times of panic the demand for cash remittances was greater than New York banks could meet, even by letting their own reserves fall seriously below the legal minimum.

At such times large banks necessarily tended to think first of their own stockholders. The entire system was based on cash reserves, and the total amount of cash could not be quickly altered. In the absence of a central bank with power to *create* reserves, only the treasury could afford relief to the New York money market in times of emergency, and such help as the treasury could give was adequate only during lesser disturbances.

Proposals for reform of the commercial banking structure included the suggestion that concentration of reserves could be lessened by establishing more reserve and central reserve cities. To achieve this objective, Congress on March 3, 1887, amended the National Bank Act to permit cities of 50,000 or more to become reserve cities upon the application of three-fourths of their national banks; cities of 200,000 or more could become central reserve

---

16 Within New York City there was a further concentration, as six or seven metropolitan banks came to specialize in this business.

cities under the same condition.[17] The amendment made no changes in the basic reserve structure. Country banks still had to keep a reserve of 15 per cent against deposit liabilities, three-fifths of which might be deposits with national banks in reserve or central reserve cities. Reserve city banks were required to keep a reserve of 25 per cent against deposits, one-half of which might be balances with banks in central-reserve cities. Banks in central reserve cities had to keep a 25 per cent cash reserve against deposit liabilities. Thus banks electing to become central-reserve-city banks could no longer count balances with New York as part of their reserves.

Within a few weeks applications of St. Louis and Chicago banks for central-reserve-city status were approved by the Comptroller of the Currency. In seeking to become ultimate holders of bank reserves, St. Louis and Chicago banks were taking a calculated risk. At one stroke they were required to double their own cash reserves, and balances due from New York would no longer count in the computation of their reserve position. The main objective of the St. Louis and Chicago bankers was to attract balances from reserve cities, which would presumably grow in number; they thought too that country banks would increase their accounts as St. Louis and Chicago became important money centers. Banks in both St. Louis and Chicago did succeed in taking some correspondent business away from New York. But they continued to keep large balances with New York banks, and in times of stress withdrew them in amounts not in keeping with their central-reserve-city responsibilities. Whatever the legal status of banks in Chicago and St. Louis, only New York banks, with access to a well-developed market for short-term funds, could actually provide central-reserve-city services.

THE ESTABLISHMENT OF THE FEDERAL RESERVE SYSTEM

Both the first and second Banks of the United States performed central-bank functions and were comparable in effectiveness to the contemporary Bank of England. In the absence of political opposition either Bank would have evolved into a fully developed, mature institution. Had other legislation not been forthcoming, it seems likely that the United States treasury might have come to perform most central banking functions, though direct treasury control of the banking system would have been a striking departure from world-wide experience up to that time. As it happened, the severe panic (and ensuing depression) of 1907 so aroused the American people to the need for basic reform that it came within half a dozen years.

The most painful manifestation of economic crisis in pre–World War I days was a scarcity of currency—of hand-to-hand money. As individuals and business firms became apprehensive about the economic future, they rushed to the banks to convert their deposits into cash. The banks, which operated on the "fractional reserve" principle, could not immediately meet demands

---

[17] The designation "central reserve city" and "reserve city" did not appear in legislation until 1887; the term *country bank* did not appear in the 1887 law but had by that time become customary.

for all their deposit liabilities. A single bank could *gradually* convert its assets into cash; given time, any sound bank could even be liquidated in an orderly fashion and its depositors and stockholders paid off in full. But in periods of panic an orderly shifting out of assets into cash was difficult if not impossible. Not only was there insufficient time, but as harried banks all tried to sell securities (their most liquid assets) at the same time, prices of securities fell drastically. For some banks the consequent losses on securities proved disastrous, even though "runs" were stopped. If, instead of selling its securities, a bank called its loans or refused to renew notes as they came due, pressure was transferred to the customers of the bank. And if these customers—business firms that had come to rely on the bank for loans in time of need—could not meet their obligations, they were forced into insolvency.

A common way of mitigating these difficulties was to "suspend" payments during crises. Before the Civil War, suspension meant that banks temporarily refused to redeem their notes or pay out deposits in specie. After the Civil War, suspension meant ceasing to pay out cash in any form —gold or gold certificates, silver or silver certificates, greenbacks, national-bank notes, or subsidiary coins. Instead of suspending, a bank might restrict cash payments to a certain maximum sum per day or per withdrawal. During the panic of 1907 such suspensions were more general and longer (over two months in some cities) than they had ever been before. In the Southeast and Midwest the resulting shortage of cash was so serious that local clearing houses even issued "script" against collateral pledged by co-operating banks in order that people could carry on business. These small-denomination "clearing-house certificates" were not issued much elsewhere, but large-denomination certificates were used by banks in cities all over the United States to make up balances due one another.

It is small wonder, then, that Americans became exercised over a recurring embarrassment felt to be entirely the fault of existing laws, even though the banking community thought the system adequate and on the whole sound. The Aldrich-Vreeland Act, passed in 1908, provided for the organization of "national currency associations" to be composed of not less than ten banks in sound financial condition. The purpose of the associations was to enable the banks forming them to issue emergency bank notes against the security of bonds and commercial paper in their portfolios. A secondary provision, which was really an attempt to stall off more positive action, established a National Monetary Commission. Made up of eighteen members of the Congress, nine from each house, the Commission sponsored voluminous studies that brought together a shelf of volumes ranging from compilations of data to superbly executed historical and analytical monographs. The report of the Commission in 1912 helped point up for the public the weaknesses of the American banking system.

The faults described by the Commission were those economists and businessmen had been writing and talking about for years. A major defect was that the economy suffered from the harmful effects of an "inelastic" currency. By this the Commission meant that the amount of coin and paper money in the economy did not expand and contract in accordance with the needs of the business community. It was argued that as business activity increased and decreased the quantity of currency ought to increase and decrease. Since during the financial panics that always accompanied the onset of depressions the cash demands of depositors could not be met by the banks, with resulting suspension of currency payments, the Commission felt that bank reserves should be "pooled" to make them readily available to all banks in times of stress.

Modern thought has pretty much debunked the importance of "elasticity" of the currency. For one thing, changes in the rate of turnover of the currency enable a given amount of cash to do more work in times of increased seasonal activity and to finance a smaller dollar amount of transactions in slack periods. Second, there is something to be said for a certain amount of inelasticity; in times of increasing economic activity, inelasticity of the currency supply damps down incipient inflation, and in periods of decreasing economic activity, inelasticity eases the accompanying deflation. Third, deposits, by the early 1900s so important a part of the monetary supply, were certainly elastic—they could expand and contract, the expansion being limited by the amount of reserves the banks held. It was at this very point that the main difficulty was encountered, for in times of cyclical stress reserves were quickly depleted.

What was needed was a central institution that could *create* reserves. Some contemporary writers thought the problem could be solved by simply putting cash reserves in a central place, whence they could be dispatched as required to various parts of the country. That is why we read so much in the literature of a half-century ago of the need for pooling reserves, though it should have been clear that reserves *were pooled* in New York.[18] But painful stringencies developed anyway, because New York banks could not create more cash. *A great central institution was needed with authority to hold the reserves of the commercial banks and to increase these reserves through its own credit-granting powers.*

Fortunately, some problems described by the National Monetary Commission and others could be solved only by establishing a central bank. Both private firms and the United States government had to pay too much for routine services. The simple process of collecting checks was in post–Civil War days a complex and expensive procedure. There were extreme examples of checks being sent hundreds of miles and through many banks

---

[18] The concentration of reserves in New York City was tremendous. By the 1900s six New York banks, with two-thirds of the resources of national banks in that city, held three-fourths of the reserve deposits of correspondent banks. During times of stress the reserves of these banks slowly dropped below the 25 per cent legal reserve ratio, falling as low as 19 per cent during the crash of 1907. While permitting this violation of the rules, the Comptroller of the Currency, as well as the banks, viewed the practice with alarm.

to effect collection of a sum drawn on a bank a short distance from the
residence of the payee.[19] Even normal procedure, however, was time-consum-
ing and costly since a bank always had to depend on some other commercial
bank to act as its agent in collection. Because there was no national collection
agency that could act to offset items in the way clearing houses did within
local urban areas, there was much unnecessary remitting of cash, frequently
over long distances. The transit departments of banks had to write innumerable letters and spend much time figuring out the best way to collect an
item, with consequent additions to operating expenses.

A central bank was also needed to help the treasury. After the demise of
the second Bank of the United States, the federal government had to maintain its own fiscal agent in the form of the treasury, which was by law required to remain aloof from the banking system. Impossibly antiquated
methods of handling government funds resulted. Even in the early years of
the twentieth century, the government had a sizeable amount of banking
business to do. The treasury continuously received and disbursed tax monies
in all sections of the United States and needed an institution to carry its
principal checking accounts. Further, an official institution was required
to handle the myriad physical details involved in government borrowing,
to advise treasury officials regarding management of the public debt, and to
act as the agent of the treasury in gold and foreign-exchange transactions.
By 1910 the need for a modern central fiscal agent was too great to be put off.

The National Monetary Commission placed undue emphasis on difficulties not of a crucial nature and failed to make explicit the need for establishing central control of the money supply. Nonetheless, its Report of 1912
brought matters to a head. Even before the Commission reported, its chairman, Senator Nelson Wilmarth Aldrich of Rhode Island, published his
Suggested Plan for Monetary Legislation, which he presented to Congress
in 1912. The Aldrich bill provided for a weak central bank, with little
government participation in its operations. It would have created a National
Reserve Association to have a head office in Washington and branches in
important financial centers, and direction of the National Reserve Association would have been in the hands of officers of large banks. The Association
would have acted only in times of emergency, and there would have been
no shifting of commercial bank reserves to the central Association. Control
of the monetary system would have been exercised by bankers, and the
public through its elected officers would have had little to say about monetary
matters. The Aldrich bill thus bore little resemblance to the Federal Reserve
plan that followed it, and it did not pass Congress for two reasons. To meet

[19] Banks in the United States customarily required "remittance charges" for payment on
checks other than those presented over their counters or through the local clearing house—
i.e., on checks presented by mail. If a bank served as a "collecting agent" for another
bank, it likewise charged for the service *unless* the bank for which it did the collecting
maintained an account with it. Thus a bank located a short distance from the drawee
bank would often send a check to a correspondent situated many miles in another direction just to avoid a remittance charge.

the demands of their constituents, the Congress that met in 1911 and 1912 insisted upon public oversight of any proposed central bank. Furthermore, the Democrats, confident that they would elect a national administration in 1912, probably wanted to delay action in order to have full credit for the establishment of a central banking institution.

Two days before Christmas in 1913 President Wilson signed the bill establishing the Federal Reserve System. Under its provisions the United States was to be divided into not less than eight and not more than twelve districts, with a Federal Reserve bank in each one. Twelve districts were decided upon, and in each a city was selected for the location of the Federal Reserve bank. Each district presumably enclosed an area homogeneous with respect to economic activity and containing sufficient resources for the organization of a strong Reserve bank. An unbelievable amount of wrangling and politicking went on over the delineation of districts and the location of Federal Reserve banks, and the cities that lost out could only hope that they might get one of the branches to be organized in the future.[20]

The system was to be headed by a Federal Reserve Board composed of seven members, including the Secretary of the Treasury and the Comptroller of the Currency *ex officio* and five others to be appointed by the President. Each Federal Reserve bank was to be run by a board of nine directors. Three of the directors, representing the "public," were to be appointed by the Federal Reserve Board, the remaining six to be elected by the member banks of the district. Of the six locally elected directors, three might be bankers, and the remaining three were to represent business, industry, and agriculture. Thus the banking community had a minority representation on the Reserve bank directorates in each district.

The Federal Reserve Act made membership in the system compulsory for national banks; state banks, upon compliance with federal requirements, might become members. Upon joining the system a commercial bank had to purchase shares of the capital stock of the Federal Reserve bank of the district up to the amount of 3 per cent of its combined capital and surplus. (Another 3 per cent *might* be required.) Thus the member banks nominally owned the Federal Reserve banks, though the annual return they could receive on their stock was limited to a 6 per cent cumulative dividend. A member bank also had to deposit with the Federal Reserve bank of the district a large part of the cash it had previously held as reserves. The act originally provided that member banks might retain a part of their reserves as cash in vault, but in 1917 the requirement was changed; after 1917 *all* the legal reserves of member banks were to be in the form of deposits with the Federal Reserve bank.[21]

---

[20] For more of this story see Ross M. Robertson, "Branches of Federal Reserve Banks," *Monthly Review,* Federal Reserve Bank of St. Louis, XXXVIII, 8 (August 1956), 90–97.

[21] All required reserves were held on deposit with Federal Reserve Banks from June 21, 1917, until late 1959, when, after a series of transitional steps, member banks could once again count vault cash as reserves.

Because much of the final monetary chapter is concerned with the development of the Federal Reserve System, we may conclude our present discussion with three observations: (1) Although the majority opinion in the United States was strongly in favor of a central bank, there was real fear of one. Consequently, twelve regional banks, centrally coordinated but presumably under a large measure of local control, were created. (2) Contrary to experience in other countries, where central banks were owned either by private individuals or by governments, Federal Reserve banks were to be owned by the institutions having the privilege of membership. To make certain that decisions would not be taken with a view to profits, dividends to member banks were carefully limited. (3) It was expected that the Federal Reserve banks would operate almost automatically and that if the Federal Reserve Act were carefully followed monetary disturbances would be very nearly eliminated. To most people the elimination of monetary disturbances was synonymous with the elimination of business fluctuations as well.

It was with high hopes, then, that the country began what was thought to be a new era in our economic life. We shall later turn to an examination of the failures, the frustrations—and the successes—that were in store.

Key Changes
in Industry

The division of labour is limited by the extent of the market.

ADAM SMITH

 During the half-century that lay between the end of one great war and the beginning of another the American economy took on most of its modern characteristics. The change that impresses, that stands out above all others, was the shift from an agricultural to an industrial economy. Until the decade of the 1880s agriculture was the chief generator of income in the United States. The census of 1890 reported manufacturing output greater in dollar value than farm output; by 1900 the annual value of manufactures was more than twice that of agricultural products. American gains in manufacturing output, relative to the rest of the world, were phenomenal. In the mid-nineties the United States became the leading industrial power among the nations, and by 1910 her factories poured forth goods of nearly twice the value of her nearest rival, Germany. In 1913 the United States accounted for more than a third of the world's industrial production.

Europeans were not less concerned than Americans to develop a solid foundation of manufactures, but in two respects American experience differed from that of the older nations. For one thing the industrial products of the United States were primarily sold in the home market; not until after the turn of the century did manufacturers begin to seek major outlets in foreign countries. Within an expanding free-trade area protected by high tariffs, enterprisers found more than satisfactory markets except in times of prolonged depressions. More important, perhaps, was the fact of considerable national self-sufficiency. In large part, western European countries brought raw materials from overseas to workers steeped in a tradition of fine craftsmanship. In contrast, "the industrial progress of the United States was the result of carrying labor to raw materials." [1] It might be added that the labor that came to the raw materials was, on the whole, unskilled and unspecialized.

Technological Change and the Increasing Size of the Firm

In Chapter 8 we traced the remarkable developments that resulted, by the middle 1850s, in widespread substitution of machine for hand methods. Invention went on apace in the period we are now considering, each contribution in turn furnishing part of a heritage for those to follow. Professor Usher has said that the process of inventing is like the process of learning. Indeed, in the United States it was a *part* of the process of learning, hastened by the needs of a young country for devices that would save labor and time and that would enable people to move quickly across great spaces.

How shall we review the technological changes that took place between two great wars? We begin by taking some examples of the introduction of machinery and changes in processes in consumer-goods industries, our objective being to discern the *kinds* of substitution of machine for hand processes that occurred. We turn then to a consideration of some technological changes of the first importance—those made in the processing of metals, particularly iron and steel. Because mechanization implies *power* mechanization, we must then direct our attention to sources of energy. And finally we must mention the better *organization* of the factory that made possible increases in labor productivity.

MECHANIZATION AND CHANGES IN PROCESSES:
NONDURABLE CONSUMER GOODS

We now pick up a thread of the previous narrative by considering first the textile industries, for it was in the processing of fibers that machines first proved themselves. In no other field had power-driven machines been so successful before the Civil War, and improvements during the latter part of the nineteenth century were in the direction of achieving greater automaticity. Ring-spinning, which had been invented some thirty years before the Civil War, was perfected and came to be the most important type of spinning in cotton mills. Ring spindles made it possible to draw, twist, and wind simultaneously so that processing was continuous.

---

[1] V. S. Clark, *History of Manufactures in the United States*, Vol. II (New York: McGraw-Hill, 1929), p. 2.

The outstanding development in the textile industries was the commercial success of the Northrup automatic loom in 1895. For decades power looms had been in general use, and operations had been made smoother as time went on. Yet two considerable difficulties remained to be surmounted after nearly a century of practical use. When the shuttle ran out of yarn, operations had to cease while a weaver inserted a new bobbin; and whenever a warp thread broke it was necessary to stop the loom by hand. Automatic looms, such as the Northrup loom, have devices that eject empty bobbins and insert fresh ones during the split-second interval in which the shuttle rests between movements across the loom. Furthermore, they stop automatically when a thread breaks, so that constant surveillance by a weaver is not necessary. After 1900 further strides were made toward automaticity. Of special importance were the tying-in and drawing-in machines that made possible the mechanical attachment of new warp threads to those already in the loom.

Because of the physical characteristics of the fiber and the uses to which the cloth is put, the woolen industry was hindered in the introduction of new methods. For example, mule spinning, which requires intermittent operation and greater floor space, remained important largely because it produced a soft, fluffy yarn. To produce in quantity the smooth, hard-worsted fabrics that would become the more valuable product of the industry, it was necessary to have mechanical combing. Only by mechanizing combing could the "tops," the long fibers used in making worsteds, be separated from the "noils," or short fibers, in sufficient quantity to make possible the rapid growth of the worsted branch. Thus in 1860 there were only three worsted mills in the United States; mechanization of combing about 1870 started an increase in production of finer cloths that did not level off until 1910 or thereabouts.

Before World War I the two great natural fibers, cotton and wool, were in no serious danger of competition. Silk, the ancient fiber of aristocrats, could be provided only in small quantities. Flax required so much hand labor that its cost kept fine linens in the luxury market only. Yet as early as 1900 it was apparent that man would eventually *make* fibers that would be either cheaper than natural fibers or better suited to his fancy. The first patent for a rayon process was obtained in France in 1884, and within the next twenty years or so the four types of rayon were in commercial production in Europe. Known originally as artificial silk, the various cellulose fibers were to come into competition first with cotton and then with wool, but they made no serious inroads until the 1920s. Commercial production did not begin in the United States until 1911, and the ensuing decade was one of experimentation in which finer filaments with greater tensile strength were sought.

Changes took place simultaneously in the clothing industries or "needle trades." We saw earlier how the sewing machine led to some factory production of clothing in the 1850s. During the Civil War mechanization of the

The system typified by craftsmen like these (who are shaving fur skins to their proper thickness in a Philadelphia workshop) steadily gave way to large-scale enterprise.

men's branch of the clothing industry increased rapidly. Standardized sizes were arrived at from measurements of soldiers taken by the army, and the problem of achieving approximate fit was thus solved. Beginning in the 1870s rotary cutting machines and reciprocating knives made it possible to cut several thicknesses of cloth at once. By 1895 sewing machines were improved to the point where, power driven, they could operate at speeds of 1,600, 2,200, and 2,800 stitches per minute, and well before World War I pressing machines were replacing hand irons. Because of style considerations women's dresses were usually made in the home or by a dressmaker until the very end of the nineteenth century, but by 1900 coats were made in factories, as were hosiery and underwear. Even with mechanization a good many hand operations remained in the making of outer garments, and as late as 1920 only half the workers in the garment industries were machine operators or helpers.

The subject of apparel leads to mention of leather and shoe production. As late as 1875 tanneries were small and located near supplies of tan bark along the seaboard states, in the mountain areas of Virginia, North Carolina, and Tennessee, and across the mountains in the Midwest. The art of making leather had not changed much since colonial days, and quality was dependent upon the hides and skins available and the skill and experience of the boss tanner. During the last quarter of the century the local tanneries tended to disappear and the scale of operations increased sharply. For one thing the discovery of a tanning concentrate made it unnecessary to locate near sources of tan bark, which was bulky and costly to transport. More important, though, was the rise of the large meat packers in the Midwest; their operations furnished the better quality "packer" hides, as distinguished from the "country" hides of the farmer and butcher, and large tanneries gravitated toward this source of supply.

During the half-century before 1860 the shoe industry had passed from the craft shop into the merchant-employer stage and was rapidly moving into factory production. It was only in the decade or so before the Civil War that store shoes were shaped for the left and the right foot; consequently, ladies and gentlemen had their footwear custom made and continued to do so for a long time. Manufacturers, however, came to realize that design, finish, and attention to size and fit were necessary to securing a broad market for factory output. In 1875 they introduced the Goodyear welt process by which soles could be attached to uppers without allowing nails and stitches to penetrate the inside of the shoe. Within the next twenty years or so machines appeared to do the work of lasting, eyeleting, heeling, and so on, and by 1914 the industry was highly mechanized.

Partly as a consequence of the early technical maturity of the industry a remarkable method of making equipment available to individual firms was established. There had been a tradition in the industry of renting machinery to operators on a royalty basis. In 1899 the United Shoe Machinery Company was formed with control of the basic machine patents. It achieved a tight control of the business that lasted for decades, and to this day the company remains dominant in the shoe-machinery industry.

In the food industries, changes were unspectacular but persistent and important. Innovations in food processing, plus rapid urbanization, led to the removal of much food preparation from the home. Consider for a moment the flour-milling industry. Even in colonial times some of the great mills were almost completely mechanized and were the earliest examples of continuous-process manufacture. Until after the Civil War there was no change in methods or techniques. Then it became necessary to devise a way of grinding the hard spring wheats of the Northwest without generating so much heat from friction that the flour became discolored and its quality lowered. Americans at first solved the problem by "high grinding"—i.e., by setting the old millstones somewhat farther apart and letting them revolve more slowly. From central Europe, however, where hard wheats had long presented a problem, came the gradual-reduction process that was to take the historic millstones out of use. In this process grain was put through a series of corrugated rollers. Roller grinding, introduced in the 1870s, had nearly superseded older methods by 1890. Costs were greatly reduced and quality of the flour much improved, but even more important, the milling industry had overcome the obstacles to grinding the hard wheats of Minnesota, the Dakotas, Kansas, and Oklahoma.

Technological changes were followed by increase in the size of mills. Greater size enabled the mill to draw its supply of wheat from a large area so that many types of wheat could be blended to get a flour of uniform quality. For the little baker's shop a standardized flour was not crucial; for the commercial baker it was.

The cracker and biscuit division of the industry was mechanized earlier than the bread-baking division and before the turn of the twentieth century had begun to expand rapidly. By 1910 it was apparent that the bread-baking division would shortly take over arduous work hitherto performed in the kitchen. During World War I the trend away from home baking of bread was rapid, but the commercial unit remained characteristically small; advances in mechanization of bakeries have been post-1920 developments.

Bread and meat have been the traditional staples of diet in the Western world. At the same time that bread made outside the home became a possibility for most consumers, a steady, safe supply of meat entered city markets. Cured pork had long been furnished to the eastern market by western packers, but fresh beef and pork were supplied by local packers. Even though they were close to the consumer, eastern processors had to confine their slaughtering to cold months because of spoilage. The West had a great cost advantage in the production of meat animals, but livestock could be transported to major markets only with prohibitive weight losses. The answer to the problems of transporting meat to the East and preserving it lay in developing some practical means of refrigerating, both in slaughterhouses and in railroad cars. By 1870 slaughterhouses had rooms refrigerated by ice, and shortly thereafter a Swift employee, by circulating air in an iced boxcar, made possible the long-distance shipment of perishable fresh beef. The bitter opposition of local packers could only briefly hinder the advent of a cheaper and more reliable source of meat. By 1880 the rise to dominance of the great national packers was well started. With the opening of national markets the big houses came more and more to utilize the output of by-products, thereby reducing meat costs. The technique of the assembly line (operating in reverse) had its first great acceptance in the relatively simple process of preparing meat animals for market.

We had occasion earlier to mention the first attempts at canning foods. By 1920 the city housewife could take from the grocer's shelves a large number of staple items in cans; indeed, except for meat specialties, the variety of canned goods was about as great at the close of World War I as it is today. The Civil War experience of Union soldiers had done much to gain acceptance of canned milk and the commoner fruits and vegetables. By the late eighties the city housewife of modest means could obtain over a counter nearly all of the things that but twenty-five years before she had laboriously "put up." The canning industry, thus firmly established, rapidly improved its operations along two main lines. More was learned about making canned foods safer and more palatable—from the chemistry and bacteriology of processing to the temperature and pressure at which different foods should be cooked. Important in bringing about typical factory production was the introduction of machine-made cans, of automatic soldering of can tops, and of machines for filling cans. By the turn of the century even the process of getting vegetables and fruits ready for canning had been mechanized.

MECHANIZATION AND CHANGES IN PROCESSES:
PRODUCER GOODS

Iron and steel. It may be well to recall for a moment what was said in Chapter 8 about the early iron industry. Between 1815 and 1850 three innovations in iron manufacture were adopted: the rolling of bars and plates, the "puddling" of pig iron (to make merchant bar), and the use of anthracite coal and then coke in the reduction process. By mid-nineteenth century there were available to machine-makers, in quantity, tough, fibrous, malleable, noncorrosive wrought iron and hard, brittle, and nonmalleable cast iron. The former was too costly for many uses and, while suitable for agricultural implements, it lacked tensile strength and could not withstand the stresses and strains that the greater speeds and heavier structures of industry were beginning to require. The brittleness of cast iron ruled it out for most purposes. There was an obvious need for a cheap, multipurpose metal with the qualities of high ductility, toughness, and ability to withstand strain without distortion.

For centuries men had known how to make steel in small quantities. As late as 1850 high-carbon steel, chiefly used in the manufacture of cutlery and certain tools, was a scarce and expensive commodity. It was made in a crucible or pot by melting wrought iron and then carefully adding carbon.[2] The steel of the future was to be a relatively low-carbon product made by the so-called *indirect* process, indirect in the sense that the iron is first reduced in a blast furnace and in a second step refined—i.e., converted into steel.

The first successful method of making steel in quantity was invented almost simultaneously by an Englishman, Henry Bessemer, and by an

---

[2] In Chapter 3 we observed that steel is a form of iron containing carbon ranging in amounts from about 0.1 per cent to 1.7 per cent. *Low-carbon* steel (less than 0.25 per cent carbon) is a *mild* or *soft* steel. *Medium-carbon* steel ranges in carbon content from roughly 0.25 to 0.60 per cent. *High-carbon* or *hard* steel has between 0.60 per cent and about 1.7 per cent carbon content. In general, as steel increases in hardness it increases in tensile strength and brittleness. With a greater carbon content than 1.7 per cent the product becomes cast iron.

American ironmaster, William Kelly. There is reason to believe that Kelly may actually have come up with the idea first, but fame and fortune fell to Bessemer. In the Bessemer-Kelly process hot air is blown through molten pig iron, the oxygen in the air igniting and burning out the chief impurities, carbon and silicon. Although Bessemer presented his idea in a paper read in 1856, several years of experimentation were to pass before commercial production was possible. And almost as soon as the first operations began in 1864, Bessemer was denounced as an impostor by some manufacturers who found that the method did not work. As it turned out, iron ores containing more than 0.05 per cent of phosphorus could not be converted by Bessemer's original process. The difficulty arose from the fact that the cylindrical pot in which the molten pig iron was refined had to be lined with a refractory material that could withstand enormous heats. If an *acid* lining of siliceous rock were used, *alkaline* impurities like phosphorus and sulfur were not removed from the ore and spoiled the metal. In the United States, where nonphosphorous ores were readily available in the experimental years, the difficulties of the "acid" process were not so great, but in Europe and England, where phosphorous ores predominated, a more satisfactory way of making steel in quantity had to be found. How the problem was solved will be discussed in a moment.

Only a little while after Bessemer and Kelly came forth with substantially the same process, another, the open-hearth method, was brought to experimental status. Inventors were trying to find a way of making cheap steel without infringing Bessemer's patents, and they were also trying to overcome some of the deficiencies of Bessemer's process. The Bessemer method was so quick that there was not sufficient time to test the steel for carbon content; the manufacturer could thus never be certain for what purposes a given batch would be suitable. The best work in the new direction was done by William and Friedrich Siemens in England and Émile and Pierre Martin in France. By 1868 the main features of the open-hearth, or Siemens-Martin, process were settled. Instead of a cylindrical converter that could be tipped like a huge kettle, the open-hearth method used a furnace with a shallow, open container holding a charge of molten pig iron, scrap iron, limestone, and even some iron ore. There were two periods of operation during which the charge was melted down and then refined.

Several considerations have made the open-hearth process more economical than the Bessemer. A large charge required about twelve hours as against ten to fifteen minutes for a Bessemer "blow," but during the long refining period open-hearth steel could be sampled and its chemical composition adjusted to exact requirements. The open-hearth furnace also had a cost advantage over the Bessemer converter in that scrap iron and iron ore could be charged with the more expensive molten pig iron. The regeneration principle, by which the open-hearth furnace made use of hot gases drawn from nearby coke ovens or blast furnaces to melt and refine the charge, was highly efficient.

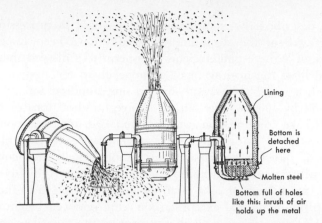

Lining

Bottom is detached here

Molten steel

Bottom full of holes like this: inrush of air holds up the metal

The Bessemer converter (top) takes a charge of from 15 to 60 tons of molten metal, depending on its size. The open-hearth process (below) takes a charge of as much as 175 tons of molten scrap iron and iron ore.

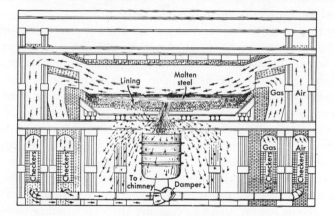

Acid linings were used at first in *both* major processes, and until a chemically different lining was devised steel could be made only from a very narrow range of ores. A third major innovation was the discovery of the "basic" process by the Englishmen Sidney Thomas and Percy Gilchrist. They reasoned that if a Bessemer converter were lined with some basic material like burned limestone or dolomite, the harmful phosphorus would be held from combination with the steel. Shortly after 1878 the basic Bessemer method was put into operation in Europe, and it has continued there as a major process in the making of "Thomas" steel. About 1880 a basic lining was adapted to the open-hearth furnace.

Only the electric furnace remained to be introduced—around 1900 in Europe and a few years later in the United States. During the period under consideration electric steels remained quantitatively insignificant, but as the demand for quality steels increased, the electric process would one day surpass the Bessemer in tons of output.

We have described in a simple way the changes in processing without which the growth of the steel industry would have been impossible. Increases in size of furnace and efficiency of operation followed these changes. In 1850 good blast furnaces averaged from seven to ten tons of pig iron a day. Twenty-five years later seventy-five to one hundred tons a day was a maximum, and by 1900 a daily output of five hundred tons or more, with markedly less coke consumption, was common. During these years methods of handling material improved greatly, regenerative heating of the blast was developed, blowing equipment was strengthened, and coke entirely superseded anthracite and bituminous coal as a fuel. A highly significant change in the production of coke occurred in the 1890s. Up to that time the elements in bituminous coal except carbon were removed by combustion in old-fashioned beehive ovens, and in the process the volatile parts were allowed to escape. The by-product coke ovens, particularly the Koppers ovens, permitted the capture of valuable gas, tar, ammonium sulfate, and other chemicals, and these elements, when sold or used, reduced costs. In addition, there resulted a great saving of heat.

This last remark serves to remind us that heat is one of the major costs of steelmaking. Perhaps the outstanding accomplishment of the industry in the period before 1920 was the integration of processes that led to great savings in heat. Thus coke ovens came to be placed close to blast furnaces to avoid heat loss. Blast furnaces in turn were placed near steel furnaces, either Bessemer or open hearth, so that molten pig iron could be delivered directly to them. Finally, converters and open hearths were situated near the roughing mills so that the first rolling could be done as quickly as possible with a minimum of reheating. There were, to be sure, other economies resulting from integration, the most notable being savings in the handling of materials and in the administration of the entire process.

It would take us too far afield to consider the vast number of innovations in the shaping of steel products, for we should have to study the details of various types of rolling mills, massive steam hammers, hydraulic presses, and the like. Two pre-1920 developments, however, deserve special mention, for their effects were to ramify throughout the whole economy. Most important was the rapid ascendancy of the basic open-hearth process for making steel. Though introduced shortly after the Bessemer method, open-hearth steel lagged far behind until the 1890s, for Bessemer steels were eminently satisfactory for rails, which constituted the first great demand for the new product. We have already noted the technical advantages of open-hearth refining. As engineers grew familiar with steel characteristics, they became convinced that plates and structural shapes made of Bessemer steel had defects that did not appear in the open-hearth product. The consequence of this preference was that some rolling mills had to build open-hearth furnaces to meet the new demand. Furthermore, costs of open-hearth processing were much lower than those of the Bessemer process, not only because scrap could be used but also because small operators could build and operate

Steel manufacture took unprecedented amounts of capital in the form of great furnaces and mechanical aids as well as skilled workmen able to judge when the time was ripe to tap Bessemer converters like these.

plants far smaller than those necessary for a Bessemer operation. Moreover, small owners did not need to fear being "held up" by the large companies that controlled the Bessemer ores. By 1910 the open hearth had clearly won out over the Bessemer converter; from this time on, the annual output of the latter actually decreased.

The second major pre-1920 development was the increasing use of alloy steels. Nothing like the volume of output of World War II and later was achieved, but the end of World War I saw the United States the global leader in ferroalloy production. Like nearly all the principal inventions in the technology of steelmaking, the idea of obtaining great hardness by bringing other metals into the composition originated in Europe. Chrome steel was known by 1821; in 1876 a process for making nickel steel was patented in France. Ten years later the Bethlehem Steel Works purchased patent rights for the latter process, and in 1890 the company was making nickel steel plates for the Navy. The decade of the nineties saw the steady introduction of alloy steels in the making of gear wheels and die castings, and by 1900 Bethlehem was producing tool steel. Besides chrome and nickel, tungsten, molybdenum, manganese, vanadium, titanium and other metals—all familiar to the modern layman—were in use by 1905; five years later over 500,000 tons of alloy steel were produced annually. To satisfy the growing demands of the machine-tool and automobile industries large amounts of the ferroalloys were likewise imported, but World War I forced American manufacturers to meet most of the requirements themselves.

Nonferrous metals. Other metals, quantitatively far less important than steel, have played a vital part in the growth of the capital goods industries. Of the nonferrous metals, copper and aluminum rank after steel in tonnage and fulfillment of essential functions.

Copper is one of the metals man has used for a long, long time. Found at first in a pure or nearly pure form, it was readily worked up into simple shapes and easily alloyed with zinc to form brass and with tin to form bronze. The uses of copper were long limited, however, to utensils, decorative pieces, tools, firearms, and the like. That copper played no major role in the life of Americans until late in the nineteenth century is indicated by the fact that the greatest annual output of the metal before 1873 was no more than 16,000 tons. Copper's properties of high thermal conductivity and resistance to corrosion made it a useful material. But because of its property of electrical conductivity, it became an essential material to United States industry when electricity was developed as a major source of power.

Deposits of pure copper were quickly exhausted. Consequently, the ores containing copper oxides and copper sulfides have constituted the chief sources in modern times. Unlike iron ores, which may contain as high as 60 per cent iron, copper ores are "rich" if they are as much as 7 per cent copper; the sulfides, which since 1910 have been the principal ores, contain 1 per cent or less of copper. Because of the low copper content of the available ores, a process of "concentration" must precede reduction, and it was the discovery around 1914 of a new way of concentrating—by the "froth flotation" method—that made practical the use of hitherto unexploited low-yield reserves. The ore is reduced and converted by processes not unlike those described for steel; but the "blister copper" that results, 99 per cent pure, must be further refined because even the slightest impurities of lead and zinc spoil the electrical conductivity of copper. This final refining is done by an electrolytic process, which has an additional advantage in that it yields by-products of gold and silver.

A striking and significant development in metals technology took place when aluminum was made available for industrial purposes. The most common of the metallic elements, aluminum long defied efforts to separate it from the minerals with which it is found. It was first obtained in a pure form early in the nineteenth century, but for many decades it remained in the "precious" class, obtainable only in the scientific laboratory. European scientists worked first on chemical rather than electrolytic processes of separating the pure aluminum. Their first major step toward success was the extraction of aluminum oxide, or alumina, from the ore, bauxite. As so frequently happens when a number of minds turn seriously to the solution of a problem, two men discovered almost simultaneously an economic method of reducing alumina. Charles Martin Hall, a young American, and Paul Hiroult, a young Frenchman, in 1886 successfully separated the aluminum by passing an electric current through a mixture of cryolite and alumina. The electrolytic process made possible production of the light metal in quantity, and commercial output began in the 1890s. At first confined to the manufacture of trinkets and cooking utensils, aluminum by the twentieth century was gaining acceptance as a structural material, sometimes alloyed with steel, and as cable for power transmission. The advent of the automobile increased the demand for aluminum and prophesied the growing need for light metals. It was not until the expansion of aircraft production in the World War I years, however, that aluminum began to take its place in the economic sun; even in 1920 it was by no means obvious that the airplane would assure it a position of major importance.

MACHINERY AND MACHINE TOOLS

Improvements in metals processing were important because they made possible rapid advances in the design of machines and machine tools. For some years after the Civil War, Great Britain led in machinery production, with the French and Germans largely copying their efforts. Until at least 1900 the English maintained superiority in making heavy machinery, whereas Americans did best in making light machine tools.

After the Civil War major improvements were made in steam engines and boilers. Far higher pressures were achieved with safety than had hitherto been dreamed of. In engines the most notable change was in maintaining even speeds at high velocities. After the middle 1880s multiple-expansion (compound) engines were generally employed for marine use, in power-houses, and in factories.

In the making of machine tools progress was made toward greater accuracy, uniformity, and simplicity of design. New England and Pennsylvania manufacturers remained pre-eminent for a while after the Civil War, each tending to specialize in a single type of machine such as lathes or planers or grinders. Within twenty-five years Cincinnati manufacturers were bidding for first place, and after 1910 the Ohio city became the most important center of machine-tool production in America.

During the 1890s there were two major technical advances: (1) machine tools were made automatic or semi-automatic and (2) compressed air and electricity were used to drive high-speed cutting tools and presses. The demands of the automobile industry and of the armament and aircraft industries during World War I brought the machine industry to maturity. V. S. Clark reports that between the end of the Civil War and the end of World War I precision in metalworking increased from a tolerance limit of 0.01 inch to 0.001 inch, and tolerances of 0.0001 of an inch had been achieved although not in quantity production. By 1919 machine tools had increased greatly in power as well as in precision. Great electrically driven shears could cut steel slabs twelve inches thick and forty-four inches wide, and huge presses could stamp out the parts of automobile bodies rapidly enough to make possible "mass" production.

SOURCES OF POWER

Between 1860 and 1920 there was a remarkable transition from reliance upon the power of wind, water, and the physical exertion of men and animals to other sources of energy. The transition had only begun in the first half of the nineteenth century. In 1850 more than three-fourths of all power was furnished by animal energy, and the energy of men produced more power than machines did. As late as the eve of the Civil War, water power was far more important than steam power in the United States.

In Chapter 8 we discussed the difficulties encountered in the introduction of steam engines. Through the 1850s there was much disagreement as to the relative costs of steam versus direct water power, but by the end of the Civil War the argument was settled. Sites on streams large enough to power early mills and embryo factories were scarce, and the available ones were frequently so out of the way that they were uneconomic as spots for industrial concentration. Furthermore, as the forests were cleared stream flows became more and more variable and could not be relied upon. Sometime during the decade of the 1870s steam surpassed water as a source of power. In addition to the reasons mentioned above, two major influences operated to secure what appeared to be the final defeat of the ancient water wheel and the more recently developed water turbine. These were (1) the ever increasing efficiency of the steam engine and (2) the opening up of vast and apparently inexhaustible supplies of coal as a result of the transportation revolution. By 1890 relatively few factories, these mostly in the textile and paper industries, used direct water power, though gristmills and sawmills still availed themselves of this source.

But another way of utilizing the force of water flow was to be devised. At the time when steam engines gained an unquestioned ascendancy, electricity came on the scene as a form of power. Like steam, electricity was not a new energy *source;* it was a new *means* of using energy generated either by the flow of water or the burning of fuel.[3] But electricity brought about a remarkable improvement in the utilization of the older sources. Electric power is flexible and divisible. The power plant can be separated from the manufacturing establishment by long distances, and cumbersome devices for changing the to-and-fro motion of the steam engine into rotary motion and then transmitting this motion are unnecessary. Furthermore, there is readily "on tap" the energy required to turn either a small motor or a large one.

---

[3] From the first, steam-generating capacity has exceeded hydrogenerating capacity. In the public mind, hydropower has been synonymous with cheap power because water-flows are a gift of nature. Costs of building dams and installing equipment make hydrogenerated electricity more expensive than steam-generated electricity in all but a few favored areas.

Electric power can be generated by the manufacturing, mining, or transportation company that uses it, or it can be bought from a company that specializes in the generation of electricity. The latter method is more common today. The construction of Edison's central power plant in New York in 1882 is considered, and rightly, a monumental event. Yet on the eve of World War I less than half the electric motors in use were driven by power purchased from a central plant. By the end of the war, however, a trend from nonutility to utility power was unmistakable.

It is hard to estimate accurately the relative importance of electricity as a form of industrial power at the end of the period we are considering. The production of electrical energy in 1920 was 40,000,000,000 kilowatt-hours, about one-eighth of the annual output thirty years later. Or what is more informative, one-third of industrial power was provided by electricity in 1920, a proportion far greater than that of any other country of the world.

Our consideration of the growing importance of electricity should not, however, divert attention from the fundamental *sources* of energy. The prime movers that generate power, whether electrical or not, must be run either by flow of water or by burning of mineral fuels. We should lose sight of a key fact of American economic history if we failed to consider the relative importance of coal, petroleum, natural gas, and water power as sources of energy. Comparison is difficult, for it involves conversion of tons of coal, barrels of petroleum, and cubic feet of gas into heat values and the conversion of water power into fuel equivalents. When the arithmetic has been done we can only conclude that the United States, like England and Germany, came to industrial greatness as a consequence of being blessed with more than adequate supplies of coal. In 1890 coal was the source of 90 per cent of energy furnished industry; in the years just before 1920 coal remained the source of at least 80 per cent of industrial energy. But petroleum was rapidly growing more important and hydropower was recovering. Within twenty-five years petroleum and natural gas would become strategic fuels, but as late as 1920 transportation and manufacturing industries were squarely in the age of coal.

TWO NEW IDEAS:
MASS PRODUCTION AND SCIENTIFIC MANAGEMENT

No sketch of what was happening in American industry between the Civil War and World War I would be adequate without some account of two new approaches to production. These closely related developments—known popularly as *mass production* and *scientific management*—had such a pronounced impact upon the economy that the man in the street quickly became aware of them. *Mass production* has come to be an almost magical expression that includes all the characteristics of modern American industry; *scientific management* implies the use in business of procedures that have a laboratorylike exactness. More sophisticated definitions may be useful.

Mass production is something more than quantity production. It implies two procedures discussed in Chapter 8—continuous-process manufacture and interchangeable-parts manufacture. It implies further a high degree of mechanization, application of power, accurate machine tools, and uniform quality of materials. During the nineteenth century American industry was acquiring these attributes, and certain industries, notably those making farm implements and bicycles, came close to the modern ideal of mass production. Yet something had to be added before American industry could achieve true mass production. Physically, it was necessary to devise mechanical means of transporting materials systematically from one stage of production to another. Intellectually, there was required a detailed planning and ordering of the assembly process by the managers. It was essential that managements have as a goal the minimization of the time consumed by workers in assembling a complex product.

During the century or more that followed Oliver Evans' attempts at continuous-flow milling, entrepreneurs moved toward the ideal of minimizing processing time. In the manufacture of carriages and railroad cars the notion of stationary assembly was applied. It remained for the automobile to offer the ultimate challenge, and it was Henry Ford who unhesitatingly accepted it. When, in 1908, he decided to produce a low-priced car, designed to furnish cheap transportation and nothing more, he devised the first progressive line production of an automobile. Under his first "stationary" system subassemblies were made at several stations, but no provision was made for continuous movement from station to station. Beginning in 1913 the Ford plant adopted the "moving assembly" that had long been used in the manufacture of simple products. Pulled along by a windlass, subassemblies were accomplished in a series of operations. In 1914 a chassis, which had formerly been assembled in twelve hours, could be put together along a 250-foot line in a little over an hour and a half. Before 1920 motor-driven conveyors were moving motors, bodies, and chassis at heights and speeds convenient to workers along greatly lengthened lines. By this time the moving assembly had spread throughout the automobile industry, the electrical industry, and the budding household-appliance industry, as well as to food processing and cigarette manufacture.

Such innovation implies a change in the concept of the managerial function. In the textile industry of the early nineteenth century, managerial duties were turned over to executives of broad background and general education. The director of activity in the factory did not have to be technically competent. He was preoccupied with seeking markets, solving financial problems, and adjusting output over the business cycle. But with the growing size and complexity of the firm consequent upon technological change, it became more and more apparent that at least a part of managerial problems were problems of engineering. By 1920 there was growing recognition that the most effective managers would be men trained in the sciences, in schools of engineering, and in the new-fangled schools of business administration, for they combined technical training with a flexible outlook gained from academic pursuits.

With increases in size of plant and complexity of layout, another variable, the worker, required analysis. To problems of efficient handling of the labor force many men, chiefly engineers, addressed systematic study. Among them the most articulate, and ultimately the most famous, was Frederick W. Taylor, who with an associate at the Bethlehem Steel Company had contributed to the improvement of highspeed tool steels. It was Taylor's thesis that worker efficiency could be improved by (1) analyzing in detail the movements required to perform a job, (2) carrying on experiments to determine the optimum size and weight of tools and optimum lifts, and (3) offering incentives for topnotch performance. From such considerations Taylor went on to develop certain principles of proper physical layout of a shop or factory, correct routing of work, and accurate scheduling of the production of orders. In brief, it was Taylor's idea, in which numerous associates and followers concurred, that in planning production old rules of thumb should be replaced by principles determined after careful analysis and measurement. In this sense guiding operations would no longer be haphazard, and management could become "scientific."

In 1911 famed attorney Louis D. Brandeis gave great publicity to the concept of "scientific management" when he argued before the Interstate Commerce Commission that what the railroads needed was not an increase in rates but an intelligent ordering of operations in accordance with scientific principles. By this time entrepreneur Henry Ford, who probably had no thought of being scientific, had put the principles into practice. The demands of World War I for increased output unquestionably set many managers to testing procedures they might otherwise have scorned as useless theory.

The laboring man could not escape the conviction that he was being driven to an inhuman speed-up of effort, that increased output was being taken out of his hide. Yet increasing productivity and the tendency of real wages to move upward left him with the uneasy feeling that there might be some merit to "scientific management" after all. Having the materials flow faster did not necessarily force a man to work faster. With improved methods the worker did not have to move as far to handle material, he made a smaller personal expenditure of energy, and he was better protected against physical discomfort and industrial accidents. In any case, by 1920 Simon Legree attempts to drive the worker were disappearing in industries experiencing rapidly increasing output.

The Concentration of Industry and the Increasing Size of the Firm

From the foregoing we might conclude (and correctly) that pressures of technological change would lead to an increase in the size of the firm. A trend toward bigness was indeed unmistakable after the Civil War. During the decade of the 1870s, while the number of manufacturing establishments remained nearly constant, the capital invested in them increased by about two-thirds and the value of their output increased by more than half. Save in a handful of industries, however, there was no startling growth in the size of the firm during this decade. But beginning around 1880, initiated by forces not entirely technological and continuing for nearly a quarter of a century, a change occurred in the structure of American industry that was awesome in its manifestations and far-reaching in its consequences. This change has been tagged with many names, none of them properly descriptive. At the time it was referred to as the "rise of the trusts." Later writers have called it the "combination movement" or the "merger movement." Whatever we call it, the trend toward bigness, toward concentration of economic power, demands the careful attention of the student of economic history.

WAYS OF ACHIEVING
INDUSTRIAL POWER

Economists find convenient the concept of the firm of "optimum" size. With reasonably free entry into and exit from an industry and with no legal limits placed upon size, the individual firm may become quite large. It may grow large horizontally by acquiring a number of plants that turn out approximately the same product, or it may integrate vertically in order to control a sequence of processes. In some industries, on the other hand, the firm may be typically small and may remain so for generation after generation. Bigness brings many advantages. A large firm can normally hire a more skilled management, it can set up a more effective marketing machinery, it can more easily and cheaply finance itself, and (up to a point at any rate) it can better withstand the vagaries of the economic climate. Moreover, a large firm can readily achieve technological economies resulting from division of labor, integration of processes, the use of large machines, and substantial research facilities. But there is a limit to the reductions in cost to be had from increases in scale. If nothing else, the pressure upon management at last brings diseconomies. One man must finally make crucial decisions, and an organization can become so vast that human capabilities are insufficient to guide complicated operations efficiently.

It was to be expected, then, that on the several economic grounds just mentioned the size of the business unit, in manufacturing and mining industries at any rate, should increase. But there was another reason why firms aspired to bigness. They wanted to gain some degree of "monopoly" control over the sale of their products. And now we have used a common word that requires some explanation, for monopoly can mean many things to many people.

Strictly speaking, a monopoly is a firm that is the sole seller of a product for which there is no close substitute. But examples of pure monopoly are hard to find. In the entire history of the United States there have been no more than a dozen monopolies of important products sold in a nation-wide market. A more meaningful term, which describes a common-market structure in our economy, is "monopoly power." Without having the market control of a single seller, a firm may nevertheless obtain so large a portion of the total sales of a good or service that it can effectively influence—or even determine—the price at which the good or service sells. For example, if a large firm produces a third of total output, smaller firms may be so fearful of aggressive action on its part that they simply "follow" the big firm in matters of price and production policy. Or half a dozen firms, each of such a size that by varying output it can affect price, may produce nearly the whole of an industry's output; in such a market, an "oligopoly" in the jargon of economics, *even without collusion among the sellers* the price charged the consumer may turn out to be what a monopolist would have charged.[4]

A firm or a small group of firms may come to dominate an industry in many ways. The least spectacular route to monopoly power is simple expansion over time of the original house.[5] Financing itself by reinvestment of its own profits or with new funds from outside the company, a firm *may* achieve monopoly power without resort to any of the devices we shall presently name. To do so it must possess some special advantage conferred upon it by law, such as a patent or special license to operate, or else it must control the whole supply of a necessary factor of production, most likely a raw material. And once a firm has achieved considerable size it may then be protected from the competition of others because of "good will" or because the size of fixed plant necessary to efficient operation has become so large that no entrepreneur, without undue risk, can jump, full-grown, into the competition.

During the last half-century, except for the decade of the 1920s, the type of growth described in the preceding paragraph has been common. Between 1880 and 1905, however, the process of achieving bigness was hastened by efforts of existing firms to combine. The devices by which combination was achieved numbered over a score, but they can be classified in three categories: (1) devices for bringing together the managements of firms in order to "share the market"; (2) devices for bringing together the managements and linking the financial structures of firms; (3) devices for bringing to-

---

[4] The problem of pricing when there are few independent sellers is a stubborn one. Whenever a seller controls such a large portion of an industry's output that he can, by varying his output, influence price, he will take into account the *reactions* of rivals to any price-cutting he may have in mind. As soon as sellers realize that price cuts will almost certainly be followed by the retaliatory cuts of rivals, the industry may well become stable with respect to price and production policy. Firms then tacitly agree to assure themselves the monopoly profits they would get by collusion.

[5] The Aluminum Company of America achieved its pre–World War II market dominance in this way.

gether the management, financial structures, and physical properties of firms so as to create a single *new* firm.

The first attempts at combination were through the relatively simple devices in category (1). In the years immediately following the Civil War the so-called gentleman's agreement was common—and not ordinarily successful for very long. Such agreements were informal, verbal arrangements chiefly made for the purpose of setting and maintaining prices, but they might also serve for adopting common policies regarding extension of credit, cash discounts, and the like. When restriction of output was desired, the stronger and formal (i.e., written) contract known as the pooling agreement earned favor, because it was difficult to agree informally on such restrictions. The pool corresponded to the European cartel; it differed from its European counterpart chiefly in the fact that under the English common law such agreements were held illegal and were not enforceable in the courts. But the purpose of the pool was the same as that of the cartel. By its means, sellers could divide a market and assign each seller a portion. They could divide the market on a basis of output, each producer to sell so many units. Or they could divide it on a territorial basis, each producer to be free to sell in his own protected area. Or they could form a "profits" pool, whereby net income was paid into a central fund and later split on a basis of percentage of total sales in a given period. Although pools were formed even before the Civil War, they did not come into their own until after 1875. During the eighties and nineties strong pooling arrangements were made in a number of important industries; producers of whiskey, salt, coal, meat products, explosives, steel rails, structural steel, cast-iron pipe, and certain tobacco products achieved great success with pooling agreements, as did the railroads in trunk-line territory.

Both gentlemen's agreements and pools "worked," at least temporarily. In fact, they were employed all during the period under discussion, and we probably have them with us today. But there were serious disadvantages in these "loose" forms of collusion. For one thing, insofar as they were successful in raising prices and achieving a "monopoly" profit, they encouraged new firms to enter the field. Too, one of the major objectives of collusion was maintenance of prices in deflationary periods, yet it was in times of falling business activity that the temptation to violate agreements was strongest. The very freedom allowed the several firms, although usually an advantage, made it possible for individual managers to exceed their assigned outputs or encroach on another's territory when the going was rough, and there was no legal recourse against violators. Inevitably, smart operators sought a foolproof method of achieving the same ends by linking the financial structures of firms as well as their managements—our category (2) above.

The first of these stronger forms to find favor was the trust, a perversion of the ancient fiduciary device whereby trustees held property in the interest of either individuals or institutions. Under a trust agreement the stockholders of several operating companies formerly in competition with each other turned over their shares to a group of trustees and received in exchange "certificates of trust." The trustees thus had voting control of the operating companies, and the former stockholders received dividends on their trust certificates. This device was so successful as a means of centralizing control of an entire industry and so profitable to the actual owners of stock that trusts were formed in the 1880s and early 1890s to control the output of kerosene, sugar, whiskey, cottonseed oil, linseed oil, lead, salt, rubber boots and gloves, and other products. But the trust form had one serious defect: agreements were a matter of public record. Once their purpose was clearly understood, such a clamor arose that both state and federal legislation was passed outlawing them, and some trusts were dissolved by successful common-law suits in the state courts.

Whereupon alert corporation lawyers thought of another way of linking managements and financial structures. Occasionally special corporate charters had permitted a company to own securities of another company, such provisions having been inserted to allow horizontal expansion. In 1889 the New Jersey legislature revised its *general* incorporation statutes to allow any corporation so desiring to hold the securities of one or more subsidiary corporations. As the trusts ran afoul of the law in several states, many of them simply obtained charters in New Jersey as "holding companies." The prime objective of centralizing control and at the same time leaving individual companies free to operate under their several charters could thus be achieved by a relatively simple device. Theoretically the holding company had to own something more than 50 per cent of the voting stock of the several subsidiaries. In practice, especially as shares became widely dispersed, control could be maintained with a far smaller percentage of the voting stock. The holding company was here to stay, though it would have to resist, off and on, the onslaughts of Justice Department attorneys.

Yet it had already seemed clear to many ambitious promoters that out-and-out consolidation of interests (in the technical sense) was preferable to any other form of combination. Strictly speaking, a consolidation takes place when two or more operating companies unite to form a *new* corporation. Some writers on corporate finance still insist upon calling this kind of combination an *amalgamation* as distinguished from a *merger,* which refers to the acquisition by an existing corporation of the assets of one or more other corporations. In the case of a technical consolidation (amalgamation) a new corporate name results from the joining together of two or more companies; in the case of a merger the ensuing corporate name is that of the company that purchases the assets of the firm or firms taken over. In either case the physical properties of two or more previously existing entities are brought together either by an exchange of old securities for new or by a cash purchase. The result is a combination of the type listed as category (3) in the classification some paragraphs back.

The Two Phases
of the Concentration Movement

Whatever the path to combination, whatever the form of organization finally selected, the large firm was by 1904 typical of American manufacturing industry. Why was bigness inevitable? How can we account for the major transformation that occurred in the last few decades of the nineteenth century and the early years of the twentieth? We have suggested that one reason was a natural movement, encouraged by competitive pressures, toward "optimum" size. Yet clearly there was another reason, a conscious aiming for monopoly power. We have now to examine the forces that impelled entrepreneurs toward control of a large part of the output of many major industries, for it is clear that a rapacious, overweening desire for monopoly profits did not suddenly sweep American entrepreneurs into great combinations.

We find a clue to the motivation toward combination in the reflection that the movement occurred in two major phases. The first was the predominantly *horizontal* combination (1879–93) in industries producing the old staples of consumption. The second was the predominantly *vertical* combination that occurred between 1898 and 1904, for the most part in the producer-goods industries but also in a few consumer-goods industries making new products for growing urban markets.[6]

As late as the 1870s America's major industries served an agrarian economy. Except for the few companies then providing metal parts and rails for the rapidly expanding railroad industry, firms in most industries simply processed agricultural products and sold them in the still small cities and to the farmers who had provided the raw materials. These firms were small, usually buying raw materials locally and selling finished goods locally, their markets protected for some distance by high costs of transportation from the plants of competing manufacturers. When, as in the case of the textile industry, firms competed in a national market, they bought and sold through commission agents, who also handled the business of other firms in the same industry.

During the 1870s and 1880s, as the railroads bonded the country together in a national market, existing small firms in the consumer-goods industries first experienced a phenomenal increase in demand for their products. Increased demand was followed by expansion of facilities in order to

---

[6] The following analysis follows closely the pathbreaking work of Professor Alfred D. Chandler, Jr., to whom we are indebted for a new interpretation of the concentration movement. For the Chandler thesis at various stages and in alternative sources see "The Beginnings of 'Big Business' in American Industry," *Business History Review*, XXXIII, 1 (Spring 1959), 1–31; "Development, Diversification and Decentralization," in *Postwar Economic Trends in the United States,* edited by Ralph E. Freeman (New York: Harper, 1960), pp. 235–88; and *Strategy and Structure* (Cambridge: Massachusetts Institute of Technology Press, 1962).

take advantage of the new opportunities. Then, shockingly and distressingly, came the realization that there was great excess capacity, with consequent "overproduction" and prices persistently tending to drop below the costs of production of most firms. To protect themselves from insolvency and ultimate failure, many small manufacturers in the leather, sugar, salt, whiskey, glucose, starch, biscuit, kerosene, and rubber boot and glove industries (to name the most important) combined horizontally into large units.[7] They then systematized and standardized their manufacturing processes, closing down the least efficient plants and at the same time creating purchasing, marketing, finance, and accounting departments to service the units that remained. By 1893 consolidation and centralization was well under way in those consumer-goods industries that manufactured staple items to which households had long been accustomed. Typical of the large firms thus created were the Standard Oil Company of Ohio (after 1899, the Standard Oil Company of New Jersey), the Distillers' and Cattle Feeders' Trust, the American Sugar Refining Company, and the United States Rubber Company.

Of the firms that became large in the first wave of concentration, most spectacular was the Standard Oil Company. It is hard for moderns to think of petroleum as primarily a consumer good, yet the fact is that until well after the turn of the twentieth century an illuminant, kerosene, was the chief petroleum product. Beginning in 1854, kerosene was manufactured from a soft bitumen called cannel coal, and by 1859 thirty-four small companies, ranged in a great semicircle from St. Louis to Portland, Maine, made "coal oil." Edwin L. Drake's successful oil strike at Titusville, Pennsylvania, in the late summer of 1859 doomed the coal-oil industry, for kerosene was much more simply extracted from liquid petroleum.

From its beginnings in 1860 the petroleum-refining business was characterized by a large number of small firms. By 1863 there were more than 300 firms in the industry, and though this number had declined by 1870 to perhaps 150, competition was vicious, and the industry was plagued by excess capacity. "By the most conservative estimates," write Williamson and Daum, "total refining capacity during 1871–72 of at least 12,000,000 barrels annually was more than double refinery receipts of crude which amounted to 5,230,000 barrels in 1871 and 5,660,000 barrels in 1872. At the same time total demand approximated crude production at $4 per barrel." [8] An industry with investment in fixed plant and equipment that can turn out twice the volume of current sales is one inevitably characterized by repeated failures (usually in waves on the downswing of the cycle) and highly variable profits for the most efficient firms. In the oil industry the Rockefeller firm, organized in 1869 as the Standard Oil Company of Ohio, was perhaps the

---

[7] As we have observed, in the various industries pools and other loose forms of organization often preceded combination into a single large company.

[8] Harold F. Williamson and Arnold R. Daum, *The American Petroleum Industry* (Evanston: Northwestern University Press, 1959), p. 344.

John D. Rockefeller, the archetype of nineteenth-century businessman, brought discipline and order to the unruly oil industry, parlayed a small stake into a fortune estimated at more than $1 billion, lived on in good health (giving away some of his millions) until age 96 on a diet of milk, golf, and river-watching.

best managed, with two great refineries, a barrel-making plant, and a fleet of tank cars.[9]

When Rockefeller made the decision to bring order to the petroleum industry is not certain. It is clear, though, that Standard's holdings grew steadily during the 1870s, largely through the acquisition of refineries in Pittsburgh, Philadelphia, and New York, as well as in Ohio. Demanding and getting rebates on oil shipments (and even drawbacks on the shipments of competitors), Standard had made considerable progress in reducing independent refining competition by the end of 1876. By 1878, Standard either owned or had under lease 90 per cent of the refining capacity of the country. The independents that remained were successful only as they could produce high-margin items, such as branded lubricating oils, that did not require high-volume, low-cost manufacture.

To consolidate the company's position a trust agreement was drawn up in 1879 whereby three trustees were to manage the properties of Standard Oil of Ohio for the benefit of Standard stockholders. In 1882 the agreement was revised and amended; stockholders of forty companies associated with Standard also turned over their common stocks to nine trustees, the value

[9] John D. Rockefeller got his start in business at the age of nineteen, when he formed a partnership with Maurice B. Clark to act as commission merchants and produce shippers. Moderately wealthy before the end of the Civil War, Rockefeller entered the oil business in 1862, forming a series of partnerships before consolidating them as the Standard Oil Company.

of properties put into the Trust being set at $70 million against which 700,000 trust certificates (par value $100) were issued. The agreement further provided for the formation of corporations having the name Standard Oil Company in New Jersey and New York as well as in other states. When the Supreme Court of Ohio ordered the Standard Oil Trust dissolved in a decree of 1892, the combination remained effective for several years by maintaining closely interlocking directorates of the major refining companies. Threatened by further legal action, company officials changed the Standard Oil Company of New Jersey from an operating to a holding company, increasing its capitalization from $10 million to $110 million so that its securities might be exchanged for those of the subsidiaries it held. All the advantages of the trust form were secured, and, at least for the time being, none of the dangers were incurred.

Thus as the American Sugar Refining Company had done in 1891, Standard went from trust to holding company after successful combination had long since been achieved. Typical of this second period, though, was another kind of consumer-goods industry, producing *new* products (or old products in a new way), for a growing urban market. Firms in these industries formed large organizations, vertically integrated except for the raw-material stage, in order to achieve economies of production and marketing. In these industries were manufacturers of fresh meat, cigarettes, and high-grade flour; included also were makers of sewing machines and typewriters. Thus, Gustavus F. Swift and his brother Edwin, after experimenting with the shipment and storage of refrigerated meat, formed a partnership in 1878 that grew over the next two decades into a huge, integrated company. Its major departments—marketing, processing, purchasing, and accounting— were controlled from the central office in Chicago. Other meat packers like Armour and Morris had to build similar organizations, and by the late 1890s the meat-packing industry was dominated by a few firms with highly centralized, bureaucratic managements. In similar fashion James B. Duke set out in 1884 to establish a national and even world-wide selling organization to market his machine-made cigarettes. In 1890 he merged his company with five competitors to form the American Tobacco Company. Less than fifteen years later American, after a series of mergers, achieved a monopoly in the cigarette industry.

Urbanization of the population led to changes in both demand for and ways of supplying consumer goods. But an even more spectacular result of the growth of cities was the increased demand for producer goods, with a consequent stimulation of output in the heavy industries like steel, copper, power machinery, and explosives. Cities meant a continually growing demand for lighting, communication, power, street railways, and copper wire for the increasingly complex electrical lighting apparatus, to say nothing of the requirements for construction materials for burgeoning skyscrapers. These demands led in turn to the formation of large firms that emphasized vertical integration and highly centralized control over vast operations.

Andrew Carnegie, here dictating to his secretary, spent his early years building up an integrated steel firm, which combined with the Morgan and Moore interests to form the United States Steel Corporation.

In steel the Carnegie Company had by the early 1890s consolidated its several manufacturing properties into an integrated firm that owned vast coal and iron deposits. While the Carnegie interests grew, other businessmen were creating powerful steel companies. In 1898 the Federal Steel Company was formed under the auspices of J. P. Morgan and Company. Its integrated operations and products greatly resembled those of the Carnegie Company, but it had the further advantage of close alliance with the National Tube Company and American Bridge Company, producers of highly finished products. The National Steel Company, created by W. H. Moore, was the third largest producer of ingot and basic steel shapes and was closely connected with other Moore firms that made finished products—the American Tin Plate Company, the American Steel Hoop Company, and the American Sheet Steel Company. When Carnegie, strong in coal and (through his Rockefeller alliance) iron ore, threatened to integrate forward into finished products, he precipitated action toward merger by the Morgan interests. The result was the United States Steel Corporation, organized in March 1901 with a capital stock of over a billion dollars. Controlling 60 per cent of the nation's steel business, United States Steel owned in addition to its furnaces and mills a large part of the vast ore reserves of the Lake Superior region, 50,000 acres of coking-coal lands, more than 1,100 miles of railroad, and a fleet of lake steamers and barges. While protecting its position in raw materials, the corporate giant was now able to prevent price warfare in an industry typified by high fixed costs.

In copper Guggenheim's Philadelphia Smelting and Refining Company began a huge integrated operation that was soon imitated by Amalgamated Copper and the American Smelting and Refining Company. In the explosives industry, after more than a generation of effective control of prices and production through the Gunpowder Trade Association, E. I. Du Pont de Nemours and Company in 1902 bought out a large number of independent companies and then consolidated them into a single, well-knit organization with centralized accounting, purchasing, engineering, and traffic departments. And so we might trace similar combinations with similar motives through a long list of "Americans," "Nationals," and even "Internationals" —American Locomotive, American Can, National Packing, International Harvester, and so on.

How shall we sum up this discussion of consolidation? One way is to inquire how many really important large firms were created during this early period of combination. A well-known study covering the years 1888–1905 gives us the information that 328 combinations were effected, of which 156 were large enough to have a degree of monopoly control in their general industries.[10] Many of these were failures, but an astonishingly large proportion are with us today as major concerns. As to the degree of dominance attained by these firms at the turn of the century we are, unfortunately, less well informed. The generally accepted estimate is that by 1904 roughly two-fifths of the manufacturing capital of the country was controlled by these three hundred-odd very large companies with an aggregate capitalization of over $7 billion. Perhaps four-fifths of the manufacturing industries had at least one representative of the 328 large firms within it.

And what of the period from 1905 to 1920? During this decade and a half the trend toward concentration slowed down greatly. As might be expected there was some failure of large firms, and prosecution under the Sherman Act resulted in spectacular dissolutions of the Standard Oil Company of New Jersey and the American Tobacco Company. Somewhere between thirty and forty new combinations of a size comparable to those of the 1888–1904 period were effected so that, on balance, there was little change. The considerable growth of two firms in the automobile industry indicated that firms producing durable consumer goods might become large. Thus was foreshadowed a resumption of widespread efforts to achieve market dominance in new industries—efforts for which promoters of the "roaring twenties" were to become notorious.

We must pause now in our consideration of the problem of bigness in American industry. We have discussed one of the chief reasons for the in-

---

[10] See Shaw Livermore, "The Success of Industrial Mergers," *Quarterly Journal of Economics,* L, 4 (November 1935), 68–96.

creasing size of the firm—changing technology. We have dwelt at some length on another and more compelling reason—the driving efforts of entrepreneurs to secure protection against the ravages of competition during a period characterized by severe fluctuations in economic activity and great uncertainty as to expectations.

How, then, shall we account for the slacking off of the combination movement between 1905 and 1920? Partly by the fact that a reasonable degree of productive efficiency was reached shortly after the turn of the century. Partly by the fact that in at least a score of key industries a substantial degree of monopoly power was already achieved. And partly by the fact that the period from 1900 to 1920 was characterized by rising prices and generally increasing business activity—by "good times."

Yet were we to be content with our analysis so far, we should leave out of account the personal and institutional forces that made the period 1860–1920 exciting and dangerous and critical in United States history. These were years in which men sought economic power and, so seeking, encountered a universal demand for social control of those who wanted to establish a strange and potentially terrible aristocracy. We are now nearly ready to consider the struggle that ensued between the seekers after economic power and the people.

To comprehend the struggle we must, however, treat briefly two topics. We must first see how trade relationships, especially those with the rest of the world, were changing, for expanding internal markets and a peculiar international isolationism helped weigh the balance in favor of the powerful. At the same time the laborer was becoming conscious of the genuine power that workers could exert when organized on a great scale. We shall examine these areas, then, before returning to a consideration of the antitrust movement.

Commerce at Home
and Abroad

Colonel Roosevelt, on horseback, broke from the woods behind the line of the Ninth, and finding its men lying in his way, shouted: "If you don't wish to go forward, let my men pass, please."

RICHARD HARDING DAVIS

Trade at Home

MAJOR FLOWS OF COMMERCE

For thirty years after the Civil War the currents of commerce were about what they had been in the ante-bellum period, largely because the old regional specializations were maintained that long. New England and the Middle Atlantic states continued to send manufactured goods west and south in exchange for agricultural products and raw materials. In the 1890s the composition of the goods-flows changed perceptibly as the North Central and Southern states began to achieve a significant amount of manufacturing output for national as well as local markets. Between 1900 and 1920 production of the industrial Northeast increased steadily but not as fast as that of the newer areas, which took advantage of ready access to rich raw material sources and westward-moving markets to reduce transportation costs.

The states of Ohio, Indiana, Illinois, Michigan, and Wisconsin specialized in making goods dependent upon the basic resources of coal and steel. Until 1900, or thereabouts, production of these newer states was typically less highly finished than that of eastern states. But with the growth of the automobile industry and with rapid additions to the list of household appliances, it became apparent that one day this section would be the formidable rival of the Middle Atlantic–New England section. We have already observed that agricultural processing industries flourished in the central states. The only major raw materials that had to be imported as time went on were lumber from the South and petroleum from the Southwest.

The South lay prostrate for at least fifteen years after the Civil War. For another half-century this stricken section was to remain almost hopelessly poor. There was, however, a way out. The way lay in an industrialization that would furnish jobs so that the excess of rural population could get off the land and incomes could rise sufficiently to give Southerners a level of living comparable to that of the rest of the country. Yet before 1920 southern manufacture was mostly of the low-value-added kind not calculated to relieve the poverty of the region. Chief among the new industries was the cotton-textile industry, which made remarkable gains after the turn of the century. Indeed, by 1920 the South had almost half the spindles in cotton manufacture and probably more than half the spindle-hours operated. Tobacco manufacture, production of food and related products, and the making of furniture had become significant southern industries by 1920. These products more and more came to be distributed in a westward as well as a northerly direction.

Cities in the Midwest and South, long established as distributing centers for the manufactures of the East, grew phenomenally as industrial workers flocked to them. Chicago and Detroit, Cleveland and Cincinnati, St. Louis and Kansas City, Memphis and New Orleans, and Atlanta and Birmingham originated shipments that went in all directions far beyond their own trade areas. By 1910 the West and South originated half as much railroad tonnage of manufactures as the East. Meantime, smaller cities within the trade areas of the metropolises and cities in the thinly populated region west of the Mississippi specialized in the mercantile function. Trade eddied about these lesser centers, which distributed goods at wholesale and retail over clearly marked, if overlapping, territories. As automobiles came into common use after 1910, large towns and cities gained business at the expense of small towns and villages; by 1920 retailers in urban centers were beginning to attract customers from distances undreamed of a decade previously. This change was reflected in new ways of distributing goods and in new marketing institutions.

CHANGES IN MARKETING METHODS

Nineteenth-century Americans resented the middleman. This feeling was a holdover from the days when any seller of goods was suspected of chicanery and the courts adjured the buyer to beware. Something of the same suspicion yet attaches to those who handle goods in the intermediate distributive processes. Upon hasty consideration it may seem that manufacturers' agents,

Mulberry Street, Manhattan, in 1910 offered its residents a great variety of groceries as partial compensation for their notoriously crowded living conditions. Dentists and diamond merchants alike touted their services.

wholesalers, brokers, jobbers, and even salesmen are unnecessary. A little reflection, however, convinces us that their contribution to the entire productive process is great. It is obvious that consumer goods are of no use if they are not where they can be consumed.

Because of the difficulties of communication and transportation until late in the nineteenth century, wholesalers were far more powerful then than they are today. The problems to be surmounted in the assembling of wares required men of great business ability. In the United States during colonial days and up to about 1840 the wholesaling function was performed by great importing merchants and by brokers and commission agents. Importers brought from the rest of the world a variety of semifinished and finished goods that were sold to jobbers or directly to city retailers and country merchants. As the output of American factories grew in the first

Standardized clothing, like the ready-made suit pieces pictured opposite, emerged from Civil War measurements of American male sizes. Economies resulting from such mass-production techniques drove down the cost of clothing, while mail-order solicitation helped broaden markets.

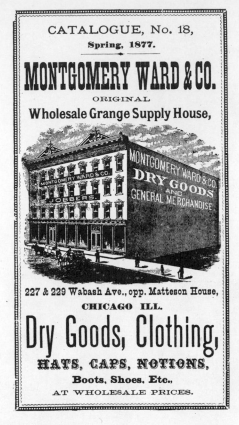

half of the nineteenth century, manufacturers found it convenient to let commission agents take their whole product and dispose of it in urban markets. The manufacturer was thus relieved of the necessity of selling his own product, though he frequently became overly dependent on his agent.

In the two decades before the Civil War, wholesaling institutions began to change. As an agent middleman the commission merchant received the goods of others for sale and was accountable to the owner for the proceeds of the sale, but he did not take title to the goods.[1] The full-service wholesale houses that evolved after 1840 bought goods on their own account from manufacturers and importers for sale to retailers, frequently on credit. In the growing cities of the Midwest successful retailers came to perform some wholesale functions along with the business of selling to consumers. As these houses grew they sometimes dropped their retailing activities altogether and concentrated on handling the output of manufacturing centers to the east. Not infrequently wholesale firms, especially those located in major distributing centers like Chicago and St. Louis, took on several lines of

---

[1] After deducting the expenses of selling the goods (chiefly transportation and warehousing costs) and his commission, the commission merchant remitted the sales receipts to the manufacturer for whom he was selling.

merchandise, but more often they specialized in a single "full line," such as hardware or dry goods.

From 1860 to 1900 full-line, full-service wholesale houses were without serious competitors in the business of getting goods from manufacturers to retailers. But as transportation and communication facilities improved after the turn of the century, the power the wholesaler enjoyed as the most effective agent for making a wide variety of manufactured products available to merchants began to shift, for manufacturers found themselves in a position to go directly to retail outlets. Wholesale houses did not decline between 1900 and 1920; actually, their sales continued to increase. But they handled an ever smaller *proportion* of goods in wholesale channels.

In the country, where retail units remained characteristically small and independent, the wholesale house kept its customers. The general store was rapidly disappearing except in villages and hamlets, as retailers in towns with a surrounding trade area began to specialize in particular lines. But this specialization of retail functions did not bring about a reduction of the traditional wholesaler's business. What hurt was the development of new types of retail outlets, typically large, and the increasing ability of manufacturers to establish strong consumer preferences through advertising.

Department stores. Of the new retailing organizations that gained definite acceptance by 1920, the department store ran counter to the trend of greater specialization in handling merchandise. As cities became bigger and more congested, the convenience of being able to do all of one's shopping within a single store had increasing appeal. Furthermore, department stores offered delivery services and credit privileges that made for convenience in an ever more complex urban existence. The early department stores of large cities evolved after the Civil War out of the efforts of dry-goods stores to replace business lost to the growing ready-to-wear trade. There was a definite division of the store into separate departments, each with its own manager, buyers, and clerks, for a line of merchandise; the separation was once so distinct that departments were frequently leased to individuals.

Department stores at first bought through wholesalers. However, larger ones like Macy's of New York, John Wanamaker's of Philadelphia, and Marshall Field of Chicago took advantage of their growing size to obtain price reductions by going directly to manufacturers or their selling agents. Because of the size of their operations, large stores with their numerous clerks had to set one price to all comers, and the old joy of higgling with a merchant over the price of an article was soon a thing of the past. So successful was the department store idea that by 1920 even a small city could usually boast of one. Small department stores bought through regular wholesale channels, and their departmentalization was so indistinct that they were much like the general store of an earlier day.

Chain stores. Middlemen participate in the series of transactions that make it possible for goods to yield their services to consumers, and their profit is the return for taking risks in the performance of this function. The fact that nineteenth-century middlemen were doing a necessary job did not mean that they were doing it as efficiently as possible. It soon became apparent to some enterprisers that costs of distributing goods in certain lines could be reduced by buying directly from manufacturers and processors. But to achieve the bargaining power to enable them to buy directly they had to have retail sales of considerable magnitude. Such sales could be obtained by combining in chains many spatially separate outlets with a centralized buying and administrative authority. Additional savings could be made by curtailing or eliminating the major services of credit and delivery.

One of the early chains, with us today, was the Great Atlantic and Pacific Tea Company, founded in 1859. From an original line restricted to tea and coffee, the company expanded in the 1870s to a general line of groceries. F. W. Woolworth in 1879 began the venture that was to make him a multimillionaire when he opened variety stores carrying articles that sold for no more than a dime. By 1900 tobacco stores and drugstores were often organized in chains, and hardware stores and restaurants soon fell under centralized managements. By 1920 grocery, drug, and variety chains were firmly established as a part of the American retail scene. A few companies then numbered their units in the thousands, but the great growth of the chains was to come in the 1920s and 1930s. Along with this growth would

F. W. Woolworth, a pioneer in chain-store merchandising, opened his first store in 1879 in Lancaster, Pennsylvania.

come innovations in physical layout and the aggressive selling practices that incurred the wrath of the independents.

The mail-order house. It is difficult for the modern resident of an urban area to imagine the thrill of "ordering by mail." Yet for many American families in the decades before World War I the annual arrival of a catalog from Montgomery Ward or Sears, Roebuck was an event anticipated with pleasure. Although Montgomery Ward started his business with the intention of selling only to Grangers, he soon included other farmers and many city dwellers among his customers. Both Montgomery Ward and Sears, Roebuck & Company had their great growth after they moved to Chicago, a vantage point from which they could sell with optimum economy of shipping costs and time to eager midwestern agrarians and to both coasts as well. Rural free delivery and the establishment of a parcel-post system were godsends to mail-order houses. By 1920, however, it was apparent that the farmer could now readily get to town to make his purchases; if the mail-order houses were to remain important merchandisers, they would shortly have to modify their selling methods.

Merchants had advertised long before the Civil War. But so long as durable and semidurable goods were either made to order for the wealthy or turned out carelessly for the undiscriminating poor and food staples were sold out of bulk containers, the field of the advertiser was limited. In fact, the first attempts at advertising on more than a local scale were largely directed toward retailers rather than consumers. Notable exceptions were patent-medicine manufacturers, the first sellers in America to advertise on a national scale. A combination of circumstances accounted for this peculiar fact. The general health of Americans in the nineteenth century was not especially good, medical facilities were not available to everyone, and there was a universal seeking for relief from aches and pains.[2] Once a nostrum gained acceptance, competitors could make inroads on its sales only after persistent and extensive newspaper campaigns. In a field where profit margins were tremendous, rewards to successful advertisers were high.

Until 1880 newspapers were the principal advertising medium, outdoor advertising constituting an alternative for some products. During the 1860s newspapers began to change their format to increase their reader appeal. Instead of placing advertising in a few lines on the front page, they used larger spaces on the inside of the paper. Beginning in the late 1870s most standard literary periodicals accepted advertising. Only *Harper's Magazine* held out against the practice until 1900, by which date *Scribner's* and *Century* were sandwiching reading material between two columns of advertising. Between 1890 and 1905 the demand for advertising space grew so rapidly that popular magazines like the *Ladies' Home Journal* and the *Saturday Evening Post* could make a fortune for their owners by enlarging the page size and interspersing advertising with reading matter.

The general level of advertising copy both as to truthfulness and to taste was if anything worse than it is today. Reputable newspapers and magazines usually refused material that was patently false or misleading. Generally speaking, the terrible vulgarities to be found in the advertising of the 1920s did not appear before World War I. Early advertisers were more patronizing than those of today, they were tactless about beseeching the lower classes to emulate the élite, and they often indulged in revolting sentimentality. Nevertheless, the approaches that today find favor with advertisers were all used more or less extensively before 1920. One way or another advertisers tried to impress upon prospective customers a brand name or trademark. Sometimes the advertiser attempted to sway his audience with lengthy argument. On occasion he tried to influence buyers by presenting the testimony of a famous personality. The silly jingle and

---

[2] There is a suspicion that the popularity of patent medicines depended in good part on their high alcohol content. Many, if not most, customers would not have touched liquor, and they may not have realized that the immediate sense of well-being derived from such medicines arose from alcohol instead of from other "beneficial ingredients."

Advertising helped expand consumer demand for new products like this all-purpose potion.

catchy slogan, which attempted to prove the worth of a product by simple assertion of its quality, were popular then as now.

By 1920 advertising was a billion-dollar industry. In some fields the increasing size of the firm in American industry was an important factor in the growth of national advertising, but advertising itself helped firms to attain size. There is some evidence that great holding companies did not budget as large a portion of their income for advertising as did the several companies that sometimes succeeded them. The case of the tobacco industry is pertinent. Until 1911, the year in which dissolution of the old American Tobacco Company was ordered, cigars and smoking tobacco were far more widely used than cigarettes. Beginning in 1912 American consumption of cigarettes grew at a tremendous rate. Various influences help to account for this remarkable change in a consumption pattern, but the coincidence of dissolution and the change in demand is too obvious to be overlooked. When several competing companies began to advertise their particular brands of cigarettes, they succeeded not so much in taking business away from each other as in selling the American public on cigarette smoking.

Nor did manufacturers in other fields overlook this possibility. By 1920 it was accepted that a firm had to advertise to maintain its share of an industry's sales. It was also realized that as competing firms carried on extensive campaigns, demand for the product of the entire industry might increase. Yet only a good beginning had been made. Two changes were to loom large in the future of American advertising. One was the radio that in a decade was to do the job of advertising far more effectively than it had ever been done before. The second was the change in the kind of consumer durables people would henceforth buy. In 1869 half the output of consumer durables consisted of furniture and house furnishings; thirty years later the same categories still accounted for somewhat more than half of the total. But after 1910, as first the automobile and then electrical appliances revolutionized American life, the share of furniture and household furnishings in the output of consumer durables declined rapidly. Household furnishings were articles that could not be differentiated in people's minds with any remarkable degree of success, though efforts were continually made to do so. On the other hand, automobiles and household appliances could be readily differentiated and presented a wonderful challenge to the American advertising man. How he accepted the challenge we shall discover later.

Foreign Trade

Between 1860 and 1920 the network of international trade took on its modern characteristics. From the new lands of the world came an ever swelling flow of foodstuffs and raw materials to support growing industrial populations and feed the furnaces and fabricating plants of industry. In exchange went the manufactured and semimanufactured products of the industrial countries, chief of which were Great Britain, Germany, and the United States.

In the great sweep of change two major forces dominated. One was the rapid improvement in methods of communication and transportation. To take three instances, the first transatlantic cable went into operation in 1866, a railroad line spanned the American continent in 1869, and the Suez Canal was opened in the same year. Most important were the railroads in various parts of the world that made possible a flood of cheap grain—from Canada, Australia, Argentina, Russia, and the Danube Valley, as well as from the midlands of the United States. In the late seventies and early eighties refrigeration on vessels made possible the shipment of frozen meats, then dairy products, and lastly fruits. To these were added the products of the tropics—rice, coffee, cocoa, vegetable oils, and tapioca.

But transportation was not the whole story. We have described previously the second major force at work—improvements in metals processing. It was not by mere chance that Great Britain, Germany, and the United States rose to industrial supremacy during the nineteenth century, for these were the countries that had coal and iron in abundance. England, which until 1875 was pre-eminent in manufactures, lost ground in the last quarter of the century to Germany and the United States. Her volume of trade increased, but her chief role came to be that of world financial leader. In iron and steel production the United States forged to the front; the United States and Germany quickly became leaders in applied fields engendered by the efforts of scientists—the electrical, chemical, and machine-tool industries.

During the last third of the nineteenth century and the first decade of the twentieth, the countries of the world became divided into two groups—

those that possessed political and economic power and those that did not. The tropical and subtropical countries of Africa, Asia, and South America, though drawn into world trade as sources of materials and (reciprocally) as buyers of cheap factory products, remained nearly stagnant at low levels of income per capita and developed little industrial power. In the temperate zones where the occident had reproduced itself—in the United States, Canada, Australia, New Zealand, and Argentina—population growth ran ahead of food production and income per capita rose rapidly. No other area, however, reached a stature comparable to that of the United States.

The dollar figures in Table 15-1, unadjusted for changes in the purchasing power of money, tell us much about the growth of United States foreign trade.[3] Since the period 1873–96 was one of falling prices, the dollar figures increased less than did the physical volume of trade. On the other hand, the period 1896–1914 was one of steady increases in prices, and from 1914–20 price rises reflected sharp inflationary pressures. Thus the physical volume of trade between 1896 and 1920 did not increase by anything like the amount indicated by the dollar figures. Nonetheless, because of World War I there was a remarkable increase in trade, especially on the export side, between 1914 and 1920. Merchandise imports almost invariably exceeded exports up to 1875. From 1875 on, exports exceeded imports in every year except three; from 1894 on there was no year in which the value of goods sent out of the country did not exceed the value of goods brought in.

Let us now observe (see Table 15-3) the major trends in the kinds of goods exchanged, classifying all exports and imports in five categories. (For a typical breakdown of these five categories, see Table 15-2.) Bear in mind that we are concerned with a percentage distribution rather than with *volume* of trade. On the export side the most striking change was in the decline of raw materials from three-fifths of the value of exports at the end of the Civil War to less than one-fifth by 1920. Crude foodstuffs swelled to nearly one-fourth the total of exports for the five-year period 1876–80, reflecting the piercing of the West by the railroads, and then fell until 1915. Manufactured foodstuffs likewise rose to one-fourth of total exports for the period 1876–80, held the proportion for twenty-five years, and then dropped in relative importance until World War I brought a small revival. A third important trend was the sustained rise of semimanufactures and finished manufactures. In the 1915–20 period these two categories accounted for about half the total value of exports.

We find the opposite movements, though not as marked, on the import side. Crude materials rose from one-tenth the value of imports after the Civil War to two-fifths the value of imports during World War I years. The chief crude materials imported—those necessary to a great industrial structure but not found in the United States—were rubber, tropical fibers,

---

[3] It is possible to adjust the dollar figures in order to take account of the changing value of money, but the procedure is tedious and unnecessary for our purposes.

Table 15-1

Foreign Trade—Value of Merchandise Exports (Including Re-exports)
and Imports, 1860–1920 (in millions of dollars)

Year	Exports	Imports	Excess of exports (+) or imports (−)	Year	Exports	Imports	Excess of exports (+) or imports (−)
1860	334	354	−20				
1861	220	289	−70	1891	884	845	+40
1862	191	189	+1	1892	1,030	827	+203
1863	204	243	−39	1893	848	866	−19
1864	159	316	−158	1894	892	655	+237
1865	166	239	−73	1895	808	732	+76
1866	349	435	−86	1896	883	780	+103
1867	295	396	−101	1897	1,051	765	+286
1868	282	357	−75	1898	1,231	616	+615
1869	286	418	−131	1899	1,227	697	+530
1870	393	436	−43	1900	1,394	850	+545
1871	443	520	−77	1901	1,488	823	+665
1872	444	627	−182	1902	1,382	903	+478
1873	522	642	−120	1903	1,420	1,026	+394
1874	586	567	+19	1904	1,461	991	+470
1875	513	533	−20	1905	1,519	1,118	+401
1876	540	461	+80	1906	1,744	1,227	+517
1877	602	451	+151	1907	1,881	1,434	+446
1878	695	437	+258	1908	1,861	1,194	+666
1879	710	446	+265	1909	1,663	1,312	+351
1880	836	668	+168	1910	1,745	1,557	+188
1881	902	643	+260	1911	2,049	1,527	+522
1882	751	725	+26	1912	2,204	1,653	+551
1883	824	723	+101	1913	2,466	1,813	+653
1884	741	668	+73	1914	2,365	1,894	+471
1885	742	578	+165	1915	2,769	1,674	+1,094
1886	680	635	+44	1916	5,483	2,392	+3,091
1887	716	692	+24	1917	6,234	2,952	+3,281
1888	696	724	−28	1918	6,149	3,031	+3,118
1889	742	745	−3	1919	7,920	3,904	+4,016
1890	858	789	+69	1920	8,228	5,278	+2,950

SOURCE: *Historical Statistics of the United States, Colonial Times to 1957*, pp. 537–38.

and metals such as nickel and tin. Crude foodstuffs showed uneven ups and
downs but did not change materially over the half-century, as Americans
imported coffee, tropical fruits, and olive and coconut oils that could be
produced domestically only at great cost, if at all. Imports of semimanufac-

Table 15-2 [a]

Major Trends in Exports and Imports

	Typical exports	*Typical imports*
CRUDE MATERIALS	Crude petroleum Coal Raw cotton	Crude rubber Raw silk Hides and skins
CRUDE FOODSTUFFS	Grains Fruits Vegetables	Coffee Tea Fruits
MANUFACTURED FOODSTUFFS	Meat Lard Prepared fruits	Sugar Meat Butter and cheese
SEMIMANUFACTURES	Iron and steel plates Lumber Refined copper	Wood pulp Copper in bars, etc. Tin in bars, etc.
FINISHED MANUFACTURES	Electrical machinery Farm implements Cotton textiles	Earthenware and glassware Woolen textiles Scientific and professional instruments

[a] The classification is that of the Foreign Trade Division of the Bureau of the Census.

tures increased somewhat, but finished manufactures declined in importance as the American productive capacity grew.

Tables 15-4 and 15-5 tell us something of the directions of our international trade. Although Europe after the Civil War became a more important customer of the United States than ever before, American exports to Europe began to decline about 1885. During the seventies and eighties Europeans took more than four-fifths of our exports; by 1920 the figure dropped to three-fifths.

Meantime, the United States remained Europe's best customer. The sharp decline in the proportion of American imports coming from Europe during the years 1915–20 was the result of a wartime disruption that permanently injured this trade. In the first twenty years of the twentieth century American foreign traders found customers in Asia and in Canada—with an interest in the Latin American market just beginning. On the import side the Asiatic countries and Canada were furnishing a great part of the crude materials that were coming to typify our imports. Already South America had achieved a substantial position as a purveyor to Americans of coffee and certain key raw materials.

The best way to understand the history of American foreign trade is to examine a series of international balance-of-payments statements to see what changes took place in the major accounts.[4] Between 1850 and 1873 the United States had a slightly unfavorable trade balance. Between 1874 and 1895 the balance shifted to favorable. From 1896 to 1914 it was markedly favorable, and from 1915 to 1920 it was enormously favorable. But, as we learned, items other than merchandise enter into the international balance of payments. A persistently favorable balance of trade may be offset by "importing" the services, the securities, or the gold of other nations. It is important to understand how, as the years went by, the people of the United States were willing to offset their consistently favorable balance of trade.

The Civil War and the years immediately after saw a continuation of high levels of income and a consequently high propensity to import goods. United States firms were paying foreigners substantial sums in interest and dividends, and on balance United States nationals were using more of foreigners' services than foreigners were using of Americans'. Table 15-6 shows that for goods and services and income on investment by foreigners Americans paid out about $1,800 million *net* during the period 1850-73. Residents of the United States were able to enjoy this net inflow of goods and services by accepting the investment of foreigners to the extent of $1,600

---

[4] We learned in Chapter 10 what an international balance-of-payments statement is and found that it is convenient to classify all items under three main accounts—the current account, the gold account, and the securities account. See pp. 227-31.

Table 15-3

Exports and Imports of Merchandise, by Economic Classes, Percentage Distribution, 1861–1920

Yearly average	Percentage of total exports of United States merchandise					Percentage of total imports				
	Crude materials	Crude foodstuffs	Manufactured foodstuffs [a]	Semimanufactures	Finished manufactures	Crude materials	Crude foodstuffs [a]	Manufactured foodstuffs [a]	Semimanufactures	Finished manufactures
1861–1865	20.0	22.1	34.4	5.7	17.8	14.1	14.3	17.5	13.6	40.5
1866–1870	57.6	9.1	13.8	4.7	14.9	11.7	13.2	19.9	13.9	41.3
1871–1875	44.9	15.5	19.6	4.7	15.3	16.1	14.1	20.1	13.6	36.1
1876–1880	32.2	23.9	24.4	4.6	14.9	18.6	18.2	21.5	12.5	29.4
1881–1885	33.8	21.0	25.5	4.8	14.9	20.0	14.9	19.2	13.7	32.3
1886–1890	38.1	15.0	25.0	5.5	16.4	22.7	15.8	16.5	15.8	29.3
1891–1895	33.7	17.2	27.2	6.3	15.6	23.6	18.7	17.9	14.4	25.5
1896–1900	26.1	18.9	24.0	9.6	21.3	29.5	15.1	15.9	13.4	26.2
1901–1905	30.3	12.2	22.2	11.3	24.1	33.4	12.9	12.4	16.7	24.7
1906–1910	31.7	8.9	18.1	14.2	27.1	34.6	11.0	11.8	17.8	24.8
1911–1915	30.7	8.8	14.3	15.4	30.7	34.9	12.8	12.6	17.4	22.4
1915–1920 [b]	18.2	9.2	17.7	15.4	39.6	40.1	12.2	16.2	17.1	14.4

SOURCE: *Statistical Abstract of the United States, 1941*, p. 533.

[a] Includes beverages.

[b] Period, July 1, 1915, to December 31, 1920.

Table 15-4

United States Exports, by Continents,
Percentage Distribution, 1860–1920

| Yearly average | Percentage of total exports | | | | | | |
| | North America | | South America | Europe | Asia | Oceania | Africa |
	Northern	Southern					
1860	6.9	8.8	4.7	74.8	2.4	1.5	1.0
1865	10.0	20.5	7.2	57.7	1.4	2.4	.8
1870	5.5	7.9	3.9	79.8	1.5	1.0	.5
1871–1875	6.4	7.2	4.0	80.2	1.0	.8	.4
1876–1880	5.0	5.4	3.3	83.1	1.7	1.1	.6
1881–1885	5.4	5.7	3.6	81.1	2.2	1.6	.5
1886–1890	5.2	5.8	4.3	79.3	2.8	2.0	.5
1891–1895	5.5	6.8	3.7	79.5	2.3	1.6	.6
1896–1900	6.9	5.6	3.1	76.7	3.9	2.3	1.5
1901–1905	8.6	6.7	3.2	72.3	5.3	2.0	1.9
1906–1910	10.2	8.7	4.6	68.2	5.5	1.8	1.0
1911–1915	14.2	7.7	5.2	64.0	5.6	2.2	1.1
1915–1920 [a]	12.0	7.7	5.5	63.2	8.6	1.7	1.3

SOURCE: *Statistical Abstract of the United States, 1941*, p. 542.
[a] Period, July 1, 1915, to December 31, 1920.

million and by accepting $200,000 in payments by immigrants and their families. (The latter are called "unilateral transfers.")

From 1874 to 1895 the American price level fell more than price levels abroad so that real bargains were to be found in the United States. Falling real incomes of many Americans kept imports down. Moreover, American agricultural commodities were offered to the world in rapidly increasing quantities. When we consider that besides the manufacturing industries of the United States were becoming progressively more efficient, it is hardly surprising that exports should have increased as they did (see Table 15-1). For these years the favorable *trade* balance was reduced by a growing tendency to use the *services* of foreigners. Even so, Americans had net credits on current account of $1,700 million, foreign investors poured another $1,500 million into this country, and Americans shipped a little gold. Offsetting the credits were more than $2 billion in interest and dividend payments to foreigners, and on balance unilateral transfers began to go the other way as immigrants sent substantial sums back to the old country.

During the prosperous years of 1896–1914 the United States came into its own as an economic power. The favorable balance of trade shot up to over nine billions, but this figure was cut to less than $7 billion by purchases

Table 15-5

**United States Imports, by Continents,
Percentage Distribution, 1860–1920**

Yearly average	Percentage of total imports						
	North America		South America	Europe	Asia	Oceania	Africa
	Northern	Southern					
1860	6.7	12.5	9.9	61.3	8.3	.3	1.0
1865	14.7	19.5	9.7	48.2	6.1	.5	1.4
1870	8.3	17.1	9.9	55.1	8.7	.4	.6
1871–1875	5.9	16.6	11.0	55.6	9.7	.7	.6
1876–1880	5.6	17.6	13.8	50.3	11.3	.9	.5
1881–1885	6.3	14.4	11.4	55.1	10.5	1.7	.6
1886–1890	5.6	13.8	11.5	56.0	10.4	2.3	.5
1891–1895	4.6	16.3	14.9	50.6	10.8	2.1	.6
1896–1900	5.0	10.3	13.2	52.6	14.6	3.1	1.3
1901–1905	5.4	13.3	12.5	51.3	15.4	.9	1.1
1906–1910	5.9	13.4	11.7	51.3	15.2	1.2	1.2
1911–1915	7.7	14.5	12.8	46.6	15.8	1.1	1.4
1915–1920 [a]	12.7	17.5	17.6	20.3	27.1	2.1	2.7

SOURCE: *Statistical Abstract of the United States, 1941*, p. 542.

[a] Period, July 1, 1915, to December 31, 1920.

of services from foreigners. Interest and dividend payments to foreign investors and the remittances of immigrants to their families were not sufficient to balance the payments without an outward gold flow and a reversal of the capital flow.

Finally, World War I wrought a change in the balance of payments of the United States. The last lines of Table 15-6 show the great favorable balance of trade created by the prodigious demand for American war materials. Until the United States entered the war in 1917, European nations financed their purchases here by selling their American securities and by shipping gold. When the United States finally took its position on the side of the Allies, continued large purchases of American goods were made possible by public loans to the Allies. At this stage in the progress of international relations there was no thought of *giving* assistance to our friends. It was expected that one day the loans would be repaid—just how no one thought to ask. During the war Americans, as private citizens, began to invest heavily in the fortunes of other countries, and in these few years received more income in the form of interest and dividends than they paid out. At last, as the −14.1 figure in the capital transactions column shows, the United States had shifted from a debtor position to a creditor position.

Table 15-6

United States Balance of International Payments, by Periods
(in billions of dollars)

Period	Goods and services net	Income on investment net	Capital transactions net	Unilateral transfers	Changes in monetary gold stock	Errors and omissions
1850–1873	−.8	−1.0	1.6	.2		
1874–1895	1.7	−2.2	1.5	−.6	−.4	
1896–1914	6.8	−1.6	−.7	−2.6	−1.3	−.6
1915–1919	14.4	1.2	−14.1	−1.8	−1.2	−1.5

SOURCE: *Historical Statistics of the United States, Colonial Times to 1957*, pp. 562–65.

The Acceptance of Protectionist Doctrines

In a Victorian world that paid more than lip service to the ideal of laissez faire, the untrammeled price system was allowed to allocate resources more than it had ever been before or ever has been since. But the United States, which, like most of Europe, had long been protectionist, became more so beginning with the Civil War. Setting up ever higher tariff walls, Americans led the way in setting a policy of controlling trade with other countries in the interests of national policy.

In 1861 maximum United States tariffs were not more than 24 per cent and averaged around 20 per cent. The national prosperity of the last fifteen years before the Civil War seemed to refute protectionist arguments that a healthy economy required high duties. Yet by 1864 the trend of nearly three decades was reversed, so sharply and positively as to put the United States on a high protective-tariff basis for nearly three-quarters of a century. There was no widespread demand for such a change in policy; only in the manufacturing centers were the old arguments for protection advanced with enthusiasm. To win the votes of the industrial East the Republicans came out for higher tariffs during the campaign of 1860. After the returns were in, but before the inauguration of Lincoln, Congress passed the Morrill Act of 1861, the first of a long series of laws levying ever higher taxes on imports. Thus the first step was taken before the war, but only when southern congressional opponents of the tariff were out of the Congress. The requirements of Civil War financing, at a time when import duties and domestic excises furnished the principal revenues, gave an excuse for raising tariffs to unprecedented highs. By 1864 the *average* level of duties was 47 per cent, and protection was granted to any commodity for which it was asked.

For twenty-five years after the war, men in both political parties attempted to reduce the "war tariffs." There were minor reductions, but the structure of duties remained heavily protective. During his first administration President Cleveland placed the Democrats squarely on the side of greater freedom of trade, but his defeat in 1888 blasted hopes of reform. The McKinley tariff of 1890 raised the average level of protection to 50 per cent, increased the articles on the dutiable list, and reaffirmed the Republican commitment to support of high tariffs. Following insignificant reductions during Cleveland's second term, the Dingley Act of 1897 raised duties to an average of almost 60 per cent. More goods, by value, now paid import tax than came in free. As might be expected, free goods were mostly raw and semifinished commodities requiring further processing, but some farm products, raw wool, and hides were placed in a protected status.

The prosperity of 1897–1914 made it easy to defend high-tariff policies. It was argued that the country was experiencing a high level of employment and economic activity *because* tariffs were high. Yet by 1900 American industry had obviously come of age. American manufacturers were competing in the markets of Europe; especially in the metals-processing industries it was apparent that most American firms needed no protection. The textile industries, which had enjoyed the benefits of high tariffs for a century, paid the lowest wages, had the most unemployment, and suffered from the rigors of competition more than any other class of producers. Moreover, it was readily demonstrable that import duties usually raised the prices of protected articles to consumers. As the populace felt the pressures of rising living costs in the first decade of the century, voters blamed tariffs, and Democratic politicians exploited this unrest. When the Payne-Aldrich bill of 1909 failed to bring any relief of high tariffs, there was widespread political protest.

In the campaign of 1912 the Democrats promised a downward revision of import duties, a revision that was carried out in the Underwood-Simmons bill of 1913. These reductions, while substantial, were not sufficient to satisfy everybody; however, iron and steel were put on the free list, and duties on cost-of-living items like cotton and woolen textiles were sharply reduced. The result was a simplified tariff structure, still of protective significance, with average duties about half what they had been for several decades. During Wilson's administration the average level of the tariffs was just a little over 25 per cent, almost the level that had prevailed in 1860.

So there was reason to hope that the United States would be willing to accept the creditor position so rapidly achieved during World War I. As long as the United States was an international debtor, her high tariffs did not harmfully disrupt international trade. The tariff may in fact have dampened fluctuations in imports as the national income changed over time and thus stabilized industrial growth in the young country. However, the United States in 1920 had to be prepared to take the output of European nations if Europeans were to pay their war debts to the United States. The economic consequences of American unwillingness to become net importers of goods and services will be examined in Chapter 22.

From 1789 almost until the end of the period we are considering, tariff-making in the United States was a legislative matter. The executive branch of the government was left no discretion in the setting of rates, and the same duties applied to imports of a given class no matter what the country of origin. Shortly after the return to protection in the 1860s it became apparent that the increasingly complicated tariff structure would require Congress to seek technical assistance in establishing rates. Furthermore, in a world in which barriers to international commerce were increasing, someone in the executive branch needed authority to make tariff concessions in order to obtain favors from other countries. And even the firmest protectionists were aware that schedules made under the political pressures continually exerted on Congress might contain serious inequities that would burden those who ultimately had to pay the tax. Both political parties at last came out for tariff-making on a "scientific" basis. Tariffs were presumed to be scientifically computed if they precisely offset the lower cost of production of a given article by a foreign country.[5]

To achieve these various objectives boards and commissions were suggested from the end of the Civil War. Nothing came of the suggestions until 1916, when Congress authorized a United States Tariff Commission. The Commission had no powers to set rates, but it could investigate and make recommendations. It was to be bipartisan, and its freedom from political bias was supposed to be a help in achieving the proper "scientific" attitudes. This body added something new to American tariff history when, in 1922, Republicans in Congress got down to the serious business of raising rates again.

The United States in an Imperialist World

Erection of trade barriers by European countries in the nineteenth century (Great Britain being a notable exception) marked a revival of national self-consciousness in the Old World. One manifestation of the revived nationalism was a "new" imperialism. During most of the nineteenth century Europeans did not seek physical expansion, for the economically and politically powerful countries were not convinced that colonies were a paying proposition. But in the early 1880s western Europeans became obsessed with a desire to own more of the earth's surface. Africa, before 1875 almost entirely unexplored and unsettled, was partitioned among the major European powers. In Asia the French took over all of Indochina, British India annexed Burma, and Britain extended her hold over the Malay states. China, avoiding physical disintegration, had nevertheless to make humiliating economic concessions to the major European powers. By the end of the nineteenth century, there was not much of the world left to colonize.

Pressures built up by the Industrial Revolution encouraged this second expansion of Europe. By 1875 output of the industries first mechanized was becoming very great. Industrialists and merchants thought that Asiatic and African markets would furnish a vent for the rapidly increasing production

---

[5] Equalization of costs, if widely attempted, would of course have nullified the gains from international specialization.

of cheap manufactured goods. The centuries-old notion that a government ought to have command over its raw-material sources also played a strong part in the colonization. Most important of all the economic reasons, however, was the profit-seeking of those with capital to invest; the frantic efforts to seize thinly populated and apparently worthless land were stimulated by hope of return from the fruits of the land or from mineral discoveries. Reinforcing the purely economic motives was desire for national glory. Private citizens took personal pride in the fact that their country owned exotic territories and dominated weak peoples. Nor could it be denied, in a day when sea power was still vital to a nation's military success, that national strength was buttressed by ownership of naval stations in widely separated parts of the globe.

The importance of economic motives in the search for colonial possessions is borne out by the fact that the nations first industrialized took the lead in late colonization. Great Britain, France, Belgium, and the Netherlands obtained the prize possessions. Germany, Italy, and Japan—the last major powers save Russia to feel the full impact of the Industrial Revolution—came out of the competition with the poorest prizes.

Meantime, the United States maintained her preoccupation with internal affairs. As long as great areas of unexploited land lay within her borders, there were no pressures for physical expansion, and inside her large free-trade area domestic markets developed rapidly enough to forestall concern for foreign markets. When America finally decided to expand, the decision had little to do with the vulgar profit motive. American imperialistic ventures were primarily the result of (1) a strong nationalist feeling engendered by a few politicians and vociferous newspaper editors and (2) the desire for an impregnable military position in the Caribbean, the Central American Isthmus, and the Pacific.

But whatever its real motives, American expansion ostensibly sprang either from pure altruism or from accidents of history. The only territory outside the continental limits acquired by the United States before 1898 was Alaska, presumed to be almost worthless. In 1893–94 there was agitation to annex Hawaii, but the American people would not stand for the high-handed methods used to depose the old Hawaiian government. Business interests generally were opposed to the needless and tragic Spanish-American War, and there was little popular enthusiasm for the conflict until a martial spirit was whipped up by an appeal to American sympathies for the down-trodden. But the quick and favorable outcome of the war forced Americans to make decisions regarding expansion outside the continental borders.

The first decisions concerned disposition of the former Spanish colonies of Cuba, Puerto Rico, and the Philippines. Cuba was given nominal independence and Puerto Rico territorial status. The Platt Amendment of 1901 so restricted Cuban independence that Cuba became in effect a protectorate of the United States. Instead of granting independence to the Philippines, the United States took them as a colonial possession. With these islands in the Pacific and a growing interest in the trade with the Orient, the United States insisted upon an "open-door" policy in China and, in general, upon economic opportunities in the Far East equal to those of the European powers. By the Hay-Varilla Treaty of 1903 the United States acquired a perpetual lease of the Panama Canal Zone from the newly independent Republic of Panama, and the completion of the Canal in 1914 assured a lasting interest in the Caribbean and Central America.

Indeed, two years before construction of the Canal began, the policy known as the "Roosevelt Corollary" to the Monroe Doctrine had been pronounced. In a message to Congress in 1904 Roosevelt enunciated a principle that was to make the Monroe Doctrine an excuse for intervention in the affairs of Latin American countries. Because, he argued, chronic weakness of a government might require some "civilized" nation to restore order and since, by the Monroe Doctrine, European interference would not be tolerated, the United States might be forced to exercise police power in "flagrant cases of wrongdoing or impotence." Europeans were not disturbed by such an assumption of international police power, but Latin Americans were. And they had reason to be apprehensive.

The United States was not long in applying the Roosevelt Corollary. When the little Dominican Republic could not meet its financial obligations, certain European states threatened to collect payments by force. Roosevelt's new doctrine required American intervention to forestall such moves. A treaty was signed in 1905 giving the United States authority to collect customs duties, of which 55 per cent was to be paid to foreign creditors. In 1916 the Dominican government tried to get out from under United States domination, and the Marines were sent in to quell the rebellion. In 1914 Haiti was made a protectorate of the United States, again with the aid of the United States Marines. American forces landed so often in Nicaragua that the matter became a standing joke.

After the 1910 revolution in Mexico against the old dictator, Díaz, American (and foreign) investors, who were heavily committed in railroads and oil, pressed for intervention and the restoration of order. President Wilson for a time encouraged Latin Americans by failing to invade Mexico with force. But "watchful waiting" could last just so long under the cries of outrage at destruction of American property, and United States citizens declared themselves unable to tolerate repeated affronts to American honor. Troops crossed onto Mexican soil in 1914 and 1917, in the latter year under the leadership of Black Jack Pershing, to seize the "bandit" Villa. With the adoption of the Mexican Constitution in 1917 the turmoil subsided temporarily only to begin again in the early twenties.

The years 1898–1918 were thus marked by both legitimate expansion and a sordid "dollar diplomacy." The former may with caution be condoned. It was inevitable that the United States, flanked by the Atlantic and Pacific, should require such outposts as the Virgin Islands and Guam. It is even possible to excuse, albeit grudgingly, the necessity of using high-

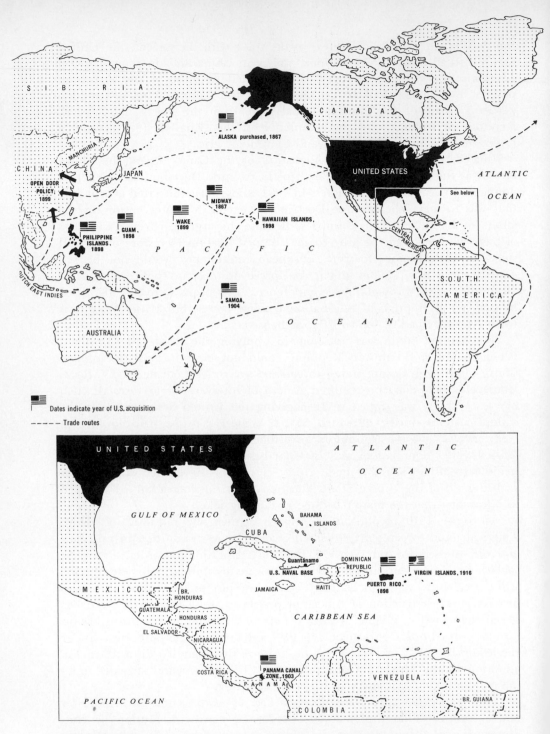

New Imperialism: A reluctant and sometimes uncertain America found colonial responsibility thrust upon it as a consequence of expanding world interests, wider-ranging trade, and growing industrial might.

handed methods to wrest the Panama Canal Zone from Colombia. It is not possible, however, to approve a diplomacy used to promote or to protect the private financial or commercial interests of the United States. If American capital was willing to take profits in the weak countries of Central America and the Caribbean, it should also have been willing to take the risks of venturing under unstable governments. Americans contended, of course, that the benighted Latins were better off with the improved sanitation, better educational facilities, and higher incomes that usually followed American intervention. Our friends to the south were not properly impressed, however, apparently preferring freedom to material gains.

The imperialistic ventures of the United States made the nation turn its attention outside itself and brought increased military strength. Offsetting these gains were the fears and hatreds built up among natural allies in Central and South America, with whose aspirations Americans should have been in sympathy. It would take a new generation of Americans and a second world war to remove a good part of the emotional conflict. Even so, the harm of two decades of harsh diplomacy has not yet been undone.

The Organization
of Labor

The first little office, which was about ten by eight, had
a door, a small window, and a brick floor. It was cold in
winter and hot in summer. The furniture was make-shift,
consisting of a kitchen table brought down from our
scanty house furnishings and a box for my chair. My
second boy, Henry, who helped me when not in school,
and who now takes great pride in the fact that he was
the first office boy of the Federation, helped to contrive
office furnishings.

SAMUEL GOMPERS

The Changing Status of American Labor

Post-1860 growth in the size of plant, firm, and industry changed the lives of American workers. As
factories grew larger and firms combined, the old
relationship between owner and worker disappeared.
The emergence of corporate organization brought
a class of professional executives in place of the
owner-managers of former years. Hired executives
felt less personal concern for the welfare of workers
and, by the same token, workers found old loyalties
to the employer dissolving.

Employer and employee could have gotten along
all right without either mutual affection or loyalty
if another emotion had not come to be a part of
the daily life of all but the highly skilled or especially favored workers. Fear, resulting from a fundamental and inescapable insecurity, was omnipresent.
Workers were afraid of many things. They were
afraid of unemployment, which could result from
technological change or from seasonal and cyclical
swings in economic activity. They were afraid of
the physical danger involved in most occupations
in a day when little was known about prevention of

industrial accidents, when insurance was almost unknown to poor families, and when neither society nor industry felt responsible for harm that befell the worker on the job. And many of the immigrants, of whom there were millions, felt lost and insecure because they were strangers.

But most of all the laborer was afraid of his lack of bargaining power. As economic units grew larger, the individual became a less important part of the productive process. Even in the skilled trades the single worker, no matter how able, could not contend long against an employer. Furthermore, employers often banded together to enforce their will. Nor was the individual worker bolstered by the sympathy of influential members of the community. Almost to a man, the business and professional classes, including clergy, presumed that right was on the side of the capitalist. Almost unfailingly the courts sided against the laborer. If a workingman wished to get along in the world it behooved him to do what he was told, to accept adversity with good grace, and above all to know and keep his place. That his place was not enviable is attested to by contemporaries.

There might be strength in union, but the worker often ran the gravest sort of risks whenever he participated in union activity. It was a rare thing to find a management not violently opposed to the collective action of labor. Union leaders or "agitators" found themselves blacklisted and unable to secure employment. Companies often summarily discharged anyone who joined a union—or even insisted that prospective employees sign "yellow-dog" contracts, i.e., agreements not to join a union. Employers hired labor spies—detectives in the guise of workers—to furnish complete lists of union members and to report union plans and strategy in detail. Often when employees threatened to strike, employers would immediately close the plant, "lock out" the workers, and wait for hunger and the pressures of angry wives to bring them to submission.

Between 1860 and 1920 unions operated in a political and social climate of almost unbelievable hostility. Americans were at least half a century behind the times in their failure to realize that the agrarian economy, in which the individual did have some measure of control over his own destiny, was fast disappearing. Business and professional people felt that the working masses would be content if they were not stirred up by a few misguided and power-hungry rabble rousers. If a man worked hard, did what he was told, and saved his money he could always rise to the top, they thought. To grant security to unions in the form of, say, a closed shop was an unconscionable interference with the rights of both employers and those laborers who wanted to remain rugged individualists.

State and federal governments stood firmly on the side of business against labor unions. It was considered a legitimate use of the police power to call out troops to break strikes. Such actions were condoned by the courts, state and federal, which proved invaluable allies of management in the struggle to suppress collective action on the part of the laboring class. Especially effective as a device for restraining union action was the injunction.

Employers could go to court to have labor leaders enjoined from calling or continuing a strike. Failure to comply with an injunction meant jail for offenders, and "government by injunction" proved to be one of the strongest weapons in the arsenal of those who would prevent effectual collective action by workingmen.

Despite these odds, labor as a class made progress between the end of the Civil War and the end of World War I. Nothing like minimum standards of social security for the majority or a minimum acceptable level of living for a huge minority had been attained by 1920. But the laborer's workweek was shorter and his earnings were greater than they had ever been in the past.

WAGES AND HOURS

Until quite recently the least satisfactory economic statistics for the years between the Civil War and World War I were those of wages, earnings, and hours of labor. Five basic data sources have long been available—the Aldrich Report (1893), the Weeks Report (1880), Bulletin 18 of the United States Department of Labor (1898), The First Annual Report of the Commissioner of Labor (1886), and the Dewey Census Report for 1890. But until these materials were subjected to formal scrutiny and analysis, historians could reach only tentative conclusions from them. Fortunately, Clarence D. Long has done the long-awaited job.[1]

What changes occurred in the hours that constituted a workweek? How did wage rates and earnings vary? In 1860 the average number of hours worked per day in nonagricultural employments was close to 10.8. By 1890, according to Long, the average workday in manufacturing was 10 hours, a decline of about 7 per cent since 1860, and people normally worked a six-day week. There were, of course, variations from the average. Skilled craftsmen in the building trades worked a 10-hour day in 1860 and probably no more than an average of 9.5 hours by 1890. On the other hand, in the textile mills outside New England, 12- to 14-hour days were still common in 1890, and workers in steel mills, paper manufacturing, and brewing stayed on the job 12 hours a day, 7 days a week.

Both daily wages and annual earnings in manufacturing increased by about 50 per cent between 1860 and 1890. Prices rose so rapidly during the Civil War that real wages fell drastically between 1860 and 1865. But from that year on the cost of living declined, not steadily but persistently, wiping out the Civil War increase and returning the dollar to its prewar purchasing power.[2] The consequence was that *real* wages and earnings in 1890 were likewise up by about 50 per cent. Daily wages in manufacturing rose from just over $1 in 1860 to $1.50 in 1890, and annual earnings changed from something under $300 in 1860 to over $425 in 1890. In the building trades

[1] Clarence D. Long, *Wages and Earnings in the United States, 1860–1890* (Princeton: Princeton University Press, 1960). See especially pp. 3–12 and 109–18.
[2] Long, p. 109.

both real wages and real earnings rose a little more, perhaps by 60 per cent. It should be realized that wage differentials among industries were great both in 1860 and 1890, the highest-wage industry paying from two to two and a half times the lowest. If we take into account the shortening of the workweek by about 7 per cent, the net increase in hourly money or real wages over the thirty-year period was about 60 per cent, or 1.6 per cent compounded annually.[3] Despite the tremendous immigration of these years, American workers made substantial gains.

What of the 1891–1920 decades? Until Albert Rees completed his corrective study in 1961, students of the period concluded that real wages showed little change between 1890 and 1914. In his classic book Paul H. Douglas had found slight gains in real wages and earnings for the entire three decades, with much of the improvement coming in 1919 and 1920.[4] Basing his estimates of money wages on data from the *Censuses of Manufactures* and the reports of labor bureaus in several states, Rees found a slightly steeper upward trend of money earnings than Douglas did. The Rees cost-of-living index for 1890–1914 rises appreciably less than the Douglas wholesale price index, so that when the money-wage series was deflated the result was a 37 per cent rise in the real earnings of manufacturing workers between 1890 and 1914, or an annual compound rate of increase of 1.3 per cent.[5] If the gains observable just after World War I are taken into account, the annual rate of increase for the three decades 1891–1920 may not be far from 1.6 per cent, or approximately the rate Long found for the preceding thirty years.

During the second thirty-year period there was continued gradual improvement in the standard workweek. By 1910, for all industry, it was 55 hours; by 1920 it had dropped to about 50. A widespread weekly work pattern was five 9-hour days plus 4 or 5 hours on Saturday morning, and the Saturday-noon siren still blows in many a small town. Again, the skilled trades were better off, having achieved a 44-hour week by 1920. Unskilled laborers, on the other hand, were still working 9 hours a day, 6 days a week, and the 12-hour day persisted in the metals processing industries.

Estimates like these have their shortcomings, but they make possible two generalizations about wages and hours. (1) For thirty years after the Civil War, despite frequent setbacks, labor made definite and substantial gains in real income. However, traditions regarding the length of the working day were hard to break down except in the skilled trades, where they showed signs of weakening. (2) Between 1890 and 1920 the increase in real wages and earnings was perhaps slightly less than in the previous period, but labor took considerable gains in the form of markedly shorter workdays and workweeks.

---

[3] Long, p. 109.

[4] Paul H. Douglas, *Real Wages in the United States, 1890–1926* (Boston: Houghton Mifflin, 1930).

[5] Albert Rees, *Real Wages in Manufacturing, 1890–1914* (Princeton: Princeton University Press, 1961), pp. 3–5.

When publicized, bad working conditions like these among very young slate pickers in Pennsylvania at the turn of the century won some middle-class sympathy for labor's cause.

OTHER MEASURES OF PROGRESS

American wage earners have always stressed gains in the form of higher wages and shorter hours as the proper criteria for judging progress. But since the early years of the nineteenth century labor has also striven for welfare gains through political activity, and by 1920, after a century of effort, some of these gains were realized.

Before 1920 there was a reversal of the upward trend in the employment of children that had set in with post–Civil War industrialization. In 1880 1,000,000 boys and girls between the ages of ten and fifteen were "gainfully occupied," and the number rose to a high of nearly 2,000,000 by 1910. In 1910 one-fifth of the youngsters between ten and fifteen had a job, and they constituted 5.2 per cent of the work force. But in 1920 the total number employed was back to less than 1,000,000, children made up only 2.6 per cent of the work force, and only one-twelfth of the ten to fifteen age group was at work.

Since hours were long and working conditions were unsatisfactory if not positively harmful, the decrease in the employment of children represented a social improvement. This improvement was primarily attributable to the successes of humanitarian groups in obtaining protective legislation at the state level. Massachusetts had a long history of ineffective child-labor legislation. The first stringent regulation did not appear until Illinois in 1903 passed a law limiting child labor to eight hours a day. State laws limiting hours of work, requiring minimum wages, and placing age limits were common by 1920, but further remedy was still required, especially in the cotton South and certain industrial states of the mid-South and East.[6] Efforts by Congress to place federal restrictions on the use of child labor were on two occasions before 1920 declared unconstitutional by the Supreme Court.

The status of women in the labor force had not improved much by 1920. The number of women gainfully employed showed remarkable increases after 1880. In that year 2,500,000 women, constituting 15 per cent of the gainfully employed, were at work outside the home. This number doubled by 1900, when women made up 18 per cent of the labor force. By 1920 8,500,000 women, comprising one-fifth of the gainfully employed, were in some pursuit other than homemaking.

The employment of women was once considered a grave social evil. We no longer think so, but up to 1920 there were two special problems in connection with the work of women that largely justified those who opposed women's work. First, women tended to be in the lowest-paid fields —such as cotton-textile manufacture and domestic service—with little opportunity to move to more lucrative and stimulating jobs. Second, wherever they worked, women were exploited in the technical sense of not getting in wages what they added to the value of the product. As with child labor, statutes prescribing maximum hours and minimum wages for women were common by 1920, and there was growing legislative concern with the physical surroundings in which work was performed. But in the mill towns of the South and the industrial cities of the North women needed the further protection of the law

In the absence of strong legal measures, the slow but inexorable forces of competition operated to open pleasanter and more lucrative occupations. As the typewriter and other office equipment became generally accepted before the turn of the century, girls found a new field in which, both temperamentally and physically, they had a comparative advantage. Sales work in city stores became a more attractive occupation than degrading domestic service. As the ancient notion that females are intellectually inferior began to fade, parents educated their daughters for professional work. Finally, World War I caused a great shake-up in hiring policy as employers, forced

---

[6] In these states especially the fight against child labor was made indirectly through increases in compulsory education ages.

to take on women as replacements for men lost to the armed services, discovered that for a wide range of occupations women could perform as satisfactorily as men.

To gauge the progress of labor, we should note developments in the field of social insurance. In an industrial society workers are vulnerable to loss of income from (1) industrial accidents, (2) prolonged and serious illness, (3) old age, and (4) unemployment. Before 1920 only the problem of insurance against loss from industrial accidents received legislative attention. Up to World War I the idea of protecting against the hazards of sickness, superannuation, and economic fluctuations was preposterous to most Americans—even though Europeans had since the 1880s begun to make systematic provision for alleviating suffering resulting from these foreseeable causes.

By the end of the nineteenth century it was apparent that simple justice required protection to the laborer against the frightful hazards of accident. We can only guess at the annual number of industrial accidents in the years before 1900, but estimates of insurance companies showed that after 1900 there were annually from 25,000 to 35,000 deaths and more than 2,000,000 serious injuries from accidents on the job. Some occupations were more dangerous than others; mining, metals processing, railroading, fishing, and stevedoring were notorious for the risks involved. Under the English common law (which had developed in a society in which the handicrafts predominated) workers had recourse against an employer in the event of an accident, but under conditions that made it unlikely for them to win compensation. To receive compensation for injuries, an employee had to bring suit against his employer. Unless he could prove negligence on the part of the employer—a difficult thing to do—he could not win his case. Furthermore, if the employer could show (1) that the employee was aware of the hazardous nature of the job when he took it or (2) that an accident was the result of the negligence of the employee or of a fellow worker (the "fellow-servant" rule), he had a good defense. And, of course, a good many workers had neither the means nor the knowledge to take the steps necessary to legal action.

Two remedies were possible. One was to pass laws providing safer conditions in hazardous occupations. The second was to abrogate the common-law rules that practically freed the employer of responsibility and to require that the employer compensate the worker for injuries. Since most employers did not have sufficient resources to guarantee indemnities, the second remedy required some form of insurance either with a state fund or with a private insurance company. In Germany (1884) and England (1897) the insurance idea was put into practice successfully, and in the United States the first workmen's compensation act was passed by Maryland in 1902. The Maryland act, like other early laws, was declared unconstitutional, but in 1914 New York and New Jersey succeeded in framing statutes that would stand up under court tests. Meantime, Congress, acting under its power to regulate interstate commerce, passed in 1908 an Employers' Liability Act, which gave

Table 16-1

The Labor Force, 1860–1920 (Persons Ten Years Old and Over) [a]

Year	Total labor force	Per-centage of popula-tion (ten years and over)	Nonagricultural pursuits		Agricultural pursuits	
			Number engaged in	Per-centage of labor force	Number engaged in	Per-centage of labor force
1860	10,532,750	47.0	4,325,116	41.1	6,207,634	58.9
1870	12,924,951	44.4	6,075,179	47.0	6,849,772	53.0
1880	17,392,099	47.3	8,807,289	50.6	8,584,810	49.4
1890	23,318,183	49.2	13,379,810	57.4	9,938,373	42.6
1900	29,073,233	50.2	18,161,235	62.5	10,911,998	37.5
1910	37,370,794	52.2	25,779,027	69.0	11,591,767	31.0
1920	42,433,535	51.3	30,984,765	73.0	11,448,770	27.0

SOURCE: *Historical Statistics of the United States, 1789-1945*, p. 63.

[a] Strictly, the table reports the number of "gainful workers"—persons who had a gainful occupation, both working or seeking work at the time of the census. See source, p. 55, for concepts.

railroad workers protection by abrogating the fellow-servant rule. In 1916 the federal government provided compensation laws for its civilian workers. With the tremendous acceleration of industrial activity that came with the war, other states hastened to put in similar plans of insurance, and by 1920 the great majority of all states had compensation laws in effect. During the war years the merits of other kinds of social insurance were debated, but no important extensions were seriously considered by Congress.

These, then, were the concrete gains to which the laboring man could point with pride. But anyone who wished could paint a dark picture of insecurity and show effectively that the worker under capitalism was not yet the beneficiary of a diffusion of the system's rewards.

Immigration and the Labor Force

In Table 16-1 is shown the number of persons ten years old and over in the labor force as of the decennial census for the years 1860–1920. The people in the labor force, as indicated in the table, were the breadwinners—including those unemployed. Not included in the labor force were house-wives, whose output of services was not valued in the market place, and students, who were presumably preparing themselves to take a place as productive workers. The rest of the population was made up of those who were too old or too young, too rich, too lazy, or too sick to work. In 1860 two-fifths of the labor force was engaged in nonagricultural pursuits and three-fifths in agricultural pursuits. By 1890 these percentages had been reversed, and by 1920 three-fourths of the labor force was in nonagricultural employment and one-fourth was in agriculture. No other single statistic is as good an indicator of the profound change that took place in the economy over these sixty years. To put the figures in a different way, while the labor force as a whole increased fourfold during the period, the number of people in nonagricultural employment increased sevenfold.

The striking growth in the total work force in great part reflected the tremendous pulling power of America for Europeans. Between 1865 and 1880 more than 5,000,000 immigrants found permanent or temporary homes in the United States, and between 1880 and 1920 the number swelled to 23,500,000. As Table 16-2 shows, there were considerable year-to-year variations, the number of immigrants invariably rising with good times and falling with bad. Peak years of inflow coincided with, or immediately preceded, the *onset* of severe depressions. Observe how peaks were reached in 1873, 1882, 1892, 1907 and 1914. For obvious reasons immigration fell off greatly during the prosperous World War I years.

Table 16-2

American Immigration, 1860–1920
(in thousands)

Year	Number of immigrants	Year	Number of immigrants	Year	Number of immigrants
1860	154				
1861	92	1881	669	1901	488
1862	92	1882	789	1902	649
1863	176	1883	603	1903	857
1864	193	1884	519	1904	813
1865	248	1885	395	1905	1,026
1866	319	1886	334	1906	1,101
1867	316	1887	490	1907	1,285
1868	139	1888	547	1908	783
1869	353	1889	444	1909	752
1870	387	1890	455	1910	1,042
1871	321	1891	560	1911	879
1872	405	1892	580	1912	838
1873	460	1893	440	1913	1,198
1874	313	1894	286	1914	1,218
1875	227	1895	259	1915	327
1876	170	1896	343	1916	299
1877	142	1897	231	1917	295
1878	138	1898	229	1918	111
1879	178	1899	312	1919	141
1880	457	1900	449	1920	430

SOURCE: *Historical Statistics of the United States, Colonial Times to 1957*, pp. 56–57.

The great source of cheap labor was immigration. Densely packed boats brought millions of unskilled workers to America, often under contracts that specified no wage increases for the first year.

In the 1880s there was a decreasing inflow of people from northern and western Europe and an increasing inflow from southern and eastern Europe. It is usual to speak of the immigration from Great Britain, Ireland, Germany, and the Scandinavian countries as the "old" immigration, and to distinguish it from the "new" immigration of Hungarians, Poles, Russians, Serbs, Greeks, and Italians. In the seventies more than 80 per cent of the immigrants came from the north and west of Europe; by 1910 80 per cent of the total were coming each year from the south and east. It is reckoned that 1896 marked the point at which a majority of those arriving annually were no longer of the "old" nationalities.

Much was once made of the presumed economic significance of this shift in the sources whence new Americans came. In ethnic characteristics the Swedes and Germans of the old immigration were not unlike the Anglo-Saxons who colonized America. Slovaks and Magyars, on the other hand, along with Russians and Italians and the other peoples from the new areas, had queer customs and spoke odd languages. And they looked different. To native-born citizens of turn-of-the-century America they seemed inferior in skills, in cultural background, and in potentialities. Even their tardiness in arriving on these shores appeared to indicate a certain lack of energy and aggressiveness.[7]

The new immigrant supplanted the old for two reasons. As economic opportunity grew in England, Germany, and Scandinavia, America became less attractive to nationals of these countries. More important, though, was the rapid improvement in transportation during the sixties and seventies. The steamship put the Mediterranean much closer to America, and railroads from the interior of eastern Europe to Mediterranean ports made possible the movement of the peasantry. There was a vast difference in the economic opportunities offered an American laborer, even an unskilled one, and those available at home to the European peasant. Once the transportation barriers were removed the suction created was irresistible; railroads, steamship companies, and American mill and factory managers hastened the movement by advertisement and financial assistance.

It is probably true that immigrants after 1880 were less skilled and educated than earlier immigrants. It may be that their different political and cultural history made their assimilation into American democracy and their organization into labor unions more difficult. Nevertheless, the economic effects of the old and the new immigration were roughly the same. New arrivals, whatever their national origins, usually went into the ranks of unskilled labor. Slovaks, Poles, and Italians replaced Irish, Germans, and Swedes in the coal fields and steel mills, and like their predecessors took the lowest position in the social strata.

What was the impact of foreigners on the American economy? Although 28,000,000 people arrived between 1865 and 1920, the ratio of foreign-born to the total population held *fairly constant at around 14 per cent*.[8] But at the end of the period more than one-third of the men employed in manufacturing industries and almost one-half of those in mining were foreign born. Moreover, the great majority of immigrants entered the labor markets of New England, the middle Atlantic states, and the states of Ohio, Michigan, and Illinois, and their numbers were concentrated in the great industrial cities of those states. Working for low wages in crowded factories and sweatshops and living in unsanitary tenements, immigrants complicated such urban social problems as slums, crime and delinquency, and municipal corruption.

American business profited greatly from the inexhaustible supply of unskilled and semiskilled workers. The steamship companies that brought them to America and the railroads that took them to their destination were the first to benefit. But manufacturing and mining companies profited most,

---

[7] *Each* immigrant group in its period of peak arrivals looked inferior; the "shanty Irish" and "dumb Swedes" of a previous generation were as much scorned. But Americans in the twentieth century seized upon the assumed "inferiority" of southern and eastern Europeans as an argument for excluding them.

[8] This rather curious fact is accounted for by the high rate of increase of the native population plus substantial outmigration during periods of depression.

An inevitable consequence of the urban crowding of workers was the growth of dark slums (like this one in Newark, New Jersey), which bred hopelessness, squalor, and crime. Conceivably, these same slums may have provided fierce incentive to their ablest residents to escape.

for they could expand their operations to supply growing markets without any increase in the costs of low-grade labor. Moreover, the influx of immigrants meant more customers for American retailers, more buyers of cheap manufactured goods, and a greatly enlarged market for housing.

The rapidly increasing supply of unskilled labor kept wage levels for great numbers of workers from rising. Therefore, insofar as established American workers could not escape from the unskilled ranks, they were adversely affected. But supervisory jobs and skilled jobs went to native white Americans, and the number of better jobs was increased as the mass of new-immigrant unskilled grew. Moreover, wages of craftsmen engaged in making equipment to be used by the masses of unskilled and semiskilled doubtless rose. And native American labor gained from lower-priced manufactured products made possible by cheap labor.

Management was convinced that unrestricted immigration was necessary to the growth of American industry. Labor was equally certain that the influx of foreigners continually undermined the economic status of native workers. From Civil War days to the end of World War I there was a constant struggle between the proponents and adversaries of immigration restriction. In 1864, at the behest of the manufacturing interests, Congress passed the Contract Labor Law, which authorized contracts made abroad to import foreign workers and permitted the establishment of the American Emigrant Company, to act as agent for American businessmen. This law had the practical effect of bringing in laborers whose status was scarcely to be distinguished from that of indentured servants. Wage earners fought this law until its repeal in 1868; from this year on there was a continuing struggle to restrict immigration generally.

First to feel the effects of the campaign for restriction were the Chinese. The influence of the Chinese on the labor market was localized almost exclusively in California, where the Workingman's Party (the "sand lotters") urged the exclusion of all Orientals. By the Chinese Exclusion Act of 1882 the first victory of the restrictionists was won. Successful in their first major effort, the restrictionists pressed on to make illegal the immigration of anyone who could neither read nor write. Acts requiring literacy tests passed Congress, but Cleveland and, later, Taft vetoed them. For many years labor had to be content with whittling away at the principle of free movement of all comers into the United States. After Chinese exclusion the next success was in outlawing the importation of "contract" workers, whose cost of passage was to be repaid out of their earnings in the United States. In succeeding laws further restrictions were imposed upon the immigration of the physically and mentally ill, vagrants, and anarchists. In 1917 Congress finally passed a literacy test, this time over President Wilson's veto. Permanent bars to the free flow of migrants into the United States were soon to be erected.

The Achievement of Permanent Organization

The outbreak of the Civil War, at once disruptive and stimulating to the economy of the North, was a blow to union efforts that had flowered in the immediately preceding years. Labor received bad publicity, too, as a consequence of the loud objections of union leaders and the labor press to the conscription law that allowed men who could pay a $300 commutation fee to escape military service. The objection against commutation fees left an impression of disloyalty of unions in the public mind, an impression deepened by isolated riots fomented by the Copperheads. The fortunes of organized labor ebbed to the point of seeming hopelessness.

The recovery of business from the initial adverse effects of hostilities was not long delayed. As war contracts were let and the salubrious effects of deficit financing were felt throughout the economy, output and incomes rose splendidly. By the middle of 1862 the depression of the early months of the war was over. During the summer prices of consumer goods began to increase, and, as almost always happens, wages lagged behind the cost of living. The reduction of real incomes became severe enough to make organization mandatory upon the workers. Because of the extreme labor scarcity that developed as men were called into the Army, the time was ripe for a renewed union effort. Unions that had managed to stay alive through 1860 and 1861 gained membership rapidly, and new unions sprang up even outside the established industrial areas. Strikes were used so successfully to obtain wage concessions that organization became progressively easier. The unsuccessful strikes were mainly those called in protest against technological innovations that threatened to destroy jobs. During the Civil War, labor became convinced that it was futile to struggle against the inevitable mechanization of industry. A great step forward was taken when leaders realized that time could not be rolled back.

Craft unions gained so much in numbers and strength that employers became concerned. By December of 1864 there were perhaps three hundred local unions with a membership of 200,000 concentrated in the industrial states of New York, Pennsylvania, and Massachusetts. City centrals reappeared as did national unions organized along craft lines. At least eleven national unions, some of them with a continuous history down to the present, were formed by 1865.

Business activity slackened after the war, and labor's position was weakened further by the return of soldiers to their jobs. Furthermore, the downward pressure exerted on wages by immigrants, their numbers swollen by the Contract Law, was not relieved by the westward movement stimulated by the Homestead Act. But the economy, after hesitating, moved on to good years in the early seventies. By 1873 there were forty-one national craft unions with a membership estimated between 300,000 and 400,000.

The craft type of union had always been advocated by conservative labor leaders, who were primarily concerned with wages, hours, and working conditions. These men knew that national organization was essential, for the great improvements in communication and transportation had given labor a mobility it had never had before. There was no point in organizing in New York City if Philadelphia workers in the same trade, not abiding by union rules, could come to New York to take the jobs of strikers. But while they recognized the need for a national association of workers in a single craft, these leaders did not advocate an all-inclusive union seeking broad social and political ends. However, the depression that followed the downturn of 1873 revealed once more, and with crushing finality, the inherent weakness of the pure national craft union. Among the first to go down was the numerically strongest of them all, the shoemakers' association known as the Knights of St. Crispin. Of the forty-one national craft unions, only eight, greatly weakened, survived six years of hard times. Was there no way to lasting labor solidarity?

"ONE BIG UNION"

Two alternative lines of action had long been urged by leaders disgusted with the periodic disintegration of the job-conscious union. One course was to catch the masses up in a new political party that would aim at overthrowing orthodox economic institutions and establishing a socialist government. The other course was to support whichever existing political party would further labor's goals within the institutional framework of capitalism. Either plan depended for success upon the formation of a single, all-inclusive union that could unite all labor elements and bring sympathizers in business and the professions into close, active alliance with labor. The more radical movement, the revolutionary establishment of a socialist government, was never able to muster sufficient support to make it a serious threat, though the socialists furnished many leaders who later furthered the more conservative cause. The alternative approach to power, through "one big union" operating within the existing governmental framework, came very close to success.

As early as 1864 a national federation of city centrals—i.e., local organizations of several craft unions—had been attempted without success. Only two years later there was started another federation that captured the imaginations of workingmen and their political allies and quickly secured 500,000 members. This was the National Labor Union (NLU), noteworthy as the first manifestation of labor's yearning for a solid front against the opposition of the business class. Originally seeking modest, purely economic objectives, this federation of city assemblies attracted a few national craft unions as affiliates. At first the Union proposed a moderate program, emphasizing arbitration of disputes and advocating strikes only as a last resort, which placated labor-haters. But radical leaders gradually injected a more idealistic fervor, and the organization came to place more emphasis on social reform. In coalition with agrarian reformers the National Labor Union went into politics on a platform that proposed an increase in the money supply, a weakening of the "money monopoly" of the banks, and the establishment of producers' and consumers' co-operatives. This growing emphasis on political activity alienated the NLU's local craft membership, and it was dissolved after defeat at the polls in 1872.

Meanwhile, in 1869 the most romantic of all American labor organizations had come into being as an association of poor Philadelphia tailors. Under the leadership of a Baptist preacher, Uriah S. Stephens, the Noble and Holy Order of the Knights of Labor had an inauspicious beginning. With all the trappings of a fraternal lodge, including a secret religious ritual, this group sought a new appeal to the workingman and a new protection for him. Besides having economic ends in common, the membership would be held together by bonds of brotherly love. Since the bitter opposition of property owners had proved so damaging in the past, the new organization would give to its members the protection of anonymity.

The basic units of the Knights were local assemblies, the first of which was formed in Philadelphia when other crafts allied themselves with the tailors. With the formation of other local assemblies, composed of either pure craft or "mixed" unions, district assemblies of five or more local assemblies were established. The district assemblies were in turn knit together by the General Assembly, governed by a General Executive Board presided over by the Grand Master Workman. Authority was highly centralized and absolute. The district assemblies controlled the local assemblies; the General Assembly in turn had "full and final" jurisdiction as the governing body of the organization. As membership increased, the Knights aspired to be "one big union," with a geographical principle of structure and a membership including skilled and unskilled, male and female, of all colors and national origins. As many as one-fourth of the members of a local assembly could be non–wage earners, and only bankers, doctors, lawyers, and purveyors of liquor were excluded from membership.

The growth of the Knights of Labor was slow during its first ten years. Its real rise began in 1881, two years after Terence V. Powderly replaced Uriah Stephens as Grand Master Workman. Neither a vigorous nor an imaginative leader, Powderly for several years intuitively steered a proper course. He understood that the mystical and secret features of the Order created suspicion in the public mind and earned the enmity of the Roman Catholic Church. Moving quickly to strip all of the secrecy and much of the scriptural language from the ritual, Powderly opened the membership to many who could not otherwise have joined.

The conjuncture of events was favorable to the expansion of the Knights of Labor. In 1877 labor agitation erupted with unprecedented violence in protest against the terrible economic hardship that accompanied the depression. Trainmen, frequently unorganized, carried out a series of strikes against railroads; work stoppages were followed by rioting and the use of police and state and federal troops to put down the disturbances. As a conquence, laboring people became convinced that against the great power of the middle class there had to be set a single powerful union and that the union would have to fight for widespread social reform. A demand for labor solidarity rose, then, just before the country emerged temporarily from depression, making a rapid organization of local assemblies possible.

The Knights of Labor may have had 20,000 members by 1881. Within five years membership reached the unprecedented total of 750,000, the great accretions coming for the most part in 1885. Although the Knights had begun as an organization opposed to strikes, it was through a series of brilliant strike victories that its great membership was won. In 1884 and 1885 the Knights were successful in a series of work stoppages against the railroads, then the most powerful business firms in the country. The acclaim accorded the union was tremendous. When, in addition, the leadership announced the attainment of an eight-hour day as the next major objective, workers rushed to join.

A peak of membership and power was reached in the spring of 1886, after which there was a decline almost as precipitous as the rise had been. Stretching their luck too far, the Knights lost a strike against one of Jay Gould's railroads and with it lost much of the prestige gained in a victory over Gould in the preceding year. When, in May of 1886, a general strike to achieve an eight-hour day failed to materialize, members lost faith. Membership slipped to 100,000 by 1890, in which year the growing American Federation of Labor won a showdown fight against a group backed by the Knights to organize the cigar trade in New York City. Though the Knights remained in existence until 1917, they were of no importance after 1900.

Thus ended labor's great experiment of the nineteenth century. Why did it fail? Certainly not because of its objectives, which were noble and worthy. In addition to such goals as equal pay for men and women, the abolition of child labor, an eight-hour day, and the payment of money wages on a weekly basis, the Knights sought even more general benefits. They wanted improvement of the educational system, the establishment of producers' co-operatives with the object of doing away with the wage system, equal status for everyone regardless of creed, sex, or color, and approximate equality of income and opportunity for all the productive members of society. In a period of economic stagnation these aims were sufficient to attract the rank and file and keep them in the organization, but in time of prosperity members would be satisfied with nothing less than efforts to raise wages and shorten hours. Yet the Knights of Labor were never adept at wage-and-hour bargaining. For one thing, its heterogeneous membership made for discord and conflict over policy; members who had learned a skilled trade saw no reason why their greater bargaining power should be wasted in an effort to secure benefits for the unskilled. Second, the concentration of power in the hands of a very few top leaders, for a time a real source of strength, turned out to be a cause of jealousy and rebellion, especially after the leadership showed no skill in the strategy of strikes. Third, the large union dissipated its financial resources on strikes, which were costly even when won, and on co-operative ventures that failed. So when an organization came along that promised the strongest element in labor a persistent fight for better wages, shorter hours, and less dangerous and unsanitary places in which to work, the uplift movement collapsed. Labor's élite—the craftsmen—took the cash and let the credit go.

THE AMERICAN FEDERATION OF LABOR

In 1881, the year in which the Knights of Labor began its rise to short-lived eminence, a new experiment was getting under way. Meeting in Pittsburgh, Pennsylvania, the leaders of six of the strongest craft unions in the country proposed a federation of national unions. The new organization, composed of printers, carpenters, glassworkers, iron and steelworkers, molders, and cigar-makers, was to be known as the Federation of Organized Trades and Labor Unions. Its leaders were Adolph Strasser, then president of the International Cigar Makers Union, and Samuel Gompers, a former radical rising to prominence as a colleague of Strasser. The original membership was less than 50,000 and did not begin to increase until the Knights of Labor drive had spent itself. In 1886, strong national unions connected with the Knights withdrew in dissatisfaction and founded the American Federation of Labor. It was then a simple matter for the two federations to amalgamate, the new organization taking the name of the American Federation of Labor. Samuel Gompers became the first president of the group that was to dominate the labor movement for half a century.

Membership grew slowly during the next dozen years, reaching 250,000 by 1898. There followed the first of two pre-1920 periods of remarkable AFL growth. By 1904, 1,676,000 workers had enlisted in the cause. A decade of slow increase ensued, membership approximating 2,000,000 in 1914. Then came the second period of rapid addition to the ranks; by the end of World War I the Federation could make a legitimate claim to 4,000,000 workers, or 80 per cent of all union members. Of the unions remaining outside the AFL the most important were the four railroad brotherhoods, which were highly co-operative. The rest contended for jurisdiction with AFL affiliates or had disaffiliated for one reason or another.

How shall we account for the substantial growth and the capacity of the Federation to weather economic slumps? Although labor leaders themselves would not place primary emphasis on the fortuitous onset of almost twenty-five years of good times, prosperity was a major element in the stability of the new organization. Between 1898 and 1920 economic activity was on the whole quite high with a rapidly growing rate of industrial output. There were only three depressed periods, from which the country emerged without serious deflation and prolonged unemployment. But credit must also be given those who planned the strategy. After long years of trial and error, labor leaders, including men with radical backgrounds like Strasser and Gompers, had discovered the principle of pushing for concrete gains in good times and plumping for such legislative action as could be achieved without participating in politics as a labor party. Furthermore, their policy, "to defeat labor's enemies and to reward its friends," meant that they played one major political party against another, a practice that probably maximized the number of favorable bills passed by legislative bodies and minimized the risk of shattering defeats at the polls.

Certainly some credit for the American Federation of Labor's remarkable prewar success must be attributed to (1) its almost uncanny ability to make suitable modifications in structure without violating craft autonomy or permitting "dual" unionism, and (2) its promotion of the trade or collective-bargaining agreement as a means toward stabilizing relations with employers.

AFL leaders, from the experiences of the preceding seventy-five years, were convinced that stable unions had to be organized by self-governing crafts. The one unifying principle of the Federation was control of job opportunities and job conditions. This principle implied an organizational unit comprised of men performing the same job who, in the absence of collective action, would compete with each other to their economic detriment. Thus the craft union could act quickly to exert economic pressure on the employer.

But craft organization also meant that there could be no more than one union to a trade. Two unions within a single craft (dualism) was unthinkable; dualism weakened solidarity and destroyed a "united front." Yet rigorous adherence to the single-craft ideal had disadvantages that became more pronounced after the turn of the century. There was, first, the per-

Labor's leadership came to be largely in the hands of Samuel Gompers (standing, left), who in 1881 sat on this first Executive Council of the American Federation of Labor.

plexing problem of setting the boundaries between different crafts; "demarcation" or "jurisdictional" disputes arose with increasing frequency. Second, problems of common interest to several crafts went unsolved because there was no basis of co-operative action. Finally, mechanization of industry and rapid immigration of Europeans made it possible for employers to substitute unskilled for skilled workers, weakening the control of single-craft unions.

To solve these problems by a wholesale turning to industrial unionism would have been to deny the principle of craft autonomy. Yet it became quickly apparent that there would have to be *some* exceptions to craft organization. As early as 1902, for example, the AFL granted a charter to an industrial union, the United Mine Workers, for it was readily apparent that in mining the numerical superiority of the noncraftsman made organization on a basis of crafts altogether unrealistic. By 1915, however, the AFL had only five industrial unions affiliated with it.

The AFL tended to solve the problem of structure by amalgamation of two or more closely allied trades. Sometimes called "material" craft unions, the amalgamated organizations brought together those who worked with the same material, such as metal or glass. Some amalgamated craft unions, like that of the plumbers and steamfitters, constituted a sensible removal of an artificial line of distinction. Other amalgamations, like those of the machinists or the meat-cutters and butcher-workers, resembled an industrial union. In any case, amalgamation went on steadily, especially after 1908. By 1915 an observer could count only twenty-eight pure craft unions in the AFL as against nearly one hundred amalgamated unions. Furthermore, in 1908 the AFL had begun to form "departments" to help its craft affiliates preserve autonomy while having some of the advantages of an industrial union. The first of these, the Building Trades Department, and later the Metal Trades Department, the Railway Employees Department, and the Union-label Trades Department, accomplished the federation at a national level of all national unions having closely related interests. Thus did the AFL, by compromise and innovation, bring its structure into accord with the changing facts of economic life.

Meantime, AFL affiliates were assuring their own continued existence and the general stability of the labor movement by obtaining increased use of the written trade agreement. Written trade agreements were rare before the late 1880s; after 1890 they gradually became an accepted outcome of collective bargaining, whether on a local or national level. The first modern trade agreement on a national level was concluded in 1891 between the National Union of Iron Molders and the Stove Founders Defense Association. It established the essential conditions of employment, set up procedures for the settlement of disputes, and provided for enforcement and for renewal of the contract. Enough collective-bargaining agreements were signed before the depression of the mid-nineties to make them a significant factor in helping the unions weather that storm. With the growth of unionism from 1898 to 1904 the written agreement became well established in key trades and industries. Such recognition was a great source of strength in the decade of slow growth that followed; the footholds secured in this way made possible a second period of increase in collective bargaining during World War I.

INDUSTRIAL CONFLICT AND EMPLOYER OPPOSITION

The gains of labor just recounted were not obtained without a serious and prolonged struggle that had not yet been decided by 1920. Employers, supported by middle-class opinion and by government authorities, took the position that their rights and the very institution of private property were threatened by the growing strength of unions.

The most violent conflict between management and labor occurred during the long, grinding deflation that lasted for nearly a quarter of a century after 1873. During the depressed years of the middle seventies blood was shed in breaking strikes by force; a climax of conflict was reached in the turmoil of 1877, which began with the railroad strikes in Pittsburgh and spread throughout the country. The brutality was not all on one side. In the anthracite regions of Pennsylvania a secret society known as the "Molly Maguires" for years terrorized the populace and committed murder and other outrages while fighting employers and strike-breakers. Generally,

The Haymarket Riot of 1886 erupted when efforts to win an eight-hour day at the McCormick Harvester Works in Chicago met with flat refusal by employers and led to police attack on strikers.

though, it was the laborer who had to fend off the physical assaults of paid thugs, state militiamen, and federal troops.

Three incidents, spaced in time so that they did maximum damage to labor's cause, stand out as examples of the most severe disputes. The infamous Haymarket affair of May 3, 1886, occurred as the tragic climax of efforts of the Knights of Labor to secure a general strike of workers in the Chicago area. A bomb thrown at policemen attempting to break up a mass meeting at Haymarket Square resulted in several deaths. Four men, probably innocent, were executed for murder, and the injustice of the punishment roused great resentment on the side of labor sympathizers. On the public platform and in the press antilabor agitators for their part used the incident as a horrible example of what radicals and anarchists could do to undermine American institutions by violence.

Six years later, just as antilabor feeling was subsiding, the management of the Carnegie Homestead Works at Pittsburgh decided to oust the Amalgamated Association of Iron and Steel Workers, then trying to organize the Homestead laborers. A strike was called, ostensibly because the company refused to come to an agreement on wage matters, and Henry Frick, a close associate of Carnegie, brought in three hundred Pinkerton detectives to disperse the strikers and maintain order. Turning the tables, the striking mob won a weird battle with the detectives, capturing several and injuring them severely. To restore order the state militia was called out, and the union suffered a defeat that set back the organization of labor in steel mills by several decades.

The Homestead episode received an adverse publicity exceeded only by that of the Pullman strike of 1894. Although the Pullman strike was led by mild-mannered Eugene V. Debs, who had not yet embraced socialist doctrines, the strife was attributed to the un-American ideology of radical leaders. Rioting spread over the entire Chicago area, and before peace was restored, this time by federal troops sent on pretext of protecting the United States mails, scores of people were killed and injured. Again the seriousness of the labor problem became a matter for widespread concern and the basis of much immoderate opposition to the cause of labor generally. On the other hand, the Pullman strike served as a warning to conservative union leaders that violence would only disrupt unions and hurt them in the public regard. Furthermore, the dispatch with which Debs and other leaders were clapped in jail (on contempt proceedings) for disobeying a court injunction against inciting union members to strike was a sobering blow. Any long-run strategy would have to include efforts both to pacify voters and to strengthen labor's position in the courts. Pre-1920 successes along both lines were, to say the least, limited.

Beginning in 1902, employers changed their tactics. They began a serious drive to sell Americans on the benefits—to employers, workers, and the public—of the open shop. To further their propaganda ends, several organizations were formed, most prominent of them the National Association of Manufacturers and the American Anti-boycott Association, both of which were assisted materially by employers' trade associations. So effective were the employers' efforts that labor leaders of all shades of political beliefs began to feel pressure to do something. The radicals, despairing of helping the unskilled through socialist political activity or through the American Federation of Labor, started the Independent Workers of the World (IWW) in 1905. At least until World War I the IWW, bent on organizing along industrial lines, was instrumental in forcing the AFL to make the structural modifications we have noted.

Gompers, able young John Mitchell of the United Mine Workers, and others favored a counter-offensive against the employers through education or propaganda. Affiliating with the National Civic Federation, an association of people with an enlightened social outlook—including wealthy eastern capitalists, corporation officers, editors, professional men, and labor representatives—AFL leaders sought to win a more favorable attitude from the electorate. The National Civic Federation maintained a division for the mediation and conciliation of disputes, tried to secure wider acceptance of collective-bargaining agreements, and preached the doctrine that greater labor responsibility would mean fewer work stoppages and a better livelihood for all. How much good the National Civic Federation did is hard to say. Doubtless it served in part to offset the organized efforts of employers, but the alliance may have lulled job-conscious unionists into ultraconservatism at a time when more aggressive policies were called for. At any rate, the core of employer opposition remained almost as solid as ever, particularly among the industrialists of the Midwest.

Nor did the judiciary show signs of increasing liberality in court opinions on statutory attempts to protect the right of workers to organize. By the end of the nineteenth century the right of labor unions to *exist* was established. Yet the right of employers to force employees to enter into antiunion contracts was upheld to the very end of the period under discussion. In the case of *Adair* v. *United States* (1908) the Supreme Court declared unconstitutional a provision of the Erdman Act that made it unlawful for any carrier in interstate commerce to discharge an employee because he had joined a union. In the case of *Coppage* v. *Kansas* (1912) a state law, similar to many state laws passed to outlaw antiunion contracts, was declared invalid. Coppage, a railroad employee, had been fired for refusal to withdraw from a union. Because his withdrawal would have cost him $1,500 in insurance benefits, the Kansas Supreme Court held that the statute protecting him prevented coercion and was valid. But the Supreme Court of the United States reversed this decision, holding that an employer had a constitutional right to require an antiunion contract from his employees; a statute contravening this right, the Court held, violated the Fourteenth Amendment in that it abridged the employer's freedom of contract.

As late as 1917 the Supreme Court of the United States decided that antiunion or "yellow-dog" contracts, whether oral or written, could be protected by injunction. The Hitchman Coal and Coke Company, after winning a strike, had hired back miners on the condition that they could not be members of the United Mine Workers while in the employ of the Company. Later, organizers for the union tried to get the men to promise that, after a certain time had elapsed, they would again join the union. In a United States District Court the Company asked for and obtained an injunction stopping further organizing efforts. The Supreme Court affirmed the decision, holding that, even though the men had not yet joined the union, they were being induced by organizers to break a contract with the employer and that the employer was entitled to injunctive protection. Surely labor had a long way to go before overcoming the centuries-long bias of the judiciary.

In 1920 labor could look back on sixty years of slow improvement. Real wages were up and hours were shorter. Children and, to some extent, women received the protection of the law. The fundamental ideas of social security were being more generally discussed, and clear-cut legislative victories had

Henry Clay Frick (shown here enjoying the fruits of his labors) obtained vital coking coal properties as a steel industry adjunct, became Andrew Carnegie's partner and later an architect of the hard line that steel leaders took with labor unions in the bitter Homestead Mill strike of 1892.

been won to reduce the hardships caused by industrial accidents. Perhaps most important of all, trade unions had become strong enough to weather future depressions without disintegrating.

On the other hand, the problems of poverty and insecurity were far from settled. A majority of the unskilled workers and their families—and certainly a large minority of the entire labor force—lived below what we should today call a "minimum-comfort" standard. Output per man-hour increased around 20 per cent per decade between 1900 and 1920, yet wage earners received no such increases in real earnings. Inequality of incomes was striking in 1920, and there seemed to be little prospect of improvement. The top 10 per cent of income receivers got one-third of the national income, the top 20 per cent at least half of it; the bottom half of income receivers received less than one-fourth of total income. In the face of the hostility of employers, trade unions could only look to government to equalize their disadvantage in bargaining. Yet the courts, so far, had indicated a hostility only slightly less than that of the employers.

One hopeful experience came out of World War I. A National War Labor Board, created to reduce the number of serious work stoppages and encourage co-operation between labor and management, actually promoted and supported collective bargaining. Furthermore, representatives of organized labor for the first time had an opportunity to participate at a high level in the executive work of the federal government. Union leaders learned then that further advances would come only as the people, through the national government, evened up the balance of power. Fifteen years were to elapse before such intercession would permanently and finally strengthen labor's position.

Progress, Depression, and the Appeal to Government

From the time of Say and Ricardo the classical economists have taught that supply makes its own demand;—meaning by this in some significant, but not clearly defined, sense that the whole of the costs of production must necessarily be spent in the aggregate, directly or indirectly, on purchasing the product.

J. M. KEYNES

We now pause to evaluate the performance of the American economy between 1860 and 1920. It seems fair to conclude that businessmen, farmers, and laborers were better off at the end of the period than they were at the beginning. But progress was interrupted from time to time by spells of falling economic activity with accompanying loss and hardship. Our problem now is to summarize the available data and comment on the efficiency with which a free capitalistic economic system performed its function of allocating resources. We shall then observe how Americans began to ask their government for protection from the rigors of economic competition.

Growth and Instability

CHANGES IN INDUSTRIAL PRODUCTION AND NATIONAL INCOME

We have emphasized the rapidity with which the United States became an industrial state between the Civil War and World War I. Two studies of the fragmentary economic statistics of the period give us a measure of the speed of economic growth in terms of industrial output.

Edwin Frickey has prepared indexes of commercial and industrial production, showing changes in manufacturing production and in transportation and communication. Between 1860 and 1914 all industrial and commercial production increased at an average annual rate of 5.38 per cent. Transportation and communication output increased at a faster rate than manufacturing output, but durable goods production increased at the fastest rate of all (see Table 17-1 and chart on p. 408).

These are remarkable average annual growth rates. As the period progressed, there was a slight retardation in the rate of growth, and if we exclude the Civil War and post–Civil War expansion (1860–73) the averages drop somewhat.[1] After making this allowance, however, we are left with an average percentage growth in all industrial and commercial production of 5 per cent for the forty years from 1874 to 1914.

William N. Shaw, in a study for the National Bureau of Economic Research, surveyed the production of finished commodities and found a comparable, though somewhat lower, rate of production increase.[2] For the period 1879–1914 the Shaw series indicates an average annual growth rate of 3.8 per cent for finished goods, including producers' durable goods. Like Frickey, Shaw found the rate of increase higher for durable than for nondurable goods.

As measured by industrial output alone, the economy made great gains in the period we are examining. Now let us broaden our basis of measurement to include, as nearly as we can, all the goods and services produced by Americans. In Chapter 10 we found that changes in the national income, adjusted for population growth and deviations in the cost of living, gave us

---

[1] Pre-1873 evidence is so thin that the annual growth rate computed by Frickey for the 1860–73 period cannot be taken too seriously.

[2] William N. Shaw, *Value of Commodity Output since 1869* (New York: National Bureau of Economic Research, 1947). Differences of product classification and methods of computation account in part for the difference in growth figures.

Table 17-1

Estimated Average Annual Percentage Growth in Production, 1860–1914

All industrial and commercial production	5.38
Manufacturing	4.95
Durable goods	5.90
Nondurable goods	4.50
Transportation and communication	5.82

SOURCE: Edwin Frickey, *Production in the United States, 1860–1914* (Cambridge: Harvard University Press, 1947).

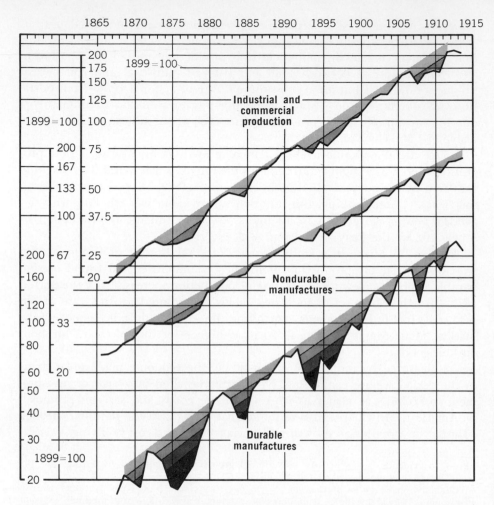

1865 1870 1875 1880 1885 1890 1895 1900 1905 1910 1915

1899 = 100

Industrial and commercial production

Nondurable manufactures

Durable manufactures

1899 = 100

Reprinted by permission of the publisher from Edwin Frickey, *Production in the United States, 1860–1914,* 1st ed., Cambridge: Harvard University Press, copyright 1942 by the President and Fellows of Harvard College. Adapted by A. G. Hart, *Money, Debt, and Economic Activity,* 2nd ed. (Englewood Cliffs, N.J.: Prentice-Hall, 1953).

Expanding Production: During the period of greatest industrial growth, the key sector was durable goods, which expanded steeply after the Civil War.

an adequate, if not ideal, yardstick. Aside from the statistical difficulties of estimation, the value of the national-income yardstick is limited by the fact that the quality and variety of goods and services consumed change over time. Moreover, the national income must be stated in dollars, and goods and services produced in the home (nonmarket output) are not included in the totals. Nevertheless, national-income estimates furnish the best indicator we have of the product that the people divided among themselves.

We turn now to Simon Kuznets' estimates of the national income. In order to "reduce detail, minimize error, and permit a clearer view of the longer-term changes," Professor Kuznets has put his estimates in decade averages. According to Table 17-2, the annual national income in the 1914–23 decade, measured in 1929 prices, was about six times what it was in the 1869–78 decade. Over the years covered, changes from decade to decade averaged about 23 per cent; but increases in the national income from year to year were by no means continuous or regular, although the table does not reveal the irregularity. Depressions, booms, deflation, and inflation were all reflected in fluctuations in income figures, though before 1920 these ups and downs were ordinarily not so marked as fluctuations in industrial production.

Table 17-3 gives us information on per-capita growth in national income. On the average, per-capita income in real terms increased about 11 per cent per decade. As the period progressed, there was a retardation in the rate of growth, but for the 1914–23 decade real per-capita income per year was two and a half times as great as it was in the 1869–78 decade.

According to Martin's estimates the national income, adjusted for cost-of-living changes, grew at an average annual rate of 4 per cent between 1859 and 1919.[3] This figure is consistent with the growth rates for industry calculated by Frickey and Shaw. The economic statistics tell us conclusively that the American economy was developing rapidly on a firm industrial basis in this period.

PROSPERITY AND DEPRESSION

But progress was not achieved without setbacks that brought hardship and suffering to great numbers of people. And in more peacetime years than not, employment and production were below 90 per cent of a full-employment output.

Let us look once again at the chart on p. 408 showing Frickey's indexes of nonagricultural production. This time we will consider industrial and commercial production, durable manufactures, and nondurable manufactures. If we connect the peaks of the curves, we have very nearly straight lines that show growth trends. Since the peaks indicate output when resources were fully employed, the trend lines trace the production potential. Inspection of all three curves reveals two extended periods—in the seventies and nineties—in which production was well below potential. In the eighties and late in the first decade of the twentieth century also there were slumps in activity not quite so pronounced but nonetheless serious.

The reader will at once note that the amplitude of swings in durable-goods output was much greater than in nondurable goods. It has frequently happened that during small slumps in durable-goods production nondurable output has not dropped at all, and year-to-year changes in durable-goods

---

[3] Robert F. Martin, *National Income in the United States, 1799–1938* (New York: National Industrial Conference Board, 1939), pp. 6–7.

Table 17-2

National Income in Current Dollars and Dollars of 1929 Purchasing Power, 1869–1923 (annual averages for overlapping decades)

	Total national income (billions of dollars)	
Decades	*Current prices*	*1929 prices*
1869–1878	6.5	9.4
1874–1883	8.4	13.7
1879–1888	9.9	17.9
1884–1893	10.9	21.0
1889–1898	11.7	24.2
1894–1903	14.5	30.1
1899–1908	19.8	37.5
1904–1913	26.1	44.8
1909–1918	36.3	50.3
1914–1923	55.3	57.2

SOURCE: Simon Kuznets, "Changes in the National Income of the United States of America since 1870," *Income and Wealth Series II* (London: Bowes & Bowes Ltd., 1952), p. 30. By permission of the publisher.

production have ordinarily been several times as great as in nondurable goods. The reasons for this difference in the time series are fairly obvious. Durable goods, whether they belong to producers or consumers, yield their service flows over long periods of time. Moreover, the replacement of durable goods is usually postponable. A machine shop can usually make an old lathe do another year, especially if business is bad. A household can put off buying a new car or refrigerator if family income threatens to fall. But as entrepreneurs and household units postpone purchases of durables, repairmen who service durables actually find the demand for their services increasing. Too, the demand for food, residential utilities, tobacco, and cheaper forms of entertainment falls slowly and in some instances may actually rise as incomes fall.

Closer inspection of our data would reveal several minor fluctuations or cycles in addition to the major ones. Yet we get the clearest idea of the nature of economic fluctuations by focusing on the big swings. Professor Hansen has described as follows the four major cycles indicated by the curve of durable-goods output.[4]

1. After an upward swing of seven years, production reached a peak in 1872 and then turned downward for four years. The trough was

---

[4] Alvin H. Hansen, *Business Cycles and National Income* (New York: Norton, 1951), pp. 22–31.

Table 17-3

Population and National Income (1929 Prices) per Capita, 1869–1923 (annual averages for overlapping decades)

Decade	Population (millions)	Percentage increase	National income per capita (dollars)	Percentage increase
1869–1878	43.5		216	
1874–1883	48.8	12.2	281	30.1
1879–1888	54.9	12.5	326	16.0
1884–1893	61.2	11.5	343	5.2
1889–1898	67.6	10.5	358	4.4
1894–1903	74.0	9.5	406	13.4
1899–1908	81.3	9.9	461	13.5
1904–1913	89.6	10.2	500	8.5
1909–1918	97.6	8.9	515	3.0
1914–1923	104.9	7.5	545	5.8

SOURCE: Simon Kuznets, "Changes in the National Income of the United States of America since 1870," *Income and Wealth Series II* (London: Bowes & Bowes Ltd., 1952), p. 55. By permission of the publisher.

reached in 1876, and output of the previous peak year was not matched again until 1878, a year in which output was still far below potential. The length of the major cycle from trough to trough was eleven years, and the decline in output of durables from peak to trough was 33 per cent.

2. Durables production again reached a peak in 1882 after an upswing of six years. On the downswing a trough was reached in three years, and after four years of depression there was recovery to the level of 1882. The length of the cycle from trough to trough was nine years, and the decline in output of durables from peak to trough was 25 per cent.

3. The upswing of the cycle of 1892 was interrupted by two mild recessions, and the peak reached after seven years was below the curve of potential (see chart, p. 408). The depression that began late in 1892 was extremely severe but was interrupted by substantial recovery in 1895. If we count 1896 as the trough year, the length of the cycle from trough to trough was eleven years, and the fall in durables output was 34 per cent.

4. The upswing of the 1907 cycle was eleven years in length and was interrupted by two recessions, the recession of 1904 being so marked that some writers consider it a major depression. The contraction of 1907–08 amounted to a 29 per cent decline in durables output, the

drop occurring in so short a time as to give an unusual shock to the economy. But recovery was quick, too, 1907 output being reached again by 1909. The length of the cycle from trough to trough was twelve years. After the recovery of 1908 the economy started on a long upsurge of production, interrupted in 1910 and 1914, which culminated in the war boom.

The construction cycles, though not altogether independent of durable-goods cycles, had movements of their own. There were three of them in the 1860–1920 period, with peaks in 1871, 1892, and 1909. The extremely severe depressions of the 1870s and 1890s coincided with sharp curtailment in building construction, and the shorter and milder depressions following 1882 and 1907 came when the building trend was still upward.

Mineral production rose and fell with rising and falling manufacturing output, but the amplitude of the swings was greater. Agricultural output fluctuations showed little relationship to industrial fluctuations, but, for reasons examined in Chapter 11, the curve of agricultural *prices* had much the same shape as the curve of industrial output.

The facts just observed about the major fluctuations in economic activity from 1860 to 1920 fit the view of economic cycles expressed in Chapter 10. Entrepreneurs, guided by present prices and expectations of future business conditions, buy new buildings and equipment and add to their inventories. But this *real investment* eventually reaches a temporary saturation point when the goods and services that fully employed resources produce cannot be taken from the market at prices that enable entrepreneurs to cover their costs. Real investment then falls, followed by a fall in incomes and retrenchment of expenditures by consumers, especially on consumer durables. If government takes no corrective steps, the economy may drag along for years with less than full employment output, revival coming at last as capital goods wear out, population grows, and innovation stimulates new demands.

Many economists have long supported a theory of "long waves" in economic activity. The Russian economist Kondratieff thought the existence of long cycles of approximately fifty years' duration "very probable." While denying any strict periodicity of such cycles, he suggested that there were long-run cumulative movements. During upswings business fluctuations would be characterized by short depressions, and during downswings depressions would be longer and more intense. No less a figure than Schumpeter gave a prominent place to the Kondratieff cycle in his analysis of fluctuations.

It is tempting to accept a theory of long waves as an explanation of a long period of "hard times" that prevailed from 1873 to 1896 and an equally long period of "good times" from 1896 to 1920. Yet the trend of output and per-capita real income was intermittently upward during both periods, a fact that seems to deny the assertion of a long cycle of economic activity. Is it possible that the testimony of laborers, businessmen, and farmers regarding the difficulties of the 1873–96 period during which they lived is not to be believed? Or that the buoyancy of the 1896–1920 period was indeed illusory?

The paradox can be resolved if we focus our attention on prices. In Chapter 10 it was observed that long upswings and downswings of *prices* appeared to affect the intensity of booms and depressions. In Chapter 11 we remarked a secular downward trend of prices from the end of the Civil War to 1896 followed by a secular upward trend of prices to 1920. Two depressions occurring during the long period of falling prices were of unusual severity and duration, whereas there was only one severe depression while prices were rising and it was of brief duration. The "waves" were therefore of prices, not of production. With generally falling prices we should expect to find slumps longer and deeper than in a period of rising prices.

But we have yet to ascertain the fundamental causes of the long price swings. In view of the heated monetary controversies of the late nineteenth century we might suspect that money was the root of the price difficulties. The chart on p. 414 shows relative changes in wholesale prices, nonagricultural production, and the money supply from 1860 to 1920. The first thing that strikes us is that the upward drifts of both the money supply and industrial production tend to be parallel, indicating about the same over-all rate of increase for the sixty years. We may therefore be inclined to rule money out entirely as a causal factor, for while the quantity of money grew with output throughout the *entire* period, prices fell for thirty years and then rose for twenty-five years. But closer inspection reveals that the money supply had either decreased or grown at an arrested rate before each of the major downturns in industrial production. Recoveries were accompanied by rapid and steady increases in the quantity of money. After 1896 the money stock increased at a faster rate than in the preceding thirty years, and between 1896 and 1914 its growth was interrupted only once.

Two monetary episodes previously described are relevant to this discussion. The monetary contraction of the 1870s was doubtless aggravated by the resumption of specie payments. In 1873 gold was at a 10 per cent premium in terms of greenbacks. By the end of 1878 gold had fallen to par, rough evidence that the United States had been forced to deflate 10 per cent more than the rest of the world to resume gold payments.[5] Doubtless the long and noisy debate over the silver question intensified the depression of the 1890s by creating some business uncertainty and by causing foreigners to withdraw funds (and thus bank reserves) at a most inopportune time. These incidents helped to make depressions longer and deeper, as did the banking crises that were inevitable concomitants of pre-1920 panics. How much they contributed to the 1873–96 downtrend in prices is uncertain.

In sum, it appears that changes in the rate of increase of the money supply and recurring monetary disturbances influenced the long price swings. We must not, however, forget that bank reserves were sufficient to

---

[5] See Rendigs Fels, "The Long-wave Depression, 1873–97," *Review of Economics and Statistics,* XXXI (1949), 69.

Total Money in Billions of Dollars   Index Numbers

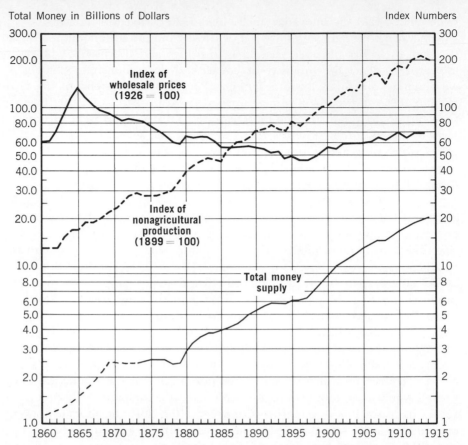

Reprinted by permission of the publisher from Edwin Frickey, *Production in the United States, 1860–1914,* Cambridge: Harvard University Press, copyright 1947, by the President and Fellows of Harvard College. Adapted by Albert G. Hart, *Money, Debt, and Economic Activity,* 1st ed. (Englewood Cliffs, N.J.: Prentice-Hall, 1948). *Historical Statistics of the United States, 1789–1945.*

Prices, Production, and Money: The wholesale price index declined after the Civil War while nonagricultural output increased dramatically and the money supply moved upward at a somewhat slower but still surprisingly vigorous rate.

permit a growth in bank deposits that kept pace with output over the 1860–1920 period as a whole. An adequate interpretation of the secular price trends must give weight to other influences.

An explanation that has received wide acceptance holds that a slowing down in the rate of growth of railroad construction was a powerful depressor in the last quarter of the nineteenth century. Surely the railroad offered a vast outlet for real investment and stimulated investment in related industries. It is true that expansion of the railroads was at a diminishing rate after 1870, but the decline was slight up to 1895. Annual construction of new mileage reached a peak in the mid-eighties and fell abruptly until 1897.

But it would be a mistake to conclude from construction figures that railroad investment was no longer a potent force in the economy.[6] Until 1918 there was an almost uninterrupted increase in railroad traffic with consequent heavy investment in equipment, especially in rolling stock. Total new and replacement investment of United States railroads rose tremendously after 1897 to a peak in 1910. Unquestionably, this expenditure, along with investment in the new street railway, electrical, chemical, and automobile industries contributed to the buoyancy that characterized the early years of the century.

We must, it seems, look for another influence on prices. We have already observed that agricultural output in the United States increased faster than industrial output for several decades after the Civil War, a period in which agriculture was far more important as a source of income than it is today. The expansion of the American West continued, and new lands in temperate zones were opened all over the world. The development of railroad and ocean transportation made possible an outpouring of agricultural products at steadily decreasing prices. It would have been astonishing if the index of wholesale commodity prices had not drifted downward under such circumstances. Not until the end of the nineteenth century, when industry began to play a clearly dominant role in the Western world, providing new employment opportunities and so generating income, could there be a rising secular upswing in prices.

To sum up, evidence available to date does not support a conclusion of "long waves" of economic activity, but there can be no question about the existence of two long price swings within the period we are studying. Even without these swings there would have doubtless been output fluctuations; but the downswing of prices from 1869 to 1896 made depressions within those years worse than they would otherwise have been, and the upswing of prices from 1897 to 1920 mitigated the effects of depressions. It has been customary to attribute the great price swings solely to monetary causes. Although monetary episodes influenced the course of economic activity, the money supply increased rapidly *throughout* the 1870–1920 period. We cannot, therefore, explain the long deflation followed by inflation in terms of monetary phenomena alone. Retardation in the total rate of railroad investment was likewise an influence but not a determining one. The great drag on prices for a quarter of a century was the massive increase in the supply of farm products relative to the demand for them. The equally great stimulant to prices for another quarter of a century was the achievement by the Western world of a rate of increase of industrial production far greater than that of agricultural production.

---

[6] Railroads accounted for 20 per cent of gross capital formation (new plus replacement investment) in the 1870s, 16 per cent in the 1880s, and about 7.5 per cent in each of the next three decades. Melville J. Ulmer, *Trends and Cycles in Capital Formation by United States Railroads, 1870–1950*, Occasional Paper 43 (New York: National Bureau of Economic Research, 1954), p. 11.

The Impetus to Economic Growth

American society was clearly an "achieving society," to use Professor McClelland's expression, and the drive for success was particularly strong among American entrepreneurs. Their efforts were reinforced by three sources of increasing productivity that assured a churning, throbbing economy, at least into the 1920s.

1. *In the North and West before 1860, and in the South after 1875, Americans were persuaded that investment in human capital—in education —paid big dividends.* By 1900 an eighth-grade education was considered essential to success, and high school was rapidly coming within the reach of everyone. By 1920 a high-school education was considered the birthright of the majority of young Americans, and college was no longer just a distant dream. With something like a one-generation lag, the investment in knowledge played a large part in the growth of the economy.

2. *The increasing size of the American market, which kept right on expanding up to 1920, led to economies of scale in manufacturing that played a significant role in productivity changes.* By 1910 the advantages of a great common market were plain to see, and regional specialization largely offset the harm done by high protective tariffs and the consequent disruption to international trade.

3. *Not much more important in long-run effect, but far more exciting in its short-run manifestations, was technological change.* Sometime around 1900 the relationship between the business world and invention took a radically different turn. Up to this time strategic inventions, which we have defined as the commercially successful ones, led to the establishment of business firms. As these firms manufactured the product made possible by invention, their engineering and technical staffs of course made improvements and refinements in the basic product. But not until the electrical industry emerged in the 1890s did it become necessary for business firms to make a formal, organized, systematic attempt to develop new products simply in order to keep ahead of other firms.

The electrical industry had had three main lines of development. The great pioneers in the arc-lighting industry—Edward Weston, Charles Brush, and Elihu Thomson—proved that lighting by electricity could be commercially successful. George Westinghouse, head of the firm bearing his name, pioneered with alternating current systems, ultimately to win acceptance over the direct-current systems advocated by Thomas Edison. Edison and his firm, Edison General Electric, had been the pioneer innovator in incandescent lighting and had developed a good business in generating equipment for both isolated and central plants.

Largely in order to obtain the much needed patents of the other company, the firms of Thomson-Houston and Edison General Electric consolidated in 1892 to form a new company, General Electric. By 1894 the two dominant firms in the industry, Westinghouse and General Electric, possessed hundreds of patents; some were obtained directly from company engineers, some by purchase from outside inventors, and some by merger with other firms. As the two leading firms expanded their lines to include nearly all types of electrical apparatus, they came more and more into conflict with each other, and by 1896 over three hundred patent suits were pending between General Electric and Westinghouse. The upshot of their legal involvements was a cross-licensing agreement that in effect enabled the two companies to use all existing patentable ideas except those owned by the small independents in the business. Within a few years many of these small firms had sold out to one or the other of the two giants.

Thus in the 1890s both major firms developed engineering staffs that systematized the search for new ideas. By 1900, as Harold Passer has remarked, "competition in reality was between the engineering staffs of two companies." We should not be surprised to learn, then, that in 1900 General Electric asked an M.I.T. professor, Dr. Willis R. Whitney, to establish a Schenectady laboratory devoted to scientific research in applied physics. Needless to say, Westinghouse shortly established a competing laboratory in Pittsburgh.

Research and development thus began as a form of business strategy in an industry that to this day remains a bellwether in this kind of competitive effort. For twenty years or so after 1900 the research and development departments of General Electric and Westinghouse concentrated largely on improving processes and equipment in the power business and to a lesser extent in the lamp business. But as electric-generating machinery became more and more complex, both major companies assured themselves of a continuing flow of a multitude of parts by purchasing or establishing subsidiary companies to make parts and components. Because the end products of the companies did not require the entire output of switches, fuses, condensers, etc., company sales departments began to market these smaller items. Moreover, research aimed at producing better components often opened new vistas. Professor Alfred D. Chandler, Jr., tells us, for example, that dissatisfaction with its insulating materials brought General Electric into the plastics business, when in 1912 its research laboratories began experimenting with resins.

But it was not until after World War I that General Electric and Westinghouse began the diversification of products that was ultimately to effect the very organizational structures of the two firms. Two fundamental decisions led to the ultimate multiplicity of products. (1) It was decided to develop and manufacture consumer appliances in order to increase the demand for electricity and thus for the heavy power machinery that was after all the original output of the two firms. (2) As the research laboratories came up with new alloys, new chemicals, and new electronic devices it was made an explicit business policy to expand the sale of these items whenever there was a prospect of long-term profitability. So General Electric formed one subsidiary to make and sell X-ray equipment and another (Carboloy, Inc.)

to sell the new metals that General Electric scientists first developed for use in generating and transmission equipment. Westinghouse, too, began the manufacture of X-ray equipment and went also into the elevator business. Not until the early 1930s, however, were both companies irrevocably committed to the proposition that competition would forever take the form of systematically discovering, perfecting, and then marketing new products and new processes.

Social Justice and the Role of Government

Whatever the causes of the great downswing in prices after the Civil War, the deflation meant continual trouble for the agricultural South and West. During the major depressions, hardship also overtook the industrial East, where labor and small businessmen bore the brunt of falling economic activity.

The depression of 1893–96 was the culmination of more than two decades of unsatisfactory performance of the American economy. The physical suffering and spiritual degradation that accompanied it were unprecedented and have only since been equaled by the Great Depression of the 1930s. During the terrible winter of 1893–94, the problem of relief reached enormous proportions in cities large and small. Some communities limited their relief projects to soup kitchens and bread lines. New York, with the biggest problem, had the co-operation of charitable societies, the bread and clothing funds sponsored by newspapers, and the low-cost food centers of philanthropists, but the city had nevertheless to provide millions of dollars of direct relief. There was a strong opinion in many cities that out-and-out relief contributed to a certain flabbiness of character in poor people, who would surely become used to getting something for nothing. Therefore, the municipality would require a day's labor in the public parks or on the streets in exchange for a weekly or daily family ration of food. Many argued for public-works projects on a state-wide scale, but such proposals were not well received. Governor Flower of New York, for example, rejected requests for a state public-works program in 1893 on the grounds that it was not the duty of government to support people and that public works for relief would lead to further paternal legislation and prodigal extravagance.[7]

Direct intervention of the federal government was proposed early in the emergency when the convention of the American Federation of Labor called for the issue of $500 million in paper money for the purpose of constructing public works. The idea was picked up by Jacob Coxey; indeed, the objective of Coxey's Army and its march on Washington in the spring of 1894 was to petition Congress for a $500 million paper issue to be spent for good

---

[7] For an absorbing discussion of the problem of relief see Samuel Rezneck, "Unemployment, Unrest, and Relief in the United States during the Depression of 1893–97," *Journal of Political Economy*, XLI (August 1953), 324–45.

roads.[8] But such governmental interference with the private economy was unconscionable in the view of most propertied people, who were supported by the testimony of a large number of respected professors of economics and sociology.

People were more interested in discussing causes and cures of the depression than in debating the merits of various relief plans. Most vociferous were the advocates of monetary reform, the controversy between the "silver lunatics" and the "gold-bugs" reaching the heights of vituperation. Proponents of protection argued that the depression of 1893 had been brought on by businessmen's fear of tariff reductions aroused by the Democratic victory of 1892, and advocates of low tariffs rejoined that this subsidy of the trusts was the very source of oppression of the poor. Labor leaders attributed the workers' plight to the greed and selfishness of employers and in particular took the managerial class to task for promoting unrestricted immigration. On this question, surprisingly, labor had the backing of the dean of American economists, Francis A. Walker, who thundered that the American standard of living and the quality of American citizenship were being degraded by "vast throngs of ignorant and brutalized peasantry from the countries of eastern and southern Europe." A few obscure writers, not accepted members of the intellectual community, thought that deflation and depression might have been the result of government fiscal policy since the Civil War. Surpluses had been the rule, the federal debt having been reduced nearly $2 billion between 1866 and 1893. But anyone who suggested deficit financing as a possible cure for depression was considered not quite bright, if not downright dangerous, for economic orthodoxy held that nothing was so damaging to business confidence as running a deficit.

No concrete proposal for mitigating slumps was enacted into law. As the decade of the 1890s dragged on toward revival and ultimate recovery, Americans seemed resigned to recurrent breakdowns of the economic machine with all the suffering they entailed. But a step was taken in the nineties, almost, it seemed, by accident, that adumbrated the inclusion in the tax system of an automatic stabilizer and a more equitable division of the tax burden in good times and bad.

THE ADOPTION OF AN INCOME TAX

In the campaign of 1892 Cleveland and the Democrats had promised tariff reform, but as debate on a new tariff bill progressed, it appeared that a coalition of Republicans and conservative Democrats would succeed in preventing a downward revision of duties. With practically no reduction in the previously existing high rates in prospect, the treasury was confronted with a continuation of the deficit that had begun late in 1892. An income-tax provision was therefore inserted in the proposed tariff bill on the grounds that revenue from another source was necessary to compensate for the loss

---

[8] Rezneck, pp. 327 and 333.

of revenue from customs duties. Conservative members of Congress bitterly fought the income-tax provision, charging that the tax was unjust, inquisitorial, and ill-timed. William Jennings Bryan in the House and William V. Allen in the Senate defended the income-tax rider with fire and eloquence. Senator Allen pointed out that according to census statistics, 91 per cent of the country's 12,000,000 families owned 29 per cent of the national wealth and that 9 per cent of the families owned 71 per cent. Other Senators of the West and South urged, as they had been doing for twenty years, that a tax on income was fair because it levied on individuals in proportion to their ability to pay and, with a part of income exempted, did not impinge on necessities. The most convincing argument of all was that the distress and unrest among low-income groups made it necessary for the rich to assume a larger proportion of the expenses of government if socialism were to be avoided.

The Wilson-Gorman Tariff Act of 1894, besides slightly reducing customs duties, provided for an income tax of 2 per cent on personal incomes above $4,000 and for a tax of 2 per cent on all corporate net income. The country was not without experience with this form of taxation, for an income tax had been in effect from 1862 to 1872 as a Civil War finance measure. Nevertheless, the Congressional action precipitated a storm of controversy exceeded in violence only by the debate over the silver question. The battle did not last any longer than it took to get a test case to the Supreme Court. Despite a previous decision that a tax on income was an excise tax and hence not a direct tax, the Court in 1895 held that the income tax was a direct tax and therefore required by the Constitution to be apportioned among the states according to population. Since the Wilson-Gorman Act had not provided for apportionment among the states, the income-tax legislation was declared unconstitutional.

This ruling of unconstitutionality did not permanently deter the advocates of an income tax. Within a decade a majority of the electorate clearly wanted a more equitable basis of taxation. In his 1908 message to Congress Theodore Roosevelt recommended both an income and an inheritance tax, and Taft came out for a personal income tax in the campaign of 1908. Early in the Taft administration a tax of 1 per cent was levied on corporate incomes of more than $5,000, and in 1909 Congress sent to the states for ratification a constitutional amendment providing for a tax on personal incomes.

With ratification of the Sixteenth Amendment early in 1913 the way was open to an income-tax law that would not be undone by the courts. Section II of the Underwood-Simmons Tariff Act of 1913 imposed a "normal" tax of 1 per cent on the taxable income of every United States citizen, giving an exemption of $3,000 to each taxpayer plus an additional $1,000 to a married person living with spouse.[9] In addition to the normal tax an additional tax

9 No exemption was allowed for minor children. Interest on government bonds was exempted, as was interest on state and local bonds and salaries of state and local officials.

Form 1040.

INCOME TAX.

THE PENALTY
FOR FAILURE TO HAVE THIS RETURN IN
THE HANDS OF THE COLLECTOR OF
INTERNAL REVENUE ON OR BEFORE
MARCH 1 IS $20 TO $1,000.
(SEE INSTRUCTIONS ON PAGE 4.)

UNITED STATES INTERNAL REVENUE.

RETURN OF ANNUAL NET INCOME OF INDIVIDUALS.
(As provided by Act of Congress, approved October 3, 1913.)

RETURN OF NET INCOME RECEIVED OR ACCRUED DURING THE YEAR ENDED DECEMBER 31, 191....
(FOR THE YEAR 1913, FROM MARCH 1, TO DECEMBER 31.)

Filed by (or for) .... of ....
(Full name of Individual.)   (Street and No.)

in the City, Town, or Post Office of .... State of ....
(Fill in pages 2 and 3 before making entries below.)

1. Gross Income (see page 2, line 12)	$			
2. General Deductions (see page 3, line 7)	$			
3. Net Income	$			

Deductions and exemptions allowed in computing income subject to the normal tax of 1 per cent.

4. Dividends and net earnings received or accrued, of corporations, etc., subject to like tax. (See page 2, line 11)..........	$			
5. Amount of income on which the normal tax has been deducted and withheld at the source. (See page 2, line 9, column A)..				
6. Specific exemption of $3,000 or $4,000, as the case may be. (See Instructions 3 and 19)				
Total deductions and exemptions. (Items 4, 5, and 6)........	$			
7. Taxable Income on which the normal tax of 1 per cent is to be calculated. (See Instruction 3).	$			

8. When the net income shown above on line 3 exceeds $20,000, the additional tax thereon must be calculated as per schedule below:

	INCOME.		TAX.		
1 per cent on amount over $20,000 and not exceeding $50,000....	$		$		
2 " " 50,000 " " 75,000....					
3 " " 75,000 " " 100,000....					
4 " " 100,000 " " 250,000....					
5 " " 250,000 " " 500,000....					
6 " " 500,000					
Total additional or super tax	$				
Total normal tax (1 per cent of amount entered on line 7).....	$				
Total tax liability...........................	$				

An unwelcome innovation to many Americans of upper-income status was the income tax. This 1914 form barely hinted at the complexity of the contemporary Form 1040, still decades in the future.

or surtax was levied progressively on income over $20,000. The maximum rate of 7 per cent (1 per cent normal plus 6 per cent surtax) applied to incomes of $500,000 or over. Adoption of the principle of progressive rather than proportional rates was hailed by reformers as a major step toward social justice, but propertied people and the conservative press spoke darkly of a first step toward complete confiscation of private property.

ANTITRUST ENFORCEMENT AND THE COURTS

The Sherman Act of 1890 was passed, it will be recalled, without fanfare or acclaim, largely because times had recently improved. But the problem of monopoly had been a source of great political turmoil, and it was to be again. As the depression of 1893 deepened, monopolies in general and the trusts in particular were blamed. Nor did the trusts escape public wrath with the onset of prosperity, for the business upturn coincided with the beginning of a second combination movement. Journalists kept their readers informed of the nefarious doings of large business firms and warned of the perils of concentration.

For nearly a decade after its passage, the Sherman Act was as ineffective as the Interstate Commerce Act of 1887 had been. The act seemed simple enough. It declared illegal "every contract, combination in the form of trust, or otherwise, or conspiracy in restraint of trade among the several states." It prescribed punishment of a fine or imprisonment or both for "every person who shall monopolize, or attempt to monopolize, or combine or conspire . . . to monopolize any part of the trade or commerce among the several states." The Attorney-General was charged with enforcing the act by bringing either civil or criminal proceedings in the federal courts. How the law should be interpreted was thus left to federal judges.

The Supreme Court did much to discourage enforcement by its decision, rendered in 1895, in the case of *United States* v. *E. C. Knight Company*. The Attorney-General had brought an action against a firm that admittedly controlled 75 per cent of the sugar-refining capacity of the country; but the Court would not apply the Sherman Act on the ground that the company was engaged in manufacture and not in interstate commerce, and that Congress intended the prohibitions to apply only to interstate commerce. The business of sugar refining, the Court held, ". . . bore no direct relation to commerce between the states or with foreign nations. . . . Commerce succeeds to manufacture, and is not a part of it." The Court further implied that the Sherman Act did not preclude the growth of large firms by purchase of property—i.e., by merger or consolidation.

In the case of *United States* v. *Addyston Pipe and Steel Company* (1899), the Court made it clear that the Sherman Act did apply to collusive agreements among firms supposed to be in competition with each other. And in 1904, in the Northern Securities Company case, the Court decided that the provisions of the act applied also to holding companies. As noted in Chapter 16, the decision in this case came as a shock to corporation lawyers who thought that the holding company form of organization was immune to antitrust prosecution.[10]

As early as 1902 Theodore Roosevelt sensed the political value of trust-busting, and in the campaign of 1904 he promised vigorous prosecution of monopolies. During his administration, bills were filed against several great companies, the most important being against the American Tobacco Company and the Standard Oil Company of New Jersey. These firms were the archetype of monopoly in the public mind, and the judgment of the Supreme Court in the cases against them would indicate the degree of enforcement that might be expected under the Sherman Act.

In decisions handed down in 1911 the Supreme Court ordered the dissolution of both the Standard Oil Company and the American Tobacco Company. The Court in both cases found that unlawful monopoly power existed and gave great weight to evidence of intent to monopolize. As an aid to discovering intent and purpose, the Court examined the predatory practices that had occurred during each company's growth and the manner in which the companies exercised their monopoly power. The oil trust, so it was asserted, had achieved its powerful position in the market by unfairly obtaining rebates from the railroads and by acquiring refining companies brought to terms after price wars. Similarly, the tobacco trust had brought competing companies to heel by price wars, frequently closing them after acquisition by purchase. Moreover, the record showed that the old American Tobacco Company exerted a strong monopsonistic power, beating down the prices of tobacco to the farmers when it was sold at auction. The Court for the first time adopted a "rule of reason" with respect to restraints of trade, and since action against all possible violators was obviously impossible, it became necessary for the Court to exercise judgment.

> Under this principle, combinations which restricted competition were held to be lawful as long as the restraint was not unreasonable. Since there is no precise economic standard by which the reasonableness of a restriction on competition can be measured, the courts examined the practices pursued by a corporate giant in achieving and maintaining its position in the market. Predatory practices were indicative of an intent to monopolize the market, and a corporate combination which achieved dominance by indulging in them might be dissolved. Those which behaved in a more exemplary manner, even though their size gave them power over the market, did not transgress the law.[11]

Standard Oil and American Tobacco were the only companies dissolved,

---

[10] Antitrust prosecution is full of ironies that suggest the tangled web that is woven when government intervenes on behalf of any group in society. In Northern Securities the Supreme Court blocked the efforts of James J. Hill to create a great regional railroad system in the northwestern quadrant of the United States. More than half a century later many transportation experts are urging such systems as the railroads' only hope of salvation.

[11] George W. Stocking, "The Rule of Reason, Workable Competition, and the Legality of Trade Association Activities," *University of Chicago Law Review*, XXI, 4 (Summer 1954), 532–33.

but even if the courts had continued ordering dissolution or divestiture it is unlikely that competition in the classical sense would have been restored. The four major successor companies to the American Tobacco Company constituted a tight oligopoly with respect to cigarette manufacture. Stock in the thirty-three successor companies of the Standard Oil Company was ordered distributed pro rata to the stockholders of the holding company, and it soon became apparent that the successor companies were not going to compete vigorously with one another. Whatever the benefits of dissolution, an increase in price competition was certainly not one of them.[12]

In two decisions handed down at the close of World War I, large companies formed by merger were effectively freed from the threat of dissolution, provided that the actions of the dominant firm were not calculated to exclude competitors from the market. In the case of *United States* v. *United Shoe Machinery Company of New Jersey, et al.,* Justice McKenna took as the basis of his decision the finding of the trial court that the constituent companies had not been *competitors,* but instead performed supplementary rather than identical functions in making shoes. The Court did not deny the monopoly power of United Shoe Machinery Company; it simply held that the company's power was not illegal because the constituent companies had never been competitive. The decision in *United States* v. *United States Steel Corporation* made the position of merged companies even safer. Justice McKenna, who again spoke for the Court, found that the corporation possessed neither the power nor the intent to exert monopoly control. The majority of the Court was impressed by the fact that examination of the history of United States Steel revealed none of the predatory practices complained of in the oil and tobacco cases. The Court took cognizance of the splendid relations of the steel company with its rivals, noting that United States Steel's power ". . . was efficient only when in co-operation with its competitors, and hence it concerted with them in the expedients of pools, associations, trade meetings, and finally in a system of dinners inaugurated in 1907 by the president of the company, E. H. Gary, and called 'The Gary Dinners.' "[13] But the corporation ". . . resorted to none of the brutalities or tyrannies that the cases illustrate of other combinations. . . . It did not have power in and of itself, and the control it exerted was only in and by association with its competitors. Its offense, therefore, such as it was, was not different from theirs and was distinguished from theirs only in the leadership it assumed in promulgating and perfecting the policy. This leadership it gave up and it had ceased to offend the law before this suit was brought."[14]

---

[12] There are ironies in the tobacco case, too. Before 1911 cigarettes were not nearly so important as they were to become after World War I changed men's smoking habits. Competitive advertising of the four successor companies unquestionably accounts for the rapid increase in women's smoking during the 1920s; institutional advertising of the staid old tobacco monopoly would almost certainly not have pushed the demand curve for cigarettes so sharply to the right.

[13] 40 Sup. Ct. 251 U.S. 417, 295.   [14] 40 Sup. Ct. 251 U.S. 417, 295–96.

Justice McKenna held that United States Steel had not achieved monopoly power despite its control of 50 per cent of the industry's output. He decided that the pattern of regular price changes over time, clearly shown by the evidence, could as well have emerged from a competitive market as from collusion. The government's assertion that the size of the corporation made it a potential threat to competition in the industry was denied. On the contrary, said the Court, ". . . the law does not make mere size an offense, or the existence of unexerted power an offense." After a decision like this one only the most optimistic Justice Department attorneys could see any point in bringing action against a firm simply because it was big.

In 1914, during Wilson's first administration, Congress passed the Clayton Act, which was intended to remove ambiguities in existing antitrust law by making certain specific practices illegal. Price discrimination among buyers was forbidden, along with exclusive selling and tying contracts, if their effect was to lessen competition. Firms could not acquire the stock of a competitor, and interlocking directorates among competing firms were forbidden, again if the effect was to lessen competition. A newly established Federal Trade Commission of five appointive members was to enforce the act, decisions of the FTC to be appealed to the circuit courts. The Commission could also carry out investigations, acting on its own initiative or upon the complaint of an injured party. If a law violation were found, the Commission could issue a "cease and desist" order, and offenders then had a right of appeal to the federal courts.

The Clayton Act was so weakly drawn as to add little to the government's power to enforce competition. Once the existence of listed illegal practices was determined, the courts still had to decide whether their effect was to lessen competition or promote monopoly. As we have just observed, by 1920 about the only practice the courts would consistently consider in restraint of trade was explicit collusion among independent producers or sellers. "Reasonable" monopoly practices of huge firms, on the one hand, and "weak" forms of collusion on the other were not subject to punishment. The useful functions of the Federal Trade Commission became the compiling of a mass of data helpful to economists and the elevation of the ethics of competition by acting against misbranding and misleading advertising. Not until it could take action on the basis of injury to *consumers* instead of on the basis of injury to a *competitor* would the public gain much advantage from its efforts.

Thus, the one great pre-1920 experiment in the social control of business achieved little. By the time a vigorous enforcement of the antitrust laws was undertaken, late in the 1930s, it was too late to do much about the problem of bigness in industry. But by then it was clear that a kind of competition not envisaged by the framers of the Sherman Act protected consumers. The effectiveness of this new competition we shall examine in Chapter 22.

Part Four:

1921 to the Present

World War I ended, the promising young song writer, Harry Donaldson, cast his lot with the just organized Irving Berlin Music Company to begin a long and mutually profitable association. His smash 1919 hit was at once question and prophetic answer: "How ya gonna keep 'em down on the farm after they've seen Paree?" How indeed? Millions of young Americans had been wrested from the placid boredom of country life to mark the beginning of the end of an agrarian society. To be sure, only a fraction of them ever saw Paris, and some got no farther than Camp Funston. But flat-headed country boy, small-town bookkeeper, and city mill worker alike had a taste of travel that broke deadly routine and at small cost. Less than a hundred thousand of them died in battle and not many more than that of influenza.

The high pitch of wartime excitement had passed, of course, and there were signs that the old provincialism could return. Isolationist sentiment had prevailed in the Congressional elections of 1918; and the press made it plain to all who could read that the intellectual in the White House would fight in vain for a genuine peace among men, even if France and Britain could be dissuaded from their vengeful course. In a dreadful intrusion on the rights of the individual, a moralistic minority secured passage of the Eighteenth Amendment, which took away a basic comfort of field hand and factory worker on the grounds that drinking was sinful and that poor people were not entitled to such luxuries anyway. A swell of religious fundamentalism was rising that would crest in the right-wing hate activities of the Ku Klux Klan, and by 1924 that wicked organization's anti-Negro, anti-Jew, and anti-Roman Catholic persecutions had become a national scandal.

The future nevertheless held a bright promise of prosperity and more fun for everybody. Women had at last gained an unequivocal right to vote, but their emancipation was broader than that. Young women in particular began to

426

chisel away the double standard of morality typical of pre-1914 relations between the sexes; the flapper of the 1920s with her boyish bob and figure was in 1919 already emerging as the girl who could smoke men's cigarettes, drink men's whiskey, play men's games, even work at men's jobs. There were many reasons why women gained their freedom, but the biggest one was that men thought they were more enjoyable that way.

The United States had entered World War I not so much because of provocation as because Americans spoke English and preserved an essentially English heritage. After all, the British blockade of Europe was actually more offensive and humiliating than the sinking of English and French vessels carrying American passengers and goods, and phony British propaganda about German atrocities should have been transparent even to prime specimens of H. L. Mencken's *homo boobiens*. What actually brought American entry into the war was the sudden agonized realization that German might would prevail in the absence of help from the United States.

Entry on the side of the Allies clearly swung the tide of battle and assured victory to the exhausted French and British. As in the Civil War, World War I witnessed little that was remarkable in the way of technological innovation except in a few industries producing strategic products like chemicals and machine tools. Indeed, the output response of manufacturing industry was on the whole nothing to be proud of. Unlike the Great War to follow a generation later, World War I did not induce radical changes in systems and processes that would overpoweringly affect American economic life.

Composer Donaldson's popular song implied that the upheaval of World War I was moral and social rather than technological and economic. With the peculiar insight vouchsafed only to artists, he foresaw the era of speakeasies and bathtub gin, of The Untouchables and the Capone mob, of Harding's Ohio gang and Coolidge's servants of big business. It would be impossible to keep the boys down on the farm, yet in the next two decades there would not really be a place for them in the city. For all their bright hopes, those who were young in 1919 would be the "lost generation" of Fitzgerald and Hemingway. The Great Depression would blight the most productive part of their lives, and the United States would not really enter the twentieth century until after World War II forced Americans to accept their international responsibilities.

Agriculture in an
Industrial Economy

The problem of agriculture is not unique. It is the leading case in a large class of problems. . . . The common characteristic shared by these problems is that, as a result of changes in the economy, the labor and capital employed in the industry cannot all continue to earn, by producing goods for sale in a free market, as much income as they formerly earned, or as much as they could earn if employed in some other use; that is—*the industry is using too many resources.*

COMMITTEE FOR ECONOMIC DEVELOPMENT

In Chapter 11 we laid the groundwork for an analysis of the modern farm problem. Now we examine the manifestations of the problem as they appeared in the 1920s and 1930s, considering then the series of legislative attempts to relieve the farmers' plight. It will next be our unpleasant task to reassess the causes of economic dislocation in agriculture and show why American farm policy has failed to secure anything like a satisfactory allocation of the resources devoted to agriculture. Finally, we consider briefly a new approach to the conservation of America's natural resources.

The Economic Position of the American Farmer

For a quarter of a century before 1920, American agriculture was moving to a stronger position in the economy. During the last six years of this quarter-century, World War I abnormally stimulated farm production and gave a tremendous boost to farm prices and incomes. Nevertheless, the World

War I improvement in the lot of the farmer was a continuation, somewhat amplified, of a trend in progress for twenty years before the war.

During 1919 and the early months of 1920 hopes for the future were rosy. Then came the blow. In mid-1920, farm prices began a precipitous drop. From an index of 234 in June of 1920 (1909–14 = 100), prices received by farmers fell to an index of 112 a year later. By the end of 1921, despite a little recovery, wheat was selling for 93 cents a bushel that eighteen months previously had sold for $2.58, and corn was down to 41 cents from $1.86. Many commodities did not suffer quite so severe a decline, but the falling off of prices was serious in all lines of production. There followed a gradual recovery, the farm price index in August 1925 standing at 159. After a small decline during 1926 and 1927, prices remained stable until the end of 1929.

The deflation of 1920 and 1921 was severe in the industrial sector of the economy but not so great as in agriculture. Prices *paid* by farmers fell to the end of 1921 and then remained stable to the close of the decade. The terms of exchange (the ratio of prices received by farmers to the prices paid by them) ran against agriculture during the break in prices and then recovered so that by 1925 they were not much below the figure of 1920. This index fell off a little during the next few years, but in 1929 it was still not far from the level of prosperous prewar years. On the whole, then, it does not seem that agriculture should have suffered much in the middle and late years of the twenties. Yet, as we shall see later, there was great agitation for remedial farm legislation during these years. Why?

The answer seems to lie in the fact that a large part of the farmers, especially in the Middle West, had incurred fixed indebtedness at what turned out to be the wrong time. During the decade 1910–20 land values had risen sharply; at the height of the boom the best lands in Iowa and Illinois sold for as much as $500 an acre. In these ten years many a high-grade farm doubled in value. To buy their high-priced properties farmers often borrowed heavily, and farm-mortgage debt increased rapidly. Long-term debt rose from $3,200 million in 1910 to $8,400 million in 1920, and as a result of distress accompanying the deflation of the early twenties reached a high of nearly $11 billion in 1923. Although a majority of American farmers may not have been burdened with fixed charges during these years, such charges undoubtedly created difficulties for a large and extremely vocal minority.[1]

The troubles of the decade after World War I were mild compared with the debacle of the next decade. With the onset of the Great Depression

---

[1] By fixed charges I mean here the payments of principal and interest that had to be met currently and at regular intervals. Farms, like business enterprises generally, have fixed costs that cannot be avoided, but these costs are certainly more burdensome when, because of thin equities, they must be met out of current income. It should be added that the balance sheets of all farms tended to change unfavorably during the 1920s, no matter what their debt positions may have been, for assets generally declined in value during the period. Thus, the equities of most farmers shrank.

farm people began to suffer economic distress that none but the old-timers would have thought possible. Consider first what happened to farm prices. The break came in the first months of 1930 and continued until a low point was reached in February of 1933. From a farm-price index of 147 in January of 1930, there was a drop to 57 in February of 1933 (1909–14 = 100). Department of Agriculture statistics show that in three years the average price of corn at central markets fell from $.77 to $.19 a bushel and the average price of wheat from $1.08 to $.33 a bushel. Ten-cent corn and twenty-five-cent wheat were common at local elevators, and five-cent cotton was the burden of the Southerner.

In terms of farm income and disparity between agricultural and non-agricultural prices the picture was just as bad. Gross farm income, which had reached a postwar high of almost $14 billion in 1929, slipped to $11 billion in 1930 and fell drastically to about $6.5 billion in 1932 (see chart below). Production expenses also fell during this time but not nearly so much as the gross-income figure, so that in 1932 the *net* realized income from agriculture was just over $1.8 billion, *less than one-third of the 1929 figure and one-half that of the bad year of 1921.* The agricultural terms

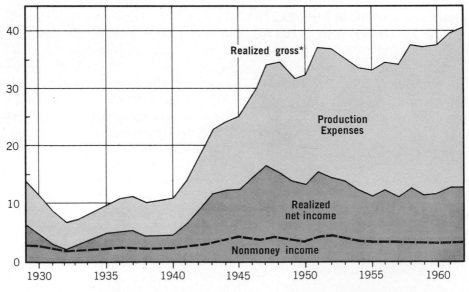

* Including government payments, beginning 1933

United States Department of Agriculture.

Farm Income: The growing gap between realized gross income in farming and the amount of cash left after heavy production expenses have been met reveals at a glance the source of much of the malaise in the American countryside, the sense of failing prospects among the marginal farmers.

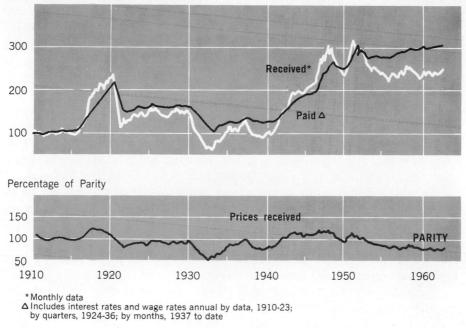

United States Department of Agriculture.

Outgo and Income: Since the early 1950s prices received by farmers have not kept up with prices paid by farmers (upper chart) so that prices received have declined as a percentage of parity (lower chart).

of exchange were adverse to an almost unbelievable extent, having dropped by 1932 to a low of 54 per cent of the level of 1920. Farmers with fixed indebtedness were unable to meet their obligations, and foreclosures were rife.[2]

Farm prices began a rise in April of 1933, climbing to 131 early in 1937 (see chart above). The recession of 1937–38 affected the agricultural sector, the index of farm prices falling back to 100, where it stood in both the first and last months of 1940. Meantime, prices *paid by* farmers recovered somewhat from a 1933 low and then remained almost stable through 1940; because farm prices recovered more than industrial prices the terms of exchange were definitely improved. From the low of 1932, gross farm income moved steadily upward to $11 billion in 1937, fell off a little for two years, and was at the $11 billion mark again in 1940.

American preparation for war, which began in 1940, did not affect agricultural markets until the next year. In 1941 the demand for farm products, both for export and for domestic consumption, increased noticeably, and United States entrance into the war late in the year gave a further impulse

---

[2] In early 1933, 52 per cent of farm debt (45 per cent of debtors) was in default.

to the trend. During World War II industrial production rose at a rate of 30 per cent a year, and agricultural production, aided by exceptionally good weather, climbed at the remarkable rate of 5 per cent per year.[3] Price controls during the war were designedly less effective for agricultural than for nonagricultural commodities; consequently, prices of farm products rose more rapidly during the war than prices of things the farmer had to buy. Contrary to the expectations of many experts, the demand for food, feed, and fiber continued high after the war. The removal of price controls in the summer of 1946 permitted all prices to shoot up, but the rise in agricultural prices was steeper than any other. From a peak in January of 1948, however, farm prices fell steadily, and by mid-1950 they were down about one-sixth from their high point. But even before the outbreak of war in Korea, prices received by farmers began to rise again, soaring to an all-time high early in 1951. From February 1951 the trend of farm prices was generally downward, with a break in the latter part of 1952 great enough to cause consternation among farmers. In 1954 farm production was more than 40 per cent greater than the 1935–39 average, and prices received were beginning a gentle drift away from parity.

Favorable prices and a high level of farm output during the 1940s and early 1950s meant that the farmer's lot was much improved from the dreary decade of the 1930s. From a peak of $16,800 million in 1947, net income dropped to just over $13 billion in 1950. Half of this loss was regained in 1951, a steady decline from 1952 to 1954 bringing net income back to wartime levels. In 1950 the dollar income of farmers was three times as great as it had been in 1940, and since the general price level did not quite double during the period, real net income had risen by 50 per cent. But the dramatic improvement in the position of American agriculture did not signal an end to concern over the level of income in agriculture. After sagging in the mid-1950s, gross farm income rose to more than $40 billion in 1962, an all-time record. Yet net income in that year stood at only $12,800 million, a billion dollars below that of 1953 and four billion dollars under the record high of 1947. Had it not been for nearly two billion dollars of *direct* government payments and rising net income per farm because of the reduced number of farms, the plight of all but the largest and most efficient units would have been desperate.

Farm Legislation

Pre-1920 attempts to help the farmer by federal legislation were not calculated to have a direct effect on prices and production. In the past forty years, however, agricultural groups have succeeded in obtaining legislation

---

[3] These figures may be compared with the average World War I industrial rate of increase of 5.7 per cent per annum and an agricultural rate of increase of 1.7 per cent per annum.

that directly affects prices received by the farmer and that, consequently, causes production to be different from what it would be in a "free" market. The acceptance by the American people of the principle that the government ought to bolster the economic fortunes of particular occupational groups or classes is of momentous importance. Farmers have not been the only beneficiaries of this emerging philosophy; but we cannot find a better example of the way in which legislation, passed at first in an effort to relieve emergency distress, has become accepted as a more or less permanent part of the economic mechanism.

The farm program has taken its present form by easy stages best analyzed by considering three subperiods. There were the years, approximately 1921 to 1933, in which ideas were being formulated. From 1933 to 1941 farm legislation was designed to achieve recovery from economic depression. With the onset of World War II new objectives developed. During the war, legislation was slanted toward the stimulation of certain kinds of farm output, and in the postwar period there has been a persistent attempt to lessen disparity between agricultural and nonagricultural income.

THE FIRST EFFORTS, 1921–1933

As early as 1919, Secretary of Agriculture Houston, who was not so optimistic as most agricultural leaders, called for a conference to discuss possible agricultural problems, but not until disaster struck in the form of sharply falling prices and incomes was this proposal seriously considered. Violent protests from farmers in the late months of 1920 led Congress to create a Joint Commission of Agricultural Inquiry in 1921. The Commission reported the obvious, that farm troubles were the result of general business depression and of a decline in exports, and recommended measures to help co-operative marketing associations, improve credit facilities, and extend research activities by the Department of Agriculture. More important was the National Agricultural Conference, called early in 1922 by the Secretary of Agriculture, Henry C. Wallace. Despite the administration's attitude, expressed by President Harding, that ". . . the farmer must be ready to help himself," a good many radical proposals were heard at this conference. In its report the idea of parity for agriculture was first made explicit, and the slogan "Equality for Agriculture" was offered. There was recognition of the fact that in times of falling demand for goods, manufacturers reduce production and lower prices slowly, while farmers maintain production and take the consequences in the form of sharply falling prices. It was argued that agriculture as a whole was *entitled* to its fair share of the national income and that justice would be done if the ratio of prices received by farmers to the prices paid by them were kept equal to the ratio that had prevailed in the years 1910 to 1914.

From 1923 to 1933 various ideas were proposed that aimed at securing parity prices or "fair-exchange value" for the products of agriculture. Senator George Norris proposed a plan unpopular with the Republican administration. He wanted to establish a government corporation that would actually go into the business of processing farm products, eliminating profits of middlemen. Then there was the plan of the National Grange to increase exports by the payment of export bounties. The bounties were not to be paid in cash, but instead in negotiable certificates, called debentures, which could be used to pay import duties and therefore would have a cash value. Toward the end of the period a group of college professors developed a "domestic-allotment" plan, which introduced the notion of limiting the amount of products farmers could produce and sell in the domestic market.

The scheme most readily acceptable to professional farm supporters and politicians was incorporated in the McNary-Haugen bills considered by Congress between 1924 and 1928. This proposal was well received because it made use of more or less traditional devices, including a high tariff on agricultural products. The fair-exchange value of each farm product was to be determined, the fair value being a price that would have pre–World War I purchasing power. This "fair" price was to be maintained in the domestic market in two ways. First, a tariff was to protect the home market from imports. Second, a private corporation chartered by the federal government was to buy a sufficient amount of each commodity to force its price up to the computed fair-value level. The corporation could in turn sell the acquired commodities. Obviously, if the purchases had been necessary to raise prices, the commodities could not be sold in the domestic market. Hence it was proposed that they be sold abroad at the world price, which would presumably be lower than the supported American price. Administrative expenses and operating losses would be shared among the producing farmers. For every bale of cotton or bushel of wheat sold, a tax called an "equalization fee" would be charged the grower. This tax would be used to defray all expenses of operating the price-support plan. The farmer would gain insofar as the additional amount of income resulting from higher prices exceeded the tax expense.

The McNary-Haugen bills were twice passed by Congress and twice vetoed by President Coolidge. Did the agitation of the twenties then secure anything for agriculture? There were some gains. For one thing the Capper-Volstead law of 1922 freed farmers' co-operatives from the threat of prosecution for violation of the antitrust laws. Also, the Federal Intermediate Credit Act of 1923 provided for twelve intermediate credit banks that would rediscount for commercial banks and other lending agencies agricultural paper maturing within three years.[4] To achieve the broader aims of price and income maintenance there were two major efforts. A naïve belief in the tariff as a device to raise prices of farm products, which had been traditionally exported, *not* imported, led to "protection" for agriculture, cul-

---

[4] Nonemergency farm credit needs were pretty well taken care of with the passage of this act, for the Federal Farm Loan Act of 1916 had established twelve Federal Land Banks to provide long-term loans to farmers through co-operative borrowing groups.

minating in the high duties of the Smoot-Hawley Act of 1929. More significant was the passage of the Agricultural Marketing Act of 1929, which was the outcome of Republican campaign promises of the previous year. The first law committing the federal government to a policy of stabilizing farm prices, the Act of 1929 worked as much as possible through nongovernmental institutions. The act established a Federal Farm Board with the primary function of encouraging the formation of co-operative marketing associations. The Board was also authorized to set up "stabilization corporations," to be owned by the co-operatives, which would use a $500 million fund to carry on price-support operations.

Had the economic conditions of the 1920s persisted, the law might have had fruitful results. With the onset of serious depression in 1930, the Federal Farm Board strove valiantly to support farm prices through its stabilization corporations, but it was a case of sending a boy to do a man's work. Between June 1929 and June 1932 the corporations bought surplus farm products only to suffer steadily increasing losses as prices went on down. The Board itself took over the operation and accepted the losses, expending in three years some $676 million in stabilization operations and loans to co-operatives. While all this was going on, the individual farmer, faced with catastrophically falling prices, maintained or even increased his output. Obviously, a new approach was called for.

THE CRYSTALLIZATION OF A FARM POLICY, 1933–1941

By the date of Franklin Roosevelt's inauguration, thinking about farm policy had undergone fundamental changes. Proponents of dumping American farm products abroad were successful in securing the dollar devaluation of 1933–34, which made dollars cheaper in terms of foreign currencies and thus stimulated demand for commodities traded in world markets. But this solution to the farmer's dilemma was not satisfactory because the worldwide depression was accompanied by extremely low world prices. American policy-makers sought a plan to raise farm prices substantially in the home market. It had become clear that supports through purchases and loans, like those attempted by the Federal Farm Board, would require enormous outlays and would probably be ineffectual unless the supply of products were restricted. As a consequence, a scheme evolved that took the central idea of the previously suggested domestic-allotment plan.

In May of 1933 the Agricultural Adjustment Act was passed. It provided for an Agricultural Adjustment Administration, popularly referred to as the AAA, which had the responsibility of raising farm prices by restricting the supply of farm commodities. The most important weapon of the AAA was the "acreage allotment." Taking into consideration prospective demand and carry-over from the previous season, the AAA would determine a total acreage of certain major crops to be planted in the next growing season. The total acreage would then be subdivided into state totals, which were in turn to be allotted to individual farms on the basis of each farm's recent crop history. For example, the base acreage for each wheat farm was to be the average acreage in wheat from 1928 to 1932. In order to secure the co-operation of the individual farmer, a direct "benefit payment," later called an "adjustment payment," was made. Wheat farmers restricting acreage received in the beginning about thirty cents a bushel on 54 per cent of their average production in the base period. The payment was made by check from the federal treasury, but in the early days of depression it seemed a little too much to expect the general taxpayer to foot the bill. The benefit payments were financed, therefore, by processing taxes paid by the first processor of any product. Thus millers had to pay a tax for each bushel of wheat turned into flour, though it was not expected that the processor would bear the burden of the tax. Instead, it was assumed that the processing tax would either be shifted backward and taken out of the farm price or shifted forward and paid by the consumer.

The original AAA scheme received a setback in 1936 when the Supreme Court, in the Hoosac Mills case, declared that the Agricultural Adjustment Act was unconstitutional because it attempted to regulate agricultural production, a power reserved to the several states. Specifically, the processing tax was declared invalid. The adverse decision did not force a discontinuance of acreage allotments, but only changed the *basis* on which allotments were made to one that presumably encouraged soil conservation.

The drought of 1936, with its attendant dust-bowl conditions, focused attention on the need for vigorous soil-conservation measures and prompted passage of the Soil Conservation and Domestic Allotment Act of that year. Under this act the Secretary of Agriculture could replace the old type of specific contract between the government and the farmer with an open offer to make benefit payments to anyone who would reduce his acreage of soil-depleting crops and take steps to conserve or rebuild the land withheld from production. But production in 1937 was very high, and there was pressure to supplement acreage reduction with even more vigorous measures.

The soil-conservation basis of acreage allotments was maintained. However, Congress in 1938 passed a new Agricultural Adjustment Act, which placed more emphasis than heretofore on the principle of giving direct support to prices. Since 1933 the Commodity Credit Corporation had operated as an independent agency with the minor function of "cushioning" prices of corn, wheat, and cotton against adverse fluctuations in demand and supply. The CCC had carried out the cushioning function by making loans to farmers on the security of their crops, most of these loans being made "without recourse." Nonrecourse loans were a heads-you-win, tails-I-lose proposition. If the CCC made an advance against a commodity and the price of the commodity fell, the farmer could let the CCC take title to the stored product and cancel the debt together with accumulated interest. If the price of the commodity against which the advance had been made rose, the farmer could sell the commodity, pay back the loan with interest, and keep any difference. Thus, loan rates became, in effect, minimum prices.

H. J. Heinz Company founder Henry Heinz stops in one of his fields to greet some of the hands, about 1900.

From 1933 to 1937 CCC operations were carried on with reference to rather vague goals so far as price objectives were concerned. In these early years no loans were made on wheat because short crops kept wheat prices around $1 a bushel. Lending on corn and cotton was nominal because of reasonably low loan rates combined with a strong tendency for prices to move upward.

The Agricultural Adjustment Act of 1938 greatly increased the power of the CCC by making it mandatory upon the directors that loans on corn, wheat, and cotton be at rates between 52 and 75 per cent of parity. The camel had got his feet into the tent. From now on Congress was to specify support prices at a certain per cent of parity prices, parity prices being defined as farm prices having the same purchasing power as those prevailing in a favorable base period. In 1938, and for many years to come, the base period for most products was 1910–14.

Mandatory supports went into effect after farm prices had dropped from their post-depression, "recovery" highs of 1937. From 1939 to 1941 the CCC accumulated great quantities of wheat, corn, cotton, and tobacco. Strengthened demand following the outbreak of war enabled the government to get rid of these stocks profitably, but holdings of wheat were large into the war years, and vast amounts of low-grade, short-staple cotton were not disposed of until even later.

Two other means of restricting the supply of farm products came into use during the thirties. One of these, the *marketing agreement,* was tried in the early experimental years, then fell into disuse, and after 1937 became important for certain fruits and vegetables and in the chief milk areas. Marketing agreements are contracts between an association of producers of a raw product and the processors of the product, and the making of the contracts is refereed by a Department of Agriculture representative. Producers and processors may set minimum prices, total quantity to be marketed, and allotment of marketings among processors. Milk producers and the city milk companies, in addition to controlling amounts of milk marketed, have made a profitable thing of establishing different prices for milk going into uses with different elasticities of demand.

Marketing quotas became important after 1936, when Congress empowered the Secretary of Agriculture to set an upper limit to the amount growers of certain crops could sell. Before such controls could be instituted the Secretary had to determine that the current supply of a basic commodity exceeded a "reserve supply." A referendum was then held, and if two-thirds of the qualified producers approved, a quota was assigned each grower. If amounts in excess of the quota were marketed by any farmer, he was subject to penalties or fines on the excess sold.

Most early efforts at raising farm prices were directed at reducing supply rather than increasing demand, but two ways of stimulating dollar sales of food and fiber by federal subsidy were quickly devised. The more acceptable of the "surplus-removal" operations have been the nutrition or direct-distribution programs.[5] Nutrition programs have taken the form of food-stamp plans, low-cost milk distribution plans, and school-lunch programs. School-lunch programs were so readily accepted by the public that they have since been authorized by separate legislation without any implications of furnishing relief. The Food Stamp Plan, in operation from 1939 to 1942, won enthusiastic supporters.[6] Stamps given to low-income families were used to purchase food from regular retail outlets, storekeepers in turn cashing the stamps at the treasury. Thus surplus commodities were given to those who presumably needed them most. The benefits to poor and undernourished people were of more importance than any inconsiderable influence such schemes may have exerted on agricultural demand.

The second, and indefensible, kind of surplus-removal operation has been the export subsidy. This method of increasing the sales of farm commodities originated in the Agricultural Adjustment Act of 1933, but not until the passage of an amendment in 1935 (commonly referred to as Section 32) did sales become significant. In that year it was provided that as

---

[5] Euphemisms designating the various forms of subsidy change as old ones wear thin and new ones come into vogue.
[6] In 1961 advocates finally secured reactivation of the Food Stamp Plan on a pilot basis in eight economically distressed areas.

much as 30 per cent of annual customs revenues might be used to finance the disposal of surplus at home and abroad.

The subsidization of exports by payment of bounties did not reach alarming proportions before World War II.[7] In the fiscal year 1939–40 amounts spent on bounties for wheat and cotton amounted to $26 million and $38 million, respectively. As we shall observe presently, expenditure of public funds on export subsidies would one day become an effective, if somewhat shady, means of adding to American farm income.

FARM POLICY DURING WORLD WAR II AND AFTER

Early in 1941 the troubles that had plagued agriculture for so long began to disappear, for to meet lend-lease and growing domestic requirements expansion of production was required. To encourage expansion, Congress passed three laws in May, July, and December of 1941. The first of these directed the CCC to support the basic crops of wheat, corn, cotton, tobacco, rice, and peanuts at 85 per cent of parity. The second, the Steagall Amendment, gave the Secretary of Agriculture authority to support the price of any *nonbasic* commodity at *not less than* 85 per cent of parity if, in the opinion of the Secretary, support was necessary to increase production of a crop vital to the war effort. The third guaranteed the 85 per cent loan rate on basic crops for the years 1942 to 1946, inclusive, putting price floors into effect for six crops for a period well into the future.

During 1942, administration thinking reflected two major concerns. Emphasis was placed on the necessity for stimulating particular *kinds* of output, notably of meats and the oil-bearing crops, and avoiding a repetition of the price collapse that followed World War I. Legislation of October 1942 set final policy for the war period and for two postwar years. The 1942 act provided *minimum* support rates of 90 per cent of parity for both basic and Steagall commodities, the supports to remain in effect for two full years beginning with the first day of January following the official end of the war. Finally, price ceilings on farm products were set at a minimum of 110 per cent of parity.[8]

---

[7] An export bounty is a payment to exporters of so much per unit of commodity to offset losses incurred in the process of buying in the artificially supported home market and selling at lower world prices. This kind of interference with international trade, a form of dumping, can be defended on the grounds that it offers the rest of the world an enhancement of real income, for other countries can enjoy the goods that are dumped. But it affects adversely the income and market positions of producers of competing commodities, hurting friendly nations in a way the United States has always considered unfair. All matters of our relationships with other countries on one side, there are always other ways to give farmers as large an income as can be obtained with an export-subsidy and taxes. For elucidation of these matters see D. Gale Johnson, *Trade and Agriculture* (New York: Wiley, 1950).

[8] There were two other provisions that some readers might wish to know about. Cotton supports were set at 92.5 per cent of parity. The Secretary of Agriculture, at his discretion, could leave wheat and corn supports at 85 per cent of parity if he felt that the higher prices would discourage livestock feeding.

Over the war period and during two postwar years price supports were not generally required. Because of the great demand for most products, agricultural prices tended to push against ceilings, but the Secretary found it necessary to set floors for some needed nonbasic commodities above minimum levels. Surplus supplies of eggs and certain grades of hogs created a problem for a while in 1944, but on the whole farm prices were subject to upward pressure. For some meats and dairy products it was even necessary to roll back retail prices in an effort to "hold the line" against inflation. In such cases, to prevent a reduction in the floor prices received by farmers, meat packers and creameries were paid a treasury subsidy equal to the amount of the rollback on each unit sold.

We have already noted that the war enabled the CCC to get out from under heavy inventories built up between 1939 and 1941. From 1944 to 1946 loans of the CCC were small. Beginning in 1944, however, egg purchases became so great as to cause embarrassment, and the support of eggs and potatoes received a fantastically unfavorable press in 1945 and 1946. But foreign demand through UNRRA and military governments, an unexpectedly high domestic demand, and the removal of price ceilings led to highly favorable postwar prices and to light CCC loan and purchase commitments. Most production restrictions on crops had been dropped before or during World War II so that by the spring of 1948 only tobacco and potatoes were still controlled.

Unfortunately, this happy state of affairs did not last long. Farm prices and income started downward in July of 1948. With the high support prices required by the Agricultural Acts of 1948 and 1949, price declines meant a return to increases in loans and accumulation of inventories. The Commodity Credit Corporation was ready, for in June of 1948 Congress had given it a borrowing authorization of $4,750 million and placed it on a permanent basis.[9] During the fiscal years of 1949 and 1950 price-support loans and inventories climbed to a total "investment" of over $3,500 million. The seriousness of the increases was indicated by the concentration of support operations in the four great staples—corn, wheat, cotton, and tobacco. In fact, corn stocks owned by the CCC or pledged to it as collateral were greater than at any previous time. Wheat inventories were about the same as those held in the previous high year of 1942. Although cotton holdings did not approach the inventories of 1939–41, they were not far from those of 1942.

---

[9] Under the War Food Administration the CCC had for a time imported needed commodities such as coffee, tea, fats, and sugar. This foreign-purchase program was begun again after the war. In addition, the Corporation in 1946 was charged with the responsibility of procuring large quantities of agricultural products to meet the requirements of both United States government agencies administering foreign relief and foreign governments and relief agencies. This "supply program" tapered off during the fiscal year ending in June 1950, largely as a result of the recovery of agriculture in western Europe. For further information consult the *Report of the President of the Commodity Credit Corporation,* which appears at the end of each fiscal year.

To understand why CCC inventories increased so in years of mild recession it will be necessary to review postwar farm legislation. A Presidential declaration that the war was officially over, made in December 1946, signaled termination of rigid wartime supports at the end of 1948. Although it had been amended several times, the basic farm law was still the old Agricultural Adjustment Act of 1938, generally felt to be in need of revision. Consequently, extensive discussion of the whole farm problem went on during 1947 and the first half of 1948, and there was much talk of writing a permanent farm bill. To testify before the House Agricultural Committee came farm leaders, government experts, and university professors. The result was the Agricultural Act of 1948, passed in haste in the last days of the Congressional session, which maintained price-support levels through 1949 at the magical 90 per cent figure for basic commodities and the principal Steagall commodities.

The contribution of the midwestern farm states to the Democratic victory of 1948 led to a lengthy reconsideration of the policy laid down by the Republican-controlled Eightieth Congress in the 1948 act. The Democrats were determined to write a new law, and it seemed for a while that a new method of subsidizing agriculture might be tried. In the spring of 1949, Secretary of Agriculture Brannan announced the plan of compensatory payments to which the press and public quickly attached his name, though its central ideas had been developing for many years in academic writings. The Brannan plan would have allowed the prices of certain perishable commodities to seek their own level in the market place, the difference between the market price and a "modernized" parity price to be paid the farmer (up to a certain maximum number of "units") with a check from the treasury. Secretary Brannan would have continued price supports for the nonperishable (storable) products by the old device of nonrecourse loans to producers. After months of heated argument, during which the National Grange and the American Farm Bureau Federation aligned themselves against such an unconcealed payment of subsidies, the House of Representatives refused to give the Brannan plan a trial run on even three commodities. Opponents of the Brannan plan won the day by castigating so straightforward a subsidy as "socialism."

In the fall of the year the Agricultural Act of 1949 was passed. The law distinguished among three groups of commodities: (1) the six "basics"—wheat, corn, cotton, tobacco, rice, and peanuts; (2) five "designated nonbasic" commodities—wool and mohair, tung nuts, honey, Irish potatoes, and milk and milk products; (3) and "other nonbasic" commodities—the rest of some 170 United States commodities. The Secretary of Agriculture was required to support the basic commodities provided they were under production controls or marketing quotas, but a rigid support of 90 per cent of parity was permanently mandatory only in the case of tobacco. After 1952 the other basic commodities were to be supported at between 75 and 90 per cent of parity, the level of support depending upon the supply of each commodity.[10] The 1949 act, like the 1948 law before it, provided a new parity formula. The "modernized" method of computing parity prices took into consideration prices received and prices paid during the most recent ten-year period instead of the relationships prevailing during the 1910–14 period. There were two exclusions in the new formula: no wartime subsidy payments were included on the "received" side and no wages paid by farmers to hired hands on the "paid" side. However, parity prices computed under the new formula could not drop more than 5 per cent per year below what they would have been under the old formula, and until the end of 1954 the parity price for any basic commodity could not be lower than under the old method of computation. In general, the new formula raised parity prices for livestock and livestock products, dairy products, poultry, and some fruits and vegetables and lowered them for grains, cotton, citrus fruits, potatoes, and eggs.

The 1949 legislation thus made use of methods devised in the preceding seventeen years for restricting the supply of farm products. However, a decision was made in favor of *flexible* price supports as against the wartime *rigid* supports, tobacco being an exception. And the new method of computing parity prices had the merit of basing the program (after 1954, at any rate) on an experience no longer that of another age and time.

Neither flexible supports nor the new parity formula became effective as planned. After the start of the Korean War, Congress amended the law to make 90 per cent support of the basics mandatory, and the old method of computing parity prices remained more favorable to farmers than the new. The war once again enabled the CCC to reduce embarrassingly high inventories and loans, total "investment" falling to $2 billion in mid-1951. The crops of 1952 and 1953, however, required an inordinate amount of support, and by August of 1954 CCC loans and inventories amounted to nearly $7 billion. Twice during 1954 it was necessary to increase CCC authority to borrow for support operations, the last change bringing total authority to $10 billion.

After procrastinating for more than a year the Eighty-third Congress at last came up with its version of a farm program in the Agricultural Act of 1954. The inner circle of Department of Agriculture officials strove valiantly to find a fresh approach to the problem of price maintenance but in the end advocated making the major provisions of the 1949 act effective.[11] Secretary Benson was especially insistent on the restoration of flexible sup-

10 Support of the "designated nonbasic" commodities was likewise mandatory upon the Secretary of Agriculture. Support levels were to be between 60 and 90 per cent of parity except for milk and milk products, which were to be between 75 and 90 per cent. Support for the rest of the nonbasic commodities was permissive. If funds were available, the storable products were to be supported at between 75 and 90 per cent of parity and the perishables at from 0 per cent to 90 per cent.

11 Wool was singled out for experimental support on the compensatory-payment basis advocated by former Secretary Brannan.

California, to no one's apparent surprise, lived up to its boastful turn-of-the-century advertisements and became the fastest-growing state in the union.

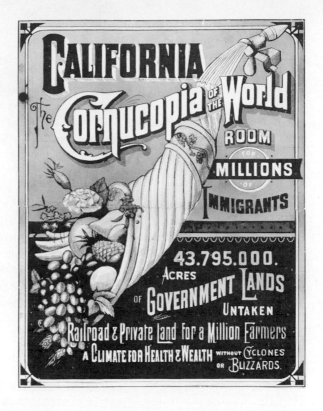

ports, which were finally set for five of the six basics at 82.5 to 90 per cent of parity.[12] The 1954 act again postponed changing to the modernized parity price formula for basic commodities; the notion that the 1910–14 period represents parity ("fairity") is too deeply ingrained to die easily. In an heroic attempt to "insulate" the massive stocks of the CCC from the market, Congress authorized the setting aside of up to $2,500 million of CCC stocks for donation or sale for enumerated worthy causes.

Unfortunately, feed grain and wheat carry-overs kept right on swelling, and other surpluses, though not as alarming, showed no signs of lessening. The Soil Bank Act of 1956 aimed at reducing supplies of the six basics by achieving a 10 to 17 per cent reduction in plowland by obtaining "voluntary" action through payments for shifting land out of production into the "soil bank." The diversion payments were based on the old formula of multiplying a base-unit rate ($1.20 for wheat, $.90 for corn, etc., to start) by normal yield per acre by the numbers of acres withdrawn. The plan made use of a phony conservation handle and at the same time tried to avoid the appearance of controlling farm decisions. The results were unbelievably bad.

---

[12] The support level of tobacco remained at 90 per cent. Price supports on milk and milk products, tung nuts, and honey continued mandatory, but all other commodities, including Irish potatoes, were simply eligible for support.

Carry-overs went right on mounting, reaching astronomic heights in 1961 after nine consecutive years of increase.

The Kennedy administration had no choice but to get hardboiled. Secretary of Agriculture Orville Freeman devised no new techniques. He simply made an honest approach to the problem by dropping all nonsense about having freedom and controls at the same time. The Emergency Feed Grain Bill of 1961 encouraged drastic reductions in acreages devoted to corn and grain sorghums by offering a whopping $1.20 a bushel in diversion payments to farmers reducing acreage by 20 per cent. Even higher payments were offered for diversion of an additional 20 per cent of feed-crop acreage. Results in 1962 were on the whole good. Although a planned reduction of 23 per cent of the 1959–60 base acreage slipped to 18 per cent, twenty million acres were finally diverted. For the first time in a decade, feed grain carry-over actually dropped in 1962, and the prospect was for continuing reduction. This modest success encouraged the administration to attack massive surpluses of wheat with a similar, though fabulously expensive, plan. Unfortunately, the wealthy farmers and their organization, the Farm Bureau Federation, secured the defeat of the wheat program at the referendum in 1963.

Causes of Economic Dislocation in Agriculture

In the present chapter we have so far been concerned to trace (1) broad changes in farm prices and income over the last four decades and (2) major changes in farm legislation during the same period. In order that these two lines of development might be presented clearly, little attempt was made to discern *causal* relationships. But such descriptive material would do little to satisfy our curiosity if it were not accompanied by some economic analysis. We now turn to the task of inquiring why for forty years agriculture has been beset with recurring problems that defy solution.

SUPPLY AND DEMAND VARIABLES IN AGRICULTURE

When we were discussing the trials and tribulations of American farm people in the late nineteenth century, we summarized the causes of their plight in a single simple proposition. This statement is equally valid as an explanation of the difficulties of the last four decades, and it may be well to repeat it in slightly different form. *The supply of farm products as a whole has exceeded the demand for them at prices that cover the costs of most farm units.* It is not inevitable that this proposition will always hold true, but it is the considered opinion of economists that it will hold true indefinitely unless there is a continuing drastic transfer of human resources out of agriculture.

What major forces have affected the supply of and the demand for farm products? Most readers could probably make a good list without further discussion, but it will be helpful to elaborate the previous brief treatment.

Let us list the secular and cyclical forces affecting supply and demand insofar as they have their play within the domestic economy. (The influences of foreign trade are considered at the end of the present discussion.)

1. The forces affecting the *supply* of food, feed, and fiber are:
   a. Acres of land devoted to crop production.
   b. The state of agricultural techniques: more specifically, the progress of mechanization and scientific applications.
   c. Unpredictable fluctuations in the weather.
   d. Time lag in production response (e.g., the hog cycle).
   e. The nature of competition in agriculture.
2. The forces affecting *demand* are:
   a. The rate of population growth in the United States.
   b. Price and income elasticities of demand for farm products.
   c. Changes in consumer tastes, the development of knowledge concerning nutritional requirements, and occupational shifts with accompanying dietary effects.
   d. The development of industrial products that compete with products of the farm.
   e. Fluctuations in industrial activity.

Supply. (a) For thirty-five years after 1920 harvested acreages remained almost stable at about 350,000,000 acres. The legislation of 1933 and the drought of 1934 resulted in a reduction to 304,000,000 acres harvested in 1934, but a gradual rise took place after that so that in 1954 the total land under cultivation was about what it was in 1920. The decrease in numbers of horses and mules was so great during the period that upwards of 60,000,000 acres of land were released from growing feed for draft animals, with a consequent transfer of land to production of commodities for human consumption.[13] After 1956 incentives to divert acreage to "conservation" purposes were substantial, and in the early 1960s acreage harvested stood at or just below the 300-million mark (see chart, p. 446).

(b) Technological innovation has gone on apace. In mechanization and the application of scientific discoveries there is no foreseeable end to the changes present knowledge may produce.

On American farms in 1920 there were scarcely 250,000 tractors of the old-fashioned, heavy type. By 1960 there were approximately 4,750,000 tractors, most of them modern, all-purpose machines that have been greatly improved over 1920 models in speed, power, and efficiency. Motor trucks in the same time increased from 100,000 to more than 3,100,000. Modern

---

[13] It might be added that engineering advances have made possible the future reclamation of much land formerly considered not cultivable. For example, in such areas as the Grand Coulee, the Central Valley of California, and other less important places, technological advance has made feasible large-scale irrigation that would have been impossible two decades ago. However, this sort of addition to the possible cultivable area does not appear to be a serious threat at the moment.

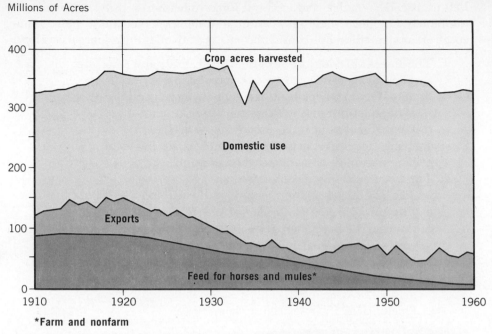

Millions of Acres

Crop acres harvested

Domestic use

Exports

Feed for horses and mules*

*Farm and nonfarm

United States Department of Agriculture.

Cropland Uses: The continuing high productivity of farms has kept the total figure of acreage nearly constant for the past half-century. Feed acreage, meanwhile, has declined steadily with the increasing mechanization of farms in all regions.

farm implements include self-propelled combines, flame cultivators, corn-pickers, cotton-pickers, and insecticide-blowers. Recently, special types of aircraft have been developed for use on huge "super farms."

The results of scientific research have been applied to agriculture with growing rapidity. The individual farm is too small a unit to carry on its own research activity; for this reason public agencies such as the state agricultural experiment stations and the Department of Agriculture have done this important work. Because both basic and applied research have been socialized, new discoveries are made available to all producers. Thus, even though a particular innovation may make equipment already in use obsolete, it will almost certainly be introduced by farmers in a position to do so, and competition may force its general adoption within a short period of time. Uninhibited innovation is in sharp contrast to that of industry, where a few firms may withhold from use a new method that would make investment in plant and equipment obsolete.

Application of scientific discoveries to agriculture was held back during the 1930s by the depression. In 1940 there was a backlog of discoveries ready to be put into general use; during World War II many of these applications were made, and innovation since 1945 has been phenomenal. The use of hybrid seed and the practice of artificial insemination have become generally accepted. New methods of pest and disease control, new ideas about fertilization, and better tillage practices have made their contribution to steadily increasing yields. The agricultural colleges and experiment stations in the several states have been experimenting to find crops peculiarly suited to the various growing regions. All in all, this major secular force increasing the supply of farm products shows no sign of slackening.

(c) Crop yields in any growing season depend to a large extent upon the weather, and the weather is unpredictable. Good and bad years may alternate. Or several ideal seasons may succeed each other to be followed by successive years of adverse conditions. Those who lived through them cannot fail to remember the terrible droughts of 1934 and 1936, years in which corn crops were 40 per cent below normal. On the other hand, the Midwest was favored by excellent weather during the war; in 1942 corn yields were some 35 per cent above normal, largely because the rains came at exactly the right time. Similarly, wheat output was more than 25 per cent below average from 1933 to 1936; in 1942 it was 44 per cent above average. The student can well imagine what difficulties would have been encountered had these production figures been reversed.

(d) Time lag in the production response of the farmer contributes to year-to-year variations in the output of agriculture. Take, for example, the hog cycle. Confronted with low corn prices, farmers are led to breed more sows and feed more pigs. A year later, when the increased numbers of animals are brought to market, hog prices fall. Farmers are then deterred from breeding sows and feeding pigs with the result that sometime later hog supplies will fall off and hog prices will rise. In the case of beef cattle there may be a lag of three or four years in response to price changes. In the production of field crops there are no pronounced cyclical variations, but output is always several jumps behind changes in demand. If, for example, there is a sharp decrease in the demand for corn in the middle of a growing season, farmers cannot respond to it until time to plant corn the next spring. The responsiveness of agricultural output to price changes is sluggish compared to that of a manufacturing industry.

(e) Time lag in production response results primarily from the length of crop and livestock production periods and from the seasonal nature of agricultural production. This complication is strongly reinforced by the nature of competition among farmers. Markets for farm products approximate most closely the purely competitive market of economic theory. For most agricultural commodities, a large number of producers sell a standardized product to a large number of buyers. Any one farmer, no matter how large an operator he may be, knows that he can increase his output of a particular commodity without having any appreciable effect upon its price. So it happens that in times of falling farm prices individual producers often try to keep their own incomes from falling by offsetting price decreases with production increases. As everyone tries to save himself, supplies are increased, prices fall still further, and producers as a whole are worse off. This response to falling prices was certainly observable from 1929 to 1932, when crop acreages increased each year. In the case of crops grown in restricted geographical areas (the citrus fruits, for example) it may be possible for growers to form an association for the express purpose of controlling production. But cotton is grown on more than half a million farms, corn on nearly 2,000,000, and chickens are raised on nearly every one of the 3,500,-000 farms in operation. Is it possible that these producers will, on their own initiative, ever "get together" on a policy of reducing output even when such a policy would seem to be in the best interests of all?

Demand. (a) Any discussion of the demand for agricultural products must begin by considering trends in the number of mouths to be fed and bodies to be clothed. As Table 18-1 shows, the rate of population increase in America slowed considerably after 1910, dropping to just a little over 7 per cent in the 1930–40 decade. Wartime prosperity reversed the downtrend, and beginning with the huge baby crop of 1947 population growth approached the turn-of-the-century rate of 20 per cent per decade, where it has stayed well into the 1960s. There are good reasons for believing that this rate of increase will be maintained, the best one being that babies born in the late 1940s will begin to form families in the mid-1960s. Yet we should not overlook the fact that in other Western countries in the twentieth century population growth has slowed down greatly, stood still, or even declined.

(b) A second major influence on agricultural demand results from the low price and income elasticities of demand for farm products taken as a whole. One of the most useful generalizations of economics is the so-called

Table 18-1

Increase in United States Population, 1870–1960 [a]

Year	Population (in thousands)	Increase over preceding census (in thousands)	(percentage)
1870	39,818		
1880	50,156	10,337	26.0
1890	62,948	12,792	25.5
1900	75,995	13,047	20.7
1910	91,972	15,978	21.0
1920	105,711	13,738	14.9
1930	122,775	17,064	16.1
1940	131,669	8,894	7.2
1950	150,697	19,028	14.5
1960	178,464	27,767	18.4

SOURCE: *Statistical Abstract of the United States*, 1962, p. 5.

[a] Excludes Alaska and Hawaii.

law of demand, which states that as the price of a good or service falls the quantity taken from the market will increase. But the law of demand says nothing about the *degree* of responsiveness of quantity changes to price changes. Following a relatively small change in price the quantity taken may increase much or little. If for example a fall in price of 1 per cent leads to an increase in quantity taken of more than 1 per cent, we say that demand is *elastic;* if a fall in price of 1 per cent leads to an increase in quantity taken of less than 1 per cent, we say that demand is *inelastic.* Whenever we wish to measure the responsiveness of the quantity demanded to *price* changes we speak of the *price elasticity of demand.*

But there is another concept of elasticity that is also useful. As the income of an individual increases, his consumption of goods will presumably increase, and we may wish to measure the responsiveness of certain kinds of purchases to income changes. Suppose, for example, that a person's income increases by 10 per cent. If he increases his expenditure on food by more than 10 per cent, we say that his *income elasticity of demand* for food is greater than one; if, on the other hand, he increases his expenditure for food by less than 10 per cent, we say that his income elasticity of demand for food is less than one.

Both price and income elasticities of demand for farm products as a whole are low. What do these low elasticities signify? Let us consider first the long-run consequence of a generally low price elasticity. The introduction of machine methods and the application of scientific discoveries enable agriculture to expand output. The increased output, since it is produced more efficiently, should be available at lower costs and consequently at lower prices. Even though incomes and tastes are unchanged, so that demand stays the same, amounts taken from the market should increase as a result of the lower prices. But because of price inelasticity of demand, increases in quantity taken will not ordinarily be proportionately as great as the price reductions, the consequence being a drop in total receipts. There will be exceptions, of course, in the case of particular commodities.[14] Yet agriculture is not in the fortunate position of manufacturing industries generally, where reductions in price following the introduction of new methods have normally led to great increases in sales to willing and eager buyers.

Just as serious in its implications has been the low *income* elasticity of demand for many of the traditional farm staples. Because of low income elasticities changes in the national income are not followed by proportional changes in money expenditures for the products of agriculture. A 10 per cent increase in the national income, for example, results normally in a less

---

[14] Much remains to be done in the statistical verification of elasticities of demand. Elasticities change, of course, over time. Studies indicate that demand is elastic with respect to price for better cuts of beef and lamb, for fruits, and for some dairy products. Demand is quite inelastic, on the other hand, for the cereal grains, for potatoes and most vegetables, and for sugar. For this latter group of products price elasticities may average as low as .25. Why?

than 10 per cent increase in the total amount spent on the output of farms.[15] There are exceptions, of course. Income elasticities for specific products may be quite high. Furthermore, as incomes of poor families rise, they may well increase their expenditures on food and clothing by an amount proportionately greater than the percentage change in income. On the other hand, income elasticities of families in middle- and upper-income groups are probably quite low with respect to goods composed of the raw food and fiber of the farm.[16]

Empirical investigations suggest that income elasticity of demand for farm products has been low for the past century and that it will become less as incomes rise further.[17] So far as the traditional staples are concerned there is little reason to think that there will ever be a reversal of this trend. However, there were signs during the war years and postwar years of rising incomes that income elasticities of certain products are much higher than had been believed. Since the war Americans have eaten, per person, more dairy products, more fruits and vegetables, and more meat, eggs, and poultry; at the same time per-capita consumption of potatoes, grain products, and sugars and syrups has fallen. Clearly, the future in farm production lies with commodities that come under the heading of "good things to eat." The foods showing per-capita increases in consumption are likely to show further increases in the future; on the other hand, the cereals will have a smaller and smaller per-capita consumption, and resources will almost certainly have to be transferred from their production.

(c) Certain foods are especially necessary to sound physical health. Adults have come to be more and more careful of their own eating habits, and we may be sure that their children will have better and better diets. Insofar as people are taught how to use food more efficiently, discoveries in the field of nutrition need not result in a greater demand for food. At the moment, however, there is little doubt that recent discoveries encourage the consumption of items requiring a relatively great amount of resources in their production. Nor, in considering demand for agricultural products, can we overlook the occupational shifts that have accompanied industrialization and urbanization. The average American does less outdoor work and more

---

[15] Contrarily, a decrease in the national income of 10 per cent would not result in a falling off of expenditures on farm commodities of 10 per cent. But over the years the national income, with only temporary setbacks, has moved rapidly upward, and it is consequently the changes in expenditure in response to income increases that interest us most. Nevertheless, low income elasticity of demand is a protection to agriculture during a depression.
[16] This is in accord with Engel's law, which states that as the income of a consuming unit increases, the proportion of income spent on necessaries will decrease and the proportion spent on luxuries and put into savings will increase. Furthermore, people who are comfortably well off tend to buy food and clothing that has gone through a lot of processing so that much of what they spend on these items goes for services rather than raw materials. Frozen foods and custom-made suits are examples.
[17] Theodore W. Schultz, *Agriculture in an Unstable Economy* (New York: McGraw-Hill, 1945), pp. 62–70.

Mechanized harvesting (like this in a Vernon, Texas, wheat field) brought vast increases in productivity, but the investment required for low-cost farming gradually ranged beyond the reach of the typical family farm.

sedentary work than his parents and grandparents did. This fact, together with the tendency of the population to contain a greater proportion of older people, has resulted in less need for the high-calorie foods. Such evidence reinforces the conclusions reached above concerning income elasticities of demand for food.

(d) The market for American farm products may be adversely affected by the development of competing products made by industry. Man-made fibers like rayon and dacron reduce the demand for wool and cotton. Insofar as such new products serve as substitutes for old the immediate effect is harmful to the producer of the old product. But the ultimate effect may be favorable in that the new material may make possible a considerable expansion in the manufacturing industry concerned, with a resultant increase in the demand for agricultural products as a whole. It is a pretty safe generalization that the harmful effects of innovation do not last long. And for foodstuffs at least, it seems quite unlikely that there will ever be any serious competition from "synthetic" products. No one has ever invented a close substitute for a good steak.

(e) It was shown in Chapter 11 that agriculture was in bad shape during those years in which industrial production did not increase at a rate both rapid and greater than that of agricultural production. The so-called golden

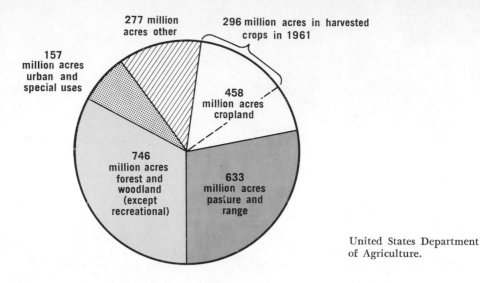

United States Department
of Agriculture.

How Land Is Used: Of the 2,300,000,000 acres of land in the fifty states, more than half remains open country; something like a fourth of this vast acreage is cropland or in urban and special uses.

era of agriculture was one in which industrial expansion was vigorous and in which industrial output increased at a rate three times as fast as that of farm output. Let us now look at the figures for (1) the interwar period and (2) the years since the outbreak of World War II.

By taking selected years we may see at a glance the pertinent data for the period of peace (see Table 18-2). Industrial production increased less than 50 per cent as compared with the 150 per cent increase that took place in the two decades before 1915. The expansion of industrial output was three times as great as that of farm output, the same as in the earlier twenty-year period. *It was not enough, however, that industry as a whole should expand at a faster rate than agriculture. The rate of increase was simply not sufficient to guarantee an adequate market for farm commodities.* Furthermore, the plight of agriculture was desperate in precisely those years of great industrial stagnation. Only a strong export demand could have saved the day, but the decrease in farm exports during this nineteen-year period was catastrophic.

The progress of agriculture from 1941 to 1948 was inevitable as the domestic economy boomed and farm exports rose rapidly (see Table 18-3). There was an upward surge in industrial production of 90 per cent to meet war needs, with a leveling off through 1949 in the neighborhood of 50 per cent above the output of the last prewar year. Equally remarkable was the rise in farm production to a level, after 1947 and up to 1951, 25 per cent above the 1940 position. Now if we recall that prices of agricultural commodities remained at high levels until mid-1948, we may raise a pertinent

Table 18-2

Indexes of Industrial and Agricultural Production, 1920–1939 (1920 = 100)

Year	Industrial production	Agricultural production
1920	100	100
1925	120	105
1930	121	106
1935	116	99
1939	145	115

SOURCE: By permission from *Agriculture in an Unstable Economy* by Theodore W. Schultz, p. 119. Copyright 1945. McGraw-Hill Book Co., Inc.

question at this point. Why did farm prices and incomes not begin to deteriorate in 1945, or at the latest in 1946, when industrial production began to fall off so sharply? Several reasons may be given. Many families, unable to obtain scarce durable goods in the early postwar years, kept expenditures on food and clothing higher than they might otherwise have done. Others doubtless drew on wartime savings to maintain a standard of living to which they had become accustomed. The removal of controls in 1946 allowed all prices to shoot up, the money incomes of the population rising much faster than real incomes. Probably the most important factor was an increase in

Table 18-3

Indexes of Industrial and Agricultural Production, 1940–1953 (1940 = 100)

Year	Industrial production	Agricultural production	Year	Industrial production	Agricultural production
1940	100	100	1947	149	116
1941	130	104	1948	155	125
1942	158	116	1949	145	125
1943	190	114	1950	167	124
1944	187	118	1951	179	126
1945	160	117	1952	185	131
1946	134	121	1953	200	131

SOURCE: *Federal Reserve Bulletin* and *Agricultural Outlook Charts*. Computations are the author's.

Table 18-4

Indexes of Industrial and Agricultural Production, 1953–1962
(1953 = 100)

Year	Industrial production	Agricultural production	Year	Industrial production	Agricultural production
1953	100	100	1958	103	110
1954	94	100	1959	116	111
1955	106	103	1960	119	114
1956	109	104	1961	120	115
1957	110	102	1962	130	116

SOURCE: *Economic Report of the President*, 1963, pp. 210, 258.

foreign demand for food, which took up the slack that would otherwise have appeared.

As industrial output faltered and foreign demand weakened in 1948, agricultural prices and income skidded. The industrial boom of 1950 and 1951 was enough to assure a rapid and sustained upturn in agricultural prices and income, and the boom was reinforced by renewed foreign demand. But as the *rate* of increase of industrial output slowed in 1951 and 1952, agricultural prices faltered and a downturn in farm exports was enough to precipitate a sharp drop in farm prices.

During the ensuing decade the nonagricultural sector of the American economy turned in a disappointing performance. For reasons to be examined later, industrial output flagged to such an extent that increases in the industrial-production index did not greatly outstrip those in the agricultural-production index. So another variable on the demand side contributed to the problems of American agriculture.

THE DECLINE OF AGRICULTURE'S FOREIGN MARKET

A high level of farm exports can sustain agricultural prices and incomes in the absence of a booming industrial sector. Over the last half-century, however, foreign demand for American agricultural products was a source of strength only during wars and their aftermath—until the American government adopted a policy of ruthless dumping of farm surpluses in foreign markets.

The strong traditional export market for American cereals and livestock products showed unmistakable signs of weakening in the early years of the century. By 1910, except for cotton, tobacco, and fruit, sales of farm commodities abroad had fallen to the level of the 1880s. World War I brought about a reversal in this unfavorable trend, and in 1919 exports equaled one-fifth of our total farm production.

The experience of the 1920s was fairly good. Through 1928 agricultural sales abroad stayed at about $2 billion per annum, a dollar volume about equal to that of 1917. Unfortunately, sustained farm exports were made possible by the willingness of Americans to take the securities of foreigners in part payment for the goods sent them. Beginning in 1929 our people became fearful of making loans abroad, and this turn, accompanying as it did the gathering strains of world-wide depression, resulted in a severe decline of exports. For domestic agriculture the ominous fact of the 1930s was this: although the total volume of United States exports increased substantially with general recovery, agricultural exports rose only a little and then fell to a half-century low of about $500 million in 1940.

Inexorable historical forces had worked themselves out. As American agriculture developed in the first half of the nineteenth century, the United States exchanged farm products for the manufactured articles of Europe. Among the items received from Europe were machines and tools—capital goods that started the young country on its way to becoming an industrial producer. As the manufacturing output of the United States increased, fewer and fewer finished articles were needed from Europe; in fact, protective tariffs effectively kept out industrial goods. America after the Civil War began to export increasing amounts of manufactured goods, and agricultural exports, though increasing in dollar volume, constituted a smaller and smaller part of total sales to other countries. Until the twentieth century, however, Europeans continued to be very good customers of the American farmer because they had invested heavily in this country, and interest, dividends, and repayments of principal gave them dollar credits with which to buy in the United States. But U.S. failure to import manufactured goods in sufficient quantities gradually caused Europe to go elsewhere for agricultural products —to Canada, Argentina, Australia, New Zealand, and Russia. Furthermore, continental farmers were beginning to demand tariff protection for *their* products.

World War I reversed the trend, though in the long run the war had a harmful effect because European nationals divested themselves of American securities and their countries became indebted to the United States. American loans forestalled the evil day for a time, but we could not long continue to sell if we would not buy. And the strong European nationalism of the 1930s, with its emphasis on self-sufficiency, secured the final undoing of our old position as a chief supplier of foodstuffs to the old countries.

The enormous exports of agricultural products in the years following World War II were made possible by loans and gifts.[18] These exports slackened considerably with the recovery of European agriculture and declining relief programs. World agricultural output in 1953 was nearly equal to prewar, and foreign countries either needed fewer imports or could get

---

[18] At the peak of the foreign-aid program in 1948–49, 60 per cent of agricultural exports were financed by United States foreign-aid programs. In 1952 and 1953 only 15 per cent of farm exports were aid financed.

them cheaper from foreign competitors, despite the fact that American export prices were lower than domestic prices. But beginning in 1954, largely under Public Law 480, the United States began a massive subsidy of the export of many commodities in excess supply. Largely because of the subsidy, exports accounted for 15 per cent of cash receipts in 1962, over half of that year's wheat and rice output and one-third of cotton production being exported in that year.

Since 1953 commercial exports of farm products for dollars drifted upward from about $2,500 million to $3,500 million in 1962. But a substantial portion of these sales (about $1 billion in 1962) were "assisted"—i.e., were made at less than domestic prices through export bounties paid largely on wheat and cotton. An increasingly large amount of agricultural commodities have been sent abroad under different government programs. In 1962 $1,600 million worth were sold for foreign currencies or given away under P.L. 480 and the Act for International Development.

Essentially, then, there has been only slight improvement in agriculture's foreign-market position, for commercial exports for dollars, *without assistance,* have not increased enough since 1953 to alleviate the problem of domestic surpluses. What is more, since 1953 present and potential members of the European Economic Community have taken the greater part of farm exports sold for dollars without any subsidy. Common Market countries have now agreed on a common agricultural policy for certain of their major farm commodities, and this policy includes the use of variable import fees as well as a common tariff against agricultural products coming in from outside countries. Unless the United States can negotiate tariff and other trade concessions, agricultural exports to western Europe may face substantial reductions.

Farm Problems and Farm Programs

Up to this point we have treated agriculture as a whole and have been preoccupied with aggregate quantities. This method has the advantage of enabling us to see fundamental problems in broad perspective and get answers otherwise unobtainable. Yet we must not overlook certain developments *within* agriculture that are matters of concern to everyone interested in its welfare.

SPECIAL PROBLEMS

There are great differences among farm units with respect to wealth and income, and an intelligent social policy must take these differences into account. As long ago as 1945, 57 per cent of the farms in the United States produced 95 per cent of the value of all farm products sold. The 1959 Census of Agriculture revealed an astonishingly similar result: commercial farms with annual sales of $2,500 and over, 56 per cent of the total, accounted for 95 per cent of sales of farm products. But these figures do not tell the story

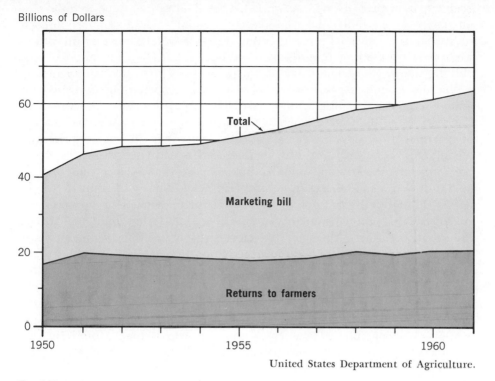

Billions of Dollars

Total

Marketing bill

Returns to farmers

60

40

20

0

1950　　　　　　　　　　1955　　　　　　　　　　1960

United States Department of Agriculture.

Food Outlays: Despite rising total expenditures by consumers on food, returns to farmers remain nearly stationary.

of recent resource shifts in agriculture. Since World War II, commercial farms with annual sales of $10,000 and over have produced an increasing share of the country's food and fiber, the output of 800,000 farms in this category being more than two-thirds of the total. On the other hand, out-migration from agriculture and reduction in number of farms has occurred largely in the categories of farms with annual sales of $2,500 and under. Between 1949 and 1959 the decline in the number of farms to 3,700,000 was almost entirely the consequence of a reduction from 2,700,000 to 1,600,000 in the number of farms with gross annual incomes under $2,500.

Despite the corrective forces at work to reduce the number of people on small farms, there continues to be a terrible problem of poverty for the two-fifths of farm families with a total money income of $2,500 or less. Some farm leaders and not a few agricultural economists dismiss the problem with the comment that low-income operators are part-time farmers. Nearly a million are, but many of them suffer privation, as do another million poor farmers who work full time to eke out a living from the soil. The problem of poverty in agriculture cannot easily be cast aside.

Consider for a moment the matter of land tenure. For generations it has been apparent that anyone who works on the land cannot hope to do as well financially as the individual who exerts an equal amount of effort in some industrial or commercial pursuit. It has always been felt, however, that there were certain offsetting rewards of a subjective but, nevertheless, real and abiding nature. Paramount among them has been the opportunity to own a piece of ground, a place of one's own. This compensation is denied the tenant farmer. Sometimes a tenant will be on his way to farm ownership, but more often than not tenancy is a sign of low income with small chance of eventual ownership. As early as 1880 25 per cent of our farmers were tenants—i.e., nonowners. By 1920 tenant farmers had risen to nearly 40 per cent, and in the early and middle thirties more than 42 per cent of farm operators were nonowners. In recent years conditions of tenure have improved substantially, and one of the most hopeful signs of progress in agriculture was the drop in tenancy by 1960 to slightly less than one-fifth of the country's farmers. Yet somewhat more than 40 per cent of operations in the major corn and wheat areas are carried on by tenants.[19]

Poverty is to be found wherever people make a living at farming, but certain areas stand out as trouble spots. One of these areas is the "one-hundredth meridian" states, which have in the past suffered acutely from unfavorable weather and are likely to experience bad weather again. The "cut-over" regions of the lake states and the Appalachian Mountains also contain many farm people who barely make a living. But the region where agricultural distress has been most severe is the South.

Present difficulties of southern agriculture have their roots in colonial days, but the method of freeing the slaves greatly increased the stresses. American emancipation was *landless* and *without compensation;* slaves were not given any land to till and owners were not reimbursed by society for their losses. With rare exceptions Negroes had nothing to contribute to the productive process but their unskilled services; landowners, when they lost their slaves, lost a great part of their investment. After the Civil War efforts were made to establish a wage system for Negro workers, but few planters succeeded in the endeavor. The newly freed Negro did not want to work in gangs under close supervision as he had done when a slave. The capital-poor landowners lacked funds to make wage payments and faced serious losses if committed to wage contracts in years of poor yields or low prices. The solution was some form of share tenancy. At best, the tenant owned his own mules and implements and became a "standing renter," paying a fixed amount of cotton or other crop at the end of the growing season. At worst, he furnished only his own labor, lived in a tenant house on the plantation, worked with the landowner's tools and animals, and shared the crop on a fifty-fifty basis. Under such an arrangement the tenant was a "cropper," dependent even for his supplies upon the local merchant. The more able

---

[19] Earl O. Heady, *Agricultural Policy Under Economic Development* (Ames: Iowa State University Press, 1962), p. 588.

and industrious Negroes, if fortunate enough to have honest landlords and merchants, came gradually to own their own land. But holdings were pitifully small and capital equipment was inadequate, to say the least. For most tenants, Negro and white, there was a kind of bondage only technically to be distinguished from serfdom.

Tenancy tied the South to cotton, for the traditional staple always had a more or less predictable market value, and landowners and merchants had to have some assurance that their advances would be repaid.[20] For seventy-five years after the Civil War southern industrial growth was painfully slow, and there was little opportunity for escape from the meager existence that farming afforded. The result was a tremendous pressure of population, both black and white, upon the land. By any standard of measurement, southern agriculture was inferior to that of the non-South before World War II, and even the remarkable gains of the last dozen years or so have not eradicated this paradox of poverty amidst the plenty of America. Three-fifths of southern farmers were tenants before the war, two-fifths of them were tenants afterward, and one-sixth of them were still croppers. Although the war effected a 25 per cent decline in the southern farm population, nearly half of the migrants came back again, and in the early 1950s southern farm families constituted approximately one-half of the farm population of the United States.[21] Despite the exodus of both Negroes and poor whites that went on during the ensuing decade, the South still had more than 1,600,000 of the nation's 3,700,000 farms, with relatively few farms in the large commercial categories. During the last twenty years there have been drastic reductions in cotton acreage, with encouraging trends toward mixed farming. But the average amount of crop land per farm is less than half the figure for the non-South, and there is one tractor to about every seven farms, compared with one for every two farms in the non-South. Only a good beginning has been made toward achieving adequately mechanized units of efficient size.

ECONOMIC EFFECTS OF FARM PROGRAMS

Technological improvement in agriculture has meant that food, feed, and fiber could be furnished in ever greater quantities to the nation and to the rest of the world. But along the way something has gone wrong. Since the Civil War there have been long periods in which agriculture has suffered from severe depression. Indeed, except for the years 1895–1920

---

[20] Consider the following statement. "Under post–Civil War conditions the production of cotton, with the use of the simplest agricultural implements and with the system of sharecropping cutting down to a minimum the necessity for capital by the man actually working the soil, afforded a means for embodying a large volume of labor in a staple product. This embodied labor could always be sold at some price without the necessity for the use of great ingenuity in developing demand or catering to it or in developing an intricate market mechanism." From Calvin B. Hoover and B. U. Ratchford, *Economic Resources and Policies of the South* (New York: Macmillan, 1951), p. 282.

[21] These figures include Oklahoma and Texas in the group of southern states.

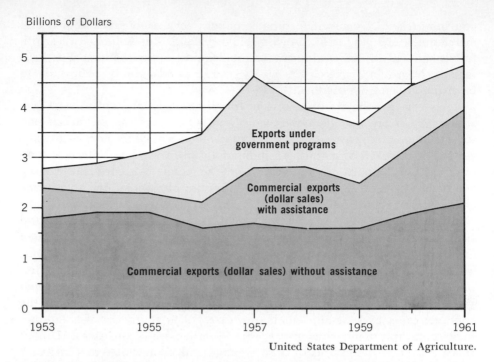

Billions of Dollars

Exports under
government programs

Commercial exports
(dollar sales)
with assistance

Commercial exports (dollar sales) without assistance

1953   1955   1957   1959   1961

United States Department of Agriculture.

Agricultural Exports: The growing role of government in promoting food shipments overseas has raised the importance of such programs to a point where
in 1961 they surpassed nonassisted shipments in dollar totals.

and 1941–52, only the most efficient producers have been able to operate at
a profit. Even in these good years the majority of people on farms have had
incomes far below the average for the United States.

We have seen how farmers and their representatives have asked for and
received help from their government. Unquestionably, the farm programs
have helped operators well down the income scale, but there is every reason
for believing that the lion's share of assistance has gone to those already
at the top of the heap. The biggest direct subsidies have gone to the biggest
producers; when acreage restrictions were put into effect, those in a position
to reduce acreage the most got the largest checks. As the government has
supported commodity prices, those with the most bushels or bales to sell
have received the chief benefits. Studies indicate that inequality of incomes
in agriculture is greater today than it was three decades ago. There has
been some recent improvement in the lot of the bottom half of the farm
population, but only because of the relief afforded by outmigration.

The facts, as we have observed them, show conclusively that a rapidly
expanding industry is essential to a healthy agriculture. Full employment
and rising incomes for workers in the nonfarm sector mean a strong and
increasing demand for food and fiber. But more than this, a greater number of

jobs in industry and commerce mean that those who cannot make an adequate living on the land will be able to earn a livelihood in the cities and towns. In a technically progressive economy, and certainly in one in which *agricultural* techniques are improving, the proportion of the total population gainfully employed in agriculture must continually fall. To put the matter another way, as man's knowledge and intelligence grow greater, fewer and fewer resources need be devoted to obtaining the necessaries of life and more and more resources may be devoted to obtaining conveniences and luxuries. This has been true in the economic history of the United States. In 1790, 90 per cent of the work force were employed in agriculture; in 1960 the figure was less than 10 per cent.[22] At its peak in 1916 the farm population was 32,500,000; in 1954 it stood at 19,000,000 and in 1961 was under 15,000,000, or 8.1 per cent of the population. Favorable as the exodus has been there are still far too many people in agriculture, especially in the South. It is not inconceivable that 2 per cent of the work force could produce all the farm products that the United States and a large part of the rest of the world could take at profitable prices. And *within* agriculture, fewer resources must be devoted to foods that merely keep body and soul together and more to those that are both nutritionally and gastronomically better.

If we accept the proposition that the fundamental cause of low incomes in agriculture lies in an excess of population on farms, it seems unwise to adopt a social policy that makes farming more attractive than it would be under a free pricing system. Insofar as past efforts at raising farm incomes have been successful, motives for moving from the land have been weakened. We have observed, however, that the benefits from both direct subsidies and price supports go largely to farmers in the best economic position. The people most likely to transfer out of agriculture are not, therefore, offered much inducement to stay. A decline in the farm population of more than 600,000 people in 1961 alone bears out this conclusion.

We may be sure that some kind of a federal farm program is going to be required for a long time. The question remains, is such interference with the price system wise or necessary? Farmers and economists have different, but not irreconcilable, answers.

In general, "commercial" farmers, represented by their organizations and by the farm bloc in Congress, continue to support federal legislation of the sort we have reviewed. They know perfectly well that acreage restrictions are of little avail over a period of years; for as soon as a farmer receives an acreage allotment he removes his poorest land from production, leaving his best acres in the restricted crop and cultivating the remaining land more intensively. They also know that price-support operations lead to the piling up of tremendous commodities stocks, which can be liquidated without lowering agricultural prices only in wartime—or by dumping them abroad. Responsible farm leaders are aware, too, that unfavorable press stories ac-

---

[22] Farm employment has dropped from 13,500,000 in 1910 to an average of 6,500,000 in 1962.

companying the accumulation of huge government-owned stocks of commodities excite public hostility to farm programs.

Yet a combination of acreage restrictions and CCC-type price supports has the unquestioned advantage of masking the amount and extent of the subsidy to agriculture. Although tying price and income maintenance to conservation is basically dishonest, the conservation idea dilutes the element of subsidy in the public mind. Moreover, Department of Agriculture outlays on the program, great as they are, do not include the higher prices paid by consumers for food and fiber as a consequence of support operations. Finally, since the subsidy is provided by a market mechanism, it seems respectable, whereas subsidy checks paid at the end of a growing season to make up an amount of income deemed necessary would seem too obvious to be tolerated. For these reasons farmers generally support proved methods of government subsidy. Within agriculture the only serious differences arising in recent years have been over the question of rigorous versus mild controls over output. The American Farm Bureau Federation, which speaks for the more affluent farmers, wants lower support prices and greater freedom to plant, for Farm Bureau membership makes huge profits on large volume. Supporting sharp restrictions on acreage combined with astronomic support prices are the small-farmer organizations, chiefly the National Farmers Union, the National Farmers Organization, and the National Grange.

Although farm organizations, with the exception of the Farm Bureau Federation, are satisfied with recent attempts to solve their problems, economists, generally speaking, are not. Many agricultural economists, definitely sympathetic to agriculture, feel that policies established over the last four decades may, in the long run, prevent a satisfactory solution to the farm problem. There has long been an objection to the ideal of "parity," partly on the ground that no group in society is entitled, by right, to a fixed portion of the real national income. But there is a stronger argument. Successful attempts to maintain prices of farm commodities in the same *relative* position over time may keep consumers from getting supplies of the things they want most. Parity prices tend to keep agricultural resources in the production of what people have wanted in the past. If some agricultural prices are not allowed to fall *relative* to others, the pattern of cultivation will remain too rigid, and the result will be chronic "surpluses" of some crops.

Although economists look with disfavor upon present types of agricultural subsidies, they agree that *some* kind of a federal farm program is necessary. Because of the nature of competition in agriculture, farmers are peculiarly vulnerable to the ups and downs of economic fluctuations. Once a farm family is established it becomes increasingly difficult to leave the farm, and there is substantial agreement that a legitimate aim of subsidy is to keep middle-aged farmers on the land until their retirement. Finally, nonagricultural firms react to falling demand in a way not open to farm units. Industrial firms restrict production, lay off a good part of their work force, and reduce prices only a little and reluctantly at that. Agriculture meets recession by maintaining output and letting prices fall, whereas industry maintains prices and lets output (and employment) fall. The way of agriculture is certainly better for consumers, but it is hard on farm people.[23] Incomes fall and the terms of exchange run badly. Furthermore, many who would otherwise migrate to the towns and cities stay on the farms; and some come back who have previously gone away, for there is at least enough to eat on the old home place. The net result is extremely low per-capita farm incomes.

Most economists agree, therefore, that a farm program directed toward combatting the evils of depression is necessary. It is one thing, however, to recommend measures that are primarily counter-cyclical in aim and an altogether different thing to advocate a permanent interference with the pricing system, to be operative in both good times and bad. A case can be made for braking the rate at which the family farm disappears and for subsidizing the training of the displaced rural poor for urban pursuits. But no one familiar with the facts of social life can advocate the artificial support of prices when a plan of compensatory payments could better maintain farm incomes at levels agreed on; for to the $5 billion annual cost of recent programs ($1 billion for storage alone) must be added higher consumer prices. Unfortunately, the recommendations of social scientists as to what public policy *ought* to be carry far less weight than the recommendations of a substantial number of voters.

Conservation of Natural Resources: The Second Stage

How we view the conservation movement depends, of course, upon our definition of the word conservation. Strictly speaking, to conserve is to preserve—to keep what one has without deterioration or decay. But conservation should mean something more than hoarding; it should refer to some "proper" allocation of resource use over time. A true conservation program *ought* to aim at checking the lessening of future productivity of a soil area, a stand of timber, a mineral deposit—or even a famed natural beauty spot. Moreover, to conserve a natural resource for *future* use it is usually necessary to make a *present* expenditure of capital and labor; it is not ordinarily enough that the resource be simply withdrawn from use.[24]

Some public expenditures of capital and labor, rationalized on the grounds that they are made in the interests of conservation, in fact amount to nothing more than an outlay to increase *present* production. The outlay

---

[23] Of course, unemployment is hard on the industrial worker, as we will consider later. Indeed one agricultural economist, Professor Peter Dorner, argues that farm-program costs and unemployment-compensation costs are incurred for precisely the same reason.

[24] For a more technical exposition of such matters see Earl O. Heady, "Soil-Conservation Programs," *Journal of Political Economy*, LIX, 1 (February 1951), 48 ff.

could be made now or a hundred years from now with no deterioration of the natural resource. Thus irrigation and drainage projects do not ordinarily prevent diminution of future production. Speaking generally, a piece of Arizona desert land can be irrigated at any time in the future and the resultant increase in production will be just as great as if the improvement were made now. *Reclamation is not the same thing as conservation.* Similarly, the application of fertilizers on level land may only increase short-run production and do nothing to prevent permanent soil deterioration.

Like any other economic problem, conservation implies choices. These choices may well be made by the private market system, as in the case of the mineral industries; the fact that the price system makes them does not mean that they are bad. On the other hand, if an expenditure is to be made for the purpose of increasing the income stream from a given resource, a complete calculation of benefits versus costs may require a consideration of "income" for which no private entrepreneur would pay anything. The conflict between development and nature preservation erupts because some values can be protected only through social action. Moreover, the problem of allocating resources for conservation objectives is simplified by considering the *natural* resource base as part of the *total* capital base of the economy. As Professor Milliman has remarked, ". . . natural resources are only part of the total stock of capital and . . . there is no a priori reason for believing that natural resource capital is any more productive than other types of capital. It is not the *origin* of capital that is important, man-made or natural, but rather its total amount and the relative productivity at the margin of alternative forms of capital." [25]

Between the administrations of Woodrow Wilson and Franklin Roosevelt the cause of conservation suffered under public management of resources. The first blow to enthusiasm for public measures came in the Presidency of Warren G. Harding. In 1915 President Wilson had set aside Naval Oil Reserve No. 3 in Wyoming. The reserve took the name of Teapot Dome from a butte located on it, and its supervision and that of the previously established California reserves were entrusted to the Secretary of the Navy. President Harding illegally transferred the administration of the reserves to Secretary of the Interior Albert B. Fall, a confirmed enemy of the conservation movement. Fall granted contracts to private oil companies, allowing them to take oil from the naval reserves to the point of exhaustion in exchange for the construction of storage tanks on both coasts. When the fraud became known, control of the oil reserves was restored to the Secretary of the Navy, but "Teapot Dome" became a rallying cry for those who wished to oppose government ownership and control of resources.

The reaction away from federal conservation that set in during the early twenties was not lessened under Herbert Hoover. Both the President and

---

[25] J. W. Milliman, "Can People Be Trusted with Natural Resources?" *Land Economics*, XXXVIII, 3 (August 1962), 201.

Conservation and the careful nurture of fields, here demonstrated in McClain County, Oklahoma, have also added to farm productivity, hence unwittingly exacerbated the farm problem.

his Secretary of the Interior, Ray Lyman Wilbur, came out flatly for the transfer to the western states of all unappropriated and unserved lands. A commission, appointed by President Hoover to make recommendations regarding future land policy, supported the proposal of cession to the states of the remaining public domain. But even Westerners, including the powerful livestock interests, were in opposition to the idea, and Congress refused to enact a bill containing the commission's recommendations.

The Forest Service did move forward during the 1920s. The policy was to cut and sell only ripe timber from the national forests. Efforts were made to introduce the most up-to-date methods of cutting and planting so that a substantial future supply would be assured. There was a remarkable improvement of the administration of the range lands within the national forests. Essentially, though, nothing new had been added to the conservation ideal since the days of Theodore Roosevelt.

There was an upward surge of the movement under the administrations of Franklin Roosevelt. Old methods were carried out with renewed vigor, and two innovations marked a new approach. First, the government took steps to conserve the soil owned by *private* individuals. Second, it was insisted that a meaningful program of conservation required the simultaneous protection of many resources within an entire region.

Along the lines of traditional policy, perhaps the most important step was the withdrawal of the remaining public domain—nearly 175,000,000 acres—until the land could be classified as to its best use. A small portion was later made available for private entry, but most of it was organized into grazing districts under the Taylor Grazing Act of 1934. Before the passage of this act stockmen let their animals feed on the great public ranges without restraint. Under the new system permits were issued to allow the grazing of a certain number of animals, the object being to restrict the number to what a given range could carry without depleting the forage. By 1950 there were fifty-nine grazing districts that included 145,000,000 acres, and in addition grazing leases were issued on scattered public domain lands and on Indian reservations. A generation after passage of the original act controversy smolders over proper disposition of these lands. There is a growing opinion that the federal government ought to reserve those areas classified as suitable for recreation, national forests, wildlife refuges, and reclamation and power projects, selling the rest to the highest bidders.

Much antidepression expenditure by the government went into conservation work. Late in 1933 Harold Ickes could remark, with truth, that the young men of the Civilian Conservation Corps had accomplished more reforestation in six months than all the federal agencies had in the preceding fifteen years. More important, funds were obtained to expand the national forests by purchasing poorly kept private forest lands, located for the most part in the Southeast. By 1950 national forest acreage was up to 180,000,000, and the government controlled in addition forested land of some 200,000,000 acres in Indian reservations, wildlife refuges, national parks, and other public holdings. By no means all of this land contained first-rate timber.

About 116,000,000 acres, or one-fourth of the United States total, was publicly owned commercial forest land divided between federal agencies, which managed 89,000,000 acres, and state and local agencies, which controlled 27,000,000 acres. The very best timber owned by the federal government is located in the West, far from markets and in inaccessible areas, and investment in roads will be necessary before it can be used. But much of the present noncommercial forest owned by the government will one day become merchantable—far sooner than it would have in private hands.

Old-line conservation efforts included some incidental preservation of the soil. It was not until New Deal days, however, that serious efforts were made at systematic conservation of agricultural land. These efforts started with the Soil Erosion Service, set up in 1933 in the Department of the Interior. In 1935 the Soil Conservation Service was established as an agency of the Department of Agriculture. Originally, contracts were made with individual farmers, the Service furnishing technical assistance and some materials, the farmers furnishing labor and the rest of the materials. Early in 1937 President Roosevelt wrote the governors of the states requesting that legislatures pass enabling acts to permit landowners and occupiers to form soil conservation districts. A model state law was enclosed which the states followed rather closely. By May 1947, all the states, as well as Hawaii, Alaska, Puerto Rico, and the Virgin Islands, had passed laws permitting the establishment of soil conservation districts when approved by a vote of the farmers within a proposed area. In 1954 about 2,500 soil conservation districts, including 80 per cent of all farms, had been organized.

A conservation district has a governing board, the members of which are called supervisors, commissioners, or directors. The board coordinates activities within a district and may give priority to critical areas. It receives applications for assistance and serves as an intermediary between the individual farmer and the Soil Conservation Service. When a farmer's application is approved by the board, a technician from SCS works with the farmer to make a comprehensive plan of conservation. A co-operative agreement, stating what the individual intends to do and what help the district will supply, is then drawn up; the only signatories are the farmer and the board. There is no coercion and there are no penalties for noncompliance. If a farmer does not do his part, he is simply dropped from the list of those receiving assistance.

The Soil Conservation Service operates, then, on the premise that what the individual needs most is "know-how." Another federal agency takes a different approach. The Production and Marketing Administration, through its Agricultural Conservation Programs Branch, assumes that what is needed to secure proper practices is financial assistance. From 1936 to 1943 the payments of this agency were disguised income subsidies. Since 1944, however, the major objective has been to encourage farmers to carry out "conservation" practices by furnishing them materials such as lime, or by making money payments that must be spent for certain approved projects. PMA outlays, although considered as conservation expenditures, often do no more than increase short-term productivity.

Any discussion of new notions of conservation must contain some mention of what may constitute the ultimate solution to the whole problem—the inclusion of major valleys in programs of great scope. There are those who argue that nothing less can bring permanently successful conservation. The evidence is not conclusive, although the Tennessee Valley Authority (map, p. 468)—one outstanding example—has unquestionably done a remarkable job of upgrading the agriculture of an entire region. Two judgments about TVA may be safely made. First, major floods are a thing of the past in the Tennessee Valley; this means that much bottom land is protected

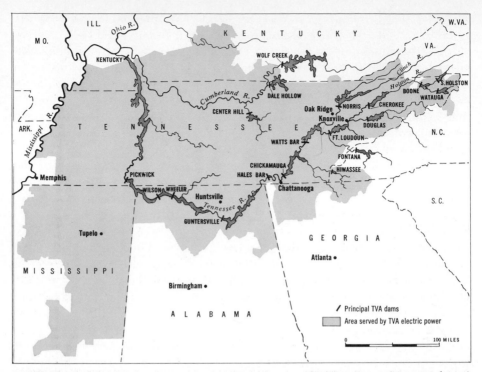

Public Power: The Tennessee Valley Authority, the New Deal's major experiment in publicly financed power, ranges through parts of six states. Its admirers call it a splendid monument to "regional planning," while its foes say it is a noxious example of "creeping socialism."

from periodic dumping of erosion debris.[26] Second, TVA has done much to prevent upland erosion. Although a unified system of dams and reservoirs can prevent *major* floods with their consequent destruction of bottom land, the problem of erosion on the uplands remains. Silting from uplands is the enemy of the reservoirs and the navigable channel; it must be stopped at the source, where the raindrop strikes the ground. Thus TVA authorities have had no choice but to work hard at securing general adoption of con-servation practices. Their program includes reforestation and afforestation, substitution of cover crops for row crops, contour plowing, and the building of check dams to prevent rapid runoff. Technical assistance and demon-stration, in co-operation with other federal agencies and with state univer-sities, has been the chief help to the landowner, but free seedlings and free fertilizer have frequently swung the balance in securing co-operation.

Rapid changes in technology, improvements in transportation, and the discovery of new mineral deposits at home and abroad have made much

---

[26] Such dumping can be devastating. The old farm of my grandparents, flooded by the Kansas River, is a complete loss, with as much as 30 feet of sand covering what was once highly productive land.

of the old conservation argument seem trivial. Yet the type of conservation originally espoused by Theodore Roosevelt and Gifford Pinchot still has its ardent proponents. For a time after World War II it appeared that there might be a resurgence of the old-time, almost religious enthusiasm for conservation, because people were concerned about the rapid depletion of mineral and timber resources that had occurred during the war. But political conservatives are more often than not opposed to conservation practices for the reason that such practices imply interference by government with private business.

With the return to office of the Republicans in 1952, the country witnessed a trend away from traditional conservation methods. In May 1953, Secretary of the Interior Douglas McKay announced that he was relinquishing the best hydroelectric site remaining on the continent—Hell's Canyon—to the Idaho Power Company, a private utility. There have been other proposals calculated to raise the ire of people interested in preserving natural resources. For example, Senator Cordon of Oregon sponsored a timber-exchange bill that would have allowed large lumber companies to take over choice acreage inside the National Forests. Another bill proposed to convert into vested rights the permissive status of stockmen whose animals graze on the public ranges. The act giving four coastal states—Texas, California, Louisiana, and Florida—the off-shore oil reserves was considered by many an anticonservation measure. The changing political climate will doubtless result in future swings in attitudes toward conservation. Hopefully, the electorate will accept the advice of a growing corps of experts specializing in resource problems.

This new breed of conservationist bases its thinking on the proposition, well documented by the massive study of Resources for the Future, that the United States is not "running out" of natural resources. For the next three or four decades the most pressing problem is likely to be that of providing standing room, including recreation areas, for a population that is (a) growing rapidly and (b) increasing its per-capita demand for outdoor recreation. Rivaling this problem in urgency are others brought on by population pressure—protection of air and streams from pollution and preserving wildlife and open spaces. But although some products will increase in cost and diminish in quality because of reduction in ore deposits and oil reserves, substitute products and changed technology will provide fairly smooth adjustments. We approach the future one day at a time and can prepare for such extreme scarcities as they finally emerge.

There will certainly be enough cropland and to spare for another half-century, though prudence suggests the maintenance of a soil area sufficient to meet possible explosive demands in the distant future. If we have limited funds to spend on conservation, they must be used to conserve and not simply to raise short-run productivity. SCS expenditures have generally met this test better than PMA expenditures, but both agencies have been guilty of forgetting that their objective is long run. Expenditures for irrigation, drainage, better rotations on level land, and the like, cannot be justified under a conservation program unless these practices do save the soil. And there is a further point to be considered. Everyone knows that soils in different geographical areas vary greatly in quality. With limited funds, it will be better, from society's point of view, to give priority to the conservation of the better soils.[27] This sounds like hard doctrine, and it is. The execution of such a policy is fraught with political difficulties, for it is easy to point out that the farmer who owns poor land needs assistance more than the farmer who owns good land. Recent conservation policy has, in fact, tended to neglect such realistic considerations.

Technical advances have made possible the reclamation of arid land that was at one time considered certain waste. Only water is needed to transform the desert. Pumps driven by 65,000 horsepower motors have been installed at Grand Coulee Dam for the purpose of lifting water 280 feet from the Columbia River into the Coulee, whence it can be diverted to irrigate vast areas. By means of complex systems of dams, reservoirs, pumps, and tunnels, the water from one river basin where there is an excess can be diverted into another river basin where there is a deficiency. The Bureau of Reclamation estimates that eventually 50,000,000 acres of extremely fertile land can be brought into production west of the Rockies. Such developments lead us to ask whether the whole problem of soil conservation should not be closely related to reclamation (i.e., soil-development) programs. Might it not be possible to increase future output more by a given investment in, say, irrigation than by the same investment in the prevention of soil erosion? The answer to these questions is that to be on the *safe* side we should decide to preserve rather than develop. If soil is allowed to erode away, it is gone forever. A compromise is suggested by the possibility of assuring "stand-by" production capacity. Marginal land in quantity could be withdrawn from production and seeded down, to be returned to use only in the case that a great population growth should one day make such a step necessary.[28]

At the moment the pressing social problem is one of getting resources *out* of agriculture. Events of the last century and a half incline us to the judgment that this will continue to be the problem requiring solution. It is all right to dream dreams about the opening of a new West. It is all right to help farmers save their land, provided it is worth saving. But until such a time as it is no longer necessary to spend annually great sums of money to support farm prices, it behooves us to consider the interrelated matters of farm production, conservation, and reclamation with a minimum of sentimentality and a maximum of cold calculation.

---

[27] There are apparent exceptions to this generalization. For example, it may be necessary to stop erosion of hopeless upland areas in order to prevent the carrying of, say, sand into lowland areas where it can be deposited on highly productive land. But of course the object in such a case is to save the better and not the worse soil.
[28] See Heady, pp. 55–57.

Government in the Transportation Business

A wanderer is man from his birth.
He was born in a ship
On the breast of the river of Time.
Brimming with wonder and joy
He spreads out his arms to the light,
Rivets his gaze on the banks of the stream.

MATTHEW ARNOLD

The title of this chapter was not chosen carelessly. Most companies within the several transportation industries of the United States are privately owned by individuals who receive profits and presumably stand losses. Yet for reasons to be examined the federal government has intruded itself into the transportation business. Americans have generously voted tax monies to build facilities for all the new and one of the old transportation industries. And the regulatory function, undertaken at the national level in 1887, has expanded to such an extent that no firm can make a major decision to invest or disinvest without the approval of a regulatory agency.

After reading this chapter, the student may conclude that government subsidy of agriculture has been a small operation compared with the subsidy of transportation. This interference with private enterprise is the result of the most remarkable feature of recent transportation history—rapid change from older to newer forms. As each new transportation form proved itself, Americans were eager to benefit from it. But under the market system resources would have been directed only to geographical areas where they gave promise of earning at least the going rate of return, and less favored areas would have been ignored. So government subsidy was required. In an age of increasing speed, the town, city, or state with access only to inferior—i.e., older—transportation facilities pressed for improvements and contributed funds to stay abreast of the economic competition. National considerations also led to strong Congressional support for investment at the federal level. Canals, then railroads, and finally highways, airways, and natural waterways have therefore received subsidies from the national government. Subsidy of the different industries has been granted without much regard for interindustry competition and with little consideration for the balance of the system as a whole.

Canals were rapidly falling into disuse before the outbreak of World War I. Almost everywhere, except on the upper Ohio and the Great Lakes, traffic on the natural waterways was dwindling. The electric street railway showed unmistakable signs of decay before 1920, as did the foreign merchant marine until wartime activity revived it. Until the end of World War I railroads were the dominant means of transportation; yet, as we look back, we can see that by nearly every test the industry had reached maturity.

Since 1920 the shift from rail to highway has loomed above all others in importance. Trucks and buses have taken business away from the railroads, trucks especially having hurt the railroads by winning the short-haul, high-grade traffic. The airlines began to compete with the railroads for passenger traffic in 1930 and by 1940 were capturing much of the long-distance, first-class passenger business of the railroads. Between the two World Wars the foreign merchant marine once again shrank, while the coastwise trade and the Great Lakes bulk traffic went on expanding.

World War II reversed the fortunes of both the railroads and the foreign merchant marine. Gasoline and rubber shortages enabled the railroads to win back passenger and freight traffic that seemed irrevocably lost to both truck lines and automobiles. The foreign merchant marine was suddenly stimulated, while coastwise shipping was reduced by the submarine menace. Airlines, despite the difficulties of adding to their fleets, continued their prewar growth, and technological advances of military aviation promised a golden future when equipment should become available. Although the older forms of transportation were given a new lease on life and achieved record high volumes of traffic, it was apparent that after the war the automobile and the airplane would again be serious and even damaging competitors.

The Federal Government and New Forms of Transportation

THE HIGHWAYS

For financial rather than technical reasons progress in highway building long lagged behind progress in vehicle manufacture. Thus, the early use

There is hardly room for houses, so extensive grow the demands of superhighway cloverleafs, as demonstrated by this interchange near Corona, Long Island, New York. Such improvements have revolutionized the inventory policies of some companies by making truck transportation rapid and dependable.

of cars and trucks was limited pretty much to city streets because of inadequate interurban roads. During World War I the private motor car ceased to be used exclusively for visiting around town and for sport, the omnibus appeared on city streets, and motor trucks replaced horse-drawn drays. Intercity bus travel and intercity motor-truck transport were not important until the 1920s.

Until the advent of the automobile, responsibility for roads belonged to local governments. During the first fifteen years of the century, states became aware of the need for supervision and coordination of the old road districts and the somewhat more modern county systems. Yet only a few states were financially able to provide a basic statewide net, let alone make adequate provision for the country roads. And there remained the problem of an interstate system. Clearly some kind of federal program was necessary.

The movement for good roads received a push from many groups. One group was the auto clubs. The first automobile show was held in 1900 in the old Madison Square Garden, and it was not long before social clubs, such as the American Automobile Club of New York and the Automobile Club of Southern California, were formed.[1] When in 1902 the local clubs federated to form the American Automobile Club, auto enthusiasts could speak with a loud voice. They were soon joined in their demands by the American Road Builders Association and its lobby and by the American Association of State Highway officials. Between 1910 and 1915 national conventions and congresses met at length to urge an integrated interstate highway system. Promoters set up booster organizations in towns along the route of the proposed coast-to-coast Lincoln Highway. But it was the farmers who pressed hardest to get out of the mud, and legislators with heavily rural constituencies, Representative Shackleford of Missouri and Senator Bankhead of Alabama, piloted the first federal legislation through Congress.

With the passage of the Federal Aid Road Act of 1916 the United States began in halting, timorous fashion to hasten the development of a national highway system. The government committed itself to spend $75 million for the building of rural post roads, the money to be spent by the Department of Agriculture over a period of five years. The national contribution was not to exceed 50 per cent of total construction cost, exclusive of bridges and other major structures, and was conditional upon the organization of state highway departments with adequate personnel authority and sufficient equipment for initial work and subsequent maintenance. The Federal Highway Act of 1921 amended the original law by requiring that the Secretary of Agriculture, in dispensing aid, give preference to states that had designated a system of highways to receive federal aid. A designated state system was to constitute the "primary" roads of the state and was not to exceed 7 per cent of the state's total highway mileage. Incidentally, Congress in the act of 1921 appropriated as much money for a single year's construction (1922) as it had for all of the preceding five.

Despite the good start more than a decade of frustration was to meet the efforts of those who had seen the light and had carried the fight for better roads. State legislative appropriations were sporadic and uneven. The traveler of the 1920s often found a smooth strip of concrete ending suddenly in a sea of mud or terminating at a stream for want of a ferry or a bridge. Within the states the most densely populated areas naturally tended to get the "primary" road designations and consequently the good roads. In the great agricultural midlands highways remained unbelievably bad as late as the early 1930s. In Kansas, for example, long after the cities of Kansas City, Topeka, and Wichita were connected by a concrete slab, travelers along the old Pike's Peak, Ocean-to-Ocean Highway, designated U.S. Highway 36, were

---

[1] F. L. Paxon, "The Highway Movement, 1916–1935," *American Historical Review*, LI (1946), 236–53.

frequently stranded. The dirt roads of Kansas still connected with Nebraska's major highways, then topped with a magnificent layer of gravel, and the county and township roads had not been noticeably improved for 50 years. Under such conditions a trip of only a few miles could not be undertaken until the weather was certain.

One blessing of the depression was the impetus given road programs by relief and recovery agencies. Roads properly came in for a good share of public expenditures undertaken to escape economic doldrums. Before 1932, federal funds had not amounted to as much as 10 per cent of total revenues for highways. In 1932 they rose to 30 per cent and shot up the next year to over 40 per cent. Not until the war came on did federal participation drop in percentage to predepression levels. Meanwhile, the concept of federal aid had expanded. After 1933 "secondary" roads—i.e., roads outside the basic 7 per cent—were included in the assistance program, and money was authorized for improving parts of highways that ran through cities and for grade-crossing elimination.

During the war years proper highway maintenance was not possible, and some major routes deteriorated rapidly. In anticipation of a rebuilding program Congress passed the Federal-Aid Highway Act of 1944, making $1,500 million available for expenditure in the three fiscal years following the end of the war. The law provided for the designation of an interstate highway system of not over 40,000 miles, this system to receive the largest single part of the appropriated funds. Secondary and feeder routes, including farm-to-market roads, came in for specific appropriations. Recognizing the seriousness of the growing congestion in urban areas, the law set aside monies for use exclusively on those segments of the basic interstate system lying within the limits of cities of 5,000 or more. The 1944 act also appropriated funds for federal roads within national parks, national forests, public lands, and Indian reservations.

In 1956 Congress authorized the Interstate and Defense Highway System. Designed to provide some 41,000 miles of limited-access, multi-lane mileage connecting the principal centers of the United States, the project was scheduled for completion in thirteen years and estimated to cost $27 billion; subsequently the period of completion was extended and the total cost re-estimated at $41 billion. By 1963 approximately one-third of the total project was finished. Financing of the interstate system was on the familiar grant-in-aid basis, with the federal government putting up 90 per cent of the money and the states 10 per cent.[2] Additional excise taxes on petroleum products, tires, and trucks were to go into a highway trust fund to finance the new system on a pay-as-you-go basis, grumblingly called a "paid-before-you-go" basis by critics.

---

[2] States barring advertising within six hundred feet of the right of way qualified for an extra federal grant of one half of 1 per cent.

Fast air travel between cities has made airports more dependent on long runways and nearby residents newly aware of the screech of a four-engine jet. Drastically shortened travel time has greatly increased the productivity of business and professional men and has changed the character of many service trades as well.

AIRWAYS AND AIRPORTS

Before 1920 the airplane had practically no economic significance. For more than a decade after the first flight of a heavier-than-air craft in 1903, the new machines were the playthings of eccentric sportsmen and scientists. World War I gave impetus to the development of engines and structures, but major improvements lay in the future. In 1918 a military airplane was used for a commercial purpose when the Post Office Department and the War Department jointly sponsored an airmail route between Washington and New York. The project was soon dropped, but in the early twenties the Post Office established airmail service between major points. When it appeared that airmail was practical, Congress in 1925 ordered all contracts let to privately owned airlines. The Air Commerce Act of 1926 marked the first federal attempt to promote civil aviation. A civil airways system was provided for, along with funds to improve navigation facilities. Meantime, sensational long-distance flights, financed by rich men, caught the public imagination, furnishing evidence of the great future of commercial aviation.

The government of the United States was expected to assist this infant industry. The first direct contribution of the federal government, aside from subsidies granted through airmail payments, was the establishment of marked routes, equipped at first with beacon lights, then with radio markers and radio range beacons. With the growth of private airline companies, route mileage rose from less than 2,000 miles in 1926 to 22,000 miles in 1935, when plans for modernization and improvement of the airways were drawn up to improve airline safety. In 1949 there were 57,000 miles of federally owned air routes operating in the United States and its territories; by 1960 this figure had soared to 220,000. The system, largely made up of "VHF" airways and "superskyways" above the 17,000-foot level, was equipped with navigational aids, instrumental approach systems, air-route traffic-control centers, an extensive weather-reporting service, and traffic control towers at major airports. From 1925 to 1961 expenditures of the government on construction, maintenance, and operation of airways were approximately $3 billion. These contributions to the airways system were made without any kind of recovery from the users of the system.

Long after the beginning of commercial aviation in 1926 the federal government felt no responsibility for airport construction except for the provision of emergency landing fields, considered part of the airways system. Until 1933, airports were built as private business ventures or as projects of municipalities wishing to grasp the opportunities of a coming air age. Municipal financial troubles accompanying the depression made investment in such long-range projects progressively more difficult, and the federal government then began to participate in such ventures as a part of the relief program. Between 1933 and 1940 the federal government contributed just over 70 per cent of the funds for airport construction, and municipalities furnished most of the rest. Because the main object of expenditure was unemployment relief, no comprehensive plan of location and design was followed, and much building was wasted. In 1940 Congress provided for a systematic extension of airport facilities, but before it could go into effect the war intervened. During the war years practically all activity was carried on at the federal level, military objectives being primary in all decisions to invest. The result was that by the end of World War II the government had provided about three-fourths of the money for all airport construction.

The 1946 Federal Airport Act attempted to put order and consistent long-range planning into airport construction. Seventy-five per cent of available funds were to be apportioned among the states on a basis of population and area; the remainder was to constitute a discretionary fund. Federal participation in small airports was set at 50 per cent of construction costs, not counting land acquisition; in large airports participation might be less than 50 per cent. Applications for federal aid could be made by any public agency at a local level, but to obtain approval projects had to be included in the current National Airport Plan of the Civil Aeronautics Administrator. The 1946 Act worked well through the 1950s, though the Eisenhower administration tried in 1958 to prevent its extension beyond June 30, 1959. But Congress did not concur in the view that the government should ". . . begin an orderly withdrawal from the airport grant program," and continued federal aid into the early 1960s.

As late as 1940, most airports did not earn revenues sufficient to meet operating expenses, let alone capital costs. With the great increase in air passenger traffic in wartime and postwar years, users more nearly paid their share of airport expenses, and nearly all major air terminals, properly managed, began to cover costs of maintenance and operation, with a few covering *all* their costs from rental payments, landing fees, aviation fuel sales, and restaurant and other concessions. Airports in small cities often failed to cover operating expenses. Yet the requirements of a national system of air transport required federal planning of minimum facilities, and the government got something else for its subsidy—free use of airports by military aircraft and space for air traffic control and weather observers.

Federal Regulation of Transportation

THE RAILROADS

Federal regulation of the transportation industries began with the railroads and has acquired there a complexity not found in water, air, or highway transportation. Before 1920 the chief emphasis was on protecting the public from discriminatory railroad rates. After 1920 the competition of trucks and automobiles brought a complete turnabout in the objectives of government control; since then the railroads, not the public, obtained the protection of the regulatory authority.

The great debate after World War I over the return of the railroads to private ownership made it clear that adjustments in the financial structure of railroads would be required if a large number of companies were to survive. Even before competing industries made their inroads on rail traffic, the railroad industry was in poor financial health, and many companies, large and small, were in desperate circumstances. Inept and sometimes fraudulent managements had settled large funded, interest-earning debts on many roads; and restrictive rate-setting by the Interstate Commerce Commission often kept companies from getting legitimate rate increases. In 1920, when the return of the railroads to their owners was imminent, additional financial problems appeared: the government had to be reimbursed for improvements to the railroads made during government seizure; funds had to be raised for modernization; and money had to be found to bring together scattered employees and equipment.

The Transportation Act of 1920 was an heroic effort to solve both transitional and long-run problems. The act guaranteed for six months after return to private operation a net income equal to that of the best six-month period under federal control. The carriers were permitted to fund at 6 per cent interest the debt owed for improvements made by the government. For loans with maturities up to fifteen years, $300 million was provided, and financial help was made available to short lines that had been especially hurt by wartime losses of traffic volume. It was felt that

Still accounting for more intercity freight traffic than any other mode of transportation in the early 1960s was the railroad, here shown taking advantage of one of the great postwar technological innovations, "piggybacking" of long-distance truck cargoes.

if the railroads were given this much assistance in the transition period, permanent policy decisions regarding rates and consolidation of companies into systems could be made to produce a sound, healthy industry.

Section 15a of the act laid out for the Interstate Commerce Commission a rule of rate-making. The Commission was instructed to set such rates as would enable the railroads, as a whole or in certain groups, to earn ". . . under honest, efficient and economical management a fair return upon the aggregate value of the railway property." The rule, we note, applied to the railroads as a whole or in groups, not to individual carriers. A perplexing problem therefore arose. Some roads were high-cost carriers and others were low-cost carriers. A rate that would yield a handsome profit to one road might net a loss to another, and there was no guarantee that the government would make up deficits. Also, different rates for the same class of service would remove some lines from competition or discriminate unfairly against certain users of the service. What was to be done?

The answer was given in the "recapture clause" of the act, which required that one-half the earnings of any railroad in excess of a fair return on the fair value of its property should be paid to the Interstate Commerce Commission. These earnings were to be placed in a contingent fund from which loans could be made to weak lines for capital expenditures or to refund maturing obligations. Carriers fortunate enough to earn more than the allowed rate of return were to retain the other half of the excess in a reserve fund from which they could pay interest, dividends, and rentals in bad years.

Another provision of the act reversed a previously settled policy toward pooling agreements, devices (discussed previously) for splitting either traffic or profits among colluding companies in some predetermined way. Long considered a monopolistic practice, pooling was henceforth not regarded as restrictive of competition if in the "public interest" and carried on under ICC regulation. Legalization of the practice reflected Congressional feeling that highway competition would effectively protect the consumer from monopolistic restrictions of the railroads.

The guide to rate-making, the recapture clause, and permissive pooling were more than transitional measures, yet they were not considered final solutions. To achieve effective control of the entire railroad industry the Commission was granted authority to consolidate roads into systems and to control the rate of investment and disinvestment. Great hopes were placed in the consolidation idea. The Commission was instructed to work out a plan whereby each individual line would be assigned to a system, and each system was to be set up so that a uniform rate scale would yield approximately the same return on the fair value of the property. After the system plans were established, hearings were to be held at which stockholders and shippers could express their views. The ICC was then to publish a final plan and assist in proposed consolidations. Any two companies could combine properties, provided that the merger was in accordance with the master plan and was agreeable to the stockholders and to the Commission.

The grandiose consolidation scheme was supported by provisions giving the Commission "exclusive and plenary" jurisdiction over the issuance of railroad securities. To this financial power was added absolute control over abandonments; after 1920 no railroad line could cease operation without permission of the ICC. Furthermore, the Commission could require the construction of new lines where traffic justified extensions and could compel the owner of a terminal to allow the use of the facility to another carrier upon payment of just compensation.

After 1920, passenger business began to decline. Freight revenues held up well during the general prosperity of the twenties; even so the financial position of the roads as a whole was not good. In only one year was the "fair-return" standard of 5.5 per cent on the "fair value" of properties actually reached by the railroads as a whole. With the onset of depression in 1929 the financial position of all the companies deteriorated rapidly. By 1931, railroad managements were demanding rate increases, just when shippers could least afford them and when competing agencies were striving desperately to take away business. The Commission could give only a little relief. With 60 per cent of their total capitalization in bonds, on which interest was payable regardless of earnings, the railroads were in a critical position. Many were saved from outright collapse only by loans from the Reconstruction Finance Corporation. Deficits of 1932 and failure to recover in the first half of the next year led to the Emergency Transportation Act of 1933.

The emergency act contained two parts. One was designed to relieve the railroads of immediate financial pressure; the other made important amendments to the Interstate Commerce Act. The emergency provisions tried to promote co-operation among the lines through three large regional committees to be guided by a Federal Coordinator of Transportation. Joint use of facilities, elimination of "wasteful competitive practices," and financial reorganizations to reduce fixed charges were suggested as necessary economy measures, but in the years of severe strain not even temporary relief was secured by these means.

Changes in the Interstate Commerce Act marked the passing of two cherished notions. The 1920 rule of rate-making was abandoned. Instead of fixing rates on the old "fair-return" standard, which had proved so difficult and expensive of enforcement, the Commission was directed to consider the need of the carriers for revenues sufficient to provide an adequate transportation service. Further, the highly controversial "recapture" clause was repealed. Railroads with high earnings had all along resisted efforts to take away their excesses over a "fair-return" standard, and weak roads that needed loans from recaptured funds could not meet the stringent mortgage requirements. No one argued to retain this foolish law.

Tenaciously, the 1933 act held to the idea of consolidation, which by then had lost its universal appeal. The combination of both strong and weak roads to form large systems was resisted, for obvious reasons, by the stockholders of the money-making lines. Labor feared consolidations because they meant a reduction in jobs. Shippers believed consolidations would result in higher rates. Yet those who dealt with the problem of financial deterioration of the roads could cling only to this one hope. They felt that failure to accept the ICC's final plan of consolidation, published in 1929, could be partially explained by technical difficulties in the way of bringing properties together. With the removal of these difficulties by the 1933 legislation, it was hoped that consolidation would begin in earnest.

The severity and length of the depression in railroading was bewildering. Ton-miles of freight and passenger-miles fell proportionately more than those of competing transportation forms. What was worse, recovery in the railroad industry lagged far behind the rest of the economy. In 1936, net income was about 1 per cent of capital, and the recession of 1937–38 brought another bad deficit in the latter year. In 1938, roads controlling one-third of total mileage were in receivership, and only the threat of war in Europe brought enough business to keep many lines out of bankruptcy. The chief source of difficulty was the depression, which bore heavily on industries furnishing the greater part of revenue-yielding traffic. Yet the failure of the railroads to respond to the general improvement must be laid to other causes. Competition from the trucking industry and the private automobile had produced a deadly effect, as had competition from pipelines and water carriers. Coal, the principal commodity carried by the railroads, was losing out to other energy sources, and shipments of building materials, also an important source of revenue, did not recover to predepression levels. The decline of foreign trade eliminated much long-haul business from the interior to the coasts. And heavy, long-term indebtedness precluded substantial cost reductions through the purchase of efficient, modern equipment.

The railroads were buoyed by World War II; to the credit of the railroad industry it must be said that the handling of traffic was as admirable as it had been sorry during World War I. Facilities for handling traffic were about the same. Cars and locomotives were fewer in number, but their capacity was greater; railroad mileage was less in 1941 than it was in 1916, but there were more sidings and more double track. The roads were helped by the fact that traffic did not all flow to one coast, by much more commodious port facilities, and by the efficient use of equipment through the car service division of the American Association of Railroads. An incentive to co-operative effort was the fearsome specter of immediate and probably permanent nationalization of the roads in the event of a breakdown comparable to that of World War I. Finally, the Office of Defense Transportation, headed by Joseph B. Eastman, did a masterful job of coordinating the entire effort. The expeditious handling of a volume of traffic about twice that of World War I stood as a first-class achievement.

Yet only a little while after the war it became apparent that the railroads were in serious, continuing trouble. The Korean War slowed the decline in percentage of freight and passenger traffic carried, but the downward trend continued on into the early 1960s. From two-thirds of intercity freight traffic in 1946, the roads slid to little more than two-fifths in 1961; passenger traffic in the meantime dropped from just under 20 per cent to less than 3 per cent of passenger-miles. In 1961 the industry earned a minuscule 1.9 per cent on its total investment of $27 billion, and railroad employment on Class I lines was only 664,000, less than one-third of the total employed in 1921.

The railroad industry's difficulties were readily attributable to a relative and even absolute fall in demand for railroad services in a period of almost uninterrupted growth in business generally. But why this catastrophic drop in demand? In part it resulted from continued erosion of the bulk-commodity traffic, the bread-and-butter stuff the railroads have always carried with an "inherent advantage." Much of the coal business, for example, disappeared as transmission of electricity over long-distance, high-voltage lines made it possible to burn coal at mine site or at a generating station along the Ohio River. The St. Lawrence Seaway has diverted enormous tonnages of grain from the eastern trunk lines to water, while iron ore has come from foreign countries to salt water's edge rather than going across country to add to domestic ton-miles. Meantime, motor carriers skimmed much of the traffic cream by moving high-tariff items swiftly across an ever improving highway net. It was not *how much* the trucks hauled but *what* they hauled that did the damage.

Recent public policy has showed some signs of recognizing the problem of the railroad industry as one of tremendous excess capacity, made worse by exciting technological innovation of the most progressive railroad companies. An industry that could handle 75 per cent more traffic with little addition to variable costs obviously needs more business, and more business will come only with substantial rate reductions. By stating a new rule of rate-making in the Transportation Act of 1958, Congress encouraged the Interstate Commerce Commission to stimulate flagging business with rates that would grab lost business back. Section 15a was amended by the following paragraph:

> In a proceeding involving competition between carriers of different modes of transportation subject to this Act, the Commission, in determining whether a rate is lower than a reasonable minimum rate, shall consider the facts and circumstances attending the movement of the traffic by the carrier or carriers to which the rate is applicable. Rates of a carrier shall not be held up to a particular level to protect the traffic of any other mode of transportation, giving due consideration to the objectives of the national transportation policy declared in this Act.

Presumably a competitor would have a hard time complaining of a railroad rate so low as to have an adverse effect on competition. Yet the last clause in the new rule would give a commissioner or judge an excuse for keeping a railroad from competing on a price basis—on the ground that such competition conflicted with the objectives of "national transportation policy."

MOTOR CARRIERS

Better highways, better trucks, and the large pneumatic tire made possible the commercial success of a new transportation form—the truck line. It was not hard to get into the trucking business. A few hundred dollars would make the down payment on a truck, and one truck was the only piece of equipment many operators owned. When the depression came on, many unemployed truck drivers from various former employments—draymen, gravel-haulers, and employees of business establishments—purchased a truck on credit and started an intercity truck "line." In this way they bought themselves a job that lasted as long as they could pay out-of-pocket expenses like gas and oil and keep up payments on the equipment. These shoestring operators neither kept books nor took out insurance, and few worried about covering all their costs. Thousands of them hauled freight, and the mushrooming industry began to suffer all the pangs of competition.

Since Americans have always been enthusiastic about the virtues of competition, it seems odd that this development in the trucking industry should have caused concern. Indeed, there were those who argued that truck lines ought to compete freely among themselves and that competition should be carried further to permit all of the various modes to strive in any way to take business away from rivals. But there were many sources of opposition to such a policy. The large, well-established operators in the trucking industry felt their profits being reduced by the undercutting of a mass of small-scale common and contract carriers. The market, as they put it, was "chaotic" and needed the quick restoration of order.[3] By 1933 the railroads were aware of the dangers of an uncontrolled trucking industry, and their executives pressed Congress for a tough law. Meanwhile, a number of trade associations and the United States Chamber of Commerce became interested, as did the professional regulators in Washington. Some of the last even urged the view that all the competing transportation industries should be welded into rational systems, each type of carrier to perform the service for which it was best suited.

But the idea of forming great regional transportation systems, made up of all different types of carriers, was abandoned in favor of a plan of interindustry competition. Each new transportation industry was nevertheless to be regulated in Washington as it approached maturity. The Motor Carrier Act of 1935 was the first major attempt to bring an industry other than the railroads under almost total regulation.

The act of 1935 became Part II of the Interstate Commerce Act, everything having to do with railroads being included in Part I. The law exempted certain types of motor carriers, such as vehicles used to carry agricultural products, trucks used by farmers in the course of their operation, and vehicles employed by railroads and airlines. Private trucks and buses—those owned and operated by firms not in the transport business —were not entirely exempted from ICC regulation but were subject to some supervision.[4] The two major categories covered by the act were the "common" and "contract" carriers.[5]

Economic regulation of any transportation facility implies the power of an authority to grant the right to operate in specified territories or over certain routes, to control rates, and to determine the kind of services to be

---

[3] To this day the first argument for regulation advanced by large trucking interests is that a regulatory authority prevents "chaos," meaning that the big companies are thus spared certain of the less pleasant manifestations of a competitive industry.

[4] Both exempted carriers and private carriers must observe certain requirements regarding safety equipment, qualifications of drivers, and maximum hours that personnel may work. Private carriers, in addition, are subject to the requirements as to accounting and reports and marking of vehicles.

[5] Common carriers stand ready to accept the business of anyone shipping commodities which they are equipped to carry. Contract carriers take shipments only under specific agreement and presumably do not hold themselves out to serve the general public. In practice the distinction between common and contract carriage is not clear for the reason that contract carriers may keep taking on contracts until they are for all practical purposes common carriers.

rendered to shippers or travelers. Thus, the Motor Carrier Act of 1935 directed the Interstate Commerce Commission to issue "certificates of public convenience and necessity" to common carriers and "permits" to contract carriers. In general, rates were to be "just and reasonable" and nondiscriminatory, but the rule of rate-making, like the one applying to the railroads, allowed the Commission wide discretion. The Commission *might* fix both maximum and minimum rates for common carriers; for contract carriers only minimum rates might be prescribed, and care was to be taken that no undue advantage should be given them over any common carriers. Tariffs had to be published, and thirty days' notice of changes in rates or classifications was required. Services had to be safe and adequate. Although these were the basic conditions imposed by the act, other provisions were included to assure *total* regulation of motor carriers, like that of the railroads. Records and accounts were to be kept and reports made as prescribed. Securities issues of large lines were placed under the scrutiny of the Commission. All the provisions governing intercorporate relationships of railroads—the control of consolidations, pooling, and the like—applied as well to motor carriers.

For a while after 1935 it appeared that the hand of the regulatory authority would weigh as heavily on the trucking industry as it had on the railroads. But after a desperate time during World War II because of tire and gasoline rationing, the motor-carrier industry expanded tremendously, and the segment that grew the most was that of the private trucks. The Interstate Highway System, by adding speed and flexibility to truck carriage, further encouraged expansion of private trucking. The consequence of the relatively slower growth of the common motor carrier was that only 35 per cent of truck traffic was regulated in the early 1960s.

THE AIRLINES

During the 1930s people were still thrilling to new speed records set by aviators. As multi-engined aircraft provided safer and more economical flights, people began to travel by air. Nor did the early airlines fail to take advantage of the adventuresome appeal of their service. They were clever about introducing an air of luxury and glamour into air travel. Hostesses were attractive girls who were also registered nurses, meals were served on a complimentary basis, and attention was lavished on the traveler; he was made to feel that he was a guest and not a paid fare. Such treatment eased the qualms of passengers who reflected on the unenviable safety records of airlines in the early years.

Regulation of the growing air transportation industry had long been under consideration by the government. By the middle 1930s three administrative agencies were in the regulatory picture—the Department of Commerce, the Interstate Commerce Commission, and the Post Office Department, the last by virtue of its power to fix rates for the carriage of mail. In 1937, legislation was proposed that would have placed commercial air transportation, along with the railroads and the motor carriers, under the jurisdiction of the ICC. This legislation failed of enactment, partly because President Roosevelt, himself an aviation enthusiast, wanted a separate commission with promotional as well as regulatory powers. Bills to this end were drawn up, and at the hearings a fourth agency, the Maritime Commission, unsuccessfully asserted its claim to control overseas lines.

The Civil Aeronautics Act of 1938 established the first real economic regulation of commercial air transport. We need not go into details of the original act, because only two years later the Civil Aeronautics Authority created by the original law was reorganized. At this time Congress established within the Authority, an agency in the Department of Commerce, the Civil Aeronautics Administration and the Civil Aeronautics Board. The CAA was to handle all matters pertaining to the airways system, enforcement of safety rules laid down by the CAB, and promotion of airline traffic. The CAB was to be in charge of economic regulation and the determination and issuance of all rules relating to safety.

From its inception the Civil Aeronautics Board has exercised an authority over the airlines similar to that of the ICC over land carriers. CAB has issued certificates of public convenience and necessity to domestic carriers and permits to lines operating between the United States and foreign countries. It has exercised authority over rates and can set minimum and maximum tariffs. Control over intercompany relationships has been complete and final. The provisions of the law have permitted a tighter regulation than that exercised over any other kind of transportation facility. Furthermore, the CAB was directed to do everything in its power to further the progress of commercial aviation. This provision has resulted in rate-making policy that until recently has protected the airlines from continuing losses and in a paternalism that has neglected altogether the welfare of competing transportation industries.

For more than a decade the CAB assured the airlines of profitable operations by means of an airmail subsidy. Although the Postmaster-General paid for the transportation of airmail, charges for the service were determined by the CAB under its authority to fix just and reasonable rates. The Civil Aeronautics Act directed the board, in fixing rates, to consider "the need of each such carrier for compensation for the transportation of mail sufficient to insure the performance of such service and, together with all other revenue of the air carrier under honest, economical, and efficient management, to maintain and continue the development of air transportation to the extent and of the character and quality required for the commerce of the United States, the Postal Service, and the United States." The board interpreted the "need" of the airlines in a sense most favorable to them. Any company that was not run dishonestly or inefficiently could obtain airmail payments sufficient to make up any operating losses and provide stockholders with a "fair" return on their investment. Under this system there was of course no way of telling for sure what portion of payments was a proper reimbursement for carrying the mail and what portion was pure subsidy.

Congress had said, in effect, that airlines could operate on a cost-plus basis. The possibility of a loss within any accounting period was not precluded, but adjustments could quickly be made to remove it. Each company's "need" was considered separately, the result being that the large, money-making lines, such as the four transcontinentals, after a time received low "service" payments per mail-ton-mile while other companies received high "need" payments. In 1948 these rates varied from sixty cents to seventy dollars a mail-ton-mile.

In 1951 the CAB began to divide payments into two parts, separating airmail pay from subsidy, and the Federal Aviation Act of 1958 made this procedure mandatory. Both feeder and major lines have since received a service rate based on line-haul and terminal charges, and feeder lines and helicopter companies have enjoyed substantial direct subsidies. Apportionment of costs among passenger, express, freight, and airmail services implies arbitrary judgments on which complete agreement would be unlikely, but there appears to be a consensus among transportation economists that airmail payments are greater than justified by costs and so involve some subsidy.

The Federal Aviation Act of 1958 recognized the growing complexity of air traffic by abolishing the old CAB and establishing a Federal Aviation Agency to exercise control over the physical facilities of civil aviation. The Administrator, who reports directly to the President, coordinates the requirements of national defense and commercial aviation and in effect has complete charge of the total aviation system. Functions previously performed by the Secretary of Commerce under the Federal Airport Act of 1946 were turned over to the Administrator, as was responsibility for the National Airport Plan and expenditures of federal aid for airport construction. The CAB still investigates accidents, reporting their causes, but it is the duty of the Administrator to carry out Board recommendations aimed at providing air safety.

DOMESTIC WATER CARRIERS

The discussion of water carriage in Chapter 12 ended on a note of doubt about the future of this transportation form. By 1915 there was a flourishing traffic only on the Great Lakes, the Ohio, and the coastwise lanes. Yet the belief persisted (and still persists) that water transport was inherently cheap and that great industrial and commercial development awaited communities, especially those in the Midwest, that could gain access to a navigable channel. Proponents of inland water transportation have been indefatigable. With the Corps of Engineers of the War Department to abet them, they have succeeded in persuading Congressmen to provide large funds to create avenues for water-borne commerce. For thirty or forty years now the rivers and harbors bill has typified pork-barrel legislation.

Domestic water transportation includes, besides traffic on inland rivers and canals, shipping on the Great Lakes and the coastwise and intercoastal routes. Some public expenditures have been required on the Lakes, chiefly to improve connecting channels, and on the coasts for harbor work and deep-water channels. The really significant sums, however, have been spent on the river systems and on the intracoastal canals along the Atlantic and Gulf coasts. By 1960 the Corps of Engineers had spent more than $5 billion on dredging channels to minimum depths, building dams and locks to maintain water depths, dredging harbors, and constructing revetments. The depression years saw an increase in this kind of activity, and since World War II expenditures have trended steadily upward, reaching annual levels of a third of a billion dollars in the early 1960s.

Although many doubtful projects have been undertaken, domestic water transportation has been greatly stimulated by government provision of facilities. Large shippers of commodities easily loaded at terminals—such as coal, oil, sulfur, sand, gravel, and even automobiles and trucks—can use the waterways profitably. In the early 1950s 5 per cent of annual intercity freight was shipped on the inland waterways, a volume about half that transported on the Lakes. Between 1925 and 1950 traffic on the Mississippi River System, which accounts for nearly half the total channel length of inland waterways, increased sixfold from about 4,500,000,000 ton-miles to over 27,000,000,000 ton-miles. In the ensuing decade traffic on the Mississippi System approximately trebled while total traffic on the Great Lakes and inland waterways increased by about one-third. In 1960 the share of intercity traffic handled by vessels on the Great Lakes and inland waterways was about what it had been ten years earlier.

Economical shipment by barge is restricted both as to area and commodities, as the experience of the Inland Waterways Corporation shows. Established in 1924, the IWC operated the Federal Barge Lines on an "experimental" basis. Originally set up to show the feasibility of river-borne commerce and to develop modern equipment, the Lines were to be sold after they had demonstrated their worth. Although the venture showed operating losses in seventeen of its twenty-nine years, much of the barge-load traffic of the federal lines was profitable. Losses were incurred on less-than-bargeload shipments that the federal lines took at more favorable rates than private operators. Similarly, shippers on the 3,100-mile system pressed for service to out-of-the-way points at rates that would not cover costs. The lines demonstrated at least the prospect of a profitable total operation, for in July 1953 they were sold to the St. Louis Shipbuilding and Steel Company for $9 million. Under the terms of the sale the new company, known as Federal Barge Lines, Inc., had to provide substantially the same service furnished by the former government line. Private operators have made the lines pay by replacing obsolete equipment, reducing personnel, divesting themselves of terminal operations, and cutting out nonpaying points of call.

In spite of new modes of travel, the canal remains charmingly inexpensive, particularly to bulk-cargo shippers. Here, near Waterford, New York, an oil tanker clears a lock in the Erie Canal, with its usual few inches to spare.

Like all other transportation agencies, domestic water carriers eventually came under federal regulation. During the 1930s there was agitation for unified governmental control over inland water carriers, though the reasons for regulation were less compelling than in the cases of the motor carriers and the airlines. By 1938 common carriers in the intercoastal, coastwise, and Great Lakes trade had come under Maritime Commission authority to fix rates, but contract carriers were excluded from regulations. The ICC had jurisdiction over the common ship carriers owned by the railroads. Thus, there were two regulatory authorities concerned with inland water transportation, and the railroads complained that their lines were much more severely restricted than those under Maritime Commission control. Furthermore, the railroads were beginning to feel the pinch of unrestrained canal and river competition and lobbied steadily for their inclusion in a comprehensive regulatory act.

Sentiment among transportation experts and members of Congress was generally favorable toward unifying legislation. The Transportation Act of 1940 transferred jurisdiction of all water carriers engaged in interstate commerce from the Maritime Commission to the ICC. Control provisions with regard to water carriers were much the same as those previously applied to railroads and motor carriers, and these provisions were made Part III of the Interstate Commerce Act. However, so many exemptions were granted that the ICC in 1943 was constrained to report its control limited to a small proportion of the water-borne commerce. If a carrier transported no more than three commodities in bulk or if the cargo were liquid in bulk, no regulation could be imposed. Furthermore, all private carriers were exempt. Since most tonnage carried by water moves in exempt categories or in private fleets, there was little left to regulate; not more than 15 per cent inland-waterway traffic was under ICC jurisdiction in the early 1960s.

THE MERCHANT MARINE

The Merchant Marine Act of 1920 presumably took the government out of the foreign shipping business. Government-owned vessels were to be sold at low prices to shipping companies that were to receive tax advantages and construction loans on favorable terms. But even though the ships moved into private hands the merchant marine continued to dwindle. An act of 1928, which tried to bolster the merchant marine by increasing indirect subsidies especially through mail payments, was of no avail. Tonnage in the foreign trade dropped from 11,000,000 in 1920 to 7,000,000 in 1929; a decade later tonnage was down to about 3,300,000. By 1935 only one-third of United States exports and imports and a negligible portion of the rest of world trade was carried in American ships. Although the American merchant fleet in the late 1930s was still second only to that of Britain in tonnage, it was slow and old; within another few years it would have been almost entirely obsolete.

For reasons of national defense, Congress in 1936 reversed the long-standing policy of not granting direct subsidies to carriers in the foreign service. The Merchant Marine Act of 1936 established a new body, the United States Maritime Commission, which was authorized to grant "construction differential" and "operating differential" subsidies. The purpose of the act was to put American shipbuilders and ship operators on an equal footing with their lower-cost foreign competitors so that the American merchant fleet would carry a substantial part of United States foreign commerce. Upon application by a qualified concern, the Commission would undertake to have a vessel built in an American shipyard, at the same time contracting to sell it to the applicant for a price equal to the cost of construction abroad. The difference between the actual cost and the estimated foreign cost was thus the amount of the "construction differential" subsidy, which was supposed to be no more than 50 per cent of the cost of construction in an American shipyard. If, however, certain features, especially useful for national defense, were incorporated in the ship, the government would stand the cost of them.[6]

The principle of the operational subsidy was the same; the Commission would make up the difference between the cost of operation under United States ownership and the cost of operation under a foreign flag. A recapture clause in the contracts enabled the government to get back half of any profits in excess of 10 per cent per year over a ten-year period.

The Commission experienced difficulty in determining foreign costs of construction and operation, but the directive of Congress in this respect was clear. The mandate to promote the merchant marine to the extent that it would carry a "substantial" part of United States foreign commerce was not so clear. In practice the Commission interpreted "substantial" to mean 50 per cent of the trade *taken as a whole*. Although an effort was made to place American carriers on all the important trade routes between the United States and foreign countries, it was not considered necessary to have one-half the commerce of *each* route handled by United States operators.

Assistance rendered to the shipping industry between 1936 and 1941 did not result in a merchant fleet large enough to transport men and supplies to the fighting fronts in World War II. The Liberty ships and Victory ships of World War II years were built on government account so that the construction and operating programs under the Maritime Commission were interrupted. After Pearl Harbor, shipyards that had been acres of weeds, rotting timbers, and rusting iron were refurbished, and new shipyards sprang up on inland waterways, in back channels, and on the Great Lakes. For the first time in the history of shipbuilding, component parts were fabricated at inland points and assembled on the coasts.

Since World War II the merchant marine has enjoyed indirect benefits of greater monetary value than the amounts received for construction and operating differential subsidies. By the Merchant Ship Sales Act of 1946 Congress provided for the sale of hundreds of high-class ships on terms especially favorable to American-flag operators. Several hundred first-rate dry-cargo vessels were sold for as low as one-third their prewar cost. Other indirect benefits have included the charter of government-owned vessels under favorable terms, guaranteed loans at low interest rates for ship construction programs, and guarantee to United States operators of half the business shipped under the European Recovery Program and the military-aid program. Direct subsidy payments have been resumed under the successor to the Maritime Commission, the United States Maritime Administration, now an agency within the Department of Commerce. The Federal Maritime Board, whose chairman is also head of the Maritime Administration, acts as a regulatory agency, determining rates, services, and practices of seagoing vessels that serve as common carriers and actually executing the subsidy contracts with shipping companies.

---

[6] Through this device the liner *United States,* costing an estimated $70 million, was made available to the United States Lines for only $28 million.

Millions of Ton-Miles

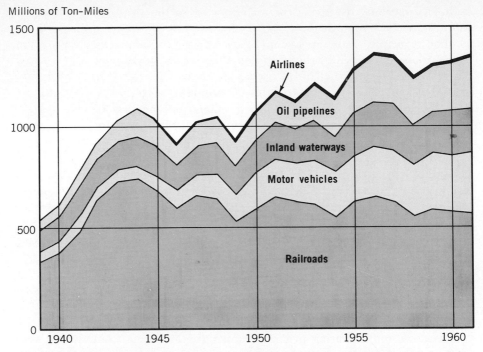

1939–58: Interstate Commerce Commission, Bureau of Transport Economics and Statistics, *Intercity Ton-Miles, 1939–1959*, Statement No. 6103. 1959–61: Seventy-fifth and Seventy-sixth Annual Reports of the Interstate Commerce Commission.

Transportation Mix: Railroads, while still the basis for more than 40 per cent of intercity freight traffic, have yielded important tonnage to trucks, inland waterways, and oil pipelines.

A Federal Program for Transportation

COMPETITION AMONG THE MODES OF TRANSPORTATION

The charts summarize the consequences of more than a generation of competition among the major transportation agencies. Gains in the shares of intercity freight traffic carried by inland waterways, motor trucks and pipelines were at the expense of the railroads. (Airline express and freight carriage has increased, but as a proportion of total freight it is still negligible and does not even appear on the chart.) Railroad passenger traffic has almost gone back to the unsatisfactory levels of the late thirties. Private autos now convey the overwhelming proportion of intercity passenger traffic. Despite the remarkable rate at which they have moved forward since World War II, airlines in 1960 accounted for little more than 3 per cent of total intercity passenger-miles.

Basic economic forces, many of them already mentioned, were unquestionably at work to bring about these results. Yet clearly intervention by the federal government distorted and twisted the resource allocation process to secure an outcome far different than the unfettered price system would have provided. The Interstate Highway System, affording rapid, flexible truck service, encouraged new concepts of regional factories linked by highways and permanently removed the railroads from competition for this high-rated freight. Soon after its opening in 1959 the St. Lawrence Seaway not only shunted business of the major railroads between Chicago and New York but diverted much traffic that would otherwise have moved out of Gulf ports. Not content with an $800 million expenditure to reduce the number of dams on the Ohio River from forty-one to fifteen, Congress appropriated $1,200 million to make the shallow Arkansas River navigable into the heart of Oklahoma. Driving the supply of transportation services always ahead of the demand for them, American public policy has removed the last vestige of market discipline by largely avoiding user charges to defray the great social costs incurred.

The transportation problem of the United States can best be brought into focus by considering the tremendous outlays made to subsidize the various modes of transportation since World War I. A good part of this

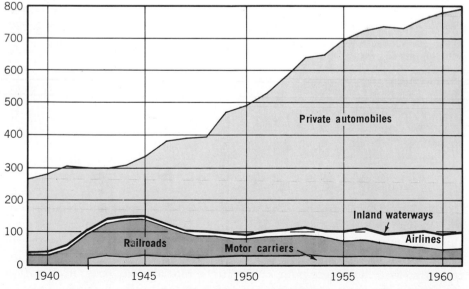

Interstate Commerce Commission, various Annual Reports.

Passenger Traffic: Private automobiles have grown to a position of overwhelming dominance since the war, as indicated by the thin slivers marking train, bus, and airplane transportation.

Table 19-1

Summary of Federal Program Funds in Direct Aid of Transportation
(in millions, figures rounded)

Subject	Program magnitude 1917 (or later) through 1960	Estimated program magnitude 1961–75
Corps of Engineers expenditures for navigation improvements	$ 5,080	$ 6,582
Tennessee Valley Authority expenditure for navigation	219 [a]	91
Coast Guard expenditures relating to navigation	1,687 [b]	4,787
Coast and Geodetic Survey expenditures for surveys and charts in aid of navigation	158	198
Federal-aid highway authorization	20,659	41,759
Federal aviation program	4,489 [c]	18,595
Merchant marine subsidies:		
Operating differential subsidy	969 [d]	1,500 [e]
Construction and reconstruction subsidy	306 [f]	341 [e]
TOTAL	$33,567	$73,853

SOURCE: *National Transportation Policy* (Doyle Report), Preliminary Draft of a Report to the Senate Committee on Interstate Commerce, Eighty-seventh Congress, first session (Washington, D.C.: U.S. Government Printing Office, 1961), p. 172.

[a] Beginning in 1935.
[b] Beginning in 1952; data for prior years was not furnished.
[c] Beginning in 1927.
[d] Beginning in 1947.
[e] Based upon computed annual average payments for five-year period from 1956 through 1960.
[f] This construction differential subsidy program started in 1936, and the reconstruction subsidy program started in 1955.

expenditure was a legitimate charge against the public treasury for social-overhead capital that would have been provided in no other way. It is hard to believe, though, that proposed outlays (see Table 19-1) can be justified except as boodle for those who lobby most effectively in Washington.

THE CONFLICT BETWEEN REGULATION AND PROMOTION

The logical inconsistencies of many of the developments recounted in this chapter are apparent without further discussion. There must be something the matter with a transportation system in which all the major agencies except railroads and pipelines are subsidized by the government. Furthermore, it is illogical to pour public funds into all forms of transportation facilities without attempting to coordinate expenditures by some accepted principle.

One half-hearted effort to bring order into the confusion was the Transportation Act of 1940. This law, as we have seen, brought domestic water transport under the partial control of the ICC. It made improvements in ICC procedures for handling the growing burden of work. Further, it made major changes in certain matters of policy directly affecting the railroads. The twenty-year-old notion of consolidation of lines according to an ICC plan was abandoned, and the Commission was directed, in making rates, to fix them without regard to protecting certain carriers. But the 1940 act was basically a statement of national transportation policy. The Commission was directed to provide "fair and impartial regulation of all modes of transportation" and to administer the law so as ". . . to recognize and preserve the inherent advantages of each." But air transport is outside the jurisdiction of the ICC, and much water and highway traffic lies outside its power. The ICC has nothing to say about how many airports shall be constructed, how many miles of highway shall be built, or how many miles of channel shall be dredged. Finally, the Interstate Commerce Commission has appeared to set rates that have, in fact, protected the railroads against other competing forms.

Indeed, both motor and water carriers have complained that the Commission approves extremely low rail rates where there is a likelihood of diversion of traffic by trucks or barges. In this way, they have argued, the agency with inherent advantages in furnishing certain types of service is kept out of the competition by the below-cost rates of the railroads. To such contentions the railroads retort that neither motor nor water carriers pay anything like the fees that they should for the use of waterways and highways and that without this subsidy their charges for the service in question would be much higher. The trucking companies assert in turn that they pay through license fees and gasoline taxes for their use of the highways, a contention hardly supported by tests indicating that heavy vehicles are destructive of the roads. Representatives of the railroad interests get in a final plea of unfair treatment with the argument that as common carriers railroad freight is entirely subject to regulatory authority, whereas the greater part of truck and water freight escapes regulation.

A solution to the problem of conflict between regulation and promotion was suggested in a 1949 report of former Secretary of Commerce Sawyer. The government, he stated,

> . . . should consider continuing its various promotional programs along lines which call for payments by the user for the various facilities. Government regulatory agencies should simultaneously consider the elimination of rates which are not closely related to the fully distributed cost of rendering the service. If action along both lines were to proceed at the same time, most of the legitimate complaints which the railroads have against their competing carriers would be eliminated and most of the legitimate complaints which water and motor carriers have against the rail carriers would be disposed of. The net result would be a more effective use of transport resources with each type of carrier performing the various services in which it had a cost advantage.

In the decade that followed Secretary Sawyer's statement there seemed to be an increasing sentiment for imposing realistic user charges. There was also a swing to the notion that less regulation and more market discipline would achieve a healthier set of transportation industries. As Professor L. L. Waters has remarked, the growth of private transportation, while leaving a few pockets of monopoly, has removed much of the need for conventional regulation; for the greatest measure of consumer and customer protection now lies in the individual's power to move himself and his goods by *private* vehicle over public highways, waterways, and air routes. Government can exercise its most effective control through determination of public expenditures on public ways. Traditional regulatory agencies have thus become a poor third in providing user protection. It follows that greater reliance can be placed on the price system by allowing the forces of competition to determine rates of investment and output in the transportation industries.

Yet common sense and experience tell us that advocates of the various transportation forms will keep on competing for public funds and thus for resources, without much regard to social need. A genuine coordinating agency should have charge of *all* promotional activity so that resource allocation may be justified on other than political grounds. Great pressure has developed for the establishment of a Department of Transportation with a secretary of cabinet rank who could face the combined problems of promotion, investment, and regulation.

But we shall not soon expect to have a different approach to transportation policy. For the outcome of complete control by a governmental commission is that the commission eventually identifies itself with the industry controlled. As long as shippers and the traveling public receive reasonably good service without seriously discriminating rates, there is not likely to be any insistence on a coordinated, rational system. Only economists and a few government career men will press for change. There is little reason to think that they will successfully make a case against the combined opposition of both the regulators and the regulated—who have usually agreed that the status quo is preferable to any sweeping change. Yet President Kennedy's 1962 plea for greater reliance on ". . . unsubsidized privately owned facilities, operating under the incentives of private profit and the checks of competition . . ." elicited some enthusiastic response from members of Congress. Good sense may one distant day prevail.

Money
and Financial Institutions
(1914 to the Present)

We shall deal with our economic system as it is and as it may be modified, not as it might be if we had a clean sheet of paper to write upon; and step by step we shall make it what it should be. . . .

WOODROW WILSON

During the half-century that has elapsed since the establishment of the central bank revolutionary changes have occurred in American financial institutions. The banking system and the country's money supply have come under a large measure of federal control. Commercial banking, once one of the riskiest of businesses, has become almost riskless. And from an almost insignificant position in the financial system the nonbank intermediaries, particularly savings and loan associations, have attained great power and influence. The story of these changes is essentially the story of government intervention—pervasive, continuous and sweeping—intervention generally aimed at making access to financial institutions the privilege of everyone.

Federal Reserve: The Evolution of a Central Bank

Toward the end of Chapter 13 we laid out the broad outlines of the structure of the Federal Reserve System at its inception. This structure appears to be essentially unchanged today. If the student were to read the original Federal Reserve Act and then all the amendments to the act, he might even get the impression that there have also been no fundamental changes in the *operation* of the System since 1914. Yet nothing could be farther from the truth. Actually, the Federal Reserve System operates far differently from the way it was planned; for the present powers of the Reserve banks are less and those of the Board of Governors much greater than anyone would have thought possible in 1914.

How did the United States get a monetary authority with a strong and persistent influence on the commercial banks and with almost unlimited powers to control the quantity of money in the economy? To answer this basic question, we must consider three separate topics. The *first* deals with the confusion, apparent for nearly twenty years, over the question of who was to control the System. Was it to be the Federal Reserve Board in Washington or a group of individual Reserve bank executives named, essentially, by the bankers themselves? The *second* topic concerns changes in the techniques of credit regulation. Under a *third* heading we shall observe what major policy decisions have been accepted by Federal Reserve authorities and by what lights decisions have been taken.

THE QUESTION OF CONTROL OF THE FEDERAL RESERVE SYSTEM

We have already paid some attention to the matter of who was to run the Federal Reserve System. To repeat, the chief coordinating (managerial) agency was the Federal Reserve Board, made up of five members appointed to the Board by the President and two other members *ex officio*—the Secretary of the Treasury and the Comptroller of the Currency. From these five appointed members were named the Governor and Vice Governor, chief executive officers of the Board. At each of the twelve Federal Reserve banks (see map), authority was centered in a nine-man directorate composed of Class A, Class B, and Class C directors. The three Class A directors might be bankers; the three Class B directors were to be engaged in commerce, agriculture, or industry and could not be connected with any commercial bank. Class A and B directors were elected by the banks; on the basis of their capitals, banks in each district were divided into three categories— small, medium, and large—and those in each category were to elect a Class A and a Class B director. The Federal Reserve Board would appoint Class C directors, one of them to be the official representative of the Board at the district level. Designated the *Federal Reserve Agent,* he was to serve as chairman of the board of directors and was doubtless intended to be the chief executive officer of the Federal Reserve bank in each district, responsible to the Board in Washington.

In Chapter 13 we had occasion to note the public nature of the controls provided, but in practice things worked out very differently. A strange dualism of authority developed that the framers of the act (and the people of the country) did not intend. How much this dualism affected the monetary

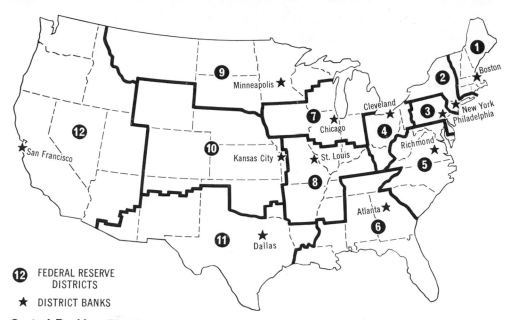

Central Banking: The Federal Reserve System was organized in 1914, when many people still feared the concept of a central bank. So twelve district Banks, now an economic anachronism, were established.

system is hard to say, but we must pay some attention to it in view of the failure of Federal Reserve to prevent the 1929–33 collapse of the banking system.

The subtle fight for ultimate control began in the opposition of bankers to reform legislation. Many far-seeing members of the banking community, especially those in New England, favored a central-banking institution with a substantial measure of public control, but typical opinion was much against it. Specifically, bankers in general were hostile toward the Federal Reserve Act, for they felt that the Federal Reserve Board had too much power and that the System would have a long-period inflationary bias. The American Bankers Association, expressing the feelings of most bank executives, condemned the measure as "socialistic." Moreover, the change had come so quickly that even those not actually opposed had misgivings about the rapidity with which the new law was put into effect. As Dean Taggart has said, "It is small wonder that the bankers of the country, as well as their customers, were bewildered when, within a few months following the inauguration of a new administration not definitely pledged to banking reform, the Federal Reserve Act was written and passed, and its provisions placed in operation in a little over nineteen months." [1]

Bewildered or not, the bankers soon found an opportunity to take over

[1] J. H. Taggart, *The Federal Reserve Bank of Boston* (Boston-New York: Bankers Publishing Co., 1938), p. 57.

the driver's seat. The Federal Reserve Act had not been clear as to just who the operating head of each Federal Reserve bank should be. Presumably, the Federal Reserve Agent, in his capacity as chairman of the board, was to be the chief policy-making officer. Since the framers of the act had purposely left undetermined the internal organization of the banks, the Federal Reserve Board had to decide who the operating head would be. The Board ruled that directors of Federal Reserve banks might elect a president or manager who could be either from the directorate or from outside. It was further recommended that the operating head be called the "governor" of the bank.

The governors of Federal Reserve banks quickly became the dominant officials at the district level, with the Federal Reserve Agents in a definitely subordinate position. It is not hard to see how this happened. Through the Class A and B directors, bankers had a majority on the boards of directors. They could pick the operating head of the Reserve bank, and they invariably selected a seasoned banker of wide experience. As it happened, the man chosen governor of the New York Reserve Bank was an exceptionally vigorous leader, hardboiled and articulate. He was Benjamin Strong, just come from the presidency of the Bankers Trust Company of New York City. One of J. P. Morgan's fair-haired young men, he was eminently acceptable to the big banks.

The New York Reserve Bank, located in the financial center and chief money market of the country, was bound to be a major influence in the new system, and its strategic importance was magnified by the dominating personality of its governor. Although Mr. Strong was not a member of the board of the New York bank, he furnished the real leadership, and from the first the directors almost routinely followed his recommendations.[2] Even the Federal Reserve Board in Washington came quickly to regard him and the other governors as the chief executives of the banks. At first the Board sent all communications to the Federal Reserve Agent; after a while it wrote to the governor, frequently not even sending an information copy to its own representative. The tendency was strengthened by the fact that salaries of the governors were ordinarily much higher than those of the Agents. Finally, the title of "governor," a common designation of the chief officer of European central banks, was a much more prestigious one than that of "agent."

The unquestioned dominance of the governors in the several banks would not have made much difference if they had remained subordinate to the Federal Reserve Board, but they did not. Even before the Reserve banks commenced operation, a Council of Governors was formed, with Mr. Strong

---

[2] My colleague, Professor E. R. Wicker, insists that I overestimate Strong's dominance of System affairs, pointing out that on occasion his directors balked at a recommended action. (For example, in the fall of 1919 they refused to approve Strong's proposal to raise the rate on member-bank advances.) I do not contend that Strong always won out; I simply feel that from 1914 to 1928 he either made or approved every *major* decision.

as its chairman. In 1916 the Council became the Conference of Governors and as such held regular formal meetings to determine policy for the System as a whole. When the Federal Reserve Board objected to regular formal meetings, the Governors' Conference began to meet informally for discussion of mutual problems.

Until 1922 a running battle for control persisted between the Federal Reserve Board and the Conference of Governors, the Board objecting in particular to meetings called outside of Washington without any notification whatsoever. In 1922, as a compromise, it was agreed that the Board would regularly summon the governors to Washington for meetings at which Board members would be present. This arrangement, which continued for a number of years, did not, however, lessen the power of the governors, particularly Mr. Strong. For at just this time it became necessary to establish a coordinating authority to supervise the open-market operations of the several Federal Reserve banks. Open-market control actually began with a small committee of governors. Although the Federal Reserve Board got its back up in 1923 and proclaimed its authority to control sales and purchases of securities, the New York bank under Governor Strong continued to dominate policy until 1929.[3] Not until 1930 did the Federal Reserve Board, after the onset of severe depression, finally assert its central controlling authority over open-market operations, a policy confirmed by the Banking Act of 1933. After nearly two decades of Federal Reserve operation, the question of ultimate authority was settled. The people wanted government control instead of banker control—and in the early 1930s they got it.

The Banking Act of 1935 clinched the matter. The Federal Reserve Board was henceforth to be called the Board of Governors, a significant change in that the new designation implied that it was henceforth to be the "board of bosses." Furthermore, the operating heads of the Reserve banks were to be termed "President" and "First Vice President" instead of "Governor" and "Deputy Governor." Individual boards of directors could still choose their chief executive officers, but their selections were to be approved by the Board of Governors. Since 1935 there has been little possibility of a return to decentralized authority.

TECHNIQUES OF REGULATION

So far, we have only described the structure of the Federal Reserve System and summarized the early contest for authority. We must now direct our attention to the evolving techniques and changing objectives of central bank control.

At this point it may be well to recall how the money supply of the United States was provided up to 1914. The government furnished money chiefly by coining precious metals and authorizing the commercial banks to issue

---

[3] Governor Strong died in the fall of 1928, but the spirit of the man was enough to lead the way for a few more months.

notes and create deposit credits. A third way, having the treasury print paper money, was also used (notably in the case of the Greenbacks), but business people feared the inflationary possibilities of this last method and wanted to avoid it.

Now in other well-developed countries of the world a fourth way of manufacturing money had come into general use by the latter part of the eighteenth century: a *central bank* was authorized to issue notes and create deposits. This method had the undeniable advantage of giving those in authority the power to create money almost immediately, if the need arose, and to destroy money if it appeared that inflation threatened. With the establishment of the Federal Reserve System the United States adopted this fourth method.

How was this money-creating process to be carried out? To understand it we shall have to pay particular attention to the matter of *reserves*—of both member banks and Federal Reserve banks.

Member-bank reserves. The reader will recall that under the National Banking Act the reserves of national banks consisted of cash in vault and deposits with correspondent banks. (The reserves of state banks generally comprised the same two kinds of assets, but the laws governing amounts and the proportions to be held in cash varied considerably under the different state laws, just as they do today.) Under the Federal Reserve Act the reserves of member banks were to be held partly as *deposits* with the Federal Reserve bank of the district in which they were located and partly as cash in vault. In 1917 Congress amended the act, establishing new reserve requirements that were to prevail for nearly twenty years. In accordance with this amendment, *the legal reserves of member banks of the Federal Reserve System were to consist solely of deposits with Federal Reserve banks.* The old classification of central-reserve-city, reserve-city, and country banks was kept, and the reserve required against demand deposits was set at 13, 10, and 7 per cent, respectively. Banks of all classes had to keep only a 3 per cent reserve against time deposits.[4] Note that these reserve percentages were much lower than those formerly required for national banks. Lower reserve ratios had the effect of easing credit considerably, but they were justified on the grounds that centralization of reserves made high reserve requirements unnecessary.

On November 16, 1914, the date set for beginning the operations of the Federal Reserve System, member banks deposited the first payment of their reserves.[5] Reserve authorities had requested that deposits be made in gold

---

[4] Under the National Banking Act no distinction had been made, for reserve purposes, between demand and time deposits. Since state laws generally required a small percentage of reserves (or none at all) against time deposits, the Federal Reserve Act set a low requirement to keep member banks from being at a disadvantage in this regard.

[5] In order to enable banks to make the transfer of reserves with a minimum of inconvenience, they were allowed a period of two and a half years and could, for a time, continue to count deposits with correspondents as reserves.

so far as possible in order that Reserve banks might establish a gold reserve, and member banks complied. Subsequent transfers were made without difficulty, and the centralization of reserves was accomplished. Such cash as a commercial bank needed to keep in its vaults to carry on day-to-day transactions did *not* count as legal reserve after June 1917. If a bank needed to add to its till money or replace cash withdrawals, it simply drew on its deposits with the Reserve bank of its district much as you or I would draw on a personal checking account. Finally, the reserve deposits of member banks were not immobilized funds but working balances that rose and fell as banks received and lost funds in the check collection process.

We have frequently mentioned the phenomenon of reserve creation. The mere *centralization* of existing reserves would have been helpful in preventing some of the difficulties of the old system, but centralization alone would have had limited usefulness. But by extending their own credit Reserve banks could actually add to a member bank's reserves. Under the original act it was presumed that Reserve bank credit would be extended by rediscounting those assets of member banks that took the form of "eligible paper"—i.e., promissory notes or bills of exchange of short maturities created as the result of an agricultural, industrial, or commercial transaction.[6] A far more important way of creating Reserve-bank credit has since come into use, but in 1913 rediscounting was thought to be the only significant method.

What, precisely, is meant by "rediscounting"? We have already observed that a bank lends money in two ways—by "loan" and by "discount." Although the distinction is a technical one, the terminology is important. A bank makes a "loan" if it gets its interest at the *end* of the lending period; it "discounts" if it *deducts* the interest when it lends the money. Suppose that the financial officer of a local department store wishes to borrow $50,000 to finance a special purchase of refrigerators. He estimates that the refrigerators will all be sold at a profit within ninety days, so he borrows the money at 4 per cent interest for that period. The bank deducts the interest, $500 (4 per cent of $50,000 for one year is $2,000; one-fourth of $2,000 is $500), at the time of making the loan, and therefore credits the store's checking account for $49,500. When the discount matures, the department store will repay the bank the principal sum of $50,000.[7]

---

[6] For the sake of simplicity we shall not consider the matter of eligible paper in detail. Originally the requirements for eligibility were extremely rigid, but the definition of eligibility has changed from time to time. Today the matter is of little importance for reasons that will shortly become clear. It is enough to observe here that for many years "eligible" paper arose from the lending activities of commercial banks as they provided *working* (not fixed) capital for business and agriculture. Industrial and commercial loans, if they were to be eligible for rediscount, could not normally run for more than ninety days from the time of rediscount; agricultural loans could run for as much as nine months.

[7] Anyone familiar with beginning economics will recall that the bank could lend the $50,000 because it had "excess reserves" in this amount. Since the department store borrowed the money in order to buy refrigerators, an authorized official will shortly write a check in that amount and send it to a supplier in payment of an invoice. The supplier will deposit the check in another bank, and when the check is collected, the lending bank's reserves and deposits will fall by $50,000.

But what is a rediscount? The framers of the Federal Reserve Act foresaw that a bank might sometimes be confronted with a legitimate demand for loans and not be able to accommodate its customers without reducing its reserves below the legal minimum. So it was provided that a member bank could replenish its reserves or, alternatively, get cash in the form of Federal Reserve notes by *rediscounting* its loans and discounts. To continue with our example: the bank that discounted the department store's note for $50,000 could, in effect, sell that evidence of debt to the Federal Reserve bank and have the proceeds credited to its own account. Suppose that the department store's note had sixty days to run and that the rediscount rate was 2 per cent. The bank could endorse the note, send it to the Federal Reserve, and receive credit for the principal sum of $50,000 less sixty days' interest at 2 per cent ($50,000 − $166.67 = $49,833.33). Now the member bank's lending ability would be restored.

Thus Federal Reserve banks were truly "bankers' banks." Shortly after the System was established, it was made even easier to get needed funds from the central bank. In 1916, an amendment was passed enabling a member bank to get an out-and-out loan from its Federal Reserve bank at the prevailing rediscount rate. Such a loan, called an "advance," could be obtained on the basis of the member bank's own note *secured* by eligible paper or by government obligations. But whether a bank rediscounted or obtained an advance, it was in effect borrowing reserves on which to do business.

It will now be apparent why so much attention has been devoted to member-bank reserves and the devices by which they could be replenished. By rediscounting or making advances to member banks, the Federal Reserve banks could ease money and credit. In its power to raise or lower the rediscount rate, Federal Reserve presumably had a real instrument of control. When Federal Reserve authorities felt that an expansion of bank loans was desirable, the Reserve banks would set the rediscount rate at a level that was low relative to prevailing interest rates. When credit was expanding at a rate that threatened inflation, the rediscount rate would be raised to a high level relative to market rates of interest. A low Reserve bank rate represented a low cost of accommodation to member banks and thus to ultimate borrowers; a high rate meant that borrowing would be expensive.

Federal Reserve bank reserves. A definite qualitative restriction was placed on the extension of Reserve bank credit. This restraint was automatic if you believed in the so-called commercial-loan theory of credit—the "real-bills" doctrine, as the English called it.[8] According to the commercial-loan theory of credit, the banking system could safely expand its loans, and thus

---

[8] In 1913, nearly everyone of importance did adhere to some variant of this theory. Adam Smith had stated it in *The Wealth of Nations,* and it was accepted almost without question throughout the nineteenth century in both Britain and the United States. For a thorough treatment of the real-bills doctrine and its influence on economic thought, see Lloyd W. Mints, *A History of Banking Theory in Great Britain and the United States* (Chicago: University of Chicago Press, 1945).

the money supply, if commercial banks would take care to make only short-term, self-liquidating loans. It was reasoned that if the proceeds of loans were used to finance the actual bringing of goods onto market—i.e., current production—there could never be trouble. Every time a bank made a loan to finance a "real" transaction, the loan would be paid off from the sale of the processed goods. Funds would then be available for carrying another manufacturer (or wholesaler or farmer) over another production period. If the "needs of business" so required, it would be all right to expand the quantity of money—since there would supposedly be an increase in total production of goods in approximately the same proportion. If, over a period of time, production were increasing, the quantity of money would increase. If, on the other hand, production were decreasing, the quantity of money in the economy would then decrease. This kind of a rise and fall in the money supply would presumably be safe. Furthermore, if commercial banks had nothing to do with providing the *fixed* capital for business enterprises, they would be properly liquid. Fixed capital should be provided, it was felt, only by the sale of securities or by plowing back the earnings of a business.

The framers of the Federal Reserve Act placed great faith in the commercial-loan theory. They felt that it was the first and great principle of safe and sound banking. But in addition to its qualitative restriction a quantitative restriction was needed. It was well enough to require that the basis of Reserve bank credit be self-liquidating paper, but it was also essential that an upper limit be placed on the secular growth of such credit by tying it to gold.

In 1913 nearly everyone who professed to know anything about money believed firmly in the virtues of the gold standard. Since the end of the nineteenth century economically advanced countries had been on gold. New methods of processing gold and the discovery of great deposits in South Africa and the Yukon-Klondike region had meant ample stocks for monetary purposes. Prosperity and economic growth had been the rule for countries adhering to the gold standard. At last it seemed that a firm set of principles had evolved for guiding central bank action and assuring a money supply of the proper size.

The original Federal Reserve Act required the Reserve banks to keep gold reserves against their major liabilities. Gold holdings were to be at least 40 per cent of the value of Federal Reserve notes outstanding and 35 per cent of member-bank deposits. Anyone who wished might own gold, and all other forms of money were to be convertible into gold. Thus private citizens would themselves impose a limitation on the potential expansion of credit, for if the dollar seemed to be losing its purchasing power, they would redeem their paper money and bank deposits in gold. Further, the Federal Reserve authorities would have a guide to policy in the gold reserve ratio. A decline in the ratio toward the legal minimum would signify either a rise in Federal Reserve liabilities or a "drain" on the gold reserve. Such a drain could be "internal," on account of the desire of Americans to hold gold, or "external," as a consequence of an unfavorable balance of payments abroad. In any case, a fall in the gold reserve ratio would be the signal for a rise in the rediscount rate and a tighter credit policy. Such action would damp down economic activity, lower domestic prices and incomes, and thus stop the flow of gold out of the country. For lower prices made it easier for foreigners to buy American goods, and lower incomes at home made it harder for people in the United States to buy the goods and services of foreigners.

As matters turned out, the restraints placed on the expansion of Federal Reserve credit didn't work according to plan. Why this was so will become apparent as we proceed.

CHANGING INSTRUMENTS OF CONTROL

One reason for the ineffectiveness of the restraints envisaged by the framers of the Reserve act lay in the adoption of a more flexible and powerful technique of controlling credit—the purchase and sale of securities in the open market. At the outset it was foreseen that the twelve Reserve banks would need earning assets, and they were empowered to purchase and sell bankers' acceptances, bills of exchange, government securities of all maturities, and short-term state and municipal warrants. We have the word of one close to all the formational activity that the framers ". . . recognized open-market operations in the classical British view of central banking as being a valuable means of making the bank rate effective." [9] Indeed, anyone familiar with European central-bank techniques would have been aware of the effect of open-market purchases and sales on the reserves of commercial banks. But the practical bankers put in charge of the System's fortunes were largely ignorant of such relationships, and anyway most of them believed that government securities inside the banking system constituted inflation. So for half a dozen years after the System went into operation reliance was placed on rediscount policy as the credit control instrument. Open-market operations were carried out only to adjust the earning assets of Reserve banks, and no provision was made for coordinating the buying and selling activities of the several banks.

It was not until the early twenties that the Federal Reserve realized that the discount mechanism by itself was not a sufficient control over bank credit. When member banks had adequate reserves and did not need to borrow, the level of the rediscount rate made no difference, and the role of the central bank was passive. On the other hand, the purchase and sale of securities in the open market enabled the Federal Reserve to affect commercial bank reserves on its own initiative. When Reserve banks bought securities, payment was made by checks drawn on themselves. Sellers of the securities deposited the checks to their accounts with commercial banks,

---

[9] H. Parker Willis, *The Theory and Practice of Central Banking* (New York: Harper, 1936), pp. 183–84.

which in turn sent them to the Reserve banks for credit to their reserve accounts. The effect was to increase both the deposits and the reserves of the commercial banks. A sale of securities by Reserve banks had the opposite effect of decreasing the deposits and reserves of commercial banks. The basis of the operations lay in the fact that by writing checks on themselves Reserve banks could *create* the funds used to purchase securities and could *absorb* funds from securities sales by destroying member-bank deposits.

As time went on the procedures and administrative organization of open-market operations took form. The securities bought and sold were shortly confined to United States governments of all maturities. In 1922 the old Conference of Governors appointed a committee to coordinate purchases and sales. The next year, after the struggle for power discussed previously, the Federal Reserve Board formed its own committee to handle open-market operations and began the practice of buying and selling for system account. In 1930 the committee was composed of one representative from each Reserve bank; the Banking Act of 1933 made this arrangement formal and designated the group the Federal Open Market Committee. By this time operations could not be carried out by any single bank without Board approval, but a Reserve bank still had the right to refrain from participation if it so desired. The Banking Act of 1935 removed this right and established the Open Market Committee in the form it has at present. It consists of twelve members, and Board dominance is assured by having all seven of its members on the Committee. The other five members are representatives of the Reserve banks elected annually by the boards of directors of the several banks, which are grouped for the purpose. Because of its strategic position in the money market, the New York bank always has a member.

In carrying out its functions that so vitally affect the welfare of the economy, the Federal Open Market Committee has the widest discretion. The law only requires that decisions be taken ". . . with a view to accommodating commerce and business and with regard to their bearing upon the general credit situation of the country." For a long time the FOMC met every three months, an Executive Committee of five meeting oftener to make interim decisions. Since 1955 the full Committee has met approximately every three weeks, and all Reserve bank presidents, whether on the Committee or not, have come to join in the pow-wow. Actual dealing is supervised by the manager of the System open-market account, a vice-president of the Federal Reserve Bank of New York. After broad lines of policy are laid down by the Open Market Committee, frequently after long and inconclusive discussion, open-market purchases and sales become a highly technical operation carried out by the New York Fed's trading desk, which has a great deal of discretion.

During the 1930s the discount mechanism permanently lost much of its importance, although it has never ceased to have some significance. The original idea of permitting member banks to rediscount only eligible paper was abandoned during the Depression decade. The 1916 change, which enabled commercial banks to obtain fifteen-day advances from the Reserve banks on their promissory notes, was fundamental. Gradually the practice of rediscounting almost disappeared, as member banks used the more convenient device of borrowing on their government securities.[10]

Emergency legislation of the early thirties liberalized the basis on which Reserve credit could be released through the discount window. The Banking Act of 1935 made permanent the authority of the Reserve bank to make advances up to four months on notes secured by *any* assets satisfactory to it. But several forces worked toward making the discount rate insignificant as a means of control. After 1934, excess reserves of the commercial banks grew to enormous proportions as gold flowed in unprecedented quantities from abroad; with excess reserves so high there was little need for banks to borrow. Even as reserve positions became tighter with the onset of World War II, the tradition against borrowing, especially of the country banks, served as a check against indebtedness at the Reserve bank.[11] But the discount rate lost its importance chiefly because the Board of Governors insisted on control of Reserve bank discount windows, via Regulation A, to such an extent that member-bank borrowing was no longer regulated by *rate changes* but by *administrative fiat*.

The Federal Reserve Act provided that each Reserve bank should set its own rate of rediscount subject to the "review and determination" of the Board in Washington. Whether an individual Reserve bank had the power to initiate a rate change or to refuse compliance with a change proposed by the Board was long a matter of controversy. By now it is well settled that the Board of Governors has the power to initiate rate changes and to insist upon adherence to established rates, even though in practice individual Reserve banks, after consultation with the Board, initiate rate changes. There will normally be only brief periods in which all twelve banks do not charge the same rate. But however great the centralization of control over the discount rate, the judgment as to whether a member bank is making "proper" use of Reserve credit remains with the Reserve banks. In this respect, more than in any other, the autonomy of the individual Reserve banks has remained as the framers of the act envisaged it.

We must consider briefly the third instrument of Federal Reserve control—changes in reserve requirements. Ever since 1917 the basis of setting

---

[10] Another reason for the disappearance of rediscounting lay in the aversion of farmers and small-town businessmen to having their promissory notes sold to a bank outside the community. When a note that had been rediscounted came due, a Reserve bank would send it back to the original lending bank for collection of the amount owing. But a stamp on the back of the paper indicated that it had been rediscounted. There was thus no way of keeping the offensive transaction secret.

[11] There is an assumption, usually valid, that banks do not like to borrow money (except, of course, from their depositors). Some banks never borrow, and some borrow only to adjust their reserve positions. However, banks have little hesitancy about borrowing when it is a cheaper way of adjusting reserve positions than selling short-term securities.

reserve requirements for member banks has remained essentially unchanged, but the power of the Board to change total requirements for the system as a whole has been increased.

Almost as soon as the 7-10-13 per cent requirements for nonreserve, reserve, and central-reserve-city banks were established, it was suggested that the Board be given authority to raise and lower these required ratios. Not until 1933 was permissive legislation forthcoming, and then only for the duration of the economic emergency and with the permission of the President. The Banking Act of 1935 finally gave the Board of Governors permanent authority to raise and lower reserve ratios. Henceforth, the longstanding ratios of 7, 10, and 13 per cent could be as much as doubled; i.e., the percentages held against demand deposits by country banks could vary from 7 to 14, those held by reserve-city banks from 10 to 20, and those of the central-reserve-city banks from 13 to 26. Reserves against time deposits for all classes of banks might be set anywhere between 3 per cent and 6 per cent. The rules established in 1935 have, with one exception, remained unchanged to the present. In the late summer of 1948 Congress granted the Board temporary power to raise reserve requirements even higher, and during the ensuing months partial use was made of this authority, which expired on June 30, 1949.[12]

During World War II and its aftermath considerable reliance was placed on selective controls over certain narrowly defined areas of credit. In this respect a change occurred in the original notion of the proper function of the monetary authority. For selective controls do not aim at a blanket effect on the supply of credit but at the use of credit in particular segments of the economy. Partly because they arbitrarily interfere with only a portion of the business community and partly because the same effects can be obtained through use of the general instruments, there has since 1952 been little disposition to invoke these meddlesome and harshly discriminating controls.

Selective controls affect the demand for credit rather than the supply of it. Those who argue for them contend that the general instruments are not effective under certain conditions. For example, in the mid-1930s there was great fear of a recurrence of speculation in the stock market, and the Board of Governors was given authority to regulate margin requirements on loans for the purpose of purchasing or carrying securities. Just before the United States entered World War II and before price and allocation controls were seriously in effect, it was felt necessary to restrict the growth in consumer credit by increasing downpayments required on durable goods and restricting maturities on installment paper. Early in the war these restrictions on consumer credit—known as Regulation W—were tightened and extended. During two periods after World War II, as inflationary pres-

---

12 Effective July 28, 1962, the almost century-long classification of "central reserve" cities was removed.

sures built up and it appeared that general credit controls would not sufficiently restrict the demand for consumer durables, Regulation W was reimposed. In the fall of 1950, under authority contained in the Defense Production Act of that year, the Board of Governors temporarily put Regulation X into effect. Regulation X raised downpayments and limited maturities on conventional loans to finance one- and two-family residences, and later the regulation was extended to cover other dwellings and new commercial construction. Since the early 1950s only Regulations T and U, which set margin requirements for securities purchases, have remained in this arsenal.

There is no question that both the general and selective instruments of control work—i.e., they are mechanically effective. The effects of the general instruments on reserve positions of member banks can be precisely measured. The results of selective controls, though less certain and less predictable, are nevertheless admitted. In short, there is nothing "theoretical" about the way the tools of reserve adjustment work. Yet the actual manipulation of the tools, the carrying out of a proper monetary policy, constitutes one of the most perplexing problems in applied economics.

If general controls—manipulation of required reserve ratios and execution of open-market operations—are, in fact, mechanically effective, why then should there be any difficulties in their use? There are several reasons. For one thing, the precise results of creating or destroying reserves, so far as the money supply and the rate of interest are concerned, are not always known. An increase in the reserves of banks that in time of full employment would result in an addition to the money supply several times as large as the reserve creation may, during a depression, have no effect at all on the quantity of money. But even when the monetary authorities can be sure of a ready responsiveness of the money supply to reserve changes, they cannot predict with certainty the effects on the output of the economy as a whole. Finally, international objectives may conflict with desired monetary objectives. Within the nearly forty years of Federal Reserve experience World Wars I and II and the Korean War meant that noneconomic considerations controlled policy a good part of the time. During the 1920s, in an effort to facilitate Great Britain's return to the gold standard, Federal Reserve followed a policy of easy money not necessarily dictated by domestic requirements, and more recently persistent deficits in the U.S. balance of payments have put the Fed in the opposite bind. Thus, during more than half of the Federal Reserve's existence policy decisions could not be taken solely with a view to domestic economic considerations.

Whatever the difficulties may be, a responsible monetary authority must take action according to some lights. Despite the frequent conflict of aims, the monetary authority has made judgments that, for better or worse, have influenced the money supply and the rate of interest. A detailed study of policy decisions and of the reasons for these decisions constitutes an advanced and, to say the least, controversial topic in the economic history of the United States that is beyond the scope of this book. It is instructive, though, to review briefly and simply the major types of policy problems and actions.

The first three years or so of System activity were devoted to organization. Then came World War I with its unprecedented requirements for treasury financing. The obvious advantages of having a central bank to assist the government in wartime did much to gain quick acceptance of the Federal Reserve System and to establish it as a permanent institution. Yet the necessity for co-operating with the treasury in securing funds for the prosecution of the first "modern" war made the attainment of some economic objectives an impossibility. The large deficits were financed by the sale of bonds. Some of these were purchased by individuals and corporations out of current income, but a greater amount was bought either by the banks themselves or by individuals and corporations with funds borrowed from the banks. The Federal Reserve encouraged the banks to lend on the security of government bonds by making reserves for this purpose available at preferential rates. Interest on the bonds took care of the interest borrowers had to pay to the banks on their loans, and exhortations to patriotism did the rest.

Armistice in 1918 did not bring an end to the problems of treasury financing. To assure the success of the great Victory Loan of 1919, Federal Reserve co-operation in extending credit to the commercial banking system was still essential. Yet as early as December 1918 Reserve authorities expressed the view that a return to "stability of prices" could be accomplished only as the banks could unload their government bond holdings on the nonbank public.[13] Prices, which had risen steadily since the outbreak of war in Europe, moved even more sharply upward in 1919. A year after the end of hostilities, rediscount rates were finally raised; in the spring of 1920 the New York Federal Reserve Bank raised its rate to an all-time high of 7 per cent and left it there for a year. Meanwhile, wholesale prices continued to rise for a year and a half after the armistice until May 1920, when they began a decline which soon became precipitate. Not until the spring of 1921, when the deflation was nearly over, were rediscount rates reduced. There was much criticism of the System on grounds that (1) general economic aims were subordinate to the interests of the treasury during 1919, and (2) it failed to recognize the seriousness of the liquidity crisis that began in the late spring of 1920.

By the end of 1922 the severe liquidation that followed the 1920 break had ceased, and an improvement in business activity promised a brighter future. The next seven years witnessed some experimentation in central-bank control that has probably received higher marks from economists and

---

13 *Federal Reserve Bulletin* (December 1918), p. 1164.

historians than it deserved. Unfortunately, neither inside nor outside the System was there a theory of central banking adequate to prevent the tragedy of 1929–33.

Beginning in the spring of 1923, open-market purchases and sales of the Federal Reserve banks ceased to be a responsibility of the individual banks. Control over these operations was centralized and the basis for making judgments about security purchases and sales changed. Henceforth, securities were not bought on System account to increase earnings of the Federal Reserve banks but to accommodate commerce and business. Between 1923 and 1929 open-market operations were on occasion used in conjunction with changes in the discount rate in the traditional "scissors" operation of central banks. When it was desired to decrease member-bank reserves, securities were sold on the open market. Banks finding their reserves decreased tended to borrow from the Federal Reserve banks, where they were met with an increase in the discount rate and thus an increased cost of accommodation. Contrariwise, to ease credit open-market purchases were executed and banks that did not find reserves increased sufficiently were encouraged to borrow from the Federal Reserve by a lower discount rate. As Federal Reserve holdings of securities fell, bills discounted usually rose, and vice versa. Indeed, Fed authorities considered the response of commercial banks to open market purchases or sales a "test" of monetary policy. If, for example, an injection of reserves was followed by an approximately equal reduction in member-bank borrowing, Reserve officials felt that the "right" amount of bank credit was outstanding.

When at the beginning of 1923 an incipient boom threatened inflationary pressures, securities were sold and the discount rate was raised. A downturn in manufacturing production occurred in the summer of 1923 and continued into 1924, when discount rates were lowered and government securities were purchased. If System policy was aimed at combatting the recession, it certainly came several months too late, and the monetary ease of 1924 is probably better explained by Governor Strong's wish to keep interest rates down and so help England back onto the gold standard. Anyway, business picked up in the fall of 1924; almost without effort 1925 and 1926 were years of stable prices, output, and employment. Then came the frustrating years of the late twenties in which the Board was confronted with conflicting objectives. Rising real-estate prices and the rapidly growing volume of security credit concerned System authorities in early 1927. But late spring brought convincing evidence that industrial production was turning down. According to Adolph Miller, the only economist on the Federal Reserve Board, European currencies were also showing weakness, a turn that might interfere with agricultural sales abroad. So an easy money policy, implemented by open market purchases and a reduction in the discount rate, was begun in May. According to Miller the policy ". . . outlined by the New York Federal Reserve Bank, or more particularly by its distinguished Governor" was brilliantly successful in the short run but allowed bank credit (always the touchstone of early System policy) to get out of hand. Despite restrictive Fed efforts begun in 1928, it was necessary early in 1929 to exert "moral suasion" in an effort to bring about a reduction in brokers' loans. But direct pressure was largely ineffective because these loans were being made in great volume by lenders other than commercial banks. In the late summer of 1929 discount rates were raised to high levels, probably at just the right time to do maximum damage.

The general liquidation that began the last week in October 1929 was met by lowering of the discount rate. Federal Reserve credit plummeted, but gold inflows steadied the volume of member bank reserves after a first sharp drop. The Fed seemed content to let reserves stay at their 1929 levels throughout 1930 and the first half of 1931. Other than lowering the discount rate to 2 per cent, the monetary authorities showed no signs of aggressive action or even of major concern.

In September 1931, swamped by a wave of depression from the Continent, Great Britain went off the gold standard. Fearing that the United States would follow suit, foreign central banks and wealthy individuals transferred funds abroad and United States gold reserves began to drop. Although American gold reserves were near an all-time peak, the Federal Reserve Bank of New York played the gold-standard game by raising the rediscount rate in an effort to raise interest rates generally and stop the external gold drain. But what was far worse, Fed officials allowed member bank reserves to fall precipitately, and the money supply continued its decline at an accelerated rate. Disaster befell the country as the Federal Reserve, figuratively wringing its hands, allowed banks to fail by the hundreds, its minions in the Reserve banks actually conniving to collect on loans to failing banks before other creditors had their chance. By June of 1933 the money supply had dropped 30 per cent from the June 1929 figure. In the 1932 Annual Report (not the 1931 Report) the Board maintained that in February of 1932 its use of open-market purchases was inhibited by the requirement that Federal Reserve notes be backed by either gold or eligible paper. Although discounts secured by government bonds were eligible collateral, the bonds themselves were not. The Board argued that if the Federal Reserve carried out open-market purchases member banks would reduce their indebtedness and, consequently, the Reserve banks' holdings of eligible paper. But this meant that more gold would be required as note collateral at a time when only $416 million of gold was not committed to some legal reserve purpose. To substantiate its position the Board remarked that the Glass-Steagall Act of February 1932 provided a remedy by permitting government securities to serve as collateral against Federal Reserve notes. The System did indeed begin first moderate and then vigorous open-market purchases, and by mid-1932 System holdings of governments were over $1,800 million, a very large figure for the time. But let it never be forgotten that in 1931, when the heat was on, Federal Reserve officials refused to inject reserves for no such technical reasons. In his diary entries for August 1931 Charles S. Hamlin, then a member of the Board, tells us that the Open Market Committee voted 11 to 1 against open market purchases of $300 million, substituting $120 million instead. The governors of the several banks, still in the driver's seat, simply could not comprehend the extent of the catastrophe, and Governor Meyer of the Federal Reserve Board was even worried about inflation.

During the banking holiday of 1933 there was another brief episode of credit tightness. Then began a period of monetary ease that was not to be seriously interrupted for twenty years. By the summer of 1933 nearly all banks were out of debt to Federal Reserve, and system-wide excess reserves were considerable. With the "golden avalanche" of the mid-thirties, brought on as Europeans sent their funds to safety, excess reserves grew steadily. In 1937, concerned over possible inflationary threats, the Board raised reserve requirements, sharply reducing excess reserves and doubtless contributing to the nasty recession of 1937–38.[14] The downturn was met by a policy of monetary ease, and excess reserves again grew rapidly until they approached $7 billion at the end of 1940.

One new policy appeared in the late thirties. In 1937 the Federal Open Market Committee purchased bonds with a view to securing "orderly" conditions in the money market. From this time on a specific objective of policy was the promotion of a stable government securities market. Upon the outbreak of war in Europe, for example, heavy purchases were necessary to keep bond prices from falling drastically. But support of the bond market at pegged prices was not attempted until after the outbreak of World War II.

The primary objective of Federal Reserve policy during World War II was to assure treasury funds adequate to meet all government expenditures. On the day after Pearl Harbor the Board of Governors announced that the treasury would be supplied with sufficient money for war financing. In March 1942 the FOMC asserted its intention of preventing a rise in interest rates on government securities during the war and pledged the co-operation of the System. The chief instrument used to assure the success of treasury financing and to keep interest rates from rising was open-market policy. The Federal Reserve stood willing to buy, without limitation, all government obligations offered at the established prices and yields. On long-term securities this meant a maximum yield of 2.5 per cent, and yields ranged downward to a low of three-eighths of 1 per cent on ninety-day treasury bills.

This wartime policy had two important consequences. The first was the virtual abandonment of controls over the System's holdings of government securities, the volume of bank reserves, and the money supply. To prevent yields from rising, the Federal Reserve had to buy all governments offered to it at fixed prices. Bank and nonbank investors alike could thus obtain

---

[14] As a result of the decrease in excess reserves brought on by the increase in reserve requirements, loans and investments of member banks declined from $33 billion on December 31, 1936, to $32 billion on December 31, 1937.

cash for their government securities at will, and there was no effective upper limit to the monetization of the public debt. Second, large government deficits and restrictions on the availability of civilian goods sharply increased liquidity in the economy, and, since anyone could shift out of government securities into cash, funds were readily available to private borrowers. As a result the entire structure of interest rates remained low.

Inflationary pressures generated during the war were checked by price controls and rationing and on the surface appeared to have no harmful effects on the economy. The demand for credit was held in check. But both households and business firms accumulated huge amounts of savings between 1940 and 1945. Over the same period the money supply approximately trebled. Households, long kept from purchasing consumer durables, and business firms in need of new capital equipment stood ready to release their deferred demands. Between August 1945 and August 1948 the cost-of-living index rose 35 per cent and wholesale prices 61 per cent. Almost two-thirds of the rise in the cost of living over prewar levels and more than two-thirds of the total increase in wholesale prices came after the end of the war.

The Federal Reserve was almost entirely helpless in this inflationary situation. Strong voices, chiefly within the treasury, argued that the obligation to support prices of government securities, though precluding efforts at monetary restraint, was paramount. The proponents of support for treasury issues desired two main objectives. First, they felt it necessary to minimize interest charges on the public debt and to assure the success of treasury refunding operations. Second, fearful of the predicted postwar depression and unemployment, they were convinced that an endless supply of credit, furnished at low cost to business, was required even during the inflation. Co-operation with the treasury in pursuing these objectives meant that central bankers had little to say about the course of economic activity. It is not astonishing that most Federal Reserve authorities were reluctant to accept the treasury lead.

Had it not been for the decline in business activity that set in toward the end of 1948, a showdown must have come before it did. During the mild deflation of 1949 the controversy between Federal Reserve and treasury quieted down. By early 1950, however, recovery set in. Even before the outbreak of war in Korea, the question of proper monetary policy in the face of renewed inflationary pressures again came under discussion. By early spring of 1951 the cost of living and wholesale prices had risen in less than a year by nearly 10 and 20 per cent, respectively. Meanwhile, the gentlemanly disagreement between Federal Reserve and the treasury threatened to become a disruptive argument.

With the continued pressure of expansionary forces in late 1950 and early 1951, it became apparent to reasonable men that some way of resolving the conflict between Federal Reserve credit policy and treasury debt management had to be found. When the controversy began to involve prices of long-term bonds, treasury and Federal Reserve officials were at last forced to come to some agreement. Early in March 1951, the Secretary of the Treasury announced the "accord," which removed some of the inconsistencies that had so long beset national fiscal and monetary policy. Briefly, the treasury agreed to refund a part of its long-term marketable obligations into long-term nonmarketable 2.75 per cent bonds. The Federal Reserve, although agreeing to maintain an orderly market and to assist in the refunding of maturing treasury issues, would henceforth be able to allow yields on short-term securities to rise enough to make discount policy effective, and support of long-term bonds at or above par was no longer required. By early 1952 short-term yields had firmed, and some bonds were selling at more than 4 per cent below par.

After nearly ten years of weakened control over the money supply, the Federal Reserve regained its traditional weapons. It was once again possible to regulate the amount of commercial-bank reserves and thus the money supply and interest rates. Fed authorities turned to with a will. The policy adopted from the date of the accord to the late spring of 1953 was one of moderate restraint, ". . . designed to limit bank credit expansion to amounts consistent with the requirements of a growing economy operating at a high level without inflation." Open-market operations were so conducted as to adjust for gains or losses of reserve funds resulting from market causes and to compensate for seasonal swings in the demand for credit. In the winter and early spring of 1953 yields on intermediate- and long-term bonds rose sharply as the treasury lengthened maturities and raised the coupon rates on new issues. Federal Reserve authorities allowed the money and capital markets to become so tight in April and May of 1953 that in June they had no choice but to engineer a sharp reversal of policy through open-market purchases and downward adjustment of reserve requirements. Through the recession of 1953–54 a policy of "active ease" brought yields on government securities back to levels prevailing at the time of the accord.

During the next two swings in business activity the central bank pursued much the same course. Fed officials began to tighten credit in late 1954, long before ordinary mortals knew that an upturn had come. Yet in August of 1957, as many indicators were forecasting the coming recession, the Fed raised the discount rate yet another notch and reaffirmed the thirty-month policy of ever tightening finance. In November 1957, well after the beginning of the 1957–58 downturn, the monetary authorities brought about a precipitate downturn in interest rates, only to start them on their way to new highs as the economy began an expansionary phase in the late spring of 1958. A more moderate reduction in rates was engineered in the mild recession of 1960–61, and in the two years of moderate upswing that followed the Federal Reserve was less disposed to jack rates up than it had been in the two immediately preceding expansion periods.

In sum, during the period 1951–63 the Federal Reserve for the first time in its history explicitly accepted a major share of the responsibility of stabilizing the economy. Massive intervention in the government securities market through open-market operations clearly had a pervasive effect on interest rates.[15] In all fairness, the monetary authorities must be given some credit for containing inflationary pressures during the middle 1950s. Yet the economy had to pay a substantial price for this service in the form of a growing liquidity squeeze, for in the period 1951–63 the money supply grew at a rate of only slightly more than 2 per cent per annum. The consequence was a steady and persistent decline in the ratio of the money supply to the gross national product.

Since 1953 Federal Reserve and the treasury have avowedly tried to maintain the "independence" of the central bank. Federal Reserve officials have largely divorced themselves from the debt management oprations of the treasury. The treasury no longer seeks or gets from Federal Reserve support for a particular range of maturities to assure the success of a new issue. Yet everyone knows that the treasury and the central bank cannot go separate ways, without regard to each other's actions. The selection of rates and maturities of new government bond issues have their inevitable effect on the money supply and the rate of interest, the very quantities that the central bank is most concerned to influence. When the treasury is marketing a new issue, the System must on occasion provide the commercial banks with reserves or accept disastrous stringency in the money market.

Following the accord the Federal Reserve System did not become independent, but it did escape the dominance of the treasury, which had begun with United States entrance into World War II. In the post-accord period both agencies have operated on a basis of free interchange of views and close co-operation. More and more, however, the Director of the Budget and the Council of Economic Advisers have had their say in the formulation of *total* stabilization policy. It appears unlikely that a central bank can ever make decisions without regard to the views of the administration currently in office, and that the interdependence of monetary policy, debt-management policy, and fiscal policy must always be recognized.

The Changing Character of Commercial Banking

THE PROBLEM OF BANK FAILURES

Between 1900 and 1920 the number of banks in the country more than trebled—from about 9,000 to nearly 30,000. Banking was a lucrative business, and bankers had impeccable social status in the community. In this period of rising price levels banking was also less risky than usual in pre–New Deal days, for assets behind bank loans tended always to increase—

---

[15] The student will get some notion of the *volume* of meddling that went on when he reflects that in the three calendar years, 1957–59, it took $36 billion of gross transactions to achieve a $1,700 million net increase in Federal Reserve credit. See Ralph A. Young and Charles A. Yager, "The Economics of Bills Preferably," *Quarterly Journal of Economics*, LXXIV (August 1960), p. 351.

The prudence and patience of the rainy-day saver is reflected in the jam-up of patrons on opening day at this New York building and loan association in 1928. Of all the nonbank intermediaries, savings and loan associations would one day show the most spectacular growth.

rarely to decrease—in value. Bank failures averaged around eighty-five a year.

During the 1920s people began to speak of the "problem" of bank failures. Beginning in 1921 the number of banks decreased by several hundred each year. Over the nine-year span 1921–29, 5,411 banks failed. Most of them were small country banks, 85 per cent of the suspending banks having total assets of less than $1 million. But the remaining 15 per cent were national banks, and some of these were among the largest banks in the country.

The wave of failures that began a decade before the economic disintegration of the early thirties was in part a reaction to the rapid bank expansion that dated from around 1900. Banks had sprung up in nearly every village and hamlet, small county seat towns often boasting three or four, and the urbanization of the twenties was bound to result in some lessening of numbers. The greatest number of failures occurred in the predominantly agricultural areas as mortgages, made on the basis of high land values, went into default. With the deterioration of assets that occurred when loans to farmers and to businesses dependent upon farmers went bad, thousands of banks had no choice but to close their doors permanently.

During the great depression the number of suspensions was so great as to threaten the collapse of the entire banking system. Frightened depositors rushed to demand their funds, and banks were forced to liquidate assets in falling markets. As business activity fell off disastrously, even the most reliable borrowers could not repay their loans. During the four years 1930–33, 8,812 banks suspended, nearly half this number going under in 1933 alone. Courageous and vigorous rescue work on the part of the Federal Reserve banks would have mitigated the disaster, but central bankers of those emergency years, except in isolated instances, were primarily concerned about the solvency of the Federal Reserve banks. They actually did not understand that theirs was the money-creating power and that Reserve banks could not fail.

Beginning in February 1932, the Reconstruction Finance Corporation (RFC) made loans to banks in danger of failure and later made loans to help in the liquidation of closed banks. To enable other banks to re-open their doors on a sound basis, the RFC was also authorized to invest in the stock of commercial banks. In all, the RFC advanced nearly $2 billion to banks and purchased almost $1 billion of bank stock.[16] Many commercial banks, especially large ones, were saved from failure by the RFC, and final catastrophe was probably averted through its vigorous lending activity.

One of the first objectives of those wanting to prevent a recurrence of economic collapse was the establishment of a plan of deposit insurance. For a century there had been experiments in ways of protecting depositors and noteholders against bank failures. The safety-fund laws of pre–Civil War days had operated with some success in a few states. Because notes were either issued by or guaranteed by the federal government after the Civil War, noteholders no longer needed protection, but the problem of protecting deposits remained. By 1907 eight states had initiated plans of deposit insurance applicable to the state-chartered banks within their boundaries. These plans did not work well because (1) the premiums charged the participating banks were too low, (2) covered banks did not include the larger and stronger national banks, and (3) covered banks did an undiversified business in predominantly rural areas. It was apparent that some kind of a federal scheme would be required if deposit insurance were to be successful.

Bank customers and most bank managements were receptive to the temporary plan of deposit insurance provided in the Banking Act of 1933. Two years later the Banking Act of 1935 contained a permanent plan that has remained essentially unchanged to the present. The administering body is the Federal Deposit Insurance Corporation (FDIC), which, having paid back an original capital contribution by the treasury and the Federal Reserve banks, gets its funds from premiums paid by insured banks and from

---

[16] A. G. Hart, *Debts and Recovery* (New York: Twentieth Century Fund, 1938), pp. 55, 295. As we saw in Chapter 19, the railroads were greatly benefited by the RFC, and insurance companies, mortgage companies, and industrial firms were likewise helped, chiefly through loans.

interest on accumulated receipts. In an emergency the FDIC is authorized to raise large sums by borrowing from the treasury and others. All members of the Federal Reserve System must participate and others may do so. In 1961 about 97 per cent of all commercial banks holding more than 98 per cent of all deposits are insured.

Until 1950 the first $5,000 of each deposit account was insured; in 1950 the coverage was raised to $10,000 of each account. Although more than half of the dollar amount of deposits are not insured under the plan, present coverage is sufficient to limit the runs on banks that formerly resulted from group panic. Perhaps of greater significance are the examining and supervisory powers of the FDIC, which have led to higher standards of banking operation among the smaller banks. No one pretends, of course, that any system of deposit insurance guarantees an impregnable banking system, but with other strengthening factors, to be noted presently, it seems unlikely that we shall again witness anything like the wholesale suspensions of another era. Bank suspensions since 1933 have scarcely been significant; since 1934 the FDIC has made disbursements of $349 million to depositors in 445 failing banks, of which $328 million was recovered.

THE CONCENTRATION OF BANKING

Even with the tremendous reduction in the number of commercial banks that occurred between 1920 and 1933, the United States was left with more than 15,000 in 1934. Since then new banks have been organized, but a larger number have gone out of business as a result of mergers and absorptions, suspensions, and voluntary liquidations. By the end of 1954 a few more than 14,000 commercial banks were operating, and a decade later there were a few less than 14,000. The American tradition of a large number of independent banks continues, but a simple counting of establishments engaged in the banking business does not tell the whole story. Since the banking holiday of 1933 there has been a pronounced tendency toward concentration in banking.

The Federal Reserve defines concentration as ". . . the transaction of a decreasing proportion of the nation's banking business by separate and independently managed banks." Specifically, concentration may be evidenced by the growth of branch, group, and chain banking, and by increases in the volume of business controlled by the largest banks in the country or in a state or section.

When a parent bank owns and operates two or more offices, either within the same city or the same state, we refer to the offices other than the parent bank as "branches." Some states prohibit branch banking. Others allow branches to be established within the city or county in which the parent bank is located, and still others permit state-wide branches. Federal law regarding branches is never more liberal than state laws. In general, it permits members of the Federal Reserve System to establish branches in their main-office cities or in their main-office states if the laws of the state

A banker's nemesis in the early 1930s was the bank run. July 1930 saw this scene at Millbury, Massachusetts, which was repeated many thousand times over in the United States as depositors lost confidence in the guardians of their funds.

in which they are located explicitly authorize the state banks to have branches. The extent to which branch banking has developed is thus determined by an assortment of state laws.

Branch banking has shown a fairly steady increase over the past half-century as indicated by Table 20-1. Roughly 70 per cent of the branches established since 1933 have been new banking offices, the remaining 30 per cent representing the conversion of banks into branches.

There are two other forms of "multiple" banking besides branch banking—groups and chains. These two types have largely arisen in an effort to avoid the branch banking laws that, even in their most liberal form, keep the branches of a bank within the boundaries of a state. A "group" of banks consists of two or more banks under the control of a holding company that may or may not be a bank. In contrast to a branch system, a group of banks may operate in several states, though some groups are intrastate and are simply substitutes for branch systems in states that prohibit branch banking. A chain of banks is similar to a group but is distinguished by control over several independently incorporated banks exercised by one or more individuals or through interlocking directorates. Chains tend to center around a major bank, much larger than the others in the chain, but there are exceptions to this generalization.

Groups and chains experienced only negligible expansion from 1933 to 1948, but there has been considerable growth of these systems since that time. Between 1948 and 1961 the banking offices of fifteen leading groups, which comprise 85 per cent of the banking offices and deposits of registered

Table 20-1

Branch Banking in the United States for
Selected Years [a]

| End of year | Number of banks operating branches | Total number of branches operated | Location of branches | |
			In main-office city	Outside main-office city
1900	87	119	25	94
1920	530	1,281	773	508
1930	751	3,522	2,391	1,131
1940	954	3,525	1,602	1,923
1950	1,404	5,056	2,211	2,845
1952	1,483	5,520	2,496	3,024
1954	1,720	6,416	2,860	3,556
1957	2,066	8,373	3,502	4,871
1959	2,351	9,835	3,983	5,852
1960	2,523	10,702	4,288	6,414
1961	2,696	11,620	4,644	6,976

SOURCE: Board of Governors of the Federal Reserve System, *Banking and Monetary Statistics* (Washington, D.C., 1943), and *Federal Reserve Bulletin*.

[a] Includes mutual savings banks but does not include banking facilities at military and other government establishments.

bank holding companies, increased by over 80 per cent. At the end of 1960 forty-seven holding companies controlled 9 per cent of the commercial-bank offices and $18,300 million of deposits—nearly 11 per cent of all commercial-bank deposits in the country.[17] Chain banking, concentrated in a few states where branch banking is prohibited, actually declined in importance between 1931 and 1945, but this form of organization seems to be making a comeback. In 1945 the Board of Governors reported that chains had about 522 banks with deposits of $4,600 million. At the end of 1961 the Association of Registered Bank Holding Companies estimated that chains included 700 banks with deposits in excess of $9,200 million.

It is possible, of course, that an undesirable concentration, in the sense of acquisition of great power by a few banks in the country, may be taking place in another way. The largest bank in the United States, the Bank of America with headquarters in San Francisco, customarily reports a volume of deposits greater than the total of deposits for all member banks in the Eighth Federal Reserve District. In fact, in six of the twelve Federal Reserve districts member-bank deposits total less than those of the Bank of America, and in two more districts member-bank deposits about equal those

---

[17] Gerald C. Fischer, *Bank Holding Companies* (New York and London: Columbia University Press, 1961), p. 47.

of the Bank of America. The National City Bank of New York and the Chase National Bank regularly show $5 billion of deposits or more.

On the other hand, the changes in the proportion of total deposits held by the one hundred largest banks of the country reflect no particular trend toward concentration. This proportion increased from less than one-third in 1923 to over 55 per cent in 1935, and, after a brief reversal, to nearly 58 per cent in 1940. During World War II the proportion fell sharply and then leveled off at a little more than 46 per cent during the 1950s, rising to 50 per cent in the early 1960s.

One more remark on the size of banks is in order. Since 1920 the number of banks has been halved while the total of bank deposits has increased more than sevenfold. On the average, then, banks are about fifteen times as large today as they were forty-odd years ago. This change is all to the good, for financial institutions usually gain strength with size. It is for this reason, too, that many people cannot become too excited over the growth of branch banking and the existence of groups and chains.

THE CHANGING CHARACTER OF BANK BALANCE SHEETS

A somewhat technical point remains to be considered, not so much for its own sake as for the light it throws on the shifting nature of commercial banking.

For a while after World War I, banks continued to do business in the traditional way. The distribution of earning assets varied from bank to bank, but usually loans based on commercial transactions greatly exceeded "investments"—i.e., holdings of securities. A glance at the chart on p. 524 gives a good idea of the relative importance of loans, government securities, and "other" securities, chiefly the bonds of private corporations. During the twenties portfolio policy remained almost unchanged. With the onset of depression and the consequent falling off of business activity, banks reduced the volume of loans greatly, increasing somewhat their holdings of

Rapid clearance of checks is assured by devices like this magnetic-ink reading machine (which also sorts the checks into appropriate piles). This installation, at New York's First National City Bank, reflects the increasing automation of banking in America.

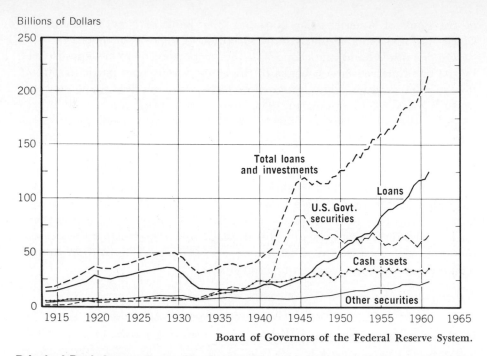

Billions of Dollars

Total loans
and investments

Loans

U.S. Govt.
securities

Cash assets

Other securities

Board of Governors of the Federal Reserve System.

Principal Bank Assets: During the Great Depression bankers became progressively fearful of loans to business, but their faith in the business community was restored in postwar booms.

governments. By 1934 the total amount of investments exceeded the amount of loans, though it was not until 1943 that the income from the former exceeded the income from the latter. By that time the value of securities owned was twice that of loans outstanding.

In 1945 it looked as though banks had changed from holders of private debt to holders of public debt. Many observers were commenting that the banking system had ceased to perform its primary function of assuring a steady flow of goods and services into the market place by furnishing short-term credit to commerce and industry. Supporters of this view contended that bank loans no longer bore a close relationship to industrial production and that there was a growing tendency for banks to keep funds idle in the form of cash assets. Bankers rejoined that safe loans could not be made during the thirties and that the government, by building its own facilities and lending directly to business during World War II, had continued to depress the demand for loans. In effect, the bankers argued, banks financed the government, which in turn financed private industry.

During the postwar years there was a rapid growth of loans as banks, to increase their profits, shifted out of the government securities that an obliging Federal Reserve, until 1951, stood ready to purchase at or above par. By late 1952 loans exceeded holdings of government securities, though

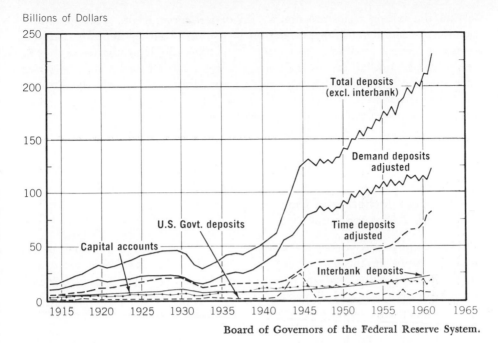

Billions of Dollars

Total deposits
(excl. interbank)

Demand deposits
adjusted

U.S. Govt. deposits

Time deposits
adjusted

Capital accounts

Interbank deposits

Board of Governors of the Federal Reserve System.

Principal Bank Liabilities: During World War II demand deposits (and thus the money supply) soared. In recent years time deposits have increased in relative importance.

other securities weighted the balance on the investment side. Even with the return toward the historical distribution of assets, particularly notable since the mid-1950s, it is apparent that the economic functions of banks have been modified. In the modern economy they have become both allocators of funds to business firms and residual lenders to the federal government. As they always have, though, banks continue to perform the vital functions of keeping most of the economy's money supply on their books and of facilitating the process of making payments by transferring deposits from one account to another.

One continuing change on the liabilities side of commercial bank balance sheets ought to be observed. The chart above indicates that capital accounts (owners' equities) have not increased since 1920 in anything like the same proportion as deposits; i.e., the ratio of capital accounts to total deposits has fallen. As far back as 1890 the ratio was one-third, and at the inception of the Federal Reserve it was one-fifth. Except for the depression years the ratio has fallen until it presently approximates one-twelfth.

Because the capital accounts represent the owner interest and the buffer that furnishes some depositor protection in the event of unprofitable operation or liquidation, some economists and bankers have expressed grave concern over this historical tendency. A more moderate and modern view is that the falling ratios are not a sign of weakness. If the assets of banks deteriorate rapidly, a high proportion of capital to either deposits or assets does not furnish significant protection, as witness the depositor losses during the wave of bank failures in the early thirties. And if we examine the ratios of capital accounts to risk assets—i.e., to assets other than cash and government securities—we find that they have not fallen very much over time. The thinner capitals of modern times do not point up a weakness of the banking structure so much as they indicate a change in the way of carrying on the business. Banks today rely to a far greater extent on the funds of depositors as a basis of profitable operation than they did even a generation ago.

The Money Supply and the Nonbank Intermediaries

By 1914, coins and currency constituted a relatively small portion of the money supply. In the past forty years bank deposits have come more and more to serve as the medium of exchange, and today cash is used for convenience only. It is still of passing interest to note the kinds of coin and paper money that have circulated in the past few decades.

COINS AND PAPER MONEY

In 1914, cash in circulation consisted chiefly of gold and gold certificates, silver certificates and silver coin, United States notes, and national bank notes. Between 1914 and 1933 the currency for which the treasury was responsible did not change much in the various categories except that, for practical reasons, gold coins went gradually out of use. It had been expected that national-bank notes would disappear from circulation after the establishment of the central bank, but national banks kept their issue out mostly for advertising purposes.[18] Not until the issuing privilege was withdrawn in 1935 did national-bank notes begin to disappear. Meanwhile, Federal Reserve notes became the major item of the currency, accounting for about two-thirds of total cash by 1936.

This proportion held until 1941. On June 30 of that year, of a total of $9,600 million cash in circulation (i.e., outside treasury and Federal Reserve), Federal Reserve notes amounted to about $6,600 million and the treasury currency to about $3 billion, mostly silver and silver certificates, United States notes, and minor coin. The remarkable increase in the cash supply that occurred during World War II and the postwar years was mostly in Federal Reserve notes. As of mid-1954, cash in circulation amounted to $30 billion, of which $25,400 million were Federal Reserve notes and the rest treasury currency; by the end of 1962 cash in circulation was over the $34 billion mark, of which $30 billion were Federal Reserve notes. The function of issuing hand-to-hand money has become almost exclusively that

---

[18] The name and city of the issuing bank appeared on the national-bank notes.

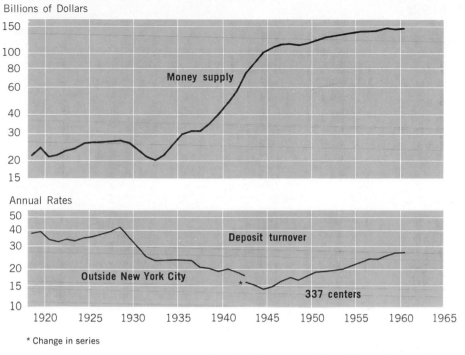

Billions of Dollars

150
100
80
60
40
30
20
15

Money supply

Annual Rates

50
40
30
20
15
10

Deposit turnover

Outside New York City

*

337 centers

1920 1925 1930 1935 1940 1945 1950 1955 1960 1965

* Change in series

Board of Governors of the Federal Reserve System.

Money Stock and Velocity of Circulation: The rate of increase of the money supply (defined by Federal Reserve as demand deposits and currency outside banks) has slowed in recent years, but deposit turnover has increased substantially since 1945.

of the Federal Reserve; except for the coinage, treasury currency is an anachronistic vestige of a day long past.

Between 1915 and 1920, currency outside banks increased over two and a half times. Between 1920 and 1940 it increased approximately 50 per cent. During World War II years currency outside banks quadrupled and, after declining gently for a few years after 1945, began a slow rise that has continued into the 1960s. Although the rate of increase would understandably be high during wartime because of accelerated business activity, the growth during the late war cannot be explained on these grounds alone. Wishing to hide skulduggery, many people required transactions to be effected in cash, and it is probable that ill-gotten gains are even now stashed away in safe-deposit boxes in bills of large denomination.

Whatever the reasons for the large amounts of cash now required by the public, decisions to hold a given amount of coin and paper money are made by the individuals in the economy. Federal Reserve cannot make people hold a greater volume of cash than they wish to hold or reduce the quantity that people consider necessary for daily business transactions. Nor do the treasury or the commercial banks have anything to say in the

Table 20-2

Total Assets of Major Financial Institutions
(millions of dollars)

End of year	Commercial banks	Life insurance companies	Savings and loan associations	Mutual savings banks	Total
1910	19,226	3,876	932	3,690	27,724
1911	20,574	4,164	1,031	3,837	29,606
1912	21,822	4,409	1,138	4,015	31,384
1913	22,683	4,659	1,248	4,170	32,760
1914	23,058	4,935	1,358	4,273	33,624
1915	27,527	5,190	1,484	4,408	38,609
1916	30,972	5,537	1,599	4,651	42,759
1917	36,747	5,941	1,769	4,810	49,267
1918	40,988	6,475	1,898	4,940	54,301
1919	47,843	6,791	2,127	5,363	62,124
1920	46,644	7,320	2,520	5,840	62,324
1921	42,208	7,936	2,891	6,160	59,195
1922	47,267	8,652	3,343	6,597	65,859
1923	49,203	9,455	3,943	7,023	69,624
1924	54,224	10,394	4,766	7,538	76,922
1925	57,475	11,538	5,509	8,025	82,547
1926	58,105	12,940	6,334	8,572	85,951
1927	61,433	14,392	7,179	9,240	92,244
1928	66,429	15,961	8,016	9,780	100,186
1929	65,621	17,482	8,695	9,873	101,671
1930	61,985	18,880	8,829	10,540	100,234
1931	51,420	20,160	8,417	11,137	91,134
1932	45,738	20,754	7,737	11,103	85,332
1933	40,640	20,896	7,018	10,758	79,312
1934	47,586	21,844	6,406	11,008	86,844
1935	52,338	23,216	5,875	11,173	92,602
1936	57,672	24,874	5,772	11,485	99,803
1937	55,475	26,249	5,682	11,562	98,968
1938	58,243	27,755	5,632	11,611	103,241
1939	65,216	29,243	5,597	11,852	111,908
1940	72,799	30,802	5,733	11,981	121,315
1941	79,104	32,731	6,049	11,808	129,692
1942	96,891	34,931	6,150	11,907	149,879
1943	114,199	37,766	6,604	13,024	171,593
1944	137,090	41,054	7,458	14,761	200,363
1945	160,312	44,797	8,747	16,987	230,843
1946	149,517	48,191	10,202	18,665	226,575
1947	155,377	51,743	11,687	19,714	238,521
1948	154,506	55,512	13,026	20,474	243,520
1949	157,462	59,630	14,622	21,493	253,207
1950	168,932	64,020	16,893	22,385	272,230
1951	179,464	68,278	19,222	23,439	290,403
1952	188,603	73,375	22,660	25,233	309,871
1953	193,010	78,533	26,733	27,130	325,406
1954	202,378	84,486	31,736	29,276	347,876
1955	210,734	90,432	37,880	31,274	370,320

matter. The monetary authority can affect the size of the money supply, but it is up to the nonbank public to determine how much of it will be held as cash.

BANK DEPOSITS

The most remarkable aspect of the growing money supply has been the secular upward movement of demand and time deposits. A glance at the chart on p. 538 or Table 20-3 confirms this observation. The increase in deposits has not been uniform, sharp upward thrusts having come during wartime and sudden drops during depressions.

It is beyond the scope of this book to discuss in detail the forces that have brought deposits to their present volume. We may say, briefly, that they came into being because the commercial banks, acting as a system, created deposits through the lending process. The ability of the banking system to lend depends, at any time, on the quantity of reserves possessed by the banks. But what determines the amount of reserves?

There are many variables that affect the quantity of reserves of the commercial banks; of these, three are so important that for all practical purposes we may neglect the others. They are the size of the monetary gold stock, the amount of currency in circulation, and the amount of Reserve bank credit.

1. *Gold no longer plays its old role in the American monetary system.* During the crisis of 1931–33 people began to hoard gold and gold certificates as they lost confidence in all other forms of money. By authority granted in the Banking Act of 1933, the President in April 1933 required all individuals and business firms, including banks, to exchange their gold and gold certificates for other cash at a Federal Reserve bank. Anyone wishing to obtain gold for export had first to obtain a license from the

Table 20-2 (continued)

End of year	Commercial banks	Life insurance companies	Savings and loan associations	Mutual savings banks	Total
1956	217,460	96,011	42,875	33,381	389,727
1957	222,696	101,309	48,138	35,215	407,358
1958	238,651	107,580	55,139	37,784	439,154
1959	244,686	113,650	63,530	38,945	460,811
1960	257,552	119,576	71,476	40,571	489,355
1961	278,561	126,816	82,135	42,829	530,341
1962 ᵖ	290,340	133,169	93,729	46,116	563,354

SOURCES: *Banking and Monetary Statistics, Federal Reserve Bulletin, 1956 Life Insurance Fact Book, Savings and Home Financing Source Book, 1956, Annual Report, Comptroller of the Currency,* and Raymond W. Goldsmith, *A Study of Savings in the United States* (Princeton: Princeton University Press, 1955–56).

ᵖ Preliminary.

treasury. The Gold Reserve Act of 1934 extended the prohibition against direct gold ownership to the Federal Reserve banks, which were required to turn gold over to the treasury in exchange for gold certificates. Henceforth, the monetary gold stock was legally owned by the treasury, and gold certificates constituted the reserves of Federal Reserve banks against their major liabilities—Federal Reserve notes and member-bank deposits. In June 1945, the original reserve ratios of 40 per cent against Federal Reserve notes and 35 per cent against deposits were changed by an act of Congress to 25 per cent for both notes and deposits. Since no one can convert his money into gold certificates, gold certificate reserves are only a legal fiction. Setting a gold certificate reserve ratio places a legal upper limit to the amount of Federal Reserve credit that can be created, but the limit can be changed by Congress at any time. Thus gold no longer serves as an automatic regulator of the money supply. But *changes* in the monetary gold stock still affect the reserves of commercial banks.

By a series of steps taken in 1933 the official price of gold was gradually raised—i.e., the official gold content of the dollar was lowered.[19] Since February 1, 1934, the treasury has stood ready to buy at a price of $35 an ounce all gold offered to it. Sellers of gold may be either foreign central banks or domestic mining companies. When a seller takes gold to a United States assay office, he is reimbursed by a check written by a representative of the United States Treasury on the treasury's account with Federal Reserve. The seller then deposits the check in a commercial bank; the commercial bank in turn sends the check to a Federal Reserve bank, which credits the commercial bank's reserve account. The Reserve bank in effect exchanges the check for gold certificates, thus adding to its own reserves. When the treasury sells gold, either to a foreign central bank or to an American importer who needs it to meet an obligation abroad, reserves of both member banks and the Federal Reserve fall.

2. *Increases in the amount of currency in circulation decrease member-bank reserves, and decreases in the amount of currency in circulation add to member-bank reserves.* When a member bank notices an increasing demand for paper and coin, it obtains additional supplies by drawing a check on its reserve account at the Federal Reserve and thus reducing its reserve balance. Contrariwise, as people return cash from circulation, the member bank deposits the redundant amount with the Federal Reserve, in this way adding to its reserve account.

3. *We have already noted that when Federal Reserve credit is created, either by open-market purchases or by advances to member banks, the reserve accounts of commercial banks are thereby increased.* When Federal Reserve contracts its credit, either by open-market sales or by taking pay-

---

[19] Redefinition of the dollar in terms of a smaller amount of gold is called "devaluation." Devaluation, as we mentioned in Chapter 18, was based on the theory that raising the price of gold would result in a proportionate increase in commodity prices.

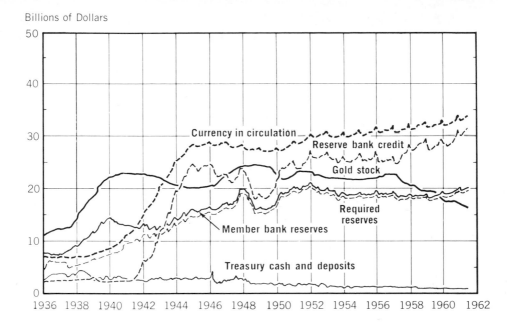

Billions of Dollars

Board of Governors of the Federal Reserve System.

Factors Affecting Reserves: Through the use of Federal Reserve credit the central bank can set the amount of member-bank reserves at any desired level.

ments from member banks, the reserve accounts of commercial banks are reduced.

Changes in the gold stock are largely dependent on international financial conditions and are thus pretty much independent of central bank regulation. Changes in the amount of cash that people wish to hold are likewise largely independent of Federal Reserve regulation. Federal Reserve credit, as the Board puts it officially, ". . . is the balance wheel between these two more or less independent factors and member bank reserves. It is the chief means by which the Federal Reserve, through influencing the volume of member bank reserves, can discharge its responsibility to regulate the volume of bank credit and the total money supply."

It is instructive to follow the course of the four factors of the monetary equation since January 1934 (see chart below). From 1934 to the end of 1941 the monetary gold stock of the United States increased tremendously. The growth of currency in circulation partly offset the gold inflow throughout these years and during 1941 more than offset it. The Reserve authorities, thinking to maintain easy money conditions during most of the thirties, left Reserve bank credit stable at about $2,500 million. The result was a large increase in member-bank reserves until the end of 1940. During World War II there was a net outflow of gold as the United States purchased strategic materials, chiefly from Latin America, and exported a vast quantity of goods to our allies under lend-lease. Currency in circulation rose rapidly during the war, reducing member-bank reserves, but monetary authorities saw to it that sufficient Reserve bank credit was available to assure ample reserves for war financing. From the end of the war until mid-1950 Reserve bank credit fell rather drastically, though net gold inflows left member reserves about what they were five years earlier (see chart, p. 531).[20] Since the accord the amount of reserves has been primarily dependent upon Reserve credit, with net reserve injections (through open-market purchases) offsetting the reserve-reducing effect of the gold outflow that began in 1958.

In general, as we have said, deposits will rise as reserves rise and fall as reserves fall. This will not always be the case, however, and it may happen that the banks in the system will wish, for years on end, to keep excess reserves. The chart on p. 524 indicates that during the stagnant thirties banks could not find safe outlets for loans to business, and excess reserves were inordinately great by 1940.[21] Thus deposits did not rise nearly as much as they might have between 1933 and 1940. During 1941 and 1942, total reserves actually fell as deposits rose, a phenomenon made possible by the huge amount of excess reserves. By 1943 excess reserves were close to a working minimum, and since that year deposits have been closely related to reserves.

So long as business activity is great, with full or nearly full employment, the correlation between reserves and deposits is high. Banks in the large cities always keep their excess reserves to a smaller figure than do country banks, and there is some recent evidence to support the conclusion that all banks now operate with smaller reserve balances than previously. In time of economic slump banks have always kept a larger volume of excess reserves than during good times, and there is good reason to suppose that as time goes on commercial banks change their propensity to hold excess reserves. For this reason the banking system's "free" reserves—i.e., excess reserves minus member-bank borrowing—may often delude monetary authorities who use this variable as their chief indication of monetary ease or tightness.

THE NONBANK INTERMEDIARIES

The money supply, strictly defined, consists of currency outside banks and demand deposits on the books of commercial banks. Money is perfect liquidity. Yet clearly liabilities of other financial institutions, the nonbank intermediaries, are so readily convertible into money that they constitute

---

[20] The fact that reserves did not increase, on balance, during this five-year period meant that the money supply could not grow much either. Federal Reserve's sanctimonious insistence that in these pre-accord years support of bond prices made it an "engine of inflation" is patent nonsense.

[21] The excess would have been much greater if the Board of Governors, beginning in August 1936, had not raised reserve requirements, doubtless helping to bring on the recession of 1937–38.

a category of financial assets closest to money in the liquidity spectrum. Largely for this reason the recent growth in volume of deposits in mutual savings banks, savings and loan shares, cash values in life insurance, equities in pension funds, etc., has captured the attention of economists and financial observers.

The nonbank intermediaries are essentially *consumer* directed. With a few obvious and minor exceptions they purport, on the one hand, to render some kind of service to household units. They will insure a life, lend money on residential real estate, invest in securities to provide for retirement income, make personal loans, and so on. On the other hand, they all accept savings, serving as a go-between that links the household unit to demanders of funds, which may be other household units or business firms.

Nonmonetary intermediaries, like commercial banks, have grown and thrived because they are profitable to someone. The notion has gained currency that financial institutions have been promoted because the wise and good men of a community wanted to do something nice for people. Originally, altruistic motivation may have been strong. But venturers have always had their psychic rewards, and we delude ourselves when we imagine that financial entrepreneurs are essentially different from other entrepreneurs. To take an example, savings and loan associations began their rapid upsurge after 1910 for reasons that had little to do with altruistic endeavors to provide decent housing for urban dwellers. Instead these institutions got their start because builders were continually thwarted in their attempts to develop mass markets by the reluctance of commercial banks to make mortgage loans available to anyone but the affluent. Lucrative insurance and abstracting businesses could be run on the side. And once the savings and loan industry could do a volume business, lending itself (with accompanying fees and charges) became extremely profitable.

It is easy to generalize about the growth of financial intermediaries, using the jargon of economics. Internal financing of household and business units, though continuing to be substantial, has in the last half-century been largely replaced by external financing—borrowing from other units. External financing may be direct or indirect; i.e., a borrowing (deficit) unit may obtain funds directly from a lending (surplus) unit, or it may obtain them indirectly from an intermediary. Intermediaries exchange their own liabilities for funds, largely of household units, which are in turn lent to businesses or household units in exchange for securities such as bonds or mortgages.

To be profitable nonbank intermediaries must operate in an environment that includes (a) homogeneity of the money supply, (b) large numbers of people (savers), (c) a growing supply of securities, and (d) a high rate of increase in real incomes so that households can enjoy the luxury of saving. A moment's reflection convinces us that for approximately a century these historical prerequisites to profitable indirect financing have been met in the United States. To be sure, particular intermediaries have benefited from special legislation. Thus New Deal laws providing for federal insurance of savings and loan accounts, plus the establishment of the Federal Home Loan Bank System to make money available to associations at subsidized rates, made savings and loan shares liquid enough to be attractive in the judgment of savers. The savings and loan business has benefited from highly favorable tax legislation, as have insurance companies and pension funds. Credit unions pay no federal income taxes at all. The list of advantages clearly subsidizing the nonbank intermediaries is almost endless.

Nevertheless, inspection of the relevant data supports the proposition that another influence, essentially impersonal and mechanistic, encourages and promotes the growth of the nonmonetary intermediaries. This influence is summed up in the following hypothesis:

> The growth of nonmonetary intermediaries is preceded and largely determined by an expansion of the money supply by the banking system; the nonmonetary intermediaries serve the cause of total economic growth by dislodging idle bank deposits and making them a part of the active money supply.[22]

In the twentieth century the most obvious and rapid increases in the money supply have occurred during the two World Wars when, as a consequence of deficit financing, there were abnormally rapid additions to the money supply. A glance at the chart on p. 535 indicates that in both of these periods assets of commercial banks grew at faster rates than those of the major competing nonmonetary intermediaries. Similarly, Table 20-3 and the chart on p. 538 reveal how in war years the total liabilities of commercial banks increased as a proportion of the liabilities of the major financial institutions selected for comparison.[23]

It is clear that the sharpest retrogression of the bank system occurred with the deflation of the Great Depression. It is also apparent that the deficit financing of the Korean episode was sufficient at least to arrest the postwar decline in the relative position of the commercial banking system. In the recession years of 1953–54 and 1957–58 total bank assets and bank liabilities rose substantially as the Federal Reserve removed restraints on the money supply, but only in the latter episode was the boost to the money supply sufficient to halt the slow decline in the relative position of the commercial banks.

The money-creating institutions grew faster than the nonmonetary institutions during periods of massive deficit financing such as occurred

---

[22] For this proposition and much of the following discussion I am indebted to my colleague Professor E. E. Edwards, who has been patient with me for many years while I have learned to accept this view. However, Professor Edwards has no responsibility for my statement of these relationships.

[23] Increasing the number of intermediaries for comparison is not likely to change the conclusions to which we come. Nevertheless, a full treatment ought to include, at a minimum, investment companies, credit unions, and private (noninsured) pension funds. The latter, for example, grew by more than $7 billion in the two years between December 31, 1958, and December 31, 1960, to reach total liabilities of $33 billion.

Millions of Dollars

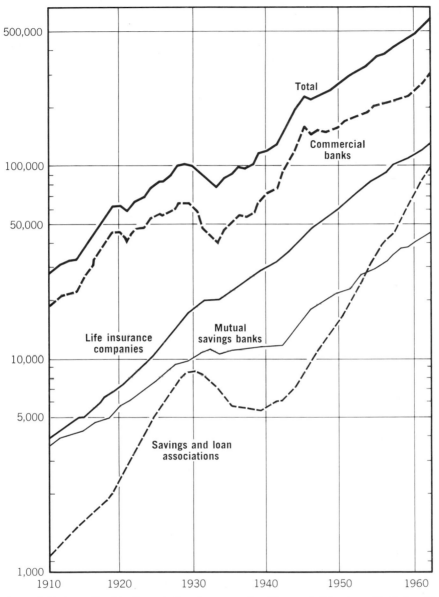

Annual Report, Comptroller of the Currency; Banking and Monetary Statistics; Federal Reserve Bulletin; Raymond W. Goldsmith, *A Study of Saving in the United States* (Princeton: Princeton University Press, 1955–56); *1956 Life Insurance Fact Book; Savings and Home Financing Source Book, 1956.*

Growth of Financial Intermediaries: For several reasons the growth of savings and loan associations since 1940 has been fantastic. Their success has led to demands by competing intermediaries and government officials for restrictive legislation.

Table 20-3

Principal Liabilities of (Claims Against) Major Financial Institutions (millions of dollars)

End of year [a]	Commercial banks			Life insurance companies	Savings and loan associations	Mutual savings banks	Total
	Demand deposits (adjusted)	Time deposits	Total deposits	Policy reserves less policy loans	Share accounts of individuals	Total deposits	
1910	8,254	3,636	11,890	2,731	759	3,392	18,772
1911	8,668	3,928	12,596	2,931	n.a.	3,526	n.a.
1912	9,156	4,313	13,469	3,107	n.a.	3,687	n.a.
1913	9,140	4,606	13,746	3,276	n.a.	3,833	n.a.
1914	10,082	4,441	14,523	3,431	n.a.	3,919	n.a.
1915	9,828	5,264	15,092	3,619	1,190	4,044	23,945
1916	11,973	6,088	18,061	3,909	n.a.	4,327	n.a.
1917	13,501	7,038	20,539	4,223	n.a.	4,417	n.a.
1918	14,843	7,207	22,050	4,590	n.a.	4,533	n.a.
1919	17,624	8,522	26,146	5,025	n.a.	4,940	n.a.
1920	19,616	10,509	30,125	5,479	1,741	5,395	42,740
1921	17,113	10,917	28,030	5,845	1,965	5,642	41,482
1922	18,045	11,592	29,637	6,308	2,210	6,002	44,157
1923	19,144	13,871	33,015	6,932	2,626	6,378	48,951
1924	20,898	15,280	36,178	7,616	3,153	6,820	53,767
1925	22,288	16,570	38,858	8,481	3,811	7,219	58,369
1926	21,721	17,508	39,229	9,462	4,378	7,683	60,752
1927	22,730	18,962	41,692	10,494	5,027	8,265	65,478
1928	23,081	19,761	42,842	11,596	5,762	8,770	68,970
1929	22,809	19,192	42,001	12,569	6,237	8,838	69,645
1930	20,967	19,012	39,979	13,424	6,296	9,424	69,123
1931	17,412	15,366	32,778	14,015	5,916	10,012	62,721
1932	15,728	13,631	29,359	14,033	5,326	9,929	58,647
1933	15,035	11,019	26,054	14,308	4,750	9,488	54,600
1934	18,459	12,213	30,672	15,372	4,458	9,738	60,240
1935	22,115	13,170	35,285	16,864	4,254	9,871	66,274
1936	25,483	14,046	39,529	18,389	4,194	10,056	72,168
1937	23,959	14,779	38,738	19,803	4,080	10,170	72,791
1938	25,986	14,766	40,752	21,106	4,077	10,278	76,213
1939	29,793	15,258	45,051	22,579	4,118	10,523	82,271
1940	34,945	15,777	50,722	24,147	4,322	10,658	89,849
1941	38,992	15,884	54,876	26,026	4,682	10,532	96,116
1942	48,922	16,352	65,274	28,114	4,941	10,641	108,970
1943	60,803	19,224	80,027	30,676	5,494	11,717	127,914
1944	66,930	24,074	91,004	33,443	6,305	13,351	144,103
1945	75,851	30,135	105,986	36,705	7,365	15,385	165,441
1946	83,314	33,808	117,122	39,805	8,548	16,835	182,310
1947	87,121	35,249	122,370	42,945	9,753	17,763	192,831
1948	85,520	35,804	121,324	46,101	10,964	18,405	196,794
1949	85,750	36,146	121,896	49,258	12,471	19,293	202,918
1950	92,272	36,314	128,586	52,533	13,992	20,031	215,142
1951	98,234	37,859	136,093	55,957	16,107	21,915	229,072
1952	101,508	40,666	142,174	59,866	19,195	22,586	243,821
1953	102,451	43,659	146,110	63,709	22,846	24,398	257,063
1954	106,650	46,844	153,494	67,776	27,334	26,359	274,963
1955	109,914	48,359	158,273	72,069	32,192	28,187	290,721
1956	111,391	50,577	161,968	76,219	37,148	30,026	305,516
1957	110,254	56,139	166,393	80,206	41,912	31,683	320,194
1958	115,507	63,166	178,673	84,416	47,976	34,031	345,196
1959	115,402	65,884	181,286	89,357	54,583	34,977	359,549
1960	115,102	71,380	186,482	93,242	62,142	36,343	378,209
1961	120,525	82,145	202,670	98,900 [b]	70,885	38,277	410,748
1962	121,700	96,700	218,400	103,800 [b]	80,378	41,334	443,912

SOURCES: *Federal Reserve Bulletin, 1959 Life Insurance Fact Book, Banking and Monetary Statistics, Annual Report, Comptroller of the Currency, National Association of Mutual Savings Banks Statistical Bulletin, Federal Home Loan Bank Board* releases, *Savings and Mortgage Statistics*, American Bankers Association, and Raymond W. Goldsmith, *A Study of Savings in the United States* (Princeton: Princeton University Press, 1955–56).

[a] June 30 from 1910 through 1922.

[b] Preliminary and partly estimated.

during World Wars I and II. This growth paved the way for rapid increases in assets and liabilities of the nonbank intermediaries. As a large money supply is created, an even larger proportion of balances lie idle. Contrary to vulgar belief, commercial banks cannot lend deposits.[24] For this reason, some force must dislodge quiescent balances if they are once again to enter the transactions stream. It is at this point that the derivative institutions begin their growth as bank depositors are persuaded to transfer funds held as time deposits and (presumably to a lesser extent) demand deposits from commercial banks to savings and loan associations, mutual savings banks, mutual funds, etc. The transfer is from institutions of greater "respectability" to those of lesser "respectability," the enticements being many—higher interest payments, greater convenience, hedges against inflation, and so on.

It seems likely that the effect of money creation during recessions has the same, if a somewhat milder, effect. Increases in the money supply that took place during the recession of 1953–54 and again during the recession of 1957–58 were probably substantial enough to be of considerable assistance to the nonbank intermediaries. It is apparent, of course, that increases in the money supply are necessary to the continuing growth of the nonbank institutions. The question is, are increases in the rate of growth of the money stock, consequent upon a "flexible" monetary policy, reflected in subsequent increases in the rate of growth of the secondary or derivative institutions? Only further observation and experience will provide answers to this question.

A word of caution should be inserted here. The removal of either a time or demand deposit from a commercial bank in order to purchase a savings and loan share or a life insurance policy has no effect on the money supply as customarily defined. For example, money used to purchase a savings and loan association share does not remain in the till of the association. As funds are received by individual associations, they are almost at once transferred in the form of a demand deposit of the association back to a commercial bank. They remain as the demand deposit of a commercial bank until they are withdrawn in the form of real-estate loans to borrowers; the proceeds of these loans are in turn redeposited in banks, as builders and other sellers of houses receive payment from buyers. To be sure, a particular bank may not receive in demand deposits what it loses in time deposits, but viewed broadly the banking system as a whole does.[25]

In short, the nonbank intermediaries serve to dislodge bank deposits and to keep them in flux. They do not have any effect on the money supply except in the vague sense that if they were not actively increasing the velocity of circulation of a given money supply the central bank might find

---

24 The sophisticated reader need not be reminded that a bank "writes up" its deposits whenever it makes a loan, whether to business or government, being prepared, of course, to pay checks drawn against these new liabilities from whatever balances it regards as reserves.

25 Against the demand deposits the banks will, of course, have to keep a higher percentage of reserves than they would against time deposits.

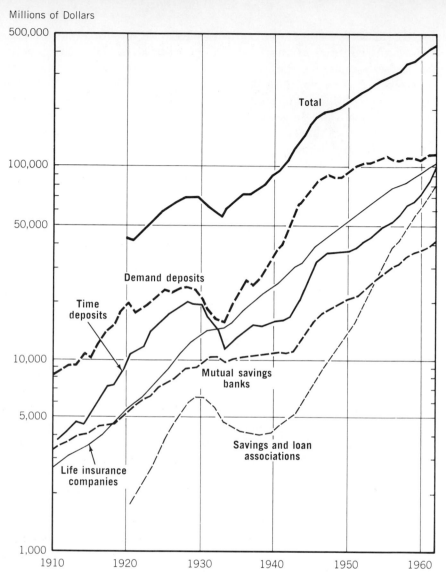

Millions of Dollars

Annual Report, Comptroller of the Currency; American Bankers Association; *Banking and Monetary Statistics; Federal Home Loan Bank Board* releases; *Federal Reserve Bulletin;* Raymond W. Goldsmith, *A Study of Saving in the United States* (Princeton: Princeton University Press, 1955–56); *National Association of Mutual Savings Banks Statistical Bulletin; 1959 Life Insurance Fact Book; Savings and Mortgage Statistics.*

Liabilities of Major Intermediaries: Life insurance companies were least affected by the blow of the Great Depression; savings and loan associations suffered most during the dismal decade of the 1930s.

it necessary to create a larger one. The fact remains that the liabilities of the nonbank intermediaries are in the category of assets known as "securities" and not "money," and money creation must antedate the issuance of these securities if the latter are to increase at a constant or increasing rate.

The Dominance
of Manufacturing

In its most general terms, the hypothesis states that a society with a generally high level of *n* Achievement will produce more energetic entrepreneurs who, in turn, produce more rapid economic development. But such a simple statement is loaded with difficulties. What, exactly, is an entrepreneur? In what sense is he crucial for economic development?

DAVID C. MC CLELLAND

Once again we come to the part of our narrative that treats of industrial change.[1] If the task of suggesting the innovation that took place between the Civil War and World War I was difficult, the present one of trying to convey some impression of developments during the past half-century seems impossible. It is important, nevertheless, to describe this broad area of industrial growth in which many find both the wellspring of American progress and a source of despair for the future.

By nearly any measurement we choose to take, manufacturing continues to dominate the American economy. The manufacturing industries presently account for a greater share of both corporate profits and expenditures for new plant and equipment than do any other class of industry (in the broader sense of the term). Despite a decline in manufacturing employment from 35 per cent of all nonfarm wage and salary employment in 1947 to 30 per cent 15 years later, manufacturing still provides more jobs than any other category of goods-

[1] In this chapter, as in Chapters 7 and 14, the adjective *industrial* refers mainly to manufacturing and mining. Unavoidably, the word is sometimes used in a broader sense.

Table 21-1

National Income by Industrial Origin, Selected Years, 1929–1960
(in millions of dollars)

	1929	1933	1940	1945	1950	1955	1960
Agriculture, forestry, and fisheries	8,278	3,713	6,247	14,889	17,923	16,084	17,286
Mining	2,048	647	1,868	2,717	5,010	5,609	5,207
Contract construction	3,808	755	2,569	4,280	11,833	17,358	21,884
Manufacturing	21,888	7,562	22,336	52,008	74,371	104,490	121,987
Wholesale and retail trade	13,358	5,485	14,337	27,997	42,707	55,000	67,963
Finance, insurance, and real estate	12,693	5,745	8,208	12,830	21,789	30,918	42,537
Transportation	6,636	3,036	5,040	10,536	13,278	15,781	17,939
Communications and public utilities	2,864	2,000	3,056	4,244	7,198	11,677	16,734
Services	10,338	5,567	8,854	14,614	23,089	33,740	49,150
Government and government enterprises	5,093	5,326	8,762	36,764	23,490	37,766	52,506
Rest of the world	810	323	357	369	1,188	1,783	2,287
ALL INDUSTRIES TOTAL	87,814	40,159	81,634	181,248	241,876	330,206	415,480
MANUFACTURING AS A PERCENTAGE OF TOTAL	24.9	18.8	27.4	28.7	30.7	31.6	29.4

SOURCE: *Statistical Abstract of the United States* (1962), p. 312, and *Survey of Current Business* (July 1962), p. 11

producing or service-producing industries.[2] Except for the years of the Great Depression, more than 25 per cent of the national income has originated in manufacturing, and of late the proportion has been nearer 30 per cent (see Table 21-1). If we include mining, so-called industrial activity accounts for well over one-third of the national income received in any year.

In short, on the basis of income generated, manufacturing today is in about the same *relative* position as agriculture was a hundred years ago. But this position was very nearly attained by the end of World War I. (Only four decades ago Calvin Coolidge remarked that the business of this country is business.) It is the purpose of the present chapter to pay attention to the remarkable aspects of industrial change since the 1920s.

In so brief a compass we shall not be able to pay much attention to particular industries. We shall try, however, to draw from recent observation of all manufacturing industries three generalizations. The first has to do with typical growth patterns, the second with technology, and the third with the size and number of firms in the several industries.

Recent Growth Patterns of Manufacturing Industries

In a well-known study published in 1934, Dr. Arthur F. Burns reached some conclusions that serve to introduce the present section.[3] He observed first what we all know intuitively—that industries rise and decline and that at any moment of time most will be growing and a few will be on the way

---

[2] *Manpower Report of the President* (Washington, D.C.: U.S. Government Printing Office, 1963), pp. 17–18.
[3] Arthur F. Burns, *Production Trends in the United States Since 1870* (New York: National Bureau of Economic Research, 1934).

down. Two interesting further facts emerged from his study. One was that, contrary to popular belief, an industry does not seem to reach a maximum size and then level off; once it ceases to grow it soon goes into a decline. A second, and more significant, fact is that as the decades pass individual industries show a retardation in their rates of growth.

This law of production trends seems to be borne out by other studies and by the testimony of men who make their living in the market place. A product when first introduced normally goes through a brief period of slow growth while it is gaining acceptance. If it gains acceptance (and many products do not), output for a time increases at an accelerating rate. But as years pass the rate of growth of output tends to decline, though retardation in expansion may be interrupted by sharp upward thrusts in demand consequent upon such causes as an outbreak of war, the shutting off of a foreign supply, or an increase in people's incomes.

The reader may think that such a proposition is really just a mathematical truism, that an initial increase in production at a rate of, say, 100 per cent per annum obviously cannot be maintained forever. But Professor Burns sought less obvious reasons and reached the following conclusions. Decline in the rate of growth of particular industries is a concomitant of rapid growth in total production. Continual introduction of new goods and services means that the demand for old ones must be restricted, and the faster the introduction of new commodities the greater the restrictive influence on old ones.[4] Specifically, interindustry and interproduct competition (about which we shall have more to say later) may have effects on a particular line of production ranging from diversion of demand to the outright undoing of an established industry. Recent examples come readily to mind. Rapid acceptance of frozen foods has adversely affected the output of canned foods. Television has hurt the motion-picture industry badly, changed radio production altogether, raised problems in the spectator sports industry, and even affected book sales and the custom of restaurants. Nor is this all. Besides the increase in number and variety of commodities, a multiplication of processes for producing a given commodity may well take place over time. Thus, steel-reinforced aluminum cable, both stronger and lighter than an electrically equivalent copper cable, has won almost the whole of the high-voltage transmission line business and is rapidly winning in the so-called secondary distribution field.

Finally, there is a persistent competition between old and new industries for the factors of production as well as for customer favor. Indeed, the very existence of an economic system implies a bidding among entrepreneurs for the use of scarce resources. Technological advances can and do reduce the restrictions imposed by scarcity of resources, but, as we have just observed, the stimulation that one industry receives from technical advances is likely to lead to retardation in competing industries.

Bearing in mind this fundamental fact of a tendency toward retardation

---

[4] Burns, p. xvi.

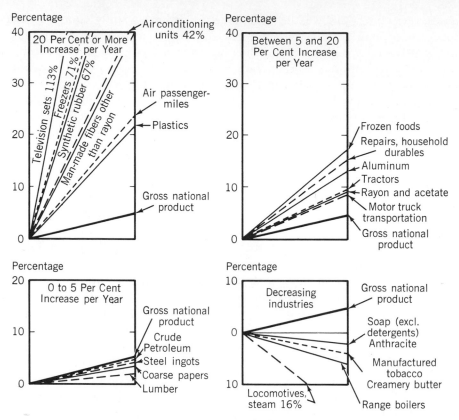

United States Department of Commerce.

Production Changes: "Sectoral" growth (in which some industries prosper while others languish) is nothing new, but its impact in the 1940–51 period was highly visible. (Compare these rates of growth with the next chart, for the 1948–60 period.)

in the growth of specific industries, we may proceed to remark some significant production trends observable since 1940. The rise in total output during the forties and early fifties averaged about 5 per cent per year, from one to two percentage points greater than the annual average over the previous half-century. In this recent period there were remarkably diverse production trends.

United States Department of Commerce economists collected data on more than 160 industries and classified them, on the basis of their experience between 1940 and 1951 (see chart above), in three groups: fast-growing, moderately or slowly growing, and declining.[5] Because total physical output for the United States increased at an average annual rate of 5 per cent

[5] For details see Louis J. Paradiso and Francis L. Hirt, "Growth Trends in the Economy," *Survey of Current Business* (January 1953), pp. 5–10.

during this period, industries were designated as rapidly growing if their average yearly rate of increase was half again as large as the composite average, or 7.5 per cent. Industries or products having an average annual rate of increase of more than zero and less than 7.5 per cent were considered moderately or slowly growing. Some industries and products, as we might surmise, showed declines.

More than sixty products fell in the rapidly growing category, including producer and consumer goods, both durable and nondurable, as well as services. Only about one-third of these rapidly growing items were new products; the rest had long been on the market. Antibiotics had the highest average growth rate, a phenomenal 118 per cent per annum. Output of television sets was almost as great, with home freezers and clothes driers next. Toward the bottom of the list were such familiar old products as sulfuric acid, asphalt, and cigarettes. But among the fast-growing industries growth rates varied considerably toward the end of the period. For example, frozen foods and phosphoric acid since 1948 exceeded their 1940–51 average rate of growth, whereas tractors, locomotives, and rayon and acetate showed a definite tendency to slow down. Such abrupt changes in growth rates remind us that we must always be careful about inferring a *future* rate of growth from any average of past rates.

Most of the industries in the intermediate group were, as might be expected, old ones. The greater part of American industrial output lies in this category. Items such as shipping containers, glass containers, and truck and bus tires were at the top of the list with increases above 5 per cent but below 7.5 per cent. Goods such as electric lamps, canned fruits and vegetables, lubricating oil, salt, and electric fans showed output increases about the same as that of the gross national product. Staple foods, such as sugar and wheat flour, and standard goods such as wool carpets and rugs, radios, and cigars had barely measurable annual rates of increase.

Paradiso and Hirt found that seventeen industries studied showed declining tendencies. Changes in consumer tastes accounted for some of the declines, as in the cases of pipe and chewing tobacco and lamb and mutton. Average annual rates of decline in the production of men's suits and overcoats were partially accounted for by changes in taste and partly by the entry into military service of a large proportion of young males during the period studied. For the most part, however, the retrogressing industries fall victim to the competition of substitute or alternative products. Radiators, convectors, and mechanical stokers were rapidly displaced as more satisfactory heating systems gained favor. Butter had an average annual decline in output of around 4 per cent since 1940, not because oleomargarine was better but because it was so much cheaper. And so it went with windmill pumps, soap, steam locomotives, and wood shingles.

It is instructive to observe how growth patterns shift with the selection of a different time span. For the period 1948–60 (see chart, p. 544), the one most recently studied by the Department of Commerce, fast-growth products

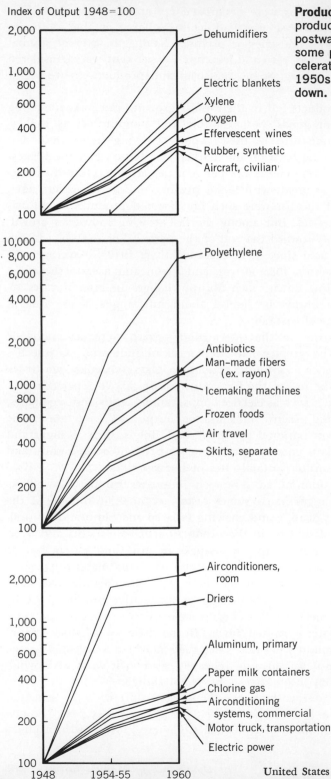

Index of Output 1948=100

Product Growth: A study of product growth rates in the postwar period shows that some products manifested accelerated rates after the mid-1950s while others slowed down.

Chart 1 (y-axis: 100, 200, 400, 600, 800, 1,000, 2,000):
- Dehumidifiers
- Electric blankets
- Xylene
- Oxygen
- Effervescent wines
- Rubber, synthetic
- Aircraft, civilian

Chart 2 (y-axis: 100, 200, 400, 600, 800, 1,000, 2,000, 4,000, 6,000, 8,000, 10,000):
- Polyethylene
- Antibiotics
- Man–made fibers (ex. rayon)
- Icemaking machines
- Frozen foods
- Air travel
- Skirts, separate

Chart 3 (y-axis: 100, 200, 400, 600, 800, 1,000, 2,000):
- Airconditioners, room
- Driers
- Aluminum, primary
- Paper milk containers
- Chlorine gas
- Airconditioning systems, commercial
- Motor truck, transportation
- Electric power

x-axis: 1948   1954-55   1960

United States Department of Commerce.

changed remarkably.[6] Of the more than seventy items in this group, 10 per cent showed uninterrupted growth at a rate of over 15 per cent per year. Outstanding examples included polyethylene and transistors. Some fast-growth products accelerated their rate of growth in the last six years of the period, some slowed their rate of growth, while others that averaged more than a 7.5 per cent rate of increase for the whole period reached a leveling stage or actually declined.

Rapidly growing industries are important to development because they give impetus to the economy. One type of output that gives the economy an undercurrent of great strength is the manufacture of household durables. For a while after its introduction, sales of a new durable increase slowly. Shortly, if it is to gain acceptance at all, the durable makes rapid gains, gains so great as to affect incomes and employment in the entire economy. Before World War I automobiles and washing machines gave a big boost to the economy. Early in the twenties electric refrigerators and radios got their start and were a buoyant force through the 1930s. Since World War II automatic washing machines, television sets, home freezers, and, most recently, room airconditioners, dehumidifiers, and driers made their mark.

One final word needs to be said about individual growth rates and the relationship of these rates to business fluctuations. Some products and services—like cigarettes and telephone service—are only slightly affected by business downturns. Others, including consumer durables generally, feel severely the effects of falling income, though they may rebound quickly after a business upturn.

The Possibility of a Second Industrial Revolution

In our discussion of technological change between the Civil War and World War I (Chapter 14), we emphasized the mechanization of industry. From Watt's first successful engine to the end of World War I, the story of technological advance was narrated in terms of the introduction of larger and more nearly automatic machines that came more and more to depend upon efficient uses of inanimate energy derived mostly from fossil fuels.

A continuation of the narrative of techniques still requires us to pay attention to machines and power. Power-driven devices that perform feats of amazing dexterity on the one hand and great strength on the other were introduced at a high rate during the 1920s and again during World War II and after. But in addition to mechanization, two other forces have recently brought important changes in our technology: these are (1) recent applications of the discoveries of science to industrial processes and (2) the development of unified systems of automatic control. So great has been the impact of the scientist, who can now actually change molecules to suit him,

---

[6] For average annual rates of growth, 1948–60, of 304 products see Francis L. Hirt, "New Light on Patterns of Output Growth," *Survey of Current Business* (September 1961), pp. 14–15.

and so fundamental have been the developments of control mechanisms that people are today speaking of a "new technology" or a "second industrial revolution." Whether or not these fancy expressions are warranted we shall have to inquire.

First a word or two about mechanization. As Dr. Harry Jerome has remarked, mechanization is many-sided. Sometimes gains in mechanization will be the result of the introduction of an altogether new machine; sometimes they will be the result of making old machines larger or faster. Not infrequently the introduction of new mechanical gadgets will be combined with the removal of discontinuities in processing. Sometimes, as Jerome has pointed out, mechanization will take place because the materials being worked up have changed; this seems to be presently true in the construction industry, for example, where metal building facings have gained acceptance. Sometimes, as in the case of mechanization of coal mining, new and powerful devices are put to work to help men do what are essentially the same old jobs.

So in the primary metals industries almost unbelievable advances have been made in the physical handling of the materials involved. Strip mining of coal, which furnishes so much of the energy necessary for metals processing, now accounts for just under one-third of total bituminous output. Mechanical mining of ores and mechanical charging of furnaces are almost universal. Continuous rolling of sheet metal, introduced in the steel industry in 1926, has become commonplace. More and more the primary metals industries have achieved uninterrupted production in huge integrated plants. In the case of steel, this means that molten iron can be converted into steel beams, sheets, and plates without the great losses of heat that were common up to 1920. And throughout the process heavy handling is done by all kinds of mechanical conveyors, from fork-lift trucks to giant cranes.

Changes of this sort are not without interest and significance. They are spectacular and are likely to come most readily to the reader's attention. But improvements in mechanization have been taking place for nearly two centuries. The question that entrepreneurs as well as economists are now asking is this: Has there been any fundamental shift in the *way* innovation takes place, with the result that its social impact may be changing? During the 1920s, as the mechanization of industry went on apace, we heard much about the problem of "technological unemployment." There is currently a renewal of this discussion, for it may well be that scientific applications have added something new to an old problem. Chemists and metallurgists can almost at will create new materials to replace old, and electronic engineers have brought the day of "push-button" control of whole processes near.

THE PETROCHEMICALS

The story of the impact of chemistry on economic life is essentially the story of the petrochemical industry. The beginnings of the industry can

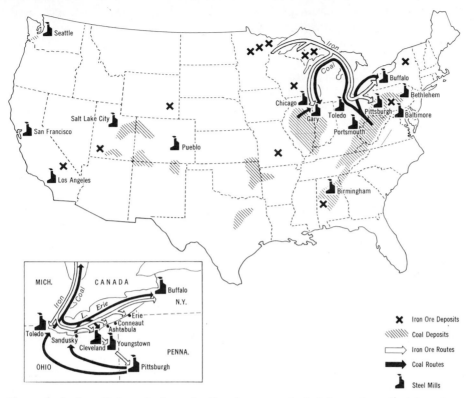

Heavy Industry: Major steel production is concentrated in centers that boast an abundance of either iron ore or coking coal or have a favorable site (usually on a waterway) to which ore and coal can be brought cheaply.

be traced from the early 1920s, when modern techniques of petroleum refining came first into use.

Crude petroleum is made up of various hydrocarbons—molecules of carbon and hydrogen atoms—in many different structural arrangements and hundreds of combinations. The process of refining aims at separating the constituent molecules and, more recently, at recombining the fractions in any desired way. Originally refiners relied on the fact that the different hydrocarbons have different boiling points so that they pass off at different temperatures in a distillation process.

By "cracking" the crude oil, heavy molecules are broken up into lighter ones, and some remaining heavy ones can then be further treated. So-called catalytic cracking, in which petroleum is subjected to heat under great pressure in the presence of a catalyst, began in the early 1920s. Polymerization, whereby the chemist arranges light molecules in chains (polymers) and thus obtains physical properties that would never occur in a "natural" state, followed only a little later; it is in a sense the opposite of cracking.

The scientific study of petroleum refining has resulted in a whole series of new products made from petrochemicals, i.e., from compounds recovered from petroleum or natural gas. Many of the important basic chemicals, such as ammonia, methyl alcohol, ethyl alcohol, and glycerol, once derived from coal or agricultural products, are now in the petrochemical group. In 1960 petrochemicals accounted for more than 30 per cent of United States chemical production by weight and nearly 60 per cent of chemical production by value. Most important of the end uses for petrochemicals, measured on a tonnage basis, is synthetic rubber. Next come automobile and aviation antifreezes and antiknock compounds, followed by the synthetic fibers (cellulose acetate, nylon, dacron, etc.) and the various plastics.

To get some notion of how new materials come from a test tube, we can consider for a moment the plastic, polyethylene. This is a white, waxy material familiar to everyone in its use for squeeze bottles and semitransparent wrap; it is also used as an alternate material for containers, primary insulators, piping, etc. Made by eight companies, including Du Pont, Union Carbide and Carbon, and Monsanto, polyethylene at the moment is ahead of the polyvinyls (shower curtains, seat covers, garden hose) and polystyrene (toys, bathroom tile, housewares) in total output. Polyethylene is made by the manipulation of ethylene, an invisible, light gas, which is obtained from natural gas or as a by-product of oil refining. Under great pressure, ethylene molecules are linked together, or polymerized, to form long chains of single molecules known as polymers. By regulating the size of the molecules a plastic that retains its flexibility at fairly low temperatures results.

THE NEW METALS

Science has also recently wrested from nature the secrets of processing metals of special importance in an age of great speed and unbelievably fine tolerances. Before 1900 only fourteen metals were in common use with two more, chromium and tungsten, just gaining acceptance in steel alloys. During the past half-century, output of most of the old metals has increased greatly, and some thirty new ones have emerged as valuable industrial materials. The interest of the public has been particularly captured by the increasing use of the light metals and the development of alloys and superalloys that withstand high temperatures.

Aluminum had become a "tonnage" metal by the end of World War I. What Alcoa did with aluminum, Dow Chemical has since done with magnesium and, very recently, Du Pont with titanium. Although all three metals are now produced in significant amounts, aluminum is far ahead in quantity of output. Total annual United States production increased from about 85,000 tons in 1920 to nearly 300,000 tons in 1940. Since then it has increased to 2,000,000 tons. Compared with the 100,000,000-ton-a-year steel industry this seems a small quantity, but when we reflect that steel is roughly three times as heavy as aluminum the amount appears larger. And as aluminum researchers develop ever stronger alloys—which can actually compete in some uses with structural steel—the optimism of Alcoa, Reynolds, Kaiser,

Massive capital equipment such as the finishing stands shown here at a U.S. Steel Corporation hot strip mill has contributed to the increasing productivity of American industry, helping to keep domestic producers competitive with foreign manufacturers, who pay lower money wages.

and Kennecott executives over their potential future markets expands.

Magnesium, lightest of the structural metals, is now in tonnage about where aluminum was before World War II—but its present production is thirty times what it was in 1940. Fabricators are learning how to handle it, and its extreme lightness gives it such a decided advantage in some uses, particularly in aircraft manufacture, that it may one day approach aluminum in sales volume. Whether titanium, in production only a decade and a half, will ever catch up with aluminum is problematical, but it has now moved into other than jet-engine applications.

Despite the glamour that attaches to the light metals, at least in part because of their uses in aircraft and space vehicles, the metals, notably the alloy-steels, that can withstand high temperatures have contributed much to economic progress. The development of alloy-steels has been continuous since the end of the last century, largely because of their usefulness in making machine tools. But the last twenty-five years or so have brought the need for new alloys that will stand up under extremely high temperatures.

By the mid-1950s power-plant boilers operated at steam temperatures of 1150° F., and mercury boilers at temperatures as high as 1220° F. Atomic reactors may require parts that can withstand temperatures of 2000° F. Some chemical processing generates heat up to 4200° F., and the blaze of the arc in an electric furnace gets up to 6000° F. The reasons for the trend toward higher temperatures are many, but they may be summed up in the statement that (1) many processes are impossible without them and (2) modern engines of whatever sort achieve efficiency as energy lost to the "sink" is reduced through higher inlet throttle temperatures.

But heat creates great technical difficulties, at least one of which is well known to every boy with an interest in airplanes. The major difficulty is high-temperature engineering failure as a result of "creep," a more or less slow yielding or deformation of materials that occurs when atomic bonds lose their cohesiveness under heat and stress. Thus, as an airplane passes the sonic barrier its skin is heated by the compressed or "ram" air in front of its leading edges, and its wings can weaken and go to pieces. Although engineering failure points are met somewhere below melting points, they cannot be eliminated simply by constructing with metals with high melting points. Corrosion resistance, tremendous centrifugal strength, proper nuclear cross section, and other characteristics may also be necessary in a particular application.

Answers to high-temperature problems have been found in the slow, trial-and-error development of alloys that will maintain desired characteristics when subjected to great stress and high temperatures. We have already noted the pre–World War I work with ferroalloys, largely directed toward improving the cutting qualities of machine tools. The ferroalloys have grown in importance over the past forty years until today they constitute over 10 per cent of total steel tonnage and are absolutely essential to the equipping and tooling of the petroleum, chemical, electrical, aircraft, and armament industries. But even stainless steel, one of the best of the steel-alloys for high-temperature work, begins to fail at 1300° to 1600° F. and beyond. Thus, although the ferroalloys have become "richer" through the years, engineers have had to resort to the superalloys of nickel-chrome-cobalt-molybdenum-columbium-tungsten that contain almost no iron.

But these superalloys take large amounts of the scarcest materials, and there is no guaranty that even they will do the jobs eventually to be required. Perhaps in the rare metals, as yet almost totally unknown, or in some new alloy of molybdenum or titanium, a material will be found which will lessen the problems of high-temperature engineering failure. Or possibly the "cermets," combinations of metals and ceramics, may yield solutions. And of course some required temperatures are so high that no material wall will hold them so that it has been necessary to experiment with charged particles in a magnetic field in the hope of perfecting a "magnetic bottle." We may be reasonably sure that the scientist will remove the blocks that nature has put in the way of technological progress.

Since shortly after World War II there has been much excitement, and not a little misapprehension, regarding extensions of automatic controls. The excitement is over the possibility that one day a few topnotch technicians and a skilled maintenance crew can run factories that, under present techniques, are manned by hundreds or thousands of skilled and semiskilled workers. The misapprehension is experienced by people who feel that automatic control of whole processes is no different from the automatic working of a single large machine or group of machines.

We can best approach the subject by recalling that automatic machines have long since been successfully operated. The governor on Watt's steam engine made use of a principle still of key importance. Oliver Evans had by 1784 constructed a completely automatic flour mill; once the wheat was dumped in the hoppers, no human hand participated in the process until lids were clapped on the barrels of finished flour. After a century or more of trying, a really satisfactory automatic loom was in operation by the 1890s.

In 1912 it took 162 machines to finish the four flat faces of 108 cylinder heads an hour; by 1946 six machines could do the same work, but they were still hand-fed. In 1953 a single, horizontal broach could outproduce the six machines of 1946. Why? Because castings were brought automatically to the broach, machining operations were automatic, and the completed heads were automatically ejected and sent by conveyor line to the next operation. By the late 1950s forty-two automatic machines, linked together by automatic transfer devices for moving engine blocks through the process, could turn out finished six-cylinder blocks in 14.6 minutes compared with nine hours in conventional manufacture.

This example reminds us that automaticity of operation of a machine lessens the expenditure of human physical effort in a manufacturing process. Sometimes the reduction of effort is so pronounced, as in the case of the cylinder heads just mentioned, that it receives excited comment in the business press. The automatic loading and unloading of multi-stage machine tools and the movement of pieces in process from one machine to another by "transfer" machines and conveyor systems (so-called Detroit automation) is certainly impressive. But, as one writer has remarked, "automated" lines like these are but a step forward in the development of machine tools and production lines.[7]

Wherein does automation differ from improvements in production lines? In what sense is it a "new" technology? The easiest way to get to an understanding of the principles involved is to recall the problems facing military officers charged with defending Britain against German planes early in World War II. The old methods of pointing antiaircraft guns by hand, taught American ROTC students as late as 1940, were obviously of little

---

[7] John Diebold, "Automation—the New Technology," *Harvard Business Review*, XXXI, 6 (November-December 1953), 64.

avail against the extreme speeds of the enemy's aircraft. Such speeds, according to Professor Wiener, ". . . made it necessary to give a predicting machine . . . communication functions which had previously been assigned to human beings. Thus, the problem of antiaircraft fire control made familiar the notion of a communication addressed to a machine rather than to a person." [8] A predicting *machine* had to be given communication functions; men reacted too slowly. A machine, given certain instructions, had to lay a gun on the target, and if the gun missed, had *itself* to make the corrections that would on the next round get a hit.

Effective antiaircraft fire was really dependent upon two advances. Some kind of self-correction had to be built into a closed system, and a way of amplifying small energy-levels into high energy-levels by other than mechanical means had to be devised. Operations were controlled by a device akin to a modern high-speed computer, and small energy-levels were amplified by a vacuum tube or electron valve rather than by complicated gears and other mechanical gadgets.

Thus was born an entirely new technology. This innovation was not simply an increase in mechanization, as some would argue, but an altogether novel concept of control, in which a machine gives orders and directs its own operations. It can be argued that automation is simply the culminating innovation that was the logical outcome of increasing automaticity of machines. On the other hand, there is merit in the contention that electronic tubes and transistors are now replacing *thought* processes rather than muscle power and manual dexterity. To be sure, someone must program the computer. But the computer then goes on to perform what were once thought processes *beyond* addition and subtraction, multiplication and division. As one executive has recently remarked, automated processes are rapidly eliminating the "blockhead" jobs on the production line and in the white-collar offices.

Modern oil refineries have most closely approached the ideal of automation so far, but products that lend themselves to continuous-process manufacture and assembly-line techniques will more and more be brought under complete automatic control. Instructions to the computer that gives the orders for the entire process are given by a taping or by punched cards. Since the system employs the "feedback" principle, the control mechanism operates on a basis of *actual* performance instead of *expected* performance. If a part is not turned out correctly, a sensory member tells the control mechanism—which allows further time for machining or rejects the part. All such feedback devices are tied together in a closed-loop system so that the assembly or manufacture of a product or of multiple products may be performed without the intervention of a human hand. To repeat, the essence of automation lies in the giving of orders by a machine and in a self-correcting mechanism.

---

[8] Norbert Wiener, *The Human Use of Human Beings* (Boston: Houghton Mifflin, 1950), p. 176.

Catalytic cracking of petroleum takes place in these giant towers at Esso's Elizabeth, New Jersey, refinery. A gentle blizzard of platinum inside the towers promotes the "fractional distillation" so that high-grade products like lighter fluid come off at the top, paraffin at the bottom.

This revolutionary approach to manufacturing will require the redesign of products and machines—even of entire processes. Redesign implies large additions to cost, and the computers that perform the logical tasks of control are inordinately expensive, running to hundreds of thousands of dollars apiece. But as the new technology has become more familiar, broad principles of design have evolved and something approaching quantity production of the control devices, with considerable similarity of parts between them, has been achieved. Furthermore, flexibility of both materials-handling mechanisms and machine tools has been attained so that a given automatic line can be shifted from the production of one product to another. There seem to be no serious obstacles to a continuing rapid increase in completely automatic production processes.

But as Professor Wiener has said, for true automatization the white-collar operations connected with production must also be mechanized. Machines that in the most modern offices perform cost accounting and other business functions must be controlled by the same mechanism that directs factory processes. The subjection of all the elements of production to computer control will almost certainly come gradually so that the problem of absorption of workers displaced by the new technology will not soon become critical. Even so, technological unemployment on a hitherto unknown scale may one day be the consequence of scientific progress.

RESEARCH AND DEVELOPMENT, DIVERSIFICATION,
AND DECENTRALIZATION

Contrary to general opinion, the systematic application of science to product and process development through R and D departments has not been widespread throughout American industry. By the early 1920s only two other industries besides the electrical, chemicals and rubber, made large outlays in this area. During the late 1920s and the 1930s the petroleum industry, the farm implement industry, and the automobile industry also began to build large research organizations. In the years immediately preceding World War II, perhaps three-fourths of the personnel in organized industrial research were in these six industries. To be sure, other industries, then as now, were spending money on the search for new products and processes. But steel, nonferrous metals, paper, textiles, and food industries have provided well below 25 per cent of the trained manpower in industrial laboratories, even since World War II.

In postwar years two glamour industries have invested considerable resources in R and D. In part because of its inevitable participation in the space race the aircraft industry has spent a great deal on research. Yet aircraft manufacturers are in effect simply spending the money for the government. Similarly, the United States government has provided well over half the funds used in the development of scientific instruments, at the same time providing the largest market for these instruments. We might add that many of the newer products of the electrical companies have likewise been largely financed by government subsidy. However, with the exception of the scientific-instrument output of the electrical companies, the assembling and process industries that originally pioneered in research and development departments have continued to provide their own funds for this kind of investigation.

Changes in money expenditures on R and D in the postwar years and changes in the proportions of research expenditures financed by industry and the federal government are both startling. From expenditures that averaged a little over $2 billion in 1946 and 1947, R and D outlays rose to an average of more than $5 billion in 1953 and 1954, to $10 billion in 1957 and 1958, to approximately $12.5 billion in 1959 and 1960. *Business Week*

Table 21-2

Research: Who Spends the Money
(in millions of dollars)

	1946–47	1953–54	1956–57	1957–58	1958–59	1959–60	1962	1969
Federal government	400	970	1,280	1,450	1,720	1,780	1,700	3,060
Industry	1,300	3,630	6,440	7,730	8,400	9,400	11,550	21,240
Colleges and universities	300	450	600	720	840	1,000	1,400	2,900
Nonprofit institutions	100	100	140	150	200	250	350	800
TOTAL	2,100	5,150	8,460	10,050	11,160	12,430	15,000	28,000

SOURCES: 1947, Defense Department
1953–60, National Science Foundation
1962–69, *Business Week* estimates

estimates $15 billion of such outlays for 1962 and projects a whopping $28 billion of expenditures in 1969. Table 21-2 shows the amount spent by the major spending units during this period.

The question of who ultimately foots the bill is a different one. The federal government pays for much of the research done by industry and, through grants, for a good deal of academic research. Industry finances research done by universities and nonprofit institutions. As the second table shows, industry roughly doubled the amount of its expenditures on research and development in the period 1953–59. But over the same span of years the federal government came close to tripling its outlays. To put the matter another way, in 1953 the United States government contributed roughly 40 per cent of research and development funds and industry supplied approximately 60 per cent. By 1959 these proportions were reversed.

Table 21-3

Research: Who Pays for It
(in millions of dollars)

	1946–47	1953–54	1956–57	1957–58	1958–59	1959–60	1962	1969
Federal government	500	2,740	4,960	6,130	6,720	7,700	8,500	11,000
Industry	1,515	2,240	3,260	3,660	4,149	4,426	6,165	16,400
Colleges and universities	75	130	170	180	196	204	225	450
Nonprofit institutions	10	40	70	80	95	100	110	150
TOTAL	2,100	5,150	8,460	10,050	11,160	12,340	15,000	28,000

No one can say, of course, how these proportions will change during the decade of the 1960s. Most informed guesses suggest that there will be a swing back toward a larger proportion of R and D outlays by industry and a somewhat smaller proportion by the federal government. One trend seems fairly well established. It is more and more the practice of both government and private industry to finance research through universities and colleges, simply because it is a less expensive procedure than setting up new facilities to take care of each problem as it comes along.

We saw on pp. 352–57 how, by the early 1900s, the typical American industrial corporation manufactured a single line of products to be sold in a national market. The usual firm then had an operating department to perform each major industrial function. Product diversification was not a business strategy, and output was uncomplicated. Organization was highly centralized, with the functional departments unified by an executive vice-president or an executive committee, which in turn reported to a president, who in turn might or might not report to the chairman of the board of directors.

But firms that adopted product diversification as a business strategy quickly found that the highly centralized structure would not work satisfactorily. Thus General Electric, after two decades of experimenting with its organization, finally had to reorganize activities along product lines. Just after World War II the company accomplished its structural reorganization by setting up major departments—apparatus, lamp, appliances, air conditioning, electronics, and chemical. Each of these departments was headed by a senior executive, a vice-president who had under his control all necessary operations and who was completely responsible for the profit performance of his department. The older functional departments, which remained at the head offices, in effect became advisory and planning departments, reporting to the president and the chairman of the board. After 1950 General Electric carried this plan even further, subdividing the six main product departments into more than seventy. Managers of these smaller departments presently have almost complete autonomy in directing production and in performing the marketing function. Although several of these smaller units are grouped under a general divisional manager, this division executive has no staff, presumably so that he will not interfere with the activities and responsibilities of those under him. Four new group vice-presidents at the very top echelon were appointed to advise those beneath them and to confer (as part of an executive committee) with the president and chairman of the board.

As Professor Chandler has demonstrated, decentralization of structure has similarly occurred in the other industries that have been active in diversifying products as a business strategy. On the other hand, companies in the metals and agricultural processing industries have been rather slow to adopt both the strategy and the organization, though there are certainly exceptions to this rule.

Table 21-4

United States Energy Production from Mineral Fuels and Water Power, 1920–1961 (in trillions of British Thermal Units)

			Mineral fuels						
					Coal		Petroleum and natural gas		
Year	Total energy	Water power [a]	Total	Total	Anthra-cite	Bitu-minous and lignite	Total	Crude petro-leum	Natural gas
1920	21,365	738	20,627	17,175	2,276	14,899	3,452	2,569	883
1930	22,119	752	21,367	14,011	1,762	12,249	7,356	5,208	2,148
1940	25,088	880	24,208	13,380	1,308	12,072	10,828	7,849	2,979
1950	34,510	1,573	32,937	14,647	1,120	13,527	18,290	11,449	6,841
1955	38,900	1,447	37,453	12,839	665	12,174	24,614	14,410	10,204
1956	41,510	1,542	39,968	13,857	734	13,123	26,111	15,181	10,930
1957	41,826	1,524	40,302	13,553	644	12,909	26,749	15,178	11,571
1958	39,132	1,693	37,439	11,292	538	10,754	26,147	14,204	11,943
1959	40,932	1,645	39,287	11,319	524	10,795	27,968	14,932	13,036
1960	41,844	1,723	40,121	11,364	478	10,886	28,757	14,935	13,822
(prelim.) 1961	41,793	1,752	40,041	10,932	452	10,480	29,109	15,206	13,903

SOURCE: *Statistical Abstract of the United States, 1962*, p. 528. Unit heat values employed are: Anthracite, 12,700 B.T.U. per pound; bituminous coal and lignite, 13,100 B.T.U. per pound; petroleum, 5,800,000 B.T.U. per barrel; natural gas, total production multiplied by 1,075 B.T.U. per cubic foot minus repressuring vent and waste gas multiplied by 1,035. See also *Historical Statistics of the United States, Colonial Times to 1957*, series M71-87.

[a] Assuming average central-station practice for each year; declined from 3.00 pounds of coal per kilowatt-hour in 1920 to .88 pounds in 1960.

ENERGY SOURCES

We close this brief treatment of technological change with a consideration of changing energy sources. What has happened since 1920 is summed up in Table 21-4.[9]

It is apparent that the American economy depends for its energy almost entirely upon the mineral fuels. Two developments of the four decades stand out clearly. The first is that both crude petroleum and natural gas have become far more important than coal, traditionally the basis of an industrial civilization. The second is that coal, which reached its peak as an energy source during World War I, dropped markedly during the thirties, and came back to a new high just after World War II, has been losing out both relatively and absolutely.

Coal has had a major role in world history and, in the foreseeable future, will continue to have. Some engineers and scientists even predict that one day we shall be almost totally dependent upon coal energy. At the moment, though, bituminous mining is a sick industry. We must not jump to the conclusion that the United Mine Workers are to blame because they have driven up labor costs. Mechanization of mining operations and the

[9] The table actually understates the growth of energy recovered from coal and other sources, because the unit heat values employed are constant whereas increasing efficiency of utilization has caused them to rise steadily over time. Thus, bituminous coal is calculated at 13,100 B.T.U. per pound, petroleum at 5,800,000 B.T.U. per barrel, and so on. If we assume, however, that the secular rise in efficiency for all mineral sources of energy has been about the same, the table gives us a good notion of the relative importance of the different sources.

favorable location of major United States deposits have kept per-ton costs lower than those of other countries. But as Professor Zimmermann once remarked, gasoline, the major petroleum product, "packs a much bigger punch" per pound or per cubic foot than does coal and has thus become "the great mover." [10] In a vast country like the United States, where flexible transportation facilities are so important and where oil and natural gas are found in relative abundance, it is little wonder that these hydrocarbons have gained the position that coal once held in the English economy.

The reader who has heard so much about the power output of the Tennessee Valley Authority and the great dams of the West may be mildly astonished to note that water power is relatively unimportant, accounting in the early 1960s for less than 5 per cent of the annual supply of energy. The fact is that, although a certain glamour attaches to dams, reservoirs, turbogenerators, and long-distance transmission lines, water power has had difficulties competitively. It will be recalled that around 1880 water was disappearing as a power source but was rescued by the development of hydroelectric plants between 1880 and 1910. After 1900, however, the growing efficiency of fuel power plants appeared to threaten the water wheel and water turbine. In fact, the number of pounds of coal required to generate a kilowatt-hour fell from 7.05 in 1899 to about 0.90 in the late 1950s.

It became apparent, meantime, that hydropower was not free simply because it fell from heaven and rolled down steep, natural slopes. Expensive dams and equipment were required to utilize it. Nevertheless, certain forces at work during the past thirty years have enabled water power to develop modestly in competition with fuel power.[11] Old industries grew up where the coal supplies were, but certain new ones—the light metals, for example—have been established where there is really "cheap" hydroelectric power. An increase in the distance of economical transmission—the maximum in the United States is now in excess of three hundred miles—has made it possible to bring existing urban centers within the orbit of hydroestablishments once far from civilization. For nearly twenty years, while the actual quantity of fuel required to generate a kilowatt-hour has declined, the cost of the fuel has risen sharply. All these things have combined to keep water power in the running. Even more important, however, has been the political appeal, apparent even before the New Deal came to power, of the control of entire river systems or watersheds. Integrated watershed control implies multipurpose dams, which in turn mean hydroelectric output. But the number of dam sites is limited, and power plants that originally relied solely on water have added steam and auxiliary power as needs grew.

Of one thing we may be sure: An ever increasing amount of coal, oil,

---

[10] Erich W. Zimmermann, *World Resources and Industries,* rev. ed. (New York: Harper, 1951), p. 495.
[11] Zimmermann, pp. 570–71.

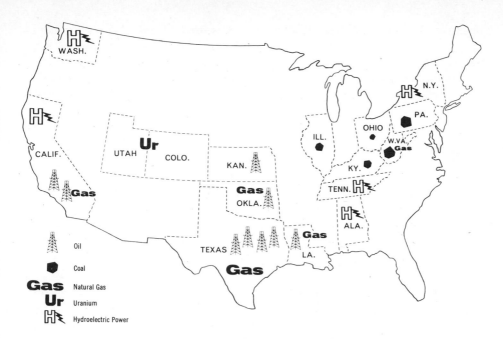

Power: Mineral and water sources of electric power fall into three main classes: hydroelectric, fossil fuel (including coal, natural gas, and oil) and nuclear. The map shows only the principal sources of such power.

gas, and water is being converted into electricity (see map). At mid-century more than one-fourth the coal and practically all of the water power were used to produce electrical energy; and roughly 10 per cent of petroleum and natural gas were used for this purpose. The amount of electrical energy consumed since 1935 has more than quadrupled, and all signs point to even more spectacular increases over the next quarter of a century.

But what of the pressure on the minerals that many have worried about for half a century? Recent history teaches us that, at least for the present, we have no cause for concern. Proven oil and gas reserves are continually being discovered. Coal supplies should last for 2,000 years. A survey of energy resources made in the early 1960s by Resources for the Future concluded that the country will still have enough coal, oil, and gas to meet its needs in the year 2000.

Nevertheless, in the long run the chief hope of plentiful energy lies in advances in technology. These may range from the design of a refractory ceramic body used in high-voltage insulators to new ways of using solar and geothermic energy. In the popular mind nuclear energy has limitless potentialities, and atomic-powered electric plants of some size have gone into operation. But many competent engineers, arguing that atomic power will not necessarily be "cheap" power, insist that coal will have to take over the major role as an energy source when petroleum and natural gas supplies begin to dwindle. Attempts to convert coal into fuel gas and oil products, begun in 1913, bore fruit as Carbide and Carbon Chemicals Company pioneered in operating the world's first commercial coal-hydrogenation chemical plant. Everything considered, problems of fuel supply and utilization have approached long-term solution during the past four decades.

The Bogey of Concentration in Industry

If we may judge from the amount of space devoted to the subject in economic journals, monographs, and textbooks, the concentration of industry continues to be regarded as a major social problem. Especially during the 1930s, when the characteristics of American capitalism were being examined with unusual intensity, were professional economists in almost unanimous agreement about the growing evils of monopoly power.[12]

It is understandable that observers of the depression scene should become concerned about the "decline of competition." In the first place, the decade of the 1920s brought a wave of business consolidation comparable in some respects to the merger movement of 1897–1904. Second, the best figures available indicated a startlingly large proportion of corporate wealth in the hands of a few firms. One study concluded that in 1933 57 per cent of corporate wealth outside the financial field was controlled by two hundred firms. Third, new and subtle ways of reducing the pangs of price competition seemed to be gaining popularity. Among these the most effective were organizations of all the producers in a field into manufacturers' institutes or trade associations. Finally, and most important, it was apparent during the depression that prices were stickier and output declines more severe in those industries where a few firms were dominant.

"MERGER FOR OLIGOPOLY" INSTEAD OF "MERGER FOR MONOPOLY"

It will be recalled from the discussion of Chapter 14 that there are several ways of achieving and maintaining a measure of monopoly power. In practice, largely as a consequence of the Sherman Law, the *safest* way of gaining market power has been to grow big by consolidation. Besides being the safest way it has almost always been a highly effective way. The third great wave of mergers, which began toward the end of World War I, had largely exhausted itself by 1929. With only a few really important combinations yet to take place in the 1930s, market structures of the major industries were pretty well cast. Professor Stigler has pointed out a funda-

---

[12] During the first flurry of excitement over growing monopoly power, which came at the turn of the century, the most respected economists considered the combination movement a normal step toward achieving economies of scale. It was the popular journalists who feared the new giants and roused their readers to the danger of monopoly.

mental characteristic of this third merger movement that helps us to place it in proper historical perspective.[13]

Stigler has shown that during the first two waves of combination the resulting firms attained very high percentages of the output of their industries, seldom less than 50 per cent. The major objective of such combinations was a high degree of monopoly power, though pure monopolies rarely resulted.[14] In post–World War I years the merged firms by and large secured much smaller percentages of an industry's output because mergers usually took place among the companies that were smaller than the dominant one. Meantime, the dominant firm, which had frequently held a near-monopolistic position, gradually came to control a smaller share of the industry's production. The steel industry best exemplified this trend. United States Steel's share of ingot capacity dropped as Bethlehem and Republic sharply increased their shares through merger. The shift from near-monopoly markets to oligopolies was also notable in cement, cans, petroleum, automobiles, agricultural instruments, and glass.[15]

Some industries that had approached the competitive norm, in that they had been composed of large numbers of firms, became oligopolies during the third merger movement. Dairy products and packaged foods were the outstanding examples of this kind of rapid change in market structure, but liquors and beverages, paper and printing, machinery and machine tools, and even motion pictures also came to be priced in markets characterized by "few" sellers.

OLIGOPOLY AND THE "NEW" COMPETITION

"Merger for oligopoly" had unquestioned success in major industries. Yet even as the country's economists viewed with alarm some twenty years ago, the end of progressively greater concentration had at least temporarily been reached. Again, a crop of mergers in the late forties and fifties brought cries of alarm from academic halls and courtrooms, but the rate of merger slacked off to ease the concern of professional antitrusters.

Contrary to widely held beliefs, there is little evidence that concentration has increased over the past three decades. Large firms have grown larger, to be sure, but in an expanding economy small firms have grown larger, too. They may even have increased somewhat their relative share of markets.

But the change from "monopolistic" to "oligopolistic" markets and the arresting of the trend toward concentration of productive capacity in a few firms may nonetheless have left an economy tethered by monopolistic restrictions. A first look at the most recent data is not altogether comforting.

---

[13] George J. Stigler, "Monopoly and Oligopoly by Merger," *American Economic Review,* XL, 2 (May 1950), 23–33.
[14] Recalling the reasons given for the first and second combination movements in Chapter 14, the reader should be sure he understands why such high degrees of control were thought necessary.
[15] Stigler, p. 31.

Table 21–5

Percentage of Value of Shipments Accounted for by the Four Largest Companies in 1958, 1954, and 1947

Industry	1958	1954	1947
Primary aluminum	(*a*)	100	100
Locomotives and parts	95	91	91
Electrical lamps (bulbs)	92	93	92
Telephone and telegraph equipment	92	90	—
Flat glass	92	90	—
Soap and glycerin	90	85	79
Gypsum products	88	90	85
Steam engines and turbines	87	87	88
Cereal breakfast foods	83	88	79
Tin cans and other tinware	80	80	78
Cigarettes	79	82	90
Aluminum rolling and drawing	78	88	94
Synthetic fibers	78	80	78
Computing and related machines	77	74	69
Motor vehicles and parts	75	75	56
Tires and inner tubes	74	79	77

SOURCE: *Concentration Ratios in Manufacturing Industry, 1958* (Washington, D.C.: U.S. Government Printing Office, 1962).
a Withheld to avoid disclosing figures for individual companies.

Consider the findings presented in a report prepared by the United States Bureau of the Census, *Concentration Ratios in Manufacturing Industry, 1958*. Table 21-5 lists sixteen industries in which 74 per cent or more of total shipments were concentrated in four firms in 1958. Table 21-6 lists industries in which concentration in four firms *increased* by ten percentage points or more in the period 1947–58. Table 21-7 is illustrative of industries in which the percentage of value of shipments accounted for by four firms *decreased* by ten percentage points or more in the period 1947–58.

There is simply no doubt that in manufacturing industries of key importance there is sufficient concentration to permit oligopoly power as orthodox economic theory defines it. How serious a problem of public policy confronts us? An answer to this question depends upon the reply to a further question. Granted the high degree of concentration, is there still an effective competition among producers? Classical economics concluded that, except in unusual circumstances, the consumer need not fear the power of any seller, that he would always have the protection of the inexorable forces of the market place. The implication of nearly all the recent literature on imperfectly competitive markets is that the built-in protective mechanism of the competitive process is gone.

We are thus confronted with a paradox. By any measure we choose to take, the American consumer has been progressively better off over the past

Table 21-6

Selected Industries Exhibiting Increased Concentration:
Percentage of Value of Shipments Accounted for by the Four Largest Companies
in 1958, 1954, and 1947

Industry	1958	1954	1947
Soap and glycerin	90	85	79
Motor vehicles and parts	75	75	56
Domestic laundry equipment	71	68	40
Bolts, nuts, washers, and rivets	50	15	20
Boilershop products	37	30	18
Paper and board products	34	25	15
Finishing textiles, except wool	26	24	14

SOURCE: *Concentration Ratios in Manufacturing Industry, 1958* (Washington, D.C.: U.S. Government Printing Office, 1962).

half-century. But how can he be if our economy is bowed down by monopolistic restrictions? How has it come about that, despite the omnipresence of oligopoly, more and more of this world's goods and services have been made available to the run of humankind?

In the early 1950s several solutions to the paradox were proposed. Professor Clair Wilcox suggested that oligopoly is not ubiquitous as alleged, but his argument—that the part of the consumers' dollar that goes to pay

Table 21-7

Selected Industries Exhibiting Decreased Concentration:
Percentage of Value of Shipments Accounted for by the Four Largest Companies
in 1958, 1954, and 1947

Industry	1958	1954	1947
Cigarettes	79	82	90
Aluminum rolling and drawing	78	88	94
Tobacco stemming and redrying	73	79	88
Distilled liquor	60	64	75
Aircraft engines	56	62	72
Electronic tubes	53	64	73
Shortening and cooking oil	49	55	59
Copper rolling and drawing	48	53	60
Wire drawing	34	36	45
Aircraft equipment	27	20	37
Paper bags	26	32	44
House furnishings	18	21	33
Poultry dressing plants	12	17	32
Metal doors, sash, and trim	10	15	63

SOURCE: *Concentration Ratios in Manufacturing Industry, 1958* (Washington, D.C.: U.S. Government Printing Office, 1962).

for goods made by oligopolies is fairly small—was promptly dismissed as a quibble.[16] Professor Galbraith contended that countervailing power—giant buyers confronting giant sellers—comes to the consumers' rescue, though, by his own admission, not effectively during inflationary periods. Other economists asserted the possibility of an effective, protective competition among commodities and among industries without, however, indicating what the limitations of such competition may be.[17]

These advocates of reliance on a "new" competition for defense against the evils of monopoly power felt that in this mechanism alone would be found the solution to a great policy problem. Their theory was that, especially since 1939, interindustry competition and to a lesser extent competition among products and processes *within* certain industries has caused oligopoly power to wane. The demand for a firm's products nowadays, they argued, is not as stable as it used to be for the reason that alternative (substitute) products of firms in *other* industries are more and more coming to be a part of the competition. But counting only the firms within the "industry" tells us very little. We must do our counting by taking *categories of uses* for the output of an industry, considering what products of other industries directly compete within these categories. This effort is not easy because it requires an understanding of many varied technologies.

Consider the aluminum industry. Before World War II the Aluminum Company of America was the classroom example of monopoly in a nationwide market. Since World War II this industry has been the best example of an oligopoly, with only three major firms, a newcomer from the copper industry, and one or two others.

It is possible to speak of a demand for "primary aluminum," but primary aluminum includes over one hundred wrought and casting alloys in many different shapes of innumerable lengths and thicknesses. In comparing the demand for these alloys with that for the other metals we must first specify uses. To be specific about the competition of aluminum with other metals in categories of uses, let us consider first the category of electrical cable and conductors. It is well known that aluminum and copper compete in this use, but it is not enough simply to remark the fact. The essence of the competition is in the "bundle of properties" of the two metals, the two bundles having marked likenesses and differences.[18] Both copper and aluminum have high electrical conductivity, but the specific gravity of alu-

---

[16] Clair Wilcox, "On the Alleged Ubiquity of Oligopoly," *American Economic Review,* XL, No. 2 (May 1950), 67–73. See E. H. Chamberlin's reply in the same issue, pp. 101–03, and J. K. Galbraith's in *American Capitalism* (Cambridge: Riverside Press, 1952), p. 42.
[17] The question of interproduct and interindustry competition received considerable attention in the early 1950s. See David E. Lilienthal, *Big Business: a New Era* (New York: Harper, 1952), pp. 47–94; Sumner H. Slichter, "The Growth of Competition," *Atlantic Monthly* (November 1953), pp. 66–70; A. D. H. Kaplan, *Big Enterprise in the Competitive System* (Washington, D.C.: Brookings Institution, 1953); and Edward S. Mason, "The New Competition," *The Yale Review* (Autumn 1953), pp. 37–48.
[18] Kaplan, p. 19.

minum is slightly less than one-third that of copper so that the mass conductivity of aluminum is twice that of copper. Thus, a steel-reinforced aluminum cable, both stronger and lighter than an electrically equivalent copper cable, can be used in longer spans with fewer supporting structures. On the basis of aluminum and copper prices prevalent in the last few years, copper has lost the high-voltage transmission line business. At the other extreme, copper with its higher electrical conductivity still has a decided advantage over aluminum where wire of fine sizes is used and space must be conserved. Between the two extremes there is a vigorous, persistent competition on a pure cost basis, where costs included are those of product design, investment in tools and dies, etc. Large motor windings, power and feeder cable, and bus in central power stations are today alternatively made from either material. In this use four firms in the copper industry and their copper and brass fabricating subsidiaries are direct rivals of the four major aluminum companies.

Consider another use category. In the field of die castings, aluminum alloys are making great inroads on zinc castings, long dominant in the field. Here there is also competition with the brasses, and more and more with alloys of magnesium and with the plastics. If we bring sand and permanent-mold castings into the use category, we must include almost any metal that can be melted—gray and malleable iron and cast steel being the chief additions to the competition, which is decided, once weight, strength, and finish have been considered, on a basis of costs, including those of dies and machining.

The rivalry between aluminum and the steels is keen in the manufacture of truck, van, and trailer bodies (where magnesium and wood are also alternative materials), and in certain construction uses. In making truck bodies the competition between aluminum and steel involves a balancing of manufacture and costs in use; the higher cost of aluminum bodies is generally much more than offset by the greater average pay loads, reduced license fees, and increased tire mileage consequent upon lower weight. In construction uses, the advantage, as in the case of industrial windows, may turn on savings in maintenance costs.

As we proceed through the main use categories of aluminum the other metals appear and reappear; as unlikely a competitor as lead is an alternate material in at least two uses (collapsible tubes and cable coverings). The plastics, too, reappear; and wood, rubber, Fiberglas, and even conventional building facings like brick and stone enter the system of alternatives.

In sum, if we consider interindustry competition, the number of competing firms rapidly moves from "few" to "many," but two exceptions should be raised. First, even after the interindustry competition has been taken into account, rivalry may be limited to a few firms. In one use—for instance, castings—the competition is with a hundred or more producers of primary materials outside the aluminum industry, but for another—such as conductors—the number may reduce to four outside the industry. It appears, however, that as we cut across industry lines conditions of rivalry are much different from those of intraindustry competition. The managers of firms usually cannot have the technological or accounting knowledge that enables them to predict reactions of other-industry rivals as well as they can those of rivals within the industry.

It may be further objected that the aluminum industry is left, after all such considerations, with a hard monopoloid core. Although there is an ever growing list of alternative materials, aluminum is still economically necessary in the manufacture of structural parts for aircraft. Many of the alloys commonly employed in aircraft manufacture have a host of applications; but the high-strength alloy used for the skin of an airplane is used for little else, and there is no feasible alternative material for airplane skins. It is conceivable that the companies in the industry could collude, tacitly or explicitly, in discriminating against the airplane manufacturing companies, especially in view of the fact that aluminum from the secondary (used) market would not be suitable for aircraft. It seems unlikely that discrimination to maintain a monopoly position in so small a market would be worthwhile, but this is a fact that has to be ascertained. To say the least, the problem of monopoly in the aluminum industry is narrowed to manageable proportions.

Although we could work through similar examples in industry after industry, and come to like conclusions, we still could not assert with complete assurance that interproduct and interindustry competition give complete protection against monopoly power. The point is that a simple counting of the number of producers within an industry is a poor way of coming to an evaluation of a competitive situation.

Two final comments are in order. (1) The competitive forces, of which we have just taken examples, work over long periods of time. It may require years for a change to be made from one process to another, from one material to another. In assessing the merits of a competitive system, we cannot base our judgment on the possibility of temporary abnormal profits. (2) After making allowances for interindustry and interproduct competition, it is possible that the monopoly core left to some industries may still be large. Again it is a question of the facts. For nearly a century, the steels have had no close competition in a large number of applications where weight, strength, and durability are of primary importance; rails, heavy structural members, pressure vessels, and heavy machinery are examples. Even as the competition takes place today, the marginal effect on the steel industry is much smaller than that in industries competing with it. For example (on the basis of data relevant at the moment), if all automobile license plates presently made of steel were to be made of another material the loss to the steel industry would be approximately 0.02 per cent of average annual output in recent years. Yet if aluminum were to gain this business for any one year it would mean an increase in output of nearly 1 per cent.

If the foregoing considerations have a certain cogency, then perhaps a re-evaluation of American antitrust policy is in order. It may be that we have paid too much attention to the bogey of concentration and not enough attention to the necessity for finding hard cores of monopoly and excising them.

Since 1937 the courts have taken the view expressed in the preceding section in only one major case. After Thurman W. Arnold became head of the antitrust division of the Justice Department, a vigorous program of antitrust prosecution was instituted that continued after Arnold's resignation. Between 1937 and 1948 more prosecutions were begun than in the entire history of the Sherman Act before 1937, and the cases instituted were largely directed toward established and notorious oligopolies. Emphasis was placed on dissolution, divorcement, and divestiture cases—i.e., on the actual breaking up of concentration in the old "trust busting" sense.[19] But though the government has won most of its major cases, the penalties imposed by the courts have been mild—for the simple reason that drastic penalties would make for units of uneconomic size.

The case against the Aluminum Company of America provides the best example of the perplexities that confront the courts in modern antitrust actions. In 1937 a complaint was instituted against Alcoa, alleging monopoly in the manufacture and sale of virgin aluminum and fabricated shapes. In 1942 the District Court held the defendant company not guilty, but in March 1945, this decision was reversed by the Circuit Court of Appeals, Judge Learned Hand giving the opinion. Judge Hand ruled that Alcoa, which at the time of the trial made and fabricated over 90 per cent of the virgin aluminum manufactured in the United States, was a monopoly. Turning away from the old dictum that "mere size is no offense," Judge Hand ruled that size, in the sense of market control, was the very essence of the offense. Even though the company had engaged in no immoral or predatory competitive practices, it was still in violation of the Sherman Act if, through normal business methods, it controlled most of the output of the industry. But having pronounced Alcoa a monopoly, the court refused to order dissolution of the company or divestiture of its assets. Instead, the court recommended that remedial measures be withheld until the effect on competition of government disposal of war-surplus aluminum plants could be determined. Further attempts by the government to force Alcoa to divest itself of assets met with little more success. In 1950, with Kaiser and Reynolds firmly established in the industry, the court held that competition had not been established in the aluminum industry; but the only relief granted was to require persons holding stock in both Alcoa and Alted, the Canadian subsidiary, to divest themselves of the stock of one corporation or the other.

In the case of *United States* v. *United Shoe Machinery Corporation* the

---

[19] Walter Adams, "The Aluminum Case: Legal Victory—Economic Defeat," *The American Economic Review*, XLI, 5 (December 1951), 915.

court concluded that United's control of the shoe machinery market was indisputable. The court further found that the company's practices had been neither predatory nor discriminatory as between different customers. Judge Wyzanski held that the United Shoe Machinery case fell "within the main thrust of the doctrine applied in the *Aluminum* and subsequent cases" and that United had violated the Sherman Act.[20] But the court refused to dissolve the company and ordered three forms of relief that would do little to weaken United's monopoly power.

At long last the courts appeared to have brought the legal concept of monopoly into line with the orthodox economic concept. But recognition of the existence of oligopoly power implies recognition of the historic inevitability of oligopoly. Modern productive methods leave no economic alternative to a few large firms in most industries, and the courts are quite aware that breaking up large firms may well lead to inefficient production. If, as suggested above, interindustry competition furnishes effective protection to consumers for most categories of goods, the Justice Department would be well advised to stop trying to add one or two more firms to industries that must always remain oligopolistic. Instead, the department might concentrate on finding products for which there are few alternative suppliers, within or without the "industry," and bring actions in these relatively few cases. Such a course would enable us to root out genuine cases of monopoly and avoid much useless and costly litigation.

In the Cellophane case (*United States* v. *E. I. du Pont de Nemours and Company,* 1953), it seemed that the Supreme Court would indeed move in the direction of considering interproduct competition when deciding on the extent of monopoly power, for the Court defined the relevant market to include all competing wrap—from brown paper to polyethylene film. Yet only four years later, in an action brought against the same company, the Court apparently reversed itself, narrowly defining the market for finishes and fabrics to include not the *whole* market but only the *automobile* market. Moreover, this second du Pont case (1957) brought the startling realization that any large corporation that has achieved size through stock acquisitions since 1914 can be required to divest itself of those holdings, no matter what the cost to the firm or how complicated the proceedings. And finally, in the Brown Shoe Company case, the Court pronounced a doctrine that bodes ill for many coming attempts at merger. In this case, the first major interpretation of the 1950 Celler Antimerger Act, the Court made it clear that "incipient" oligopoly would be prevented, for in the action at bar there was no serious contention that Brown's acquisition of the McKinney Shoe Company constituted a serious move toward oligopoly.[21] It seems all too clear that the law has now caught up with the economic theory of a generation ago. Unfortunately, theory has moved on ahead.

---

[20] *United States* v. *United Shoe Machinery Corp.,* 110 F. Supp. 295.
[21] David Dale Martin, "The Brown Shoe Case and the New Antimerger Policy," *American Economic Review,* LIII, 3 (June 1963), 340–58.

Domestic and
Foreign Markets

Capitalism is thus a scheme for hitching self-interest to
public service. The system rests implicitly on the assumption not that men are moved only by selfish motives, but
that selfish motives are more dependable than other motives and that the only way to get most men to work hard
and consistently is to appeal to their cupidity.

JOHN ISE

In last chapter's discussion of competition among
manufacturers no mention was made of a kind of
rivalry always present in the business world. The
businessman, when confronted with evidence of
practices that limit competition or at least cushion
its impact on competitors, inevitably rejoins that
he "competes for the consumer's dollar." This proposition is one economists have always recognized as
having a certain validity. As an introduction to our
chapter on the recent growth of American markets,
it will help to appraise the assertion.

Taking the broadest possible view, we can accept
the idea that each entrepreneur does, in fact, contend with all other entrepreneurs for part of the
custom of household units. We know that consumers
will make certain minimum outlays in several main
categories of expenditures; i.e., each family must
spend part of its income on food, part on clothing,
part on housing, and so on. But does competition
for the consumer's dollar within *categories* of expenditure restrict the power of sellers to charge
"monopoly" or "oligopoly" prices? Does this kind
of competition keep sellers from foisting shoddy
merchandise on unwary buyers? Does this type of
rivalry explain the growth of certain kinds of mar-

kets? The answer to each question appears to be yes, but to see why we must develop a classification of consumer expenditures based on human needs or wants.

For generations there has appeared and reappeared in economic literature the notion that the theory of consumption should focus on the service flow that a consumer good yields over time rather than upon the good itself. The only thing that human beings can consume is a service. Since Irving Fisher insisted upon this formulation more than half a century ago, several writers (notably Professors Knight and Boulding) have recognized the validity of the concept. Most economists, however, have preferred to consider discrete goods rather than their service flows in treating the developing forces of competition.

One of the great scientific contributions of economics suggests that there may no longer be any reason for not relating economic ends to human wants as modern psychology views them.[1] It appears possible to classify the service flows of consumer goods in accordance with the needs (wants) of the human organism. A convenient classification of needs, one acceptable to psychologists generally, is that of viscerogenic and psychogenic needs. The former are primary needs arising from man's neurophysiological make-up. The healthy organism tends to maintain itself in a state of neurophysiological equilibrium but is subject to continual pulls away from equilibrium. Whenever the organism is in a state that throws it off balance, a need to restore balance—to achieve homeostasis—arises. Thus, the need for oxygen, water, food, excretion, avoidance of heat and cold, and the like require certain service flows, some of which are noneconomic, for their satisfaction, for the restoration of balance. The psychogenic or secondary needs—those occasioned by tensions dependent on conditions outside the body such as the need for play, for superiority, for achievement, for recognition, for exhibition, for order, for dominance—give rise to the demand for a large part of the services that a modern economy provides.

An attempt to link up human demands for service flows with the needs (wants, tensions) they remove is outside the scope of this book. An example, however, illumines the nature of competition among both sellers and buyers. Household appliances in general satisfy the biological need to economize activity. An electric refrigerator and a vacuum sweeper, for example, both provide a service flow that enables the members of a household unit to avoid expenditure of energy. The refrigerator makes it unnecessary to empty water pans and chip ice with a pick; the sweeper makes it unnecessary to wield a broom or a rug beater. But the difference in operations performed by the two appliances does not mean that there is no competition between

---

[1] C. Reinold Noyes, *Economic Man in Relation to His Natural Environment,* 2 vols. (New York: Columbia University Press, 1948). The same approach was suggested a century ago by Richard Jennings in *The Natural Elements of Political Economy.* For a discussion of his treatment of the "sensations of consumption" see Ross M. Robertson, "Jevons and His Precursors," *Econometrica,* XIX, 3 (July 1951), 234–37.

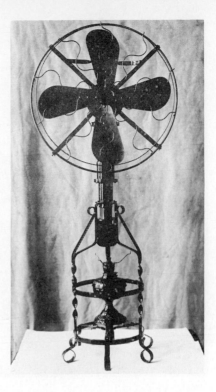

Airconditioning — Before: Until electricity made its inroads in the 1890s, this kind of kerosene-powered fan cooled off overheated Americans by redistributing, not eliminating, hot summer air.

them. From the point of view of the individual allocator of income one way of conserving effort may be clearly preferable to the other. The fact remains that he has a wide choice of alternatives. In this sense there is a close, direct rivalry among producers of goods that seem to be widely separated in the scale of choices. Thus a rough count shows some 250 manufacturers of nationally sold household appliances in the so-called laborsaving category, enough to assure competition in the classical sense.[2]

One complication may be mentioned. It will ordinarily be unusual for the service flow of a good to satisfy only one need. Although our example largely avoided this complexity, more often than not the service flow will be directed at a constellation of needs. Thus, the service flow from dress satisfies not only the obvious physiological needs but also helps to satisfy the need for recognition, for exhibition, for status, and so on. In a subsequent section of this chapter we shall call attention to the efforts of sellers to "differentiate" a product, to create in the minds of buyers reasons for preferring *their* product over that of rival sellers. The notion of product differentiation can be made more meaningful if we think of differentiation as an attempt on the part of sellers to enlarge the constellation of wants toward which the service flow of a product is directed.

---

[2] Over the past half-century it appears that appliances have also competed with the manual labor of domestics, who formerly performed the chores of washing, ironing, rug-beating, etc.

Airconditioning — After: The modern airconditioner has made city living more tolerable, electric utilities happy to find a way to smooth out the summer slump in demand for electrical current.

The readiness with which one service flow may be substituted for another thus leads to a much closer competition among functionally unlike goods than we would at first imagine. On the demand side of markets there exists another force that stimulates a vigorous, churning rivalry. The growth of the institution of consumer credit and of modern forms of urban residential credit have enabled the household unit to economize with greater precision than was possible before World War I. Since the early 1920s household units have more and more been able to refine their immediate acceptance of service flows from durable goods in the present and to plan future acceptance of these flows with some precision—for the simple reason that durable goods need not be paid for in one sum. A much larger number of bidders are consequently brought into the market for manufactured goods and houses, stimulating competition on the buyers' side.

Professor Scitovsky has attributed to the ignorance or inexpertness of buyers a considerable source of oligopoly power.[3] Ignorance, he has argued, enables a firm to seize and hold the custom of buyers who, through lack of knowledge, will not stop buying its products, and entry into an industry is thus limited; further, such ignorance is inevitable in a civilization of advanced technology.

---

[3] Tibor Scitovsky, "Ignorance as a Source of Oligopoly Power," *American Economic Review*, XL, 2 (May 1950), 48–53.

Ignorance lessens competition, it is true, but the kind of ignorance that lessens competition is not the kind that troubles us today. Surely in the producers' market technical knowledge is more and more readily available to the small firm. And it is almost equally certain that we cannot view consumers as mental defectives unable to tell a good cook stove from a bad one. A little reflection tells us that the emphasis of the modern educational system on "practical" training, which many people presently deplore, makes for a rather knowing bunch of customers—who are pretty good at selecting a television set even if they cannot parse a sentence or do a problem in ninth-grade algebra. There is little evidence that American firms—especially the very large ones—foist bad products on people incompetent to make choices. In fact, the evidence is quite the other way around.

The Market for Consumer Durables and Houses

Generalizations like the foregoing lead on to a question of importance to anyone interested in economic change. Have there been any basic shifts in attitudes of consumers toward the several types of service flows? Unfortunately, we do not have sufficient data to permit categorical statements, but some trends seem clear enough.

As we remarked in Chapter 18, Americans have of late been eating "better" foods from the standpoint of both nutrition and taste. The proportion of disposable income spent on food increased during World War II. Contrary to expectations, this proportion has not declined much since the war because housewives have shown a preference for "convenience" items into which a lot of processing has gone. Thus, when a woman buys soluble or "instant" coffee, prepared cake mixes, frozen fruits and vegetables, and canned baby foods, she is purchasing a labor-saving service flow in addition to the food itself.

The percentage of income spent on clothing seems to have fallen somewhat since the 1930s. Even so, there has recently been greater variety in apparel, both as to weight and design, and convenience, comfort, and style have become much more important to the buyer than they were even a generation ago.

But we can make a more general observation. Since 1900, and especially since 1920, Americans have more and more tended to spend their incomes on goods and services (upon service flows) that are dispensable in the short run.[4] People are buying items that enable them to economize effort and attain prestige in the eyes of friends and associates. These purchases have taken the form of more "convenient" things (such as the processed foods mentioned above) and of more services rendered directly by human beings (household domestic service excepted) such as medical care and legal advice. We can also observe a probable secular tendency to devote a greater part

---

[4] Simon Kuznets, *Economic Change* (New York: Norton, 1953), p. 282.

of consumer expenditure to housing, household entertainment equipment, and automobiles.

We shall focus special attention on consumer expenditures for durable goods and houses. Our reason for singling out these expenditures is that they are closely related to the rate of capital formation in the economy and thus to the forces that make for strength and stability.

CONSUMER DURABLES AND CONSUMER CREDIT

If a college student of today were taken back through time to observe American middle-class homes of forty years ago, what would impress him most? At first, a certain drabness, an absence of color and light, an ungraceful assortment of furniture (overstuffed), and an ornate décor might remind him of the home of an elderly relative remembered from childhood. But with a little living in the house the sense of dinginess and bad taste would pass, and he might then be struck with an undeniable fact of life in the twenties. The members of the household worked much harder at entertaining themselves and at keeping house than they do in the 1960s. Even though more of the housework was passed on to a full-time maid, it was nevertheless there to be done.

But new durable goods were already beginning to change living patterns. By 1921 two labor-saving household appliances were gaining rapid acceptance—washing machines and electric refrigerators. A 1921 washing machine was an ungainly contraption, not much improvement over a washboard so far as saving of human energy was concerned. An electric refrigerator of the mid-twenties, its elaborate cooling mechanism in the basement, made almost as much noise as the Essex in the driveway, and an icebox probably did a better job of keeping food. By 1925 electric and gas ranges were making serious inroads on sales of kerosene cook stoves and wood- and coal-burning kitchen ranges. Parents who brought their children up properly provided a piano to further the family's cultural progress, and a player-piano and phonograph were not uncommon. Radios, most of them still tuned with three dials, were just becoming the center of the family's evening interest but were not yet dependable sources of entertainment.

Households had always contained durable goods, of course; the early 1920s simply witnessed a change in their kind. In 1869 half of the output of consumer durables consisted of furniture, a proportion that still held thirty years later. As the automobile revolutionized American life and mechanization spread to the home, the share of furniture and furnishings in consumer durables production fell off rapidly. Automobiles and electrical appliances not only replaced older durable goods (such as horse-drawn carriages and iceboxes), but also brought about an *increase* in the share of consumers' expenditures going to durables. Automobiles and accessories, which accounted for half of the increase in output of consumer durables between 1910 and 1919, accounted for considerably more than half of the increase between 1920 and 1929. The 1920s were also characterized by a

Domestic Joy, 1919: Early radios, like this Aeriola, Jr., appealed to the insider's instinct by providing each listener with his own set of confidential earphones. Speakers came quickly, however, to make radios the chief source of living-room entertainment by the late 1920s.

rapid growth of radio production. Output of consumer electrical appliances rose from less than $100 million in 1920 to $543 million in 1929, two-thirds of the increase resulting from rapid acceptance of radios. By 1929 the composition of expenditure for durables was as shown in Table 22-1. Until 1948 the proportions remained quite stable, but the postwar period has seen a decline in the relative importance of household items (except hi-fidelity radios and phonographs, records, television sets, and musical instruments). In spite of the continual introduction of new and highly acceptable electrical devices, the share of these goods in the total dollar expenditures of consumers has fallen. The remarkable successes of mechanical refrigerators in the 1930s and home freezers, automatic washers, and room airconditioners in the post–World War II period just about offset the leveling off or decline in demand for established items. On the other hand, there has been a definite rise in the proportion of income spent on items, from hi-fis to boats, aimed at making leisure time more fun.

Recent changes can be measured in terms of percentage distribution of personal consumption expenditures. Table 22-2 merits inspection. Clearly, the proportion of consumer expenditures going to durable equipment has been consistently high since the end of World War II, though it should be noted that the percentage for 1929 (and probably for the years immediately preceding) was not much lower. Second, the table shows how sensitive to both depression and war expenditures on durables have been. The purchase

Domestic Joy, 1964: Television continues to exert its fascination on Americans of all ages, particularly on children. Some estimates say that children average thirty-five hours a week viewing time in the winter months.

of durables is postponable, and during extended periods of falling incomes the percentage drop in demand for consumer durables is about the same as the drop in demand for producer durables. During World War II most consumer durables were available only in greatly reduced quantities, with marked lessening of quality, and many disappeared from the market.

To sum up, since 1920 consumers have chosen to consume a higher proportion of their income in the form of durable goods, a tendency that has probably increased since the end of World War II. When we consider the *stocks* of durables in households the reasons for thinking that there has been a secular change in consumer attitudes become compelling. The per-capita value of consumer durables was $358 in 1929. Ten years later it was slightly less (in 1929 prices), as depreciation during depression years exceeded new acquisitions. During the 1940s, despite wartime restrictions and rapid growth in the population, per-capita holdings increased at an annual rate greater than that of the twenties. By the early 1950s the average per-capita value of consumer durables (in 1929 dollars) was at least half again as great as it was in 1929.[5]

How shall we account for this apparent shift in attitudes? A number of

[5] Raymond Goldsmith, "The Growth of Reproducible Wealth of the United States of America from 1805 to 1950," *Income and Wealth, Series II* (London: Bowes & Bowes, 1952), pp. 310–11, 327–28.

Table 22-1

Composition of Expenditures for Durables, Selected Years (in percentage of total)

	1929	1939	1948	1949	1951	1960
Furniture and household equipment [a]	50.0	51.3	50.9	45.2	46.1	42.0
Automobiles, tires, and parts	34.5	32.0	32.8	39.4	39.6	42.0
Other consumer durables [b]	15.6	16.8	16.2	14.8	14.4	16.0
TOTAL	100.0	100.0	100.0	100.0	100.0	100.0

SOURCE: *Survey of Current Business*, July 1952 and July 1961; also *National Income Supplement*, 1951 edition. (Note: Because of rounding, figures may not add up to totals.)

[a] Includes musical instruments, television sets, and phonographs as well as nonfurniture items such as floor coverings, china, tableware, and drapes.

[b] Composition of this category varies but presently includes such items as wheel goods, durable toys, sport equipment, boats, and pleasure aircraft.

studies have demonstrated what we have long known intuitively—that expenditures on durables are closely correlated with income changes. As people become richer they spend a greater portion of their incomes on goods yielding services that relieve work or monotony and increase personal and family prestige.

But we must look a little further. The purchase of durable goods requires at a particular moment of time a relatively large outlay for a future flow of services. There is nothing to prevent families with sufficient incomes from saving up in order to make the outlay, and some of them do. But experience has shown that the majority of American households find it difficult to save the full purchase price of major durables before buying. Even when they replace large items, relatively few consumers have an amortization fund to draw on. As noted above, consumer credit is a device, though not necessarily the only one, that puts the consumer's desire for capital goods on a competitive basis with his desire for nondurables and services. As distinguished from convenience (charge account) credit, it enables the consumer, at any moment of time, to increase his purchases over and above what they would be if he depended upon his savings.

Starting about 1850 sewing machines, furniture, pianos, and sets of books were sold by installment contract. During the first two decades of the twentieth century, installment credit gradually became respectable, and by 1920 the most conservative merchants were offering easy payment plans. Data for the 1920s are sketchy, but studies indicate the substantial use of installment credit early in the decade. By 1926 nearly two-thirds of new-car sales and three-fourths of furniture sales were on time; the proportion of installment sales to total retail sales was thought to be from 13 to 15 per cent. Even if we allow for some inaccuracy of estimation, it is apparent that installment credit was well established by 1929.

Table 22-2

Percentage Distribution of Personal Consumption Expenditures, 1929–1961

Year	Durables	Nondurables	Services	Nondurables and services
1929	11.9	47.9	40.2	88.1
1930	10.3	48.1	41.6	89.7
1931	9.1	47.3	43.6	90.9
1932	7.5	46.2	46.3	92.5
1933	7.6	48.0	44.4	92.4
1934	8.2	51.5	40.3	91.8
1935	9.2	52.2	38.6	90.8
1936	10.2	52.6	37.2	89.8
1937	10.4	52.5	37.1	89.6
1938	8.9	52.8	38.3	91.1
1939	9.9	51.9	38.2	90.1
1940	10.9	51.7	37.4	89.1
1941	11.9	52.7	35.4	88.1
1942	7.8	57.1	35.1	92.2
1943	6.5	59.0	34.5	93.5
1944	6.2	59.5	34.3	93.8
1945	6.7	60.1	33.2	93.3
1946	10.8	57.7	31.5	89.2
1947	12.5	56.5	31.0	87.5
1948	12.7	55.4	31.9	87.3
1949	13.6	53.3	33.1	86.4
1950	15.6	51.1	33.3	84.4
1951	14.0	52.5	33.5	86.0
1952	13.2	52.4	34.4	86.8
1953	14.1	50.7	35.2	85.9
1954	13.6	50.1	36.3	86.4
1955	15.4	48.6	36.0	84.6
1956	14.3	48.7	37.0	85.7
1957	14.2	48.3	37.5	85.8
1958	12.7	48.3	39.0	87.3
1959	13.9	46.9	39.2	86.1
1960	13.6	46.2	40.2	86.4
1961	12.9	45.9	41.2	87.1

SOURCES: *Business Statistics: 1961 Biennial Edition*, and *Survey of Current Business* (various issues).

From 1929 through 1938 the proportion of installment sales to total sales ranged between 38 and 55 per cent at furniture stores and between 49 and 59 per cent at household-appliance stores. About 60 per cent of all automobile sales were made on time throughout the decade, a ratio of automobile installment sales to total automobile sales that came to be accepted

Status Symbol, 1923 A.D. This sleek Stutz told the world what it thought of itself on its spare-tire cowling. "It's a Great Car," the slogan boasted.

as normal. Post–World War II experience confirmed this estimate of normalcy. After household units spent the cash saved during the war for the specific purpose of buying durable goods when they should become available, the percentages that obtained in the 1930s were approximately equaled.

Installment credit has special economic significance because it fluctuates with purchases of durables, particularly of automobiles, and hence is subject to sharp cyclical movements. As shown in the chart on p. 580 (top), installment credit extended exceeds that repaid over periods ranging up to two years, with recurrent drops in the rate of extensions to or below the rate of repayments. Since extensions of credit exceed repayments during upswings of business activity, and since repayments tend to exceed extensions during the early part of downswings, some economists have repeatedly voiced concern over the destabilizing effects of installment credit. Moreover, as the lower chart indicates, total consumer credit and installment credit outstanding keep moving, with minor periodic setbacks, to new highs, standing at $63 billion and $48 billion, respectively, early in 1963. But how high were these dollar amounts *relative* to income? To obtain a rough indication of the ability of people to carry debt, a comparison is frequently made between installment credit repayments required in any year to that year's disposable income. In the late 1950s and early 1960s this ratio fluctuated in a narrow range about 13 per cent, a few percentage points above pre–World War II

Billions of Dollars

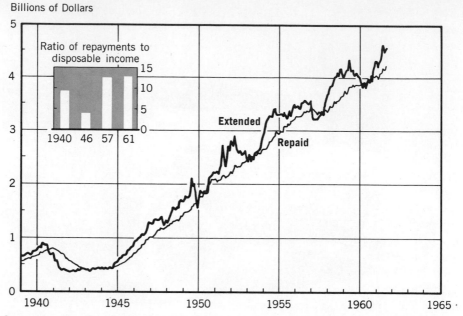

Consumer Credit: Borrowing and repayments have scaled an ever-increasing slope since the war. In the postwar period repayments have exceeded borrowings only during slumps in economic activity.

Billions of Dollars

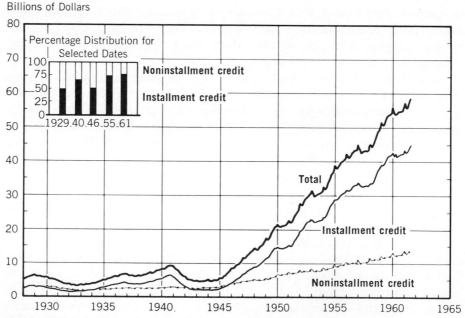

Kinds of Credit: Since the mid-1950s installment credit has amounted to roughly three times noninstallment credit (charge accounts, noninstallment personal loans, etc.).

Board of Governors of the Federal Reserve System (both charts).

levels. After an examination of the forces affecting the level of residential mortgage debt, we can hazard a judgment about the "burden" of indebtedness carried by American households.

The Great Depression and World War II placed such restraints on residential construction that between the early 1930s and the early 1950s housing standards did not keep up with increases in real income. During this period, though the number of high-income families increased, the number of high-value houses actually decreased; and while the great middle-income group of families trebled, houses of the value in which this group lived in 1929 increased by less than a third.[6] Nevertheless, by the early 1960s the postwar building boom, combined with a gradually rising consumer propensity to spend money on housing, had succeeded in reversing the trend toward deterioration of the housing stock.[7] Plainly, though, middle-class Americans did not require the amenity of space (inside and out) so cherished by their forebears.

One reason for the developing preference for smaller, easier-to-keep houses was that in combination with electrical gadgets they made more free time available to the housewife and her spouse. Another deterrent to the building of large houses has been the greater percentage rise, since the 1920s, in the price of cubic feet of housing space than in the prices of other things the consumer buys. Too, a house represents the largest single outlay that a family ordinarily makes. Financing thus becomes a major consideration, and if institutional arrangements are such that financing of inexpensive homes is favored, inexpensive homes will be built. As we shall see, federal influence on the urban residential mortgage market has encouraged building of low- and medium-priced houses.

In 1900 a little more than one-third of nonfarm residents owned the dwellings in which they lived; the nation was definitely a nation of renters. By 1920 about two-fifths of urban families owned their homes, and during the housing boom of the twenties this proportion did not change much. To their sorrow many lost their homes in the early thirties, but the decennial census of 1940 showed a return to what was coming to be considered a normal proportion of homeowners. Then came what appeared to be a sudden shift in consumer attitudes. During the forties and early fifties the number of owner-occupied urban units rose rapidly, and by early 1951 the

---

[6] Gilbert Burck and Sanford S. Parker, "The Insatiable Market for Housing," *Fortune* (February 1954), pp. 103–04.

[7] Between 1948 and 1960 housing expenditures shifted upward in both dollar and real terms. In 1948 housing expenditures comprised 10 per cent of the consumer budget; by 1960 the proportion had risen to 13 per cent. In recent years American families have also been willing to spend a larger proportion of their incomes on household operation. See Louis J. Paradiso and Mabel A. Smith, "Developments in the Consumer Market," *Survey of Current Business* (January 1961), pp. 14–16.

Percentage

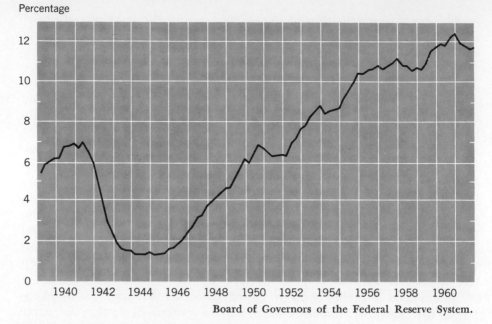

Board of Governors of the Federal Reserve System.

Buying on Time: The postwar phenomenon of installment purchasing has taken a higher and higher proportion of household income. The ratio of consumer installment credit to disposable personal income hovered in the early 1960s about the 12 per cent mark.

proportion of the urban population owning homes stood at about 54 per cent. In the ensuing decade the percentage of home-owning families increased to 62.5 per cent. It should be observed, however, that whereas in 1900 30 per cent of the homes were mortgaged to 40 per cent of their aggregate value, in the early 1960s more than 60 per cent were mortgaged to more than half their aggregate value.

The rise in owner occupancy is the result of many forces of which three are predominant. One major factor has been the long period of sustained high levels of income with accompanying large increases in liquid asset holdings and distribution changes in favor of lower income groups. Another is the subsidy to home owning provided by the Federal income-tax laws, which graciously allow interest as a personal deduction. Perhaps most important has been the availability for urban real-estate financing of vastly increasing supplies of credit on easy terms. Urban mortgage debt increased more than ninefold between the end of 1945 and the end of 1962; in mid-1963 mortgages on one-to-four family houses stood at the astronomical figure of $176 billion.

Under pre-1933 financing methods such an increase in home-ownership would have been impossible. Through the 1920s the typical mortgage loan was short-term, running three, five, or at most ten years. Loans were limited to a maximum of 50, 60, or 66⅔ per cent of appraised values with the result that high-interest second and even third mortgages were common. Although there was some experimenting with amortized mortgages, particularly by savings and loan associations, lump-sum payments or partial amortization with "balloon" payments at maturity were the rule. Interest rates on first mortgages were high, ranging on most loans from 6 per cent in the money centers of the East to 8 per cent in the South, the Southwest, and the West. Rates on second mortgages were considerably more. High rates were in part the result of the uninsured risk inherent in loans to individuals; in part they reflected the absence of a steady national market for mortgages and the lack of institutions that could assist lending firms to meet withdrawal of investors' funds in times of economic stress.

In a rapidly expanding economy the weaknesses of the old mortgage instrument were apparent. During the 1920s there were sporadic attempts by lending institutions and state governments to broaden the mortgage market and to moderate the terms on which home loans were made. None of these were effective, however, and it remained for the federal government to institute a program that would enable a large part of middle- and low-income families to enter the housing market. The effects of federal housing legislation cannot be precisely measured, but there is no doubt that by aiding the flow of credit available to borrowers at low interest rates and on a monthly amortization basis, the federal government has increased the aggregate demand for housing.

The federal housing program had its inception during the grinding deflation of the Great Depression. As in so much of the legislation of the 1930s the laws affecting urban mortgage financing mixed the motives of "relief, recovery, and reform."

Relief came first. With foreclosures rife during the early thirties, steps were taken to aid (1) the institutions that had committed a good portion of their assets to urban mortgages, and (2) the mortgagors who were losing their homes at an unbelievably high rate.

To help the home-lending institutions Congress in 1932 created the Federal Home Loan Bank System, which included eleven regional banks and their member institutions under the supervision of a Home Loan Bank Board. Membership was open to all qualified institutional lenders, including savings banks and insurance companies, but in practice the savings and loan associations, which promoted the legislation, have constituted by far the greater part of the membership. The chief function of the Home Loan Banks was to provide liquidity to member institutions by making loans to them on the security of mortgages.

In 1933 Congress came to the direct aid of homeowners threatened with loss of their properties and further assisted lending institutions by creating the Home Owners Loan Corporation (HOLC), also under the supervision of the Home Loan Bank Board. Provision was made for direct loans to individuals about to lose their homes. These loans were for fifteen-year periods at an interest rate of 5 per cent and were to be amortized on a

Levittown, Long Island, typifies the rapid growth of suburban housing in the United States since World War II. This denuded scene was photographed just as construction was being completed. Today, the lots are well shaded and the houses distinguished by personal changes made by their owners.

monthly basis. The HOLC made no new loans after June 1936, but in less than three years of active lending the agency refinanced more than a million homes and disbursed nearly $3 billion in exchange for defaulted mortgages.

Other means of increasing the supply of funds available for mortgage lending were effected at about the same time. The act that established the HOLC also provided for the chartering of federal savings and loan associations, the treasury being authorized to subscribe up to 50 per cent of the shares of any one association. In 1934 the Federal Savings and Loan Insurance Corporation (FSLIC) was established with capital provided by the HOLC. A tremendous psychological bulwark to savers, the FSLIC received premium payments from member institutions and insured the accounts of shareholders up to $5,000 (later $10,000).

Early legislation made the Home Loan Bank Board the major agency for stimulating a flow of money into urban real estate finance. In 1934, with the creation of the Federal Housing Administration, emphasis changed from relief to recovery. To stimulate new lending a scheme of mortgage insurance was devised whereby private lending institutions could make first-mortgage loans on one- to four-family dwellings and large rental properties with substantially less risk than formerly. A plan of insuring loans for repairs to real property, at first considered purely temporary, became a part of the permanent plan. Over the three decades of its existence the Federal Housing Administration has added considerably to the scope of its operations.

From the first, the FHA insured mortgages with loan-to-value ratios as high as 80 per cent, low interest rates, and amortization over twenty years. In 1938 the FHA was permitted to insure up to 90 per cent of the appraised value of newly constructed homes selling for $6,000 or less. In 1941 Congress passed Title VI of the National Housing Act to encourage house building in defense areas by making FHA insurance available, and after the war low-priced housing was made available under Title VI to veterans of World War II. In addition, the Federal Housing Administration insured loans to finance low-cost rental housing, co-operative housing for military and atomic-energy personnel, and programmed housing in designated critical defense areas. Thus the accomplishment of social aims, such as securing inexpensive housing for veterans or war workers and improving the quality of rental properties for the general populace, became a part of the FHA concept.

The National Housing Act of 1934, which established the Federal Housing Administration, also provided for *privately* owned national mortgage associations in order to create a secondary mortgage market on a national scale, but no attempts were made under this early law to form such associations. In 1935 the RFC Mortgage Company, owned by the Reconstruction Finance Corporation, began the purchase of mortgages on urban commercial properties. Not until 1938, however, was legislation passed aimed at government sponsorship of a secondary residential mortgage market. In that year the Federal National Mortgage Association (FNMA) was set up with RFC capital. Although FNMA—dubbed "Fanny May"—was not of major importance at the time of its establishment in 1938, it did furnish a market for FHA loans by buying them whenever and wherever private capital was unavailable and by selling them at a premium in certain areas at appropriate times. A decade later FNMA became a major influence in urban residential financing.

From the beginning of the depression emergency there was considerable interest in the provision of low-rental housing to underprivileged families. So-called public housing began with efforts by the RFC and later by the Public Works Administration to make loans to private housing companies. When these attempts met with little success, another way was taken to provide adequate dwellings for low-income groups. In 1937 the United States Housing Authority (USHA) began the practice of making loans to local public housing authorities established by municipalities. Through this New Deal public housing program the government thus added reform to the earlier objectives of relief and recovery.

With the onset of World War II the necessity of providing houses for war workers superseded all other objectives. Government funds for wartime housing were appropriated directly, and as noted previously private construction was financed through FHA under Title VI of the National Housing Act. In 1942 the major federal housing agencies—the Federal Home Loan Bank Board, the Federal Housing Administration, and the Federal Public Housing Authority (formerly USHA)—were combined under the National Housing Agency. Its function was to centralize and coordinate, presumably for the duration of the war, the financing and construction of both public and private housing.

In 1947, under the President's Reorganization Plan No. 3 of that year, the first peacetime housing agency was created ". . . with the responsibility of coordinating the principal housing programs and functions of the Government, and of providing a focal point for cooperative effort by Government and private enterprise in solving housing problems." [8] At the outset the Housing and Home Finance Agency (HHFA) included the Office of the Administrator, the Home Loan Bank Board, the Federal Housing Administration, and the Public Housing Administration. The chief officers of the component agencies comprised an Executive Council; this group, with representatives from other interested agencies, made up the National Housing Council. In 1950 the Federal National Mortgage Association was transferred to the HHFA from RFC. In 1955 the Home Loan Bank Board was made a separate agency. As the Federal Home Loan Bank Board it has jurisdiction over the Federal Home Loan Bank System, the Federal Savings and Loan Insurance Corporation, and federally chartered savings and loan associations. The present composition of the HHFA is shown on p. 587.

No account of postwar housing legislation can avoid some emphasis on the Servicemen's Readjustment Act of 1944, which made provision for the guaranty by the Veterans Administration of first- and second-mortgage loans made by private lenders to veterans for the purchase of homes. Under the original act the Administrator of Veterans Affairs could guarantee 50 per cent of a loan up to a maximum of $2,000; in the next year the maximum guaranty was increased to $4,000. Under Section 505a of the original act it was possible to combine an FHA loan with a VA-guaranteed second mortgage for the down payment, and a veteran could finance a $20,000 home without any cash outlay. The combined FHA-VA loan was eliminated effective October 20, 1950. Thereafter, it was only possible to obtain a VA guaranty of 60 per cent of the value of a property to a maximum of $7,500, though a veteran could, of course, obtain straight FHA financing.

The initial impact of federal credit aids on urban residential construction and finance is shown by three indicators.

1. From 1935 through 1952 about 4,250,000 new dwelling units were financed with mortgage loans insured by the FHA or guaranteed by

[8] Housing and Home Finance Agency, *First Annual Report* (1947), pp. 1–27.

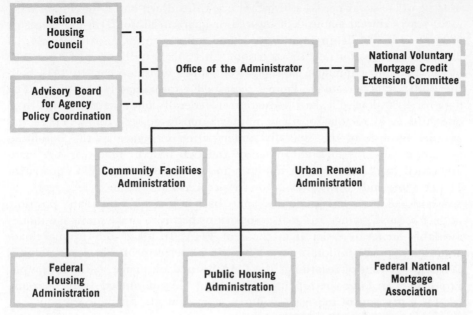

Housing and Home Finance Agency.

Housing Aid: Federal intervention in behalf of home-buying has resulted in the rapid expansion of home ownership among Americans of all but the highest income levels. Of key importance in this development, needless to say, has been the Housing and Home Finance Agency, organized as indicated above.

the VA. This number represented about 40 per cent of all new dwelling units built during the period and equaled more than one-half of the entire volume constructed during the 1920s. Of the 4,250,000 new dwelling units nearly 3,000,000 were financed with FHA and VA loans made during the seven postwar years 1946 to 1952.

2. Construction of privately financed rental units became almost entirely dependent on FHA insurance, running to more than 90 per cent of all such units in the postwar years 1946–52.

3. About 43 per cent of all residential mortgages held by institutions carried government insurance or guaranty at the end of 1952.

For a while, then, the outstanding fact of the federal housing program in the post–World War II period was the rapid growth of FHA and VA loans. A high rate of population increase, an even greater rate of family formation, and restrictions on wartime building led to a tremendous demand for both new construction and existing dwellings. Institutional investors, after years of extremely low yields, were more than willing to meet the accompanying demand for funds to finance home purchases. All that was needed was an "easy-payment" type of contract for potential homeowners with equities insufficient for buying a house on "conventional" terms, which in the early postwar period still meant one-third down and a maximum term of 20 years. Annual amounts of insured or guaranteed nonfarm mortgages of $20,000 or less built up rapidly to $5,600 million in 1950, of which $4,700 million was loans for new construction. This $5,600 million was 34 per cent of the amount of nonfarm mortgage recordings for that year. In 1951 both the dollar and percentage figures remained approximately the same. The data for 1952 showed a sharp reduction in federally underwritten loans from one-third to about one-fourth of nonfarm mortgage recordings. There was another upsurge of the federally underwritten mortgage in the mid-fifties as Korean veterans took advantage of the G.I. bill; in that year VA loans accounted for 25 per cent of nonfarm mortgage recordings, FHA loans for 11 per cent, and conventionals for 64 per cent. In the next few years the conventional loan has gradually come back to its old dominant position, largely because savings and loan associations began to make mortgage money available on terms easier than those of FHA. In 1961 conventional loans accounted for $25 billion of recordings, or 79 per cent of that year's volume. With 15 per cent of recordings the FHA-insured mortgage maintained some importance in large metropolitan areas, but VA-guaranteed loans, accounting for 6 per cent of mortgage volume, seemed at last on their way out.

The chart below shows what has happened to urban real-estate debt compared with other types of consumer debt. At 26 per cent of disposable per-

Kinds of Debt: Mortgage indebtedness still predominates among all kinds of consumer obligations in the United States, soaring toward the $200 billion mark in the mid-1960s.

Board of Governors of the Federal Reserve System.

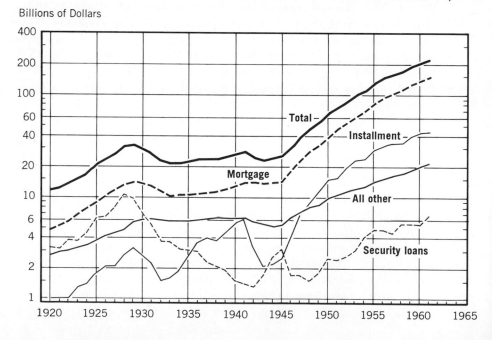

Billions of Dollars

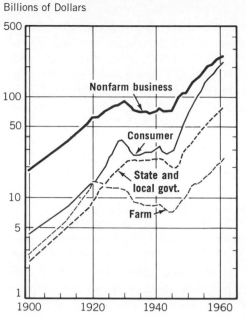

Billions of Dollars

Nonfarm business

Consumer

State and
local govt.

Farm

Nonfederal Debt: The breakdown of nonfederal debt dramatizes the fading importance of farm finance, the rapidly growing importance of consumer obligations.

Board of Governors of the Federal Reserve System.

sonal income (i.e., personal income less personal taxes, fees, and other personal payments to governments), home mortgage debt at the end of 1953 was about at the level of the mid-1930s. Since 1953, home mortgage debt has steadily increased as a proportion of disposable income, amounting to 44 per cent of D.P.I. at the end of 1962. As this chart clearly indicates, except for the years of the Great Depression and World War II, since the turn of the present century consumer indebtedness has increased at a much faster rate than the debt of nonfarm business, state and local governments, and farmers.

Before joining those who worry about consumer indebtedness we should recall three things. (1) Amortization and interest charges on purchased homes are in lieu of rent, and payments are more often than not less than rental payments would be. (2) The income left to most household units today after meeting the basic expenses of food, clothing, and shelter is much larger than before World War II. From this "discretionary" income people may safely commit a larger portion for consumer durables. (3) The debt of consumers is in strong hands. Most consumer debt outstanding has typically been owed by middle- and upper-middle-income families and by people with prospects—by young (under forty-five) married couples with children. There seems to be little evidence that the American consumer has moved in recent years to an insecure position with respect to his indebtedness.

Marketing Methods and the Customer

No description of the way in which household units have spent their money can leave out of account the marketing institutions by which consumers are brought face to face with their alternatives. Before World War I the dominance of the orthodox wholesaler in the marketing process was seriously threatened. "Large-scale retailing" had made its successful appearance, the independent retailer was already being put to it to achieve a more efficient operation, and manufacturers were settling on the best ways of getting their products before a public with which they had no direct contact. Pervading the entire distribution process was a growing respect for the effectiveness of advertising.

THE WHOLESALING OF CONSUMER GOODS

In Chapter 15 we saw how manufacturers began in the late nineteenth century to go around the wholesaler to retail outlets. The "general merchandise" wholesaler, with his warehouses of heterogeneous goods in many lines, had declined rapidly before World War I and was no longer to be a significant figure in the marketing process. As of 1920, however, the full-service, full-line wholesale house, furnishing goods in a particular line such as hardware, groceries, or drugs to retailers over great regions and even nationally, was still in a commanding position. Perhaps the major trend in wholesaling over the past thirty-odd years has been the lessening relative importance of these great houses and the increasing relative importance of the specialty wholesaler, or "short-line" distributor. The specialty firm, which confines its range of activity to a portion of the products within a single line of merchandise, has fitted into the changing scene by developing a high degree of expert knowledge from which small retailers can benefit.

We must not conclude that the decline in importance of the traditional wholesale house meant a reduction in the total flow of goods through wholesale channels. There has simply been a change in the way goods move from manufacturers (or from farm and mine) to the retailer. During the 1920s there was a substantial change in the wholesale *structure* as the wholesaler proper lost ground to manufacturer's sales branches, agents and brokers, assemblers and country buyers, bulk tank stations, and chain-store warehouses in that order. Since 1929 the relative position of the different types of establishment has remained so nearly the same that for our purposes we need not trace the changes. The total volume of wholesale trade has fluctuated with changes in business activity, moving secularly neither upward nor downward.

Wholesale houses have continued since 1929 to handle about two-fifths of the wholesale business as measured in net sales. This group is still the most important to perform wholesale functions, but within it the old order has passed in most lines. A few of the great, traditional names remain: Belknap and Simmons in hardware, Liggett and Reid, Murdock in groceries, Butler Brothers and Rice-Stix in dry goods, and so on. In fact, the full-line houses have retained most of the business in hardware and more than half of it in drugs. But inroads have consistently been made on the full-line wholesaler, to some extent by the limited-function companies (drop shippers, cash-and-carry wholesalers, and wagon distributors), but largely by the specialty firms that serve a small geographic area. The specialty wholesalers handle an assortment of items within a line (coffee, tea, and condiments instead of "groceries" or cutlery instead of "hardware"), they can furnish fresh or new goods with great speed, and they know their particular field of merchandising thoroughly.

Wholesaling has changed in kind because of the great structural shifts in retailing. It has been the growth in the size of the retail firm that has brought about the present-day orientation of the marketing process toward the manufacturer-retailer axis.

LARGE-SCALE RETAILING

Department stores were well established by 1900 and were popularly accepted in the first decade of the century. Between 1910 and 1920 it was the turn of the mail-order companies to make great gains. By 1919 the chain stores showed signs of being a potent marketing form, and in the 1920s they became a major force in retailing. How have these store types fared since?

It is all too easy to think of the department store as a fading institution, but we must not yet count "the big store" out as a merchandising form. During the twenties and thirties department stores maintained a constant proportion of retail sales, indicating that they were just about holding their own in the economy. World War II with its shortages restored some of the advantages of shopping under one roof, the result being an increase in department-store business to about 10 per cent of retail sales, a gain of perhaps two percentage points. Since 1947, department stores, although not without a struggle, have moved slowly back to their pre–World War II position. Increasing traffic congestion in the downtown areas of cities, the rise of suburban shopping centers, and the expansion of variety chains and mail-order companies into broader fields have been the chief factors working against the independent department store. Yet many of them have shown unexpected resilience in the face of changing competitive situations. Ownership groups have bought control of stores in several cities, thus bringing the advantages of tremendous buying power to many of the independents, which have continued to operate under their well-known old names. More recently alert managements have gone along with the suburban trend by establishing branches, some of them rivaling the central-city store in volume. To fight the discount houses, with their emphasis on plain décor and a minimum of service, department stores have either met discount-house prices in their old locations or opened new and less pretentious outlets for the purpose of discounting. A final irony of this competition has been the opening of flossy, new central-city stores by the discounters; like every other major retailing form before them, they have finally succumbed to the compulsion to become respectable.

Mail-order houses, as such, have done better in recent years than we might think, but only because they have changed their business methods to suit the times. Since 1929 the mail-order business has stayed fairly constant at roughly 1 per cent of retail sales, this in spite of the disappearance of many of the reasons for ordering from a catalog. A number of companies specializing in a single line or a few items have sprung up. The application of new advertising techniques to catalog illustrations and the opening of "catalog stores" in small towns have helped the older houses maintain volume. But the two great mail-order firms have in addition completely changed their sales methods. In 1925 Montgomery Ward established its first retail store in Marysville, Kansas, and Sears quickly tried the same experiment. In the following decade and a half these retail stores came to number in the hundreds, and more than half of the "mail-order" business was done over a counter. At the end of World War II Sears boldly expanded by building great department stores in readily accessible sections of major cities. Montgomery Ward, because it was timorous in carrying out its expansion program, lost ground to such an extent that in 1950 its sales were less than half those of its major competitor. During the ensuing decade Sears, Roebuck and Company became the fifth largest employer in the United States with a dollar volume of retailing of more than $4 billion a year, a retail sales figure exceeded only by A & P.

Mention of the great grocery chain reminds us that the past thirty years have witnessed a widespread acceptance of the chain principle of merchandising. Between 1919 and 1929 chain sales rose from an estimated 4 per cent of retail sales to something less than 25 per cent, a proportion that has not varied much since in good times and bad. Since 1929, however, the number of retail units in chain organizations has declined, possibly by as much as a third, as the trend has been toward fewer stores with greater volume. There has also been some shift in the use of the chain form in various lines of business. The opening of department stores by Sears and Montgomery Ward has been reflected statistically in a definite spread of chains to the department-store, dry-goods, and general-merchandise field. Chain growth has been especially marked in drugs, shoes, women's ready-to-wear, and jewelry, while only moderate gains have been made in variety merchandise, food, and automobile accessories and equipment. At the same time, there has developed a high degree of concentration within chain-store groups, as the six largest concerns in each field have attained a preponderance of chain sales in the general merchandise (department store), variety, grocery, and drug lines.

Chains have unquestionably found a place in American economic life from which they will not be dislodged. The principle of the chain has been adopted by some independent retailers. In an effort to obtain some of the advantages of vertical integration, independent retailers in most lines pioneered by the chains have achieved some success in setting up informal buying pools and voluntary chains. Nevertheless, the historical trend toward distributor integration was slowed greatly, if not actually halted, twenty-five years ago. The spectacular growth in *absolute* volume of the big merchandisers should not cause us to forget that their *relative* strength has not changed much since before the Great Depression.

Limited-line stores of widely varying size under independent ownerships have continued to do more than half the retail business in the United States. Independents have located in the suburban shopping centers that have sprung up so conspicuously since World War II. Although the chains pioneered in the development of the supermarket, independents have competed successfully as supermarkets in the grocery business, success often leading to expansion into a local group of several stores. Supermarket merchandising has also had metropolitan-area success in stores selling higher-priced goods such as clothing, appliances, and even automobiles. In an age in which deference is paid the specialist, specialists in the retail field have been able to hold their own. For they, like the large-scale retailers, can successfully differentiate their product.

THE DIFFERENTIATION OF PRODUCTS

Professor Chamberlin has said that a product is differentiated ". . . if any significant basis exists for distinguishing the goods (or services) of one seller from those of another." At the beginning of this chapter it was suggested that products are differentiated by the device of enlarging the constellation of service flows they provide. Differentiation may be achieved by adjusting the conditions surrounding the sale of the product or by varying the quality or appearance of the product itself.

Thus a good is differentiated spatially when prospective customers are able to economize physical effort in getting it. Independent retailers have traditionally operated neighborhood stores in order to reap the rewards of this type of differentiation, and they are still able to do so in the suburban shopping center, with its parking space for thousands of automobiles. In other respects the retailer may be equally successful in differentiating his establishment and the product (or products) he sells. He can give "tone" to his establishment; [9] he can carry goods of nationally known manufacturers or assiduously push "private" ones; he can appeal to those who wish a certain personal quality in their dealings with merchants as well as to people who simply wish to be waited on in anonymity.

Successful differentiation of a product sold in the nation-wide market ordinarily requires large outlays for advertising. Consumers must be persuaded that there is a good reason for buying one brand of cigarettes or cornflakes or washing machines rather than another. Advertising is effective if for any reason—rational (i.e., understandable) or not—it convinces buyers that one brand of any item is clearly preferable to another. As early as 1910 the annual volume of expenditure on advertising reached $1 billion; by 1920 the figure reached $2 billion, and by 1929 the estimated outlay passed $2,500 million. Advertising fell off greatly during the 1930s to an

---

[9] The tone may be one of spare frugality (Robert Hall's "plain pipe racks") or calculated opulence (Tiffany's). It is the difference in appeal that counts.

annual average of perhaps $1,700 million, only to rise rapidly in the forties and early fifties to nearly $8 billion in 1953. A decade later advertising outlays passed the $12 billion mark.

One of the advantages of size to a manufacturing firm is that it can afford to spend large sums on advertising to gain acceptance of its product on a national or regional scale. The requirement to advertise is thus a force making for a large optimum size of the firm.

This very fact makes it possible for small retailers to compete successfully with large ones. Much of the impact on buyer consciousness has been made through the manufacturer's efforts; the items that the retailer sells have been largely differentiated by the high-powered national advertising of television, radio, and magazines. The independent retailer need only inform the public of his existence and depend upon his location and the tone of his establishment to bring him a profitable volume of trade. Thus successful differentiation of products by the great firms in oligopolistic industries helps to account for the unexpected strength of the small outlet in the recent competitive struggle with the large retailers.

The United States and the Rest of the World

In Chapter 18 we found it necessary to discuss certain aspects of recent foreign trade in order to understand current agricultural difficulties. We may now expand our previous discussion and add some pertinent detail.

The chart opposite gives us a good idea of changes in the volume of American foreign trade and of its constitution by classes of goods. From a post–World War I high of $8 billion, merchandise exports fell to less than $2 billion in the trough of the depression. Merchandise imports, which had been consistently above $4 billion during most of the 1920s, almost ceased during the depression years. The war and postwar years marked a spectacular revival in foreign trade.

As befitted a highly industrialized nation the United States continued to specialize in the export of finished manufactures, with crude materials and semimanufactures next in importance. On the import side crude materials and semimanufactures (to be worked up into finished goods) have been the most important. Crude foodstuffs, mostly items that cannot be grown in the United States, have remained over the years a stable class of imports. A glance at the export-import chart shows that our imports of finished manufactures have fallen far short of our exports of these items, though the manufacturers of western Europe and Japan have recently been competing strongly in the sale of finished goods to Americans.

THE BALANCE OF PAYMENTS

Table 22-3 summarizes the United States' balance of payments from 1920 to 1945. For the period 1920–33 we had a favorable balance on goods and services account of nearly $8 billion, and income on investment abroad,

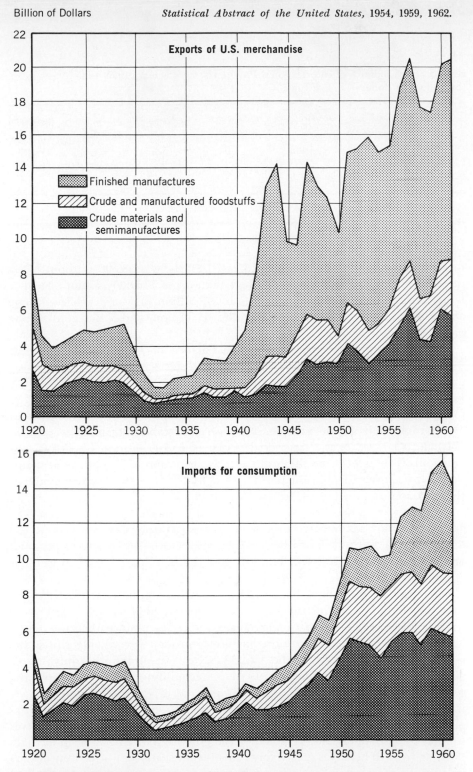

International Trade: The broad pattern that emerges from American import and export figures is that the country largely buys raw materials abroad and sells manufactured goods in return. The United States consistently enjoys a favorable balance on current account.

Table 22-3

United States Balance of International Payments, by Periods, 1920–1945
(in billions of dollars)

Period	Goods and services net	Income on investment net	Capital transactions net	Unilateral transfers	Gold	Errors and omissions
1920–33	+ 7.8	+8.5	−7.0	− 5.1	− 1.4	−2.8
1934–40	+ 2.8	+2.3	+7.4	− 1.3	−14.9	+3.7
1941–45	+36.7	+1.8	+0.8	−41.6	+ 1.9	+0.4

SOURCE: *Historical Statistics of the United States, 1789–1945*, p. 242.

including war debt payments to the United States, was $8,500 million. Thus the total credit balance of the United States was $16,300 million. Such a large credit balance was made possible by $7 billion of American investment abroad, unilateral transfers of more than $5 billion, and a net gold inflow of $1,400 million.

The effect of the depression on the balance of payments is apparent. The American export balance of goods and services dropped sharply as did income on investment. The international capital flow was reversed as Europeans, disturbed by political turmoil and impending war, sought refuge for their funds. Official figures show a capital transfer to the United States of approximately $7,400 million. However, the capital transfer was probably much larger, for the large credit item of $3,700 million for errors and omissions is thought to be the result of miscalculation of capital movements. For the seven-year depression period, gold flowed into the United States in the astronomical amount of nearly $15 billion.

For the war period, 1941–45, the huge credit balance on goods and services account was approximately offset by unilateral transfers of more than $40 billion. Unilateral transfers after 1941 no longer consisted solely of personal and institutional remittances, but were for the most part large government grants under lend-lease.

The postwar years have been so important in international relationships that we shall find it instructive to examine an abbreviated year-by-year statement of the balance of payments (see Table 22-4). Since 1946 the American balance-of-payments position has gone through remarkable shifts. Between 1946 and 1949, when the United States was almost the only source of supply of industrial goods required for rebuilding western Europe, the surplus position averaged $2 billion a year. From 1950 to 1956, inclusive, the United States averaged a deficit in her international payments of approximately $1,500 million annually, as Europeans provided for themselves (thanks to vast American aid) some of the goods imported in the immediate postwar years. There was a payments surplus of nearly half a billion dollars in 1957, as the United States had a surplus on current account (goods and

Table 22-4

U.S. Balance of Payments Position, 1946–1961 [a]
(millions of dollars)

NOTE: Payments deficits, increases in liabilities to foreigners, and gold sales are shown by (−).

Year	(1) Recorded receipts [b]	(2) Recorded expenditures [c]	(3) Net balance on recorded transactions	(4) Net unrecorded transactions	(5) Net payments position	(6) Change in liquid dollar liabilities to foreigners [d]	(7) U.S. gold sales
1946	+14,735	−13,004	+1,731	+195	+1,926	+1,303	+623
1947	+19,737	−15,714	+4,023	+936	+4,959	+2,110	+2,849
1948	+16,789	−16,790	−1	+1,179	+1,178	−352	+1,530
1949	+15,851	−16,534	−683	+775	+92	−72	+164
1950	+13,954	−17,526	−3,572	−30	−3,602	−1,859	−1,743
1951	+19,045	−19,858	−813	+470	−343	−396	+53
1952	+18,246	−19,843	−1,597	+505	−1,092	−1,471	+379
1953	+17,287	−19,685	−2,398	+296	−2,102	−941	−1,161
1954	+18,193	−19,876	−1,683	+167	−1,516	−1,218	−298
1955	+20,349	−21,944	−1,595	+446	−1,149	−1,108	−41
1956	+24,235	−25,846	−1,611	+643	−968	−1,274	+306
1957	+27,094	−27,374	−280	+748	+468	−330	+798
1958	+23,349	−27,206	−3,857	+380	−3,477	−1,202	−2,275
1959	+24,012	−28,621	−4,609	+783	−3,826	−3,095	−731
1960	+27,470	−30,230	−2,760	−1,040	−3,800	−2,111	−1,689
1961	+28,893	−30,731	−1,838	−616	−2,454	−1,712	−742

SOURCE: U.S. Department of Commerce.

[a] 1961 data are preliminary.

[b] Sum of exports of goods and services (less goods shipped under military grant), and, from 1950 to date, direct and long-term portfolio investment by foreigners.

[c] Sum of imports of goods and services, net unilateral transfers (less military aid grants) and net outflow of U.S. capital. Payments of subscriptions to international institutions amounting to $3,385 million in 1946 and 1947, and $1,375 million in 1959 are excluded from totals of recorded expenditures and gold sales.

[d] Short-term liabilities to foreigners and long-term, U.S. Government securities. Prior to 1950, includes direct and portfolio investment in the United States by foreigners.

services) of nearly $6 billion, largely attributable to massive exports of United States commodities during the Suez crisis. Beginning in 1958, the United States deficit position averaged a whopping $3,400 million annually through 1961, and while this average was reduced considerably in 1962 and 1963 it was still high enough to cause official concern.

To summarize, from the end of 1949 to the end of 1961 the American balance-of-payments deficit was $23 billion. It was made up by an outward gold flow of $8 billion and an increase in foreign-owned short-term dollar assets of $15 billion. There was no problem through 1957 because deficits could be made up with relatively small gold sales abroad, actually considered a desirable reallocation of the free world's monetary gold stock. But the payments deficit of nearly $14 billion in the four years 1958–61 resulted in a $6 billion reduction in the United States monetary gold stock, and subsequent efforts to reduce the drain were only partly successful.

With the monetary gold stock down to $16 billion in early 1963, the United States still had 40 per cent of the free world's monetary gold supply. Of this amount nearly $12 billion was held as monetary reserves under the rule requiring the Federal Reserve to "back" Federal Reserve notes and member bank deposits with gold certificates in the amount of 25 per cent of these liabilities.[10] Viewers-with-alarm pointed out that only $4 billion in gold was left to meet a potential $21 billion liquidation of foreign-held dollar assets. But of course the United States was an international creditor to the tune of more than $27 billion, and if foreign central banks caused the United States needless embarrassment, the American central bank and treasury could retaliate. After all, the United States continued in the 1960s to be the strongest economy in the world—by a tremendous margin—and her balance-of-payments deficit was solely the consequence of doing far more than western Europeans were willing to do to protect the free world.

INTERNATIONAL ECONOMIC POLICY

Mention of foreign commitments reminds us how vast have been the changes in the international outlook of Americans since 1920. At the end of World War I Congress would not hear of cancelling the war debts of our former allies except through repayment. Although the United States during the twenties "forgave" a portion of the interest on European war debts, payments were received until the depression forced suspension, and Congress was irate over the default when it came.

American attitudes toward war debts typified the narrow economic isolation of the 1920s. Nowhere was our international thinking so clearly expressed as in the tariff laws passed after World War I. Protectionists were clearly in the ascendancy before the end of World War I. Agitation for higher duties came largely from a new group of "infant" industries ("war babies") that had sprung up to produce goods, such as chemicals and dyes, formerly made by Germany. The Emergency Tariff Act of 1921 was quickly followed by a permanent measure, the Fordney-McCumber tariff of 1922, which brought average duties up to about 33 per cent. During the 1920s, conservatives gave the high tariff much credit for the prevailing prosperity, forgetting that the high level of United States exports was made possible only by the willingness of Americans to lend abroad. With the downturn of economic activity in 1929, it was thought that serious depression might be avoided by raising tariffs still higher. In 1930, after a year of debate, Congress passed the Hawley-Smoot tariff, which raised average duties to 40 per cent. Although representatives of foreign nations officially protested and the country's leading economists urged a veto, President Hoover signed the bill into law.

Many competent observers considered the Hawley-Smoot tariff a cause of the deepening of the depression. The act was the signal for reprisals by other countries in the form of general tariff increases and import quotas, and it served notice to the world that the United States would adopt a course of selfish nationalism. In the campaign of 1932 the Republicans, maintaining that protection had brought prosperity, promised even higher duties and more of them. The Democrats rejoined that tariff-making by Congress

---

[10] Congress could of course reduce this percentage at any time.

had only succeeded in contributing to the deterioration of world trade and that a plan of negotiating with other nations to secure reciprocal trade agreements should be instituted.

In 1934 the Reciprocal Trade Agreements Act was passed by large majorities in both the House and Senate. It permitted the President for a period of three years to reach agreements with other countries whereby tariff concessions would be mutually granted. Congressional approval of agreements was not required, but the President's tariff-reducing power was limited to 50 per cent of then-existing rates of duty. In 1937, in 1940, and in 1943 the Trade Agreements Act was renewed by Congress without major amendment, and between 1934 and 1945 agreements were negotiated with twenty-nine countries.

In 1945 the act came up for renewal again, and this time the authority of the President was broadened. He could henceforth reduce tariffs up to 50 per cent of the rates prevailing on January 1, 1945; duties that had already been lowered 50 per cent from the 1934 levels could then be lowered another 50 per cent. As the Randall Commission reported in 1954, "The year 1945 marks the legislative high-point of the trade liberalization program that had been set in motion in 1934. Since that time amendments to the Trade Agreements Act have been restrictive, rather than expansive, of the President's power." [11]

Specifically, when the Republican-controlled Congress had an opportunity to review the program in 1948, the act was renewed with a so-called peril-point amendment. This provision required the Tariff Commission to specify rates of duty below which, in the Commission's opinion, tariffs could not be cut without injury to business. Although the President could lower a tariff below the peril point, Congress had to be notified and given the reasons for such an action. In 1949 the Democratic Congress repealed the peril-point amendment, but when the act came up for renewal in 1951, the administration was defeated on this question. The act was renewed for only two years, the peril-point provision was reinserted, and a new "escape clause" provided machinery for suspension of agreements to which particular industries objected. In 1953, after much controversy, the Trade Agreements Act in its modified form was extended for one year pending the report of a temporary Commission on Foreign Economic Policy (the Randall Commission). Pursuant to a recommendation of the Randall Commission, the administration requested a three-year extension of the act, but Congress grudgingly permitted only a one-year extension. As one writer has put it, periodic legislative battles over renewal of the Trade Agreements Act became an honored ritual. "After vigorous combat, the administration has purchased a small addition to its bargaining power by agreeing to amendments restricting the President's use of his authority and providing redress for injury caused by import competition. Each side has emerged from the

---

[11] Commission on Foreign Economic Policy, *Staff Papers* (February 1954), pp. 265–66.

periodic confrontation with less than it desired, yet convinced it had won a victory." [12]

Between 1934 and 1947, in return for tariff concessions from other countries, the average United States tariff level was reduced about one-fourth. But reciprocal trade agreements have their limitations, for they apply only to tariffs and do not remove quantitative restrictions on imports such as quotas. According to the Randall Commission, "we needed a bargain under which we undertook to lower American tariff rates while other countries agreed not only to give reciprocal tariff concessions but also to give up quantitative restrictions as a protective device. By and large, however, the bargain on quotas could not be negotiated. Many countries were willing to guarantee that protective quotas would not be placed on the particular commodities on which they had made tariff concessions to the United States; a few others were willing to guarantee minimum quotas to the United States on some items. But these concessions, taken all together, did not materially affect the quota system." [13] Agreements to outlaw quantitative restrictions could not be achieved because no country felt that it could give up its quota system unless all other countries did, and a bilateral agreement with the United States was not suitable for securing such a guaranty.

The need for multilateral negotiations led to the proposal by the United States for a multilateral trade organization. In 1947 the General Agreement on Tariffs and Trade (GATT) was concluded as a means of furthering international trade co-operation. Originally there were twenty-three contracting nations; by 1963 the number had grown to fifty and included all the major countries of the free world. Under GATT's auspices several important tariff conferences have been held, and the resulting agreements have been made parts of the General Agreement on Tariffs and Trades. The principal result of the multilateral negotiations has been to cut the level of United States tariffs another one-fourth from 1934 levels. Using the rates effective January 1, 1960, the average ad valorem equivalent of duties collected was about 12 per cent. Few countries had lower rates.

With the formation in 1958 of the European Economic Community, tariffs once again became a major problem of public policy. The Common Market was formed for the precise purpose of lowering trade barriers among the six powers signing the Treaty of Rome—Belgium, the Netherlands, Luxembourg, France, Italy, and Germany. Among the Six all barriers to trade would ultimately be removed, and free transfer of labor and capital across national boundaries would be permitted. But the Six would establish a common system of tariffs applicable to the rest of the world, including the United States. As the success of the Common Market became apparent in the early 1960s, it was obvious that the United States would have to pursue

---

[12] Peter B. Kenen, *United States Commercial Policy: A Program for the 1960's* (Washington, D.C.: U.S. Government Printing Office, 1961), p. 3.
[13] Commission on Foreign Economic Policy, pp. 270–71.

Overseas expansion of American corporations has created such improbable sights as beret-clad Frenchmen checking German-made gauges on American-made machines. This scene is at U.S. Tire and Rubber Company's plant near Paris.

trade policies aimed at linking her own great common market with that of western Europe. To this end Congress passed the Trade Expansion Act of 1962, which gave the President authority to lower or remove entirely tariffs on products in which the United States and Common Market countries have 80 per cent of the world's trade and to lower tariffs up to 50 per cent on other goods. With ministers of most of the GATT countries in attendance, the United States and Common Market representatives in 1963 began the slow and often frustrating process of negotiating mutually advantageous tariff reductions.

As important as the removal of barriers to trade was the willingness of Americans to contribute to the postwar reconstruction of western Europe and to assist in the development of the low-income nations of the free world. The fundamental change in old-fashioned, isolationist attitudes was explicitly made during World War II. In the Anglo-American Mutual Aid Agreement of 1942 the contracting parties agreed that in the payment of lend-lease claims "the terms and conditions thereof shall be such as not to burden commerce between the two countries, but to promote mutually advantageous economic relations between them and the betterment of world-wide economic relations." During the war the United States also signed at Bretton Woods the two agreements that established the International Monetary Fund and the International Bank for Reconstruction and Development. In anticipation of the "dollar shortage" expected after the war, the fund was established to maintain stability of exchange rates and to provide for orderly devaluations of currencies, internationally agreed upon, when they should appear necessary. It was hoped that the International Bank, through direct loans and by guaranteeing loans of private lenders, would stimulate international investment in productive projects.

Americans contributed about $40 billion of goods and services to their allies through lend-lease and thus removed the burden of war debts from postwar Europe. The United States quota in the fund was $2,750 million, and the ultimate subscription to the bank's capital could exceed $3 billion. During the two years immediately following the war the United States spent almost $4 billion in direct relief through the United Nations Relief and Reconstruction Administration (UNRRA). Another $3,200 million was distributed in emergency relief through the armed forces, and grants were made to countries like Greece and Turkey threatened with political disorder. Finally, a loan to Britain of $3,750 million was made to see that country through its postwar restoration. Many Americans thought these measures, amounting to nearly $17 billion, pretty substantial and expected them to be enough.

But they were not enough. So much of western Europe's productive capacity was destroyed or obsolete that the major industrial countries could not raise output sufficiently to secure a tolerable standard of living for their peoples. The severe winter of 1946–47 and poor European harvests in the immediate postwar years added to physical suffering. It became apparent in 1947 that the United States must step in to bolster the economies of western Europe or face the prospect of Communist governments in the free countries, especially in Italy and France. Secretary of State Marshall in 1947 proposed the European Recovery Plan which popularly bore his name, and the United States embarked on a vast program calculated to make the sixteen participating countries and Western Germany self-supporting. In the four years of its operation the Marshall Plan sent more than $10 billion, nearly all in outright grants, to western Europe. A large part of this amount went to restore the plant and equipment of a defeated enemy. In October 1951 all forms of aid were placed under the Mutual Security Agency. During the fiscal years 1951–53 foreign aid was almost as great as it was under Interim Aid and Marshall Aid, but there was a pronounced shift from economic to military aid.

Although the people of the United States were altruistically motivated to provide a postwar total of nearly $80 billion in economic assistance to the rest of the world, foreign aid has not been bad for either business or agriculture. By 1952 our exports amounted to over 20 per cent of world exports, but no one pretended that such a level of foreign trade could persist without subsidization. In the early 1960s American exports of goods and services amounted to a little more than 5 per cent of the national income, or nearly 10 per cent of the total production of movable goods. The "big four" of American exports—industrial machinery, automobiles, chemicals, and grains—relied on foreign customers for a large part of total sales. Imports, while constituting something less than 5 per cent of our national income, furnished many critical raw materials in addition to foodstuffs that most consumers would not wish to do without.

The major aim of foreign economic policy has recently been to strengthen the economies of our allies and thus to aid in the common cause against Communism. Foreign trade is of much less direct economic importance to the United States than it is to most of the countries of the free world. But even if foreign trade should cease to be dominated by policy aims, it is likely that the contribution of foreign trade to the American level of living and to the sales of individual industries will keep Americans from going back to the protectionist doctrines of only a generation ago.

Labor's Progress in an
Industrial Economy

Go, songs, and come not back from your far way;
   And if men ask you why ye smile and sorrow,
Tell them ye grieve, for your hearts know To-day,
   Tell them ye smile, for your eyes know To-morrow.

FRANCIS THOMPSON

Every major producing group in the United States has made great gains since 1920, but none has made such firm and unquestioned advances as labor. Real earnings have risen steadily. Hazards to income, though far from being removed, have been greatly reduced by social insurance and social assistance. American trade unions have continued to function as the basic, controlling institutions in the labor movement, though they have lately shown signs of losing the momentum gained in the 1930s.

So we begin the last chapter in the history of labor with a more optimistic assertion than the one that characterized the 1860–1920 period. The gains of labor between the Civil War and World War I were halting and tentative. World War I, accompanied as it was by government intervention in labor affairs, brought improvement; but the economic position of the worker was not bettered much by the prosperity of the 1920s, and the labor movement deteriorated rapidly between 1920 and 1932. Not until 1933, when labor leaders were forced to accept governmental assistance in achieving their objectives, did labor begin an almost uninterrupted advance on all fronts. Indeed, labor's progress since 1933 must be attributed largely to the abandonment of the principle, accepted by conservative unionists at the end of the nineteenth century, that only through union action could the interests of wage-earners be protected. Discarding the policy of "voluntarism," labor's version of laissez faire philosophy, labor leaders first accepted and then demanded the intervention of government in securing protective legislation.[1]

So rapid was the revolution by which labor came from a weak to a strong position that between 1946 and 1948 a public reaction set in. Few begrudged American workers their gains in real earnings or security, nor were many under the illusion that the problem of urban poverty had been eliminated. There was, however, a growing fear that trade unions had become too powerful. A great national union, contending with a major producer in an industry, could by striking against only one firm sharply curtail output of a necessary product. Or a whole industry could be brought to a standstill, as happened to the railroads and the bituminous coal industry in 1946. The effects on the economy of widespread work stoppages could be disastrous, and the question arose whether the public itself did not need protection. People sympathetic to labor's cause inquired if there were not some better way of settling disputes than to rely on the willingness of a large company or a large union to endure a shutdown. Some of labor's friends and many of labor's enemies expressed concern that the rights of union members were being encroached upon by union leaderships. And the managerial class complained that employee unfair practices as well as employer unfair practices should be defined and outlawed.

Thus labor found itself in the trap that some of the old-time union leaders had cautioned against. For if government could at one time intercede on *behalf* of labor, it could later move in to weigh the balance in favor of management. Legislation passed since World War II has gratified those who viewed labor's rise to power with alarm. Ardent labor supporters have considered the same legislation an affront to union leadership and a threat to the very existence of strong organization. To make our own evaluation of recent laws, we shall find it necessary to examine the history of public policy since the early 1930s. For background we must acquaint ourselves with recent changes in labor's economic position and with the growth of American unions.

The Economic Position of the Worker

WAGES AND HOURS

Fortunately, data on earnings and hours for the 1920–62 period are more reliable than figures available for earlier years. Our problem is to generalize in such a way that a clear impression of change emerges. Earnings and hours have not moved by the same percentage for different categories of workers, and within categories of workers geographical differences in wage rates have

---

[1] David J. Saposs, "Voluntarism in the American Labor Movement," *Monthly Labor Review*, LXXVII, 9 (September 1954), 967–71.

persisted for a long time.[2] We may, nevertheless, reach some pretty solid conclusions from inspection of the available indexes.

Let us look first at hours changes. Consider the length of the standard workweek rather than the average number of hours worked per week, for the average figure reflects the overtime hours of boom years and the enforced "short weeks" of depression years. During World War I the 48-hour workweek was accepted in many manufacturing industries, and by 1920 some unions had managed to obtain a half-holiday on Saturday. Not until 1930, however, was a 48-hour week standard for most occupations. Pressures to "share the work" helped shorten the straight-time week during the 1930s. The Fair Labor Standards Act of 1938, covering industries engaged in interstate commerce, set a maximum standard workweek of forty hours and permitted overtime work at the rate of time and a half. In 1940 half a day's work on Saturday was still not uncommon, but the end of World War II saw its virtual disappearance. By 1950 the forty-hour week was standard, and in some industries and in offices many workers were becoming accustomed to a thirty-five-hour week.

Nearly everyone has had more income to enjoy in his increased leisure time. A glance at Table 23-1 enables us to estimate the improvement. The base year is 1926, and since wages and earnings did not change much during the late twenties, we can compare the position of workers in that prosperous period with their position in recent prosperous years. Between 1926 and 1952 average weekly earnings of wage earners in manufacturing nearly quadrupled. In the meantime consumer prices rose approximately 70 per cent. If we take into account the rise in the cost of living, we get increases in real weekly earnings in manufacturing of more than 120 per cent (see column 3). Moreover, wages and earnings figures understate labor's material gains, for in the post–World War II period workers have received "fringe benefits," such as paid vacations and company pension plans, that have an ascertainable money value.[3]

A closer inspection of Table 23-1 reveals interesting relationships in two short periods. During the Great Depression wages fell moderately; earnings dropped more severely because of the great reduction in number of hours worked. Yet because of the decrease in consumers' prices real wages declined only slightly in one year, 1932, and average real earnings fell only mod-

[2] Economists have always taken the North-South wage differential for granted. But even though this differential is accepted, care must be exercised to specify occupations. Wages of unskilled workers in the Southeast have probably remained lower than wages of comparable workers in New England, but wages of office workers and skilled laborers in the Southeast have risen relative to New England wages so that the differential has in many cases disappeared. See, for example, Lloyd Saville, "Earnings of Skilled and Unskilled Workers in New England and the South," *Journal of Political Economy*, LXII, 5 (October 1954), 390–405.

[3] Not counting paid holidays and paid vacations, the value of fringe payments rose from an estimated $3,800 million in 1946 to $20,600 million in 1962, an increase of 700 per cent. A large portion of these benefits go to salaried personnel as distinguished from wage earners.

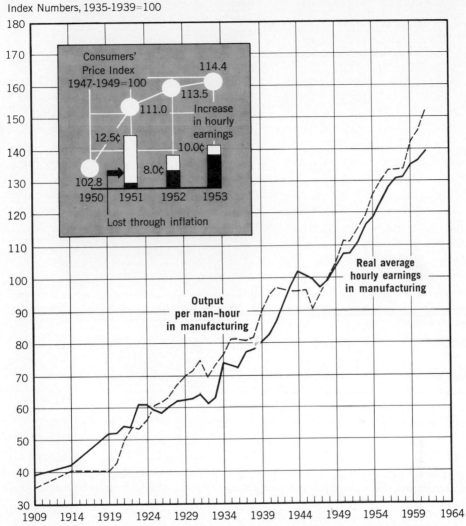

Index Numbers, 1935-1939=100

Consumers'
Price Index
1947-1949=100

114.4

113.5

111.0

Increase
in hourly
earnings

12.5¢

10.0¢

8.0¢

102.8

1950   1951   1952   1953

Lost through inflation

Real average
hourly earnings
in manufacturing

Output
per man-hour
in manufacturing

With permission from National Industrial Conference Board; Joint Economic Committee, *Productivity, Prices, and Incomes,* 1957, pp. 61 and 151; *President's Economic Report,* 1963, p. 209; John W. Kendrick, *Productivity Trends in the United States,* National Bureau of Economic Research (Princeton: Princeton University Press, 1961).

Productivity and Pay: Output per man-hour has accelerated somewhat since the turn of the century, and real hourly earnings have gone up nearly as fast. Spurts and lags suggest that wages rise faster than output only in times of booming prosperity.

erately. Such figures do not reflect, of course, the great burden imposed on the unemployed, who had no earnings at all. The sharp inflation that occurred between 1945 and 1948 was accompanied by a 25 per cent increase in money wages, but real wages held nearly constant as the cost of living rose even more.

Table 23-1

Real Average Weekly Earnings of Production Workers in Manufacturing (1926 = 100)

Year	Index of average weekly earnings of production workers in manufacturing	Consumer price index	Index of real average weekly earnings of production workers in manufacturing
1919	89.6	97.9	91.5
1920	106.7	113.4	94.1
1921	90.0	101.0	89.1
1922	87.3	94.7	92.2
1923	96.6	96.4	100.2
1924	97.1	96.7	100.4
1925	98.9	99.2	99.7
1926	100.0	100.0	100.0
1927	100.4	98.1	102.3
1928	101.3	97.0	104.4
1929	101.5	96.9	104.7
1930	94.3	94.4	99.9
1931	84.7	86.0	98.5
1932	69.2	77.2	89.6
1933	67.9	73.1	92.9
1934	74.6	75.7	98.5
1935	81.7	77.6	105.3
1936	88.4	78.4	112.8
1937	97.6	81.2	120.2
1938	90.5	79.7	113.6
1939	96.8	78.6	123.2
1940	102.2	79.2	129.0
1941	120.0	83.2	144.2
1942	148.7	92.2	161.3
1943	175.0	97.8	178.9
1944	186.9	99.4	188.0
1945	180.0	101.7	177.0
1946	177.8	110.3	161.2
1947	202.7	126.3	160.5
1948	219.6	136.0	161.5
1949	222.8	134.7	165.4
1950	240.7	136.0	177.0
1951	262.5	146.8	178.8
1952	275.7	150.1	183.7
1953	290.8	151.3	192.2
1954	291.5	151.9	191.9
1955	310.4	151.5	204.9
1956	324.5	153.7	211.1
1957	334.2	159.0	210.2
1958	338.7	163.4	207.3
1959	358.1	164.8	217.3
1960	364.0	167.3	217.6
1961	374.6	169.0	221.7

SOURCES: *Historical Statistics of the United States, Colonial Times to 1957*, and *Statistical Abstract of the United States, 1962.*

Table 23-2

Average Weekly Earnings, Wage Earners, Salaried, and Trade and Telephone
Employees, for Selected Years, 1929–1952 (in dollars and cents)

Year	Wage earners [a]	Salaried [b]	Trade and telephone [c]
1929	27.14	34.78	28.41
1933	18.59	29.42	21.78
1937	25.25	32.57	24.90
1939	25.44	33.04	25.30
1944	45.27	43.63	33.16
1946	45.83	49.14	39.59
1949	56.75	57.57	49.10
1952	69.24	66.63	56.86

SOURCE: Reprinted from "The Comparative Economic Position of Manual and White-Collar Employees," by Robert K. Burns, in *Journal of Business*, XXVII, No. 4 (October 1954), 260, by permission of The University of Chicago Press. Copyright 1954 by The University of Chicago.

[a] Occupations or industrial groups included are mining, building construction, wage earners in manufacturing, local railways and bus lines, electric light and power, wage earners on steam railroads, hotels, laundries, cleaning and dyeing plants.

[b] Occupations or services included are salaried employees in manufacturing, clerical employees in steam railroads, insurance, security dealers and exchanges, state and local government (nonschool), teachers, federal government.

[c] Included are wholesale trade, retail trade, telephone.

A well-known study enables us to compare changes in money earnings for major classes of workers.[4] Before 1929 salaried workers were much better paid than wage earners, but a second great white-collar group, employees in retail and wholesale trade and in the telephone industry, had earnings only slightly higher (see Table 23-2) than those of wage earners. The depression of the 1930s hit wage earners hardest, their earnings dropping by 30 per cent. Trade and telephone workers suffered a drop of about 25 per cent, and the earnings of salaried workers dropped by 15 per cent. At the trough of the depression earnings of salaried employees were 60 per cent greater than those of wage earners, and earnings of the trade and telephone group were 17 per cent greater. But with recovery the advantage of salaried employees began to disappear, and by 1939 the relationships of 1929 were approximately restored. By 1943 wartime demand for production workers had brought wage earners' weekly income ahead of the income of salaried workers. Postwar increases for salaried employees put them ahead again in 1946, but the boom years of 1947 and 1948 brought the manual-earnings figure nearly to equality. The high level of industrial production in 1951 and

[4] The following passage draws heavily upon Robert K. Burns, "The Comparative Economic Position of Manual and White-Collar Employees," *Journal of Business*, XXVII, 4 (October 1954), 257–67.

1952 once again put the wage earners ahead. Meantime, though money earnings of the trade and telephone group had advanced at a higher rate since 1943 than those of the other two groups, the average of manual workers exceeded that of the trade workers by 20 per cent. More recent evidence suggests no substantial change in these relationships.

Thus since the depths of the depression, wage earners overcame the income superiority of salaried people that existed before 1929. Many influences have favored the manual worker. The expansion of public educational facilities at all levels has made training for white-collar pursuits available to an ever larger proportion of the labor force, and the increase in competition for white-collar jobs has of course kept salaries down. The increasing entry of women into the labor force has further swelled the ranks of clerical and sales personnel, particularly at lower-paid levels. Immigration restrictions since the early 1920s and a desire on the part of parents to shift their children out of blue-collar occupations has doubtless reduced the supply of manual workers. Finally, we have here as convincing a piece of evidence as can be found that unions can raise earnings in those occupations where they are strong.

In two respects the white-collar employee continues to hold an advantage over manual workers. His earnings are more stable because his workweek, unlike the wage earner's, does not fluctuate with his firm's production schedule. Moreover, the incidence of unemployment is not nearly so great in the salaried as in the wage occupations. Manual workers, despite remarkable improvement in earnings, remain peculiarly vulnerable to economic fluctuations.

SOCIAL SECURITY

In Chapter 16 we took as one of the measures of labor's progress before World War I the enactment by the various states of laws regulating child labor and women's work. In recent decades such legislation has lost much of its protective significance, as compulsory education laws have kept children in school longer and federal legislation has regulated employment of firms engaged in interstate commerce. Since 1936 federal law has set minimum ages for children working on public contracts and, by the Fair Labor Standards Act of 1938, has prohibited the shipment in interstate commerce or to foreign countries of goods produced by companies employing "oppressive child labor." Oppressive child labor has in general meant employment of minors under sixteen years of age, except in hazardous occupations, where eighteen is the lower limit.

A brief summary of state enactments serves to remind us of the great variety of provisions that results when the states have supervisory authority. By 1930 all but four states regulated the hours of children in manufacturing, and about two-thirds of the states had laws covering children in other occupations. By 1960 twenty-three states had established sixteen years as the basic minimum age for employment during school hours, but twenty-seven states still set a minimum age of fourteen or fifteen for work during school hours. The laws of the several states also vary widely in regulating or prohibiting night work, hazardous work, and excessive hours of work in addition to school.

Laws regulating women's work have been directed toward protecting the health of present or prospective mothers rather than toward abolishing women's work. They were at first intended to reduce the number of hours in the working day. By 1920, some states had passed statutes requiring a weekly day of rest, prohibiting or reducing night work, and limiting homework. By 1940, forty-three states and the District of Columbia had made some attempt to limit daily or weekly hours for women, and the number of protecting states remained unchanged a decade later. The laws vary so in their provisions that they defy classification. Half the states and the District of Columbia have set a maximum of eight hours a day and/or forty-eight hours a week in one or more industries. Most of the industrial states of the East have provided the forty-eight-hour standard, but in seven states and Puerto Rico there is no limit on the workweek and in a dozen more a fifty-four- to sixty-hour week is possible. Especially in the Southeast have excessive hours and onerous working conditions remained a problem in service and other establishments clearly in intrastate trade.

Before 1932 some of these simple regulatory laws plus the workmen's compensation acts marked the only tangible social gains of labor. Against loss of income from any cause other than industrial accident, workers had no protection except the buffer of their savings, organized charity, and payments from the relief agencies of states and their subdivisions. The burden of relief during the Great Depression soon overwhelmed charitable organizations and local governmental units, with the result that the federal government, largely through the PWA and the WPA, had to take over the job. This experience with federal relief convinced a majority of Americans, on both economic and ethical grounds, of the necessity of a permanent plan for coping with severe losses in income.

A few leaders in government, business, and the universities had long argued that a comprehensive program of social security was requisite to the adequate functioning of a modern industrial economy. Yet as late as 1930 there was little public sentiment for social-security legislation. Americans believed that the individual ought to be self-reliant and objected to compulsory action by the government. In agriculture, where the need for social insurance was not so pronounced, there was understandable opposition to additional taxes for such insurance. The astonishing fact is that organized labor itself did not support social insurance (except workmen's compensation) before 1930; as late as 1931 a national AFL convention refused to endorse unemployment-insurance legislation. A not inconsequential opposition came also from private insurance companies, which sought to prevent, or at least modify, government insurance of social risks.

Four years of economic disaster removed all serious obstacles to major legislation. Whatever the philosophical objection to a social-security program may have been, certain hard facts of life were undeniable. Nearly four out of five income-receivers were dependent upon paid employment for their livelihood. There were many hazards to the continuity of income, some of which seemed to be increasing in severity as the economy became more specialized. Income interruptions included being laid off, getting sick, being injured on the job, getting too old to meet the demands of modern industrial life, and, of course, death. Finally, the *incidence* of income interruptions, although uncertain and uneven, fell most heavily upon low-income people who were least able to prepare for them.

The Social Security Act of 1935, as since amended, has met social risks through application of the *insurance* principle and the *assistance* principle. Under social insurance programs the individual acquires a *right* to income because he has paid premiums or premiums have been paid on his behalf by an employer. The Social Security Act of 1935 provided for a federal old-age and survivors insurance program and for a federal-state system of unemployment insurance. It further provided for *assistance* to the needy aged, needy and dependent children, and the needy blind, and recent amendments have added other groups. Assistance programs involve grants-in-aid to the states, the federal government meeting half the administrative costs and somewhat more than half of the assistance payments. Federal assistance programs still involve relief; although the programs are on a more just basis of payment than in former days, under them the individual must demonstrate need and he is always a supplicant rather than an applicant.

Social insurance has emancipated millions of workers from the fear of one day being "on the county." The only strictly federal part of the system is the old-age and survivors program. Under it, until 1950, the worker contributed 1 per cent of his first $3,600 of wages and his employer paid an equal amount. In 1950 the rate was raised to 1½ per cent, and in 1954 the first $4,200 of income was made taxable. Subsequent legislation raised the contributions of both employer and employee to 3⅝ per cent upon the first $4,800 of income, the tax on both employer and employee to rise to 4⅝ per cent by 1968. Nine types of benefits are paid, the most important ones going to retired covered workers at age sixty-five, to widows and widowers of covered workers, and to the wives and children of deceased workers. By 1950 the top primary benefit of $85 had become hopelessly inadequate because of rising living costs; subsequent increases have raised maximum benefits for single persons retiring in the future to $127; since the wife of a retired beneficiary is eligible to receive half his old-age benefit if she is sixty-five or older, a married couple over sixty-five years of age can have a maximum retirement income of $190.50. More gratifying to supporters of strong social insurance programs have been recent increases in coverage. By 1950, 35,000,000 persons, or about 60 per cent of the work force, were covered by old-age and survivors insurance. Amendments of 1950 brought another 10,000,000 workers under the program, including previously excluded

Future job openings will increasingly demand highly trained specialists and those with administrative and professional skills, thus penalizing still further youths like those shown above, who have dropped out of school before completing their education.

regular agricultural and household employees and most of the urban self-employed, and in 1954, a second 10,000,000 were added. More than 90 per cent of the labor force were covered in 1964.

Less extensive in its aims, but a powerful short-run help to unlucky households, has been the program of unemployment insurance. Largely to circumvent legal difficulties, unemployment insurance is provided through state systems. The Social Security Act of 1935 secured state action by levying a 3 per cent tax on the first $3,000 of wages paid by employers in all but a few business occupations. If, however, an employer paid contributions to an approved state unemployment insurance system, he could "offset" the payments to the state system against all but 10 per cent of his federal tax. If a state did not establish a system, employers would have to pay the 3 per cent tax and workers would still have no benefits. All states quickly passed laws that, despite diverse methods of calculating benefits and formulas for taxing employers, achieve reasonably uniform results. All tax receipts must be turned over to the federal treasury for credit to the unemployment insurance trust fund, and payments are made through public employment offices of the individual states. Benefits under the program are scarcely large enough to encourage idleness among most workers, average weekly benefits in 1962 amounting to $34.02 and average benefit periods to 14.1 weeks.

Our discussion of social insurance actually began in Chapter 16, where we considered the earliest workmen's compensation acts. After the Supreme Court upheld three different types of act in 1917, state after state passed either compulsory or elective workmen's compensation laws.[5] During the last thirty years most laws have been expanded to include occupational diseases as well as injuries "arising out of and in the course of employment," and all states have provided death benefits.[6] Under these laws a covered employer is required to obtain insurance with a private company or a state fund, or furnish proof of ability to provide self-insurance. Although private insurance has probably been more expensive than insurance with state funds, private insurance companies have continued to receive more premiums and disburse more benefits than state funds and self-insurance together.

Thus the only major income hazard not increasingly covered by social insurance is that of nonoccupational sickness and nonoccupational accident. Largely because of the opposition of the medical profession, which has insisted that such insurance is a step toward "socialized medicine," proposals for national health insurance plans have had hard sledding. But one day a satisfactory solution to this problem will be found.

The benefits of social insurance have extended beyond the prevention of individual privation and suffering. The worker has benefited, as he was intended to, but so have others. Private insurance companies, which once objected to old-age and survivors insurance, have found that social insurance encourages the purchase of private insurance by providing a start toward an adequate program. Unemployment insurance benefits have doubtless mitigated the effects of falling incomes at the onset of recent slumps, for cash payments have automatically bolstered consumer spending power. And though they are not an automatic countercyclical device, payments to retired people and widows with young children have been a stabilizing force in the economy, for they have kept personal incomes from dropping when age and death regularly take their toll.

THE THREAT OF UNEMPLOYMENT

Our favorable conclusions regarding improvement in the economic position of labor since 1920 must not lead us into thinking that the problem of security has been solved. Excessive unemployment, actual or threatened, has been a source of grave concern in about half of the peacetime years since 1920. Rising real wages are only of academic interest to those who can find no wages to earn, and unemployment insurance benefits do not sustain a household over a long period of joblessness.

---

[5] In 1948 Mississippi completed the list of states. In twenty-six states, employers may reject the act, but if they do they cannot plead the old common-law defenses in the event that an employee is injured.

[6] In 1960, twenty-nine states, the District of Columbia, Puerto Rico, and the Federal acts covered all occupational diseases. Only Mississippi and Wyoming have no provision for occupational diseases, the remaining nineteen covering only listed diseases.

A person is said to be involuntarily unemployed when he is willing and able to work and cannot find a job for which he is trained. Some kinds of involuntary unemployment, often referred to as *frictional* unemployment, are unavoidable in a free economy. People constantly change jobs, and firms go out of business or move their plants and warehouses. Some businesses have seasonal ups and downs in employment. Technological unemployment occurs as innovations throw people out of work, and older people so separated from their jobs may never make another permanent connection. And there are always marginal workers, who because of approaching old age or mental or physical disabilities, find themselves continually moving into and out of the work force. Frictional unemployment cannot be lightly dismissed but it does not reflect a malfunctioning of the economy. Serious unemployment is the mass unemployment that results from sudden, drastic declines in economic activity.

The 1920s were fairly free of cyclical unemployment after the depression years of 1921 and 1922, when unemployment may have amounted to 11 and 7 per cent, respectively, of the labor force. But the 1930s were dismal years of joblessness. No two estimates of the extent of unemployment agree. The Bureau of Labor Statistics data, accepted as conservative, show one-fourth of the civilian work force of approximately 48,000,000 without jobs at the trough of the Great Depression. For ten straight years, 1931–40, more than one-tenth of the civilian labor force was unemployed, and for most of these years the ratio was one-sixth or more. Such figures do not, of course, take into account the severe amount of underemployment that persisted because of short workweeks and work-sharing plans, nor do they reflect the great numbers of people who worked far below their appropriate levels of ability and training. (See Table 23-3.)

Unemployment of such magnitude left the administration of Franklin D. Roosevelt no choice but to devise a massive program of relief. No other kind of activity so clearly typified the New Deal, and the remedies prescribed were the object of conservative scorn. Hastily devised and poorly administered as some of them were, they marked a change from the grudging RFC loans and the "trickle-down" theories of the Hoover administration and were approved by the great majority of the electorate.

The Federal Emergency Relief Administration (FERA) was established in May 1933 to make grants to state and local agencies for direct relief and work projects on public property. A few months later the Civil Works Administration (CWA) was created under the FERA to undertake the first large-scale work program. CWA workers repaired streets, painted buildings, and improved parks under the supervision of public officials. The first "permanent" plan of relief was provided by the National Industrial Recovery Act, which created the Public Works Administration (PWA). Administered by Harold L. Ickes, Secretary of the Interior, the PWA granted funds and made loans to states and municipalities for the construction of such public works as highways, post offices, and school buildings. Work done under

Table 23-3

Estimated Unemployment, 1929–1943

Year	Average annual number unemployed in thousands	Percentage of civilian labor force
1929	1,550	3.2
1930	4,340	8.7
1931	8,020	15.9
1932	12,060	23.6
1933	12,830	24.9
1934	11,340	21.7
1935	10,610	20.1
1936	9,030	16.9
1937	7,700	14.3
1938	10,390	19.0
1939	9,480	17.2
1940	8,120	14.6
1941	5,560	9.9
1942	2,660	4.7
1943	1,070	1.9

SOURCE: Bureau of Labor Statistics.

PWA programs was performed by private contractors, who were not required to hire laborers from the ranks of the unemployed. It was felt that even though the program might not help unemployment directly, large expenditures (amounting to more than $3,000,000,000) would stimulate the economy and at least indirectly provide employment.

The national work-relief program came to full flower in 1935 with the establishment of the Works Progress Administration under Harry Hopkins. The object of the WPA was to provide work directly to the unemployed. In an effort to avoid a "dole," WPA created projects that used the services of painters, authors, sculptors, and musicians, as well as manual workers. More than half of total WPA expenditures were on public works. Because it operated under its own administrative staff rather than through private contractors, the WPA was accused of competing with private industry, and its projects were derisively described as boondoggles. Nonetheless, WPA provided an enormous amount of relief in a way that allowed people to maintain their self-respect.[7] Not until 1942 was it possible to liquidate the agency.

---

[7] At the peak of its activity in 1938 the WPA employed about 3,300,000 workers on its projects. Employment on undertakings supervised by PWA, the Civilian Conservation Corps, and the National Youth Administration brought the total of government "relief" jobs to well over 4,000,000 in 1938.

The rate of unemployment, a growing domestic concern, has risen to successively higher plateaus since the Korean War. As here (Muskegon, Michigan, in 1961), those unemployed most frequently are the semiskilled, the older workers, and the very young who have not yet succeeded in getting a job.

The problem of unemployment vanished during World War II, and, to the relief of national administrations, did not reappear for several years after the war. But as the recession of 1949 deepened, unemployment passed the 4,000,000 mark, dropped seasonally, and got uncomfortably close to 5,000,000—7.5 per cent of the labor force—in February 1950. A fall in unemployment before the outbreak of the Korean conflict was encouraging, coming as it did without the stimulus of a rearmament program. But a rather serious decline in industrial production beginning in July 1953 again brought increasing joblessness, and by March 1954 unemployment exceeded 3,750,000, nearly 6 per cent of the civilian labor force. From the middle 1950s on the concern of economic policy-makers was the stickiness of the unemployment rate during economic expansions (see chart, p. 618). In the boom of 1955, nineteen months after the trough of the 1953–54 recession, unemployment was 3.4 per cent of civilian work force. In 1959, fourteen months after the trough of the 1957–58 recession the rate of unemployment was still 5.6 per cent, and in early 1964, thirty-six months out of the trough of the 1960–61 recession, the figure was a frustrating 5.5 per cent.

Economists, employers, union leaders, and government officials disagree as to what constitutes a tolerable amount of unemployment. There has long been a substantial opinion that regards unemployment up to 3 or 4 per cent of the labor force as unavoidable during peacetime. This amount of unemployment from "accepted and normal" causes is no less hard on the

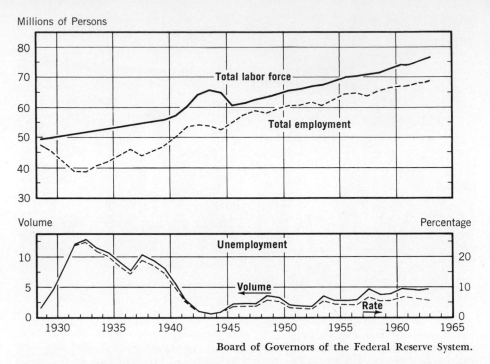

Millions of Persons

Board of Governors of the Federal Reserve System.

Workers and Nonworkers: While the total labor force has risen with population growth, the unemployed have increased in number in the postwar period, and particularly in the 1950s.

workers involved than cyclical unemployment, but it is possible to mitigate its short-run impact through social insurance. But when unemployment reaches or passes the 5 per cent mark, chronic joblessness appears in the durable goods industries, and political pressures for remedies build up in urban areas. A figure much in excess of 5 per cent of the civilian labor force leads to a clamor for "permanent" solutions to a problem that just won't go away.

The Labor Movement and Government Intervention

THE GROWTH OF AMERICAN UNIONS

Membership in American unions, which in 1920 exceeded 5,000,000, dropped precipitously to 3,500,000 in 1923 and remained nearly constant until 1929. Even the depression brought no further great losses, total membership amounting to just under 3,000,000 in 1933. The American Federation of Labor membership meantime fell from about 4,000,000 to 2,200,000.[8]

The depression of 1920–21, unsuccessful postwar strikes, and a renewed

---

[8] Irving Bernstein, "The Growth of American Unions," *American Economic Review*, XLIV, 3 (June 1954), 301–18.

wave of employer antagonism contributed to the first sharp drop. Equally devastating to union progress and union morale was the capitulation of labor to company welfare programs designed to entice workers away from their own organizations into company unions. But the inertia of the 1924–29 period must be primarily attributed to two other causes. The price level remained almost constant as money wages rose moderately, with the consequence that the greater part of labor felt warmly comfortable in the general atmosphere of gratitude toward business big and little. More important, the powerful AFL unions, their members especially well off during the building boom, took no interest in organizing the growing mass-production industries.

A sign of the low level to which union energies had fallen under a feeble and unimaginative leadership was the apparent resignation of workers at the onset of the depression to the national disgrace of depression unemployment. But before the new administration had been in power a year, the more vigorous union leaders sensed that the government would encourage organization and that the attitude of the country toward unions had changed as people became disillusioned with business. Especially successful in their organizational efforts were the powerful and able leaders of the industrial unions that had evolved within the AFL: John L. Lewis of the United Mine Workers, Sidney Hillman of the Amalgamated Clothing Workers, and David Dubinsky of the International Ladies Garment Workers.

By the mid-thirties a conflict within labor over the question of proper union structure had grown to major proportions. The move to organize the new mass-production industries—steel, automobiles, rubber, and electrical equipment—was inevitable; but the older unions hampered such organization by insisting that their craft jurisdictions remain inviolate and by raiding the membership of the new industrial unions. In 1935 eight industrial unions formed the Committee for Industrial Organization within the AFL, and in 1936 they were suspended from the federation. Three years later the CIO became a separate entity, the Congress of Industrial Organization.

Conflict continued between the two great federations, but the competition seemed only to spur the growth of membership. There was defection, to be sure. After interminable controversy over policy, John L. Lewis resigned from the presidency of the CIO, and in 1942 withdrew the United Mine Workers. Unsuccessful in getting other unions to coalesce about him, Lewis rejoined the AFL in 1946 only to disaffiliate the next year. Meanwhile, CIO leaders made no secret of their contempt for AFL's lack of militancy and failure to participate aggressively in political activity, and AFL leaders looked with concern on CIO's violent break with conservative unionism. But complacency and inertia no longer beset the labor movement. In 1955 the AFL and CIO, prodded into unity by a hostile public opinion and punitive labor legislation, merged to form the AFL-CIO.

Estimates of union membership since 1920 are shown in Table 23-4. The periods of the New Deal and World War II brought rapid growth, and

Table 23-4

Union Membership, 1920–1960
(in millions)

Year	Number	Year	Number
1920	5,048		
1921	4,781	1941	10,201
1922	4,027	1942	10,380
1923	3,622	1943	13,213
1924	3,536	1944	14,146
1925	3,519	1945	14,322
1926	3,502	1946	14,395
1927	3,546	1947	14,787
1928	3,480	1948	14,300
1929	3,461	1949	14,300
1930	3,401	1950	14,300
1931	3,310	1951	15,900
1932	3,050	1952	15,900
1933	2,689	1953	16,948
1934	3,088	1954	17,022
1935	3,584	1955	16,802
1936	3,989	1956	17,490
1937	7,001	1957	17,300
1938	8,034	1958	17,029
1939	8,763	1959	17,100
1940	8,717	1960	17,049

SOURCE: U.S. Bureau of Labor Statistics and estimates of author.

membership continued to increase steadily in the early 1950s. A membership in 1953 of nearly 17,000,000 or 28 per cent of the civilian labor force was by itself an impressive statistic.[9] It seemed more so upon the reflection that 75 per cent or more of the employees in manufacturing, mining, construction, and transportation and public utilities were working under collective-bargaining agreements. Yet as it turned out 1953 membership was close to the peak of 1956, and in the early sixties there was little reason to be sanguine about a near-term upward movement from labor's "organizational plateau."

There were many reasons why phenomenal growth should have occurred between 1933 and 1953.[10] An addition of 15,000,000 people to the civilian labor force meant a rising "organizable potential." Joining a union became socially acceptable in many geographical areas where formerly it had not

[9] Roughly 50 per cent of the total membership was in AFL affiliates, 30 per cent in CIO unions, and the remainder in unaffiliated unions.
[10] Bernstein, pp. 313–15.

been. Increasing homogeneity of the labor force made the job of union organizers easier, for differences of language, religion, and educational background did not sharply separate American workers as they once did. But the fact remained that the pro-labor attitude of government in the thirties broke down the barriers to organization in the new mass-production industries and hastened the growth of trade unionism.

Since the early 1950s there has been a reversal of these favorable trends. As observed in Chapter 21, the past decade or so has seen a shift from blue-collar to white-collar employment that has meant a constant or slightly falling organizable potential. Forces that once made for homogeneity of the work force have been working recently to move many of labor's partisans into the upper middle class, which, with some obvious exceptions, is not sympathetic to labor's cause. Public misapprehension of the complex relationships between prices and wages, together with press and legislative exaggeration of union corruption, have created suspicion and resulted in declining support at the polls. But it was the change in national labor policy beginning in 1947 that really did the damage by making it difficult to organize in smaller firms, in the retail and service trades, and in the South. To the subject of post-1930 labor policy we must now turn.

Throughout the 1920s employers continued to use effectively the anti-labor instruments developed before World War I. They discriminated, in hiring and firing, against employees who joined or organized unions. The hated yellow-dog contract, adjudged constitutional by the Supreme Court, was commonly employed to prevent union membership and to serve as a basis of civil suits against unions that persuaded employees to violate the contract. Most useful of all weapons was the injunction, by which a court could forbid, at least temporarily, such practices as picketing, secondary boycotts, and the feeding of strikers by the union.

Except for legislation that applied only to the railroad industry, Congress refused to interfere by statute with labor relations until 1932. The Norris–La Guardia Act of 1932 was a first great step toward removing the barriers to free organization. Largely procedural in character, the act had the effect of modifying or eliminating the worst abuses of the labor injunction. The yellow-dog contract was eliminated by making it nonenforceable in the federal courts, and issuance of injunctions was greatly restricted. Moreover, as a result of a liberal definition of the term *labor dispute,* unions were freed to engage in organizational activity. Specifically, the term was defined in such a way as to permit *secondary* activity in the form of boycotting and picketing by other than employees as distinguished from the narrower concept of *primary* activity only. By the act the government granted to workers the *opportunity* to organize but did not positively intercede to assure that they could secure the benefits of collective bargaining.

The first positive assertion of the right of labor to bargain collectively was contained in Section 7a of the National Industrial Recovery Act, but no means of enforcing the statement of principle were provided. Two years later the NIRA was declared unconstitutional, on grounds that had nothing to do with the labor section, and Congress replaced Section 7a with a much more elaborate law of labor relations. This was the National Labor Relations Act, usually referred to as the Wagner Act after its sponsor, Senator Robert F. Wagner of New York.

The Wagner Act proceeded from the explicit premises that inequality of bargaining power between individual employees and large business units depresses "the purchasing power of wage earners in industry" and prevents ". . . stabilization of competitive wage rates and working conditions," and that denial of the right to self-organization creates industrial strife. The act established the principle of collective bargaining as the cornerstone of industrial relations in the United States and laid upon management the obligation to recognize and deal with a *bona fide* labor organization in good faith. Furthermore, it guaranteed workers the right to form and join a labor organization, to engage in collective bargaining, to select representatives of their own choosing, and to engage in concerted activity. Negatively, the Wagner Act outlawed a list of "unfair" managerial practices that had had the effect of denying worker rights. Henceforth, employers could *not:*

1. interfere with, restrain, or coerce employees in the exercise of their rights of self-organization and collective bargaining,
2. dominate or interfere with the formation or administration of any labor organization or contribute financial or other support to it,
3. encourage or discourage union membership by discrimination in regard to hiring or tenure of employment or condition of work, except such discrimination as might be involved in a closed-shop agreement with a *bona fide* union enjoying majority status,
4. discharge or otherwise discriminate against an employee for filing charges or testifying under the act, or
5. refuse to bargain collectively.

The Wagner Act was no mere statement of principles. It established a National Labor Relations Board (NLRB) of three members that had genuine powers of enforcement. Upon complaint of unions and after hearings, the Board could issue cease-and-desist orders to employers adjudged guilty of unfair labor practices. If employers did not comply with orders, the NLRB could turn to a United States Circuit Court of Appeals for enforcement. The Board further had power, on its own initiative or at the request of a union, to supervise a free, secret election among a company's employees to determine which union, if any, should represent the workers.

Labor hailed the Wagner Act as its Magna Charta. When the Supreme Court declared the law constitutional in 1937, there were no remaining barriers to the rapid organization of labor. But before the question of constitutionality was settled, many employers openly violated the act with consequent increasing turbulence in labor relations. Animosity between the suspended CIO unions and the AFL grew, leading to jurisdictional conflicts that the NLRB spent much time settling. As industrial strife seemed to be increasing rather than decreasing, there were public demands for amendments to the act, and employers complained bitterly of the one-sidedness of the law.

The Wagner Act was never intended to be a comprehensive code of labor relations. It did not even define "collective bargaining," nor did it cover the problems of jurisdictional disputes, "national emergency" disputes, and secondary boycotts. Had World War II not intervened, basic amendments to the act would doubtless have come before they did. The war placed the national problem of labor relations nearly in abeyance. Through the National War Labor Board, established in 1942, wage rates were stabilized; wages rose during the war by about 13 per cent, or a little less than other controlled prices. With financial pressures removed, labor and management were persuaded to give up strikes and lockouts in exchange for representation on the War Labor Board. Work stoppages occurred, particularly in 1944; but man-days lost were only a small percentage of total working time, and Presidential seizures of struck industries, although well publicized, were few. Normal two-party collective bargaining procedures were often circumvented by reliance upon co-operative decisions of regional offices of the Board.

With the end of the war much overtime disappeared, and earnings fell as prices held firm or edged up. The heat was on labor leaders to secure wage increases, which were not forthcoming without a struggle. The widespread work stoppages of 1945–46 alienated large segments of the electorate. Employers complained loudly that they were being caught in the jurisdictional disputes of rival unions and that labor itself was guilty of unfair practices. There was a growing belief that the power of unions was being used to infringe the rights of individual workers. After the Republicans won control of Congress in 1946, no time was lost in drawing up a long, technical bill that significantly amended the Wagner Act. The new law, passed in 1947 over President Truman's veto, was called the Labor-Management Relations Act and became familiarly known as the Taft-Hartley Act.

The Taft-Hartley Act reflected a belief that the individual worker should be protected by public policy not only in his right to join a labor organization but also in his right to refrain from joining. The closed-shop agreement, under which the employer hires only union members, was outlawed. Union-shop agreements, which permit nonunion members to enter employment but require them to join the union within a certain time after starting on the job, were permitted. However, enforcement of union-security provisions was limited to cases of nonpayment of dues, and, more important, the law permitted the states to outlaw *all* forms of union security, including the union shop.

Mass labor meetings like this one at the Chrysler Corporation in 1950 (members are listening to United Auto Workers' president Walter Reuther) are becoming less typical of American labor strategy.

The Taft-Hartley Act, unlike the Wagner Act, further assumed that the interests of the union and the individual in the union are not identical. It took the view that many union members are "captives" of the "labor bosses," a position especially offensive to a great part of organized labor. For example, the act provided that a union could not negotiate a union-shop provision in collective-bargaining agreements unless a majority of workers in the unit voted for it. In 1951, after 46,000 separate polls in which security provisions won 97 per cent of the time, the requirement of NLRB-conducted union-security elections was dropped, and a large number of doubters became convinced that union leaders commonly reflect the wishes of their memberships.

The most important features of the act were those purporting to regulate unions in the "public" interest. A union seeking certification or requesting an investigation of unfair labor practices had to submit to scrutiny of its internal affairs by filing financial statements, and its officers were required to sign non-Communist affidavits. The right to strike was modified by providing a "cooling-off period" after notice of termination of contract, and the President was given authority to postpone strikes for eighty days by injunction. More significant in "evening up" the one-sidedness of the Wagner Act was the outlawing of certain union unfair practices. Since 1947 it has been unfair for a union:

1. to restrain or coerce *employees* in their right to join or refrain from joining a labor organization, or to restrain or coerce *employers* in the selection of employer representatives for purposes of collective bargaining or adjustment of grievances,
2. to cause or attempt to cause an *employer* to discriminate against an employee,
3. to charge, under a valid union-shop agreement, an "excessive" initiation fee,
4. to refuse to bargain collectively with an employer where the union involved is the certified bargaining agent,
5. to "featherbed" the job—i.e., to cause an employer to pay for services not performed, or
6. to engage in, or encourage employees to engage in, a strike where the object is to force one employer to cease doing business with any other employer. This provision banned the secondary boycott.

After twelve years of almost complete freedom, labor found the Taft-Hartley Act harshly restrictive. Dire warnings were heard of the coming decline of trade unionism in America. Labor's leadership was incensed at the offensive language and punitive spirit of the act. But many of the provisions looked worse in print than they proved in practice. The injunction clause, for example, stirred memories of the days when the courts granted injunctions at the request of private parties; in the hands of a President of the United States, acting in an emergency, the injunction was no longer a destructive weapon. Regulation of internal union affairs was only a nuisance and an interference with private business.

However, some of the new requirements for rigorously admissible evidence of unfair employer practices doubtless retarded organization, especially in the South. By 1963, nineteen states had passed antilabor legislation in the form of "right-to-work" laws. "Right-to-work" legislation, by making it illegal to enforce the union-shop provisions of an agreement within the state concerned, kept unions in continuous organizing efforts and were a source of friction among union and nonunion workers.[11] American labor would continue to fight for revision of the Taft-Hartley Act.

As the decade of the 1950s closed, labor's public relations showed no signs of improvement. Indeed, the Labor-Management Reporting and Disclosure Act of 1959 (the Landrum-Griffin Act) suggested that Congress would

---

[11] The only "right-to-work" state with serious pretensions to consideration as an industrial state was Indiana. In general, managerial fear of union-security provisions is a pretty good indication of an inept and insecure managerial corps.

discipline the whole of labor in order to protect against the machinations of a few corrupt leaders. In any case, the law tightened restrictions on secondary boycotting and organized picketing, required detailed reporting of all financial transactions of unions with their officers and members, and required secret-ballot elections of officers, whose terms of office were carefully restricted. No one could object to the provision preventing felons and Communist-party members from being union officers for five years after conviction, nor could there be serious reservations about the new rules restricting free-wheeling use of union funds. But in the so-called bill of rights for union members it was once again clear that Congress viewed the interests of union leaders and the rank-and-file as irreconcilable—a view scarcely supported by overwhelming evidence of worker loyalty to their leadership.

If unions had lost political potency in recent national elections, it was not for lack of political activity. AFL-CIO, with its political-action arm, was vigorously trying to reward labor's friends and defeat its enemies. The federation had a large staff of trained economists, busy testing labor's economic gains against changes in productivity and formulating clever arguments to substantiate new demands on managerial prerogatives. Lurking always was the fear of another serious depression, but there were reasons to think that no responsible political party would permit anything more than minor slumps in economic activity. What these reasons were we shall see in the final chapter.

Depression, Prosperity, and the Demand for Full Employment

For each historian brings to the rewriting of history the full range of the remembered experiences of his own days, that unique array that he alone possesses and is.

J. H. HEXTER

In the uncommonly pleasant summer of 1929 Americans were congratulating themselves that a way to unending prosperity had been found. The flow of goods and services had reached an all-time high, industrial production having risen 50 per cent in a decade. Most businessmen were satisfied with their profit positions, and workers were content with the moderate gains in wages and earnings that enabled them to enjoy the luxury of automobiles and household appliances. Farmers grumbled about price weakness in agricultural products; but it was traditional that they should, and anyone could see that mechanical inventions had made life on the farm easier than ever before. Besides, anyone really wanting to become rich had only to purchase the common stock of thriving enterprises and put his shares in safekeeping, secure in the knowledge that they would appreciate in value.

There was no reason to expect that prosperity and production would not go on increasing. The political climate was favorable to the business venturer, then high in public esteem as the provider of material well-being. Herbert Hoover, a successful businessman and distinguished public servant, had been elected to the Presidency, and although some people thought him a bit inclined to the liberal side, it was generally felt that he would be a temperate and judicious leader. Equally reassuring was the stability of the economies of western Europe. War damage had been repaired, the gold standard had been restored, and the problem of reparations seemed near solution. Hope was high for a return to the free international movement of goods and capital that had characterized the rapid economic growth of the two decades before World War I.

How quickly the dream of lasting prosperity was broken we all know. Even as the summer of 1929 passed, there were signs, for those who would read them, that all was not well. Toward fall a perceptive few did read them, with the consequence that a wave of selling engulfed the stock market late in October. The psychological impact of falling securities prices would not alone have set the economy in a precipitous downturn, but it loosed other forces that had been gathering. Recession, then depression, and finally almost complete breakdown of the economic system followed.

We have already had much to say about the Great Depression and the remedial legislation required to combat it. But we have not yet measured it, nor have we explicitly examined its causes.

The Great Depression and Its Cure

In the four years 1929–33 the American economy simply went to pot. The gross national product in current prices declined 46 per cent, from $104.4 billion to $56 billion; in constant prices the decline was 31 per cent. Industrial production fell by more than half; wholesale prices were off one-third and consumer prices one-fourth. But the most horrible statistics of all were those of employment and unemployment. Civilian employment dropped by almost 20 per cent and unemployment rose from one and a half million to at least thirteen million. Conservatively, one-quarter of the civilian work force was unemployed, but extensive part-time employment and underutilization of skills meant that the real unemployment rate must have been close to one-third. Fully half the nation's breadwinners were either out of work or seriously reduced in circumstances.

The profile of durable goods production since 1920 (see chart, p. 629) reveals more clearly than words the magnitude of the business drop of the early 1930s. From a peak of nearly 40 in 1929 (1957 = 100), the index of durable goods output fell to 9 in 1932. At the trough of the depression, in March 1933, the durable goods index stood at 8; output of durables had fallen 80 per cent. Nondurables dropped much less, from an index of something over 40 to about 28.

The intensity of the depression was distressing, but its seeming endlessness brought frustration and despair. Forty years had passed since the long

Ratio Scale 1957 = 100

Board of Governors of the Federal Reserve System.

American Industrial Production: Industrial production by the early 1950s had surpassed the titanic output levels reached during World War II, confounding those who thought postwar stagnation was inevitable.

depression of the 1890s. The depression of 1920–21 had been sharp and nasty, with a decline in durables output of 43 per cent. But it had behaved as a depression should; i.e., it had come and gone quickly, with complete recovery of manufacturing production in less than two years. In the Great Depression, on the other hand, manufacturing output did not reach the 1929 level until late 1936; it stayed somewhat above the 1929 level for nearly a year but dropped again and did not climb back to the pre-depression peak until late 1939. Durable goods production did not regain the 1929 peak until August 1940, more than eleven years after the beginning of the depression.

THE CAUSES OF DEPRESSION

For more than thirty years economists have been asked to explain the economic crisis that beset not only the United States but the rest of the world as well. A satisfactory explanation requires us to distinguish between the forces that brought a downturn in activity and those that turned a business recession into utter disaster.

Schumpeter found the seeds of downturn in industrial events of the first decade of the twentieth century that, because of World War I, could not have their full effects until the twenties.[1] Chief of these events was the development of mass production of durables. The purchasing power of American households had to increase at a high rate to keep up with increases in output. The relatively new institution of consumer credit doubtless enabled manufacturers to sell their automobiles, radios, and refrigerators in greater volume than would otherwise have been possible. It was necessary, though, that earnings keep up with the increasing output per man-hour of labor—i.e., with increasing productivity—and the evidence is that they did not. We cannot measure exactly the discrepancy between increases in productivity and increases in real earnings, but in view of the rapid mechanization of industry during the twenties it must have been substantial. Between 1923 and 1929, productivity in the new manufacturing industries may have risen three times as fast as real wages. In any case, it now seems apparent that by the end of the twenties domestic markets were incapable of absorbing the nearly full employment output of industry.

Hindsight enables us to detect two drags on the economy that prepared the way for a depression. Most important was the decline, from 1925 onward, in both residential and nonresidential construction. The boom in building activity that began in 1918 had doubtless helped the economy out of the slump of 1920–21; the downward phase of the same building cycle, coinciding as it did with other weaknesses, was a major depressing influence. What was a gentle slide in construction from 1925 to 1927 became a marked decline in 1928.

---

[1] J. A. Schumpeter, "The Decade of the Twenties," *American Economic Review* (May 1946), p. 4.

The second drag on the economy came from the agricultural sector. During the twenties the trend of world agricultural prices was downward. In the farm belts, where indebtedness incurred for the purchase of land remained high, there were in the late twenties widespread complaints among businessmen that sales to farmers were falling. In the great agricultural midlands few manifestations of boom psychology appeared after 1926.

A mild downturn in durables output in the spring of 1929 and a drop in nondurable production in the summer could well have been expected, but nothing catastrophic portended. The blow came with the break in the stock market during the last week in October. Normally, economists do not consider fluctuations in the stock market as a *cause* of business fluctuations, though many recognize an indirect effect of market swings on the attitudes of entrepreneurs and consumers. The 1929 break, however, must be viewed as an exception to the general rule because participation in the market was so widespread among business decision-makers. The New York *Times* index of twenty-five industrial stocks, which early in 1924 had stood at 110, climbed by January 1929 to 338 and by September to 452. It was almost impossible to buy a common stock that did not rise rapidly in value, and investors quickly accumulated paper fortunes that many of them converted into real fortunes. The optimism engendered by these gains permeated the business community and led to the conclusion that permanent prosperity had been achieved. When the break came, the shock to the economy was indescribable. Paper fortunes disappeared; and so did a great many real ones, as people who had taken great profits on some issues were required to put up more margin to save their other stockholdings. The terrible realization that a new era had not dawned, that the businessman was not infallible, brought on a pervasive pessimism that no amount of cheerful public statements could relieve. After falling to 275 within a week of the first drop, the market recovered only to slide another fifty points by mid-November. Whether the psychological trauma or the reduction in the supply of investment funds did the greater damage we do not know, but within a year of the crash industrial production was down more than 25 per cent.

The devastating impact of the stock-market crash came in the early stages of the depression. Public morale might have improved and the market might have regained some buoyancy had it not been for the structural weakness of the banking system. Three waves of bank failures, each timed to have a particularly unsettling effect, shook the economy. The first came at the end of 1930 and the beginning of 1931, just when there were faint signs of an upturn. The second came late in 1931, after the Federal Reserve System had raised the rediscount rate to stanch an outward gold flow. The third, and most disastrous, began in mid-1932 and continued to the point of paralysis and breakdown in the late winter of 1932–33. Each wave of failures resulted in the destruction of deposits in suspended banks and caused other banks to contract their loans as fast as they could. Equally important, the wholesale breaking of trusted banks drove home to the public

Wall Street—Black Friday, October 29, 1929: Investors milled around in confusion in the planked street (subway construction was going on) as the extent of the disaster inside the New York Stock Exchange (right) came clear. Ultimately, $50 billion in paper valuations disappeared.

as nothing else the terrible seriousness of the depression. In part, as we observed in Chapter 20, the bank failures can be laid to stupidity and gross neglect of duty on the part of the individual Federal Reserve banks. Another chunk of blame can be laid to the shocking ignorance of the Board late in 1931. A final difficulty lay in the faulty structure of the commercial banking system. Since early in the nineteenth century Americans had insisted upon small, weak banking units that were largely required to provide their own liquidity; as values fell, these banks simply lacked the staying power that a few giant chains, whose fortunes were not tied up with any one community, would have had.

Most economists would agree that the forces so far examined played a major role in inducing and deepening the depression of the 1930s. Other influences have been given varying weights. One view, perhaps not so common as it once was, is that the Federal Reserve System's easy-money episodes of 1924 and 1927 fed the flames of stock-market speculation and thus led to disaster. But it can as well be argued that the policy of restraint adopted in late summer of 1929, by driving up interest rates and causing banks to turn away some borrowers, precipitated the crisis. The answer probably is that, considering the gathering strength of the other forces at work, Federal Reserve policy did not make much difference one way or another in *inducing* the depression. Some writers have emphasized the sharp drop in American exports as a causal factor, but the drop seems to have been as much a result as a cause of the depression. In 1930 imports fell about as much as exports, so that the American net favorable balance on goods and services account was $1 billion, or about what it had been since the mid-twenties. In 1931 the favorable balance fell to about $500 million. No one would deny that a decline in the American export balance had a depressing effect on the economy, but the magnitude of the fall was actually not very great.

As Americans suffered through the first two years of the depression, they analyzed, in everyday language, the causes of the trouble they were in and suggested cures. Some of the analysis was astonishingly accurate, and many of the remedies proposed, had they been tried, might well have prevented the precipitate drops in income and employment that characterized the late stages of the depression. But remedies potent enough to do much good required a radically different approach to public finance and a revolutionary

Compassionate concern for the unfortunate was one mark of the New Deal, and it was a trait especially marked in the First Lady, Eleanor Roosevelt, who is shown in 1933 going over the plans of a Project for Rehabilitation of Destitute Coal Miners with construction engineers in West Virginia.

concept of the role of the federal government in time of economic crisis. The administration of Herbert Hoover, elected to office on promises of a safe, conservative program, was simply incapable of the radical, imaginative leadership that alone could save the day.

The common judgment that the Hoover administration did nothing to combat the depression is as erroneous as the notion that it was the cause of the depression. Within the limits of economic orthodoxy and somewhat beyond, steps were taken to restore equilibrium. We have already considered the principal legislative and administrative measures taken by the Hoover administration. Monetary policy was idiotic, but the ignorance of the central bank was the ignorance of American economics generally. Although the Reconstruction Finance Corporation came chiefly to the assistance of large businesses, the very formation of such an agency marked a sharp break with tradition. Support of agricultural prices by the Federal Farm Board was equally revolutionary. Indeed, the only criticism of these measures is that they did not go far enough. The major deficiencies of the Hoover administration were persistent refusal to establish a federal program of work relief and failure to carry out a fiscal policy of conscious and aggressive deficit financing.[2] Too much reliance was placed on maintaining confidence through public testimonials of leaders in business and government and not enough on measures to raise incomes and correct the deflation.

It looked for a while in the late summer of 1932 as though the tide might have turned. But banks continued to contract loans, and the deflation ground on. The Republican defeat in the fall may have frightened some conservatives, but more unsettling were the five leaderless months before the inauguration of Roosevelt on March 4, 1933. Bank runs spread to the largest institutions, and on February 14 the leading banks of Detroit closed. In little more than two weeks nearly half the states followed Michigan in declaring "bank holidays" or severely restricting banking operations. Industrial production was now at about 40 per cent of potential, one-fourth of the nation's breadwinners had no work, and unknown numbers of people were literally starving to death.

THE NEW DEAL

Under such circumstances a change in administrations was bound to help, and the vitality and self-confidence of Franklin D. Roosevelt were reassuring. The economy needed more, however, than psychological uplift. The most pressing need was for relief of destitute families. Scarcely less important was the necessity of reversing the falling price trend (of "reflating," as the current phrase had it) and of raising incomes of the major classes of producers—farmers, urban workers, and businessmen.

---

[2] From mid-1930 on, the treasury ran a small deficit because tax revenues fell with declining incomes. But the deficit occurred in spite of efforts to prevent it. In fairness it should be noted that Franklin D. Roosevelt promised during the campaign of 1932 to cut federal expenditures by 25 per cent and so balance the budget.

Grim hopelessness came to mark the quarter of the population that was out of work and the two-thirds that occasionally felt hunger as the Great Depression deepened. "Hoovervilles" like this shanty town sprang up in New York's Central Park and on the banks of the Potomac across from Washington.

In foregoing chapters we have examined most of the legislative measures by which the President and Congress tried to achieve recovery. A federal program of unemployment relief was put into effect immediately through FERA and CWA, followed by PWA, and mortgage relief prevented further loss of homes and farms by foreclosure. Runs on banks were stopped by first declaring a banking holiday and then reopening banks certified to be sound; and gold hoarding was ended by the simple device of requiring everybody to turn monetary gold over to the treasury in exchange for some other form of money. Late in 1933 the devaluation of the dollar was begun, for by raising the treasury's buying price of gold—i.e., by lowering the gold content of the dollar—officials expected to make dollars "cheaper" and raise prices. These specific measures, plus a Federal Reserve policy of easy money, were intended to push the price level back up. But beyond these measures the fundamental readjustment of farm income and the industrial wage-price structure was attempted in the two major agencies of the early New Deal—the AAA and the NRA.

Agricultural poverty sent thousands fleeing from the southwest to California, with belongings piled in the family jalopy. A nation that "drove to the poor house in an automobile," as Will Rogers said, had to change some of its babies' diapers on hard-surfaced roadways.

The AAA plan for raising farm prices and incomes through acreage restrictions was considered in Chapter 18. Up to now, though, we have mentioned only those sections of the National Industrial Recovery Act that established the PWA and asserted the right of labor to bargain collectively. The chief purposes of the act were to raise prices and wages, spread work by reducing hours, and prevent price-cutting by competitors trying to maintain volume. A National Recovery Administration under the direction of General Hugh Johnson supervised the preparation for each industry of a "code of fair practice." Deputy administrators, presumably assisted by representatives of employers, labor, and consumers, prepared the codes, which were really agreements among sellers to set minimum prices, limit output, and establish minimum wages and maximum hours of work. Pending the approval of basic codes, the President issued a "blanket code" in July 1933. Sellers signing the blanket code agreed to raise wages, shorten the maximum workweek, and eschew price-cutting; in return, they could display a "blue eagle" and avoid being boycotted for not doing their part. By 1935, 557 basic codes were approved. In practice labor representatives participated in the construction of less than 10 per cent of the codes, and consumer representation was negligible. Employer representatives found it convenient to work through their national trade associations and manufacturer's institutes, with the consequence that prices were set with a view to profit maximization in the manner of a European cartel. The possibility of such an outcome was recognized in the NIRA, which suspended antitrust laws.

The effectiveness of the NIRA and other New Deal measures, especially in the early phase, will forever be debated. Obviously, a combination of measures ultimately turned the tide. For whatever reasons, the gross national product rose from a low of $56 billion in 1933 to $72,500 million in 1935, and prices of all wholesale commodities increased by a third, regaining the level of late 1930. Manufacturing output jumped after the institution of NRA, as merchants added to their inventories in anticipation of price increases. But production lapsed again, and by mid-summer of 1935 the index was no higher than it had been after the first NRA spurt. Unemployment, though reduced, was still far too great, and most manufacturing firms were operating at less than capacity.

Early in 1935 there was a growing feeling that the lift the economy experienced had come chiefly from income injections via the deficit-spending route. It was with little regret, then, that New Dealers saw the passing of NRA, declared unconstitutional by the Supreme Court on the grounds that Congress had illegally delegated legislative powers to the President. A marked rise in the index of physical production within a few months after the demise of NRA confirmed the view that an excess of government spending over government receipts, the difference made up by borrowing, increased people's incomes. At this stage, however, the use of a budget deficit as an antidepression weapon had not become official administrative policy. There was much talk of "pump-priming," through expenditures for relief and public works, but the administration was reluctant to abandon Democratic campaign pledges of a balanced budget and an end to Republican "extravagance." Nevertheless, there was a deficit in the 1936 administrative budget of nearly $4,500 million, by far the largest on record, and the cash deficit for the fiscal year ran about $3,500 million.[3]

---

[3] The administrative or conventional budget of the United States records only receipts and expenditures of funds owned wholly by the federal government for the budget period (fiscal year) running from July 1 to June 30. But to weigh the impact of treasury surpluses and deficits on the economy it is necessary to know how much will be taken away from people in taxes and how much will be turned back as cash expenditures. Economic analysts therefore find it convenient to prepare a "cash-consolidated" budget, which includes receipts and expenditures of trust funds such as old-age and survivors insurance, unemployment insurance, and railroad retirement but does *not* include expenditures not paid to the public, such as interest on the government securities in which the trust funds are invested. A third way of recording federal transactions is known as the national income accounts budget, which measures the impact of taxing and spending on U.S. income and output. Like the cash-consolidated budget it includes trust-fund transactions; it excludes loans and repayments of loans and records business taxes when they are accrued rather than when they are paid.

Roosevelt's charm and buoyance did much in itself to soften Depression's psychological impact. His broad grin made his theme song, "Happy Days Are Here Again," believable to a shaken nation.

The upswing that began in late 1935 continued through 1936. By early 1937 total manufacturing output exceeded that of 1929, and prices and wages were rising briskly. Although unemployment remained severe—between seven million and eight million at the peak of 1937 activity—government officials and economists were persuaded that prosperity had returned and that inflation threatened. Expenditures for relief and public works were cut, the cash deficit for the calendar year 1937 falling almost to zero. Federal Reserve authorities, by raising the reserve requirements of member banks to maximums authorizd by the Banking Act of 1935, drastically reduced excess reserves of commercial banks, forcing a reduction in bank loans and investments of one billion dollars in 1937. It soon appeared that such policy decisions were ill-advised. Industrial production reached a post-1929 high in May 1937 and then turned downward. Bank loans and commodity prices followed, and the weary process of deflation began again. Retail sales fell off, unemployment increased, and payrolls declined substantially. Adding to the general gloom, the stock market started a long slide in August that brought stock prices in March 1938 to less than half the peak of a year previously.

In 1937, as now, many attributed the renewed onslaught of depression to the reform measures introduced and passed in 1935 and 1936. Social-security legislation and the new freedom granted labor in 1935 came in for some hard words. But most of the criticism was directed toward the hostile political climate in which, it was asserted, vigorous business expansion was impossible. In the state of the union message of 1936, President Roosevelt had castigated "the royalists of the economic order" who, he said, opposed government intervention in economic affairs and received a disproportionate amount of the national income. Tax legislation of 1935 and 1936, directed toward preventing tax avoidance and making the tax structure more sharply progressive, was especially resented by people of means. In 1935, estate and gift taxes were increased as were individual surtaxes, and taxes on incomes of large corporations were raised along with the excess profits tax. Most hated of all taxes was the undistributed profits tax of 1936, a surtax imposed on corporations to make them distribute profits instead of holding them so that individual stockholders could avoid personal taxation.

Distrust of New Deal reforms in general and of tax policies in particular may have weakened individual incentives to carry out real investment and thus contributed to the downturn of 1937–38. If so, the expansive policies carried on by the government, beginning in April 1938, soon overcame the fears and reservations of business decision-makers. Following an explicit recommendation of the President to increase the national income through fiscal policy, Congress provided increased appropriations for the WPA. Federal Reserve reverted to an easy-money policy, and bank loans began to grow. No more tax reforms were introduced, and the only reform measure of any consequence passed in 1938 was the Fair Labor Standards Act. Business picked up in the early summer of 1938, and toward the close of the year recovery was well under way.

Not until the end of 1939, however, was total industrial production back to 1937 peak levels, and the output of durables did not reach the 1937 level until well into 1940. After Hitler's success at Munich in September 1938, the threat of approaching war stimulated military buying, and purchases of foreign governments, particularly Great Britain, grew steadily after the outbreak of war in 1939. Meanwhile the federal government had no scruples about providing adequate work-relief. Net income injection on government account—i.e., the cash deficit—was nearly $3 billion in fiscal 1939 and again in 1940; in fiscal 1941 the cash deficit was almost $5 billion. During 1940, for the first time in more than a decade, the economy showed signs of achieving full recovery. Employment and payrolls rose with the rapid increase in industrial production. Prices remained stable through 1940, but at the close of the year wage rates were beginning to firm, a sign that full employment might once again be realized.

THE CURE FOR DEPRESSION

The return of something like genuine prosperity in 1940 led a majority of the electorate to give the New Deal credit for escape from mass unemployment and faltering production. There is no question that a program of positive action—any action—was sufficient to bring about an upturn in 1933 and 1934. From 1935 on, however, it became pretty clear that output and incomes were rising because of net income injections by the government. Had these income-increasing injections been made more vigorously, in spite of fears of a rising national debt shared by most conservatives, the American economy would doubtless have bounded ahead much sooner.

Anyone unconvinced on this point has only to look at the budget, income, and production figures for the World War II period. In fiscal 1942—i.e., from July 1941 through June 1942—cash outgo of the treasury exceeded cash income by more than $19 billion. In the next fiscal year the cash deficit was $54 billion, and in succeeding years $46 billion and $45 billion. Income-generating government expenditures of this magnitude did what seven years of New Deal spending had not done. The gross national product—i.e., the total value of output sold in the market place—more than doubled in five years from $100 billion in 1940 to $211 billion in 1944. In the same five years industrial production almost doubled, the index rising from 67 in 1940 to 127 in 1944, and durables output increased more than two and a half times. To some extent these gains were illusory because prices rose moderately, many consumer durables disappeared from the market, and the quality of available durables and many nondurables declined. But there was nothing illusory about the disappearance of unemployment, which even during 1941 had *averaged* 5,500,000, or 10 per cent of the civilian work force. At the close of 1941 unemployment was down to 3,500,000, and a year later had dropped to 1,500,000. For two years during the war unemployment from all causes never exceeded 1,000,000.

It troubles most of us to attribute material gains to war. The immorality of international conflict should not, however, blind us to the fact that World War II lifted the American economy out of stagnation and serious malfunctioning. There was nothing "artificial" about the wartime boom. The same effect could have been achieved, of course, by crisscrossing the country with superhighways and building hospitals, schools, and underground urban parking facilities. In the sense that war expenditures were for destruction and not for things people wanted and needed the war was "wasteful." At the same time the war overcame the waste of idle men and idle physical plant. The money value (at constant prices) of the goods and services foregone during the 1930s because the productive machine worked so far below potential just about equaled the money cost to Americans of World War II.

The rapid increase in federal expenditures, which during the war generated more than a third of the gross national product, led inevitably to great inflationary pressures. As output began to rise during 1940, there was so much unemployment of people and manufacturing facilities that goods were forthcoming without a rise in prices. Toward the end of the year certain types of labor were in short supply, and as the economy moved toward full employment in 1941, wages and other prices began to move upward. Informal price control during 1941 did not prove effective enough to check the inflation, and on January 30, 1942, the previously established Office of Price Administration was given legal authority to put a rigid clamp on most prices. In April, OPA issued the first maximum price regulations, which froze prices at the level prevailing during March 1942. But ceilings could not be placed on food until agricultural prices reached 110 per cent of parity, and wages were not yet under effective control. Consequently, prices continued their upward movement for several months after the first general regulation was imposed. In October wages were placed under the control of the National War Labor Board, and by the spring of 1943 agricultural prices were so close to their maxima that a final "hold-the-line" regulation almost stopped further price increases for two years.

Everything considered, OPA regulation was remarkably effective. During World War II retail and wholesale prices rose about 35 per cent, and half of this increase occurred before statutory price controls were instituted in 1942. The success of price regulation was partly attributable to the sense of fair play of most Americans, who submitted with reasonably good grace to necessary rationing. As incomes continued to increase, the demand for goods and services at ceiling prices exceeded supply; with the pricing mechanism in abeyance as rationer, goods would have gone in great quantities to those rich enough to store them, to the first people standing in line, or to old and favored customers. A point system of rationing very scarce goods—gasoline, tires, fuel oil, sugar, coffee, meats, and canned and packaged foods—was therefore established. It did not work perfectly, but no one expected it to. Black markets appeared, especially toward the end of the war, in gasoline and meats. As time went on, manufacturers dropped less profitable lines and items, often quite essential to creature comfort, and specialized on high-margin luxury products. OPA officials frequently missed their estimates as to probable supplies, and some local rationing boards were lenient while others were tough. Most people felt, however, that the annoyance and occasional inequities of price control and rationing were unavoidable considering the size of the undertaking.

With many materials in far from sufficient supply to assure adequate production of armament, planes, ships, vehicles, and electronic equipment, the pricing mechanism could not be relied upon to establish a system of priorities among producers. Businesses were gradually subjected to controls that made harassing consumer controls seem only mildly restrictive in comparison. A succession of agencies was created to cope with the problem of allocating scarce materials. Finally, in January 1942, the War Production Board was created under a single administrative head with sufficient authority to allocate materials and production facilities and administer priorities. There was still need, though, for coordination of several agencies that directly affected total output. The War Manpower Commission, for example, which was responsible for the effective mobilization of the nation's labor resources, supervised the placement of workers in war industries and passed on broad categories of draft deferments. The Office of Defense Transportation under-

Final cure for the Great Depression was massive government spending, especially on war materiel like this B-17F Superfortress being inspected before shipment at Long Beach, California, in 1943.

took to weld into a single, effective system the country's domestic transportation facilities. To unify the entire productive effort, with final authority to allocate resources in their competing uses, the Office of War Mobilization was created in May 1943. For the rest of the war period the economy was run with ruthless efficiency to achieve victory over the enemy.

In winning the war Americans incidentally learned how to cure a major depression. But at what cost? Certainly not at any real economic cost, as real incomes and savings rose to unprecedented highs. Nor was there any burdensome *financial* cost, except in individual instances where thriving businesses were hurt, high-salaried workers became low-paid military men, or fixed-income receivers were pressed by rising prices. Because a little more than half of total war expense was financed by treasury borrowing, the national debt increased to astronomical figures. But somewhere along the way people began to realize that large public borrowing only caused technical difficulties of debt management to financiers and economists. Many who in 1937 predicted national bankruptcy when the debt should reach $50 billion, watched complacently as it passed the $100 billion mark, then the $200 billion, and finally approached $300 billion. Three key facts were becoming apparent. Because the debt was internally held, Americans, either as individuals or through their financial institutions, acquired assets in the form of government securities to offset the liabilities of their government. Because of rapid growth in the national income consequent upon deficit financing, both the physical and financial assets of individuals and businesses were increasing at a tremendous rate. Finally, because the government had the money-creating power, no one needed to fear national insolvency; the Federal Reserve could always provide banks with reserves for the purchase of securities issued to refund any part of the debt as it came due.

Yet there was a cost, one that weighed heavily on a people used to registering free choices in the market place. Once resources were fully employed, repeated income injections brought the threat of runaway inflation, and the price system could not be depended upon to allocate the factors of production in ways consistent with winning the war. To secure a great end, Americans submitted to a web of controls that would have been intolerable under less pressing circumstances. Price ceilings, rationing, and allocation of materials by fiat were necessary to successful prosecution of the war, but they warned business firms and private citizens of the serious implications of total government intervention in the allocation process.

The Prospect Before Us

Economic forecasters of the early 1960s cheerfully predicted a gross national product of $800 billion for 1970 and a trillion-dollar economy by 1975. These assurances for the future were both comforting and gratifying. But it is not ordinarily the business of either the economist or the historian to make long-range quantitative predictions, for ordinary mortals are not gifted with prescience. A great war, unforeseen innovations, a shift in the propensity to save or to consume, the degree of international co-operation, changing birth-control practices—these and many other influences may change the course of economic growth.

Yet our study of economic history would be something less than satisfying if it did not help us to judge the kind of economic organization and the level of economic performance Americans will accept in the future. It has been our special concern to observe the growing demands of different groups for government protection of their special interests. We have emphasized the sweep of forces that explain the abandonment of the nineteenth-century liberal ideal of the least possible governmental interference in private affairs. Were changes in the concept of the role of the state in economic life only manifestations of the economic and political unrest of the 1930s, we might anticipate some lessening of federal controls. But demands for much of the

New Deal legislation had been long growing. The first spur-of-the-moment, experimental laws have been modified and recast; but they have been retained, and their purpose of solving problems with roots deep in the past is still the same.

The farm problem, for example, did not come suddenly on us in 1930. Farmers have always been peculiarly vulnerable to shifts in business conditions. In part their troubles are the result of a liberal land policy that they themselves were largely instrumental in securing. But long-time adverse influences on the supply of, and demand for, agricultural products are not the fault of the farmer, and there is nothing he can do about the highly competitive markets in which he sells his products. The electorate has therefore agreed to price and income proctection for farmers. The methods of providing protection have altered, and we may expect further changes. There is even a possibility that the good sense of country people will lead ultimately to acceptance of the plan of compensatory payments discussed in Chapter 18; for the present price-support mechanism only helps make rich farmers richer, while doing little to maintain the family-size farm and relieve agrarian poverty. One day we may see the adoption of a farm plan that is primarily contracyclical in purpose, with the old notion of maintaining parity prices and incomes disappearing. But within the foreseeable future we will have a federal farm program of one kind or another.

The labor problem has been with us for two centuries and will persist as long as we maintain a reasonably free capitalistic economy. There is simply no avoiding disagreement between labor and management as long as each is permitted to bargain. The argument that trade unionism has not been as successful in improving wages, hours, and working conditions as union members and leaders commonly have supposed carries little weight with organized labor, and we may anticipate continuing efforts to increase union membership in the unorganized occupations. But the conflict between powerful unions and great companies seems likely to lessen as the process of education goes on. Labor leaders, advised by competent professional staffs, are well aware that they can demand and get only such gains as increasing productivity will permit. Employers, equally well advised, are likely to become less resistant to passing on the benefits of increased productivity which, as tight labor markets recur, the forces of competition assure labor anyway.[4] There are no signs, however, that the public will soon allow itself to be at the mercy of contending giants which, while testing each other's strength, can bring the economic machine to a standstill. Nor is the public likely to tolerate violence, whether gangsterism in a few union leaderships or employer use of armed hoods to resist an organizing drive.

---

[4] Real product per man-hour in the private economy and real hourly earnings in manufacturing have increased at nearly the same rate since 1910. Not infrequently, though, as in the late twenties and the late forties, productivity and earnings moved in opposite directions, to the detriment of the worker. Trade unions contend that it is their chief business to force employers to keep earnings responsive to productivity changes.

This side the millennium we may expect government to remain the arbiter of the continuing contest between big labor and big business, according to rules that favor one side or the other as the country's political complexion shifts.

The future of government intercession to control monopolistic practices is not quite so clear. There is no question that antitrust prosecution has been consistently more vigorous since Thurman Arnold instituted his program in 1937. Furthermore, the legal and economic concepts of monopoly have coalesced, as at least two federal judges have employed the theoretical models of monopoly and oligopoly in rendering decisions.[5] Unfortunately, as we have observed, the restoration of competition in the sense of "atomizing" an industry composed of one or a few firms is physically impossible and, if it were possible, economically undesirable. And it boots us nothing to increase the number of firms from one to four, as in the case of the aluminum industry, for prices and output remain about the same when there are "few" competing firms as when there is one. Dissolution is no more effective a remedy today than it was forty-odd years ago, as Judge Wyzanski's decision in the United Shoe Machinery case affirms. As I argued at length in Chapter 21, the courts and the Justice Department can effectively root out socially objectionable cases of monopoly control only by defining use categories and searching out those categories in which there is no interindustry or interproduct competition. For a long time to come, however, the orthodox view will prevail. Many people believe that monopolistic behavior has been inhibited simply by the threat of antitrust prosecution, and there is evidence that collusion in industries composed of many firms has often been prevented by Justice Department action. The decision in the Brown Shoe Company case suggests that the Supreme Court will stand in the way of mergers, even though oligopoly is only "incipient" in an industry plagued by the ills of competition. Americans are likely to continue in favor of a "big-stick" approach to the problem in preference to the "scalpel" approach discussed in Chapter 21.

If we were to continue through the entire list of instances in which the federal government has intervened in the private sector of the economy, we should find upon examination that, almost without exception, continued intervention is certain. There is no longer any serious objection to old-age and survivors insurance, unemployment insurance, federal insurance of bank deposits and savings and loan shares, federally underwritten residential mortgages, and rural electrification. No really important voices have been raised to question the advisability of federal subsidy of the air, truck, and bus lines. On the question of public power national opinion vacillates with swings in political sentiment, but in the regions directly affected a swift end to his public career faces the legislator opposing federal multi-

---

[5] See the discussion in Chapter 21 of the decisions of Judge Hand in the Aluminum case and Judge Wyzanski in the United Shoe Machinery case.

purpose dams, steam-plant construction, and power preference to municipalities and REA co-operatives. In fact, there have been in the past few
years only two major examples of federal withdrawal from interference with
the private-market mechanism. The Reconstruction Finance Corporation,
an emergency agency, was liquidated after twenty years of operation. Of
more consequence have been recent changes in trade policy. In each of the
three decades since 1934 Congress authorized the President to reduce tariffs
as much as 50 per cent, and the average United States tariff on dutiable
goods is presently the lowest in our history.

Concerning the wisdom of individual pieces of economic legislation
there is much controversy among economists. The hard political fact remains that the American people, for the reasons we have examined, have
by democratic processes chosen to protect various groups from the hardships
of unrestricted economic competition. All the signs indicate that the protection will be continued. Moreover, it is almost certain that the economy
is better off than it would have been without government intervention. I
have argued that the apparatus of competition functions very well in spite
of attempts to interfere with it, and there is much to be said for the view
that economic growth has actually been encouraged by class and group
legislation.

THE POLITICAL DEMAND FOR FULL EMPLOYMENT AND GROWTH

Since World War II the evidence has grown that Americans consider
the performance of the economy unsatisfactory if for more than brief periods
there is less than full employment. Consequently, the federal government
has been required to assume another responsibility, one with serious implications.

The goal of eliminating wide fluctuations in economic activity has only
recently been accepted by the American electorate. To be sure, from the
founding of the first Bank of the United States in 1791 to the establishment
of the Federal Reserve in 1913 there were attempts to mitigate the effects
of business recession by fiddling with the money mechanism. But as I argued in Chapter 20, during the first two decades of the Federal Reserve
System's history the money managers had no clear notion of a monetary
policy aimed at broad stabilization objectives. The failure of the System
to prevent the Great Depression and, worse, its inability to bring about
revival disillusioned economists and laymen alike. People began to wonder
if they had not been a little weak-headed in attributing so much importance to money as a causal factor in fluctuations.

The prosperity of World War II years convinced nearly everyone that
the secret of permanent prosperity lay in a fiscal policy directed toward
preventing unemployment. Congress in 1945 even considered a bill that
would guarantee full employment by placing a $40 billion "annual invest-
ment fund" at the disposal of the Secretary of Commerce. Senator Murray,
its author, said that the bill was a ". . . legal acknowledgment that the

national government assumes the responsibility for prosperity in peacetime. The Federal Government is the instrument through which we can all work to accomplish full employment and high annual income." After much argument and word-juggling, a revised version of the original "full-employment" bill was passed as the "Employment Act of 1946." Full employment was no longer explicitly required; instead it was to be the federal government's responsibility to ". . . promote maximum employment, production and purchasing power." The adjective *maximum* was purposely ambiguous, but the entire statement was generally taken to mean that the government would act quickly to shore up the economy in case a severe recession threatened. A Council of Economic Advisers, with an adequate professional staff, was added to the Executive Office of the President. The President, assisted by the Council, was directed to submit to Congress at least annually a report on current economic conditions, with recommendations for legislative action. The statute further provided that the House and the Senate form a standing Joint Committee on the Economic Report, which would study the report of the President and Council of Economic Advisers, hold hearings, and itself in turn report to Congress. Although no "investment fund" was provided, an agency was established that would keep watch and systematically inform Congress and the President of economic change.

We have already seen how the fears of a major postwar depression proved groundless and how instead inflation for a time proved to be the problem. The recession of 1948–49 caused uneasiness as industrial production dropped 10 per cent, and the gross national product fell $11 billion, or 4 per cent. The administration moved quickly, however, to award military contracts in "distressed areas," and though unemployment went above 5 per cent of the work force for several months, revival came so quickly that public clamor for action never reached much of a pitch. The Korean War assured at least three more years of prosperity, though there was a slump in consumer durables sales in 1951.

During 1953 the key indicators took an unfavorable turn. Industrial production, the gross national product, construction contracts, and manufacturers' new orders dropped, and unemployment jumped in the last quarter of the year. Because these changes did not all come at once and were not precipitate, their impact on income earners was neither sudden nor severe. But as the throbbing boom of the early 1950s faded, a pessimism that had not shown itself in 1949 pervaded the country. The magnitude of the drop was approximately the same. In about nine months industrial production fell 10 per cent, the gross national product declined 4 per cent, and manufacturing employment went off 10 per cent. There was much talk of another "inventory recession" like that of 1949, but it was clear that entrepreneurs had some good reason for reducing inventories. This widely forecasted recession was plainly triggered by a fall in national-defense spending and so in total government spending, which declined by $11 billion per annum between the second quarter of 1953 and the second quarter of 1954. Since there was a $10 billion drop in gross investment, mostly in inventories, the gross product would have declined more than $21 billion had there not been offsetting expenditures. Fortunately, state and local governments spent more during the year, exports exceeded imports, and personal consumption expenditures increased, the total offset amounting to a little over $7 billion.

Now this was far from a serious decline. Compared to the full-blown depressions of former years the 1953–54 recession seemed small indeed. It nevertheless aroused great concern. Unemployment in many manufacturing areas exceeded 10 per cent of the local work force, and many families exhausted their unemployment insurance benefits before there were clear signs of improvement. The fact that the economy leveled off for several months during the summer and fall of 1954 was little comfort to those who knew that output could not stand still if net additions to the work force of about 750,000 people a year were to be absorbed.

The administration, reassured by the Council of Economic Advisers, took no drastic steps to combat the recession by fiscal means. A moderate cash deficit, partly the result of tax remissions, had a stimulating effect. A Federal Reserve policy of "active ease" was undertaken before most informed people were aware that the business indicators had taken a turn for the worse. Nevertheless, as Professor John P. Lewis has remarked, "In the days of routine instability this would have been just the sort of situation calculated to launch the various downward cumulators in the economy— the multiplier, the accelerator, self-confirming price expectations, and credit contraction—into a progressive, interacting erosion of demand." [6] It was apparent that there were strong sustaining forces in the economy. A continuing rapid increase in population and a substantial rate of household formation created demand for consumer goods; indeed, the most important resistance to this recession was consumption, as personal income remained insulated from the general decline in spending and income. Even the distribution of the population among age groups was favorable, for the babies of the postwar boom were growing up to eat more food and wear more clothing. To such long-term natural supports were added the automatic stabilizers, which almost immediately operated to counteract the downward movement in economic activity: unemployment insurance payments, a reduction in the total tax bill as the incomes of individuals and corporations declined, the support of falling agricultural prices, and even some increase in social-security payments.

After a four-year respite from inflationary pressures, prices began a steady rise in mid-1955 that continued until early 1957, the increase amounting to about 8.5 per cent in this brief period. Inflation became the pressing domestic problem of the day, and Fed authorities doubtless increased public vexation by intemperate references to both the causes and the dangers of

---

[6] John P. Lewis, *Business Conditions Analysis* (New York: McGraw-Hill, 1959), p. 331.

inflation. What was worse, Federal Reserve continued its tight-money policy well past the point of economic downturn in the late summer of 1957, not reversing itself until November. There followed a recession of unnecessarily substantial proportions, the deepest of the postwar period. By the spring of 1958 the gap between output and capacity reached $40 billion, and unemployment at 7.5 per cent of the civilian labor force was burdensome and frightening.

The remarkable resiliency of the American economy was once again evidenced by a rebound that began in April, 1958. But the recovery through 1959 was halting and disappointing, and when the indicators took another adverse turn in 1960 the frustration of policy-makers knew no bounds. Once again the recession was short-lived, and after a trough reached in February of 1961, the economy began its longest sustained rise in the post-Korean years.

Recurrent recessions were annoying. But a greater cause for concern was the persistent failure of the economy to produce at anything like its vast potential at peaks of expansion phases. There was a preoccupation among academic and government economists with the problem of economic growth, and the divergence between the rate of increase of aggregate output and the rate of increase of the economy's productive capacity was viewed with increasing alarm.

Actually, recent performance of the American economy has been quite good by historic standards. Whether we take the last seventy-five years or the last fifty years, the annual rate of increase of real output has averaged astonishingly close to 3 per cent. If we take shorter periods, we can find a series of years in which the economy grew at startlingly different rates. For example, from 1947 to early 1953 constant-dollar GNP grew at an annual rate of 5 per cent. On the other hand, from mid-1953 to the first quarter of 1958 the growth rate was little better than one per cent. Depending on the use to which we wish to put our figures, we can select any other span of time. Thus during the years 1929–63 the growth rate of the economy was 3 per cent a year; from 1946 to 1963 it averaged about 3.35 per cent (see chart, p. 650).[7]

To be meaningful any reference to a rate of economic *growth* must be made in the context of a long span of years. It is for this reason that repeated complaints of famed Presidential advisers about a slackening rate of growth have for many a naïve ring; opponents of this view argue that the problem of unemployment is one of short-run stabilization and not growth.

The extent to which the economy actually achieves adequate growth

---

[7] In 1958 the trend line drawn through quarterly GNP data for the period 1946–58 rose at an annual rate of 3.8 per cent. There is no question that the rate of increase of real GNP slackened in the late 1950s and early 1960s. The point I would insist upon is that the short-term problem of economic fluctuations must be distinguished from the long-term problem of economic growth.

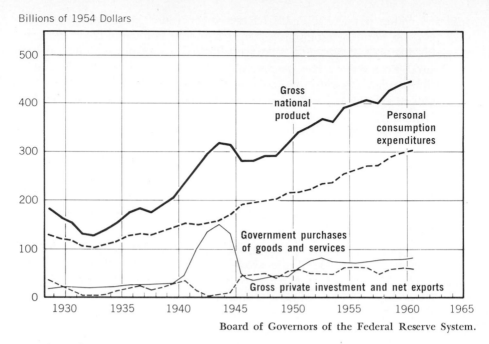

Billions of 1954 Dollars

Gross
national
product

Personal
consumption
expenditures

Government purchases
of goods and services

Gross private investment and net exports

Board of Governors of the Federal Reserve System.

American Output: Gross national product shows a reasonably satisfactory rate of increase since the war, but in the early 1960s there was widespread concern that the growth rate seemed to be slacking off.

breaks down into two issues: First, there is the matter of the rate at which, and the steadiness with which, productive potential or capacity expands. This expansion is a function of (1) growth in the available labor inputs, which in turn depend on the available labor force and average working hours, and (2) advances in labor productivity (i.e., increases in output per man-hour). Labor productivity in turn depends upon the quantity of capital and, in the broader sense, of "technology," when the latter is understood to include, besides technical production processes, advances in human knowledge and improvement in the quality of management.

Second, the economy's growth performance depends on whether we succeed in generating enough aggregate demand (i.e., expenditures on final product, or actual GNP) to keep using our growing capacity up to its potential—without trying to overuse it and thereby inducing an excess-demand inflation.

A recent publication enables us to summarize the relative importance of the forces affecting capacity as they have operated in the past generation. In a recent CED study, for the three-decade period 1929–57, Edward F. Denison has weighted individual sources of growth as follows: [8]

[8] Edward F. Denison, *The Sources of Economic Growth in the United States and the Alternatives Before Us* (New York: Committee for Economic Development, 1962).

1. Changes in employment and working hours accounted for 27 per cent of total growth. Denison notes that the "increase in employment would have contributed an amount equal to 34 per cent of the actual growth rate had hours not been shortened, but the shortening of hours provided an offset equal to 7 per cent of the total growth rate." It is worth noting that had the shortening of hours not led to an increase in the amount of work done per hour (presumably because of greater efficiency resulting from more leisure) the offset would have been not 7 per cent but 18 per cent.
2. Because the members of the work force at the end of the period were much better educated than those at the beginning of the period, the quality of the labor force was improved so much over the three decades that it contributed 23 per cent of the total growth of national product.
3. The utilization of women in jobs where they can work to maximum capacity plus the fact that, on the average, women now stay in the labor force longer and thus become more experienced and effective workers has added four percentage points to the growth rate in the three decades.

In sum, changes in the quantity and quality of labor were responsible for 54 per cent of the economic growth of the 1929–57 period. For the rest:

4. The increase in capital inputs contributed 15 per cent of total growth of which two-thirds, or 10 per cent, was the contribution of the increase in services provided by buildings (other than nonfarm residences) and by equipment.
5. The increase in all kinds of knowledge about production, by permitting more to be produced with a given quantity of resources, contributed 20 per cent of total growth.
6. Economies of scale made possible by the increase of the size of the national economy contributed 9 per cent of economic growth during the three decades.

The five sources named thus contributed an amount equal to 98 per cent of the growth rate; miscellaneous items netted an additional 2 per cent. Within the institutional framework of the American democracy, growth of capacity in the period studied resulted from increased employment, more education, more capital, the advance of human knowledge, and economies of scale associated with the emergence of the national market. If we would stimulate the rate of growth of the economy we must pay attention to this set of variables.[9]

---

[9] Other studies check out closely with Denison's. Kendrick, for example, estimates that approximately half of the average annual rate of increase in output for the period 1889–1957 is explained by the growth in labor and capital. Other variables in his estimates are education, research, and technological development.

Unfortunately, the public-policy steps likely to stimulate increases in capacity do not always satisfy public demands for action. Increased investment in education is likely to bring the greatest return in the long run, but the time lag in its effectiveness (sometimes as much as a generation) discourages those concerned about slack in the contemporary economy. Significant structural changes, such as training young people for skilled instead of "blockhead" jobs and transferring human resources from declining to growing industries, likewise take time and patience. Moreover, a surging, booming demand for goods and services stimulates research and its applications (innovation) and facilitates the transfer of people from low-productivity to high-productivity industries.

And so we come inescapably to the conclusion that high levels of aggregate demand are absolutely essential to the kind of economy that minimizes social tensions and maximizes the rate of economic growth. The responsibility for maintaining high demand levels must ultimately belong to the federal government. The problem of economic stabilization, which started out as one of shoring up flagging demand in the short run, has become one of commitment to long-run goals of full employment and adequate diffusion of welfare. Those who have read this book with care should be able to defend the proposition that growth, not inflation, has been the persistently pressing problem of the American economy—just as those who have really done their homework can feel little nostalgia for the good old days, wonderful as they must have been for the gifted few who won out in the competition.

THE DILUTION OF ECONOMIC PROGRESS

Economic progress is concerned with means, not ends. Economic progress implies that its beneficiaries can get what they want more easily than they or their ancestors did previously. However much we may long for a golden age long past, however nostalgically we may yearn for the charm of candles and coaches instead of electric lights and automobiles, we in America are demonstrably better off than our forebears of a century ago. Moreover, Americans have made greater strides out of the past than has any other people. With little more than 6 per cent of the world's population and less than 7 per cent of its land area, Americans now produce and consume more than a third of the world's annual production of goods and services. American factories turn out nearly half of the world's yearly output of manufactured goods. The income of Americans probably exceeds the combined incomes of everyone living in Europe and the Soviet Union and is certainly greater than that of all the people of Asia.

One way of measuring the economic achievement of the United States is to compare what an hour's work will buy in America with what it will obtain in other countries of the world. On this score, the United States has an edge on Canada, a considerable advantage over Great Britain, and a tremendous advantage over the Soviet Union. Or if we wish to compare present-day output with our own past output, equally impressive figures are available. During the past century productivity has increased so fast that the average American worker produces nearly eight times as much per hour of work as his great-grandfather did in 1860. And work is clearly less burdensome than it has ever been. One man with his power-driven mechanical equipment can do as much work in a forty-hour week as three of his ancestors could do in the seventy-hour week common a hundred years ago. Leisure time has at least doubled since 1910, as American workers in the past half-century or so have taken about two-thirds of national productivity gains in the form of goods and services and about one-third in the form of increased leisure.

Some of the benefits of increasing mechanization have spread to the home and are available to almost the entire spectrum of income groups. Nearly every American house is now wired for electricity, and more than 90 per cent of them are equipped with electric refrigerators, electric washers, and television sets. Other appliances and, perhaps more important, private baths or showers and private flush toilets are available to more than three out of four American homes. More than three-fourths of all families own at least one automobile and one-sixth own two or more. By 1960, the number of weeks of vacations had doubled in the post–World War II period to more than eighty million weeks a year. Those who did not spend leisure time in travel could add to real income by engaging in do-it-yourself projects about the home or could read, play musical instruments, listen to phonograph records sold in astronomical numbers, or simply restore vitality by loafing on a patio or in air-conditioned comfort.

If in the early 1960s life in America was becoming less arduous, it was also spent in better physical health and was certainly longer. When the United States became a going concern in 1789, the life expectancy of a white baby at birth was a little more than 30 years. By 1900, a white male child could be expected to live 48.2 years; by 1960 life expectancy for the same baby had climbed to something over 67 years. Female babies could expect to live a few years longer in both 1900 and 1960—three years longer in 1900 and little short of six years longer in 1960. Non-white babies did not have the same life expectancy, but their gains since 1900 have been greater than those for whites, and it is reasonable to expect that life expectancy for non-whites will continue to make relatively large increases.

At mid-twentieth century, American citizens were still confronted with the age-old problem of making adequate medical facilities available to everyone. Clearly, great advances were being made in the effectiveness of both medicines and the practitioners of medicine. It was plain, too, that advances were being made in the availability of health services to the population. Most important of these gains was in the extension of hospital, surgical, and medical expense coverage. As late as 1940 only ten million Americans had any kind of hospital insurance (i.e., any kind of prepayment of hospital costs that one day must be met by nearly everyone). In 1960 more than 130 million persons had such protection, more than 120 million were protected against surgical expense, and perhaps twenty-five million were protected against the hazards of major medical costs. Moreover, Federal old-age, survivors, and disability insurance benefits by 1960 exceeded $12 billion a year. And if the number of doctors per 100,000 of population had remained constant for more than a decade, physicians were plainly more efficient (if less personal) in treating patients than they had been in the whole history of medical science.

Many would argue that a "bathtub index" is not a measure of either the welfare or the nobility of a people. There are of course other criteria, perhaps not mensurable in the sense of those just enumerated, but nevertheless identifiable. Consider, for example, the opportunities available to the majority of Americans for advancement—for becoming somebody. The shortest way to achievement is to start with capital at the beginning of one's career, and we have remarked earlier that it is helpful to inherit or marry capital. But nowadays the most important single kind of capital is education, and Americans have better educational opportunities than any other people of the world.[10] Human capital in the form of educated people is rapidly becoming as important as industrial and commercial capital.[11] For most of our citizens the discounted value of their expected income is the most important kind of capital they own. The American culture, by supporting a broad-based educational system and making it widely available to people of all walks and conditions of life, has in this way given vitality to enterprise in the economy. Wealth is thus more equitably distributed among people, and vertical mobility within economic organizations, particularly within the modern corporation, has been promoted.

As a consequence of the fluid nature of the American society, based largely on the availability of education, individuals tend to transfer their human capital from areas in which incomes are low to those in which incomes are high. Moreover, people are more readily able to move from those occupations requiring heavy manual labor to those requiring specialization and skills. This shift has brought about a remarkable reduction of the wage differential between labor and the professions. Doctors, lawyers, teachers, and most managers are now paid, relative to unskilled labor, far

---

[10] The quality of primary and secondary education is seriously bad in many parts of the United States, and higher learning in some institutions is not as high as it should be. Everything considered, though, Americans have tremendous educational opportunities. There is no longer any reason, financial or otherwise, why an able boy or girl should not go to college. If there is any doubt about the difference that college education makes to economic progress, one need only observe the differences in progress between the United Kingdom, where less than 5 per cent of eligible young people go to college or university, and the United States, where more than one-third have that privilege.

[11] Professor Theodore Schultz of the University of Chicago has estimated that the capitalized value of the education embodied in the work force was about $900 billion in 1957 and that it has been growing at an annual rate of 4.5 per cent. Another estimate indicates that in 1958 the total stock of reproducible wealth had a value of $1,400 billion and is growing at an annual rate of about 4 per cent.

less than they were a century ago. Largely for this reason the old class-income system is disappearing, and doctors and university professors can no longer employ from one to three full-time servants.

More important, perhaps, is the fact that leadership positions in society are now available to individuals whose families were in modest circumstances. To be sure, we have always had our Horatio Alger successes, and such figures as we have support the proposition that birth still confers advantages on those who aspire to top business positions. Nevertheless, because of the impetus furnished by education and the number of openings afforded by multiple management, business careers offer almost unlimited opportunities to the sons of farmers, laborers, clerks, and salesmen—opportunities that were simply not available even a generation ago. There is no guarantee that those in modest circumstances can make it to the top of the business and professional world in one jump, but it is common to see the transition made in no more than two generations. To put the matter another way, the essentials that build American leadership—not just education, but cultural activity and travel and the opportunity to do interesting work—are as readily available to the second-generation farmer as to the second-generation business executive. The "privileged" are no longer distinguished by the way they eat, drink, house, and transport themselves; these goods and services are fairly comparable for a large majority of the population. Much innovation largely aimed at benefiting the consumer has indeed increased the productivity of the lower and middle-income groups more than the upper. Prepared cake and bread mixes, frozen fruits and vegetables, dehydrated soup mixes, and the like relieve the woman who has no help *relatively* more than the woman who does have help. The new fabrics with their time- and energy-saving qualities of upkeep likewise save the leisure of the poor housewife more than that of the rich. By the same token, it is doubtful that there have been significant improvements in the production of yachts or villas—or, for that matter, of the personal services of butlers, cooks, and housemaids—typically purchased by upper-income groups.

There is a similar egalitarian trend in the distribution of leisure time. As we have just seen, leisure is an increasingly important commodity. Paradoxically, leisure is becoming more and more the cherished possession of lower- and middle-income families. Farmers have an average workweek of forty-five hours, factory workers one of forty hours. But managers and proprietors work a fifty-three-hour week, the longest reported by the Bureau of the Census, and upper echelon executives and professional men find a seventy-hour week not unusual.

By whatever measures we choose to take, the performance of the American economy over the span of three and a half centuries has been spectacularly good. We have observed in detail how economic change occurred. In the churn and eddy of forces over which men had no control in any meaningful sense, there invariably arose the Perceptive Entrepreneur, who made the crucial product innovation or introduced the strategic cost-reducing invention. Competition then assured the extension of innovation; for the judgment of creative entrepreneurs was substantiated by profits in the market place, and the profitability of an innovation was hard to disguise.

Economic progress did not occur as a process of adding layer upon layer of capital to be used in combination with a fixed amount of land and a work force that grew in quantity but not in quality. The nicest sort of discrimination was required of the businessman for whom only one bad judgment might be one too many. The pressures of competition were two-fold: there was the lure of great gain as the reward for risk-taking and the threat of failure and loss of one's entire capital if new methods and new ideas were not promptly adopted upon proof of their profit potential. The forces of competition exerted both a pull and a push.

The resulting development of the American economy stands as a magnificent achievement, and we do well to mark the steps of its evolution and the sources of its vitality. Yet we should be naïve, not to say dishonest, did we fail to note those shortcomings of American society that seriously dilute the gains of economic progress. They persist in spite of, and to some extent *because* of, economic progress. At this juncture we border on the province of the applied economist, whose business it is to resolve problems and so ease the cares of the world. Yet economic historians a generation hence will judge the total performance of the American economy by the success with which private enterprisers and public officials restore the disadvantaged as beneficiaries of capitalist progress.

In large part because sheer competence is so unequally distributed there are inevitably those who cannot stand the pressures of competition. The consequence is a sticky, frustrating problem of poverty. Anyone with eyes to see can testify to the existence of poverty, both rural and urban. Poverty means that despite the diffusion of welfare that we have so easily demonstrated, there remain great numbers of our people who live in deprivation and penury. These are the unfortunate poor, who snatch only bits of the good life. It is hard to know just who the poor are; for some set greater store by this world's goods than others do, and no one can say that this family with $3,000 a year of income is less happy than that one with $6,000. The distressing fact remains that something like one-fifth of our people have incomes below minimum levels of comfort and decency. In 1960 between ten and eleven million multiple-person families had annual incomes of less than $4,000, and four million unattached individuals had incomes of less than $2,000. Thirty-eight million members of an "affluent society" lived in urban blight and agricultural decline. These were the poor, who lived in substandard housing, survived on bad diets, and had little hope of bettering their lot. For a long time to come the American poor would need help wherever they could find it.

Separable from the problem of poverty, though contributing to it, is another—the structural dislocation of the young and the old who simply cannot fit themselves into the requirements of a technologically changing economy. Many of the young have never been placed in productive work, and too many of the old have been too easily displaced. The unplaced and the displaced are for the most part unskilled workers: clerks, farm laborers, day laborers in industry, manufacturing operatives. The correlation between hard-core (as distinguished from cyclical) unemployment and lack of education is too obvious to be questioned. About one-fourth of the unemployed in the early 1960s had less than an elementary-school education and more than two-thirds had less than a high-school education. To put it another way, the rate of unemployment among professional and technical workers was about 1.5 per cent; among unskilled workers it was 20 per cent.

Now as we have been at pains to show, the stresses and tensions of low-income households have more and more been mitigated by the intervention of government, for it has become an accepted role of government to modify the impact of competitive forces. This intervention, as we have seen, spans the whole of economic life, but nowhere has it been more remarkable than in direct outlays on welfare. Before 1933 the shabby treatment accorded unfortunates and the unwillingness of Americans to undertake social insurance programs was little short of scandalous. In 1890 total social-welfare expenditures were an estimated $318 million or 2.4 per cent of the gross national product. By 1913 the figure was $1 billion or 2.8 per cent of the gross national product, and by 1929 it had risen to $4,300 million or 4.1 per cent of the gross national product.[12] The common impression that the "welfare state" began in the 1930s is borne out by the data. Social-welfare programs in 1935 required a $6,700 million outlay, 9.8 per cent of that year's GNP and a little more than half of governmental expenditures at all levels and for all purposes. Though such expenditures fell both absolutely and relatively during World War II, they have steadily risen since the end of the war, amounting to $58 billion or approximately 11.5 per cent of GNP in 1961. Contrary to a common impression, total expenditures of the federal government on social welfare are consistently less by several billion dollars a year than total state and local expenditures. The gap may be narrowing; nevertheless, the welfare state, if indeed it is upon us, is more responsive to local needs and susceptible of closer local supervision than is generally supposed.[13]

---

[12] These data are taken from Series N 1-29, "Social Welfare Expenditures Under Civilian Public Programs: 1890–1956," in U.S. Bureau of the Census, *Historical Statistics of the United States, Colonial Times to 1957*, pp. 189 and 193. Included in the category of social-welfare expenditures are all social-insurance programs, public aid, health and medical programs, vocational rehabilitation, institutional care, school lunch programs, child welfare, public housing, and education. A definition of welfare programs that includes education may seem too broad, but the use of this concept is dictated by the need for a generally accepted and continuous time series.

[13] In the early 1960s welfare expenditures held at 28 per cent of all federal expenditures, whereas in recent years welfare expenditures have consistently amounted to approximately 60 per cent of all state and local expenditures. Again, we must remind ourselves that the educational component of this series is large for state and local governments.

Postwar Wall Street, represented by high-speed tapes, regained most of its lost prestige, reflected the restored graces of the businessman in general and securities dealers in particular.

There are those who view government expenditures on welfare with equanimity; indeed, this group contains a large number of articulate advocates of much greater expenditures than are presently undertaken. On the other hand, an equally vocal group insists that growing welfare expenditures serve not to buttress the capitalist economy but to weaken it. The uncontested fact is that an estimated 14 per cent of the gross national product now goes to public and private philanthropy. Despite these massive outlays a residual problem of great human need remains.

It should be observed, too, that governments at all levels serve more than the negative role of palliating social ills. Whether we like it or not, government is a positive generator of income, more than one-fifth of the gross national product currently originating in government purchases of goods and services. There is much to be said in support of the argument that lower tax rates, by leaving more income available for private expenditures, would stimulate the economy (and, paradoxically, increase total tax revenues). But few knowledgeable economists would recommend substantial reductions in government expenditures. For the fact is that a reduction in public purchases of goods and services would by no means guarantee an offsetting rise in private expenditures, and it is hard to recommend any lesser stimulus to an economy that has recently showed a persistent tendency to flag.

In particular, rapid and drastic reduction in defense expenditures from the current rate of nearly $60 billion a year would be disastrous. The defense establishment now provides direct employment for one out of every 10 workers in the labor force, and military spending provides from 10 to 30 per cent of personal income in a dozen states. Some companies are dependent on the Defense Department for 99 per cent of their sales, and many of the most distinguished firms in the country sell 25 per cent or more of their output to the federal government. Two-thirds of scientific research presently carried on in the United States is financed by the Defense Department, the Atomic Energy Commission, and the National Aeronautics and Space Administration. Only the weak-headed and the unsophisticated would suppose for a moment that the American economy could maintain anything like its present stability in the absence of federal government commitments of great magnitude.

John F. Kennedy brought to the American Presidency good nature and warmth and vibrant energy. He invested the office with high intellectual quality, bequeathing a legacy of excellence that would help his successors chart a surer course.

Since the settlement at Jamestown the American market system has performed its allocating function with a high degree of efficiency. Americans admire this impersonal mechanism, in part because freedom of economic choice is consistent with freedom of political choice, and in part because freedom of choice assures more rapid advance over a wide range of economic activity than does an authoritarian system of resource allocation, however efficient such a system may sometimes be in achieving specific, short-run goals. For the scarcest of all resources is administrative ability of a high order, and the market mechanism is often a better guide to action than conscious administrative decisions. There is much evidence that markets do not make mistakes in allocating resources as often as fallible human beings, and there is plenty of evidence that the market mechanism assures creative innovation of a high order.

The hard fact remains that a substantial number of Americans are threatened now in a new and terrible way. For them there is no longer the specter of unremitting toil but instead the equally dread possibility that there will no longer be enough work to maintain dignity and self respect. For let us make no mistake about it! The Second Industrial Revolution is replacing thought processes as well as muscles, and the neurophysiological equipment of human beings will not be much needed in many future productive processes. Under these circumstances the price system becomes less and less reliable as resource allocator. Now the historic necessity is to transfer dislocated human resources to the production of services still in demand and to do it with minimum trauma through the cooperative efforts of government and business. The problem presses so that much of the old distrust of government intervention is likely to fall away in the excitement of fighting desperately for the cause of maintaining human values.

Suggested References

The bibliography that follows contains only a part, though hopefully an important part, of the literature in economic history. In compiling this list I have avoided an ostentatious padding aimed at impressing my professional colleagues. At the same time I have tried to include enough material to facilitate the preparation of term papers and other individual or classroom projects. The list is separated into categories that correspond approximately to the major topics of the text.

I should say a word about the basis for selecting these materials. In the first place, they are all books. As the footnotes will attest, *History of the American Economy* owes a great debt to journal articles, but including the journal literature would have made for an unwieldy and perhaps too specialized bibliography. For similar reasons a mass of government documents, invaluable to historians generally, was reluctantly omitted. Finally, the towering works of political, social, and cultural history—which must always inform the thinking of the economic historian—were left out for the purely practical reason of conserving space. Books on the list are there because I have found each one to contain something of value, though they range in quality from potboilers to exquisite examples of literary craftsmanship.

The serious student of history soon learns to pursue the will-o'-the-wisp of historical fact through one footnote reference after another, and the following bibliography will give him a start on his way. Anyone requiring a further boost can begin with the five-volume *Index of Economic Journals,* published in 1961–62 by Richard D. Irwin, Inc., under the auspices of the American Economic Association. Major articles are also indexed quarterly in the periodicals section of the bibliography published each issue by the *American Economic Review,* particularly under the heading "Economic History; Economic Development; National Economies." Alternatively, the student can go directly to the indexes of *The Journal of Economic History, The Economic History Review, Business History Review,* and *Explorations in Entrepreneurial History* (recently revived and currently being published at Earlham College in its Second Series). Needless to say, *The American Historical Review* and *The Mississippi Valley Historical Review* contain articles and enormous bibliographies of use to the economic historian. But so, for that matter, do a literally countless number of periodicals to which those with antiquarian bent contribute their unending researches.

I will be happy to correspond with any student or professor seriously seeking bibliographical assistance.

The Nature of Economics
and History

ECONOMICS

Boulding, Kenneth E., *Economic Analysis,* 3rd ed., New York: Harper, 1955.
Brown, E. H. Phelps, *The Framework of the Pricing System,* London: Chapman and Hall, 1936 (rep. by University of Kansas Student Union Book Store, 1951).
Friedman, Milton, *Price Theory,* Chicago: Aldine, 1962.
Hicks, J. R., *Value and Capital,* 2nd ed., Oxford: Oxford University Press, 1946.
Knight, Frank H., *The Economic Organization,* New York: Kelley, 1951.
Leftwich, Richard H., *The Price System and Resource Allocation,* New York: Holt, Rinehart & Winston, 1961.
Marshall, Alfred, *Principles of Economics,* 8th ed., New York: Macmillan, 1949.
Noyes, C. Reinold, *Economic Man in Relation to His Natural Environment,* New York: Columbia University Press, 1948. 2 vols.
Robbins, Lionel, *An Essay on the Nature and Significance of Economic Science,* 3rd ed., New York: Macmillan, 1952.
Robinson, E. A. G., *The Structure of Competitive Industry,* New York: Harcourt, Brace & World, 1932; rev. ed., Chicago: University of Chicago Press, 1959.
Samuelson, Paul A., *Economics,* 5th ed., New York: McGraw-Hill, 1961.
Schumpeter, Joseph A., *The Theory of Economic Development,* Cambridge: Harvard University Press, 1949.
Veblen, Thorstein, *The Theory of Business Enterprise,* New York: Scribner's, 1904.
Wicksteed, Philip H., *The Common Sense of Political Economy,* London: Routledge and Kegan Paul, 1933. 2 vols.

HISTORY

Altick, Richard D., *The Scholar Adventurers,* New York: Macmillan, 1950.
Becker, C. L., *Everyman His Own Historian,* New York: Appleton-Century-Crofts, 1935.
Cheyney, E. P., *Law in History and Other Essays,* New York: Knopf, 1927.
Johnson, Allen, *The Historian and Historical Evidence,* New York: Scribner's, 1926.
Langlois, C. V., and C. Seignobos, *Introduction to the Study of History,* tr. by G. G. Berry, New York: Holt, 1909.
Malin, James C., *Essays on Historiography,* privately published, Lawrence: Kansas, 1946.
Mathews, Shailer, *The Spiritual Interpretation of History,* Cambridge: Harvard University Press, 1916.
Nevins, Allan, *The Gateway to History,* New York: Appleton-Century-Crofts, 1938.
Robinson, James Harvey, *The Mind in the Making,* New York: Harper, 1921.
Rogers, J. E. Thorold, *The Economic Interpretation of History,* New York: Putnam's, 1909.
Salmon, Lucy M., *Why Is History Rewritten?* New York: Oxford University Press, 1929.
Sée, Henri, *The Economic Intrepretation of History,* New York: Adelphi, 1929.
Seligman, E. R. A., *The Economic Interpretation of History,* 2nd ed., New York: Columbia University Press, 1924.
Taylor, Hugh, *History as a Science,* London: Methuen, 1933.
Teggart, Frederick F., *Theory and Processes of History,* Berkeley and Los Angeles: University of California Press, 1960.
Trevelyan, George Macaulay, *Clio, a Muse,* New York: Longmans, Green, 1913.

Agricultural History, the Westward Movement, and the Plantation Economy

AGRICULTURAL HISTORY

Barger, Harold, and H. H. Landsberg, *American Agriculture, 1899–1939: A Study of Output, Employment, and Productivity,* New York: National Bureau of Economic Research, 1942 (Publication No. 42).

Bidwell, P. W., and J. I. Falconer, *History of Agriculture in the Northern United States, 1620–1860,* Washington, D.C.: Carnegie Institution of Washington, 1925 (Publication No. 358).

Edwards, E. E., "American Agriculture—the First 300 Years," *1940 Yearbook of Agriculture,* Washington, D.C.: Government Printing Office.

Gates, Paul W., *The Farmer's Age: Agriculture 1815–1860,* New York: Holt, Rinehart & Winston, 1960.

Gray, Lewis C., *History of Agriculture in the Southern United States to 1860,* Washington, D.C.: Carnegie Institution of Washington, 1933. 2 vols.

Heimann, Robert, *Tobacco and Americans,* New York: McGraw-Hill, 1960.

Hulbert, A. B., *Soil: Its Influence on the History of the U.S.,* New Haven: Yale University Press, 1930.

Johnson, D. Gale, *Trade and Agriculture,* New York: Wiley, 1950.

McCormick, Cyrus, *The Century of the Reaper,* Boston: Houghton Mifflin, 1931.

Rasmussen, Wayne D., *Readings in the History of American Agriculture,* Urbana: University of Illinois Press, 1960.

Rogin, Leo, *The Introduction of Farm Machinery in Its Relation to the Productivity of Labor in the Agriculture of the United States During the Nineteenth Century,* Berkeley: University of California Press, 1931 (Publications in Economics, Vol. IX).

Schultz, Theodore W., *Agriculture in an Unstable Economy,* New York: McGraw-Hill, 1945.

—— *The Economic Organization of Agriculture,* New York: McGraw-Hill, 1953.

Shannon, Fred A., *Economic History of the United States,* Vol. V, *The Farmer's Last Frontier: Agriculture 1860–1879,* New York: Farrar and Rinehart, 1945.

Shepherd, Geoffrey S., *Agricultural Price and Income Policy,* 3rd ed., Ames: Iowa State College Press, 1952.

Tostlebe, Alvin S., *The Growth of Physical Capital in Agriculture,* New York: National Bureau of Economic Research, 1954 (Studies in Capital Formation and Financing, Occasional Paper 44).

THE WESTWARD MOVEMENT

Abernethy, T. P., *Western Lands and the American Revolution,* New York: Appleton-Century-Crofts, 1937 (Virginia University Institute for Research in the Social Sciences, Institute Monograph No. 25).

Adams, Ramon, *The Old-Time Cowhand,* New York: Macmillan, 1961.

Atherton, Lewis E., *The Cattle Kings,* Bloomington: Indiana University Press, 1962.

—— *Main Street on the Middle Border,* Bloomington: Indiana University Press, 1954.

—— *The Pioneer Merchant in Mid-America,* Columbia: University of Missouri Press, 1939.

—— *The Southern Country Store, 1800–1860,* Baton Rouge: Louisiana State University Press, 1949.

Billington, Ray A., *Westward Expansion,* 2nd ed., New York: Macmillan, 1960.

Chittenden, Hiram Martin, *The American Fur Trade of the Far West,* Stanford: Stanford University Academic Reprint, 1954. 2 vols.

Clark, Dan E., *The West in American History,* New York: Crowell, 1937.

Clark, T. D., *Pills, Petticoats and Plows: The Southern Country Store,* Indianapolis: Bobbs-Merrill, 1944.

Coman, Katherine, *Economic Beginnings of the Far West,* New York: Macmillan, 1925.

Dale, E. E., *Cow Country,* Norman: University of Oklahoma Press, 1942.

———— *The Range Cattle Industry,* Norman: University of Oklahoma Press, 1930.

Defebaugh, J. E., *History of the Lumber Industry of America,* Chicago: American Lumberman, 1906–07.

Dick, Everett N., *The Sod-House Frontier, 1854–1890,* New York: Appleton-Century-Crofts, 1937.

Hibbard, B. H., *A History of the Public Land Policies,* New York: Macmillan, 1924 (Land Economics Series).

Hulbert, A. B., *Soil: Its Influence on the History of the United States,* New Haven: Yale University Press, 1930.

Innis, H. A., *The Fur Trade in Canada,* rev. ed., Toronto: University of Toronto Press, 1956.

Ise, John, *Our National Park Policy: A Critical History,* published for Resources for the Future, Inc., Baltimore: Johns Hopkins Press, 1961.

———— *United States Forest Policy,* New Haven: Yale University Press, 1920.

———— *United States Oil Policy,* New Haven: Yale University Press, 1926.

Lavender, David, *Bent's Fort,* Garden City: Doubleday, 1954.

McFarland, R., *A History of the New England Fisheries,* Philadelphia: University of Pennsylvania Press, 1911 (Publications in Political Economy and Public Law No. 24).

Paxson, F. L., *History of the American Frontier, 1763–1893,* Boston: Houghton Mifflin, 1924.

Prucha, Francis Paul, S.J., *American Indian Policy in the Formative Years: The Indian Trade and Intercourse Acts, 1780–1834,* Cambridge: Harvard University Press, 1962.

Robbins, R. M., *Our Landed Heritage: The Public Domain 1776–1936,* Princeton: Princeton University Press, 1942.

Tower, W. S., *A History of American Whale Fishery,* Philadelphia: University of Pennsylvania Publication, 1907.

Treat, P. J., *The National Land System, 1785–1820,* New York: Treat, 1910.

Turner, F. J., *The Frontier in American History,* New York: Holt, 1921.

———— *The Significance of Sections in American History,* New York: Holt, 1932.

THE PLANTATION ECONOMY

Bancroft, Frederic, *Slave Trading in the Old South,* Baltimore: Furst, 1931.

Cairnes, J. E., *The Slave Power,* 2nd ed., New York: Carleton, 1862.

Dow, G. F., *Slave Ships and Slaving,* Salem, Mass.: Marine Research Society, 1927.

Elkins, Stanley M., *Slavery: A Problem in American Institutional and Intellectual Life,* Chicago: University of Chicago Press, 1959.

Hart, A. B., *Slavery and Abolition,* New York: Harper, 1906.

Hedges, James B., *The Browns of Providence Plantations: Colonial Years,* Cambridge: Harvard University Press, 1952.

Olmsted, Frederick L., *The Cotton Kingdom,* 1861, ed. by A. M. Schlesinger, New York: Knopf, 1953.

Phillips, U. B., *American Negro Slavery,* New York: Appleton, 1918.

———— *Life and Labor in the Old South,* Boston: Little, Brown, 1929.

Stampp, Kenneth M., *The Peculiar Institution: Slavery in the Ante-Bellum South,* New York: Knopf, 1956.

Transportation

Abbot, W. J., *The Story of Our Merchant Marine,* New York: Dodd, Mead, 1919.

Barger, Harold, *The Transportation Industries 1889–1946,* New York: National Bureau of Economic Research, 1951 (Publication No. 51).

Clark, A. H., *The Clipper Ship Era, 1843–1849,* New York: Putnam's, 1910.

Cochran, Thomas C., *Railroad Leaders, 1845–1890, The Business Mind in Action,* Cambridge: Harvard University Press, 1953.

Dearing, C. L., *American Highway Policy,* Washington, D.C.: Brookings Institution, 1941.

Dearing, C. L., and Wilfred Owen, *National Transportation Policy,* Washington, D.C.: Brookings Institution, 1949.

Duffus, R. L., *The Sante Fe Trail,* New York: Longmans, Green, 1930.

Fogel, Robert William, *The Union Pacific Railroad,* Baltimore: Johns Hopkins Press, 1960.

Grodinsky, Julius, *Transcontinental Railway Strategy, 1869–1893,* Philadelphia: University of Pennsylvania Press, 1962.

Harlow, A. F., *Old Towpaths,* New York: Appleton-Century-Crofts, 1926.

Hoyt, Edwin P., *The Vanderbilts and Their Fortunes,* Garden City: Doubleday, 1962.

Hulbert, A. B., *Paths of Inland Commerce,* New Haven: Yale University Press, 1920.

Kirkland, E. C., *Men, Cities, and Transportation,* Cambridge: Harvard University Press, 1948. 2 vols.

Leonard, W. N., *Railroad Consolidation Under the Transportation Act of 1920,* New York: Columbia University Press, 1946 (Studies in History, Economics, and Public Law No. 522).

MacGill, C. E., and others, *History of Transportation in the United States Before 1860,* Washington, D.C.: Carnegie Institute of Washington, 1917.

McKee, M. M., *Ship Subsidy Question in United States Politics,* Northampton: Smith College, 1922 (Studies in History, Vol. VIII, No. 1).

Mencken, August, *The Railroad Passenger Car,* Baltimore: Johns Hopkins Press, 1957.

Miller, J. A., *Fares, Please!* New York: Appleton-Century-Crofts, 1941.

Morrison, John H., *American Steam Navigation,* New York: Sametz, 1903.

Puffer, C. E., *Air Transportation,* Philadelphia: Blakiston, 1941.

Ripley, W. Z., *Railroads; Rates and Regulations,* New York: Longmans, Green, 1912.

Rosskam, Edwin, and Louise Rosskam, *Towboat River,* New York: Duell, Sloan and Pearce, 1948.

Ulmer, Melville J., *Trends and Cycles in Capital Formation by United States Railroads, 1870–1950,* New York: National Bureau of Economic Research, 1954.

Financial History

Alhadeff, David A., *Monopoly and Competition in Banking,* Berkeley: University of California Press, 1954.

Allen, Frederick Lewis, *The Great Pierpont Morgan,* New York: Bantam Books, 1949.

Bach, G. L., *Federal Reserve Policy-Making,* New York: Knopf, 1950.

Balinky, Alexander, *Albert Gallatin: Fiscal Theories and Policies,* New Brunswick: Rutgers University Press, 1958.

Barrett, Don C., *The Greenbacks and the Resumption of Specie Payments, 1862–1879,* Cambridge: Harvard University Press, 1931 (Harvard Economics Studies, Vol. XXXVI).

Behrens, Kathryn L., *Paper Money in Maryland, 1727–1789,* Baltimore: Johns Hopkins Press, 1923.

Bolles, Albert Sidney, *Financial History of the United States,* New York: Appleton, 1885. 3 vols.

Bourne, Edward G., *The History of the Surplus Revenue of 1837,* New York: Putnam's, 1885.

Bray, Hammond, *Banks and Politics in America from the Revolution to the Civil War,* Princeton: Princeton University Press, 1957.

Bullock, C. J., *Essays on the Monetary History of the United States,* New York: Macmillan, 1900.

—— *Finances of the United States, 1775–1789,* Madison: University of Wisconsin Press, 1895 (Economic, Political Science, and History Series, Vol. I, No. 2).

Catterall, Ralph C. H., *The Second Bank of the United States,* Chicago: University of Chicago Press, 1903.

Chaddock, Robert E., *The Safety Fund Banking System in New York, 1829–1866,* Washington, D.C.: Government Printing Office, 1910.

Columbia University Council for Research in the Social Sciences, *The New York Money Market,* ed. by Benjamin H. Beckhart, New York: Columbia University Press, 1931–32. 4 vols.

Conant, Charles A., *A History of Modern Banks of Issue,* New York: Putnam's, 1896.

Davis, A. M., *The Origin of the National Banking System,* Washington, D.C.: Government Printing Office, 1910–11.

—— *Colonial Currency Reprints, 1682–1751,* Boston: Prince Society, 1910.

Dewey, D. R., *Financial History of the United States,* New York: Longmans, Green, 1934.

—— *State Banking Before the Civil War,* Washington, D.C.: Government Printing Office, 1910.

Dillistin, William H., *Bank Note Reporters and Counterfeit Detectors, 1826–1866, with a Discourse on Wildcat Banks and Wildcat Bank Notes,* New York: American Numismatic Society, 1949.

Dunbar, Charles F., *The Theory and History of Banking,* New York: Putnam's, 1922.

Eccles, Marriner S., *Beckoning Frontiers,* New York: Knopf, 1951.

Fforde, J. S., *The Federal Reserve System, 1945–1949,* New York: Oxford University Press, 1954.

Friedman, Milton, and Anna J. Schwartz, *A Monetary History of the United States, 1867–1960,* Princeton: Princeton University Press, 1963 (National Bureau of Economic Research, Studies in Business Cycles 12).

Gibbons, James S., *The Banks of New York, Their Dealers, the Clearing House, and the Panic of 1857,* New York: Appleton, 1858.

Goldenweiser, E. A., *American Monetary Policy,* New York: McGraw-Hill, 1951.

Goldsmith, Raymond W., *The Share of Financial Intermediaries in National Wealth and National Assets, 1900–1949,* New York: National Bureau of Economic Research, 1954 (Studies in Capital Formation and Financing, Occasional Paper).

Golembe, Carter H., *State Banks and the Economic Development of the West, 1830–1844,* New York: Columbia University Press, 1952.

Gouge, William M., *A Short History of Paper Money and Banking in the U.S. Including an Account of Provincial and Continental Paper Money,* Philadelphia: Usbick, 1883.

Govan, Thomas Payne, *Nicholas Biddle,* Chicago: University of Chicago Press, 1959.

Grayson, Theodore J., *Leaders and Periods of American Finance,* New York: Wiley, 1932.

Greef, Albert O., *The Commercial Paper House in the U.S.,* Cambridge: Harvard University Press, 1938.

Hacker, Louis M., *Alexander Hamilton in the American Tradition,* New York: McGraw-Hill, 1957.

Hardy, C. O., *Credit Policies of the Federal Reserve System*, Washington, D.C.: Brookings Institution, 1932 (Institute of Economics Publication No. 45).

Harris, S. E., *Twenty Years of Federal Reserve Policy*, Cambridge: Harvard University Press, 1933 (Harvard Economic Studies, Vol. XLI).

Hart, Albert Gailord, *Debts and Recovery*, New York: Twentieth Century Fund, 1938.

—— *Money, Debt, and Economic Activity*, 2nd ed., New York: Prentice-Hall, 1953.

Hedges, Joseph Edward, *Commercial Banking and the Stock Market Before 1863*, Baltimore: Johns Hopkins Press, 1938.

Helderman, Leonard C., *National and State Banks*, Boston: Houghton Mifflin, 1931.

Hepburn, A. B., *History of Currency in the United States*, rev. ed., New York: Macmillan, 1924.

Holdsworth, John Thom, and Davis R. Dewey, *The First and Second Banks of the United States*, Washington, D.C.: Government Printing Office, 1910.

Howe, Frederic C., *Taxation and Taxes in the U.S. Under the Internal Revenue System, 1791–1895*, New York: Crowell, 1896.

Huntington, A. T., and Robert J. Mawhinney, *Laws of the United States Concerning Money, Banking and Loans, 1778–1909*, Washington, D.C.: Government Printing Office, 1910.

James, Frank C., *The Economics of Money, Credit and Banking*, 3rd ed., New York: Ronald, 1940.

—— *The Growth of Chicago Banks*, New York: Harper, 1938. 2 vols.

James, Marquis, *The Metropolitan Life: A Study in Business Growth*, New York: Viking, 1947.

Larson, Henrietta, *Jay Cooke, Private Banker*, Cambridge: Harvard University Press, 1936 (Harvard Studies in Business History, Vol. II).

Laughlin, J. L., *History of Bimetallism in the United States*, 4th ed., New York: Appleton-Century-Crofts, 1897.

Lester, Richard Allen, *Monetary Experiments, Early American and Recent Scandinavian*, Princeton: Princeton University Press, 1939.

Levinson, Leonard Lewis, *Wall Street, A Pictorial History*, New York: Ziff-Davis, 1961.

Lewis, Lawrence, Jr., *A History of the Bank of North America*, Philadelphia, 1882.

Linderman, Henry R., *Money and Legal Tender in the United States*, New York: Putnam's, 1878.

McKee, Samuel, Jr., *Alexander Hamilton: Papers on Public Credit, Commerce and Finance*, New York: Columbia University Press, 1934.

Members of the Staff of the Board of Governors of the Federal Reserve System, *Banking Studies*, 1941. 3 vols.

Miller, Harry E., *Banking Theories in the United States Before 1860*, Cambridge: Harvard University Press, 1927 (Harvard Economic Studies).

Mints, Lloyd W., *A History of Banking Theory in Great Britain and the United States*, Chicago: University of Chicago Press, 1945.

Mitchell, Wesley, *A History of Greenbacks*, Chicago: University of Chicago Press, 1903.

Nettels, C. P., *The Money Supply of the American Colonies Before 1720*, Madison: University of Wisconsin Press, 1934 (Studies in the Social Sciences and History No. 20).

Noyes, Alexander D., *Thirty Years of American Finance (1865–1896)*, New York: Putnam's, 1898.

—— *The War Period of American Finance (1908–1925)*, New York: Putnam's, 1926.

O'Connor, James F. T., *The Banking Crisis and Recovery under the Roosevelt Administration*, Chicago: Callaghan, 1938.

Payne, Peter L., and Lance E. Davis, *The Savings Bank of Baltimore, 1818–1866,* Baltimore: Johns Hopkins Press, 1956.

Ratchford, B. U., *American State Debts,* Durham: Duke University Press, 1941.

Ratner, Sidney, *American Taxation,* New York: Norton, 1942.

Redlich, Fritz, *The Molding of American Banking: Men and Ideas,* New York: Hafner, 1947 (Part I), 1951 (Part II).

Riefler, Winfield W., *Money Rates and Money Markets in the United States,* New York: Harper, 1930.

Ripley, William Z., *The Financial History of Virginia, 1609–1776,* New York: Columbia University Press, 1893.

Shultz, W. J., and M. R. Caine, *Financial Development of the United States,* New York: Prentice-Hall, 1937.

Smith, Walter B., *Economic Aspects of the Second Bank of the United States,* Cambridge: Harvard University Press, 1953 (Studies in Economic History Series).

Sumner, William G., *The Financier and the Finances of the American Revolution,* New York: Dodd, Mead, 1891. 2 vols.

—— *A History of American Currency,* New York: Putnam's, 1878.

Taus, Esther Rogoff, *Central Banking Functions of the U.S. Treasury, 1789–1941,* New York: Columbia University Press, 1943.

Taylor, George R., ed., *Jackson vs. Biddle; The Struggle Over the Second Bank of the United States,* Boston: Heath, 1949 (Problems in American Civilization, Vol. 3).

Upham, Cyril B., and Edwin Lamke, *Closed and Distressed Banks,* Washington, D.C.: Brookings Institution, 1934 (Institute of Economics Publication No. 58).

Walters, Raymond, Jr., *Albert Gallatin: Jeffersonian Financier and Diplomat,* New York: Macmillan, 1957.

Warburg, P. M., *The Federal Reserve System,* New York: Macmillan, 1930. 2 vols.

Warren, G. F., and F. A. Pearson, *Prices,* New York: Wiley, 1933.

Watkins, Leonard L., *Bankers' Balances,* New York: McGraw-Hill, 1929.

Watson, David K., *History of American Coinage,* New York: Putnam's, 1899.

Industry and Commerce

INDUSTRIAL DEVELOPMENT

Alderfer, E. B., and H. E. Michl, *Economics of American Industry,* 2nd ed., New York: McGraw-Hill, 1957.

Allen, Frederick Lewis, *Lords of Creation,* New York: Harper, 1935.

Ashton, T. S., *The Industrial Revolution, 1760–1830,* London: Oxford University Press, 1961.

Barger, Harold, and S. H. Schurr, *Mining Industries, 1899–1939: A Study of Output, Employment and Productivity,* New York: National Bureau of Economic Research, 1944.

Berglund, Abraham, *The United States Steel Corporation,* New York: Columbia University Press, 1907.

Bining, A. C., *British Regulation of the Colonial Iron Industry,* Philadelphia: University of Pennsylvania Press, 1933.

Bishop, James Leander, *A History of American Manufacturers from 1608–1860,* Philadelphia: Young, 1868. 2 vols.

Bolles, Albert S., *Industrial History of the United States,* Norwich, Conn.: Henry Bill, 1881.

Borenstein, Israel, *Capital and Output Trends in Mining Industries, 1870–1948,* New York: National Bureau of Economic Research, 1954.

Boulding, Kenneth E., *The Organizational Revolution,* New York: Harper, 1953.

Bowden, Witt, *The Industrial History of the United States,* New York: Adelphi, 1930.

Bridenbaugh, Carl, *The Colonial Craftsman,* New York: New York University Press, 1950.

Burlingame, Roger, *Engines of Democracy: Inventions and Society in Mature America,* New York: Scribner's, 1940.

Burns, A. F., *Production Trends in the United States Since 1870,* New York: National Bureau of Economic Research, 1934.

Clark, V. S., *History of Manufacturers in the United States, 1607–1914,* Washington, D.C.: Carnegie Institution of Washington, 1916–28. 2 vols.

Clow, Archibald, *The Chemical Revolution,* London: Batchworth Press, 1952.

Cole, Arthur Harrison, *The American Wool Manufacture,* Cambridge: Harvard University Press, 1926. 2 vols.

Collins, J. H., *The Story of Canned Foods,* New York: Dutton, 1924.

Coman, Katharine, *The Industrial History of the United States,* New York: Macmillan, 1918.

Copeland, M. T., *The Cotton Manufacturing Industry of the United States,* Cambridge: Harvard University Press, 1912 (Harvard Economic Studies, Vol. VIII).

Creamer, Daniel B., *Capital and Output Trends in Manufacturing Industries, 1880–1948,* New York: National Bureau of Economic Research, 1954 (Studies in Capital Formation and Financing, Occasional Paper No. 41).

Defebaugh, J. E., *History of the Lumber Industry of America,* Chicago: American Lumberman, 1906–07. 2 vols.

Frickey, Edwin, *Production in the United States, 1860–1914,* Cambridge: Harvard University Press, 1947 (Harvard Economic Studies, Vol. LXXXII).

Gras, N. S. B., *Industrial Evolution,* Cambridge: Harvard University Press, 1930.

Grebler, Leo, *The Role of Federal Credit Aids in Residential Construction,* New York: National Bureau of Economic Research, 1953.

Habakkuk, H. J., *American and British Technology in the Nineteenth Century,* Cambridge: Cambridge University Press, 1962.

Hartley, Edward N., *Ironworks on the Saugus: The Lynn and Braintree Ventures of the Company of Undertakers of the Iron Works in New England,* Norman: University of Oklahoma Press, 1957.

Hazard, B. E., *The Organization of the Boot and Shoe Industry in Massachusetts before 1873,* Cambridge: Harvard University Press, 1921 (Harvard Economic Studies, Vol. XXIII).

Hendrick, B. J., *Life of Andrew Carnegie,* Garden City: Doubleday, 1932. 2 vols.

Jerome, Harry, *Mechanization in Industry,* New York: National Bureau of Economic Research, 1934.

Kennedy, E. D., *The Automobile Industry,* New York: Reynal and Hitchcock, 1941.

Kuhlmann, C. B., *Development of the Flour-Milling Industry in the United States,* Boston: Houghton Mifflin, 1929.

MacLaren, Malcolm, *The Rise of the Electric Industry During the Nineteenth Century,* Princeton: Princeton University Press, 1943.

Mantoux, Paul J., *The Industrial Revolution in the Eighteenth Century,* New York: Harcourt, Brace & World, 1935.

Mee, John F., *Management Thought In A Dynamic Economy,* New York: New York University Press, 1963.

Rae, John B., *American Automobile Manufacturers,* New York: Chilton, 1959.

Roe, Joseph Wickham, *English and American Tool Builders,* New Haven: Yale University Press, 1916.

Roll, Erich, *An Early Experiment in Industrial Organization, Being a History of the Firm of Boulton and Watt, 1775–1805,* New York: Longmans, Green, 1930.

Rosen, S. McKee, and Laura Rosen, *Technology and Society: the Influence of Machines in the United States,* New York: Macmillan, 1941.

Shaw, William Howard, *Value of Commodity Output Since 1869,* New York: National Bureau of Economic Research, 1947 (Publication No. 48).

Thompson, Holland, *The Age of Invention,* New Haven: Yale University Press, 1921.

Tryon, Rolla M., *Household Manufactures in the United States, 1640–1860,* Chicago: University of Chicago Press, 1917.

Unwin, George, *Industrial Organization in the Sixteenth and Seventeenth Centuries,* London: Case, 1957.

Usher, A. P., *History of Mechanical Invention,* New York: McGraw-Hill, 1929.

Usher, A. P., *The Industrial History of England,* Boston: Houghton Mifflin, 1920.

Ware, Caroline F., *The Early New England Cotton Manufacture: A Study in Industrial Beginnings,* New York: Houghton Mifflin, 1931.

Wiener, Norbert, *The Human Use of Human Beings: Cybernetics and Society,* Boston: Houghton Mifflin, 1950.

Williamson, Harold F., *Winchester, The Gun That Won the West,* Washington, D.C.: Combat Forces Press, 1952.

Williamson, Harold F., and Arnold R. Daum, *The American Petroleum Industry: The Age of Illumination, 1859–1899,* Evanston: Northwestern University Press, 1959.

Woodworth, J. V., *American Tool Making and Interchangeable Manufacturing,* 2nd ed., New York: Henley, 1911.

Zimmermann, Erich W., *World Resources and Industries,* New York: Harper, 1933.

FOREIGN AND DOMESTIC COMMERCE

Ashworth, William, *A Short History of the International Economy, 1850–1950,* New York: Longmans, Green, 1952.

Bailyn, Bernard, *The New England Merchants in the Seventeenth Century,* Cambridge: Harvard University Press, 1955.

Baxter, William T., *The House of Hancock; Business in Boston, 1724–1775,* Cambridge: Harvard University Press, 1945.

Beckman, Theodore N., and Nathanael H. Engle, *Wholesaling,* 3rd ed., New York: Ronald, 1959.

Beer, G. L., *Commercial Policy of England Toward the American Colonies,* New York: Columbia University Press, 1893 (Studies in History, Economics, and Public Law, Vol. III, No. 2).

Bloomfield, Arthur I., *Capital Imports and the American Balance of Payments, 1934–39,* Chicago: University of Chicago Press, 1950.

Buck, Norman S., *The Development of the Organization of Anglo-American Trade, 1800–1850,* New Haven: Yale University Press, 1925.

Clark, T. D., *Pills, Petticoats and Plows: The Southern Country Store,* Indianapolis: Bobbs-Merrill, 1944.

Condliffe, J. B., *The Commerce of Nations,* New York: Norton, 1950.

Craven, Wesley F., *Dissolution of the Virginia Company: The Failure of a Colonial Experiment,* New York: Oxford University Press, 1932.

Depew, C. M., ed., *One Hundred Years of American Commerce,* New York: Haynes, 1895. 2 vols.

East, R. A., *Business Enterprise in the American Revolutionary Era,* New York: Columbia University Press, 1938 (Studies in History, Economics, and Public Law No. 439).

Einzig, Paul, *The History of Foreign Exchange,* New York: St. Martin's, 1962.

Gibb, George Sweet, *The Whitesmiths of Taunton,* Cambridge: Harvard University Press, 1946.

Harrington, Virginia D., *The New York Merchant on the Eve of the Revolution,* New York: Columbia University Press, 1935.

Hayden, J. R., *The Philippines: A Study in National Development,* Toronto: Macmillan, 1942.

Hidy, Ralph W., *The House of Baring in American Trade and Finance; English Merchant Bankers at Work, 1763–1861,* Cambridge: Harvard University Press, 1949.

Hill, H. C., *Roosevelt and the Caribbean,* Chicago: University of Chicago Press, 1927.

Hotchkiss, George Burton, *Milestones of Marketing,* New York: Macmillan, 1938.

Hower, Ralph M., *History of Macy's of New York, 1858–1919,* Cambridge: Harvard University Press, 1943.

Hughes, J. R. T., *Fluctuations in Trade, Industry and Finance, A Study of British Economic Developments, 1850–1860,* Oxford: Oxford University Press, 1960.

Johnson, Emory R., and others, *History of Domestic and Foreign Commerce of the United States,* 2nd ed., Pittsburgh: Carnegie Press, 1915.

Knight, M. M., *The Americans in Santo Domingo,* New York: Vanguard, 1928 (Studies in American Imperialism).

McCain, W. D., *The United States and the Republic of Panama,* Durham: Duke University Press, 1937.

McMaster, John B., *The Life and Times of Stephen Girard,* Philadelphia: Lippincott, 1918.

Mikesell, Raymond F., *Foreign Exchange in the Postwar World,* New York: Twentieth Century Fund, 1954.

Nearing, Scott, and Joseph Freeman, *Dollar Diplomacy,* New York: Viking, 1925.

Pares, Richard, *Yankees and Creoles: The Trade Between North America and the West Indies Before the American Revolution,* Cambridge: Harvard University Press, 1956.

Porter, Kenneth W., *The Jacksons and the Lees: Two Generations of Massachusetts Merchants, 1765–1844,* Vol. I, Cambridge: Harvard University Press, 1937.

—— *John Jacob Astor, Business Man,* Cambridge: Harvard University Press, 1931.

Presbrey, Frank S., *The History and Development of Advertising,* Garden City: Doubleday, 1929.

Rippy, J. F., *Latin America and the Industrial Age,* New York: Putnam's, 1944.

Schlesinger, A. M., *The Colonial Merchants and the American Revolution,* New York: Columbia University Press, 1918 (Studies in History, Economics, and Public Law No. 182).

Sellers, Leila, *Charleston Business on the Eve of the American Revolution,* Chapel Hill: University of North Carolina Press, 1934.

Stuart, G. H., *Latin America and the United States,* 4th ed., New York: Appleton-Century-Crofts, 1943.

Taussig, F. W., *Tariff History of the United States,* 7th ed., New York: Putnam's, 1923.

Thorp, Willard H., *Trade, Aid, or What?* Baltimore: Johns Hopkins Press, 1954.

Viner, Jacob, *International Trade and Economic Development,* Glencoe, Ill.: Free Press, 1952.

MONOPOLY AND CONCENTRATION OF INDUSTRY

Alhadeff, David A., *Monopoly and Competition in Banking,* Berkeley: University of California Press, 1954 (Bureau of Business and Economic Research Publications).

Allen, F. L., *Lords of Creation,* New York: Harper, 1935.

Berle, Adolf A., Jr., *The 20th Century Capitalist Revolution,* New York: Harcourt, Brace & World, 1954.

Berle, Adolf A., Jr., and G. C. Means, *The Modern Corporation and Private Property,* Chicago: Commerce Clearing House, 1932.

Bonbright, J. C., and G. C. Means, *The Holding Company*, New York: McGraw-Hill, 1932.

Boulding, Kenneth E., *The Organizational Revolution*, New York: Harper, 1953.

Burns, A. R., *The Decline of Competition*, Columbia University Council for Research in the Social Sciences, New York: McGraw-Hill, 1936.

Chandler, Alfred D., Jr., *Strategy and Structure*, Cambridge: Massachusetts Institute of Technology Press, 1962.

—— *Giant Enterprise: Ford, General Motors, and the Automobile Industry*, New York: Harcourt, Brace & World, 1964.

Davis, Joseph S., *Essays in the Earlier History of American Corporations*, Cambridge: Harvard University Press, 1917.

Fetter, Frank A., *The Masquerade of Monopoly*, New York: Harcourt, Brace & World, 1931.

Josephson, Matthew, *Robber Barons: The Great American Capitalists, 1861–1901*, New York: Harcourt, Brace & World, 1934.

Kaplan, A. D. H., *Big Enterprise in a Competitive System*, Washington, D.C.: Brookings Institution, 1954.

Machlup, Fritz, *The Political Economy of Monopoly*, Baltimore: Johns Hopkins Press, 1952.

Moody, John, *The Truth About the Trusts*, New York: Moody, 1904.

Myers, Gustavus, *History of Great American Fortunes*, Chicago: Kerr, 1910. 3 vols.

Nevins, Allan, *John D. Rockefeller: The Heroic Age of American Business*, New York: Scribner's, 1940. 2 vols.

Regier, C. C., *The Era of the Muckrakers*, Chapel Hill: University of North Carolina Press, 1932.

Steffens, Joseph Lincoln, *Autobiography of Lincoln Steffens*, New York: Harcourt, Brace & World, 1931. 2 vols.

Stocking, George W., and Myron W. Watkins, *Monopoly and Free Enterprise*, New York: Twentieth Century Fund, 1951.

Tarbell, Ida M., *History of the Standard Oil Company*, New York: Macmillan, 1925. 2 vols.

Labor

Abbott, Edith, *Historical Aspects of the Immigration Problem*, Chicago: University of Chicago Press, 1926 (University of Chicago Social Service Series).

Ahearn, Daniel J., *The Wages of Farm and Factory Laborers, 1914–1944*, New York: Columbia University Press, 1945 (Studies in History, Economics, and Public Law No. 518).

Beard, Mary, *A Short History of the American Labor Movement*, New York: Macmillan, 1927.

Bell, Spurgeon, *Productivity, Wages and National Income*, Washington, D.C.: Brookings Institution, 1940 (Institute of Economics Publication No. 81).

Brissenden, P. F., *The I. W. W., A Study of American Syndicalism*, 2nd ed., New York: Columbia University Press, 1920 (Studies in History, Economics, and Public Law No. 193).

Bureau of Labor Statistics, *History of Wages in the United States from the Colonial Times to 1928*, Washington, D.C.: Government Printing Office, 1929.

Clark, M. R., and S. F. Simon, *The Labor Movement in America*, New York: Norton, 1938.

Commons, J. R., *Documentary History of American Industrial Society*, ed. by J. R. Commons and others, Cleveland: Clark, 1910–11. 10 vols.

Commons, J. R., and others, *History of Labor in the United States*, New York: Macmillan, 1918. 4 vols.

Daugherty, Carroll R., *Labor Problems in American Industry,* 5th ed., Boston: Houghton Mifflin, 1941.

David, Henry, *History of the Haymarket Affair,* 2nd ed., New York: Russell & Russell, 1958.

Dempsey, Bernard W., *The Frontier Wage: The Economic Organization of Free Agents,* Chicago: Loyola University Press, 1960.

Douglas, Paul H., *Real Wages in the United States, 1890–1926,* Boston: Houghton Mifflin, 1930 (Pollak Foundation Publication No. 9).

—— *The Theory of Wages,* New York: Macmillan, 1934.

Ely, R. T., *The Labor Movement in America,* New York: Crowell, 1886.

Foner, Philip S., *History of the Labor Movement in the United States,* Vol. I, New York: International Publishers, 1947.

Jenks, J. W., and W. J. Lauck, *The Immigration Problem,* New York: Funk and Wagnalls, 1912.

Kuznets, Simon, and Ernest Rubin, *Immigration and the Foreign Born,* New York: National Bureau of Economic Research, 1954.

Millis, Harry A., and Emily C. Brown, *From the Wagner Act to Taft-Hartley,* Chicago: University of Chicago Press, 1950.

Millis, Harry A., and Royal E. Montgomery, *Economics of Labor,* Vol. III: *Organized Labor,* New York: McGraw-Hill, 1945.

Mills, Frederick C., *Productivity and Economic Progress,* New York: National Bureau of Economic Research, 1952.

Perlman, Selig, *A History of Trade Unionism in the United States,* New York: Macmillan, 1922.

Rees, Albert, *Real Wages in Manufacturing, 1890–1914,* Princeton: Princeton University Press, 1961.

Saposs, D. J., and B. T. Saposs, *Readings in Trade Unionism,* New York: Macmillan, 1927.

Smith, Abbot Emerson, *Colonists in Bondage,* Chapel Hill: University of North Carolina Press, 1947.

Solomon, Barbara M., *Ancestors and Immigrants, A Changing New England Tradition,* Cambridge: Harvard University Press, 1956.

Stephenson, G. M., *History of American Immigration, 1820–1924,* Boston: Ginn, 1926.

Ware, Norman J., *The Industrial Worker, 1840–1860,* Boston: Houghton Mifflin, 1924.

—— *The Labor Movement in the United States,* New York: Appleton-Century-Crofts, 1929.

Wolman, Leo, *Growth of American Trade Unions 1880–1923,* New York: National Bureau of Economic Research, 1924 (Publication No. 6).

Woytinsky, W. S., and associates, *Employment and Wages in the United States,* New York: Twentieth Century Fund, 1953.

Wright, David McCord, ed., *The Impact of the Union,* New York: Harcourt, Brace & World, 1951.

Economic Growth and Fluctuations

Cole, A. H., *Wholesale Commodity Prices in the United States, 1700–1861,* Cambridge: Harvard University Press, 1938 (International Scientific Commission on Price History). 2 vols.

Collman, Charles A., *Our Mysterious Panics, 1830–1930,* New York: Morrow, 1931.

Fellner, William J., *Trends and Cycles in Economic Activity: An Introduction to Problems of Economic Growth,* New York: Holt, 1956.

Fels, Rendigs, *American Business Cycles, 1865–1897,* Chapel Hill: University of North Carolina Press, 1959.

Frickey, Edwin, *Economic Fluctuations in the United States,* Cambridge: Harvard University Press, 1942 (Harvard Economic Studies, Vol. LXXIII).

—— *Production in the United States, 1860–1914,* Cambridge: Harvard University Press, 1947 (Harvard Economic Studies, Vol. LXXXII).

Galbraith, John Kenneth, *The Great Crash,* Boston: Houghton Mifflin, 1955.

Goldsmith, Raymond W., *Income and Wealth of the U.S., Trends and Structure,* Cambridge, England: Bowes & Bowes, 1952.

—— *A Study of Savings in the U.S.,* Princeton: Princeton University Press, 1955.

Gordon, Margaret S., *Employment Expansion and Population Growth,* Los Angeles: University of California Press, 1954.

Grebler, Leo, *Capital Formation in Residential Real Estate, Trends and Prospects,* Princeton: Princeton University Press, 1956.

Hansen, Alvin H., *Business Cycles and National Income,* New York: Norton, 1951.

Harris, Seymour E., *Inflation and the American Economy,* New York: McGraw-Hill, 1945.

Kuznets, Simon, *Cyclical Fluctuations,* New York: Greenberg, 1926.

—— *National Income, A Summary of Findings,* New York: National Bureau of Economic Research, 1946 (Twenty-fifth Anniversary Series No. 1).

—— *National Product in Wartime,* New York: National Bureau of Economic Research, 1945 (Publication No. 44).

Jenks, Leland H., *The Migration of British Capital to 1875,* New York: Knopf, 1927.

Kendrick, John W., *Productivity Trends in the United States,* Princeton: Princeton University Press, 1961.

Lewis, W. Arthur, *The Theory of Economic Growth,* London: Allen & Unwin, 1955.

Martin, Robert F., *National Income in the United States, 1799–1938,* New York: National Industrial Conference Board, 1939.

Matthews, R. C. O., *A Study in Trade Cycle History, Economic Fluctuations in Great Britain, 1833–1842,* Cambridge: Cambridge University Press, 1954.

McGrane, R. C., *The Panic of 1837,* Chicago: University of Chicago Press, 1924.

Mills, Frederick C., *Productivity and Economic Progress,* New York: National Bureau of Economic Research, 1952.

Mitchell, Wesley, *Business Cycles; the Problem and Its Setting,* New York: National Bureau of Economic Research, 1927 (Publication No. 10).

Morris, Bruce R., *The Problems of American Economic Growth,* New York: Oxford University Press, 1961.

National Bureau of Economic Research, *Trends in the American Economy in the Nineteenth Century, Studies in Income and Wealth,* Vol. 24, Princeton: Princeton University Press, 1960.

North, Douglas C., *The Economic Growth of the United States, 1790 to 1860,* Englewood Cliffs, N.J.: Prentice-Hall, 1961.

Primm, James N., *Economic Policy in the Development of a Western State, Missouri, 1820–1860,* Cambridge: Harvard University Press, 1954.

Robbins, Lionel, *The Great Depression,* Toronto: Macmillan, 1934.

Rostow, W. W., *The Process of Economic Growth,* New York: Norton, 1952.

—— *The Stages of Economic Growth,* Cambridge: Cambridge University Press, 1960.

Schumpeter, Joseph A., *Business Cycles,* New York: McGraw-Hill, 1939. 2 vols.

Slichter, Sumner H., *Economic Growth in the United States,* Baton Rouge: Louisiana State University Press, 1962.

Smith, Walter B., *Fluctuations in American Business, 1790–1860,* Cambridge: Harvard University Press, 1935.

Sprague, O. M. W., *History of Crises under the National Banking System,* Washington, D.C.: Government Printing Office, 1910.

Thorp, W. L., and H. E. Thorp, *Business Annals,* New York: National Bureau of Economic Research, 1926 (Publication No. 8).

Van Vleck, G. W., *The Panic of 1857,* New York: Columbia University Press, 1943.

General

Aitken, Hugh G. J., ed., *The State and Economic Growth,* New York: Social Science Research Council, 1959.

Andreano, Ralph, ed., *The Economic Impact of the Civil War,* Cambridge, England: Schenkman, 1962.

Andrews, Charles M., *The Colonial Period of American History,* New Haven: Yale University Press, 1934.

Angle, Paul M., ed., *The American Reader,* New York: Rand McNally, 1958.

Beard, C. A., *An Economic Interpretation of the Constitution of the United States,* New York: Macmillan, 1913.

Beard, Miriam, *A History of the Business Man,* Ann Arbor: Ann Arbor Paperbacks, University of Michigan Press, 1962. 2 vols.

Beatty, Richmond C., *William Byrd of Westover,* Boston: Houghton Mifflin, 1930.

Beer, George L., *British Colonial Policy, 1754–1765,* Gloucester, Mass.: Peter Smith, 1958.

—— *Commercial Policy of England Toward the American Colonies,* New York: Columbia University Press, 1893 (Studies in History, Economics, and Public Law, Vol. III, No. 2).

—— *The Old Colonial System, 1660–1754,* Gloucester, Mass.: P. Smith, 1958.

—— *The Origins of the British Colonial System, 1578–1660,* New York: Macmillan, 1908.

Berle, Adolf A., Jr., *The 20th Century Capitalist Revolution,* New York: Harcourt, Brace & World, 1954.

Bining, Arthur C., *The Rise of American Economic Life,* New York: Scribner's, 1943.

Bogart, E. L., and C. M. Thompson, *Readings in the Economic History of the United States,* New York: Longmans, Green, 1916.

Boorstin, Daniel J., *The Americans, The Colonial Experience,* New York: Random House, 1958.

Bridenbaugh, Carl, *Cities in Revolt; Urban Life in America 1743–1776,* New York: Knopf, 1955.

—— *Cities in the Wilderness—The First Century of Urban Life in America, 1625–1742,* New York: Knopf, 1955.

—— *Myths and Realities; Societies of the Colonial South,* Baton Rouge: Louisiana State University Press, 1952.

—— *Rebels and Gentlemen; Philadelphia in the Age of Franklin,* New York: Reynal and Hitchcock, 1942.

Brown, Ralph H., *Historical Geography of the United States,* New York: Harcourt, Brace & World, 1948 (Yale Institute of International Studies).

Brown, Robert E., *Charles Beard and the Constitution: A Critical Analysis of "An Economic Interpretation of the Constitution,"* Princeton: Princeton University Press, 1956.

Bruce, Phillip A., *Economic History of Virginia in the Seventeenth Century,* New York: Smith, 1935.

Callender, G. S., *Selections from the Economic History of the United States, 1765–1860,* Boston: Ginn, 1909.

Cameron, Rondo E., *France and the Economic Development of Europe, 1800–1914,* Princeton: Princeton University Press, 1961.

Carus-Wilson, E. M., ed., *Essays in Economic History,* New York: St. Martin's, 1954.

Chitwood, Oliver P., *A History of Colonial America,* New York: Harper, 1948.

Clapham, J. H., and Eileen Power, eds., *Cambridge Economic History of Europe from the Decline of the Roman Empire,* Cambridge: Cambridge University Press, 1941–52. 2 vols.

Clark, Colin, *The Conditions of Economic Progress,* 2nd ed., New York: Macmillan, 1951.

Clough, Shepard B., *The Economic Development of Western Civilization,* New York: McGraw-Hill, 1959.

Clough, Shepard B., and Charles W. Cole, *Economic History of Europe,* rev. ed., Boston: Heath, 1946.

Cochran, Thomas C., and William Miller, *The Age of Enterprise,* New York: Macmillan, 1942.

Deane, Phyllis, and W. A. Cole, *British Economic Growth, 1688–1959,* Cambridge: Cambridge University Press, 1962.

Editors of Fortune, *U.S.A.—The Permanent Revolution,* New York: Prentice-Hall, 1951.

Fiske, John, *Old Virginia and Her Neighbours,* Boston: Houghton Mifflin, 1897. 2 vols.

Flügel, F., and H. U. Faulkner, *Readings in the Economic and Social History of the United States, 1773–1829,* New York: Harper, 1929.

Freeman, Ralph E., *Postwar Economic Trends in the United States,* New York: Harper, 1960.

Gras, N. S. B., *Industrial Evolution,* Cambridge: Harvard University Press, 1930.

—— *An Introduction to Economic History,* New York: Harper, 1922.

Gras, N. S. B., and Henrietta Larson, *Casebook in American Business History,* New York: Crofts, 1939.

Hacker, Louis M., *Major Documents in American Economic History,* New York: Van Nostrand, 1961. 2 vols.

—— *The Triumph of American Capitalism,* New York: Simon and Schuster, 1940.

Hamilton, Earl J., *American Treasure and the Price Revolution in Spain, 1501–1650,* Cambridge: Harvard University Press, 1934.

Hartz, Louis, *Economic Policy and Democratic Thought: Pennsylvania, 1776–1860,* Cambridge: Harvard University Press, 1948.

Heaton, Herbert, *Economic History of Europe,* New York: Harper, 1936.

Hopkins, J. G. E., and Florett Robinson, *Album of American History,* New York: Scribner's, 1960.

Hoskins, Halford L., *British Routes to India,* Philadelphia: Longmans, Green, 1928.

Jensen, Merrill, *The New Nation; A History of the United States During Confederation, 1781–1789,* New York: Knopf, 1958.

Jewkes, John, D. Sawers, and R. Stillerman, *The Sources of Invention,* London: Macmillan, 1958.

Josephson, Matthew, *The Robber Barons,* New York: Harcourt, Brace & World, 1962.

Keirstead, B. S., *The Theory of Economic Change,* New York: Macmillan, 1949.

Kirkland, E. C., *A History of American Economic Life,* rev. ed., New York: Appleton-Century-Crofts, 1939.

Kuznets, Simon, *Economic Change,* New York: Norton, 1953.

—— *National Product Since 1869,* New York: National Bureau of Economic Research, 1946 (Publication No. 46).

Lambie, Joseph T., and Richard V. Clemence, eds., *Economic Change in America,* Harrisburg, Pa.: Stackpole, 1954.

Landes, David S., *Bankers and Pashas,* Cambridge: Harvard University Press, 1958.

Lane, Frederic C., ed., *Enterprise and Secular Change,* Homewood, Ill.: Irwin, 1953.

Latouche, Robert, *The Birth of Western Economy; Economic Aspects of the Dark Ages,* New York: Barnes & Noble, 1961.

Leech, Margaret, *In the Days of McKinley,* New York: Harper, 1959.

Leontieff, W., *The Structure of the American Economy, 1919–29,* Cambridge: Harvard University Press, 1941.

Lopez, Robert S., and Irving W. Raymond, eds., *Medieval Trade in the Mediterranean World,* New York: Columbia University Press, 1955.

Lord, Walter, *The Good Years,* New York: Harper, 1960.

Martineau, Harriet, *Society in America,* 2nd ed., London: Saunders and Otley, 1839. 3 vols.

McDonald, Forrest, *We The People,* Chicago: University of Chicago Press, 1958.

Miller, John C., *Triumph of Freedom, 1775–1783,* Boston: Little, Brown, 1948.

Miller, William, ed., *Men In Business,* New York and Evanston: Harper and Row, 1962.

Mumford, Lewis, *The City in History: Its Origins, Its Transformations, and Its Prospects,* New York: Harcourt, Brace & World, 1961.

Nettels, Curtis, *The Roots of American Civilization,* New York: Appleton-Century-Crofts, 1938.

Nevins, Allan, *Ordeal of the Union,* New York: Scribner's, 1947. 2 vols.

Pohl, Frederick J., *Atlantic Crossings Before Columbus,* New York: Norton, 1961.

Power, Eileen, *Medieval People,* Garden City: Doubleday, 1954.

Reeves, Dorothea D., *Resources for the Study of Economic History,* Boston: Harvard Graduate School of Business, 1961.

Richards, Gertrude R. B., *Florentine Merchants in the Age of the Medici,* Cambridge: Harvard University Press, 1932.

Roosevelt, Franklin Delano, *The Public Papers and Addresses of Franklin D. Roosevelt,* ed. by S. I. Rosenman, New York: Harper, 1941–45. 4 vols.

Saltzman, L. F., *Building in England Down to 1540,* Oxford: Clarendon Press, 1952.

Schlesinger, A. M., Jr., *The Age of Jackson,* Boston: Little, Brown, 1945.

Schumpeter, Joseph A., *The Theory of Economic Development,* Cambridge: Harvard University Press, 1934.

Scott, William R., *The Constitution and Finance of English, Scottish, and Irish Joint Stock Companies to 1720,* Cambridge: Cambridge University Press, 1912. 3 vols.

Scoville, Warren Candler, *The Persecution of Huguenots and French Economic Development, 1680–1720,* Berkeley: University of California Press, 1960.

Shannon, F. A., *America's Economic Growth,* 3rd ed., New York: Macmillan, 1951.

Slichter, Sumner H., *The American Economy,* New York: Knopf, 1938.

Sombart, Werner, *The Quintessence of Capitalism: A Study of the History and Psychology of the Modern Business Man,* New York: Dutton, 1915.

Soule, George, *Economic Forces in American History,* New York: Dryden, 1952.

——— *Economic History of the United States,* Vol. VIII, *Prosperity Decade from War to Depression, 1917–1929,* New York: Rinehart, 1947.

Steiner, George A., *Government's Role in Economic Life,* New York: McGraw-Hill, 1953.

Tawney, R. H., *Religion and the Rise of Capitalism,* New York: Harcourt, Brace & World, 1952.

Tunnard, Christopher, and Henry Hope Reed, *American Skyline, The Growth and Forms of Our Cities and Towns,* Boston: Houghton Mifflin, 1955.

Weber, Max, *The Protestant Ethic and the Spirit of Capitalism,* New York: Scribner's, 1930.

Williamson, Harold F., *The Growth of the American Economy,* 2nd ed., New York: Prentice-Hall, 1951.

Williamson, Harold F., and John A. Buttrick, eds., *Economic Development: Principles and Patterns,* New York: Prentice-Hall, 1954.

Wright, Chester W., *Economic History of the United States,* 2nd ed., New York: McGraw-Hill, 1949.

Index

Cycle theory of business, 409–15
Cyclical unemployment, 615

D Dabney, Charles, 319
Dabney, Morgan & Company, 319
Da Gama, Vasco, 26
Dallas, Alexander, 168
Dartmouth College case, 243, 287 n.
Dawes Act (*1887*), 251
Death benefits, 614
Debs, Eugene V., 403
Debt, imprisonment for, 217; kinds of, 588; nonfederal, 589
Decentralization of industry, 554–56
Declaratory Act, 88
Deere, John, 258
Defense Department, U.S., 659
Defense Highway System, 128 n.
Defense Production Act (*1950*), 510
Deflation, 429, 534
De Grasse, F. J. P., Admiral, 96
Delaware, settlement of, 40
Delaware and Hudson Canal Company, 134
Demand variables in agriculture, 449–54
Dempsey, Bernard W., 22 n.
Denison, Edward F., 650
Department stores, 363–64, 591
Deposits, bank, 529–32
Depressions, 161, 214, 280, 295, 411, 418–19, 618; causes of, 630–34; cure for, 639–43; *see also* Great Depression
Desert Land Act (*1877*), 251
Dias, Bartolomeu, 26
Díaz, Porfirio, 379
Differentiation of products, 593–94
Dingley Act (*1897*), 376
Disability insurance, 654
Distilleries, *see* Breweries and distilleries
Distillers' and Cattle Feeders' Trust, 353
District of Columbia, 611
Diversification in industry, 554–56
"Dollar diplomacy," 379
"Domestic allotment" plan, 434
Domestic market: consumer durables, 573–81; from 1921 to the present, 569–94; houses in, 581–89; marketing methods and the customer, 589–94; products, differentiation of, 593–94; retailing, large-scale, 591–93; wholesaling of consumer goods, 590–91
Domestic trade: colonial period, 78–79; from 1783 to 1860, 231–34; from 1861 to 1920, 359–68; pattern of, 231–33; raw materials, character of, 233–34
Dominican Republic, 379
Dornier, Peter, 463 n.
Douglas, Paul H., 385
Dow Chemical Company, 548
Drainage projects, 464, 470
Drake, Edwin L., 353
Drake, Sir Francis, 29
Dred Scott decision, 116
Drexel, Anthony, 317, 319
Drexel, Morgan & Company, 319
Dubinsky, David, 619
Duck, Stephen, 18, 19
Duke, James B., 355
Du Pont de Nemours & Company, E. I., 357, 548
Dust-bowl conditions, 436
Dutch East India Company, 27, 37, 38
Dutch West India Company, 38

E Economics, history and, merging of, 3–12
Edison, Thomas A., 416
Edison General Electric Company, 416
Education, 217, 272, 416, 654; *see also* Colleges

Edwards, E. E., 534 n.
El Camino Real, 126 n.
Electrical appliances, *see* Household appliances
Electrical energy, 558–59
Electrical industry, 416–18
Electric furnace, 339
Elevated railways, 299
"Eligible paper," 503
Elizabeth I, of England, 31, 33
Elkins Act (*1903*), 293
Emancipation of slaves, 115, 124, 247, 458–59
Embargo Act (*1807*), 109, 184–85, 200
Emergency Feed Grain Bill (*1961*), 444
Emergency Fleet Corporation, 301
Emergency Tariff Act (*1921*), 598
Emergency Transportation Act (*1933*), 481
Employers' Liability Act (*1908*), 388–89
Employers opposition to trade unions, 401–04
Employment, 460–61, 539
Employment Act (*1946*), 647
Energy sources, industrial, 557–60
Engineers Corps, U.S. Army, 487, 488
England and the English, 24, 26, 27, 28–29, 30, 36, 45–47, 49, 81, 96, 104–05, 146, 148, 184, 194, 195, 224, 227, 300, 338, 339, 368, 377, 378, 388, 513; colonial policy, American commerce and, 69–95; immigrants from, 210, 391, 392; regulation of Americans, 84–95
English Civil War, 47, 52
English East India Company, 89, 90
Enlarged Homestead Act, 251
Equal Rights party (Loco-Foco), 173
Erie Canal, 112, 115, 130, 131, 132, 136, 186, 232, 298, 489
Erie Railroad, 138, 281
Estate tax, 639
European Economic Community, 600–01; *see also* Common Market
European Recovery Program, 491, 602; *see also* Marshall Plan
Europeans, medieval, 19–26
Evans, George Henry, 218, 219
Evans, Oliver, 65, 67, 134, 194, 197, 346, 551
Excess profits tax, 639
Export bounties, 434, 439, 456
Exports: agricultural products, 454–56, 460; "big four," 603; by continents, percentage distribution (*1860–1920*), 373; by economic classes, percentage distribution (*1861–1920*), 372; trends in, 371; value of (*1860–1920*), 370
Extractive industries, 57–62, 184

F Factories: development of, 187–202; emergence of, 199–202; production, prerequisites to, 193–98; wage earners and, 207–09
Fair Labor Standards Act (*1938*), 606, 610, 639
Fall, Albert B., 464
Fallen Timbers, Battle of, 105
Farms and farmers: economic position of, 428–32; employment, 460–61; income, 261, 430, 431; increase in number of (*1860–1920*), 262; problems and programs, 456–63
Farm legislation, 432–44; farm policy, crystalization of (*1933–41*), 435–39; farm policy during World War II and after, 439–44; first efforts (*1921–33*), 433–35
Farm policy: crystallization of (*1933–41*), 435–39; during World War II and after, 439–44
Federal administration of railroads, 296–98
Federal-Aid Highway Act (*1944*), 475

Lumbering, 203
Luther, Martin, 33

M Macaulay, Thomas B., 10
Machinery, development of, 343–44
Machine tools, 195, 343–44
Madison, James, 161
Magellan, Ferdinand, 26
Magnesium, 548, 549
Mail-order houses, 365, 591–92
Mail subsidies, 300–01
Main Line, the, 131, 133 n.
Manchester, Massachusetts, 200
Mann, Abijah, 174
Mann-Elkins Act (1910), 294
Manufacturing, see Industry
Maritime Administration, U.S., 491
Maritime Commission, U.S., 486, 489, 490, 491
Market ratio, 152, 153
Markets, see Domestic markets; Foreign markets
Marketing methods, changes in, 360–65; customer and, 589–94
Marketing quotas, 438
Marshall, Alfred, 249
Marshall, John, 243
Marshall Plan, 602
Martin, Emile and Pierre, 338
Martin, Robert F., 237–38, 409
Maryland, 164 n., 388; colonial agriculture in, 51; settlement of, 32, 48
Mason and Dixon's line, 115 n.
Massachusetts, mint established by, 72; settlement of, 33–35, 48
Massachusetts Bank, 155, 156
Massachusetts Bay Company, 34
Mass production, 345–47, 362
Mass unemployment, 615
Maximum Freight Rate case, 292, 294
McAdoo, William Gibbs, 296, 297
McChord, C. C., ICC Commissioner, 296
McClelland, David C., 416; quoted, 539
McCormick, Cyrus, 258
McCormick Harvester Works, 402
McCulloch, Hugh, 309–10
McKay, Donald, 144
McKay, Douglas, 469
McKenna, Justice Joseph, 424, 425
McKim, Ann, clipper ship, 144
McKinley, William, 315
McKinley tariff (1890), 376
McKinney Shoe Company, 568
McNary-Haugen bills, 434
Meat-packing industry, 114, 202, 335, 336
Mechanics' Union of Trade Associations, 214
Mechanization: of agriculture, 258–60; of industry, 332–43, 546
Member-bank reserves, Federal Reserve System, 502–04
Mencken, H. L., 427
Mercantile system, English, 45–47, 79, 91
"Merchant-employer system," 68
Merchant Marine, 143–46, 300–01, 472; regulation of, 490–91
Merchant Marine Act (1920), 490; (1936), 490
Merchant Ship Sales Act (1946), 491
Mergers, 560–61, 645
Merrimack Manufacturing Company, 196, 200
Metals industries, 546, 548–50
Mexican Cession, 101, 116
Mexico, 379
Miami Canal, 132
Michigan Central Railroad, 129
Middlemen, 360–61, 364

Migration, westward, 107–15; northern, 111–15; southern, 109–11
Milk and milk products, 256
Miller, Adolph, 512–13
Mill industries, 65–68, 187, 336
Milliman, J. W., 464
Mineral fuel, energy produced from, 557, 558
Miners and mining, 253, 254
Mint Act (1786), 150
Mint ratio, 152, 153, 178
Mississippi River, 140, 141, 232, 298
Mississippi River System, 488
Missouri Compromise (1820), 115, 116
Mitchell, John, 403
Molasses Act (1733), 86, 88
"Molly Maguires," 401
Monetary unit, adoption of, 147–54
Money supply, 318, 413; bank deposits, 529–32; banks and (1834–60), 173–81; changes in, 317; circulation, velocity of, 527; colonial period, 70–75; from 1834 to 1860, 173–81; from 1863 to 1914, 307–17; from 1921 to the present, 526–38; nonbank intermediaries and, 532–38
Money trust, 317–22
Monongahela River, 298
Monopoly power, 348–49, 350, 423, 560 n.; merger for, 560–61
Monroe, James, 168
Monroe Doctrine, 379
Monsanto Chemical Company, 548
Montgomery Ward & Company, 270, 365, 592
Moore, W. H., 356
Morgan, John Pierpont, 319–22
Morgan, Junius Spencer, 317, 319
Morgan & Company, J. P., 320, 356
Morgan & Company, Junius S., 318–19
Mormon Trail, 126 n.
Morrill Act (1862), 272, 375
Morris, Robert, 148, 154, 155
Morris Packing Company, 355
Morse, Samuel, 280
Mortgage loans, 582–89
Motor Carrier Act (1935), 484, 485
Motor carriers, 472, 482–85, 495
Muller, Herbert J., 1 n.
Munn v. Illinois, 289–90
Murray, Senator James E., 646
Mutual funds, 537
Mutual Life Insurance Company, 320
Mutual savings banks, 536, 537
Mutual Security Agency, 602

N National Aeronautics and Space Administration, 659
National Agricultural Conference (1922), 433
National Airport Plan, 477, 487
National Association of Manufacturers, 403
National Bank Act (1864), 303–04, 305, 322, 323, 324, 502
National banking system, growth of, 304–07
National City Bank of New York, 523
National Civic Federation, 403–04
National Conservation Commission, 275
National expansion, 26–29
National Farmers Organization, 462
National Farmers Union, 462
National Forests, 273, 466, 469, 475
National Grange, 269–70, 289, 434, 441, 462
National health insurance plans, 614
National Housing Act (1934), 585
National Housing Agency, 586
National Housing Council, 586
National income, from 1869 to 1923, 410;

National income, from 1869 to 1923 (cont.)
  industrial production changes and, 406–09;
  population and (1869–1923), 411
National Industrial Recovery Act (NIRA),
  615, 622, 636, 637
National Labor Relations Act, 622–23
National Labor Relations Board (NLRB),
  622
National Labor Union (NLU), 396
National Monetary Commission, 326–27, 328
National War Labor Board, 405, 641
National Packing Company, 357
National parks, 466, 475
National Recovery Administration (NRA),
  636, 637
National Reserve Association, 328
National Steel Company, 356
National Trades' Union, 214
National Tube Company, 356
National Union of Iron Molders, 401
National Youth Administration, 616 n.
Natural gas, 345, 557, 559
Natural resources, see Conservation program
Naval Oil Reserves, 275, 464
Navigation Acts, 47, 66, 84–85, 224
New Amsterdam, 38–39, 46, 78; see also New
  York City
Newcomen, Thomas, 189, 190
New Deal, 639, 640
New England, agriculture in, 115; colonial
  agriculture in, 56–57
New England Bank, 165
New England Protective Union, 219
Newfoundland, 49
New Hampshire, settlement of, 41
New Harmony, Indiana, 219
New Jersey, 39, 55, 388
Newlands Act (1902), 273
New Mexico Territory, 116
New Orleans, Louisiana, 49, 141, 232, 233
New Orleans, S.S., 141
Newport, Rhode Island, 66, 83
New York, 37–39, 174, 186, 303, 388
New York Barge Canal, 298
New York Central Railroad, 281, 319
New York City, 79, 83, 95, 166, 177, 214,
  215, 218, 231, 233, 281, 304, 324, 327 n.
New York Life Insurance Company, 320
New York Stock Exchange, 310, 632
Nicaragua, 379
Nickel steel, 341
Nonbank intermediaries: growth of, 535; lia-
  bilities of, 538; money supply and, 532–38
Nonferrous metals, 342–43
Non-Intercourse Act (1809), 185
Norris, George, 433
Norris-La Guardia Act (1932), 621
North, Douglass C., 230
North Carolina, settlement of, 40–41
Northern Pacific Railroad, 280, 318
Northern Securities case, 422–23
Northrup loom, 333
Northwestern Alliance, 270
Northwest Territory, 104, 105, 112, 114, 116,
  117
Note-brokers, 164
Nuclear energy, 559
Nutrition programs, 438

O Occupational diseases, 614
Office of Defense Transportation, 482, 641–
  42
Office of Experimental Stations, 272
Office of Price Administration, 641
Office of War Mobilization, 642
Off-shore oil reserves, 469
Oglethorpe, James Edward, 37, 41

Ohio Canal, 132, 232
Ohio River, 107, 111, 112, 126, 140, 141,
  197, 298, 299, 472, 482, 493
Ohio Territory, 126, 130
Old-age insurance, 388, 612, 654
Old Colony Trust Company, 320
Oligopoly, 349; competition and, 561–66;
  merger for, 560–61
"Open-door" policy, 379
Open-hearth furnace, 338, 341
Open Market Committee, Federal Reserve,
  507, 514
Open shop, 403
Oregon Territory, 100–01
Oregon Trail, 127
Oswego Canal, 130
Owen, Robert, 217, 218–19

P Pacific Railway Act (1862), 276, 278
Pack trains, 125
Panama, 277, 279, 379
Panama Canal, 301, 379
Panama Canal Zone, 379, 381
Panic of 1837, 213–14; of 1857, 244; of
  1873, 318; of 1907, 321, 326
Paper mills, 66
Paper money, 72–73, 75, 83, 97, 170, 182;
  from 1921 to the present, 526–29; gold
  certificates, 313–15; silver certificates, 311–
  13; state of, 177–78
Papin, Denis, 189
Paradiso, Louis J., 543
Parish, David, 168
Parity prices, 441, 442, 462
Partnerships, 246
Passer, Harold, 417
Patent medicine, 366n.
Patent Office, U.S., 198
Patents, 198–99, 417
Payne-Aldrich bill (1909), 376
Peace of Paris (1763), 49, 59
Peale, Charles Wilson, 154
Penn, William, 32, 37, 39–40
Pennsylvania, colonial agriculture in, 55;
  settlement of, 39–40
Pennsylvania Land Bank, 73
Pennsylvania Railroad, 138, 281
Pershing, John J., 379
Peter Cooper (locomotive), 135
Petrochemicals, 546–48
Petroleum, 345, 353–55, 547–48, 550, 557
Philadelphia, Pennsylvania, 64, 65, 66, 79, 83,
  136, 150 n., 155, 169, 201, 218, 231, 396
Philadelphia and Lancaster Turnpike, 128
Philadelphia Convention (1787), 98
Philadelphia Smelting and Refining Company,
  357
Philip II, of Spain, 27
Philippines, 378–79
Phillips, U. B., 119
Phoenix, steamboat, 134
"Piece of eight," 71, 72 n., 74
Pilgrim Fathers, 33, 34
Pinchot, Gifford, 273, 275, 469
Pipelines, 492, 494
Pitt, William, 88
Pittsburgh, Pennsylvania, 141, 398, 402
Pittsburgh Cordwainers case, 213
Plankroads, 128–29
Plantation economy, 115–24
Plastics industry, 417, 565
Platt Amendment (1901), 378
Plow, development of, 258
Plymouth Company, 31, 33, 34
Packet ships, 144
Pontiac, Chief, 92
Pools, 350

St. Lawrence Seaway, 482, 493
St. Louis, Missouri, 231, *232*, 281
St. Louis Shipbuilding and Steel Company, 488
Salsbury, Stephen, 248
San Bernardino of Sienna, 20 n.
Santa Fe Trail, 125 n., 127
Santee Canal, 130
Sault Ste. Marie Canal, 298
Savage, Chief Justice, 215
Savannah, Georgia, 233
Savannah and Charleston Railroad, 138
Savery, Thomas, 189, 191
Savings and loan accounts insurance, 534
Savings and loan associations, 533, 534, 535, 536, 537, 538, 584
Sawmills, 59, 65, 66, 187, 344
Sawyer, Charles, Secretary of Commerce, 495
Schiff, Jacob H., 320
Schmoller, Gustav, 12
School lunch programs, 438
Schultze, Theodore, 654 n.
Schumpeter, J. A., 412, 630
Science, application to agriculture, 260, 272, 446–47; research, 659
Scientific management, 345–47
Scitovsky, Tibor, 572
Scots-Irish immigrants, 49
Scotus, John Duns, 21 n.
Scoville, Warren Candler, 23 n.
Sea Island cotton, 54 n.
Sea products, colonial period, 59–61
Sears, Roebuck & Company, 365, 592
Sea transportation, 75–77
Secession, 117
Securities, railroad, 284–86
Seneca Canal, 130
Serious Fall in the Value of Gold (Jevons), 12
Servicemen's Readjustment Act (*1944*), 586, 588
Seven Years' War, 87
Sewall, Samuel, 83
Sewing machine, 198, 333–34
Share tenancy, 458–59
Shaw, Lemuel, 215
Shaw, Leslie M., 323
Shaw, William N., 407, 409
Shenandoah Valley, 49, 77
Sherman, John, 313
Sherman Act (*1890*), 357, 422, 423, 560, 567, 568
Sherman Silver Purchase Act (*1890*), 313, 315
Sherman Station, Wyoming, 282
Shipbuilding, colonial period, 66–67
Shipbuilding Trust, 320
Shoe industry, 64, 68, 202, 335
Siemens, William and Friedrich, 338
Silk culture, 51
Silver and silver certificates, 311–13, 317
Singer, Isaac, 198
Sixteenth Amendment, 420
Slater, Samuel, 199–200, 201
Slaughtering industry, 114
Slave prices, 119, 120
Slaves and slavery, 42, 44, 53, 55, 59, 81, 82, 223; economics of, 117–21; emancipation of, 115, 124, 247, 458–59; plantation economy and, 115–24; social and economic consequences of, 121–24
Slave trade, foreign, 115
Sleeping cars, 277
Slums, 393
Smeaton, John, 189
Smith, Abbott Emerson, 43
Smith, Adam, 8 n., 11, 504 n.

Smith-Hughes Vocational Education Act (*1917*), 272
Smoot-Hawley Act (*1929*), 435, 598
Smuggling, 86, 90, 115
Smyth v. *Ames*, 295
Social Circle case, 292
Social insurance, 388, 611, 612–14, 657
Socialized medicine, 614
Social justice, government and, 418–25
Social security, 610–14
Social Security Act (*1935*), 612–14
Society of Journeyman Tailors, 215
Soil Bank Act (*1956*), 443
Soil conservation, 466–67
Soil Conservation and Domestic Allotment Act (*1938*), 436
Soil conservation districts, 467
Soil erosion, 470
Soil Erosion Service, 467
Sombart, Werner, 12
South America, trade with, 371
South Carolina, 49; settlement of, 40–41
Southern, John, 191
Southern Alliance, 270
Southern Pacific Railroad, 280
Sovereign of the Seas, clipper ship, 144
Spain and the Spaniards, 23, 24, 26, 27, 30, 36, 49, 97, 184
Spanish-American War, 378
Spanish dollar, 73–74, 148, 149
Spinning jenny, 192, 193
Squatting and squatters' rights, 105–06
Stagecoach travel, 77, 128
Stamp Act (*1765*), 87, 88
Stamp Act Congress (*1765*), 88
Standard Oil Company of New Jersey, 353, 355, 357, 423–24
Standard Oil Company of Ohio, 353, 354
State Bank of Illinois, 162
State banks, 173, 174–77, 179; capitals of, 161–63; characteristics of (*1811–34*), 161–64; notes of, 163–64; number of (*1819–62*), 175; resurgence of, 304–07; surge of banking, 174–77
Steagall Amendment (*1941*), 439
Steamboats, 134, 140–43, 145, 146
Steel industry, 62, 337–42, 356–57, 547, 561
Steam engine, 189–91, 197, 260, 344
Stephens, Uriah S., 396, 397
Stephenson, George, 134
Stephenson, Robert, 134
Stigler, George J., 561
Stillman, James, 320
Stock companies, 270
Stock-Raising Homestead Act (*1916*), 251
Stockton and Darlington Railway, 134
Story, Joseph, 243, 244
Stourbridge Lion (locomotive), 134
Stove Founders Defense Association, 401
Strasser, Adolph, 398, 399
Streetcars, 299
Street railway companies, 299, 472
Strike-breakers, 401, 403
Strikes, 214, 215, 383, 394–95, 397, 401–03, 618
Strong, Benjamin, 500–01, 512
Stuyvesant, Peter, 38
Subsidies: agricultural, 462; airmail, 486, 487; income, 467; land-grant, 283–84, 288; mail, 300–01; transportation, 471; *see also* Export bounties
Subway trains, 299
Suez Canal, 368
Suffolk Bank system, 165–66
Sugar Act (*1764*), 87–88
Supply variables in agriculture, 444–49
Supreme Court, U.S., 116, 275, 287 n., 289,

A 4
B 5
C 6
D 7
E 8
F 9
G 0
H 1
I 2
J 3

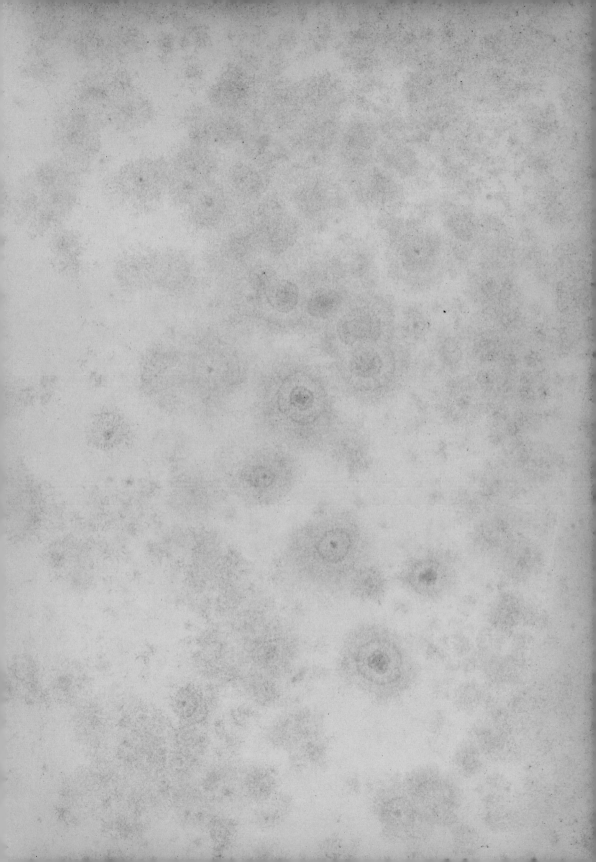